# THE TEACHING OF HIGH SCHOOL ENGLISH

*To the thousands who helped*

# PREFACE

The Fifth Edition of *The Teaching of High School English* is a textbook for students preparing to teach the English language, composition, and literature in junior and senior high schools. At the same time it is a reference book for in-service teachers, many of whom have used the first four editions as sources of innumerable and varied specific suggestions and helps.

We have stressed application more than theory, particularly after the first few chapters. We have described hundreds of tested classroom procedures. Some of these we have drawn from our own years of teaching in junior and senior high schools, colleges and universities, but we have drawn still more from the teaching experience of others and from both old and recent research and classroom experimentation. As a glance at the footnotes will reveal, at least half of the cited articles and books appeared during the past few years—since the publication of the Fourth Edition.

More than half of the Fifth Edition is new. Revision and often rewriting, additions and deletions, were necessary because of the constant changes in English teaching and in teaching conditions. For instance, today we hear much about reformulation of objectives, about proficiency tests and the tyranny of testing, about "mainstreaming." The excitement over British emphasis on oral English and on relatively unstructured programs has diminished but has not vanished. Research in the teaching of written composition has greatly increased. The search for especially effective organization(s) and emphases in secondary school language instruction still continues. Teachers are constantly experimenting, too, in choice of literary selections and ways of interesting students in them.

The environment—the political, economic, and cultural climate in which schools function—has altered, too. Inflation has increased school costs like all others, and in some places has resulted in a demand for less costly materials and procedures. Gains in civil rights, including those of women as well as of minority groups, continue though at an irregular pace, and sometimes influence a curriculum. New life-styles are evident and may quickly give way to still newer ones; one result is that schools must teach flexibility and adaptability yet still make students aware that some values and ideals can and must remain intact, for some truths are permanent.

Literally millions of words have been written and spoken during the past decade about the teaching of English in the changing environment. From the several millions of those words that we ourselves have read or heard, and from our own observation and participation in the affairs of the profession during that period, we have culled the approximately one-quarter million words in this book.

Our indebtedness is mainly to the hundreds of teachers from whom we have drawn examples, ideas, and inspiration—to those with whom we have had personal contacts, and to others whom we have seen on a podium or seen reflected in the pages of a book or a journal. They are the sources of most of the several hundred items in the Idea Boxes and the basis of much of our thinking.

Our specific thanks go to the following people for their valuable reviews of the new edition: Daniel Donlan, University of California, Riverside; Edmund Farrell, University of Texas, Austin.

**J. N. Hook**
**William H. Evans**

*January 1982*

# ABOUT THE AUTHORS

J. N. HOOK has long been associated with the University of Illinois, where he received his doctorate and served for a number of years as Professor of English and Counselor in the Teaching of English. Dr. Hook has also played a significant role in the improvement and advancement of English teaching throughout the nation, having served as Executive Secretary of the National Council of Teachers of English, Coordinator of Project English for the U.S. Office of Education, and director of a number of federal projects aimed at improving the preparation of teachers of secondary school English and stating its performance objectives. He is the author of *History of the English Language* (Scott Foresman, 1975), *The Grand Panjandrum* (Macmillan, 1980), and *Family Names* (Macmillan, 1982) as well as a number of high school textbooks.

WILLIAM H. EVANS brings to this book 30 years of experience in teaching English. A teacher in high school and junior college, a supervisor of English in a large school system, and a teacher of English and education in five universities, he has served as a speaker and consultant in this country and several others. Also active for the National Council of Teachers of English, he has served on its executive committee and has been chairman of its Conference on English Education, the national organization in his speciality. As a teacher educator, he has coordinated English Education on three university campuses, has served on the board of the American Association of Colleges for Teacher Education, and has been chairman of the Associated Organizations for Teacher Education. His writings include professional books, textbooks and standardized tests, and many articles on teaching literature, language, composition and reading. He is the editor of *The Creative Teacher* (Bantam Books, 1971).

FIFTH EDITION

# THE TEACHING OF HIGH SCHOOL ENGLISH

**J. N. HOOK**
*Professor of English, Emeritus*
*University of Illinois at Urbana-Champaign*

**WILLIAM H. EVANS**
*Professor of English and Education*
*Purdue University*

1807 1982

**John Wiley & Sons,** *New York • Chichester • Brisbane • Toronto • Singapore*

Copyright © 1950, 1959, 1965, 1972, 1982, by John Wiley & Sons, Inc.

All rights reserved. Published simultaneously in Canada.

Reproduction or translation of any part of
this work beyond that permitted by Sections
107 and 108 of the 1976 United States Copyright
Act without the permission of the copyright
owner is unlawful. Requests for permission
or further information should be addressed to
the Permissions Department, John Wiley & Sons.

*Library of Congress Cataloging in Publication Data:*

Hook, J. N. (Julius Nicholas), 1913–
   The teaching of high school English.

  Includes bibliographical references and index.
  1. English language—Study and teaching
(Secondary)  I. Evans, William Howard, 1924–
II. Title.
LB1631.H56  1982     428'.007'12     81-19682
ISBN 0-471-08923-0     AACR2

Printed in the United States of America

10 9 8 7 6 5 4 3 2 1

# CONTENTS

xi

# 1

## THE
## TEACHING
## OF
## ENGLISH:
## STILL
## SEARCHING
## AND
## GROWING

## ROOTS IN THE ANCESTRAL CLASSROOM

### THE FIRST FUNDAMENTALS

Early American colonists came to the New World not only to prosper financially and to find freedoms which they felt they could not enjoy in their homeland, but also to establish a way of life based on their ethnical and ethical traditions. In their preindustrial society, they worked by hand with simple tools. The church was their guiding institution, the family their most important social unit. Because they had to build their economy largely from the land and from the skills of their craftsmen and merchants, land, common sense, and education became prime commodities. Rites of initiation and imitation were important. Passing on ethnical and ethical traditions was essential, but so was teaching practical skills and crafts. Therefore, it was necessary to think of young men as apprentice scholars and apprentice workers. *Influence of Religion ↓*

The first colonists relied on British primers to teach fundamentals at home, in reading schools, and in dame schools. Serving as first readers, these primers typically contained an alphabet, a syllabarium, a creed, a catechism, prayers, and devotional exercises. The popularity of these little books led to the publication of several colonial editions. *The New England Primer,* first printed by Benjamin Harris between 1686 and 1690, became the most successful colonial reader. For the first 100 years after its publication it was the principal text for piety, virtue, and beginning reading; even for the next 100 years it was reprinted frequently.

1

# THE RISE AND DECLINE OF THE CLASSICAL TRADITION

Fundamentals of the classical tradition were soon emphasized by the Latin grammar school, a secondary school designed primarily to prepare students in the classical grammars and literatures required by the first colleges. At Harvard College, students (then called ''scholars'') could ''under no consideration use their mother tongue within the limits of the college, unless summoned to deliver in English an oration or some other public exercise.'' To be certain that ''scholars'' would be prepared for its rigorous classical program, Harvard College accepted only applicants who were ''able to understand Tully or such like classical Latin author *extempore,* and make and speak true Latin in Verse and prose *suo ut auint marte;* and decline perfectly the paradigms of nouns and verbs in the Greek tongue. . . .''[1]

In these early secondary schools, the stress in all subjects was upon individual instruction. Classes like those of today were not common until the middle of the nineteenth century. In the Latin grammar school, each student progressed individually. The recitation was generally just that—a re-citation in which the student repeated more or less verbatim what was in the book. The emphasis in these schools was steadily upon memory, not upon interpretation, and only seldom upon creation.

Narrowness of curriculum finally killed the Latin grammar schools. After 1751, they were gradually supplanted by academies, which—in Massachusetts and some other states—the law required every large town to establish. The courses offered by academies were diverse. Subjects which today might be labeled English included biography, composition, declamation, extemporaneous speaking, grammar, moral philosophy, penmanship, pronunciation, and rhetoric. All these were usually taught as separate courses, with little concern for orderly development or avoidance of overlapping. With the addition of English composition came the inclusion of certain approved books by English authors to serve as models. This marked the first entrenchment of certain English classics in the curriculums of American secondary schools.

In general, though, it was the lingering influence of the defunct Latin grammar school, plus changing college entrance requirements, that caused classics of English literature to be widely studied in the academies. The Latin grammar school had fostered the tradition of teaching certain selections from Latin and Greek authors; the academy, with its emphasis upon the vernacular, substituted English (not American) classics for the ancients. Johnnies-come-lately such as Burns, Scott, and Wordsworth were ignored in most schools, although the students sometimes smuggled in and read surreptitiously some little volume by a man named Byron. Through their entrance requirements, the colleges gradually reinforced the tendency of secondary schools to teach selections from a limited list of accepted writers.

2

In writing and speech, the academies specialized in grammar, rhetoric, and declamation. The grammar taught in the academies presented a perversion of the English language, for which grammarians and textbook makers were chiefly to blame. Representative of these men was Lindley Murray, whose influential grammar was published in 1795. Murray and his like assumed that English is similar in nearly all respects to Latin, and therefore referred to such things as dative case, ablative case, gerundives, and so on, disregarding the fact that the English language simply does not possess some of the forms that they tried to find. The result of teachers' following these pseudo-learned grammarians was numberless hours spent by students in parroting nonsense. The students "knew grammar" when they finished, but what they knew—and happily forgot—were definitions that were often inaccurate, paradigms that were valueless, and mistaken linguistic conceptions that would have been foolish if not impossible to apply.

The teaching of rhetoric was often better conceived than that of grammar. Some teachers, of course, were satisfied with mere verbalism, and praised the student who could echo the definitions of synecdoche, litotes, amphibology, and anaphora. Others demanded slavish imitations of the "polished periods" of Addison. Some overemphasized the four forms of discourse—exposition, narration, description, and argumentation—which are seldom found entirely separated. But many taught methods of organization, suggested ways of improving sentence structure, and offered constructive help to the student searching for the exact word. Some of America's most vital political documents and most vivid pieces of literature came from the quill pens of men who had learned rhetoric in academies.

The methods used in the academies were dictated to some extent by the aims, which were summarized this way by the New York Regents in 1839: "The great purpose of education [is] to store the mind with useful knowledge." Note the verb *store*. Schools were not to teach students to observe, to interpret, to reason, or to apply; they were only to pour facts, grain by grain, into students' minds. Dickens calls schoolman Thomas Gradgrind "a kind of cannon loaded to the muzzle with facts, and prepared to blow the pupils clean out of the regions of childhood at one discharge."

# RESPONDING TO THE GROWING NATION
## THE UNEASY GROWTH OF A FLEDGLING SUBJECT

The rapidly growing middle class in the young nation demanded a more practical secondary school program than the academies had provided. The people felt that the states should support public secondary schools to educate anyone who wanted to enroll, not just those who planned to attend college, and they envisioned a school which would continue the common-school education provided for all in the lower grades so that the working and industrial members of society would have a broader education.

Boston, cultural pioneer of American cities, led the revolt when in 1821 it established an "English classical school," later to be named the "English high school." English literature, mathematics, science, history, and logic superseded Latin and Greek in this school, as in most of the few other high schools opened elsewhere before the Civil War. These schools, unlike the majority of the academies, were supported and controlled by the public. They did not become numerous until after the Civil War, but by the school year 1896–97 there were 5109 public high schools in the United States, in addition to more than 2000 private high schools.

Throughout the nineteenth century, English as a fledgling subject struggled to broaden its literature program. The moral tradition in the schools still greatly influenced the selection of works. Because fiction and drama seemed to appeal to the imagination rather than to moral values and truth, they had an especially difficult time in the schools. Shakespeare's works were often considered indecent, even brutal—a product of the "grossness" of the age in which he lived.[2] Americans who saw in education a strong cultural and political force for social change were afraid that imaginative literature in the schools could erode the traditional foundations of the society.

College entrance requirements gave English its first recognition as a subject in the high schools. The colleges, which had dominated the curriculum of the academies, insisted throughout much of the nineteenth century that candidates be "well acquainted" with English grammar, English composition, and the English classics. Harvard, for example, began to require applicants to write a short composition, which had to be "correct in spelling, punctuation, grammar, and expression, the subject to be taken from such works of standard authors as shall be announced from time to time." Entrance requirements such as these had much to do with establishing the subject matter content—rigid though it tended to be—for English in American high schools, especially in the New England area. Toward the end of the nineteenth century, the National Education Association and the National Conference on Uniform Entrance Requirements adopted an "open list" of books to be read for college entrance, but the eastern colleges interpreted this decision as a ploy by western colleges and resisted it for many years. The creation of the College Entrance Examination Board in 1900, while shifting some attention from uniform college lists to uniform national examinations, only served to strengthen the influence that prescriptive book lists had on high school curriculum well into the 1920s.

Indirectly, rigid college entrance requirements proved to be one of the greatest blessings which English teaching has had. It was resistance to the dictates of entrance requirements, first in the New York State Association of English

THE TEACHING OF HIGH SCHOOL ENGLISH

Teachers, and later in the English Round Table of the Secondary Section of the National Education Association, that led James Fleming Hosic and others in the summer of 1911 to pass a resolution at NEA asking for the establishment of "a national council of teachers of English." In December, about 65 English teachers from twelve states joined Hosic in Chicago and formed the National Council of Teachers of English. When the meeting ended, NCTE had its first president (Fred Scott) and secretary (Hosic), other first officers, the names of several working committees, and a journal, which was to be founded at Hosic's expense. The first issue of the *English Journal* appeared in January, 1912. By NCTE's first birthday, 19 English groups around the nation had affiliated, bringing national membership to about 5000.

## REORGANIZING AND EXPERIMENTING BETWEEN THE WARS

The growing national strength of NCTE gave English teachers an active role in the reorganization and experimentation that took place in secondary education between the two world wars. High school English assumed its newly found national voice in *Reorganization of English in Secondary Schools* (1917), a report issued by the National Joint Committee on English of the NCTE and the NEA (and guided by James Hosic). This monograph became a manifesto for English teachers who had resisted uniform college requirements and had sought independence for their programs, and it gave at least lip service to "literature closely enough connected with the daily life and thought of the pupil to secure his attention and create an interest upon which to build." The main intent was to provide some flexibility for the student not planning to go to college.

The following year, Clarence Kingsley and his NEA Commission on the Reorganization of Secondary Education issued *The Cardinal Principles of Secondary Education,* which stressed these seven objectives: health, command of fundamental processes, worthy home membership, vocation, citizenship, worthy use of leisure, and ethical character. This report, together with the one issued under Hosic's direction, gave considerable thrust to an emerging English curriculum based on the cultural, vocational, social, and ethical growth of students. To these emphases, patriotism engendered by World War I added a new thrust: the teaching of American ideals as reflected in American literature.

Influenced by the philosophies of William H. Kilpatrick, Boyd H. Bode, and other "progressive" curriculum makers, high school English teachers soon became heavily involved in developing their own "learning experiences" for students. In 1929 the NCTE directed its newly elected president, Ruth Mary Weeks, to create a curriculum commission to study trends and suggest a "pattern curriculum" that could give programs some stability and direction. Six years later, through the work of this commission, NCTE published *An Experience Curriculum in English,* a collection of "experience-centered" teaching units designed to help students to develop the self-direction they would need to cope successfully with America's rapid industrial, social, and economic change. Another NCTE monograph, *A Correlated Curriculum* (1936) invited English teachers to employ "project methods" which could bring content from various subject areas into a core of common learnings so the student "as a dynamic whole" could "in the midst of living" meet and solve problems of "immediate significance." Resulting experimentation with core courses and projects revitalized interest in the subject areas in some schools, but in too many it caused great confusion. Unstructured correlations, which occurred spontaneously in the English classroom, led to unnecessary duplication of learnings from subject to subject, or led students and teachers far away from expected learnings. In *Conducting Experiences in English* (1939), a collection of narratives from teachers who had tried units in *An Experience Curriculum,* an NCTE committee echoed a growing concern over unstructured classes in which the student did whatever he or she wished to do while the teacher hoped the student's English skills would improve. Apparently the rich and meaningful experience often turned out to be shallow and meaningless. The following observation made by Robert C. Pooley in May of 1939 reflects the growing anxiety felt by English teachers after two decades of experiences, explorations, correlations, patterns, and socialization:

*Within twenty years we have had to meet, study, and assimilate several new psychologies, at least one new sociology, and a score of isms. We have had to grapple with such concepts as "the child centered school," the activity program, the socialized recitation, the project method, integration, correlation, two- and three-track plans, and the unit plan. The progressive movement has waxed fat in the last two decades. All these movements and schemes have added immeasurably to the science and art of teaching. But they have bred doubts, fears, and insecurity where once there was confidence.*[3]

High school English had indeed learned from these experiences, but it still faced—with all of secondary education—the problem of providing a sound general education for the rapidly rising high school population.

## CAN ENGLISH BE NEW, ACADEMIC, ELECTIVE, STUDENT-CENTERED, ACCOUNTABLE, *AND* BASIC?

### REACTING TO "LIFE ADJUSTMENT"

The search for a common core of general education inspired the Progressive Education Association to conduct the Eight-Year Study (1932–1940), which had much to do with the "life adjustment movement" of the 1940s and 1950s. Further experiments with cores, correlations (especially with social studies), and "common learnings," which now centered around "developmental tasks" and

6

the "needs of youth," made some leaders in English teaching concerned that English would lose its identity as a subject. Writing in the *English Journal* (April 1942), George Henry asked, "Is English on the Way Out?"[4]; Charles Glicksberg (June 1945) pointed to "a movement now under way to absorb English within the field of social studies. . . ."[5] Curricular integration, especially with broad social emphases, had caused English teachers to fear that their subject would lose whatever recognition it had finally gained as a high school subject.

These emphases on social concerns and human development in the 1930s and 1940s also prompted many English teachers to again ask their national organization for guidance. In response, the NCTE appointed a Commission on the English Curriculum "to discover ways in which the knowledge now available of the nature and uses of language, and of the problems of American and world society can be used in American education for the improvement of teaching the language arts, to the end that young people may be better prepared to deal effectively with the critical problems of life in the mid-twentieth century." *The English Language Arts* (1952), first of five books subsequently issued by the Commission, suggested concentrating more on sequential learnings than on topics for correlations and core classes. More important than "topical" organization were the "maturing powers to be attained in thinking, speaking, listening, writing, and reading." Improvement in these skills through the grades was in the Commission's view a very significant contribution to education in a democracy. The four "strands" of reading, writing, speaking, and listening became the focus for *Language Arts for Today's Children* (1954) and *The English Language Arts in the Secondary School* (1956).

## THE PROBLEM OF IDENTITY

Throughout English teaching, the high school teacher has faced the problem of identity. Struggling under the dictates of college entrance requirements, high school English could not exert its independence. Caught up in progressive movements before and after World War II, English seemed to many to be no more than a tool in the service of other disciplines, especially the social studies. For many years local committees of English teachers had written to their national organization asking such questions as: What shall we do about grammar? What is the relationship of English to a core program? Shall we have separate courses in English and speech? How should the literature program be organized? What shall we do about radio, television, newspapers, magazines?

Each decade has brought new trends, but many questions have remained the same. Even the oldest and wisest English teachers can recall moments when they first asked these perennial questions: What am I really supposed to teach? Why am I teaching this? Will it do my students any good? The questions have been inescapable. Teachers who have tried to brush them aside for the moment have been faced by students who have asked, "Why do we have to learn this stuff?" "What good is it?" "Are we going to do anything important today?" And for the teachers who have managed to find the answer in class, there has been the returning absentee who has asked, "Did I miss anything important?"

In the decade of the 1950s, two pedagogical questions focused on identity: Should English continue as a tool subject in helping to meet the immediate needs of students? Should English assert itself as a "fundamental liberal discipline" and focus more vigorously on language, literature, and composition in the classroom?

Tired of doing a balancing act between curriculum makers who stressed life adjustment and those who stressed academic reform, high school English teachers were probably relieved when the NCTE, the Modern Language Association, The American Studies Association, and the College English Association held a series of Basic Issues conferences on English in 1958. For almost a decade many of their classroom practices had been severely criticized by such books as Bernard Bell's *Crisis in Education* (1949), Mortimer Smith's *And Madly Teach* (1949), Albert Lynd's *Quackery in the Public Schools* (1953), Arthur Bestor's *Educational Wastelands* (1953), Robert Hutchins's *The Conflict in Education* (1953), and Rudolf Flesch's *Why Johnny Can't Read* (1953). American education was also made to feel guilty about Russia's launching of Sputnik (1957). Why hadn't Americans put a rocket into space first? Was our educational system only second-rate?

The basic issues conferences stressed two points: that the English curriculum should center on subject matter, and that the curriculum should be "sequential and cumulative from kindergarten through the graduate school." The aim apparently was to give the most able students a solid subject matter background for college, and to make the subject matter also challenging to the less able ones. It is interesting to note that of the 28 teachers included, only three were from high schools, although several others were former high school teachers.[6]

The views of the basic issues conferences were given a considerable boost by Jerome Bruner's book *The Process of Education* (1960), which stated that "any subject can be taught effectively in some intelligently honest form to any child at any stage of development."[7] Stressing an inductive approach in which very young children could begin learning by discovery much as scientists do, Bruner developed the concept of a "spiral curriculum," which could carry students to increasingly complex and mature understandings.

Many English programs, prompted by Bruner's philosophy, went to extremes that seemed almost by design to overlook the importance of students in the learning process. Rather than to conceptualize English teaching in a way that made it even more relevant to the student—the most important person in the whole process—reformers proceeded to take English, *the discipline,* apart piece by piece, and then tried to design pedagogical spirals and inductive lessons that

THE TEACHING OF HIGH SCHOOL ENGLISH

would help teachers to teach those pieces to children scientifically. It was not enough to look at pieces previously isolated as reading, writing, speaking, and listening. High school students studied grammar by examining structured jabberwocky, and by going about with tape recorders collecting samples of spoken English, generalizing about these samples in class, and writing descriptive rules based on personal conclusions. Many students studied lexicography by compiling their own dictionaries. Students also approached literature as mini-scholars trained in the ways of the "new criticism" to read closely and to explicate the text. Specialists in English were busy trying to create a whole generation of specialists in English.

In fairness to the many sincere and effective teachers in this movement, it should be noted that their teaching probably broadened students' understanding of language; it may have even intrigued a few. Some language programs, like those developed at the University of Minnesota, did indeed carry the promise of building greater appreciation and understanding of the nature and uses of English. But in too many cases the intensive study of linguistics and literature often intimidated teachers, who took crash institutes simply to survive in the new world of "New English." Even more regrettable is the fact that some of these teachers intimidated their own students by thrusting much of this new information at them in lectures and assignments.

Inquiry after inquiry in English, especially in linguistics, soon resulted in many more things being disassembled, questioned, and labeled in the classroom. When faced by three grammars rather than one, some school systems tried to teach all three. The result was great confusion for many students. During an evaluation of a school that taught all three grammars in the mid-1960s, one of the authors of this book discovered that students couldn't answer the question, "What is a grammar?" One girl said that when she was in junior high, she thought she had started to know what grammar was, but then her first high school English teacher told her she had learned the wrong kind.

The greatest renewal of scholarly interest in high school English in the 1960s came through the huge federally supported research and curriculum-making enterprise called Project English.[8] At no other time in the history of English teaching had so many college professors and so many high school teachers worked together in so many institutes, summer workshops, and high school classrooms. Language, literature, and composition—which made up the academic tripod—were structured in syllabus after syllabus, guide after guide. It was a time for structuring the unstructured and restructuring the structured; models, charts, tables, and other constructs appeared frequently. In spite of so much external structuring, Project English advanced the profession in many important ways. It brought school and college teachers much closer to understanding each others' goals and circumstances, created much more intellectual curiosity about English as a subject, and gave English teachers much more confidence as researchers and experimenters. On the other hand, some of the resulting projects placed too much faith on subject matter alone. Most high school teachers know that to do so is to be naive. There is nothing inherently wrong with designing programs that teach subject matter to students; problems arise, however, when structures imposed by the discipline do not take into account, or may even impede, a student's very personal approach to learning. In effect, subject matter cannot always determine method in teaching.

It must have become increasingly clear to teacher-scholars of the 1960s that the times were wrong to build a subject matter model for English curriculum. Social and political unrest was causing dissent and violence. In November 1963 President Kennedy was assassinated; in June 1968, Senator Robert Kennedy, presidential candidate, was also assassinated. In April 1968, Dr. Martin Luther King was assassinated, and racial violence rocked 126 U.S. cities. U.S. involvement in the Vietnam War further divided the nation. In the words of John Gardner, at that time Secretary of HEW "Today all seem caught up in mutual recriminations—Negro and white, rich and poor, conservative and liberal, dove and hawk, Democrat and Republican, labor and management, North and South, young and old." It was a time for introspection and exhortation; it was a time to examine one's humanistic consciousness, to speak out against injustice, inhumane acts, and violence. English teachers turned to thematic units that explored the alienation of youth, justice and injustice, civil disobedience, the consequences of war, and the rights of minorities in the society. Against such a background, subject matter content lost some of its momentum in determining teaching method. The personal and social problems, needs, and interests of students again became central in teaching. If English teachers could "turn students on" by appealing to their strongest concerns and interests, perhaps students would want to improve their English skills. In 1966 English teachers in America took a close look at the British model, which concentrated more on students' growth than on subject matter, and felt encouraged as they returned to student-centered thematic and topical units, minicourses and electives. Elective programs flourished, English teachers apparently unmindful that back in 1936 their predecessors had reached the conclusion that "under the elective system, students go through school with the most scattered and lopsided views of life. . . ."[9]

## THE PROBLEM OF CREDIBILITY

The 1970s could be called the age of disenchantment. Soaring inflation, economic recession, unemployment, crippling taxation, a decline in the hard-work ethic, a widening gap between management and labor, a decline of responsibility as brother's keeper or as "good Samaritan," an increasing sense of personal alienation and helplessness, increasing evidence of polluted food and a polluted environment, depletion of traditional energy sources, increasing violence in the streets and schools, and a declining faith in the institutions of law, government, school, marriage, and family, are just a few of the many concerns that tended to lower the morale of many citizens.

It is difficult for average citizens to know how to halt inflation, reduce unemployment, effect more equitable national taxation, or bring about honesty in the national government. But citizens do know how to reduce local taxation and to exercise greater control over local education. It is at the levels of state, county, city, and town that citizens can register their vote of no confidence in the "system." It is here that they can refuse to fund more than the "basics" in local governments and schools; it is here that they can insist on accountability for money spent.

In the early 1970s it became very clear that taxpayers were not going to support bond issues to pay for new buildings, social services, and more teachers. In fact, school boards found that they could not easily get the funds to renovate older buildings. Teachers who resigned or retired were often not replaced. Thousands of new English teachers found that school systems could not afford to employ them. Some schools played the game of taking the most promising beginner among hundreds who applied for the same opening, and then letting this person go before being tenured so that another very promising beginner could be employed at the lowest salary possible. Teacher morale declined sharply, and teachers' organizations—also hit hard by inflation—acted much more aggressively in behalf of teachers, and mounted increasingly ingenious membership drives.

The public also attacked school programs with greater vigor. When reports of declining scores on standardized tests were highly publicized in the press, the public challenged elective programs, "open" classrooms, "liberal" teachers, "controversial" books, the teaching of "values," and a host of other practices and materials that they felt stood in the way of basic education or threatened traditional beliefs in God, home, and country.

## LOOKING BACKWARD TO BASICS

During the late seventies, and early eighties, English, like other subjects in the high schools, faced a difficult dilemma. The people demanded a more solid, more "basic" education, and better qualified teachers; in short, they wanted a stronger program. But they were unwilling—reportedly unable—to pay for it. School boards that would not pay higher salaries for the best qualified teachers among the thousands without jobs asked administrators to economize even further by trimming all extras, "frills," and "nonessentials" from programs. Some demands, as the following list illustrates, went far beyond restricting content and method:

1. Emphasis on reading, writing, and arithmetic in the elementary grades. Most of the school day is to be devoted to these skills. Phonics is the method advocated for reading instruction.
2. In the secondary grades, most of the day is to be devoted to English, science, math, and history, taught from "clean" textbooks, free of notions that violate traditional family and national values.
3. At all levels, the teacher is to take a dominant role, with "no nonsense about pupil-directed activities."
4. Methodology is to include drill, recitation, daily homework, and frequent testing.
5. Report cards are to carry traditional marks (A, B, C, etc.) or numerical values (100, 80, 75, etc.) issued at frequent intervals.
6. Discipline is to be strict, with corporal punishment an accepted method of control. Dress codes should regulate student apparel and hair styles.
7. Promotion from grades and graduation from high school are to be permitted only after mastery of skills and knowledge has been demonstrated through tests. Social promotion and graduation on the basis of time spent in courses are out.
8. Eliminate the frills. *The National Review,* a conservative journal, put it this way: "Clay modeling, weaving, doll construction, flute practice, volleyball, sex education, laments about racism, and other weighty matters should take place on private time."
9. Eliminate electives and increase the number of required courses.
10. Ban innovations (a plague on them!). New math, new science, linguistics, instruction by electronic gadgets, emphasis on concepts instead of facts—all must go.
11. Eliminate the schools' "social services"—they take time away from the basic curriculum. "Social services" may include sex education, driver education, guidance, drug education, and physical education.
12. Put patriotism back in the schools. And love for one's country. And for God.[10]

This list tells teachers not only to place the highest value on facts, but also to stop short of allowing students to question facts critically or to use them to discover or support concepts. The human condition as treated in literature is to be avoided. So is imaginative, divergent, creative thinking. What, then, is left? Does the teacher stress memorizing rules of grammar and identifying and labeling sentence parts? Memorizing lines from literary classics, also authors' names and titles of their major works? Writing or reciting stock book reports? Reading plays by turns around a class? Diagramming sentences, "covering" a "clean" literature anthology, holding oral spelling bees, lecturing to students period after period, or covering themes with red ink? Does the teacher give longer homework assignments and lower grades simply to make the community believe that English is again difficult? Teachers of English have followed that path, and they have found the going dull and unproductive.

## FOOTNOTES

1. John Franklin Brown, *The American High School,* New York: The Macmillan Company, 1917, p. 13, quoting from ''New England First Fruits,'' in *Old South Leaflets,* No. 51, p. 2.
2. Arthur N. Applebee, *Tradition and Reform in the Teaching of English: A History,* Urbana, Ill.: NCTE, 1974, p. 22.
3. ''Varied Patterns of Approach in the Teaching of Literature,'' *English Journal* 28, May 1939, p. 342.
4. P. 288.
5. P. 309.
6. Applebee, p. 218.
7. Jerome Bruner, *The Process of Education,* Cambridge, Mass.: Harvard University Press, 1960, p. 13.
8. Finally responding to requests from the profession for federal support, the Congress in 1961 authorized the Cooperative Research Branch of the Office of Education to administer limited funds for English under Public Law 531. Funding was later expanded. The first director of Project English was J. N. Hook, who was followed by Erwin Steinberg, John Gerber, and Lewis Leary.
9. *A Correlated Curriculum,* p. 1.
10. Ben Brodinsky, ''Back to the Basics: the Movement and its Meaning,'' *Phi Delta Kappa* 58, March 1977, p. 522.

# 2

---

## THE
## TEACHER
## AND
## THE
## TASK

## WHAT MAKES A GOOD ENGLISH TEACHER?

During the mid 1960s, a research team of nearly 20 specialists in English and English education spent two and a half years studying the English programs of 158 high schools in 45 states to find out why during a five-year period students from half the schools had won the NCTE Achievement Award but students from matched schools also "highly regarded in their regions" had not won this award. In addition to analyzing questionnaires from 1331 teachers and 13,291 students, project directors led a team of 17 observers who made 306 on-site visits to all 158 schools.

Two characteristics finally emerged at the top of the list: the intellectual climate of the school, and the quality of the English teachers. Apparently, as far as English teachers were concerned, the first characteristic depended upon the second. The final report makes this observation: "The successful English programs seem to rely on a nucleus of outstanding English teachers who inspire the greater number of mediocre or nondescript members of the department."[1] Professional competence, dedication, enthusiasm, and professional interest in the subject and in the students—qualities that these teachers clearly demonstrated— apparently set the intellectual tone for colleagues and students.

This fact was not surprising when it was verified in the 1960s; nor would it be a surprising fact if found today. The effective teacher is still the most significant factor in the high school English program. What makes a good teacher? In the opinion of the authors of this book, the following qualities are essential ingredients.

### HUMAN QUALITIES

English teachers deal with people in teaching literature, in instruction in language, in guidance to students as they put together sentences, paragraphs, and longer pieces to communicate with people. But English teachers hope also that students develop as *humane* persons who will care about the well-being of others. It is this kind of humaneness which the teacher must teach by example. The teacher "teaches respect by being respectful; humaneness by being humane; reasonableness by being reasonable; and truthfulness by being truthful."[2] In setting such examples, the teacher is not in any way teaching secular humanism; the teacher is concerned about the welfare of human beings, and seeks to make a contribution to the betterment of society by helping students to develop as persons of goodwill, not just as efficient readers, writers, speakers, and listeners.

In accepting this kind of role as humanist, the English teacher should not act superior to students in any way. Only through an accident of chronology is the teacher older, more experienced and better trained in some one phase of knowledge. Every student in the classroom is better informed concerning some subjects than is the English teacher. Humaneness therefore also depends upon humility.

## RESPECT FOR ONE'S WORK

Although always ready to grant that the work of others can be equally significant, the successful English teacher nevertheless has a deep sense of the value of teaching. The English teacher does not teach commas simply because the course of study says to do it, or teach Shakespeare because Shakespeare is always taught in English, or teach oral English in anticipation of avoiding lessons on days when students make speeches. Students know which teachers respect their work and which teachers do not. In reflecting on his experiences in high school English, a college freshman identified two types of teachers. His former teachers will be called Mr. Jones and Mr. Smith, but the rest is in the student's own words:

> *I learned much more from Mr. Jones than I did from Mr. Smith, because Mr. Jones worked for the class. Mr. Smith didn't. Many times Mr. Jones let students hand a paper in three times; Mr. Smith didn't. Mr. Jones talked to me about my plans for the future; Mr. Smith talked to me about "Saturday Night Live" [a TV show]. Mr. Jones prevented a student from failing by helping that student in his spare time; Mr. Smith didn't. Mr. Jones scolded the principal for bringing his paycheck during class; Mr. Smith scolded the principal for bringing him his paycheck ten minutes later than usual. Mr. Jones cared; Mr. Smith didn't.*

## RESPECT FOR HUMAN DIFFERENCES

Most English teachers today do not need to be reminded to respect people who are unlike themselves. The point here is not to generalize about whether the nation is a melting pot, a salad, or a pluralistic society; rather it is to accept each student as an individual, to avoid generalizations, and to help that individual to realize his or her linguistic, humanistic potential. Teachers sometimes find themselves teaching students whose economic, social, cultural, and ethnic environments seem like alien worlds. The resulting dismay and confusion is a kind of "culture shock." Teachers frequently find themselves teaching students who do not seem to value learning. Faced by more students who won't learn than who can't learn, the teacher encounters a kind of academic shock. Teachers also find themselves teaching students who are in some way handicapped and therefore need special help. Faced by the challenge to do everything possible to "mainstream" these students—that is, involve them as actively as possible in learning activities with other students—the teacher can feel also disabled. But in working with such great diversity—whether it is cultural, educational or physical—the teacher must overcome feelings of inadequacy. Special knowledge and training will help, but the teacher must first respect the worth of the student as a person who has the right to an equal opportunity in education.

## ADAPTABILITY

John Holt has written,

> *What children need, even just to make a living, are qualities that can never be trained into a machine—inventiveness, flexibility, resourcefulness, curiosity, and, above all, judgment.*[3]

Students' success in developing such qualities clearly depends in part upon having teachers who possess the qualities. And many teachers do. They do not simply move through a routine of pouring knowledge from their own brimming pitchers into the students' cups.

In short, the successful English teacher is adaptable. Perhaps one teacher grew up in New York City and is teaching in Littleville. Another was born on a Nebraska farm and is teaching in Los Angeles. Possibly the school has had three different principals in the past three years. Maybe at nine o'clock the teacher has had a class of mainly college-preparatory students, and at ten o'clock a class of ninth graders who read a simple poem by John Masefield the Incomprehensible. The day before the big game, the teacher can relate some of the items in the lesson to the only topic that at the moment interests nine-tenths of the class, and yet help the students to learn as much as usual. When the class mood is a happy one, the teacher can be happy too, and when war or death or other shadows emerge from the nebulous world that students often successfully ignore, the teacher can be interested in hearing students' opinions.

Every teaching and learning act is an experiment. As with scientific experiments, teaching has its design, its form, its structure. But also like the best experiments, it must be constantly willing to test untested assumptions, and it must not claim results before they are certain. Every teaching act has its uncertainty, its risk. A teacher must accept the uncertainty of teaching and be willing to do a little fishing. Robert Hogan explains it this way:

> *Sometimes we are fishing. We don't know if we are going to catch any-thing, or what it is we will catch if we do make a strike. Today we are going into a class with our gear: "Stopping by Woods" and a couple of questions we hope will spark a discussion which will enliven for the students and ourselves the experience of that poem. After school, we'll stop by the lounge with our fellow fishermen and swap stories about how it went and maybe we will trade suggestions about bait and try again tomorrow. Next week I am going hunting—I am going to try again to set up a discussion in which 90% of the students (that is, except for two incurably shy ones and Georgia, who is still living through her private hell) will respond relevantly to the comments of their classmates (90% of the time) and loud enough for everyone to hear (100% of the time) with a minimum of intervention from me (their comments to exceed mine by at least four to one.) But tomorrow—tomorrow I am going fishing. Because to teach English is to spend part of one's time fishing.*[4]

Of course successful fishermen know that conditions must be favorable for fishing. A fisherman may not be able to change the weather to create ideal conditions, but a teacher can do much to create a classroom climate most favorable for the kind of fishing Hogan describes.

## ALERTNESS

Related to adaptability—prerequisite to it—is alertness. The successful teacher is physically, mentally, socially, and politically alert. Being on the alert is being constantly alive, constantly aware of possibilities. It is seeing, not simply look-ing at; it is listening, not simply hearing; it is doing, not simply verbalizing. And it is constantly testing one's own potentials, as well as those of students, through constant experimentation in teaching and learning.

Teaching is a cognitive activity, and it is an imaginative activity. But it is also a moral activity, a social activity, and a political activity. The English teacher must be alert to all that this implies. Unfortunately, some teachers are not this alert. In extreme cases, their classrooms might be compared with ice cubes frozen in a tray. English can indeed seem to be unaware of the outside world, even unaware of what is going on in other English "cubes" in a school. This metaphor somewhat exaggerates the problem, for in many schools it is far from the truth. But many English teachers are not alert to the intellectual, imaginative, moral, social, and political contexts and implications of English teaching. The question "What does this have to do with anything?" is certainly not answered by simply opening a textbook, a syllabus, or a planbook. These things can, when taken too seriously, draw English too much into itself. A few years ago, the

American Association of Colleges for Teacher Education addressed itself to the problem of preparing teachers for the "real world." Where should teachers be if not in the real world? It is when they try to make unreal worlds for themselves and their students that they and their students become most vulnerable and are in greatest danger of becoming confused and injured by abuses of language in the real world.

An alert teacher is more likely to be an honest teacher, and honesty is much needed in the classroom because it is much needed everywhere else in the real world. To be alert is to learn; and the more the teacher knows, the more inclined the teacher will be to encourage different points of view and to avoid half-truths or superficial, convenient, didactic answers.

## SENSE OF HUMOR

The teacher, being truly human, has a sense of humor. Learning is apparently something like digestion. A person digests more readily if mealtime is enjoyable, but if a person is tense at meals, food causes indigestion. A classroom is similar to a dining room; the teacher is the host.

So the successful teacher says in effect, "In my classroom, smiles will not be unholy or laughter blasphemous. I'll try to be good fun in class. It's a happy coincidence that *human* and *humor* are so much alike. What lifts human beings above the other animals? A musician may say that it's musical ability, a scientist may say that it's the ability to think inductively and deductively, a linguist that it's flexible use of language, a minister that it's religion, and a historian that it's knowing the events of the past. But American adolescents and their teachers know that humans truly became human the first time they ever laughed at anything more subtle than another's misfortune. It's human to have a sense of humor. A class shouldn't become riotous, but a few laughs per day do any class good. And the teacher, too. As somebody once said, 'He who laughs—lasts.'"

## PROFESSIONAL ATTITUDE

The capable teacher is professional in outlook. That means dedication to the profession of teaching English. It means wanting to improve the profession, to help others who are in it, and to bring other capable persons into it. It implies trying to improve working conditions in the profession but not whining about them or boasting about how much money could have been made in industry. Being professional means subscribing to professional magazines, attending worthwhile professional meetings (without using out-of-town meetings mainly for socializing, shopping, and sightseeing), and backing worthy professional activities. It includes following a carefully formulated code of professional ethics. And it means regarding English teaching as a means of enriching the minds and spirits of youth.

It also carries the responsibility of explaining, not arrogantly justifying, the goals of English teaching to the public. Marjorie Farmer offers some suggestions for communicating "with the plain, everyday public—in plain everyday English." She says,

> *Talk to the parents of your students, talk to your students and to the members of your community. Write letters to the editors of your local newspapers. Write articles for periodicals that serve a general audience, as well as for the profession and the scholarly journals. Make phone calls to your local talk shows when literacy education is being questioned—not only to defend our position, but to clarify, to inform, and to learn. Volunteer to speak on education at meetings of community groups. Write to your federal, state, and local legislators about providing adequate support for education. Serve on committees of your local [NCTE] affiliate. Run for office. Talk to school board members. Talk to taxi drivers. Persuade. Inform. Convince. And listen, read, reflect on what others are saying about our work. . . .*[5]

## ACADEMIC AND PROFESSIONAL QUALIFICATIONS

Even though personal qualifications are important, no one can deny the need for a well-stocked mind and for familiarity with educational principles and procedures. Professor Ralph Boas, writing in the *English Leaflet* long ago, commented, "There is something fatal about the human mind which particularly affects teachers, so that all too often one finds enthusiasm and vitality without any sound basis in scholarship, or else pedantic scholarship without any real imagination or human sympathy."

Like Professor Boas, you no doubt have observed many instances of the dichotomy of which he spoke. But you have probably not been so unfortunate that you have failed to meet teachers who combined praiseworthy personal qualities with exact and extensive knowledge and with ability to share that knowledge. They are the blue-ribbon teachers in our profession.

In 1976 the National Council of Teachers of English published *A Statement on the Preparation of Teachers of English,* which defined English "not only as a body of knowledge and a set of skills and attitudes but also as a process, an activity—something one does (i.e., one uses and responds to language, in a variety of ways in a variety of contexts)."[6] Pointing to "affective values of English" as stemming from a "new conviction" of English teaching in the 1970s, this statement lists seven desirable attitudes that an English teacher should reveal in the classroom and in work with individual students. Respect for individual students and for their language, and a willingness to help students to "grow as human beings" by helping them to "increase their power to use and respond to language both creatively and responsibly," become unifying elements in this list. In addition to having these attitudes, an English teacher should be aware of changes in the teaching profession and of changes in the world at large. The teacher's knowledge should include language acquisition, analysis of discourse, composing processes, reading, literature, nonprint media, resources for teaching, language in society, curriculum design, testing, and research. A teacher's goal in planning, organizing, teaching, and evaluating in the classroom should be to help students to "create discourse" and "respond to discourse" as effectively as possible.[7]

## THE TASK

### CONCEPTUALIZING THE TASK

Several theories exist among English teachers as to the nature of the task. The most catholic of these is the *carpe diem* theory. In brief, this says that any task involving the use of language is apropos and may be introduced at any time that seems suitable. "The idea that 'English' includes whatever one does with language (maybe even whatever one does with symbols)"[8] characterized many of the elective programs and "open classrooms" during the early to middle 1970s. Arthur Daigon defines the task through defining English as *anything*.

> *English is anything, yes anything, that requires disciplined employment of the language, for speaker, or writer, or reader, or listener. To claim the valid domain of our subject is English itself is, to me, absurd, for certainly we must English about something. To teach literature well, for instance, we must deal intelligently with a myriad of supposedly non-English disciplines. When we talk of human behavior, or mores and motives, of stereotypes and precedents, of passions and values, we are talking psychology, sociology, anthropology, history, and philosophy. . . .*[9]

According to this view, the task is to employ any material, any method, any idea, and any issue that will "increase insights into the vital areas of living." It is assumed that increased interest "in themselves and in the worlds they perceive" will lead students to "improve proficiency in manipulating language and other media." "Why bother with literature at all?" proponents ask. The traditional statements of English impose upon students much that does not interest them. The title of one article sums up the task: "Hook-Up, Plug In, Connect: Relevancy Is All."[10] Rather than to impose upon students what they *ought* to know, the teacher should begin first with what they *want* to know" and . . . worry about what they *ought* to know later."

20                          THE TEACHING OF HIGH SCHOOL ENGLISH

Related to some extent to the *carpe diem* theory is the *personal growth* theory applied widely in British schools and employed with less success in American schools. The task is essentially to provide a rich environment and then to get out of the way and allow the student to grow. "Growth through English" is essentially up to the student, but the teacher is always a supportive resource person and respondent. John Dixon describes the task in this way:

> *In an English classroom as we envision it, pupils and teacher combine to keep alert to all that is challenging, new, uncertain and even painful in experience. Refusing to accept the comfortable stereotypes, stock responses, and perfunctory arguments that deaden our sensitivity to people and situations, they work together to keep language alive and in so doing to enrich it and diversify personal growth.*[11]

The personal growth model is both student-based and experience-based; the task is to confront students with the experiences of life and to encourage discourse about those experiences. To quote Dixon again, "Each pupil takes from the store what he can and what he needs. In so doing he learns to use language to build his own representational world and works to make this fit reality as he experiences it."

Another theory holds that the English teacher's task is to improve *communication*. Communication is divided into two parts:

**COMMUNICATION**

| *Sending* ↔ Thinking ↔ *Receiving* |
| --- |

Each of these is in turn subdivided:

**COMMUNICATION**

| *Sending* ↔ Thinking ↔ *Receiving* | | | |
| --- | --- | --- | --- |
| Speaking | Writing | Listening | Reading |

This four-part division does not necessarily mean, though, that each section will be equally emphasized in the classroom. Thinking, often called the fifth language art, bonds all four parts together as a meaningful process. Reading is broadly enough defined to include the reading and study of literature, to which some proponents of the communication theory would devote perhaps as much as half of the time. Writing and speaking both involve study of the language (as do listening and reading), but because writing skills seem to take longer to develop than do speaking skills, teachers tend to devote more attention to the language of writing. However, those who support the communication theory are wary of spending much time studying *about* language. Consequently, they often tend to neglect substantive study of language (its history, dialects, etc.).

Defining communicating as "overcoming a differential between sender and receiver," James Moffett raises some interesting points about the process. He distinguishes between the processes of decoding (listening and reading) and encoding (speaking and writing); and he places coding at three levels: conceptualization (experience into thought), verbalization (thought into speech), and literacy (speech into print). He says that the "really difficult learning issues will be at the level of verbalization, where meaning is involved, not at the level of literacy." "Schools," he stresses, "should focus on thinking, to match thought with speech, and verbalizing, to match mind with mind." The productive and receptive activities should be better balanced in schools, he points out. The problem is the "bias toward reception." "One obvious reason for this imbalance," he explains, "is that students' production of discourse cannot be uniformly programmed, processed, and tested the way that material fed into students can be." Much more emphasis, he says, should be given the productive activities of speaking and writing (i.e., *making* discourse, and putting thoughts into language).[12]

The *tripod* theory says that instruction should encompass language, composition, and literature as equal partners in the English curriculum. Language includes study of such things as history, grammar, usage, semantics and "doublespeak," lexicography, and dialectology. Composition refers especially but not exclusively to written work. Literature means literary materials, not today's newspaper or an article in *Popular Mechanics*. During the 1960s, especially in institutes for teachers, this tripod theory was emphasized, and until the Dartmouth Conference shifted the focus of English from content to learner, it was the focal point for much curricular revision.

In mathematics, unified field theory refers to a concept of Albert Einstein concerning electromagnetism and gravitation. We may borrow the term for English to designate the belief that English is and should be a unified field, addressed to enhancing students' experiences with and through language, and using those experiences to gain insights into themselves and the society in which they live. The definition of the unifying force, however, has been debated. Some professional leaders argue that language or rhetoric is the unifying force, and that English curriculum should be language-centered, whereas others assert that literature should be the center. Those favoring the emphasis on language or rhetoric advocate intensive and extensive study of the English language, much writing on language topics, and much literary study concerned with the author's use of language and rhetoric. Those who favor a literary center contend that writing should be mainly on literary topics, and that students may best improve their use and appreciation of language by wide and deep reading. Despite such differences of opinion, though, the belief that English is a seamless garment rather than a mixture of three or four or many things has attracted considerable attention.

## THE POINT OF VIEW OF THIS BOOK

It is not intended here to arbitrate among these theories, and indeed they are not mutually exclusive. A teacher may be in a school where the departmental philosophy is essentially any one of the five, or some combination of them; or there may be no clear philosophy.

Any one of the five could support successful teaching and learning; conversely, any one of the five, if abused, could lead to poor teaching and very little learning. The first, stressing as it does the employment of *anything* that could motivate the student to listen, speak, read, and write (not necessarily in that order) seems to call for considerable teaching skill and experience, as well as broad knowledge and many available resources. The personal growth model is the foundation-stone of much modern instruction in England, and it has attracted attention in the United States since the Dartmouth Conference. Like the *carpe diem* approach, it demands special teaching skill and suggests the need for various resources. The communication approach involves of course more than the simple sending and receiving of "messages"; it involves "formulating thought into words" and "interpreting words into thoughts." At its highest levels, it demands, in Moffett's view, "the utmost in intellectual activity." This approach also demands much of the teacher and the students; as in the case of the other two, aimless openness could lead to its downfall. The last two theories mentioned differ from one another more in emphasis than in essentials. The tripod theory pays relatively little attention to speaking and listening, much to literature and written composition and language as subjects for intensive study; the unified field theory says that speaking, listening, writing, and reading may all be studied through their common denominator, language or rhetoric, or through their common greatest exemplification, literature. The tasks that these theories suggest focus on the subject matter of English. Overzealous teaching of subject matter can usurp the student's right to be an active learner.

The point of view of this book is somewhat eclectic. It may be summarized as follows:

1. English is one of humanity's tools, not important in itself. (Similarly, a hammer or a space rocket is a tool made by humans, important only when it is used.) The importance of a language lies in its use for determining and furthering the ends of an individual and of society.
2. Objectives for English-learning are necessary. Lack of objectives is aimlessness. Whatever objectives there are must focus primarily on the student; they

must also stress the interaction of student and content, of student and student, of student and the society in which the student lives.

3. Planning is better than planlessness. But plans should never be so tight that they admit no flexibility; the concept of serendipity should be clear in every teacher's mind.

4. The functioning of the English language should be given daily attention, sometimes as a thing in itself, often as a key to the clarity and effectiveness of composition and literature.

5. Students should be encouraged to read and discuss the best literature they are capable of understanding reasonably well.

6. Students should have regular practice in *using* the language through a planned but flexible sequence of oral and written compositions. Knowing about the language is important. But using the language effectively is far more important.

Although this book does not advocate any theory that places interest in subject matter above the interests and needs of students, it discusses the English teacher's tasks in detail under the headings of reading, literature, composition, language, listening, speech, and film and other media. Such categories are still preferred by most English teachers when speaking of the tasks of teaching and learning in the classroom, so they are considered apropos here. A few introductory remarks about these tasks appear in the pages that follow.

## THE TASK OF TEACHING LANGUAGE

### Determining the Purposes of Linguistic Instruction

When, in past centuries, Latin was the center of the curriculum, a Latin teacher assumed a rather clear-cut responsibility: teaching students to conjugate verbs and decline nouns, translate from Latin into English, and compose in Latin. Hour after hour was given to reciting *hic, haec, hoc,* and the like.

For many years English instruction was strongly influenced by the Latin procedures. Despite the fact that English differs from Latin in being largely uninflected, students laboriously conjugated verbs, declined nouns, and parsed sentences—parsing consisting mainly of detecting everything detectable about each word, as well as a few things that had to be accepted on faith. The process was largely useless and purposeless, but teachers *assumed* that such kinds of drill taught students what they needed to know about the language.

The conjugators and the parsers have almost disappeared, but a few of their replacements are little less sinful. These are the teachers who believe, or act as if they believe, that definitions and identification are the chief purposes of language study. Their students learn to parrot the textbook definitions: "A sentence is a group of words expressing a complete thought. The subject of a sentence tells what the sentence is about.'' The students identify, identify, pinning labels on every word.

> *Theirs not to reason why.*
> *Theirs but to do—or try.*

More enlightened teachers, steadily increasing in number, recognize two basic reasons for teaching the English language, one cultural and one utilitarian. The cultural reason is that language is a uniquely human possession. Through its use people have attempted to express their emotions, their strongest beliefs, their highest ideals. With it they have learned to inform and to deceive. It can be as descriptive and interpretive as a painting, as beautiful and moving as music, as sky-reaching as architecture. Knowledge of the qualities of language is essential to cultural roundness and solidity; the person who does not know them has a gap in education that knowledge of no other type can fill.

The utilitarian reason for teaching the English language is that the nation's work, the world's work, is dependent upon language. No type of industry or occupation listed in the yellow pages of the telephone book could long survive without language. The coming of automation and computers, the reduction of the number of blue-collar workers, and the even greater increase of white-collar employees have made clear and accurate use of the language even more essential than before. The promotion of a person is now quite often dependent upon how well he or she communicates.

Every English teacher has the task of spelling out the details of these purposes and of examining the content and procedures of the work in language to make sure that they are relevant to students' goals.

## Teaching How Language Works

Definition and identification reveal relatively little about the language, although obviously a knowledge of basic terms makes it easier to discuss sentence elements. Especially needed is manipulation of words, phrases, and clauses. Such manipulation, involving the rearrangement of the sentence parts and the substitution of different words and constructions, can do more than anything else to show students the changes in meaning and emphasis that are possible (See Chapter 8 of this book.)

Part of the manipulation consists of work in semantics. Sentences are shifted from reportorial language to affective (emotional), and vice versa. Denotations and connotations are studied. The omnipresent role of metaphor is discussed.

In addition, a study of the history of the language helps to reveal pertinent characteristics of today's English. For example, knowledge of the medieval shift away from numerous inflections tends to clarify why word order is now so important. The growth of complex sentences, replacing many simple and compound structures, has led to the possibility of more precise expression today. The addition of progressive verb forms has lent further enrichment. Most dramatic of all, at least from the students' point of view, is the steady growth of vocabulary through the centuries, with borrowings from every continent and almost every nation.

## Choosing a Grammar

A grammar is a system that describes how the language works—its sounds, word forms, and word groups. Three or more systems of grammar and a number of variations of each are available to today's teacher. These differ as to purpose and emphasis. Traditional grammar, with its eight parts of speech and Latin-derived concepts and terminology, is still the most familiar variety. It is still favored because teachers cling to the hope that somehow, sometime, traditional grammar will improve students' speaking and writing. Faced by cries for ''basics,'' these teachers use traditional grammar as a kind of security blanket. Structural linguistics stresses the language of speech as primary, with the written language as a derivative; instead of parts of speech it describes four form classes and about a score of kinds of function words. In teaching this grammar, teachers usually urge students to practice the sounds and patterns that structural linguists have described. Through ''pattern practice'' and ''substitution drills,'' they have encouraged students to imitate this observed linguistic behavior. Students are taught to assign a label to a word only after noting that the word does indeed appear in the structural ''slot'' which carries that label. Generative (or transformational) grammar in its early stages was based upon the assumption that most English sentences are transformations of a few basic ''kernel'' sentences. Later theorists differentiated ''surface structure'' and ''deep structure,'' the latter holding that one's intuitive sense of structure as a native user of the language guides transformations from deep to surface structures. The process of generating verbal structures from thoughts involves a sense of choices and possibilities, based on concepts of *how* one can express thoughts in English.

Grammarians investigate and describe the structural features of language. Each grammar, therefore, has its own descriptive system, its own reason for being, its own integrity. English teachers often become frustrated when grammarians or scholars of grammar refuse to suggest ways in which the effective use of language might be taught through teaching a particular grammar. But why should they expect grammarians to do this? A modern grammarian is interested in describing language, not prescribing it. This is where the rift occurs. Teachers have by tradition been prescribers; they have wanted to tell students how to improve. If a grammar is not prescriptive, a teacher will try to make it prescriptive. Thus, the temptation to reduce both structural grammar and trans-

26

formational grammar to sets of rules. As with traditional grammar, teachers have tended to teach these newer grammars deductively from rules to examples.

Research studies show that, in general, teaching grammar in the schools has not significantly improved the writing and speaking of students, yet the pragmatic teacher still wants to help students to make these improvements. Should the teacher abandon all instruction in grammar? No, grammar describes how English works; by studying it, students can at least realize that their language is systematic. Also, the promise of helping students to use English more effectively may still exist for a teacher who stresses these approaches: (1) teach grammar *inductively,* by encouraging students to observe the way language works and by helping them generalize about it; (2) stress the constant making and building of sentences, exploring with students the possibilities available in English; (3) Draw from any English grammar a term, description, or insight that will give students the best chance to visualize how English works. The task described by these statements calls for skill in inductive teaching and for considerable knowledge about the several English grammars.

## Understanding Dialect, Usage, and Other Things about Words

The English teacher has the task of helping each student to understand the fact that he or she has an idiolect and a dialect, and that there is nothing inherently good or bad or right or wrong about differences in these. An English teacher should not attempt to eliminate any of these differences, but rather to give students truthful information about them so they will accept them as interesting characteristics of their diversified and changing American English language. Teaching about dialects, then, has much to do with eliminating negative attitudes and myths, and establishing positive attitudes and verifying facts.

Usage is a matter of choice. A writer or speaker can put *don't* or *doesn't* in the same position in a sentence. There is nothing *wrong* about a usage that is not considered appropriate by the majority of society's leaders and by those who make a living writing and speaking through the mass media. Anything not considered ''standard'' by such people is not wrong; however, they do not consider it appropriate. Problems arise when a speaker uses words that are not understood by the listener, or that seem inappropriate, even offensive. Another task for the teacher, then, is to help students to understand that they will sometimes need to make adjustments in their language in view of their purpose, their audience, and the occasion. This is quite the opposite of telling students that anything goes. To tell students this, is to tell them an untruth. The present attitude suggests two tasks: to help students to become well informed about dialect and usage and to help them to speak and write clearly, effectively, and appropriately (i.e., to use the language that works best in view of purpose, audience, and occasion).

THE TEACHER AND THE TASK

27

*Vocabulary*

Students usually enter school fascinated by words. It is unfortunate that for many this interest diminishes. To a very significant extent, the teacher is the key. The task is clearly to do everything possible to interest students in words. The teacher can do much to create the kinds of classroom climates that will expand vocabulary. New words become most meaningful when they come from new experiences; vocabulary expands as experiences vary and expand. The movement from experiences to thoughts to words should be kept alive with activity.

Knowing words is also knowing about their power to influence thoughts and actions. A teacher should help students to become more aware of the power of words. Words can serve as the means to accomplish whatever ends the speaker or writer wishes to accomplish; thus, they serve persuaders of all kinds. Especially abusive to clear thinking and effective communication are those words and expressions used to conceal the truth (see ''Doublespeak,'' Chapter 9). Teachers should encourage students to develop word consciousness as a part of the concern for the welfare of all human beings.

## THE TASK OF TEACHING COMPOSITION

''Composition'' is defined here to include both oral and written attempts to convey information, opinions, or emotions. It covers both factual and imaginative presentations. It includes the mechanics of paragraphing, punctuating, and capitalizing, and it considers morphology, syntax, and semantics to the extent that they affect communication. It also considers the human content of composition—the personal expressions of voice, point of view, thought, creativity, and style.

### Helping Students to Find Something to Say

Good teachers of English have always been concerned at least as much with substance as with mechanics, but in the past few years the insistence upon solid content has steadily increased. No longer is a student's paper given a top grade simply because it has no misspellings, poor sentences, or solecisms; top grades are reserved for papers that say something significant, that say it clearly and convincingly. Significance and authenticity are much more likely to come through when a student knows and cares about a topic.

Students who complain that they have nothing to talk or write about are usually those who are not interested in a topic or who have never learned to marshal their resources for attack upon a topic. They stare out the window and finally turn in a blank or nearly blank paper. A skilled teacher makes certain that all students *can* write or talk about a topic, whether it is assigned or chosen. The teacher motivates the students to want to express themselves.

A first task for the teacher is to help students to learn to uncover in their own minds, or in other sources, whatever bits of information are relevant. Most students also need help in developing their own sense of voice and point of view. They need to realize that they have experiences, knowledge, and attitudes which permit them to look at a topic in ways that the teacher cannot legitimately view it. They also have feelings that will lead them to select words which the teacher would not select.

To help a student build this kind of authenticity and confidence as a writer-person, the teacher may need to meet with the student briefly from time to time to ask questions such as, "What do *you* know about this? *How* do you see it? How important is this to you? How important should it be to your listener or reader? How do you *feel* about it? Do you want to say this to a certain listener or reader? What are you *really* trying to say?" Students often need to respond to such questions as these in order to choose topics that are significant to them and are focused enough so they can accomplish their purpose with imagined listeners and readers. Teachers often say that the biggest tasks are helping students to find something personally significant to say, and then helping students to "get their heads straight" about the possible ways of saying it most effectively. Knowing that this is done best through a one-to-one approach, teachers organize some class sessions as writing "labs," so they can move from student to student to offer help when students need it most—*as* they move through steps in the composing process.

Helping students to find something to say often begins with <u>providing experi-</u>ences that will stimulate authentic feelings, thoughts, and especially beliefs, which the students will want to speak and write about. Films, pictures, posters, guest speakers or performers, incidents acted out by students, discussions of literature, literature read interpretatively, debates, music, pantomime and creative dramatics, discussions of incidents at school or in the community, sounds, objects to feel or taste or smell, provocative articles and editorials from magazines and newspapers, and the creation of other kinds of compositions (such as collages, mobiles, and slide-tape presentations) can all provide experiences which will generate ideas.

Experiences that pose problems are especially helpful. For example, students might find descriptive writing more interesting if shown an object which they can't identify. If they don't know what it is, they can't describe it by simply calling it by its name; they must look closely. "Primitive" objects used by people in past generations (an old boot jack, a butter mold, a hand corn planter, a cherry pitter) will often serve this purpose. Students can be asked to describe the object clearly enough that a reader who does know what it is could identify it. In another exercise, students can describe buildings or street intersections in their city or town, or places in their school, clearly enough that other students who have been there can identify these structures and places. The "What Is It?" paper, which describes something but does not name it, forces the student to use descriptive language.

## Teaching Principles of Organization

The tail light of an automobile doesn't belong in front; a spark plug isn't inserted in the exhaust pipe. The parts of a composition can be put together as methodically as the parts of an automobile. The effectiveness of the whole, even its clarity, depends in large measure upon the arrangement of the parts—the organization.

Teachers have used "process" papers to help students see the results of poor organization. In writing such a paper, the student describes a process which another student is to perform by reading the paper. It might be to assemble something, take something apart, perform a pantomine, or simply to get out of a seat, walk across the room, do something, return to the seat, and sit down. When each paper is put to this test, good or poor organization becomes immediately apparent; accuracy, clarity, legibility, detail, and punctuation are just a few of the other qualities that this exercise will stress.

In assisting students with organization, the teacher's role is again that of questioner, listener, and responder. Some students find outlining useful, but they usually need help in sorting out their facts and ideas as they construct the outline. A teacher must remember, however, that not all students are helped by this process. Many writers, even professional ones, must write first, not only to discover what they want to say but how they want to say it.

## Teaching Structure and Style

Within the framework of the good composition, the sentences march or trip toward an inevitable conclusion. In the poor composition, they plod or stumble or wander or reverse themselves.

The teacher's task is to help the student to see that each sentence can make its contribution to an entire paragraph, and each paragraph its contribution to a larger unit. Each clause, phrase, or word, each figure of speech, serves a purpose. Correctness of spelling, punctuation, verb forms, and the like is taught because incorrectness detracts from the receiving of the message; the message is of major importance, and nothing must be allowed to prevent its reception. Sentence structure is taught because not all possible forms of sentences are equally good for all purposes. Style is taught because some structures and some words are appropriate for certain purposes but not for all. Transitions are taught because they are signposts that remind the reader of what has been said and help the reader to anticipate what will be said and how it will be said.

Some teachers think that the best way a student can learn this kind of information is by listening to lectures or by reading handouts or pages in a grammar and composition book. This is not true. Short lectures, illustrated with interesting examples and followed by a class discussion can be somewhat helpful on occasion. So can readings. But students do not learn writing best by hearing about it or reading about it; they must *do* it, and they must be able to talk about what they

THE TEACHING OF HIGH SCHOOL ENGLISH

are doing when the problems of discovery, arrangement, and all the rest are immediate and pressing. The task of teaching structure and style cannot be accomplished very well from the front of the room, nor with assigned readings, nor with red ink. The teacher must get out among students, asking questions, listening, responding, and offering suggestions that focus on immediate problems. Teachers have not found this easy to do, but most who have tried it have become more skillful in perceiving problems and asking the best questions on the spot. Students who work this closely with their teachers generally write with much stronger involvement.

## THE TASK OF TEACHING READING AND LITERATURE

The English teacher's task as a reading teacher falls mainly within developmental reading, and extends somewhat into corrective reading. As a teacher of developmental reading, the English teacher tries to help each student to read as effectively as possible those materials normally assigned in English. This involves teaching vocabulary, sentence structure, and literary styles and forms; helping students to read for details, relationships, main ideas, and implications; helping them to adjust their reading rates to their purposes and to the different demands of different materials; and encouraging them to be much more active readers.

Obviously many students need special help before they can accomplish goals implied by the tasks just outlined. Many enter secondary schools with severe reading deficiencies. For a variety of reasons, they have not learned some of the most basic skills of word attack, their reading vocabulary is inadequate, their experiences in reading have been narrow and discouraging, and their attitudes are poor. They have been told countless times that they cannot read well enough and they believe they never will be able to do so. Sullenness, uncooperativeness, and disruptive behavior have served as their defense mechanisms for several years. Although these students will not acknowledge it, many of their protestations are cries for help.

Through more careful diagnosis, some individualized instruction, and a positive attitude, the English teacher can help many poor readers to reach their potentials. Offering, high interest reading materials on a reasonable level of difficulty is only one of many kinds of help an English teacher can give the handicapped reader.

A teacher's individual help is extremely important, but so is participation in classroom activities and discussions. Class participation can broaden the experiences which handicapped readers will take to the reading that they are able to do. Even visually impaired students can benefit from such participation. But the teacher cannot just stand by and hope that a physically handicapped or learning-disabled student will join in. Mainstreaming will do little good if the current is too swift, if handicapped readers are allowed to languish in placid pools, or, worse yet, if they are allowed to stay on the bank. Many handicapped readers fear rejection by other students more than rejection by a teacher. The English teacher must have a serious discussion with any student who rejects a poor reader who may wish to participate or who is asked by the teacher to participate with others.

Teaching literature is teaching reading. Effective instruction in literature can turn many nonreaders into readers and many poor readers into excellent readers. The reverse is also true. Ineffective instruction in literature can rob even the most able students of any desire to become serious readers.

There are of course many approaches to teaching literature. No clear proof exists to indicate that one approach is better than the other. The best teachers do not stick by one but use several in accomplishing the task. Each has merits if used judiciously, but each can be deadly if used exclusively day after day, month after month. Six basic approaches are defined briefly below:

1. The *historical,* in which the emphasis is upon the author and the background of the selection.
2. The *sociopsychological,* which emphasizes the social and psychological aspects of the selection.
3. The *personal,* which stresses the personal experience that a reader has with a selection and tries to preserve the integrity of the personal response.
4. The *value-seeking,* which considers the moral or other values of the selection.
5. The *cognitive,* which attempts to uncover the meaning(s) intended by the author.
6. The *analytical,* which attempts a study of the selection on the basis of its literary characteristics.

Whatever the approach, the primary goal of teaching literature is always pleasurable reading for students. The teacher is a resource person, a guide, a listener, a responder, who shares literature with students. Together the teacher and the students try to become sharper observers of life as revealed in literature. It is through such keen observations of life's realities in literature that students have the best chance of developing a personal sense of the qualities in a selection that can stimulate their minds and give them pleasure.

## THE TASK OF TEACHING LISTENING

Much is said about developmental reading, but little if anything is said about developmental listening. Listening, like reading, is a receptive skill. The listener, like the reader, can translate experience into thought on several levels. For example, the listener receives details (who, what, where, when, how many, what kind), sorts them out, senses relationships (This caused that . . .), generalizes (This means . . .), and considers applying these personal generalizations to future

32

thoughts and actions. Many years ago W. W. Hatfield, in the *English Journal,* pointed out other similarities:

1. Purposeful listening, like purposeful reading, is more successful than that which is without purpose.
2. Listening, like reading, is of various types, each of which must be mastered through practice.
3. Careful listening, like careful reading, involves attending (giving one's mind) to what is being communicated.
4. Semantic dangers (problems in word meaning) are even greater in listening than in reading.

Preoccupied as they often are by teaching literature, English teachers would do well to realize that there is far more to teaching English than meets the eye.

## THE TASK OF TEACHING FILM AND OTHER MEDIA

Years ago, a film was considered just an audiovisual aid. Many English teachers today can recall badly worn films of *Julius Caesar, Pride and Prejudice,* and *A Tale of Two Cities,* with their streaks and scratches and their wailing sound tracks. It was almost miraculous if one of these brittle and much-mended films ever made it through without breaking again and again. When ordered, they often arrived long after the original selection had been taught. The best teachers showed them reluctantly or sent them back unopened; the worst teachers used them as interludes and fillers. Filmstrips, which were more likely to belong to the department, usually provided background material to literature or examples of how to punctuate a sentence.

Film history, the film as art, the film as literature, and film-making have not gained general acceptance as high school subjects. Nevertheless, the use, study, and making of film have gained somewhat. During the early 1960s, English teachers became more interested in film as a vehicle for expression; they began to acknowledge its artistic integrity, its forms, its rhetorical techniques, and its ability to reveal life to the listener and viewer. For two decades, English teachers have experimented with film as *experience.* Short films, often without sound, have provided the stimulus for class discussions about feelings, conflicts, convictions, and actions as aspects of human experience and behavior. Teachers who have recognized film-making as a composing process have invited students to express their ideas by writing scripts; by using light, angle, and distance to establish mood and to suggest theme; and by editing the whole to create greater unity. Teachers who have witnessed abuses of both language and thought in many commercial films have used these films in lessons on semantics. Teachers who have sensed the dangers in drawing unsound inferences have used such films to stimulate critical thinking.

*T.V. influences*

No other form of media is now so pervasive as television. The educational impact of childrens' programs, the violence of Saturday morning cartoons, and the persuasive power of commercials for toys and sugar-coated cereals exert great influence on children. People of all ages tend to use television more often than any other appliance in their homes. It has become an incredible force for change in the society. Leading news commentators are possibly more influential than top leaders of Congress. Some jury trials have been televised live. Candidates for public office reach millions instantly and simultaneously. Riots, coronations, funerals, religious services, assassinations, floods, tornadoes, hurricanes, and other significant events are brought into our homes. English teachers, then, must take up the challenge of helping students to evaluate the impacts of television as experience—to question the quality of programming, as well as its verbal and nonverbal messages. For teachers interested in semantics, television offers many rich examples.

Our simulsensory awareness of our whole multimedia environment warrants close attention. Surrounded as they are by cassettes and tapes, TV cable, computers, citizens' band radios, stereos, instantly developed prints and motion picture films, TV video recorders for home use, news and weather satellites for instant worldwide TV viewing, and many other devices, students have learned to respond in simulsensory fashion to the stimuli. This orientation is quite different from the linear one imposed by a classroom lecture or a book; often the two conflict. A student may attempt to listen to stereo records or tapes, watch TV, talk to a friend on the telephone or base-station CB, and complete an English assignment all at the same time. Some students will admit that doing all of this simultaneously is counterproductive, but many say that they *can* study best in the midst of loud, pulsating sounds from radio, stereo, and television.

*Discuss this?*

English teachers should be concerned about the possibly adverse effects of media on the reading habits of students. A student with a television set in his or her room may indeed lose interest in reading and develop generally ineffective study habits. Problems of this kind demand understanding and close cooperation among teachers, parents, and students. English teaching must make its own adjustment, though; teachers should not narrowly and stubbornly adhere to linear teaching techniques and linear instructional materials. If the media are producing different orientations to learning, and if students can learn effectively by electronic media, English teachers must experiment with film and other media, not as audiovisual aids, but as effective vehicles for communication.

## THE TASKS THAT ARE SHARED

Many of the tasks described above are best accomplished by a teacher who has considerable knowledge and skill in the teaching of high school English; some can be accomplished as well—if not better—by teaming up with teachers in other fields; but all depend on support from students, parents, school board members, and other professionals in the school and school system.

Expressions such as "every teacher is a teacher of reading" and "all-school English" should be taken seriously. Teaching reading cannot be the task of just a *Note!* reading teacher in a school—if a school is fortunate enough to have one. Teaching speech communication cannot be the task of the speech teacher alone—if the school is fortunate enough to have one. Teaching writing cannot be the task of the English teacher alone—even if the school is fortunate enough to have only English majors teaching the subject. It is only through mutual support and cooperation that English can accomplish its goal of helping each student to read, write, speak, listen, and think as effectively as possible.

This does not mean that every teacher *is* a teacher of English. The simple fact is that few teachers of other subjects know enough about language and literature to teach them. They have necessarily specialized in other subjects and have had insufficient time, even if they had the will, to master English in addition to their speciality. In two ways, however, the teachers of other subjects may and should reinforce the work of the English teacher, just as the English teacher is constantly reinforcing or supplementing their work. One of the ways is for these other *✗* teachers to let students know that they regard good English as important. They can insist on good organization, correct spelling, accurate punctuation and capitalization, and usages in accord with those most generally approved today. They can also encourage clear speaking and careful listening. Second, the *Vocabulary* teachers of other subjects have the responsibility of teaching the vocabulary, spelling, and special reading skills required by their subjects. They are responsible, for instance, for definition, pronunciation, and spelling of such words as *theorem, enzyme, appellate,* and *pizzicato.* The mathematics teacher is responsi- *Special reading* ble for instruction in reading an algebra problem—very different from reading a short story. The social studies teacher is responsible for instruction in reading graphs—very different from reading poetry. To such an extent every teacher may be a teacher of English.

---

 ✗ **THE IDEA BOX**

The Idea Box, which is found at the end of this chapter and each succeeding one, has three purposes: (1) To suggest teaching devices of proved worth, besides those discussed in the chapter itself; (2) to mention other aids, materials, articles, or books that offer additional help; and (3) for classes of prospective teachers to provide items (sometimes controversial) for discussion. A very large proportion of the articles summarized are in the *English Journal,* both because that magazine is readily available and because it emphasizes the practical as well as the theoretical.

As Louis Zahner once said, "... no classroom practice is sound unless it stems from sound theory and can be traced back to it." The practices in the Idea Box appear to be based on sound theory, though it cannot be claimed that all are of equal merit, and certainly some are controversial, or even contradictory of others. The Idea Boxes contain many more tactics and techniques than any one teacher can or should try. However, from the riches each teacher may select the ideas that best fit his or her temperament and the needs of the classes. What will work well for one teacher in one situation may work less well in other circumstances, but every idea presented here has been used successfully in somebody's classroom.

The items in the Idea Boxes following Chapters 2 and 3 are less specific than those in the rest of the book because of the broad topics of these two chapters.

### "TOWARD A NEW ENGLISH TEACHER"

Have English teachers taken Aristotle much too seriously and used a "half-brained approach" in teaching? G. Lynn Nelson of Arizona State University alludes to recent research which "suggests that the left brain perceives analytically, linearly, and logically," and that "the right brain perceives holistically, intuitively, and imaginatively." The "new English teacher," then, will find scientific support in seeking a balance and synthesis between cognitive and affective goals. The new teacher will not feel so compelled to choose between formal, basic instruction and informal, creative instruction. The best teaching will stress both.[13]

### WHAT MAKES AN ENGLISH TEACHER AN ARTIST?

Knowledge of the subject, breadth of general knowledge, knowledge of ways to organize and present subject matter, intelligence, creative ability, knowledge of ways to evaluate teaching and learning, and practice, practice, practice. These are the qualities which enable an English teacher to become not simply an artisan (or skilled laborer) but an artist who has deeply affected students—"... what they have learned has left an indelible impression upon their attitudes and behavior."[14]

### DO YOU REALLY KNOW WHO YOU ARE?

To be aware of style as an English teacher—hair style, clothing style, teaching style, life style—is to be aware of only the superficial, the surface. It is important for an English teacher to "be easy" with these superficial qualities and allow them to change. But to be truly "authentic," an English teacher must "move to the deeper levels of the self, through self-acceptance, self-confrontation, and self-prizing." A white teacher, for example, should have the same "quiet pride in his or her own tradition" as the black teacher in the black tradition. "If we can develop an easy assurance about our own worth, tempered with an awareness of our own frailty, we can avoid destructive pride and foolish defensiveness." The task, then, is to become not just a person as teacher, but a teacher as person.[15]

## THE ENGLISH TEACHER AS PR PERSON

Ken Donelson confronts the stereotype of English teacher as "hard-nosed, intolerant, red-pencilled, unsympathetic, asexual, frustrated, a bastard (or bitch) with impossibly high standards. . . ." and appeals to English teachers to do a "public relations job." The myths will persist unless English teachers "educate other English teachers about the changing role of English with today's students, and [educate] parents about their children, their reading, their needs, and their interests."[16]

## ELECTIVES REQUIRE MORE THAN A TECHNICIAN

The English teacher as technician is not very effective in planning and teaching electives. Convention and guesswork will not do; the teacher must strive to learn as much as possible about "the nature of response to literature, the composing process, and the nature of language learning." The teacher will need to develop expertise in planning: This means developing objectives which are "valid in terms of theories of the subject matter, appropriate to the interests and abilities of the students involved, and clear enough to permit the teacher to evaluate the effectiveness of instruction." The teacher will also need to know how to select and sequence materials to accomplish these goals. In the classroom the teacher should be a careful listener and an interactive guide. Finally, the teacher must evaluate the cognitive growth and the attitudes of students continually, and must engage in self-evaluation at every step. Elective programs have not freed teachers to be better technicians; they have freed them to be better teachers.[17]

## IS THE ENGLISH TEACHER AN INTELLECTUAL GUIDE OR A POLICEMAN?

A teacher who enters the classroom eager to excite students about Faulkner's writings may have to switch roles many times between that of intellectual guide and that of classroom executive, a critical director and supervisor of all classroom activities. Susan Edgerton claims that because these conflicting roles cause much anxiety for the teacher they should be studied more carefully by teacher educators and school administrators. Student teachers, she believes, should get a better "sociological perspective" on the many "debilitating problems and tensions" which can frustrate a teacher who is dedicated to "the pursuit of knowledge."[18]

## WHAT? MORE RESPONSIBILITIES?

As an English teacher with over 25 years experience, Ken Donelson admits that English teachers already face "an impossible task"; nevertheless, he lists 11 tasks among the many which a good teacher "ought" to do." Abstracted from his article, these appear below as a list:

1. We need teachers who are aware of incredible numbers of books of many sorts [adolescent literature, best sellers, regional literature, classics, etc.].

2. We need teachers willing to spend less time talking about the joy of reading and more time giving young people a chance to discover how much fun reading can be through electives or blocks of time devoted to free reading.
3. We need teachers eager and able to read material aloud.
4. We need teachers aware of real language controversies facing readers and speakers and writers now, *not* phony or manufactured issues.
5. We need teachers who recognize that more nonsense has been written about the virtues of knowing grammatical terminology for its supposed carry-over to reading and writing than any other area of English.
6. We need teachers concerned about the manipulative power of language to help young people understand how that power affects them.
7. We need teachers who teach composition, not assign compositions.
8. We need teachers knowledgeable about using films in the English classroom.
9. We need teachers who are equally unwilling to hold on to the old or to grab on to the new.
10. We need teachers who will carefully determine texts and supplementary materials in terms of the departmental philosophy, the needs and interests of students, the enthusiasms of teachers, and the community mores and practices.
11. We need teachers acting as individuals and acting collectively as a department who will be able to publicize and explain, not defend, the work of English teachers.[19]

## WHAT IS LITERATURE, AND WHAT SHOULD WE DO WITH IT?

Dwight L. Burton of Florida State University, a long-standing spokesman for the teaching of literature in high school, makes several important observations about teaching literature today. Films, tapes, slides, and other media can serve effectively as vehicles for nonprint forms of literary art, but these must not replace the original works of such writers as Swift, Hemingway, Donne, and Frost. Oral reading and improvised dramatic activities can heighten comprehension and awareness of effects. The study of literature is a rich springboard for noncritical writing, interpretive and critical writing, and imitative writing. All literature instruction is guided by one basic objective: "to lead students to experience literature as a way of knowing."[20]

## ENGLISH: NOT A SUBJECT, BUT A MEANS

G. Lynn Nelson sees the English teacher's task as addressing the problem of the adolescent's struggle toward the clarification of experience and the establishment of self-esteem. Literature study can help; so can writing. "Literature is man's attempt to sort out and to come to terms with the world of his experience and with his own place in that world." But our teaching and testing of facts about reading and writing only create a kind of pernicious anemia. We produce no students struggling to clarify experience; we produce only anemic readers and writers. "It is as if we were to put a great larder of food before hungry people, allowing them only to smell the food, and then have the audacity to test them on how it smelled—*and all the while they were starving.*"[21]

## UNILATERALLY DEVELOPED PROGRAMS ARE DOOMED TO FAILURE

An English program developed in isolation will never get off the ground. On the other hand, one initiated by teachers and their students and carried step by step through established administrative paths has a very good chance. Eight major steps to a successful program, as outlined by Ray Hancock, Chairman at Marion Senior High School (Illinois), are: (1) professional initiation (staff or supervisory level); (2) teacher-student interaction; (3) administrative sanction; (4) program budget (cost and extra funds); (5) the professional plan (formal proposal and program development); (6) school board consideration; (7) implementation; (8) program evaluation and review. Hancock's thorough discussion of each step is based on experience.[22]

## THEMATIC "CONTRACTS" IN JUNIOR HIGH

After using "thematic, integrated language arts contracts" in the junior high for several years, Shirley M. Jones reflects on their advantages and disadvantages. In September, all students in a particular grade worked on the same contract, which served for orientation and evaluation. After the teacher had surveyed their abilities in reading, speaking, and writing as they worked through this contract, she guided students in their choices of individual contracts from a set of 65. Students who had signed up for work that was obviously too difficult could "transfer credit for a part of one contract at a more reachable level." Advantages came through a higher interest in reading, integrated use of all language arts, appeal to students' interests, self-pacing of work by students, and much variety within a structured approach. Disadvantages came through less group interaction, some students feeling overwhelmed by reading the two or three books that each contract required, lack of consistency and persistency of skill development, and the enormous amount of time demanded of teachers.[23]

## A LITTLE GRAMMAR IS A GOOD THING

Believing that even the "new" grammar texts, if taught exhaustively to students, can present much information which is confusing and unnecessary in the schools, Mark A. Neville, former NCTE president, identifies how much is enough. Helpful "elementary knowledge" would include two basic features: sound and significant. In Dr. Neville's words:

> It will feature five simple sentence patterns, and their parts: subject, predicate, complement, and modifier. It will emphasize again and again that a word is a part of speech *only* when it is used in a sentence, thus eliminating such useless trivia as "*Gold* is a noun used as an adjective in the sentence, I have a gold watch." It will concentrate on the forms of pronouns and verbs and their uses so that future TV commentators will not feel uneasy in their uses of the personal pronouns in the nominative and objective cases, will use *myself* as a reflexive, rather than as a subject or object; and will gain mastery of the principal parts of verbs and tense forms, active and passive voice.[24]

## CAN EVERYONE SUCCEED?

"Mastery learning" is based on the assumption that "with the exception of a small minority of students with physiologically based learning problems, all children are capable of academic success as traditionally defined." "Mastery teaching" is designed to guarantee "mastery learning." The teacher expects all students to complete a unit of work successfully within a specified length of time. Any students who do not pass the unit test(s) are given "corrective" assignments and retested until *all* pass the work of the unit. Essentially, no student is allowed to fail.[25]

## "WHAT'S NEW IN ABILITY GROUPING?"

Very little. This is the view of Barry J. Wilson and Donald W. Schmits, who studied the research from the 1920s to the present and conducted their own survey of teachers' attitudes toward "homogeneous ability grouping." Using a questionnaire which was given to teachers in 1924 and again in 1929, the researchers found most teachers supporting the practice today, just as they did in years past. Two-thirds of the 100 teachers in the current sample, however, stated that they were not familiar with research on the topic. The implication is that although most teachers still favor such grouping, they know very little about it. The writers conclude that teachers may be influenced mainly by their classroom experience and by the apparent logic of ability grouping. The conclusion from reading the literature is that research shows no convincing proof that ability grouping is conducive to learning.[26]

## DOES TELEVISION VIEWING PRODUCE POOR READERS?

Yes, it does, concludes Jackie S. Busch, who studied the TV viewing habits and reading habits of 595 students from grades two through twelve. "In most respects," her study agreed with one done by Wilbur Schramm in 1961 on 6000 children. Some benefits occurred in early grades, especially in vocabulary, but most students reached the saturation point by age twelve. By the seventh grade, TV begins to have a negative effect. In the Busch study, high-ability students turned their attention briefly from a book to a TV program but continued reading. Low-ability students, however, became totally absorbed in TV programs, and "for the most part, found reading boring and tedious." Eighty percent of the low-ability junior high students in this study said, "If it's on television, it must be right." Eighty-five percent of these low-ability students said that "there was no point in reading a story if you could see it on television." High school students, regardless of ability, agreed that "most people are too lazy to read a book" and "enjoy seeing the story."[27]

Unfortunately, parents do very little to limit the TV viewing of older children. The "Ninth Annual Gallup Poll of the Public's Attitudes Toward the Public Schools" reported that in 1977 parents of children age 12 and under were evenly divided on limiting or not limiting TV viewing time, but that 70 percent of the parents of children 13 years and over placed no definite time limit on viewing.[28] It is interesting that parental supervision declines just at the point when TV viewing can be most detrimental to reading improvement, especially among low-ability students.

## LISTENING AND AUDING

Allen Berger and Anne Werdmann of the University of Pittsburgh describe some classroom activities to stress *listening* (which refers to anything we can hear) and *auding* (which refers to recognizing and interpreting spoken symbols). The authors have arranged these under the first letters of the words *listening* and *auding*. Consider each abbreviated item below an open-ended invitation to use your imagination to create a useful lesson:

### LISTENING

*L*istening signs placed around the room can promote awareness.

*I*nterference can be used to advantage by having students list all of the sounds that distract them during the day.

*S*timulate interest in a unit on sounds. . . .

*T*ape record sounds to provide practice in listening.

*E*xperiment with responses to music.

*N*oises of all types can be reproduced by the students and categorized according to type, source, distance, and effect.

*I*nventing sound stories provides practice in using sounds creatively.

*N*ovel use of puppets and flannel boards can enhance attentive listening.

*G*ames provide interesting practice in listening.

### AUDING

*A*ssemble a book of stories and poems written and illustrated by the students as outgrowths of listening activities.

*U*nderstanding feelings accompanying messages. . . .

*D*irections given orally provide useful practice in attentive listening.

*I*nterpretation of films can be used to further creative listening.

*N*ews reports from radio and TV provide models of speaking and reporting techniques.

*G*oal setting can be used to develop conversational skill and courtesy.[29]

## FOOTNOTES

1. James R. Squire and Roger K. Applebee, *High School English Instruction Today,* New York, Appleton-Century-Crofts, 1968, p. 21.
2. Ronald T. Hyman, *Ways of Teaching,* 2nd Edition, Philadelphia, J. B. Lippincott Company, 1974, p. 26.

3. "Why We Need New Schooling," *Look,* January 30, 1970, p. 52.
4. "On Hunting and Fishing and Behaviorism," in *On Writing Behavioral Objectives for English,* J. Maxwell and A. Tovatt, eds., Champaign, NCTE, 1970, p. 129.
5. "The Imperative for 1978—Communicate," *English Journal* 67, January 1978, p. 21.
6. *English Education,* Summer 1976, p. 197.
7. Edward R. Fagan, "Guidelines and Geodesic Domes," *English Education,* Summer 1978, p. 237.
8. "A Statement on the Preparation of Teachers of English," *English Education,* Summer 1978, p. 197.
9. Arthur Daigon, "The Curriculum Game," in *Challenge and Change in the Teaching of English,* A. Daigon and R. T. LaConte, eds., Boston, Allyn and Bacon, 1971, pp. 21–22.
10. Charles F. Greiner, *English Journal* 58, Jan. 1969, pp. 23–29.
11. *Growth Through English,* Reading, England, National Association for the Teaching of English, 1967, pp. 12–13.
12. James Moffett and Betty Jane Wagner, *Student-Centered Language Arts and Reading, K–13,* Second Edition, Boston, Houghton Mifflin, 1976, pp. 9–17.
13. *English Education,* Spring 1977, pp. 131–138.
14. Oscar M. Haugh, "A Portrait of the English Teacher as Artist," *English Education,* Summer 1978, pp. 247–252.
15. Allan A. Glatthorn, "Teacher as Person: the Search for the Authentic," *English Journal* 64, Dec. 1975, pp. 37–39.
16. "The Fear of English Teachers," *English Journal* 63, May 1974, pp. 14–15.
17. George Hillocks, Jr., "The English Teacher as Curriculum Maker," *English Education,* April/May 1974, pp. 238–248.
18. "Teachers in Role Conflict: The Hidden Dilemma," *Phi Delta Kappan,* Oct. 1977, pp. 120–122.
19. "Some Responsibilities for English Teachers Who Already Face an Impossible Job," *English Journal* 66, Sept. 1977, pp. 27–32.
20. "Well, Where Are We In Teaching Literature?" *English Journal* 63, February 1974, pp. 29–33.
21. "Toward Teaching English for the Real World," *English Journal* 63, Sept. 1974, pp. 45–49.
22. "Curriculum Change in English: A Process of Improvement by Cooperative Change," *English Journal* 63, April 1974, pp. 46–48.
23. "The Evolution of a Language Arts Program for Pre- and Early Adolescent Students," *English Journal* 66, April 1977, pp. 47–51.
24. "Instrumental English," *English Journal* 67, Oct. 1978, pp. 10–12.

25. Edward B. Fiske, "Mastery Teaching: Until All Are Caught Up," *The Education Digest,* Dec. 1976, pp. 5-7, condensed from the *New York Times,* Aug. 29, 1976.
26. *Phi Delta Kappan,* April 1978, pp. 535-536.
27. "Television's Effects on Reading: A Case Study," *Phi Delta Kappan,* June 1978, pp. 668-671.
28. *Phi Delta Kappan,* Sept. 1977, p. 45.
29. "Listening and Auding—Activities and Research," *English Journal* 67, May 1978, pp. 36-39.

# 3

## PLANNING—
## FOR
## THE
## YEAR,
## THE
## MONTH,
## AND
## THE
## DAY

## CONSIDERATIONS IN PLANNING

### PLANNING IS ESSENTIAL

Many people are familiar with the novelty sign THINK AHEAD. The word *Think* appears in large bold letters, and so does the beginning of the next word; but then, because most of the space has been used up, the last two letters are much smaller and dip downward abruptly in order to squeeze into the little room left. This sign is popular because it humorously reminds us of a common failing— starting out thinking we know exactly what we want to do, but then realizing a little late that we have not taken something very important into consideration.

Like the designer of the sign, an English teacher can encounter serious difficulties by starting out without much forethought. In fact, English teaching may contain more unknown factors than most other occupations. English is taught in many different settings; it is controlled by many different philosophies and points of view; and it is taught to the eager, to the not so eager, and to self-professed English-haters.

Some undergraduate English teaching majors are distressed to learn that English has no national blueprint, no master planbook, to guide a teacher. Later, as student teachers, they soon discover that because teachers use many different formats for their units and daily plans, models discussed in a college methods class or shown in a methods book are likely to be different from ones used by the experienced teachers who direct their student teaching. The truth is that an ideal curriculum, unit plan, or lesson does not exist in the profession. Nor does an ideal teaching method. Consequently, no evidence exists to show consistently that a certain kind of plan leads to the most effective teaching and learning.

44

As disconcerting as these facts may appear to the beginning teacher, they don't discourage experienced English teachers from planning in ways they think best. Few experienced teachers write a unit that details all activities for the next two or three weeks, and few translate units into detailed lesson plans. When they encounter new material, however, they often jot outlines, with directions and other annotations, in daily planning books; or they may make extra mental notes while driving to or from school, which they jot down later as reminders. Throughout their planning, many teachers may behave much as writers who, before putting ideas on paper, carry thoughts around constantly, walking them about and thinking them through. Teachers are more likely to write full units and extensive daily plans when contributing to a syllabus or a guide for their school or school system. All of this doesn't mean that they think beginning teachers should plan as they do. In fact, most who supervise student teachers believe that a beginning teacher *Note* should write rather detailed plans. Whether experienced teachers write notes and outlines or extensive units and daily plans, one fact seems clear: they consider planning to be essential, and they do it in some form constantly.

## PLANS COME IN DIFFERENT PACKAGES

Planning in secondary English takes place on several levels. It also stems from many kinds of needs and philosophies, and it takes many forms. National committees of English teachers occasionally write and edit curriculum materials. *Thematic Units in Teaching English and the Humanities,* edited by Sylvia Spann and Mary Beth Culp (NCTE, 1975) is one such example. Also published by NCTE with the help of English teachers have been *Aids to Curriculum Planning* (1973), which contains useful excerpts from some of the best state and local guides in the nation, and *Recommended English Curriculum Guides K–12* (1979), an annotated list. English teachers and curriculum coordinators within a *state level* state occasionally develop a state guide to give their colleagues different ideas and better direction for their own units and plans. A state English council or association may, with the help of a committee or the editor of its journal, issue special monographs or bulletins on curriculum planning. Examples are *Elective Programs in English* (1972) and *Some New Ways of Looking at the English Curriculum* (1973), topical issues of the *Arizona English Bulletin,* edited by Kenneth Donelson. Teachers in city or county school systems occasionally pro-*City- County* duce local guides and syllabuses. Most often these are done in local in-service workshops by groups of teachers selected by system administrators or by members of local English clubs and councils. English departments or groups of *Schools* English teachers within individual schools also plan together to improve their programs. It is at this level that the most effective group planning takes place. Teachers planning together within a community and a school they know well, for students they also know well, can produce plans that are especially effective and realistic. Also of course, individual teachers write plans of various kinds. In very small schools, only one or two teachers are responsible for the entire English program. Whether teachers are in a large school or a small one, though, they demonstrate some of the same behaviors as they plan. Some teachers revise old plans carefully and write new ones often; others rely heavily on "tried-and-true" units and daily plans, which they modify only slightly, if at all. Some teachers use only parts of plans published by school systems or by commercial textbook publishers; others follow such aids closely.

## PLANS ARE FOR STUDENTS

James Moffett and Betty Jane Wagner, in *Student-Centered Language Arts and Reading* K–13, make the following case for plans that demand more student participation and judgment:

> *Our traditional classroom has not had* **enough** *structure, in the sense of enough structures. One lesson plan for all each day, one sequence for all each year—that is not to structure* **more;** *that is simply to let a single structure monopolize the learning field. This monopoly prevents individualization and makes it difficult for learners to develop judgment, which requires that they be structuring in school, not* **structured** *by school. Structuring is choosing. Judgment is choosing. Comprehending, composing, making sense of the world—these are structuring. For one thing, we can't stop a child from structuring. (We have already tried it that way.) The wisest choice for educators to make is to place student structuring at the center of school life. School should be harder and more fun.*[1]

Flexibility in planning is essential if teachers are to organize learning environments that demand thoughtful and creative uses of language. To provide these opportunities, the teacher must, as Moffett suggests, have plans, not *a plan.* Learning is more likely to take place when students have opportunities to determine for themselves why they are acquiring certain skills or studying certain details, relationships, and main ideas.

## PLANS SHOULD BE FLEXIBLE

In view of the many difficulties that one teacher and over 150 students encounter in trying to accomplish expected goals in just one week, it is no wonder that many teachers think of the planbook as a survival log, a place to map strategies to head off chaos, even anarchy. Teachers feel that they must think first of their sanity as they try to chart sensible and reasonable paths through the maze of grading periods, modules, minicourses, unscheduled assemblies, fire drills, intercom announcements, school-wide testing programs, yearbook picture-taking, band trips, Wednesday's schedule on Tuesday, shortened periods, eliminated periods, and so on. In spite of such changes and interruptions, English teachers are expected to show how well their students have learned a wide variety of facts, concepts, and skills from one grading period to the next throughout the year.

Because they are surrounded by so many things to teach in the midst of so much tumult, teachers are tempted to chop up everything into convenient blocks of time to guarantee that everything will be "covered" and tested in time to issue grades. This one-thing-at-a-time thinking gives rise to spelling days, vocabulary days, book report days, and to dividing a 15-chapter novel into a chapter a day for three weeks. It also creates the temptation to divide textbook content into as many daily lessons as time will permit. This in turn creates the need to be through nineteenth-century literature by April or *Romeo and Juliet* before Christmas vacation. One might suppose that only the inexperienced beginning teacher locks into this kind of revolving lazy Susan. The truth is that some experienced teachers do the same thing; these are the narrow-minded, the entrenched, the diffident, the uninterested, and the battle-fatigued teachers.

A bits-and-pieces plan is no plan at all. It does not allow the various aspects of subject matter to work together for the student. Literature is not the source for writing and speaking that it could become. Language study is reduced to the passive recognition of structures and rules for structures. An occasional book report takes care of individualized reading. Certainly it is tempting to break up English into small manageable bits that are taught to all students at certain times, but doing this does not take the students far enough into reasoning and critical thinking, and it does very little to give them the needed practice in using their language to say or write something personally meaningful. A bits-and-pieces plan also does not allow much room for individualized teaching and learning. Both teachers and students face problems; they make choices, and they need to communicate as effectively as possible. Both need the room to work toward solutions as individuals. They need the flexibility to choose and pursue their own alternatives.

Nothing about curriculum design guarantees flexibility. The most elaborate phase elective program can degenerate into a rigid curriculum. Team-teaching plans break down when team members see themselves as contributing specialists with no collective responsibility for helping students to see how and why their contributions fit together and point to important concepts. Large blocks of time can be easily chopped up into unrelated bits until the result is block-of-time blockage and a constipated curriculum.

In the interests of flexibility in planning, two tips seem especially valuable. First, teachers should be independent, resourceful, creative, and thoughtful, but not plan in a vacuum. They should consult texts, manuals, curriculum guides, and professional journals for assistance in making decisions. Further, they should participate frequently in shoptalk and in planning sessions with fellow teachers, and participate in professional organizations. Secondly, teachers should think more about what students can do to learn and less about what they can do to fill up the time during a class period. Some beginning teachers plan lessons like scenarios, complete with exactly what they think they should say to students. No wonder they panic when they finish lecturing 15 minutes before the end of the period, or when they hear the bell before they have finished the lecture or have given the assignment. Lesson after lesson acted out in front of the class might seem to a teacher to be a successful run of professional performances, but only two outcomes are certain: the lesson will wear out the teacher, and the students will wear out their seats.

## PLANS SHOULD HAVE CLEAR AND SIGNIFICANT OBJECTIVES

Before writing objectives, teachers should know what their individual students are already able to do. The process also begins with a clear vision of the kinds of behavior that these individual students should be able to demonstrate once they have reached their goals.

Most teachers in training have heard that considerable controversy exists over the language that should be used in writing objectives. Many administrators want "behavioral" objectives, which describe specific, demonstrable behaviors for individual students, not groups, and often include specific levels of mastery. Some teachers find such objectives presumptuous. To these teachers, the objectives seem to imply absolute guarantees of the stated performances. Other teachers may object to classifying human behaviors as though they can be learned and evaluated separately. These teachers also question whether changes in attitude and feelings, which are considered to be very important in teaching English, can be identified through observing overt behavior.

These points are well taken, but they should not prevent teachers from understanding the intent of the movement toward behavioral objectives. For years teachers wrote objectives without realizing that no one else reading them could visualize clearly what students were expected to accomplish. Traditional objectives, which used key phrases such as *to know, to appreciate, to understand,* could not be clearly pictured by the reader. How could anyone see knowing, appreciating, or understanding? Not all objectives should be stated in "behavioral" language, but those that can be phrased this way carry two advantages, provided they are done well: They establish clearer directions for instruction and they focus on the individual student in teaching and learning. (See IDEA BOX for two helpful books.)

Clarity is not very important, though, if the objective itself is trivial or counterproductive. The following objective probably isn't worth the effort to write it: "Given a list of the names of four leading English poets from the Romantic

period, and a scrambled list of representative lines from their poems, the student will correctly match all names and lines with 100 percent accuracy.'' The principal fault of this objective isn't its behavioral language; it is its insignificance. *yes*
Teachers should look at the writing of behavioral objectives which can be misused and abused. A list of trivial behavioral objectives doesn't necessarily prove that the form is at fault. Like other types of writing, an objective in any form should also assume a voice, have a clear purpose, be constantly mindful of the intended audience, be appropriate, be about something significant, and be clear and direct.

## PLANS SHOULD HAVE SOUND RATIONALES

The definition of a rationale may be clearer if we return briefly to an objective. As we noted earlier, an objective states as clearly as possible what a student should be able to do as a result of instruction. A rationale explains why it is important and valuable to the student to be able to do this. A teacher usually does not try to justify each objective separately in writing. Instead, the teacher will *For each* write a paragraph or two at the beginning of a collection of daily plans or a unit to *unit* explain why it is important for the students to be able to reach all of the objectives stated below. As anyone writes objectives, it is helpful to imagine that a student is asking, ''What good is this?'' or ''Why do I have to learn this?''

The process of fixing constantly on the value of objectives for students is complicated by the fact that people disagree about the importance of these objectives. Because most disagreements have more to do with teaching methods, student activities, and the subject matter content used than with objectives themselves, disputes arise more frequently over means than ends. A principal or a parent may ask why students are reading newspapers, writing plays, working in groups, reading ''occult'' literature, or making a film.

In anticipation of such questions, a rationale would explain the value of the objectives for *students,* and then could go on to explain how and why the methods, activities, and selected content effectively assist students as they attempt to reach the goals. If done well, statements of this kind are very useful because they state the teacher's position clearly, and they look at the student rather than the critic. When teachers, administrators, parents, and school board members look at students together rather than at each other during controversy, their chances of helping the student improve greatly. When disagreements arise, there is only one focus: the student's best interests.

## A PLAN SHOULD BE WELL ORGANIZED

A unit or daily plan can include activities for a class, small groups, pairs of students, and individuals. Some activities can be done in common—with the entire class participating—and some can be individualized. Students can interact with a teacher, and students can interact with each other. Students can be told, and students can have the freedom to discover. The teacher can teach, and students can teach. Activities can be done sequentially, and they can be done simultaneously. Throughout so much variety, the teacher's role should still be clear: it is to guide students as effectively as possible toward the goals.

The most convenient approach of course is to organize all activities so students will go through them together. Most of us can remember an English teacher who frequently said, ''I'm afraid we have no time left for discussion. Take out your grammar books, please.'' Perhaps another teacher had a list such as this on the board for us as we walked into the room: (1) Be seated before the bell, (2) Take out homework: questions one through five, page 105 in anthology, (3) Discuss ''Walden,'' (4) Review for unit test, (5) All themes due Monday.

Now let's try to recall or imagine another class. Four or five students are working individually, six are working in three pairs, and the remaining 25 are in five groups. They are reading and discussing pieces of literature that range from poems to novels, and they will spend the remaining 30 minutes and all of their English periods for the next two or three days presenting, defending, reacting to, and adding to different points of view on the question of whether the American West was won, ravished, or stolen. One or two students will address the class and lead a discussion. Each group will attempt to show that the position taken by another group is or is not valid. A pair of students will support or counter the position made by a group by presenting evidence gathered in the school library. Throughout the process, students will share diverse views found in numerous pieces of fiction and nonfiction, and they will have pooled their thinking. They will reach a number of generalizations. These activities might generate debates, argumentative essays, investigative papers, original poems and short stories, and a slide-tape documentary complete with composed and edited commentaries. Further critical reading, critical listening, and face-to-face interaction could result from their sharing so many views.

The major differences between these types of classes should be fairly clear. In the first two examples, the class moves on schedule from one activity to the next. This is generally a closed system, although it could provide some opportunities for individuals to do assigned tasks. The other class is more open and more flexible, and many activities go on simultaneously. Both are directed by the teacher, but in the second one students have wide choices as they work toward objectives in ways and with materials that interest them. The first moves much more quickly toward objectives. Evaluation will probably be more objective in the first class than in the second.

These differences should not indicate to a teacher that the choice in planning is always between tight linear plans with predetermined goals and ''open'' plans with considerable freedom and the likelihood of undetermined outcomes. Planning and teacher direction are essential in all successful teaching and learning. There is nothing inherently restrictive about activities in a linear order. Nor is there anything inherently chaotic about activities in an ''open'' arrangement. Weaknesses lie in extremes and routines. Sometimes teachers should ask students to move on to another activity. Whole classes should occasionally work on sequenced activities together. But students must also have frequent opportunities to explore and to make their own decisions. There is freedom in discipline, and discipline in freedom. Teachers must allow students to discover this fact as they learn.

## PLANS SHOULD INCLUDE APPROPRIATE EVALUATION

### Diagnosis

Faced with five or six classes—perhaps 130 or 180 students—the beginning teacher may feel a temporary bafflement. How can a teacher get to know these young people? How can a teacher know who they are and what they need to learn? *about the learner*

The principal's or counselor's files will probably yield some information concerning the age, background, academic records, test scores, and so on, of most of the students. It is usually inadvisable, though, to spend much time in studying these records until one gets to know the students fairly well in class. The mere reading of 100 or so sets of data will leave no clear impression about individuals unless one is already somewhat familiar with each student. Therefore, except for a brief preliminary examination of the records, the files may be ignored for a few weeks. Then, if the teacher wishes specific information about individuals, he or she may ask permission to consult the files again. What the teacher finds there should be taken with some salt, however, and should not be regarded as final.

For example, the file may show that freshman Dan had difficulties in passing some of his subjects in the seventh and eighth grades, that his IQ is 97, and that disciplinary action was once taken when Dan stole a hand calculator. To the teacher, Dan has seemed a pleasant, well-behaved boy who is capable of doing at least average work. In this instance, the teacher's judgment may be more reliable than the recorded comments and statistical data, for the simple reasons that data aren't always accurate and that adolescents change rapidly. Perhaps Dan, in a moment of adolescent irresponsibility, did steal a calculator; he should not, however, be regarded as a confirmed thief whose every movement must be watched. Perhaps his IQ is slightly below normal, but psychologists today are aware that IQ test scores are not entirely reliable and that IQ may change somewhat over a period of years. The process of growing up may have caused Dan's troubles in eighth grade English; perhaps now he is mature enough that these troubles are lessened. In other words, data of the sort usually found in the principal's office need to be supplemented by personal observation; these data may be of considerable value at times, but they should never lead a teacher to decide that one student is hopeless, that another is a genius, or that a third is doomed to mediocrity.

The advice just given is of great importance. Studies made in the late 1960s suggest strongly that students tend to live up to teachers' expectations. Students whose teachers have been informed that they are capable of making great strides often do make great strides. Other students, whose teachers are told that they are "hopeless," often do act as though they have no hope, and they accomplish little. The teachers' pre-established attitudes ("prejudiced" attitudes in the etymological sense of prejudging) are frequently revealed unintentionally or unconsciously to the students, and they tend to react in the ways that the teachers have shown they are expected to react.

Within a classroom the teacher has a number of ways of learning about individuals. The teacher should learn students' names quickly, for obvious reasons. Sometimes the easiest way to do so is to make a temporary seating chart at the first class meeting. Fifteen or 20 minutes' homework studying each chart plus a quick review before class can help a teacher to call each student by name in a few days. Group work or writing "workshops" or "labs" will get a teacher out into the class among students during the first days. In these closer face-to-face contacts with individual students, the teacher should make a point to use each student's name as often as possible. The students will be pleased that they have so quickly lost their anonymity; they will be happy that they are not addressed as "the boy in the green shirt" or "the last girl in the row" or "yes, you"; and they will immediately gain respect for the teacher.

After learning students' names, the teacher may begin making mental notes of individuals' characteristics. The notes are for the sake not of classifying but of understanding. Thus the teacher may note that George seems sullen in class and rather hostile toward the other students; the teacher will then be on the alert to discover the reasons for George's attitude and eventually to plan a strategy to make him more cooperative. Just making a point to say, "Hi, George," as he passes in the hall or as he enters the classroom, may help. Helen, another student, may appear to be unusually intelligent and well informed but possibly a "loner." The teacher may search for ways to involve Helen in small group work and in class discussions so that her intelligence can benefit both Helen and the rest of the class.

How a student talks, reads aloud, or listens is important. How willing a student is to contribute to class discussion, what information a student brings to class from home or neighborhood, how the student reacts to a literary selection—all these are important bits of evidence. Particularly valuable is noting what and how a student writes. In a page or two of a student's writing, one can find much more than the fact that the student does not know how to punctuate or to spell "there."

THE TEACHING OF HIGH SCHOOL ENGLISH

One may discover ambition, hopes, fears; much background; glimmerings of a *autobiography* developing philosophy of life.

Besides learning about students from administrators' data and from observation in class, the teacher may—and should, whenever time permits—talk with the students individually. The subject of conversation is relatively unimportant; it may be about schoolwork, but it may also be about football or clothes or microcomputers or anything else. From such conversation the teacher may draw valid conclusions that will help in planning and teaching.

## EVALUATION

The word *evaluation* stirs images of "pop" quizzes, which check up on reading progress; short-answer questions on authors' names, titles, dates, literary terms, quoted passages, literary background, periods, genres; words and phrases to underline and to identify; essay tests, which often appear as part of a unit test or semester examination; oral and written book reports; themes and research papers marked up with red ink. Such images appear because these are the traditional evaluative instruments that have been used for decades by strong teachers, mediocre teachers, and weak teachers.

We know, however, that the effectiveness of any test depends mainly on the knowledge, insight, and talent of the teacher who constructs it. A "pop" quiz does not have to serve as an ax; it can ask a stimulating question and produce answers that will support excellent class discussion. Not all short-answer questions need ask for regurgitated facts; a teacher can use short-answer formats creatively. Multiple-choice questions can ask students to find comparisons, contrasts, and cause-and-effect relationships; they can also be used in pairs or in sequences of three or more to test progressive thinking toward solutions. Blanks, which are used in the Cloze Procedure, can test the student's ability to use contextual clues in literal and figurative passages. A true-false choice can direct the student to a pair of multiple-choice questions that ask the student to select the statement closest to expressing his or her reason for making that choice. The same back-up can be required after a student chooses "agree" or "disagree." Choosing among options in a multiple-choice item can take the student to another part of the test where that choice leads to another set of questions. In this way, a kind of dialogue is set up between the student and the test as the student takes positions in search of a valid generalization. The procedure might be similar to branching in programmed instruction. Worksheet formats don't have to ask for underlining and identification of "parts of speech." They can invite students to make choices in language, as in sentence combining, or to build original sentences and compare them with model sentences which have been built using the same instructions. Videotapes and audiotapes can serve as vehicles for questions.

Groups or individual students can give book reports that are not restricted to author's name, title, plot, most exciting incident, and a personal commendation. Writing can vary as to type, length, purpose, tone, formality, audience, and other matters. A piece of writing can be written for one kind of reader and then rewritten for another.

English teachers should of course try to develop new testing instruments. The question should not just be "What behavior can I test with a test item I have used many times?" but just as often, "What kind of test item can I change or invent to truly test this kind of behavior?" Sometimes the teacher can adapt a test format generally used outside the field of English. Inventories and questionnaires provide useful information about students' experiences and interests. Semantic differential scales can be used to determine changes in attitude before and after instruction. Individual students can use checksheets to evaluate and record their own progress throughout units of work. Using descriptions of observable behavior expected at various points during a unit, a teacher can develop checksheets to guide observations and to provide useful descriptive data.

In addition to improvising and adapting, the teacher should also try inventing. One of the shortcomings in evaluation is that teaching produces cognitive and attitudinal changes which existing English tests do not measure effectively. In class, students often discover methods of inquiry in reading literature; they should have a chance to demonstrate these skills on tests. Unfortunately, many creative teachers who use inductive methods to progressively "test" a student's skills of inquiry throughout class sessions later fall back on traditional mastery tests which measure only knowledge of facts and predetermined generalizations.

Another shortcoming of evaluation is that once teachers post grades they often lose track of the student work that produced the grades. Consequently, they cannot examine the work later for signs of change. Students should be encouraged to keep samples of their work in individual folders, and teachers should review these folders from time to time to get a more thorough understanding of progress before issuing grades. Students can also dig into their folders frequently to improve their work and note their own progress.

## GRADING

The basis for evaluating the work of individuals is often determined by the administration. In some schools no student who attends class with fair regularity is permitted to fail. In others a grading curve must be followed by all teachers: perhaps 15 percent A's, 20 percent B's, 30 percent C's, 20 percent D's, and 15 percent F's. In such a system the top 15 percent must be given A's, even though some do not deserve this mark of distinction, or even though more than 15 percent have displayed consistent excellence; similarly, 15 percent must fail, even though they may have been fairly successful in reaching the objectives of the course. The inequities of this system should be obvious. In other schools, written comments are used rather than grades; at the end of the course the student *pass-fail* either is or is not given credit. Much could be said in favor of this plan, although some teachers complain that it destroys the initiative of potentially superior students to whom grades are an incentive. In still other systems the administrators have other rules of thumb concerning grading, rules which of course the teacher should be allowed to question in fair and open discussions.

Beginning teachers tend to give too many high grades, especially at the start of the year. Some feel that they won't be popular with students if they give lower grades. Then, as the year moves on and their understanding of the students increases, they lower the grades, to the detriment of class morale. Beginning at the other extreme can lead to trouble, too. A large number of F's is usually a greater criticism of the teacher than of the class. If many students fail to try, the teacher is not supplying adequate motivation. In such cases, the teacher should engage in strenuous introspection to discover what change of tactics is in order. It is much better to grade honestly at the outset, giving students grades that reflect their performance (always accompanied by praise when deserved, and by constructive suggestions for improvement).

As a rule, the quality of work that a student does in the last few weeks of a term should have greater bearing upon the final grade than should the work of the first few weeks. When improvement is obvious, the last efforts, not the first ones, truly reflect achievement. In the case of themes that students have improved through revision, averaging first and last efforts is very unfair.[2]

*True!*

It is too bad that grades must be given, because it seems unfair to reward or mark down any student because of innate characteristics or home environment. The student has no control over these, but they have a large share in determining whether his or her grades are high or low. But many administrators and parents say that grades must be given, colleges ask about class rank, businesses inquire about grades, and many students feel cheated unless their achievement is capsulated in a symbol. Emphasis upon "accountability" gives even further support to issuing such symbols. Those who dislike and distrust grades (preferring written statements or fairly detailed checklists, which more accurately and more realistically describe a student's performance) may agitate for change. In the meantime, they can try to make grading as fair as the system permits.

## PLANNING UNITS

Answers to the question "What is a unit?" may vary widely. One teacher said, "I'm teaching a unit on Frost's 'Death of the Hired Man' today." To her a unit meant simply having students read and discuss a single poem and perhaps bring in some related material. More typically, though, the term *unit* refers to an organized study, lasting from one week to eight weeks and centered upon a given theme or topic, to which everything in the unit is in some way related.

Some units are devoted almost entirely to composition, others to literature study or to oral work. Some may center on drama, on dramatic re-creation, on the short story, on the paragraph, on the history of the English language in America, or on any of hundreds of other things. It is most often characteristic of a good unit, though, that it combines work in reading, writing, listening, and speaking. Even though it may center upon, say, eighteenth-century satire, it provides students with an opportunity to talk and write and hear, and to look at the language as language and not just as literature.

The number of possible subjects for units, as has just been implied, is limitless. Often a concept is central, such as "Caution vs. cowardice," "Literature on death and dying," or "The essence of tragedy." A linguistic item may be the focus: "English in Chaucer's time," "Emotive and reportorial language," "English is changing," "Do you speak a dialect?," and so on. Skills may sometimes be stressed as in "Reading for greater comprehension" or "Learning to build better sentences." A large number of unit topics are suggested in The Idea Box.

Even teachers who do not use the term *unit* generally employ some kind of planning. If they did not, the work in the English classroom would probably consist of many unrelated snippets. But, as we have discussed earlier, the amount of planning may vary widely.

It was once the practice of some teachers (often at the bidding of administrators) to plan the organization of a unit to the last detail. Their lesson plans within the unit indicated that 5 minutes would be devoted to this, 10 minutes to that, and so on. The teacher gathered every scrap of material in advance and even arranged a bulletin board display to announce the unit to students as they walked into the room Monday morning. The class moved in rigid conformity to schedule, regardless of whether or not the desired outcomes had been reached.

Then, under the leadership of a few "progressive" educators, some teachers went to the other extreme, that of planlessness. In effect, they appeared before their classes, asked "What shall we do today [or during the next four weeks]?" took a vote, and did whatever the majority of students said they wanted to do, regardless of its apparent suitability to usual aims of an English course. If the students wanted to read and discuss comic books, they did that; if they wanted to spend their time in planning for a school function, they did that.

Of course there was learning in both the carefully planned and the virtually unplanned units. Students learn in spite of themselves and their teachers. But the present tendency is toward planning that is flexible enough to permit some alteration in accord with legitimate student requests, unexpected developments, or students' needs that are discovered as the unit progresses. Experienced teachers know that a unit can run into trouble if it specifies what will be done on

Monday, Tuesday, Wednesday, Thursday, and Friday of each week for weeks ahead. In most schools, the chance of doing on Friday what is scheduled for that day is remote indeed. Besides, a unit setup like that generally ignores students. If the teacher is optimistic enough to think that activities planned for five days ahead will take place after four full periods with students, then perhaps "Day One," and "Day Two" are more reasonable labels. "Day Six" may not turn out to be Monday of the second week, but at least it will be the sixth day spent on the unit. Neither approach is really flexible, though. The best arrangement might be to compile lists of activities for stages in the unit: those that could begin the unit, develop it, and bring it to a close. Some activities within each stage would be appropriate for the entire class, some for groups, and some for individuals. The teacher draws from these lists in making up plans for two or three days ahead. This arrangement may make joint planning by teachers and students easier.

Joint planning exists in various modifications in some schools. Student participation in such planning is most likely to consist of assistance in selection of specific learning activities, or perhaps in choosing between two or more equally appropriate topics for units. When students have had some voice (a genuine voice) in such decisions, their motivation is likely to be better. Some teachers therefore give students much opportunity to choose individual and group behavioral objectives, to choose and gather materials, and to be creative in designing activities. A number of teachers like to employ student committees, each of which is responsible for part of the work of the unit.

More than books should be used in most units. Films, slides, filmstrips, videotapes, and audiotapes often fit in. The making of a film or a slide-tape presentation by students may be useful for teaching principles of plotting, characterization, and writing of dialogue. Sometimes radio or TV programs are appropriate. Magazines, newspapers, and radio or TV scripts may often be used. Occasionally a field trip is desirable. Outside speakers, or teachers in other departments, may be invited to talk to the class. The students' own activities may be varied. The good unit does possess much variety, life, and interest. It is as a rule infinitely preferable to the old day-to-day assignment routine: "Tomorrow study pages 58 to 67."

Details of unit planning vary, but the following description of a written plan may serve as a general framework. The scope is broad, like that found in units written for other teachers and placed in curriculum guides, but it suggests the kind of detail and flexibility that student teachers might build into their units to anticipate the unforeseen contingencies of student teaching.

1. *The Title Page*. If the unit has a title page, it probably will include not only the title of the unit but the subject and grade level, the name of the school or school system for which it was developed, the name of the teacher who developed it, and the date it was completed.

2. *Introduction.* This statement, often only a short paragraph in length, is informative. It may tell the reader whether the unit was designed to be taught in an inner city or in a small rural community. It may also say whether it anticipates or follows other units in a total program for the semester or course. Facts in the introduction should help the reader to understand the rationale, objectives, and activities that follow. For example, the paragraph may contain sentences such as these: "This unit, which is called 'Who Doesn't Have a Dialect?,' is the first of three mini-units in the course, Our Changing American English. It is designed for a ninth-grade class of mixed abilities and mixed cultural backgrounds in a large inner-city school."

3. *Rationale.* This statement, often a paragraph in length, focuses on the value of the learnings for the *student*. It seeks to answer this question frequently asked by students: "What good is this?" It also anticipates parents or school administrators who may ask, "Is the student really learning something worthwhile?" In effect, then, the rationale justifies the behavioral objectives; it explains why it is important for the student to be able to do those things.

4. *Time Allotment.* Sometimes this information is included in the introduction. This is a short statement that tells how much time is set aside for the unit, with some allowance for interruptions and developing students' needs and interests.

5. *Objectives.* This is a list of desired outcomes, often including both general and specific student behaviors. Remember that the focus is on *student* behavior. Many school systems now prefer the language of behavioral objectives. However worded, they should be clear, brief, and to the point. They must also focus on the rationale. Don't aim students out of the picture with huge amorphous statements or lists of trivial behaviors.

6. *Student Activities.* These are short descriptions of activities that will encourage students to learn effectively. The mainstreaming of students into classrooms demands a very close look at all differences that could affect learning. It is wise to show what provisions will be made for different backgrounds, abilities, and interests. These activities form the basis of separate, more detailed lesson plans which develop each activity or group of activities fully enough for a day's classwork. They sometimes fall under these three headings:

    (a) Beginning activities. This list is of "initiating" or "introductory" or "motivational" activities intended to arouse students' interest and support and provide essential background.

    (b) Developmental activities. These are the principal learning activities that will help students to reach their objectives.

    (c) Closing activities. This list includes those activities that will bring the unit to a close: committee reports, projects, written work, talks, summaries, and so on. The focus is on recapitulation, synthesis, generalization, and evaluation.

7. *Evaluation of Outcomes*. Stated here are ways to evaluate student performance. Evaluation is not limited to a final test. The list will probably include diagnostic tests, progress tests, and mastery tests. Of course not all tests need be limited to pencil and paper. The focus is on continual evaluation.

8. *Materials*. This is a list of reading materials, media resources, school and community resources, and so on that students must or may use in their unit work. Sometimes this list is placed earlier in the unit, possibly between objectives and student activities.

9. *Professional Resources*. This is a list of materials of value to the teacher in teaching the unit: books, articles in professional journals, media resources, school and community resources, and so on.

## PLANNING LESSONS

A lesson plan is a fairly detailed outline of the work proposed by the teacher for a single class period. Some department heads, supervisors, or principals require that lesson plans be turned in for a week or two weeks in advance, so that in case of the teacher's illness a substitute will know what is to be done. In other schools no such requirement exists. The point of view in a daily lesson is that of a teacher who hopes to give each student the fullest opportunity to accomplish the stated objectives in the time allowed.

Some plans are poorly done. One may be skimpy, whereas another may be too ambitious. Yet another may be so rigidly teacher-centered that it overlooks many things that students can and should do. A lack of flexibility and a poor sense of timing cause many problems. Taking attendance, distributing materials, giving directions and explanations, changing from one kind of activity to another, moving about in the room, answering questions, helping individual students, and making assignments all take time, so they must be taken into account.

Ordinarily it is desirable for beginning teachers to make more detailed lesson plans than experienced teachers need. For the experienced teacher a statement that covers the purpose, the materials, and the main points to be included is usually enough. As mentioned earlier in this chapter, many experienced teachers, in fact, carry their lesson plans in their heads. But the beginner will feel more comfortable and probably do a better job after outlining each lesson rather carefully, even though he or she should expect to be flexible in following the plan.

Many different formats are used in the schools. The requirements followed by teachers, the length of a period, the size of a class, known abilities and interests, known difficulty of instructional material, the teacher's attitude about writing plans, and many other factors affect the detail and arrangement of a plan.

No outline can cover all lesson plans. However, the following format may serve as a useful guide:

Teacher's name _____ Date _____
Class _____ Grade _____ Period _____
Title of unit (if lesson is part of a unit)
Title of lesson
Previous assignment (if any)
Objective(s)
Material(s)
Activities
Evaluation (if any)
Assignment (if any)

Listed below are some questions to ask while writing a lesson plan. They attempt to keep three points of view in mind: the students, the teacher, and another teacher who may have to follow the plan.

*Identification.* Can anyone see these at a glance: teacher's name? date? class? grade level? period or block of time?

*Topic and subject.* Is the lesson part of a unit? If so, is the title of the unit clearly stated? Can anyone tell where this lesson belongs in the unit? Can anyone clearly tell what the lesson is about? Its subject? Its focus?

*Purpose.* Can anyone easily visualize what students are expected to be able to do during and following instruction? Does this plan help students to learn something significant in English? Is the plan based upon a defensible rationale?

*Materials.* Are instructional materials clearly identified: titles, pages, bulletin board displays, media materials and equipment, handouts, student work from previous assignment, and so on?

*Activities.* Can anyone easily visualize what students will be doing throughout the period? Does the lesson build upon a previous assignment? If so, is the assignment followed up in this lesson? Do sequenced activities follow one another in a logical order? Are simultaneous activities organized to help students to reach their goals individually or by collaboration? Do students have opportunities to learn for themselves, or is the teacher getting in the way? Does the lesson provide enough variety? Motivation? Is it challenging? Is the lesson realistic? Can students accomplish their goals with these procedures and instructional materials in the time provided? Is the plan flexible enough? Does it provide any alternatives for students who may lose interest, for those who may need extra help, or for those who can easily do more than the basic work outlined? Will there be enough time to give directions, move from one activity to the next, reach concepts through collaboration, give a necessary assignment, and so on? Is the teaching method generally inductive or deductive? Why?

*Evaluation.* Will evaluation be formal or informal? Will the teacher be the only one to evaluate change, or will students evaluate each other's performances or their own? Are the testing instruments most effective or just most convenient? Will students be able to see for themselves how much they have learned?

*Assignment.* Will the assignment be clear to another teacher? Will all students easily understand it? Does it logically follow this lesson? Is it the kind of assignment that students will be able to do only after going through this lesson? Is it helpful reinforcement or application of knowledge and skills learned today? Is it necessary preparation for the next lesson? Must it be done in class or out of class? Why? Must it be done at all?

---

### THE IDEA BOX

#### ANTIQUE VEHICLES AND BANDWAGONS

We need teachers who are equally unwilling to hold on to the old or grab on to the new. We need teachers acting as a department to develop departmental philosophies of English teaching, to define clearly what they mean by English, and to develop rationales for teaching English. Those written documents, and I believe they *should* be written out, should be made available to the public and to students. I'm appalled to discover departments hanging onto the old (diagramming, for example) for no better reason than that it has been done so long it is somehow mystically good for kids. I'm equally appalled to find departments clamoring to get onto the latest curriculum bandwagon (electives or a return to the basics, for example) without first determining whether the concept or curriculum change fits into the departmental philosophy, definition, and rationale. Further, I believe the philosophy, definition, and rationale must constantly be re-examined to determine whether its past validity makes current sense.[3]

#### "THE EJ CURRICULUM CATALOG"

Susan Koch has compiled much more than an annotated list of units and electives; under the headings of Objectives, Materials, Course Sequence (or Activities), she offers full-page descriptions under these titles: "Dreams and Nightmares," "Twain and Vonnegut," "Death: the Last Taboo," "Gods and Goddesses: Exploring Greek Mythology," "Thinking About Things," "American Ethnic Studies," "Nobel Prize Winning World Literature," "The Eskimo and His Literature," "Hang-Ups," "Literature from Prison," "Women's Literature," "People in Crisis," "Working," and "Kwaps," (an elective course on cops and crime).[4]

## THINKING: THE NEGLECTED LANGUAGE ART

Denny Wolfe, Jr., Director, Division of Languages, State Department of Public Instruction, Raleigh, North Carolina, urges teachers to help students to develop their "powers of meaning-making." To develop the intuitive, perceptual, and pictorial thought of the brain's right hemisphere, Wolfe suggests "word association games, stories for which students can make up their own endings, miming activities, exploring and inventing communication codes"; to develop the logical, linear, rational thought of the left hemisphere, he suggests deductive reasoning from generalizations found in "venerated" literature to the particulars of the human condition, and he suggests inductive reasoning from particulars to generalizations, using processes of inquiry in class discussions. It is also critical, Mr. Wolfe says, for students to "identify appropriate metaphors" so they can understand more fully what social institutions and other "things" about them "stand for."[5]

## THE ENGLISH CLASSROOM: DEFINITELY NOT CHAOTIC

Reporting responses from 595 secondary English teachers, Professor Candida Gillis of Michigan State describes the average class as being quite conventional. Here is how she describes it for today's student:

> Your class stresses literature and writing. You study subjects such as how writers use language, themes in literature, spelling and vocabulary, "standard" usage, how to write thesis and topic sentences, and how to organize paragraphs. You write exposition, narratives or personal experience, and interpretations and analyses of literature. You read many short stories and novels, and your text is an anthology. You spend time in class talking freely about the literature, discussing study guide questions, and writing."[6]

## "TEACHING CONDITIONS IN SECONDARY SCHOOL ENGLISH"—1977

1. "A typical secondary school English teacher can expect to teach 5 classes in a 6 or 7 period day, with 26 to 30 students per class."
2. "The larger the school, the higher the load is likely to be."
3. "In the great majority of schools, English teachers are responsible for the school yearbook, for the school newspaper, and for speech and drama clubs, as well as for such general duties as chaperoning, patrolling corridors, and monitoring lunchrooms."
4. "In the random sample [96 schools], 81 percent of high school English teachers had more than two preparations per day."

These are just some of the results of an NCTE study of teaching load and teaching conditions done in 316 schools during the spring of 1977 and reported by Arthur Applebee.[7]

## "NO HOMEWORK: A STUDENT'S RIGHT!"

Jerry F. Kotnour of Orchard Ridge Middle School, Madison, Wisconsin, raises the question of the student's right *not to do* "add on" assignments, such as reports and lengthy reading assignments, at home regularly throughout the year. Claiming that "the results or values of homework assignments are usually minimal" for students, Mr. Kotnour points to the usual practice of giving everyone in a class "the same assignment, regardless of abilities, interests, or outside commitments."[8]

## ARE WE ENGLISH TEACHERS UNIQUE?

Greg Larkin of Brigham Young University in Laie, Hawaii, claims that we English teachers are not unique in ways that many of us have claimed. For instance, "we are not alone in being champions of the humanities." Teachers of art, philosophy, and several of the sciences share our values. "An integration of language and thought" is our unique offering. "To see language as the uniquely human gift that it is and to appreciate it in all of its forms—from the blundering, self-conscious freshman theme to the heights of a Dickens novel, from the efficient style of a well-written business letter to the economy of Hemingway's prose—this is what we promise ourselves, our students, and our profession."[9]

## ADVICE TO THE ENGLISH TEACHER: SOMETIMES SILENCE IS NOT GOLDEN

Silence often serves only to aggravate critics who cry for literacy in the English classroom. English teachers must be honest enough to admit that they know little about teaching the basic skills of reading and writing. But more importantly, they must speak out with a loud voice in the media and at back-to-school-nights for programs that will train and support teachers of all subjects to do the job right, even if these programs could cost billions. So says Stephen Dunning in "The Public and English Teachers: An Adversary Relationship?"[10]

## MULTICULTURAL LITERATURE: SPECIAL CONSIDERATIONS IN PLANNING

Teaching literature which uses the American English language to express beliefs that are not necessarily Anglo-American has special curricular and pedagogical implications. Anglo-Americans can find the experiences of the Afro-American, the Amer-Indian, or the Chicano so distant that a teacher who is introducing multicultural literature to examine moral consciousness will have to carry these students through such prereading activities as role-playing and stereotype inventories. "Black American pride, American Indian pride, Chicano pride, Puerto Rican Pride, and newly aroused white ethnic pride" as expressed in this growing body of literature should not be pushed at students; teachers should design programs that will introduce this multiethnic literature at appropriate stages of their students' cognitive development, so that students will be able to make their own judgments about the literary concepts, sociological concepts, and psychological concepts in it. Lester S. Golub of Pennsylvania State University offers useful guidelines in "The New American Revolution: Multi-Cultural Literature in the English Program."[11]

## A RATIONALE FOR THE THEMATIC APPROACH TO THE TEACHING OF ENGLISH

In their preface to *Thematic Units in Teaching English and the Humanities* (NCTE, 1975), Sylvia Spann and Mary Beth Culp of the University of South Alabama make some statements that teachers might find useful as they develop their own rationales for thematic units:

> We are ... dedicated to the use of a humanistic, thematic approach to the teaching of English. We have experimented with other approaches and have discussed the advantages and disadvantages of each, but in our experience a concern with values has been the most successful way of getting students involved in English the way they are involved in life—questioning, reflecting, probing, wondering, and sometimes rebelling. An English program which uses language arts as a vehicle for exploring the problems and questions inherent in the human condition seems to us the most valid as well as the most practical approach.
>
> Our feelings are not, however, based merely on our personal preferences and philosophies; they derive also from our observations of society and of our students in particular. Any perceptive teacher has observed that adolescents are attempting to develop values in a confusing world. A thematic approach gives them an opportunity to integrate all of the language arts in relation to a theme or a problem, as they do in real life.
>
> In answer to the charge that in a thematic approach a student misses some of the classics and is exposed to 'inferior' literature or non-literature, simply because it happens to fit the theme, we would reply that no one book will save a student, help him to grow up, or teach him the valuable lessons of life; the habit of careful and thoughtful reception and transmission of communication concerning values is possibly the most valuable skill our students will need. In a world of future shock such a skill assumes more and more significance.

## PLANNING STUDENT INTERACTION IN JUNIOR HIGH

John Bushman of the University of Kansas suggests several "ice breakers" for junior high students who have come from different elementary schools and may not know each other. Here are two examples: 1. Each student goes around the class asking which classmates can sign an information sheet opposite statements like "A person who has a quarter in his pocket," and "A person who likes licorice." 2. Students pair off, interview each other, and then introduce each other to the rest of the class. Also noting that students often fail to "delve into the core of the topic" during group discussion, even when they know each other, Mr. Bushman suggests helping them to use key statements and questions.

*Elaboration:* "Could you go into that a little further?" Also, "I would expand on that idea by saying. . . ." *Clarification:* "What exactly do you mean?" And, "Do I understand you to mean. . . .?" *Comparison:* "That is an interesting statement. How does that compare with what was previously said?" Also, "I would compare that to . . ." *Contrast:* "How would you contrast your idea to the one (name of student) gave previously?" Also, "In contrast to your statement, I think . . ." *Justification:* "How would you defend that statement against . . ." And, "What assumptions are you basing that on?" *Evaluation:* "My reaction to that idea is . . ." Also, "What do you think of that idea?"[12]

THE TEACHING OF HIGH SCHOOL ENGLISH

HELPING THE PUBLIC UNDERSTAND THE AIMS OF LANGUAGE PROGRAMS

In the September 1976 issue of the NCTE *SLATE* newsletter, Elizabeth McPherson suggests the following strategies in response to the public's questions and complaints about language programs:

1. Emphasize that practice in using language by sharing experiences, role-playing, and other devices, is a better route to flexibility and effectiveness than having a teacher correct mistakes. In other words, discussions of appropriateness, clarity, and intelligibility are more useful than "chasing errors."
2. Explain that drills in usage are more likely to teach nervousness and self-consciousness than change in language. Such drills can teach people to fill in the blanks or name the parts, but seldom teach them to speak or write better.
3. Remind parents that schools can supply only a small part of the language learning that goes on. Children spend only seven hours a day in school for five days a week; the rest of their waking hours they are bombarded with language that seems more real to them than the language they hear in the classroom.
4. Ask for specific examples from people who are troubled about how language is taught. Deal with each objection separately rather than attempting a general defense of what we do.
5. Remind people that the National Assessment results showed that mechanics (usage choices, spelling, syntax, etc.) have not declined but have slightly improved; what declined were sentence flexibility, creativity, and coherence—just the qualities that we're trying to teach.
6. Make clear what standardized tests actually measure and what the scores actually mean. Explain what a "norm" is, what a "percentile score" is.
7. Show parents some actual assignments and explain what those assignments aim for. Invite them to visit classes and see that most activities are actually more demanding than older methods.
8. Urge school boards and legislators to provide classes small enough that every student can have the language practice necessary for real progress.
9. Demonstrate that what's "basic" about English is the ability to communicate. Successful communication can take place in many different ways, in many different situations, and depends on the good will of the listener as well as on the skill of the speaker.

## "SEVEN WAYS TO INVOLVE STUDENTS IN CURRICULUM PLANNING"

One way to reduce the apprehension which hangs over an English department when it launches a new program is to find out what students think about proposed changes. "As motivators for curriculum change," students can not only react to the whole idea of a different program, but can also suggest new courses, even new titles for their reading. "As respondents to opinionnaires," students can tell the department whether they generally react positively or negatively, and they can help the department to detect specific strengths and weaknesses. "As evaluators of strands of courses," they can comment on the value of each unit, on the clarity of assignments, the appropriateness of reading selections, and many other matters. "As evaluators of single courses," they can tell a teacher if they felt objectives were realistic. "As course designers," they can help to identify objectives, materials and activities for a unit within a course. "As team writers of course descriptions," selected students can review course descriptions and suggest changes. Finally, "as reviewers of textbooks and materials," teams of students can use criteria to "select and test" materials. Often in the process, students will recommend topics and themes which teachers have not considered for future units.[13]

## PREPARING SMALL GROUPS FOR CRITICAL JUDGMENT

Small groups often develop a new confidence in their group communication skills, but if the task is critical judgment of literature, they will need background in critical points of view. Juanita Dudley of Purdue University concludes that "the self-discovery method is only as good as the teaching that precedes it—that, in short, mere exposure to 'the best' will not necessarily inculcate a taste for quality." She acknowledges the value of spontaneous discussions when students are learning a process or an activity, but if they are to make critical judgments about literature, "the most cohesive groups in the world may, without an adequate frame of reference, come to egregious conclusions."[14]

## A THEMATIC UNIT ON OLD-TIME RADIO

Rose A. Nack of Saguaro High School, Scottsdale, Arizona, has used a thematic unit entitled "Understanding One's Parents Through Old-Time Radio" to increase vocabulary, develop listening skills, make students aware of language change, and involve students in the imaginative writing of radio scripts. Apparently students can also come to understand themselves more clearly in this unit. One student made this observation in an "opinion paper" at the close of the unit: "I'm not saying that we're exactly like the kids of yesterday, but we're not as different as many kids think we are."[15]

## READ: THE HALLMARKS OF A GOOD CURRICULUM GUIDE

A good curriculum guide is READABLE, EFFICIENT, ADAPTABLE, and DEPENDABLE. It is clear and concise, and as free as possible of educational jargon. It is easy for busy teachers to use, because most important points are logically organized and easy to find and follow. It offers suggestions, not commandments; teachers can easily adapt the suggestions "to fit their own teaching talents and the needs of their own students." Finally, teachers will be able to "find useful information that will be transferred easily into the classroom." Charles and Nancy Neff, Indian Hills School District, Cincinnati, Ohio, offer these valuable tips in the introductory pages to *Aids to Curriculum Planning: English Language Arts K–12*, Bernard O'Donnell, ed.[16]

## SUGGESTED TOPICS FOR UNITS

Topics for units are endless. The headings and specific topics listed here are only representative. The choice of topics depends upon students' grade level and inter-

THE TEACHING OF HIGH SCHOOL ENGLISH

ests, the relationship to other work of the course, the material covered in earlier years, the amount of time available, the significance of the topic for these students, and the availability of material.

Many of the suggested topics can be developed with a central literary core (perhaps to include some works suggested by students). Writing and other individual work, as well as discussion and class projects, can be built into nearly all of them. Some topics require considerable library and community resources and much use of those resources by students; others may be based upon readings in an anthology or in readily available paperbacks.

### THE CONCERNS OF PEOPLE

The Family

True friendship

Courage and heroism

Honesty and fair play

Why war?

Alienation and isolation

Multicultural awareness

What price conformity?

All kinds of humor

Taking sides

Nobody understands me

Planning a career

What price happiness?

Growing up in America

Making it in the city

Law and order

Sentiment and sentimentality

Death and dying

I have my rights

People in fear (anger, crisis, conflict, etc.)

### OUR COUNTRY AND ITS LITERATURE

With the explorers

Life in colonial days

The Revolutionary era

The early American short story

The world of Hawthorne (or another literary figure)

Literature looks at politics and government

Smog and smokestacks

American folk heroes

Afro-American literature (or Amer-Indian, Indian, white ethnic, Chicano, Puerto Rican, Eskimo, etc.)

Radicals of American literature

Women in American literature

Taking the myths out of American literature

Manifest destiny, or how the West was won

### OTHER PARTS OF THE WORLD

Literature of the African nations

Americans abroad

What can Greek and Roman literature tell us today?

Humor (imagination, love, etc.) in British (French, Spanish, etc.) literature

Riders on this planet together

Searching for roots in world literature (genealogy)

Themes of Hindu literature

## THE QUALITIES OF LITERATURE

"The play's the thing

Why poetry?

Literature of fantasy

"My dear Watson"

Science fiction

Historical fiction

What is a ballad?

What makes a good short story?

The structure of novels

Legends and lore

American non-fiction

Backgrounds to literature

## SKILLS

Reading for understanding

Reading aloud

The art of conversation

How to study

Telling stories

How to read a newspaper

The art of interviewing

Getting to know the library (media center or resource center)

Really listening

## THE ENGLISH LANGUAGE

Words that influence people (semantics)

Public (military, commercial) double-speak

Truth? in advertising

Verbal and nonverbal communication

Sexism (or racism) in language

Modern conventions in usage

British English and American English

The story of British English

The story of American English

How the English sentence works

What can happen to a word

American dialects

How people (places) got their names

## ENGLISH—NOT IN A VACUUM

Technical writing

Literary prophets (stories about the future)

Literature and music (painting, film, etc.)

English in your life's work

English for fun and leisure

Is science getting ahead of us?

Basic English for daily living

## MEDIA TECHNOLOGY AND MASS ENTERTAINMENT

Violence, sports, and low comedy (a critique of TV)

Radio back when

Do computers have a language?

Making it with—or without—the media

Is TV making poor students?

What's happening on radio?

Daily, including Sunday

Film as an art form

The power of the media

What's next in media? (A guess at the future)

The modern magazine

Are the media changing language?

Media by the people, of the people, and for the people. (Is mass entertainment for the masses?)

Film-making

68                                  THE TEACHING OF HIGH SCHOOL ENGLISH

## ON BEHAVIORAL OBJECTIVES

Two books seem especially helpful to the secondary English teacher: John C. Maxwell and Anthony Tovatt, eds., *On Writing Behavioral Objectives*, NCTE, 1970; J. N. Hook et al., eds., *Representative Performance Objectives for High School English*, New York: Ronald Press, 1972. The first presents a balanced view (pro and con) through position papers written by various leaders in the English teaching profession. The second book is a guide or manual for English teachers to use in writing objectives for lessons and unit plans. Many sample objectives are offered under these headings: Sending and Receiving Non-Verbal Messages, Speaking and Listening, Language, Reading and Responding to Literature, Writing, and Exploring the Mass Media.

## SETTING GOALS AND ORGANIZING LEARNING ENVIRONMENTS

Two useful books for setting goals and organizing learning situations are Henry B. Maloney, ed., *Goal Making for the English Teacher*, NCTE, 1973; and James A. Smith, *Classroom Organization for the Language Arts*, F. E. Peacock Publishers, Inc., 1977. The first is a collection of behavioristic and humanistic points of view about ends and means in teaching English. The second, although written mainly for elementary school teachers, has some excellent ideas for organizing English in the middle school and junior high.

## KNOWING MORE ABOUT PUBLISHED TESTS

In view of increasing interest by parents and administrators in accountability and competency testing, it is critical for English teachers to become better informed about the advantages and disadvantages of published tests in English. This book should be especially valuable: Alfred H. Grommon, ed., *Reviews of Selected Published Tests in English*, NCTC, 1976. Walter Loban, William Jenkins, J. N. Hook, Richard Braddock, and Alan C. Purves offer detailed critical reviews.

# FOOTNOTES

1. Boston: Houghton Mifflin Company, 1976, p. 28.
2. Further discussion of the grading of written work is included in Chapter 10.
3. Ken Donelson, "Some Responsibilities for English Teachers Who Already Face an Impossible Job," *English Journal* 66, Sept. 1977, p. 31.
4. *English Journal* 66, Sept. 1977, pp. 53–66.
5. "Thinking as a Language Art: Balancing the Curriculum," *The High School Journal*, Feb. 1978, pp. 247–253.

6. "The English Classroom 1977: A Report on the EJ Readership Survey," *English Journal* 66, Sept. 1977, p. 20.
7. *English Journal* 67, March 1978, pp. 57–65.
8. *The Education Digest,* May 1978, pp. 31–33.
9. "The False Mask of English Teachers," *English Journal* 70, March 1981, pp. 34–36.
10. *English Journal* 64, Sept. 1975, p. 9.
11. *English Journal* 64, Sept. 1975, pp. 23–26.
12. For further suggestions see "Achieving Student Interaction in Creative Junior High, Middle School Programs," *English Journal* 66, April 1977, pp. 67–72.
13. Bernarr Folta, *English Journal* 63, April 1974, pp. 42–45.
14. "A Farewell to Serendipity: Small Groups in the College Literature Classroom," *English Education,* Spring 1978, pp. 175–185.
15. *Statement: The Journal of the Colorado Language Arts Society,* Feb. 1973, pp. 4–8.
16. ERIC Clearinghouse, Urbana: NCTE, 1973.

# 4

## THE
## IMPROVEMENT
## OF
## READING

## IS THE ENGLISH TEACHER QUALIFIED?

An English teacher can teach developmental reading in the English classroom more effectively than a reading specialist. This statement may sound preposterous to many English teachers, but it is not at all far-fetched if one looks directly at what is involved in helping students to read as well as possible in English. Mainly it involves helping high school students with vocabulary, sentence structure, specialized language styles and forms, and with literary appreciation and comprehension. These should be familiar matters to the teacher who will be asked to do the job. Let's look at them a little more closely.

To read more efficiently, students in English will need to enlarge their reading vocabulary. For them, building the reading vocabulary will include increasing word recognition; attacking new words structurally and interpretively: inferring meanings from lexical, syntactic, factual, and semantic clues; and interacting with words that relate to their experience and to the text itself. Needed is a teacher with a fairly extensive general vocabulary, a specialized vocabulary often encountered in the content of English studies, a special interest in words, and some knowledge of how to work with words.

To extend the quality of their reading in English, students will need to apply their grammatical knowledge. Distinguishing grammatical structures from ungrammatical ones will be important, but students will find their reading much more demanding than this. In their reading, they can expect to see words which will signal syntactic relationships not only within sentences but from sentence to sentence and from paragraph to paragraph. In the language of literature, especially poetry, they will encounter language which deviates from the norm

71

phonologically, grammatically, and semantically. In any elaborate prose, they will find sequences, contrasts, comparisons, ellipses, repetitions, extensive parallelisms, balanced sentences, and intricate word patterns. Clearly the teacher's job will require a fairly strong background in linguistics and considerable experience in applying this knowledge of English grammar to reading.

Reading in English will also require students to understand the language, the style, and the specialized forms of essays, short stories, biographies, plays, poems, and novels. Trained reading teachers try to help students to read more effectively in the genres, but many do not have extensive knowledge of literature.

Perhaps nothing aids reading comprehension in English more than enjoyment and high interest. Therefore, teaching reading in the English classroom calls for a teacher who enjoys reading widely in English and who feels especially moved by certain works. In other words, the teacher should be an enthusiastic and a thoughtful reader of literature. The object is to set a good example for student readers.

Obviously the teacher's qualifications and responsibilities will be far reaching. If it is any comfort, though, he or she will not be expected to teach reading skills of all kinds. Teachers in other subjects should assume the primary responsibility for reading improvement in the technical parts of those fields; reading specialists should assume primary responsibility for helping students who have the most serious reading disabilities. The English teacher's major role in reading will be to help students to improve their reading of materials in the class.

Will the best-qualified teacher please come forward. Good! Now, here are a few things you should know. Let's begin with some basic principles.

## BASIC PRINCIPLES

### FIRST PRINCIPLE: READING IS COMPLEX, AND IT INVOLVES THINKING

If reading consisted merely of "cracking the code," of understanding and applying sound-letter relationships to pronounce words, readers would not be able to progress beyond reading one word at a time. Each word would present its own reading problem, distinct from the one before it, and it would make little difference if a reader stopped in the middle of a sentence. Readers would have to read everything aloud, or at least they would have to listen mentally to an innner voice constantly pronouncing sound-letter combinations. If this were the case, they would never be able to progress any faster than they could subvocalize or move their lips.

Fortunately, reading does not have to move along in this fashion. It is learned as an interrelationship of several skills. It is a thoughtful, conscious though seemingly automatic, integrated process somewhat like that of walking, skiing, riding a bicycle, swimming, or driving a car. Discovering clusters of meaning from clusters of printed or written symbols requires a coordinated effort. And like the other processes mentioned, it involves adjusting one's performance to prevailing conditions, not a condition; there are things to do together, not one thing to do at a time. As with these other processes, reading may be done slowly, deliberately, and seriously; or like the others, it may be done in any way that pleases the doer. The skillful reader, like the skillful swimmer or driver, develops confidence, flow, rhythm, coordination, and flexibility with experience. Kenneth Goodman defines the reading act in the following way:

> *Reading is a sampling, selecting, predicting, comparing, and confirming activity in which the reader selects a sample of useful graphic clues based on what he sees and what he expects to see. The graphic symbols are not processed one by one or in a strictly serial manner. Rather the reader samples from the print on the basis of predictions he has made as he seeks meaning.*[1]

As a thinking process, then, reading goes beyond the decoding of symbols to integrating and applying the meanings of those symbols. It goes as far as discovering what an author is thinking, and then discovering one's own thinking in the process. This kind of thinking prompts many questions about what is read. In a short story, play, or novel, a reader realizes that he must not only ask, "What happened?" but also, "Why did this happen?" and, "What does this have to do with the character's problem?" As a result of asking questions of these kinds, the reader may not only understand the theme of the work, but may wonder what that idea has to do with his own life. Literal or concrete reading leads to critical reading, and critical reading leads to creative reading.

Thinking readers are participating readers. As such, they have purposes and assume active roles. They try to discover who is speaking in literature, and they listen attentively to that voice, but they also assume their own postures and voices in responding. As they open their minds to the art and ideas of an especially skillful writer, they probe, question, grasp, pull back, reconsider, and probe again.

## SECOND PRINCIPLE: THE READING RATE IS ADJUSTABLE

Rapid reading, or "speed reading," as some people call it, has become almost a fetish. It is understandable to want to read faster, but it is unwise to want to read everything at top speed. The best reader can read very rapidly, but he or she adjusts the rate according to purpose and according to the kind of material. Purposes and demands differ between an informal essay and a formal one, and between the sports page in a newspaper and a chemistry textbook. Francis Bacon, a famous Renaissance scholar, was apparently such a reader. In his essay

"Of Studies," he very wisely said, "Some books are to be tasted, others to be swallowed and digested; that is, some books are to be read only in parts, others to be read, but not curiously, and some few to be read wholly, and with diligence and attention." This observation is as apt today as it was when Bacon made it.

One task for the English teacher, then, is to help students to read at rates that are appropriate to the purposes for reading and to the demands of the materials. To this end, the teacher can try to provide a wide range of reading materials and can stress the desirability of different reading rates. A literature program which is limited to a single anthology usually does not offer students sufficient range to develop this kind of flexibility. Fortunately, though, a variety of reading materials is available for use in English, especially in paperback format.

## THIRD PRINCIPLE: EVERYONE IN THE ENGLISH CLASSROOM CAN READ BETTER

As any experienced English teacher knows, a class is a mix of motivations, emotions, linguistic abilities, self-concepts, physical characteristics, attitudes, experiences, social conditions, economic conditions, cultural and ethnic identities, work habits, personalities, values, intellects, and so on. All of these factors affect reading, and in many cases are affected by reading. They also act in clusters, affecting one another.

Depending upon a student's cluster of some of these factors, he or she might be called advantaged or disadvantaged, or perhaps culturally different or linguistically different. Of course any such label is tenuous; it is relative to many contexts and open to many interpretations.

Because these factors are relative, the teaching of reading should also be relative. It should not work toward a common level. Let us suppose that Steve, Aaron, Franklin, Marie, Juanita, and Jo-Mei now read with different degrees of success. This is true even after reading instruction in the elementary and middle schools. And it is true because of a number of factors. The important fact to keep in mind is that the English teacher must help each student to improve in the skills in which he or she is least proficient. Let's look at these students a little more closely and consider what might be done on an individual basis to help them.

Steve, who is a word-by-word reader, might need to stop moving his lips. He might also need to increase his sight vocabulary, to concentrate more on extracting ideas from his reading materials, to practice with timed selections, to preread by skimming and scanning, and to realize that he should adjust his rate as he changes the purpose and the reading material. Aaron, who is not a word-by-word reader, does not vocalize or move his lips, and has command of a much larger sight vocabulary, can still benefit from some of the activities that will help Steve. He may also need to concentrate more on finding ideas and on developing versatility and flexibility. Aaron will probably make better progress with critical reading than will Steve, but this fact should not be a reflection on Steve's effort.

Franklin and Marie also need developmental help of the kinds just mentioned, but much more serious problems stand in the way. Franklin seems to lack skills in basic word attack. He cannot use phonics successfully in pronouncing words, and he seems unaware of basic structural clues to word meanings. When reading orally, he skips words, mumbles through them, or substitutes other words. Marie refuses to read, so it is extremely difficult to determine what her problems are. In such cases, corrective or even remedial teaching may be required. The words *corrective* and *remedial* are not labels for different kinds of reading, just for different degrees of help needed.

What can an English teacher do to help Franklin and Marie? In a small school the task usually falls directly on the shoulders of the English teacher. The teacher must look more closely at the results of standardized test scores to get a general idea of areas of difficulty and then develop and administer a much more helpful kind of instrument—the informal reading inventory. (Details about this kind of instrument are given later in this chapter.) As the inventory reveals problems more clearly, the English teacher can use some of the instructional strategies that are used by elementary and middle school teachers. The focus will be on word-attack skills, building a larger sight vocabulary, and finding literal meanings. High-interest, low-difficulty materials should be used, although high school students will not respond if they are embarrassed by using materials which much younger children use.

In a large school, the English teacher can often turn to a reading specialist for help. This specialist might assist in diagnosing difficulties or might work in the classroom with the English teacher. The specialist might also accept small groups of students from the English class in a reading classroom or clinic at prearranged times for special help. Such cooperation is clearly in the best interests of students; professional jealousies or misunderstandings must never stand in the way.

Now let's turn to Juanita and Jo-Mei. They appear to have special reading problems because they are still struggling to read English as a second language. They will not necessarily be slower learners; in fact, their potential for learning may be extremely high. They may be survivors of indifference in earlier grades in the same school system, and they may have done remarkably well in view of the sociolinguistic and psycholinguistic problems encountered so far. Traditional testing, geared to American English speakers and readers, has never identified their abilities to *read*. The English teacher usually has no idea, for example, of their ability to read in their native languages. If new to English, they can be extremely frustrated and anxious; if not new to English, they can be discouraged and turned off to the point of giving up.

What can an English teacher do to help them? First the teacher must provide a comfortable classroom that will encourage these students to respond to whatever help is given. Then the English teacher can provide more opportunities in oral communication through structured conversations and oral pattern practices. These are reinforced by words, phrases, sentences, and pictures on flash cards and other teaching materials. Like Franklin and Marie, these students will need help in attacking words, building a sight vocabulary, and finding literal meanings. As they improve, they should work with high-interest, low difficulty materials which will enable them to encounter some of the same topics and ideas that other students will find in regularly assigned materials. In searching for good transitional materials, though, the English teacher should also look for literary value.

The English teacher should be aware of special problems that can arise in working with students who are trying to read English as a second language. The teacher can feel more disadvantaged than the student. English teachers who don't know the phonology, syntax, vocabulary, intonation, or spelling of both languages cannot take into account the ways in which the student's intuitive sense of the first language is likely to interfere with reading English. The same sounds may exist in both languages but have different ranges. Words in both languages can have the same form but different meanings. Similar symbols can represent different sounds. And if this is not enough to worry about, sounds in one language may not exist in the other. The same can be true for word order and symbols for the alphabet. To this list of problems can also be added stylistic, idiomatic, and semantic differences deeply rooted in contrasting cultures. A student who is not aware of such differences may become embarrassed when reading English orally.

Although an English teacher can do much to help Juanita and Jo-Mei, the teacher should not attempt the task alone. Other students in class can help, particularly if they know both languages. So can specialists in reading and teachers in other subjects. Teachers with special training in teaching English as a second language could of course provide invaluable assistance. As programs that train such teachers increase to meet this growing demand, specialized help will be more readily available.

Students like Steve, Aaron, Franklin, Marie, Juanita and Jo-Mei, as well as those with problems not described here, can be found in English classrooms all over the country. As we have seen, the English teacher can help them to read better. The task is not easy: it requires understanding, patience, flexibility, creativity, cooperation, and hard work. It also requires doing whatever one can to motivate the student.

## FOURTH PRINCIPLE: TO READ WELL, ONE MUST WANT TO READ WELL

Unless Steve and Marie can be led to realize that reading can bring them to something that they want or need, they will probably never learn to read well. And if Aaron complacently believes that he knows all about reading, his improvement is not likely to be great. Motivation, then, becomes a key.

For all motivation, the English teacher needs to consider why some students do not want to read at all. Lance Gentile and Merna McMillan have listed ten factors which seem to cause teenagers to reject reading:

1. *By the time many students reach high school they may equate reading with ridicule, failure, or exclusively school-related tasks. Often these youngsters have never experienced joy in reading.*

2. *Some pupils are not excited by ideas. Many are driven to experience life directly rather than through reading.*

3. *A great number of adolescents do not want to sit, and in some cases are incapable of sitting, for prolonged periods of time.*

4. *Adolescence is a time of intense egocentricity. Teenagers are preoccupied with themselves, their problems, families, sexual roles, and material possessions.*

5. *Many young people demand to be entertained. They have developed little understanding or appreciation of intrinsic rewards, such as the sense of personal accomplishment that comes through prolonged effort.*

6. *A lot of these students are pressured at home as well as in school to read! read! read! Persistent stress proves counterproductive.*

7. *Many young people grow up in an atmosphere void of reading material. The "significant people" in their lives may not read or have any appreciation for learning by reading. These values are handed down.*

8. *Reading may be considered an "antisocial" activity.*

9. *Many classroom texts and supplementary reading materials are dull to look at.*

10. *Some adolescents view reading as a part of the adult world and automatically reject it.*[2]

In the midst of so much rejection, a teacher can become easily discouraged. These five axioms for motivating better reading, and the suggestions that accompany them, should prove helpful:

**Axiom 1. Each student should understand the personal advantages of reading.** As is true for adults in the population, the number of students who don't and won't read is considerably larger than the number who can't read. Many students can't even think of a book that they would like to read. For those who claim that there is nothing in reading for them, the teacher can provide a wide variety of practical reading materials which could relate to immediate interests and the need for information. These could include newspaper ads, driver manuals, do-it-yourself kits, recipes, bus schedules, yellow pages from the telephone directory, and TV schedules.[3] To this list Judith Barmore and Philip Morse have added greeting cards, comic strips, sheet music, record jackets, parts catalogs and repair manuals, posters, souvenir pamphlets, advertising circulars, ads for record and book clubs, pins, buttons, bumper stickers, game instructions, directions for assembling items, travel brochures, placemats from restaurants, jokebooks, paperback catalogs, photograph albums, and road maps.[4] Information about jobs and careers, local laws and ordinances, police procedures and regulations, students' legal rights, and many other materials could be included.

Materials such as these can serve as prompters for students who refuse to read, but they do not in any way substitute for a literature program. Like questionnaires and inventories, they serve to identify students' interests. Noting a show of interest, an alert teacher will capitalize on it by offering, not just suggesting, works which will allow the student to pursue that interest. Some of the most reluctant readers can be guided step by step from materials such as those mentioned above to literature of increasing quality. In the process, the teacher can encourage the student to talk about how reading has aided the pursuit of a personal interest.

Clear and convincing testimony of the fact that even the most reluctant readers will respond to literature which interests them has been given by Daniel N. Fader and Elton B. McNeil (1968) in their research-based book, *Hooked On Books: Program and Proof*. Fader, an English professor, had designed and piloted a program which surrounded reluctant readers with a wide variety of interesting reading materials, mainly magazines and paperbacks, and encouraged them to write freely in journals. McNeil, a psychology professor, subjected this program to research which involved an experimental group of boys at the W. J. Maxey Boys' Training School at Whitmore Lake, Michigan, and a control group at another last-chance midwestern school. The boys in both groups had been in trouble repeatedly with the law and had rejected everything that schools stood for. The boys in the experimental group (who had been given Fader's program) far outstripped the boys in the control group in several ways. Teachers and librarians observed a significant movement from cartoon books to books generally considered to have substance and literary quality. On the Verbal Proficiency Test, the Maxey boys did so well that McNeil characterized the results a "runaway performance." Boys in the control group "were unable to maintain their unsatisfactory performance of the year before."[5] The boys at Maxey also revealed a more positive attitude than the other group toward their own reading and writing, as measured by attitude scales developed for the project.[6]

The "best" students in school can also be reluctant readers. Even the most capable readers sometimes fail to see that literature can do anything worthwhile for them. The fault can lie in the reading matter itself. Perhaps a selection does not lie close enough to interests, experiences, social backgrounds, cultural identities, anxieties, aspirations, thoughts, and emotions. The most capable readers also seek personal engagements with books, and will widen and strengthen their reading performance if encouraged to read books that interest them.

No teacher can assume, however, that the fault always lies with the book. Sometimes a book is not taught in a challenging way. If a teacher's questions in class discussions or in individual conferences fail to go beyond simple recall, a student may feel that the book has very limited value. A student who thinks that the purpose of reading literature is to remember bits of information for a class discussion or a test, becomes bored and develops a low opinion of the quality of the reading material. Even the most capable students can be heard to say that some books wouldn't be half bad if it were not for teachers who do all kinds of annoying things that get in the way of reading. Often too much is said about a book. And that which *is* said is sometimes so trivial that it wastes a student's time. Many capable students will not see the need to go beyond literal reading into critical and creative reading if not urged to do so by critical and creative questions.

*Axiom 2. Each student should know how well he or she reads.* This implies that students' reading should be tested at regular intervals. It is extremely unwise, if not illegal, to post students' scores or to distribute them publicly in any way, but each student should be told privately what test scores show about his or her own reading. Students with a low score should be given encouragement and help. Students with a high score should be shown that further improvement is possible and desirable.

Ways should be designed to help students monitor their own progress. The practice of keeping individual writing folders for students is generally endorsed as a procedure that supports the workshop or laboratory approach in teaching writing. This practice is not so common in reading, but it can be just as useful. The results of questionnaires and interest inventories; records of wide, individualized reading; exercises in skimming, scanning, and vocabulary development; and scores from diagnostic and progress tests can be kept together in each folder. To protect each student's right to privacy, these folders can be kept in a locked file cabinet or closet.

*Axiom 3. Each student should know that reading can be improved.* Students who read very poorly often give up. Those who assume that they have been typed failures at reading, can easily conclude that there is no way to improve. Those who assume that they are good readers frequently give up, too. If they assume that they read well enough to maintain the high grades they value, they may not see the need to read better. They may even assume that acting as though they want to improve will in some way reflect negatively on their ability as students. Some capable readers avoid taking elective courses in developmental reading or asking an English teacher for assistance because they believe it will look bad "on their records," or will be considered a sign of weakness by peers or parents.

An English teacher cannot of course allow students to make assumptions that block or inhibit improvement in reading. Students who feel that they cannot improve or do not need to improve have no real motivation, and without motivation there will be little improvement. It is therefore the teacher's task to help students to break out of self-defeating cycles. A well-informed, caring, stimulating teacher is without doubt the most important outside factor in reading improvement. .

*Axiom 4. Reading materials should be appropriate.* Peter L. Sanders lists these six guidelines to appropriateness:

1. *The only works worth teaching have an artistic dimension.*
2. *Works should be selected for their probable appeal.*
3. *The subject matter of the works selected should be acceptable to the local community.*
4. *The works selected should reflect ethnic diversity.*
5. *There should be variety in content, style, and theme.*
6. *There should be a range in conceptual and linguistic difficulty.*[7]

The common belief that works should have artistic dimension has raised many questions about the worth of literature which has been written for adolescents. This is as it should be. Burton, Carlsen, Dunning, and others who have examined adolescent books for their value as transitional literature agree that such literature should be examined closely and that only those works of highest quality should be chosen.

Looking for quality does not mean requiring that all materials, especially those read independently by students, must be "Literature." Adolescent novels, with their demonstrated appeal in high school paperback book clubs, serve as a useful barometer for the teacher who watches for conditions favorable to further growth in reading. Students drawn to these books for outside reading are at least reading, and a reading student can be more easily led to better materials than can a nonreading student. G. Robert Carlsen observes that "the book that has the best chance of weaning the teenager between the ages of twelve and fifteen away from sub-literature is the adolescent novel."[8]

Carlsen provides helpful guidelines in the form of "The Stages of Reading Development." Noting that adolescents "will read books of great language difficulty if the subject lies close to their interests, and reject even simple books about subjects that bore them," Carlsen identifies "three transformations" that readers between the ages of 10 or 11 and 18 go through in selecting content which interests them. In early adolescence they find greatest satisfaction in animal stories, adventure stories, adolescent mystery stories, tales of the super-natural, sports stories, growing up around the world, home and family-life stories, slapstick, and settings in the past. Reaching the age of 15 or 16, teen-agers apparently prefer the nonfiction account of adventure, biography and au-tobiography, historical novels, mystical romance, and the story of adolescent life. Those who are finishing their last two years of high school are interested in the search for personal values, books of social significance, the strange and unusual human experience, and transition into adult life.[9]

THE TEACHING OF HIGH SCHOOL ENGLISH

After reviewing some of the research on reading interests, Alan Purves and Richard Beach (1972) concluded that students' interests are "most associated with the content of a work rather than its form or style," and that "most students prefer plain, suspenseful fare." Cautioning against hasty generalizations, though, these reviewers suggest that the teacher "look more deeply at the needs and drives of students in the classroom."[10]

There are many ways in which an English teacher can discover these interests that can greatly affect reading. Observations, discussions with individual students, class and group discussions, oral and written reports, library check-outs, personal writing, and entries in journals all help a teacher to gather this kind of information. These methods should be supplemented by a teacher-made reading inventory, which provides a more structured approach to information-gathering. This instrument will be described in some detail later in the chapter.

By gathering useful information and providing appropriate reading materials, an English teacher is taking two very important steps toward helping students feel motivated. If the teacher takes another step at this point, it should be to help students taste some real success in reading something that interests them. Success is of course the greatest motivator of all. First questions in an informal conference should be the kind the student has the best chance of answering. Reading assignments should be easily attainable, and the student should not feel hurried or pressured. Although it is not advisable to put much faith in the value of reading machines, advancing rate as measured by a reading accelerator, pacer, tachistoscope, or controlled reader can give students a psychological boost. At least they may begin believing that they can do better than they thought possible. If students have not worked with such a machine, the innovation of doing so may create a "Hawthorn effect" sufficient to carry them beyond their feelings of defeat or self-satisfaction. The cause and effect relationship between "I want to" and "I can" is not always convincing or workable; often a student must go from "I can" to "I want to."

***Axiom 5. The classroom atmosphere should be pleasant.*** All efforts described above will work best if the classroom environment is friendly and free from tension. Even in a rather gloomy, unattractive building, the attitude of the teacher can make a class cheerful and cooperative. The teacher also sets the tone. The way a teacher interacts with students greatly affects the way students interact with books.

## FIFTH PRINCIPLE: MANY TEACHERS SHARE IN THE RESPONSIBILITY FOR IMPROVING READING

If there is any one feature of the total reading program about which the experts agree, it is that all high school teachers have a share in the responsibility of teaching reading, even though the major part of the burden falls upon the teacher of English. In summarizing the experts' idea of an all-school developmental program (which no school yet claims to have achieved) Margaret J. Early lists 10 points. Note that teachers of subjects other than English have responsibility in numbers 1, 3, 4, 5, and 7, and possibly in one or two more:

1. *Continuous instruction in reading skills from kindergarten to grade 12 for* **all** *pupils.*

2. *Integration of reading skills with other communication skills: writing, speaking, and listening.*

3. *Specific instruction by subject-matter teachers in* **how to read and study** *in their special fields, using the basic reading materials of their courses.*

4. *Cooperative planning by all teachers so that skills will not be overlooked or overstressed.*

5. *Adjusted reading materials in all subjects for slow, average, and superior students.*

6. *Guidance in free reading.*

7. *Emphasis on the uses of reading as a source of information, as an aid to personal and social development, and as a means of recreation.*

8. *Corrective or remedial instruction for seriously retarded readers.*

9. *Measurement of growth in skills by means of standardized and informal tests; study of students' application of techniques in all reading tasks.*

10. *Evaluation of the uses of reading through study of the amount and quality of voluntary reading; study of effect on achievement in all school subjects; effect on percentages of drop-outs.*[11]

Examples from several subject fields may make this point more specific. Social studies teachers should give suggestions on how to read and study social studies materials, and should teach students how to interpret maps, graphs, and charts. H. Alan Robinson has identified these seven major patterns of writing in the instructional materials used in social studies: topic development, enumeration, generalization, sequence, comparison or contrast, effect-cause, and question-answer.[12] Knowing these patterns, students in social studies could skim text chapters in advance in order to organize more carefully their reading of them. Music teachers, in addition to teaching the reading of music, should be sure that students can read and understand such terms as *pianissimo* and *glissando*. Teachers of health and safety should teach necessary technical vocabulary.

Teachers of science and math also must assume special responsibilities. "A major task of the reader of instructional materials in science is to understand a host of details which often add up to a generalization, an abstraction, a theory."[13] Understanding illustrations of how that theory is tested, and then following directions which ask the reader to perform a process or conduct an experiment to test the theory require exact and careful reading. Mathematics involves a specialized vocabulary, symbol systems, graphics, and its own written strategies. According to Robinson, "strategies for reading and studying math must concentrate on patterns of presenting concepts and principles as well as on the solving of mathematical problems."[14]

Even this brief overview of some of the reading tasks in content fields outside English should serve to dispel the myth that the English teacher is responsible for teaching all reading skills. All teachers should teach skills appropriate to their fields, and all teachers should cooperate to make reading uniformly valued throughout the school.

## SIXTH PRINCIPLE: THERE IS NO SINGLE RIGHT WAY TO TEACH READING

Perhaps this principle is a corollary of the first, that reading is complex. Research has shown repeatedly that students may improve their reading abilities when taught by discrete methods or combinations of methods. Unfortunately some researchers or experimenters, loving their own brainchildren best, have tended to make exaggerated claims for the methods they have used successfully. Thus machine users, for instance, have urged that reading accelerators or pacers be lined along the walls like slot machines in Las Vegas. Some advocates of speed reading seem to place great importance on running a finger down or across the page to force the reader to read as rapidly as possible. Some persons who favor phonetics would apparently ignore everything else. Some who think that small vocabularies are poor readers' biggest handicaps would spend day after day on vocabulary-building devices. Some have found that extensive reading, unaccompanied by any formal instruction, may result in considerable gains, and hence have argued that all that is needed is to turn children loose in a library. And so on, ad infinitum.

The significant point is that there is a degree of truth in most of the claims. However, each of the dozens of recommended methods is likely to lead to a special—and rather limited—sort of improvement. The best program, then, it would seem, would be a balanced one that borrows some parts from each of the proved methods.

# READING IN REGULAR ENGLISH CLASSROOMS

On the high school level much of the teaching of reading takes place in regular English classes, most often in connection with the study of literature. Chapters 5, 6, and 7 of this book treat in some detail the teaching of literature; if the recommendations in those chapters are followed, improvement in reading ability will result. There are, though, some procedures and techniques that a teacher may consciously employ to improve students' general reading abilities. It is the purpose of this section to discuss those procedures and techniques. Much more experimentation is necessary, however, before we shall know the very best ways of incorporating reading instruction in the regular English program while still teaching adequately everything else that must be included. Perhaps as much as 95 percent of the research thus far reported has dealt with special classes or individual problems rather than with reading in the regular English class.

The well-balanced English program includes some reading done in common by the whole class or by sizable groups within the class and also reading done by individuals or by small groups. In this section we shall concern ourselves especially with reading in common, but in so doing we shall include many techniques that an English teacher should find useful in working with small groups and with individual students.

## GATHERING INFORMATION

A reading program is likely to be most effective if the teacher knows how well each student already reads, if students' interest is aroused, and if students' probable difficulties with assigned and unassigned selections are anticipated. Both formal and informal evaluations can be used to gather this information.

### Formal Evaluation

Some schools as a matter of general practice give all entering students a reading test. Some give such tests annually, to measure each student's growth; others give them at the beginning and end of each school year. These tests, which are often given as part of a comprehensive standardized battery encompassing several subject fields, often reveal subtest scores under such headings as vocabulary, comprehension, rate, and locational skills. If a content analysis is supplied by the test publisher, it should provide a further breakdown by identifying certain test items under headings such as word recognition, word comprehension, sentence comprehension, recognizing important details, recognizing main ideas, drawing inferences, and so forth. Standardized tests present scores as rankings which give a teacher some indication of how each student's performance compares with standards established by other students in the nation.

After using the same standardized test a number of times, school systems sometimes develop local norms based on standards which their own students have set by taking these tests. Local norms enable teachers and administrators to compare a student's performance with that of other students in the same system. Although local norms provide information, they can lead to practices that are clearly not in the best interests of students. For example, if local students have set standards far above the national norm, students who score below that local level, but still above the national norm, can be typed locally as "below average," even

THE TEACHING OF HIGH SCHOOL ENGLISH

"slow." Consequent instruction sometimes does not challenge them to do what they are capable of doing.

In drawing conclusions from scores on a standardized test, a teacher must be cautious. The teacher should examine the test itself to see to what extent it has asked students to perform in ways controlled by the reading content in English classes. Subtest scores should also be examined cautiously because the number of items under a particular skill is often too small to produce a reliable result. If answer sheets are available after machine processing, teachers can examine a student's responses for clues to reasons for incorrect choices. An analysis such as this, though, can also reveal weaknesses in test items. A teacher should know, too, that although a score may provide general information, in all likelihood that score would have varied somewhat if the student had taken several equated or matched forms of the same test. In other words, the score is an approximation within a reasonable range. This is true because formal test-taking poses sets of conditions or variables that can affect a score. Students who have different feelings and attitudes about test-taking, and who vary in their testmanship or test-taking ability, pose others. Finally, a teacher should be careful not to allow test results to focus great attention on competition with other students. Improvement in reading is an individual matter; a student makes the most satisfactory progress when he competes with himself.

If your school uses formal tests regularly, you should take advantage of the information that is available. Do not look only at the total scores, but also at the scores on various parts of the test. Even though these scores may not be highly reliable for reasons stated above, they may help to locate specific weaknesses and provide a rough profile of each student's reading performance.

If your school does not have an established and consistent testing program in reading, perhaps you can arrange one for your classes. It is probably best to plan to give different forms of the same test at the beginning and end of the same year. The comparison may please you or humble you, and may affect your teaching in subsequent years.

Do not be reluctant to talk with your classes about the kinds of things that reading tests measure—and why. Analysis of the parts may help your students to understand more clearly the components of reading skill.

In setting up a testing program, whether formal or informal, one needs to safeguard the rights of students. No longer can teachers and school administrators assume that they have the right to freely administer IQ tests, standardized reading tests, questionnaires and inventories, attitude scales, and psychological screening instruments. No longer can teachers freely examine a student's cumulative records or exchange information with other people about test results and classroom performance. No longer can teachers display test scores or class grades or leave them where others have access to them. The teacher should be sure that a procedure is in keeping with current school policies regarding a student's right to privacy. (Sometimes such policies have been reviewed carefully by the attorney for the school board.) In some cases, the teacher will definitely need the written permission of parents to gather or use personal information.

### Informal Evaluation

Although a formal testing program can provide helpful information, it is not as useful to the English teacher and the students as careful observation and informal tests and inventories. Because the English teacher's observations and tests can identify specific weaknesses and strengths in reading content materials in current use in the classroom, they provide incomparable information. This information is the most valid and most reliable that an English teacher can use in deciding what help to give. It is also the most useful to have when considering the referral of students for remedial and corrective help. It is the English teacher who observes Juan holding a book a few inches from his eyes; Sue moving her lips with every word; Eric stopping every few minutes to look around the room or out through the window; Inez rubbing her eyes; and Sam often doubling back to the material above or on a previous page, even with the easiest material. Any one of these behaviors can signal a serious problem.

A student *may* have a serious reading problem if he or she demonstrates one or more of the following behaviors:

1. Shows a lack of interest in reading.
2. Reads slowly, often word-by-word, even with easier materials.
3. Moves lips, moves head back and forth, or stops eye movements often.
4. Cannot answer questions about details, relationships, and ideas.
5. Cannot state the main idea of a paragraph.
6. Cannot summarize orally what is read or write a précis of it.
7. Has difficulty using a table of contents, an index, a glossary, footnotes, and overviews in a text.
8. Has poor study habits.
9. Mispronounces, skips, repeats, or stumbles through words.
10. Reverses pronunciations, saying *was* for *saw*.
11. Pauses and appears confused quite often in reading orally.
12. Substitutes words or guesses them.
13. Squirms, fidgets, moves book around, thumbs back or ahead, looks around the room often.

Any observant teacher could add to the list. As any wise teacher knows, however, such a list also contains some of the same dangers as a family medical book. Too much concentration on stated symptoms can magnify them unrealistically and lead to unfounded anxieties.

86

As mentioned earlier in this chapter, the English teacher can gather useful information by constructing and administering an interest inventory. This instrument is actually a questionnaire which asks about a student's special interests, hobbies, goals, work and travel experiences, books and magazines liked, movies and television programs liked, pets at home, school subjects liked, school subjects not liked, number of books read within the last year, attitude about reading, attitude about libraries, and many other things which can help a teacher to recognize possible reading interests.

Other valuable information can be gathered through an informal reading inventory constructed and administered by the teacher. This is a collection of tests that determines a student's ability to read materials assigned in regular English classes. In one such test, the teacher selects paragraphs of increasing difficulty and asks the student to read them aloud. While the student reads orally, the teacher marks errors on a double-spaced copy of the same selection, noting such things as omissions, substitutions, mispronunciations, repetitions, insertions, difficulties with word attack, hesitations, and apparent disregard for punctuation. The teacher usually follows up with a few questions about details and ideas in the passage read.

The English teacher's informal reading inventory may also include vocabulary tests; directions for writing a précis of a longer piece, such as an essay; directions for writing paraphrases and outlines; timed and untimed comprehension tests; informal textbook inventories; paragraphs and essays needing titles; sentences and paragraphs that are alike or different in facts, ideas, purpose, or tone; and paragraphs from which words have been removed.

Unlike standardized tests, these teacher-made instruments have the validity that comes from basing them on English materials actually used in the classroom. An informal textbook inventory could check the students' abilities to read their literature anthologies or language texts, and to use aids in those books, such as the table of contents, index, glossary, footnotes, bibliographies, introductory passages and overviews, summaries, guide questions, questions for discussion, suggestions for projects, and various editorial comments. Constructed as a diagnostic survey, this instrument becomes an openbook test. Questions on the test can be answered only by referring to specific parts of the text itself. It is surprising that more teachers do not construct and administer informal textbook inventories. Many students, even seniors, lack a working knowledge of the tools and overall structure of basic textbooks used regularly in their English class. Some cannot read these texts well enough to do their assignments.

Another test in the teacher's informal reading inventory deserves special mention here. Called the Cloze test, it is quite helpful in determining the difficulty level of instructional materials. The teacher removes every fifth or tenth word from paragraphs chosen randomly from the text and asks students to replace them using only the context of surrounding words as clues. Sometimes the teacher provides clues, such as the first letter of a missing word, the first and last letter, or short blanks which indicate the number of missing letters. Because the difficulty of a passage affects a student's ability to supply the missing words, the teacher can consider the test a measure of the difficulty of that passage for the student. The reliance on contextual clues also alerts the student to the importance of using them in reading. On the basis of degrees of success with this procedure, the teacher can assign reading material which is more appropriate in difficulty for individuals, groups, or classes. Douglas Thomas and Thomas Newkirk use a passage containing 50 blanks to determine students' reading levels.

*Students who fill in 61% or more of the blanks are reading at the "independent" level; they can read the material without teacher assistance. Students replacing 41–60% correctly are reading at the "instructional" level; they can read the passage, but may need some prereading assistance in areas such as vocabulary. Those students scoring less than 40% are reading at the "frustration" level; the material is simply too difficult for them.*[15]

### Anticipating General Difficulties and Needs

It is not possible to anticipate all of the difficulties and needs of individual students in reading, or to anticipate how much all students will be able to improve. However, a teacher can reduce some of the problems by providing anticipatory assistance while teaching English. The amount of such assistance should be greater, as a rule, for young students and slow learning groups than for older students and quick learners. Of course every rule has its exceptions.

Suppose that reading tests or the teacher's observations have revealed that a class had difficulty in understanding organization and grasping main ideas. A brief outline duplicated or placed on the board, may be of considerable help. For a variation, especially useful with exposition, the numbers of main and supporting points may be supplied, with the students to fill them in: I.... A.... B.... II...., and so on. Or a list of key questions, each pointing toward the main idea of a selection, may be prepared.

Also especially helpful with exposition is a structured overview of a selection, which the teacher leads students through step by step. The hope is that students will be able to structure overviews of selections on their own. As we shall see below, the procedure is like skimming, except that it delves more deeply into some matters as it progresses.

As a first step, the teacher will begin by noting the title, asking questions about the possible meanings of key words. If the author or an editor has supplied a short statement to interest or tease the reader (usually italicized above the title to one side), the teacher asks about its possible meaning and clues. Next the teacher will read the first paragraph or two, or ask a student to do so, and will try to find out whether students know what specific subject the author plans to address; what

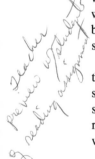

88

background facts or qualifying conditions the author thinks the reader should know about the subject; how important the subject seems to be to the writer; how many subordinate points or parts of the subject the author will discuss; and how the writer plans to carry out his or her purpose. The teacher may then show students how to skim through paragraphs in the body of the selection looking for the key or topic sentences in light of what was learned earlier. The last paragraph or two will receive a closer skimming in view of everything discovered so far.

After the first sweep, as described above, students might be guided through the selection again to look for meanings on four levels: details, relationships, main ideas, and application. On the first level, the student will be urged to ask, "Who? what? where? when?"; on the second level, the student will ask, "What does this have to do with that?"; on the third level, "What does it all mean, according to the writer?"; and on the fourth level, "What does it all mean to me, and what can I do with the information or idea?" Along the way, the student should try to determine how difficult the entire selection will be to read in detail. It may have many details or relatively few. Many unfamiliar names or terms may appear, as may facts, numbers, and percentages. Relationships may occur among several details, not simply between two or sets of two. Relationships may be drawn in nonchronological or nonlinear fashion. The main idea may be directly stated in the beginning, supported in rather obvious ways, and expanded and reinforced rather obviously near the end. However, the main idea may be presented subtly; it may be implied or suggested in a highly satirical or symbolic selection. Applications may involve complex clusters of facts and ideas that a reader must consider personally. The important thing about all this, however, is the ability to anticipate details and ideas without a teacher's help. Therefore, the English teacher should ask students repeatedly to skim selections on their own in the ways just described. Written or duplicated charts and guidelines covering points just mentioned can aid in a weaning process by which the student develops a personal strategy for previewing a selection.

The English teacher should know that the structured overview will not work equally well for all students. Richard Smith and Karl Hesse (1969) report that prereading assistance can have a positive effect on the attitudes of poor readers and on their ability to grasp main ideas. Apparently, though, it is not as helpful for good readers, who seem much more able to organize their thinking before and during reading without such intervention. In fact, good readers are likely to find that strategies different from their own can cause confusion.[16]

### Anticipating Problems with Vocabulary

There are differences of opinion about trying to anticipate difficulties with vocabulary. Some teachers like to pick out a few of the important "hard" words and define them in advance. Others argue that new words are best learned in context. You may want to experiment to see which method you prefer. Any general work that the class does in vocabulary building (see Chapter 9) is valuable for reading as well as for writing, speaking, and listening. This fact should not be surprising, for reading is not an isolated act; it reinforces the other language arts and is reinforced by them.

Knowing some facts about when and how students acquire and use words is a prerequisite for teaching reading. A student who enters first grade with relatively large and flexible listening and speaking vocabularies has an advantage in developing a reading vocabulary. The student as a beginning reader has the task of developing "strategies for associating printed representations of words with pronunciations and meanings that he has stored."[17]

For various reasons, some high school students have very low reading vocabularies. In some cases, their sight vocabulary is to low that they cannot instantly recognize all of the 220 common sight words on the traditional Dolch list. Word recognition skills taught earlier, such as consonant digraphs and blends, vowels, final consonants, inflectional endings, compounds, prefixes, roots, spelling patterns, configurations, and many more, play important roles later. But so do the ability to foresee or anticipate words which could appear in reading material on a certain subject, and the ability to use contextual clues to meaning.

The good reader usually has larger than average listening, speaking, and writing vocabularies; effective strategies for decoding written words; strategies for interpreting word meanings from nearby words and from larger contexts; and a larger than average sight vocabulary. Harold L. Herber makes this observation about a reader's vocabularies:

> For most people (depending on their occupations and interests) the relationship of the listening, reading and speaking vocabularies stabilizes, with listening and speaking larger than reading. Again, one often hears words he does not use in his conversations, and he both hears and speaks words he might not recognize in print.[18]

With the English teacher's help, students should be able to recognize in print more and more of the words in their listening and speaking vocabularies. As Herber indicates, the word hoards will be higher in listening and speaking. But the English teacher can help each student to close the gap.

## Anticipating Difficulties with the Genres

A wise English teacher not only anticipates the difficulties that students may have with words but also with the language constructs and styles of various forms of fiction and nonfiction. Poems, plays, short stories, novels, essays, and biographies present their own reading problems. They are structured in different ways to accomplish different purposes, so they must be read in different ways to be understood and appreciated. Reading problems which stem from the structure, purpose, and art of a work, and from the reader's purpose for reading it, should be given attention as the literary form is introduced. And these problems should be met with repeated readings in that genre. Some of these problems are discussed briefly below.

## Poetry

Characteristics of poetry which frequently present reading problems are its irregular length of line; use and nonuse of capitalization and punctuation; irregular and often inverted sentence structure; compressions; rhythmic, audial, and conceptual juxtapositions; images and figurative expressions. As any experienced teacher knows, capitalization at the beginnings of lines in some poems can cause students to think they are reading a list of separate sentences, varying in length from many words to one. This keeps them from sensing the natural ebbing and flowing of the language from comma to comma and from semicolon to semicolon before reaching a period. Reading as they do, line by separate line, they fail to grasp relationships and consequently meanings. Students with such basic difficulties not only have problems finding meanings discussed in class, but in finding their own meanings. They simply do not read a poem well enough to be able to account for the whole of it in any meaningful way.

## Drama

Drama is not written to be read; it is to be visualized. It is to be felt through viewing and participating. Accustomed to a running narrative which is told someone, the reader of drama also expects to find settings, characters, and actions described as they develop. But this does not happen. Instead, the reader finds actions and setting printed in italicized directions. Accustomed to reading what someone says before seeing that person's name, student readers are often confused by constantly encountering the name before the saying. Accustomed to reading about one situation or event after another in linear fashion, students are often confused by characters simultaneously acting and reacting all in the round, so to speak.

## The Short Story

As a short, compact piece of prose fiction that concerns human beings in conflict, the short story is an appealing genre for adolescent readers; yet it is not necessarily the easiest genre to read. Some students do not realize as they read that the well-written story avoids lengthy descriptions and explanations. Rather, it develops setting, characters, actions, conflict, and theme by indirection. Consequently the adolescent reader must be able to find and use clues which are suggested, implied, repeated, compared, and contrasted in ways that contribute to single impressions. The reader has to be able to find such things in single words; to do so he must use his imagination to fill in the explanations that are not actually there. Beginnings and endings can also cause difficulty. The reader may drop into the middle of an unexplained situation at the beginning and seem to drop off at the end without being told exactly how everything was resolved. The reader will encounter still further difficulties in many very contemporary stories. These include unconventional uses of time, place, point of view, story teller, and language. Although these may be artfully arranged to contribute to single impressions, the reader must be able to do some unconventional thinking to understand what they can mean.

## The Novel

The very length of a novel is enough to discourage many adolescent readers. Some students, whenever required to read a novel, spend a great amount of time looking for one that is interesting, easy, and short. Perhaps they want to find in a novel the same kind of swift, violent action or superficial situational comedy that they find on television. These students do seem distressed by the unhurried pace of the novel as it develops setting and characters, moves back and forth in time, brings in new characters, tells what happens to each one of them, and encompasses years, even a lifetime or more. As they read, students must also recall characters, main plot, and subplots as they reappear; keep these straight, yet see their relationships; recognize the problem, the climax, and the final solution or resolution; and do this often within the framework of language and style used in a much earlier time, or within the framework of experimental language and style used today.

## Biography and Autobiography

Like the novel, the genre of biography and autobiography can seem difficult because its products are often book-length. Also like the novel, it presents background information, builds settings, presents a main character, presents other characters, sometimes includes dialogue, moves from place to place, and encompasses several decades. It may tend to be rather objective, based on confirmed historical fact, or it may blend fact with fiction, based in part on the author's imagination and bias. Some modern biographers who treat controversial public figures try to build human interest through describing motives, inner feelings, and character traits. Such treatment may give the reader the feeling that the biography is an exposé. When writers insert documents or allude to sensitive facts to create the impression that their revelations are really ''inside'' ones, critical reading is called for. Furthermore, because adolescent readers often do not realize how widely two biographies about the same person can differ, having them compare two such works can promote skills of critical reading.

## The Essay or Article

No genre receives as much attention in reading instruction as the essay or article. This is largely true because it is usually short and informative. Teachers and composition books also give it much attention. Some direction is necessary, but the danger of all of this is that the student can get a view which is narrow and overstructured. Limited information about *the* structure of the essay, often breaking it down into a step-by-step schematic including the introduction, the body, and the conclusion, can mislead students into believing that every essayist will tell them what to expect, state it, and tell them what was said. Narrow instruction in essay writing can also lead students to assume that the best essays are serious in tone and informative or argumentative in nature.

Such myths do little to prepare students for reading essays. As readers, students must be ready for a considerable variety of subject matter, purpose, structure, style, and mood. Reading teachers and authors of reading texts also perpetuate another unfortunate myth. Because essays and articles are so popular as selections to test reading rate and comprehension, students can get the false impression that they should all be read as fast as possible. No genre offers greater variety. For the student reader, the best preparation is flexibility, a willingness to adjust to the essay or article at hand.

The student should also know that the essay is a highly personal form. The writer who tries to express an opinion as clearly as possible may reveal much personal information. The writer may also invite collaboration with the reader, as a fellow observer, a partner in conversation, an opponent in friendly debate. In other words, the writer asks the reader to look at a main concern and to judge whether personal opinions about it are reasonable.

## Unusual Classroom Techniques

Sometimes unorthodox teaching devices increase motivation and contribute to reading improvement. For example, junior high students in a program sponsored by the Duke University Reading Center were asked to do all of the reading necessary to assemble projects in the "65-in-1 Electronics Project Kit" sold by Radio Shack. All of the kits came with extensive instruction booklets, which contained diagrams, drawings, and simplified explanations. The hope was that students would learn to follow directions, understand cause and effect, use a table of contents, understand specialized words, use an index, understand technical terms, use charts and diagrams, get main ideas, attack words, and read with a purpose. Twenty minutes was the maximum time that even the slowest reader needed to complete a project. After completing a project, the student was almost always eager to read in the instruction booklet to discover how and why it worked. Interest was so high that the teacher could take the students through "less interesting but necessary drills" by using the "lab" work as a reward.[19]

Using the newspaper to motivate reading isn't a new approach, but Ira Epstein recommends something out of the ordinary. He suggests taking students to a library where a microfilm collection will permit them to read what happened on the days they were born. Guide questions about clothing styles, stock market listings, leaders in government, the weather, events of great historical importance, movies, TV programs, prices, and many other things can stimulate reading. Epstein also suggests comparative reading along these points by providing a copy of the most current newspaper. Students find out that life styles, the economy, and public attitudes have changed.[20]

Have you ever thought of using horoscopes to teach students to follow directions in reading? Barbara McCullough and Gene Towery of the University of South Florida claim that it can work. After reading factual information about astrology, students set up their own hypotheses about the validity of astrological predictions, find and record the zodiac signs under which they were born, read their horoscopes for several days, make a list of predicted happenings, make a list of actual happenings, compare the two lists, and test their hypotheses against their data. Directions for following this procedure are observed carefully. Also suggested is a game called "Horoscope Trail," which students play by throwing dice, reading directions, and moving their "personal zodiac markers."[21]

On the premise that "one capsule a week [is] a painless remedy for vocabulary ills," Barbara Crist surveyed her students to find ten topics of highest interest to them. Food, sex, sports, sleep, entertainment, money, personality, family, study, and politics came out on top. While exploring each topic with students in a conversational way, the teacher introduced words that students had perhaps seen or heard but had been reluctant to try. Under *Food,* students later paired off to discuss their words with classmates, and then followed up with short compositions entitled, "I Like to Eat." Students became so involved that they prepared for subsequent "rap" sessions by digging into the dictionary and thesaurus.[22]

## THINKING AND TALKING ABOUT WHAT WAS READ

In the discussion and other activities that follow the reading of a selection, the students concentrate their attention upon the selection and related items. But the teacher has an eye on the future reading of the students, and uses the present selection as a base for future operations. That is, he or she uses it to develop skills that the students will find useful in later reading in the course and in reading they may do throughout their lives.

The points and methods of attack will differ according to the needs of the class. With some groups the steady emphasis will have to be upon simple comprehension and relation of each selection to the students' lives. With other students the stress may be upon some of the more advanced skills—"depth reading," as one teacher has called it. Here is a brief discussion of a few of the reading-improvement techniques that have been proved workable.

### Understanding Details

The study of details can stimulate thinking about causes, conditions, motives, feelings, problems, conflicts, and main ideas. The following questions about

THE TEACHING OF HIGH SCHOOL ENGLISH

Steinbeck's *The Pearl* should serve to illustrate this point. After Kino finds the large oyster, why does he open his small ones first? Why do the neighbors react the way they do when Juana asks for the doctor? How does Kino feel as he knocks on the doctor's gate? Why does Kino later strike the doctor's gate so hard? If Kino distrusts the doctor, why does he allow him to treat Coyotito? Why is it unthinkable to destroy someone's canoe? Why is a rifle so important to Kino? How does having the pearl change Kino as a person? How does it change other people? Soon after Kino's hut is burned, a windstorm comes. How does the storm help Kino and Juana? The moon rises just before Kino can attack the trackers at the pool. How does the moonlight cause or change events? Toward the end of the novel, why does Juana refuse to throw the pearl away? Why does she hand it back to Kino?

## Paraphrasing

When a selection seems rather difficult for students, a small amount of paraphrasing may be necessary. Suppose, for instance, that the class has read Wilfrid Gibson's poem "The Ice-Cart." Although this is not a difficult piece, some slow students may not understand it. A brief summary by one of the students, perhaps like the following, may help. "The narrator, working in a hot office, sees a man delivering ice and imagines that he himself is suddenly transported to a polar region, where he sees white bears, swims with seals, and then lies on an ice floe while gentle snow falls upon him, covering him deeper and deeper as he sleeps peacefully. Suddenly the iceman cracks his whip, and the narrator awakes in the grimy heat." More detailed paraphrase may be used to clarify particular lines or groups of lines. For instance,

> ... I was swimming, too,
> Among the seal-pack, young and hale,
> And thrusting on with threshing tail. . . .

may require paraphrase to make clear the point that the narrator dreams that he himself actually *is* a seal.

## Mastering New Words

The words chosen for class discussion will vary with the class. The principle behind the choice is this: Which of the probably unfamiliar words in this selection will be of particular use to the students in this group? For instance, in the long first paragraph of Lamb's rather well-liked "Dissertation upon Roast Pig," these words may be unknown to many students: *obscurely, Mundane Mutations, designates, mast* (i.e., nuts and acorns), *lubberly, Younkers, conflagration, antediluvian, new-farrowed, utmost, consternation, negligence, premonitory, nether, retributory, cudgel, callous,* and *ensued.* Instead of spending most of the class hour in defining all these words, it may be more profitable to select three or four (perhaps *obscurely, utmost, negligence,* and *ensued*), discuss their meanings, and have students construct original sentences with them. Some of the words (*Mundane Mutations, mast, lubberly,* and *Younkers*) your students may never encounter again and never need.

As often as possible, meanings should be figured out by the students, using contextual clues. "The following dialogue ensued" usually reveals the meaning of *ensued.* "His nether lip" is obviously either his upper or his lower lip, and, because moisture overflowed it, it must be the lower. Students are more likely to remember words whose meanings they have deciphered for themselves than they are those that have been defined for them by teacher or dictionary.

Students should be encouraged to ask questions about word meanings, word relationships, word peculiarities. "Are there any words in the paragraph that you do not understand?" is a good opening. And perhaps it need not be mentioned that the teacher should not discourage questions by making every question the occasion for student labor: "Look it up in the dictionary, George." Dictionary use is of course important, but too often teachers have unintentionally employed the dictionary as an apparent punishment for curiosity. And curiosity is the most vital ingredient in motivation.

### Understanding Allusions and Figures of Speech

Teenagers often have difficulties with allusions and figurative language. To many of them, one teacher reported, such expressions as "Herculean effort," "crossed his Rubicon," "built a better mousetrap," "old school tie," and "the shot heard round the world" are meaningless. Daniel Webster's "brow like a mountain" doesn't denote intelligence to them; "As soon as she left, she was the life of the party" doesn't seem funny; "clippership clouds" are commercial planes; "mahogany-faced sea captains" are only red-faced; and "His nose was a topographical error" has not even one meaning, let alone two or three.

The teaching of figurative language may be somewhat more difficult than it once was, because, although the basic rhetorical figures remain the same, their possible content has been infinitely enlarged. Many of our students are literal-minded, perhaps because much in their environment encourages literalness: constant emphasis upon the tangibles of science, matter-of-fact newspaper accounts, prosaic TV dramas, and endless analysis of sentences in English classes. It seems important, though, to teach what the basic figures are and to talk about them when some of their more interesting examples appear.

The teaching of allusions becomes much more difficult every year, and no systematic approach appears feasible. Even 100 years ago human knowledge was much less than it is now, and the possible content of allusions was consequently much less. It has been estimated that the sum total of human knowledge is now doubling every ten years. Think, then, of how many more things a modern author may allude to. Only an omniscient person could unfailingly grasp allusions.

If we define allusions more narrowly—perhaps restricting them to classical and Biblical—we can study myths in school and the Bible in church school, and thus familiarize students with Orpheus and Lazarus. Otherwise we must content ourselves with examining the content of each allusion as it appears.

## Finding Main Ideas   *Teach as Objective*

Authors and editors are usually rather generous in supplying aids to understanding. Titles, chapter titles, headings, subheadings; paragraphing, transitions, "arrow words" (such as "especially significant"); use of additional space for important points; heightened style; mechanical devices (such as italic or boldface type)—these are some of the helps offered to the reader. But many high school students, and adults too, remain largely unaware of such bounty.

Particularly when dealing with expository material, the teacher may seize the opportunity to point out some of these aids. Simple questions are useful: "What do you suppose the author will discuss under this heading?" "Why does she use three paragraphs to discuss this topic?" "Why is this sentence italicized?"

Also of value in helping students to find main ideas is calling for one-sentence summaries of paragraphs, then one-sentence summaries of groups of related paragraphs, and then one-sentence summaries of entire expository selections. Class discussion of why one summary is better than another should follow.

## Drawing Conclusions

Nobody can write everything about anything. If it were possible, it wouldn't be artistic. Something has to be left to the reader, who works with the writer to draw from words their threads of thought. An artistic writer does not insult the reader by telling too much. Seldom does the writer say, "The moral of all this, dear reader, is that . . ." The writer makes only certain things clear and explicit, and leaves implicit what the reader presumably already knows or can deduce.

Unaided, few adolescents are adept at between-the-lines reading. They see what the author sets before them, and no more, just as they see cornflakes on the breakfast table without awareness of farmers, tractors, marching rows of corn, corn pickers, trucks, elevators, trains, dietitians, ovens, packaging machines. To help them see more than words on a page requires patience, skillful questioning, tolerance of differing opinions—and a teacher who can read beneath the surface.

What, for instance, is Thurber driving at in "The Secret Life of Walter Mitty"? A student said, "Mitty's wife henpecked him so much that she drove him crazy, that's all." "Is he crazy?" the teacher asked. "No," said some students, "he's just a dreamer." "Do you ever dream of being a great athlete, a great doctor, a great actor, or anything else?" "Yes, of course, maybe we all dream a little,'' the students admit. ''Does Thurber seem to like Walter Mitty?'' ''Yes, but he seems a little contemptuous of him, too.'' ''Does Thurber think it's bad to daydream?'' ''No, only if it's overdone.'' And out of such inductive discussion, such Socratic questioning, the students conclude that Thurber is saying that it is human nature to dream great dreams, to imagine that we are someone else, and that dreaming is not bad unless it is carried to such an extreme that it becomes madness—that it is less bad to dream you are a dozen great men than it is to be sure you are Napoleon.

Often, especially in nonfiction, it is desirable to have students draw conclusions about the attitude and the purpose of the author, or even about his or her probable honesty. This is often called critical reading. For instance, in an article on a political question, the students may find as much as possible about the author, try to discover whether the author would have any reason to weight arguments unfairly, and examine the arguments carefully to see whether any important considerations have been omitted.

### The Profundity Scale

Oliver Andresen has described the use of a ''profundity scale'' by means of which students estimate, or at least talk about, the amount of profundity or depth in a selection.[23] This scale recognizes five possible interpretational levels or planes: physical, mental, moral, psychological, and philosophical. Although admittedly almost every piece of literature exists simultaneously on all five planes, there are some stories that stress physical action—event after event after event, with little intellectualizing. In others, intellectual activity (not just hitting someone in the nose) is involved in solving the character's problems. ''Some more profound stories are meaningful at the moral and psychological levels, while a few can be shown to have universal philosophical meanings relating to essential problems such as the nature of man, of life or of history.'' Discussion of these levels may assist the student who observes only the physical happenings.

### Understanding Human Beings

An important segment of drawing conclusions is drawing conclusions about human beings. One of the virtues of wide and intelligent reading is that it can introduce us to a much greater variety of persons than we are ever likely to know in real life. But authors do not tell us about all these actual and fictitious beings. Instead they show them to us, and from the persons' actions and their words we must try to understand them; from such understanding may come truths that we can apply to our own lives, our own relationships with others.

In *Giants in the Earth*, Rölvaag shows Per Hansa, Norwegian pioneer in the Dakota territory, and Beret, his wife. He shows Per Hansa performing brave acts, but he does not tell us that Per Hansa is brave. He lets us observe Per Hansa talking to the land and the land talking to him, but Rölvaag does not say, ''This man is a poet.'' He lets us know that Per Hansa is disgusted because Hans Olsa does not get up and work despite his frozen legs, but Rölvaag does not say that Per Hansa is not really cruel—that it is just difficult for him to realize that many are less strong than he. Beret weeps and worries and makes dire predictions and indulges in mystic fancies; Rölvaag does not tell us that she is basically kind and delicate and loving but obsessed with terrible fears of an unfamiliar world. The reader must live with Per Hansa and Beret in the book and learn about them as he would in real life, draw conclusions about them as he would if he shared their roof. He may or may not come to admire and love them, but if he lives with them, he will attain much understanding of them, of others like them who drove their oxen toward the sunset, of his own ancestors, of himself, of his friends who have strengths and failings like those of Per Hansa and Beret.

## Understanding Literary Devices

In addition to reading for meaning, all classes to some extent—and able classes in particular—may be led to an understanding of certain literary forms and formalities. In poetry, for instance, they may note that a sentence does not necessarily end with the line, but they may see also the musical effects of rhyme and alliteration and assonance, the purpose of repetition, the reasons for and the effects of the extreme condensation characteristic of much poetry. In short stories they may observe the author's technique in plotting, the way the author flashes bits of the setting on our mental screen, the things he or she does *not* say.

## Working from Experience to Response

Many procedures just discussed will work more effectively if the teacher begins with something that is familiar and personally important to students. The professional literature on reading in English bears this out repeatedly. Geraldine LaRocque suggests that a brief prereading discussion with a class about the experience of having to leave a friend, a place, or a thing behind as a result of moving from place to place can help students to ease into a poem that deals with someone's loss.[24] Stephen Dunning suggests that students who know nothing about metaphors can profit from thinking about some which they use. According to Dunning, ''the metaphor of speech and song'' prepares students for the ''tougher, tighter metaphor of poetry.''[25] S. Alan Chester recommends moving from the simple to the complex, from students' experiences with their own language to their experiences with the language of poems. For example, as preparation for Frost's poem ''Design,'' Chester has asked students to write their own single-word responses to words and phrases such as ''white satin'' or ''snow-drop.'' Following this, he has sought oral definitions for words such as *kite, kindred, character, heal-all,* and *design.* Throughout accompanying discussions, his students have explored the nature of word associations, including puns.[26]

Suzanne Howell suggests word-association tests, using words from a short story taught, to help students to see that "a writer's experience determined his use of a word; a reader's experience affects his response to the word." After asking students to jot down "feelings, thoughts, and associations" that the story "Sentry" brought to mind, Howell found that each response contributed some insight into the story.[27]

Let's consider the justification of <u>working from experience to response.</u> It encourages a much more active collaboration between reader and writer. When response to a personal experience is carried to a text, it can enlighten response to the text; in turn, enlightened response to the text can further enlighten response to personal experience. As a result, students have a better chance of accounting for the "whole" of a text in a way that is personally meaningful and satisfying.

Students who engage in the kind of procedure just described are in a stronger position to ask and answer textual questions which will improve their reading. Even traditional questions such as "Who is speaking in the work?" and "What is the occasion?" can take on more personal meaning. So can, "What is the speaker's problem?" But students must have freedom if they are to stop, look, question, hypothesize, and explicate on their own. They will ask questions that are more meaningful to themselves as readers if the teacher makes it clear that they will have room in class discussions to say what they want to say whenever they find something that seems personally significant.

## READING OUTSIDE THE CLASSROOM

### GUIDED FREE READING

According to a famous statement by John C. Dana, the 12 rules for improving reading are the following:

*(1) Read. (2) Read. (3) Read some more. (4) Read anything. (5) Read about everything. (6) Read enjoyable things. (7) Read things you yourself enjoy. (8) Read, and talk about it. (9) Read very carefully, some things. (10) Read on the run, most things. (11) Don't think about reading, but (12) Just read.*

As teachers we are less interested in turning out graduates who have read than we are in turning out graduates who read. But students won't keep reading unless reading brings satisfaction. That means that during the school years we must cultivate in our students the habit of reading by giving them the opportunity to read widely in materials they can enjoy.

In some schools, extensive reading is completely free; that is, students may read anything and in any amount they desire. In others, it is almost completely guided, with the teacher making the selections. The happy medium is apparently "guided free reading," in which students choose from a long but carefully selected list representing various types and levels of difficulty. Both the teacher and librarian may offer specific suggestions to individual students. They steadily recommend books just a little above the level of those the students are now reading, and encourage them to avoid restricting themselves to one kind of subject matter.

Methods of conducting guided free reading vary. The most nearly typical procedure seems to be to set aside part of each class hour, or part of a week or other period of time, in which the students read whatever they select from the books and magazines that have been made available. In some classes there is no follow-up; in others there is class or group discussion regarding any topics of interest. For such a reading program to be successful the students must be surrounded by appropriate books and magazines, they must be led to read because reading is fun, and they must be taught by a person who is well read, quick to offer suggestions, but willing to slip unobtrusively into the background as the young people explore the variegated joys of reading.

Also frequently employed is the procedure of relating both in-class and out-of-class reading to the unit being studied. In some ways this is preferable, especially because the reading is likely to be purposeful and because subsequent class discussions will have unity and afford opportunities for all to participate.

## PROVIDING MATERIALS FOR EXTENSIVE READING

In a decreasing number of schools, the English teacher simply tells students, "Go to the library and pick out a book for your next book report." Modern schools leave less to chance. They encourage reading in class, but also set aside an occasional class period for reading in the library. During library periods, many different procedures may be followed: permitting browsing, spending periods with different kinds of books, giving library instructions, suggesting books, conferring with some students while others browse. To make the atmosphere for reading more attractive, some libraries have recessed reading pits replete with attractive cushions, while others have reading "lounges" with sofas and comfortable chairs.

Fair Haven Middle School in New Haven, Connecticut, created the "Book Nook Look." Seventh and eighth grade students found a part of their library "set aside with a circle of bookcases or NOOKS, each containing books of various reading levels assorted under appealing modern-day topics that are extremely hard to resist." Attractive LOOK signs invited students, who went to the library for one reading period each week, to read books on subjects ranging from women's rights and futurism to spine tinglers and career guidance.[28]

Classroom libraries are also important. The books, perhaps 50 to 200 in number, are changed at rather frequent intervals and may be "advertised" in ways such as those suggested in the Idea Box. These books may be borrowed by the teacher from the school library or, if sufficient funds are available, may be purchased for classroom use and circulated from room to room. Teachers use the results of reading interest inventories to choose books. The paperbacks, if wisely chosen, are a boon to schools with little money; publishers of these books make an effort to print titles that teachers want and students enjoy.

More students purchase and trade books. Paperback book clubs offer students opportunities each month to order books that interest them. Student organizations sometimes operate school bookstores to make paperbacks more available, and to earn money they can spend in service to the school. Paperback distributors set up combined book exhibits and run book fairs in schools. Some local bookstores specialize in trading and selling used paperbacks. Community organizations find it profitable to hold book bazaars. And of course inexpensive paperbacks turn up in greater numbers at the Salvation Army, Goodwill, and local garage sales. As a result of this increased flow of inexpensive used paperbacks, more adolescent readers can afford to purchase books.

## GETTING FEEDBACK ON OUTSIDE READING

Unfortunately some schools seem to spend much time simply checking up on outside reading. ''Book-report days'' are still among the most detested in those schools where students make written or oral reports according to antiquated formulas. But, because some teachers want records to help in guidance and to pass on to the teacher who will have the class the next year, they feel a compulsion to continue the system of reports.

Many approaches may be used to avoid the dull routine patterns for reports. Here are a few tested devices:

1. A small group of students reads the same book. The chairperson and teacher prepare a list of thought questions to be answered independently before the class. Differences of opinion may lead to discussion and create class interest in the book.
2. ''. . . a bright-eyed bookworm with wide reading experiences might be asked for a careful statement of theme, a high-level analysis of some character's motivation, a discussion of some structural aspect of the author's craftsmanship, or a comparison with another piece of literature. Most important, reporting must not be a case of either this or that for an entire class.''[29]
3. Students who have read books on similar topics (occupations, animals, history, etc.) exchange information about their books before the class.
4. A student tries to ''sell'' a book to another student, who believes that he would not like it.
5. ''Conversation circles'' with a student chairperson discuss books on similar topics.

6. The class prepares a "newspaper" with stories based upon books read.

7. On a spindle, each student places the name of a book he or she has read. By the next day, the teacher has added a pertinent specific question concerning the book. In class, the student answers the question.

8. Students may work out dialogues, monologues, pantomimes, short plays, or television dramatizations, pertaining to the book read.[30]

9. Students prepare appropriate book jackets including "blurbs." Advanced students write reviews, criticisms.

10. "Tell the story again from the viewpoint of another character in the story." "Show how color or key words or ideas run through the story. Discuss their purpose and effectiveness." "Place yourself in the protagonist's position and relate how plot would have been affected with you as the hero." "Imagine the character in the book in a different setting. . . . Change mood, time, or setting and show how it affects characters and plot.[31]

11. One of the simplest and best methods of providing a motivated check on reading is to have the students record whatever reading they do, together with a brief comment. The Cumulative Reading Record (NCTE) is ideal for this purpose. The teacher encourages the students to bring into class discussions references to their reading, just as adults do. Because the teacher notes carefully what each student has been reading, he or she may frequently address to a student a question upon which recent reading should throw some light. The class soon learns to expect and welcome such casual questions, and reads more carefully because of them. At the same time, students are learning that their outside reading may be related to many topics of discussion. Thus they gradually acquire a more adult view of reading than they may gain from some other devices.

## SPECIAL READING INSTRUCTION

Up to this point, we have examined the teaching of reading as it is done in English. The approach in the English classroom is largely developmental, but it necessarily includes some corrective reading. In teaching students to read English materials as well as possible, the English teacher has to assume some responsibility for both diagnosis and prescription. Most English teachers have the qualifications to do this fairly well; under the teacher's direction, students with a wide range of reading abilities can improve their skills.

Although developmental reading, together with some corrective measures, within the English classroom can do much to improve the reading of all students, it is not sufficient to provide special help that is sometimes needed. In addition to the work in English, some students need further diagnosis and a sustained, intensive course taught by a teacher with more training in reading. Some large high schools provide this assistance through a well-organized reading program which includes a reading specialist or consultant, a reading center, several trained classroom teachers, and an in-service program to assist and train all classroom teachers. Smaller schools may rely mainly on the classroom teacher to teach special classes in reading. In some such cases, a reading consultant employed by the school system goes from school to school to offer help. But in other cases, the responsibility for special instruction in reading falls solely on the classroom teachers.

## PROGRAMS VARY WIDELY

In a free society, with local control of schools, it is to be expected that organizational patterns will differ widely, because of peculiar local conditions and also because of the varying beliefs and understandings of administrators and leading teachers. Olive B. Niles, who has studied reading programs throughout the nation, has observed: "Organizational structure for the teaching of reading is presently very fluid in the schools, so much so that it is difficult even to identify trends, much less evaluate them."[32]

She does point to several trends, however. One is a movement away from tracking or homogeneous grouping. This has happened largely in response to social and legal pressures from ethnic groups. Another trend is more attention to individualization of instruction. Increasing in popularity are individually prescribed programs which move students step by step through skill development. Modular scheduling, reading electives, and independent study programs are providing greater individualization and sharper focus on specialized facets of reading. Some schools have tried team teaching in reading, but this practice is not without its problems because of the traditional separation between subject matter teachers and school-wide reading teachers. "Reading teachers have a very hard time relating themselves to the traditional kind of departmental organization because their goals are basically different."[33]

## THE CHANGING ROLE OF THE READING SPECIALIST

Traditionally the reading specialist in a secondary school has worked apart from classroom teachers, contacting them about accepting individual students, and then giving these students special instruction in another part of the building. Most English teachers have had very little knowledge of what the specialist was doing with their students.

It is likely that the reading specialist will continue to give special help to some students. This will probably continue to take place in a reading room or clinic, supplied with special materials and equipment, where students will go by referral for additional diagnosis and intensive, expert instruction. But, according to Albert Harris, it is probable that the reading specialist will spend "more time as a consultant to the teachers, less time in direct remedial work with children." Apparently, "more children will have their needs met within the classroom. Like the LD [Learning Disabled] teacher, the reading specialist seems to be moving toward becoming a resource person and helper to teachers."[34]

## THE READING CENTER

Robert Karlin describes the kind of reading center which supports a school-wide reading program:

> *Some junior and senior high schools set aside one large room or a suite of rooms that serves both as the center for reading instruction and as headquarters for the reading consultant. Conferences can be held with teachers and students there. It may contain a professional library in reading for the staff, and it may also contain a wide variety of interesting reading for both students and teachers. Sometimes the center adjoins the school library so that there is a smooth flow from the center to the source of books.*[35]

## VARIOUS TYPES OF SPECIAL CLASSES AND GROUPS

### Classes for Deficient Readers

These are usually classes for readers whose reading levels are one or more years below their apparent ability, as measured by intelligence tests and other means. For instance, if a ninth grader with an IQ of 100 is reading at sixth or seventh grade level and if he seems to have no serious visual or other handicaps, he would be a candidate for such a class. Such readers are numerous.

Ordinarily, the special classes for such students are treated as temporary substitutes for regular English work. For instance, 20 ninth graders are put into the special class for a semester or at most a year, and they receive English credit for the reading course. Perhaps ideally they should take both English and reading, but most school programs are too crowded to permit such doubling up. At the end of a semester or a year, if the teaching has been successful, most of the students will have made sufficient gains that they will have approached their potential as of that time. For instance, ninth grader Carol, IQ 90, may have started the term with sixth grade reading ability and finished it with eighth. That, for Carol, would represent her present potential. If her IQ were 100 or 110, though, it would be hoped that she would reach the ninth grade reading level or above as a result of the corrective instruction.

In this type of special class, the teacher attempts to find, through diagnostic tests, the major reading weaknesses of the individuals and of the whole class. Geared to the entire class is instruction in those reading skills in which most of the students are deficient. This instruction is supplemented by some individual assignments and activities, intended to help students overcome weaknesses not shared by the majority.

Organization of such classes varies considerably. Here are a few examples of patterns followed in some schools:

1. Noncredit reading laboratory—selected students sent there two or three hours a week, during study periods; individualized instruction, geared to specific needs of each student.
2. Workshop—taken for credit either in addition to or in place of English; enrollment limited to 15 or 20 per period; both group and individual instruction.
3. Reading period—one period a week taken from regular English class, for intensive work on reading improvement.
4. Concentrated work on reading—typically a three- or four-week period, sometimes in summer, when other work is laid aside for group and individual work on reading problems.
5. Daily reading session in English—15 or 20 minutes a day devoted to instruction and practice in reading.
6. Elective reading course—student initiative, both for electing the course and planning work for self-improvement; this may be a six- or nine-week module.

### Classes for Seriously Disabled Readers

Among the eighth grade students in one school are Clayton and Dolores, with reported IQ's of 76 and 78; Joachim, who has just arrived in the United States and knows no English; Blanche, with a serious speech defect; Glenn, with a serious visual defect; Bill, with an alcoholic father and an irresponsible mother, no interest in school, and a record with the juvenile courts; and Louise, who has never been more than five miles from home and who is responsible for most of the care of several younger brothers and sisters. All feel lost in regular classes, yet their needs are obviously not the same. No single formula will help all of them, but the school cannot afford the individual tutelage that might make each of them a better reader, a better student, a more productive adult.

Some schools would put Clayton and Dolores and other mentally handicapped children into special classes called "General English" or something else; in those classes the work would be sufficiently simple that the slow learners could succeed with it reasonably well. Clayton and Dolores can hardly be expected ever to read up to their grade level; their potential, as eighth graders, is probably about fourth grade level. Their other language skills are likely to be comparable.

Other schools would keep Clayton and Dolores in regular classes, and in small high schools there may be no other solution. In that case the teacher must realize that much of the work will pass over their heads, but that many special assignments within their reach are possible. Dolores and Clayton may profit especially from well-conceived group work. They may also have special abilities that can be developed and that can bring them enthusiastic acceptance by their classmates.

If the school has enough students like Joachim, the new arrival, they may be put together into a class for foreign students. Much work is now being done to improve the teaching of English as a second language. New York City, in particular, has worked out detailed plans for teaching the large number of Puerto Ricans and others to whom English is almost an unknown language. Los Angeles and other places in the West and Southwest are also working steadily on methods of teaching their Spanish-speaking students in particular. Because the techniques are specialized ones often involving much aural-oral laboratory work, they cannot be described here adequately.

Blanche and Glenn, with their severe defects in speech and vision, probably need first some specialized doctors' care that few schools can provide. The school can, however, help in making arrangements with appropriate local, county, or state authorities. Then Blanche and Glenn may be placed in a class small enough for considerable individual help. (Writing in the *Saturday Review,* former Senator Abraham Ribicoff once said, ". . . when one large metropolitan hospital recently gave medical examinations in a ghetto junior high school, 20 per cent of the students were found to have hearing and sight problems. Because nobody had ever examined them before, many had spent half their public school lives in schools for the retarded.")

Bill has an emotional problem caused by family troubles. A psychologist who works with the school may be helpful. So may a teacher, if the teacher can find one small opening in Bill's armor, one interest that can be capitalized upon, one subject that Bill is willing to read a little about. If Bill's intelligence is about normal, he may well be placed in a corrective reading class for a while. Otherwise he may be helped in a "General English" class or even in a regular one.

Louise, the student with limited experience, obviously needs reading materials that will give her some insights about the rest of the world. She might find herself in the same class with Bill. Both of them may profit from and find interesting some stories about other young people with problems similar to theirs.

Severely handicapped children like the seven we have just observed pose the biggest problem that teachers encounter. Many such children, though, can be sufficiently helped that they can contribute to society. The teaching and other assistance that they need are expensive, but it is better to spend a few hundred dollars annually on Bill now than to spend a few thousand dollars a year to rehabilitate him later. It is more economical to spend generously for the others now than it is to maintain them as public wards later.

The grouping and teaching of seriously disabled students is beginning to change. Those who are educable, including some who have been segregated from the main body of students and placed in "special education" classes, are being placed in classes with students who do not have such serious disabilities. Under a procedure called "mainstreaming," handicapped students are placed in the "least restrictive environment" for learning that can be provided. The following excerpt is from the editorial comment which prefaces a recent quarterly journal on reading:

> It is with a genuine sense of gratitude that we note the continual progress of **mainstreaming** students whose achievement, nature, or background may be different from the majority. We have come a long way since the days of tracking, inflexible grouping, and isolating those who seemed to present a challenge to the success of the instruction. Modern teachers in-training cannot believe the crudity of treatment of disabled readers which prevailed in the first third of this century.[36]

### Classes for the Gifted

Among reading programs offered by the Detroit Great Cities Project Experimental Schools has been an experimental one for college preparatory sophomores. The Fort Wayne, Indiana, school system has offered an elective course which college bound students in particular are urged to take. In Gouverneur, New York, the rather small high school has offered "efficiency classes" for sophomores, juniors, and seniors who are in the top fifth in intelligence. These classes were intended to help the most able students reach their potential. From such students the majority of tomorrow's leaders will probably come, yet in most schools they have insufficient opportunity to grow as much as they are able. Gouverneur's efficiency classes stressed efficient reading and study skills. Each student selected five fields of specialization, and, under guidance, read extensively in these fields and concurrently was given instruction in developing the reading skills in which he or she was least advanced.

Other schools are conducting different experiments in an attempt to find ways of taking down the bars that surround the most able students. These experiments are among the very significant ones in twentieth-century America.

## DEVICES USED IN SPECIAL CLASSES

Only a book devoted solely to reading can explain in detail the various methods and devices employed. Reading disability alone is the subject for books of several hundred pages. Here we can look at just a few devices, in summary form, under three headings.

### Learning Methods of Word Attack

Phonics teaches children to "sound out" many words. The phonics approach works best with words that are already in their listening and speaking vocabularies. In addition to learning the usual sounds of letters, the students need to learn the sounds of such consonant combinations as *bl, st, str, ng,* and *gr,* and such diphthongs as *aw* and *ou.*

Obviously, though, we do not want the students to have to sound out the same word again and again. Perhaps they use their knowledge of phonics and learn the word *belong,* let us say. They should, later, through the use of flashcards and similar elementary techniques, be helped to recognize *belong* at a glance. Still later they may be helped to read at a glance a group of words, such as *belong to me,* in which the word appears.

Some words like *garage, night,* and *science* are particularly troublesome. With such words, some reading specialists emphasize visualizing, writing, and memorizing. The teacher prints the word on a card and reads it orally for the students. The students look carefully at the word, close their eyes, and try to "see it" in their memories. Then they open their eyes, look at it, and "name" it orally. Sometimes students will need to go through this process several times before they can write the word from memory without the card. Several words taught in this fashion are reviewed and then tested in passages read orally by the students.

Research indicates that readers have particular difficulty with vowel discrimination.[37] This fact should point to the need for continued emphasis on short and long vowels in the lower grades.

### Increasing Speed

Slow, word-by-word readers often fail to grasp the meaning because the phrases and clauses never take shape in their minds. They may understand "John-and-Paul-came-to-the-bridge," but if the sentence contains a few more phrases and clauses, they lose the entire thought. Speed in itself is not a very important goal, but when tied to comprehension, it is.

Students should be told how one reads. Kenneth Goodman describes the visual act of reading in this way:

> *When someone reads, his eyes must stop and fix at points along the printed line in order for the graphic display to be in focus. At the point of fixation there is a small area of sharp focus surrounded by a larger area which is out of focus to various degrees but still seen. It is this surrounding area which is the peripheral visual field.*[38]

Goodman's research indicates that "words are not likely to be pulled in from the peripheral field unless they fit in some ways with the semantic and syntactic clues the reader is processing and the predictions he is making."

It is of course not best to emphasize the reading of phrases and clauses out of context, but one device which reading teachers use is that of flashing phrases and asking students to take each in at a glance. Sometimes entire reading selections are arranged by phrases vertically on a film strip and placed in a machine that flashes the phrases at a predetermined speed. Students must "read" the phrases faster than they can verbalize the individual words in them.

Reading in which the students force themselves to read at their top speed is often productive. For this purpose the material selected should be very easy, preferably two grades or more below the student's reading level. It should be on a subject interesting to the student. Because reading is, to quote Goodman, "a sampling, selecting, predicting, comparing and confirming activity," the selection should be easy enough and interesting enough to allow students to engage in this process successfully. With such material the students can be encouraged to engage in self-improvement, keeping time charts and figuring out their own reading speeds.

The usefulness of tachistoscopes, pacers, and other machines has been hotly debated. Undeniably, students who are interested in mechanical devices are fascinated by them, so motivation is made easier. Undeniably also, their use can result in greatly increased speed. However, doubters say that the increased speed is not uniformly transferred to reading done without the machine, that just as great gains may be made by reading easy material at top speed, that the acquired high speed is not necessarily retained, and that after several years the gains in comprehension, which accompanied the machine-made increase of speed, may disappear. The upshot of the discussion appears to be that machines are useful, especially for motivation, but not indispensable.

---

**THE IDEA BOX**

IMPROVING COMPREHENSION

Frederick B. Davis listed the following types of comprehension: defining words as used in the context, understanding the pattern of organization, identifying the main thought, finding answers to questions discussed in the passage, drawing inferences, recognizing literary devices, identifying the tone or mood, and determining the writer's purpose or viewpoint.[39]

Direct questioning, on whichever of these types a class is ready for, is often the best and simplest approach; for example, "What is the main thing the author says about seashells?" "What is the meaning of *sound* as the author uses it?" "Can you figure out the meaning of *bivalve* from the way the author describes it?" "What does he say causes the roaring that we hear when we hold a large shell to our ear?" "How many kinds of shells does he name?" "What shows you that the author loves the sea?"

Many variations are possible, including the writing of a title for the passage, writing a "headline" about it, thinking of another possible pattern of organization,

---

THE TEACHING OF HIGH SCHOOL ENGLISH

adding to what the author says, choosing the best summary sentence, reducing each of the author's sentences to a word or phrase, and discussing how the passage would have been different if the author's purpose or viewpoint had been different.

## THREE KINDS OF READING

Reading may be: (1) literal, what an author says; (2) interpretive, what an author means; (3) applied, relationship of what an author says to the reader's own experience. Although a good reader may perform all three acts simultaneously, less experienced readers need to be guided through the steps in order.

## READING FOR REAL LIFE

Ron Reis, who teaches at Hammond Middle School, Howard County, Maryland, helps potential dropouts to improve their reading through a "Curriculum for Real Life," which includes reading materials under topics such as "Financial Responsibilities, Social and Familial Responsibilities, and Prevocational and Vocational Skills." Specific reading assignments are made under a teaching unit like "Making a Major Purchase." Functional literacy and career education are combined in this interesting experiment.[40]

## READING ON WHEELS

John N. Mangieri and John Readence describe a unique way to take reading assistance to geographically isolated rural schools. Using a converted motor home called "The Apple Crate," instructors from the Ohio University Teacher Corps Project take a reading lab to the students. This rolling lab is well supplied with interesting reading materials and audiovisual equipment.[41]

## RATE IS RELATIVE

Brenda G. Smith, a teacher of English and reading at Kiski Area Senior High in Vandergrift, Pennsylvania, offers sensible advice to teachers trying to interpret speed reading scores. The score is relative to several factors: type of rapid reading (was it skimming or scanning instead of rapid reading of an entire selection?); comprehension (was comprehension only 50 percent?); familiarity with the reading material; reading sophistication; length of time given students; and the general readability of the material.[42]

## WHAT IS READING IN DEPTH?

"When a high-school student has read a work in depth, he has, in the first place, simply understood the words; he has translated the imagery into lively sensory impressions; he has participated vicariously in the feelings of the characters; he has explored the work for its ethical or social or psychological outlook, which he has evaluated for its truth; and most importantly if he is to continue reading, he has enjoyed himself."[43]

## RANK ORDER OF READING DIFFICULTIES

When 827 college students and adults were asked to rank their reading difficulties in order of importance, this was the result: (1) word-by-word reading, (2) vocalizing, (3) backtracking, (4) daydreaming, (5) monotonous plodding (not changing speed), (6) rereading, (7) word blocking (unfamiliar words), (8) clue-blindness (ignoring headings, key phrases, etc.), (9) finger following, (10) word analysis (giving a word more meaning than context necessitates), (11) head swinging, (12) number attraction (being stopped by a number).[44]

## NEWSPAPER HEADLINES

"From newspapers select short, interesting items with better than ordinary headlines. Number the headlines and corresponding articles for purposes of identification, cut off the headlines, and distribute the articles, giving easiest reading matter to poorest students. Headlines are kept at the teacher's desk. Each student reads his article and writes an original headline for it. As the teacher calls numbers, each student reads his article and the headline he has written. Then the teacher reads the one which was in the newspaper. The class compares them and makes comments. Students seem to enjoy a lesson of this type and do good work with it." (Mary Halloran, Braintree, Mass.)

## ADDITIONAL TECHNIQUES IN TEACHING READING SKILLS

1. Usually tests of reading speed should be accompanied by tests of comprehension, since speed without adequate understanding has no merit. However, at monthly or bimonthly intervals, students may time themselves in reading selections of comparable difficulty (selections chosen by the teacher). They may thus discover whether their reading is becoming more rapid. The teacher may, if she or he wishes, have the class answer questions to test comprehension.
2. Asking questions as one reads is probably the best way to remember, suggests Delwyn G. Schubert. A quick survey of a chapter before reading may help one to perceive relationships that otherwise would be missed. Giving oneself a quiz after reading is also helpful.
3. A student's ability to read humor understandingly is a good guide to level of comprehension and general maturity.
4. Students are given paragraphs of simple instructions for doing something that may be performed in the classroom. Each does exactly what his instructions tell him. They may write these for each other.
5. Students read an untitled paragraph. Each suggests an appropriate title and defends her or his choice in discussions.
6. To assist visualization, students may draw or describe suitable pictures to accompany certain scenes in fiction. They draw upon words and passages in the scenes to support their pictures.
7. Direct experience helps to clarify meaning. Thus, one class visited a newspaper plant and then read articles on how newspapers, magazines, and books

are printed. The material was comprehensible because the students had something tangible to which to relate the words on the page.

8. To clarify sentence meaning, one student may read a sentence, and two others may restate its idea in two different ways.

9. To increase power to understand details, students may read a passage that contains many sensory images, and find words or phrases suggesting pictures, odors, sounds, tastes, or feelings.

10. For the same purpose, the teacher may supply a paragraph and three or four questions, one of which is not answered in the paragraph.

11. Students should frequently answer thought questions, not merely factual questions, based on paragraphs or articles.

12. Students may read two short articles about different inventions (or people, countries, etc.) and then decide how they are alike and how they differ.

13. Students read a fable and then decide what familiar proverb it illustrates.

14. From a few clues in a paragraph, students decide what the setting is, or who the chief character is, or the approximate date of the incident.

15. In one column are several half-sentences: in a second column are the half-sentences needed to complete the first ones. Students are to find in the second column the words that logically complete each sentence.

16. Important tools in reading are the library catalog and *Reader's Guide to Periodical Literature*. Perhaps the best way to teach their use is to employ teacher-made or student-problems, such as ''Where can you find information about space shuttles?''

17. To improve skill in locating information, the teacher prepares specific questions answered in various reference books. Students use the indexes, tables of contents, etc., and find the answers as quickly as possible. If the teacher desires, the class may be divided into teams for an information-finding contest.

18. To improve skill in scanning and skimming, students are given a limited amount of time to find in a magazine a specified item of information, or to prepare for writing a brief summary that will give the central idea and chief supporting points. The length of time permitted may gradually be shortened.

19. Have students rapidly examine a chapter in any one of their texts, preferably a chapter with subheadings. Ask them to list 6 to 10 questions that they believe the chapter would answer. At another time you may have them draw up a skeleton outline of a chapter, and perhaps fill in the outline with the most important details.

20. Using a chapter with subheadings, ask students to indicate what is probably the chief question answered under each subheading. Then have them find and write the answer to that question.

21. Students read a paragraph, write an already familiar fact or idea related to the paragraph, and then point out how the two are related.

22. Useful films and filmstrips on reading, using the library, and similar topics are available from Coronet, Encyclopaedia Britannica, Inc., and other sources.

23. To improve students' ability to read critically, try constructing some relevance tests. Write a statement about any topic, and below it write three to five other

statements. Students are to decide which of these statements are relevant to the first one. Similarly, to improve use of the card catalog, *Reader's Guide,* and indexes, you may write a statement and then ask under which of several suggested topics the students would look to find further information, or students may prepare such items.

24. Critical reading may also be improved by asking questions concerning plausibility: "Does _____ seem to be a real person such as you might meet?" "Could this event have happened?" "Would it be probable?"

## LINGUISTICS AND READING

The possible application of linguistic principles to reading has attracted attention for some time. Recent applications include attention to the native language of students reading English as a second language; the "black English" of the English-speaking black student; the linguistic reasons for miscues (such as omitting words or word parts, inserting words, substituting words, and doubling back); and exercises in sentence combining to improve reading comprehension.

## SKILLS THAT CAN BE TAUGHT SEPARATELY

Frederick B. Davis has identified the following reading skills that can be given separate emphasis: (1) recalling word meanings; (2) finding answers to questions; (3) drawing inferences from the content; (4) recognizing a writer's purpose, attitude, tone, and mood; and (5) following the structure of a passage.[45]

## FACTORS IN READING POWER

Research by Jack A. Holmes and Harry Singler at the University of California at Berkeley found that the following elements account for 55 percent of differences in *speed* of reading: visual verbal meaning, understanding of spoken English, knowledge of homonyms, inductive reasoning, and literary interest. The following elements accounted for 75 percent of the differences in reading *power:* verbal analysis, understanding of spoken English, vocabulary in context, vocabulary in isolation, visual verbal meaning, tone intensity, and effective study planning. The high rank of understanding of spoken English in both lists suggests that considerable class talk (the British method) may indeed be of significant help.

## "SKIMMING PRACTICE"

Irwin Weiss uses *Reader's Digest* articles to provide practice in skimming. The title, first sentence in paragraphs, and concluding paragraphs are especially important.[46]

## "USING THE SCHOOL MAGAZINE WITH RETARDED READERS"

Poor readers may improve both their reading and their writing when they use the school magazine in which their contributions are welcome. They read it much more willingly than they do anthologies.[47]

## AN EXAMPLE OF GUIDED FREE READING

On "reading days" in an inner-city school, students in Lorraine Goldman's classes choose freely (and noisily) from the extensive classroom library. The book report system requires each student to answer in writing one thought-provoking question about his or her book.[48]

## BOOK SAMPLING

When students are choosing a book to read, David Sohn recommends that they examine the cover, read the blurbs, read pages 1, 50, and 100 (or 1, 100, and 200), and then, if still interested, take the "thirty-page chance" by reading the first 30 pages. They may reject the book after any step.[49]

## THEY READ ALL PERIOD

For six weeks Ann W. Ackerman's nonacademic seniors did almost nothing but read—any books they wanted. Thirty-four students read 253 books; 13 said, "I'll probably read more than in the past," and 7 said, "I have learned to enjoy reading for the first time (or again)." Thirty-three said "yes" to "Do you think six weeks of reading each year would be a good idea for Grades 9 through 12?"[50]

## MOTIVATING OUTSIDE READING

1. Raise the question, "What are the adventure zones in our world?" Get answers referring to things other than places. Then encourage reading in these zones.
2. "A touch of comedy may go further than a casual suggestion from a teacher. Post a large 'Bugs Bunny' poster which reads 'How about a Good Book, Doc?' Cards describing good books can be inserted in a window in the poster. Or one might have the cartooned figure of a diver; above it, 'Thinking of Taking the Plunge? Try Poetry.' Post below it some titles of quickly read poems." (Elaine Charles, Central High School, Grand Rapids, Michigan)
3. On the bulletin board put book reviews, pictures, and newspaper clippings referring to books. Better, let students do so.
4. "I post on the bulletin board 'best sellers' (not necessarily current books) that I recommend for the particular age group." (Marguerite Chamberlain, Franklin, N.H.)
5. The teacher's reading of brief, carefully selected excerpts from a book may make young readers eager to read it for themselves.
6. After reading books about various countries, Ruth Raymond's students in Keene, New Hampshire, hold discussions on such topics as Interesting People We Meet in Books, Problems Solved, Description of a Scene, Maxims and Aphorisms, Humorous and Witty Lines, Customs of the Countries.
7. Students might construct and explain collages, mobiles, and posters that symbolize something meaningful in a book.
8. One thousand pupils at National Hawthorne Middle School, Bayside, New York, were asked two questions: "What has a teacher of yours done to interest

you in reading?'' ''What could a teacher of yours do to interest you in reading?''
A few of the 25 most frequently cited responses were as follows: Let us choose
our own book. Tell us interesting stories. Let us act out exciting scenes from
stories and plays. Play records that tell stories. Have free reading periods. Tell
us the beginning of interesting stories. Take us to the school library. Have a
classroom library. Bring book clubs, such as TAB and XEP, to the attention of
students. Let us tell the class about exciting books that we have read.

## STATE-WIDE EMPHASIS ON READING

It is not uncommon for some state school systems, as well as some large city
systems, to require classroom teachers to know how to teach reading. Often one
college course is sufficient proof, although in some cases the number of credit
hours is not specified. Dorothy Piercey, Coordinator for Secondary Reading Education, the Arizona State Board of Education, conducted a national survey in 1971–
1972 and again in 1973–1974 to determine trends in state requirements. Eight states
required reading training for secondary certification according to the first survey,
three for English teachers only. Fifteen required it two years later, and this time
seven required it for English only. Arizona headed the requirements with two
courses: one a methods course, and the other a practicum with high school students
in the field. The researcher points to the national emphasis on the ''Right to Read''
and on accountability as main factors in this trend toward stiffer requirements.
Apparently, she notes, some states have ''much faith in their English teachers'' as
reading teachers.''[51]

## PAPERBOUND BOOKS IN PRINT

This quarterly catalog, published by the R. R. Bowker Company, lists most paperbound books (of American publishers) currently in print. It is essential for any
school library and useful in making selections for classroom libraries. Other books
from the same company include *Textbooks in Print* (annual) and *The Literary
Marketplace* (concise information about publishers, annual).

## YOUR OWN READING RECORD

After reading a book, article, or story that they may wish sometime to call to the
attention of a student or students, some efficient teachers spend 5 minutes in writing
pertinent bibliographical information on a 4″ by 6″ card, along with a brief summary or interpretive comment. A collection of such cards can be invaluable.

## ARE YOU A GOOD READING MODEL?

For a period of 4½ years, researchers measured the reading skills of almost 350
elementary, intermediate, and secondary school teachers from 35 states. When the
reading performance of the teachers was compared to that of the college freshmen
who had established norms on The Cooperative English Reading Test, 96 teachers
scored lower than half the freshmen in vocabulary, 171 scored lower than half the
freshmen on comprehension, and 195 read slower and with less understanding.[52]

In another study, 34 high school teachers of seven subjects were interviewed. Most required reading assignments, which they said most students completed, and most said that most of their students had no noticeable reading problems and liked to read. Fourteen teachers said that their students did not read their assignments. Picking up on this figure, researchers questioned 300 students in the classes taught by the 14 teachers. Of these students, 52 percent said they liked to read; 81 percent that they did not read assignments; 98 percent said tests were based on lectures and discussions rather than reading; 73 percent said they were not required to discuss their reading assignments; 95 percent said they were just assigned pages with no stated purpose for reading; 95 percent said the teacher brought in no outside books to interest them; 33 percent said their teacher didn't like to read, and 47 percent didn't know.[53] Results such as these must be viewed with caution; they should not form the basis for broad generalizations. However, they do indicate the need for teachers to ask whether they are good reading models for their students.

# FOOTNOTES

1. "Influences of the Visual Peripheral Field in Reading," *Research in the Teaching of English,* Fall 1975, p. 210.
2. "Why Won't Teenagers Read?" *Journal of Reading,* May 1977, pp. 649–653.
3. J. Estill Alexander and Ronald Claude Filler, *Attitudes and Reading,* Newark, Delaware: IRA, 1976, p. 42.
4. "Developing Lifelong Readers in the Middle Schools," *English Journal* 66, April 1977, pp. 59–60.
5. New York: Berkley Publishing Corporation, 1968, p. 211.
6. Fader and McNeil, p. 207.
7. "Reading and the English Teacher—With a Reasonable Degree of Certainty," *English Journal* 64, April 1975, p. 18.
8. *Books and the Teen-Age Reader,* New York: Bantam Books, Inc., p. 41.
9. Carlsen, pp. 21–30.
10. *Literature and the Reader,* Urbana, Illinois: NCTE, 1972, p. 108.
11. "About Successful Reading Programs," *English Journal* 46, Oct. 1957, p. 395.
12. *Teaching Reading and Study Strategies: The Content Fields,* Boston: Allyn and Bacon, Inc., p. 135.
13. Robinson, p. 99.
14. Robinson, p. 160.
15. "Filling in the Blanks: Using the Cloze Procedure for Teaching Basic

Skills," in *Classroom Practices in Teaching English 1977–1978: Teaching the Basics—Really!*, Urbana, Illinois: NCTE, 1977, p. 10.

16. "The Effects of Prereading Assistance on the Comprehension and Attitudes of Good and Poor Readers," *Research in the Teaching of English*, Fall 1969, p. 176.

17. Richard Arnold and John Miller, "Reading: Word Recognition Skills," in *Reading: Foundations and Instructional Strategies*, ed. Pose Lamb and Richard Arnold. Belmont, California: Wadsworth Publishing Company, Inc., 1976, p. 322.

18. *Teaching Reading in Content Areas*, Englewood Cliffs, N.J.: Prentice-Hall, Inc., p. 152.

19. Ward Mitchell Cates, "An Electrifying Approach to Teaching Reading or How I Galvanized 'Em in the Reading Class," *English Journal* 63, Nov. 1974, pp. 97–98.

20. "What Happened on the Day You Were Born?" *Journal of Reading*, Feb. 1977, pp. 400–402.

21. "Your Horoscope Predicts: You Can Teach Students to Follow Directions," *Journal of Reading*, May 1976, pp. 653–659.

22. "One Capsule a Week—a Painless Remedy for Vocabulary Ills," *Journal of Reading*, Nov. 1975, pp. 147–149.

23. "Evaluating Profundity in Literature," *Journal of Reading*, May 1976, pp. 387–390.

24. "Developing Special Skills for Reading the Genres," *Reading Improvement*, Fall 1977, p. 183.

25. *Teaching Literature to Adolescents: Poetry*, Glenview, Ill.: Scott, Foresman and Company, 1966, p. 20.

26. "Integrating the Teaching of Reading and Literature," *Journal of Reading*, Feb. 1976, pp. 360–366.

27. "Unlocking the Box: An Experiment in Literary Response," *English Journal*, 66, Feb. 1977, pp. 37–42.

28. Nicholas P. Cruscuolo, "Seven Creative Reading Programs for the Secondary Schools," *English Journal* 64, Feb. 1975, p. 77.

29. Stephen Dunning, "Everybody's Doing It—But Why?" *English Journal* 47, Jan. 1958, p. 33. Dunning stresses the need to have book reports reflect "common purposes that both teacher and student can hold as honest, valuable, and realistic."

30. For details on scripts, see Donald Noble, "Television Script Book Reports," *English Journal* 49, April 1960, pp. 259–261.

31. These and other suggestions are taken from Howard S. Roland, "Alternatives for the Book Report," *English Journal* 51, Feb. 1962, pp. 106–113.

32. Kenneth S. Goodman and Olive B. Niles, *Reading: Process and Program*. Urbana, Illinois: NCTE, 1970, p. 52.

33. Goodman and Niles, p. 53.

34. "Ten Years of Progress in Remedial Reading," *Journal of Reading,* Oct. 1977, p. 33.

35. *Teaching Reading in High School,* Second Edition, Indianapolis: Bobbs-Merrill Company, Inc., 1972, p. 340.

36. Ken VanderMeulen, "Editorial Comment," *Reading Horizons,* Summer 1977.

37. Robert Marzano et al. "Sound Discrimination and Reading Comprehension in Middle School Students," *Journal of Reading,* Oct. 1976, p. 36.

38. "Influence of the Visual Peripheral Field in Reading," *Research in the Teaching of English,* Fall 1975, p. 210.

39. *Education Summary,* Aug. 12, 1967.

40. "A Curriculum for Real Life Skills," *Journal of Reading,* Dec. 1977, pp. 208–211.

41. "A Mobile Reading Lab for Rural Schools," *Journal of Reading,* Feb. 1977, pp. 398–399.

42. "Speed Reading Scores in Perspective," *Journal of Reading,* Nov. 1975, pp. 128–130.

43. Bruce E. Miller, *English Record,* Dec. 1963.

44. John W. Purcell, "Poor Reading Habits: Their Rank Order," *The Reading Teacher,* March 1963, p. 353.

45. *Reading Research Quarterly,* Summer 1968.

46. *English Journal* 56, Jan. 1967, p. 135.

47. Alice B. Conroy, *English Journal* 53, Nov. 1964, pp. 624–626.

48. "Reading and Reporting," *English Journal* 58, Feb. 1969, p. 236.

49. *Media and Methods,* Feb. 1968.

50. "Reading for Pleasure and Profit," *English Journal* 58, Oct. 1969, p. 1042.

51. Dorothy Piercey, "Should English Teachers Teach Reading? The State Department Says, 'Yes.' " *Arizona English Bulletin,* Nov. 1974, pp. 37–40.

52. Lance M. Gentile and Merna McMillan, "Some of our Students' Teachers Can't Read Either," *Journal of Reading,* Nov. 1977, pp. 145–148.

53. Billie Jo Rieck, "How Content Teachers Telegraph Messages Against Reading," *Journal of Reading,* May 1977, pp. 646–648.

# 5

---

## LITERATURE: APPROACH RESPONSES AND AVOIDANCE RESPONSES

## LOOKING AT TEACHING

Variety High School occupies the entire block between 65th and 66th streets. Like most large city schools, it has an English department that is too large to act decisively as one unit day after day, so the teachers on each grade level have their own chairperson and function as a curriculum committee. The department usually meets briefly during the week before students arrive in the fall, and the grade level committees meet toward the end of each 9-week grading period. During these meetings, teachers sometimes talk about their 9-week tests, or about how they should spend the small amount of money allotted to them for consumable materials, or about some new policy or admonition passed down to them. One or two, like Mr. Loadem and Ms. Assignem, may try to grade papers. Rarely do teachers in any group discuss teaching methods. Then, off they go to their classrooms for nine more weeks to do their things in their own ways, perhaps effectively, perhaps not so effectively.

It is now fifth period on Monday, and all the doors down *A* Hall are closed. The little window in the door for A-101 contains a picture of the Tower of London.

We turn the knob and slip quietly inside. Sixty eyes in 30 heads in five rows follow us to our seats in the back of the room.

A tall, thin man in a gray suit looks out over the tops of his glasses and takes attendance while his students look at the chalkboard and copy "Reading Schedule for *Death of a Salesman*." Just to the right of this information, the board is covered by a projection screen. Chalked off in a small box in the upper left-hand corner of the board is a small piece of information: "English III, Mr. I. Tellem."

120

After he clips his attendance slip to the outside of his door, Mr. Tellem begins:

"I trust that all of you have copied the reading assignments. We'll have to move through this play by Thursday. As you can see, that means only two days on each act. The test, part short-answer and part essay, will be on Friday. *Death of a Salesman* is not an easy play, so I hope you will read it carefully and listen carefully in class. If you don't, you'll miss some of the motifs in the play—I'll say more about these in a few minutes.

"I'll expect you to take notes carefully, too. You'll find them very valuable as you prepare for my test.

"Today I'll lead off with a short lecture on motifs to look for as you read. When I finish, I'll raise the screen so you can copy a structural outline of the play. It should also help.

"Ready, now? Notebooks out? Pens or pencils out?

"*Death of a Salesman* is a play with several important motifs. . . ."

At this point, only a few faces turn as we try to slip out as quietly as we entered.

The little window in the door for A-102 contains a picture of children running through a field of tall grass and flowers. As we go in, the door bumps a boy, but he pays no attention. A girl gives us only a quick glance as she hurries by. Tenth-grade students—some in bare feet—are standing, walking about, sitting on desks, and sitting on the floor. Five sit around a table, cutting pictures from magazines; three sit on the floor among brightly colored pillows, reading, writing, and munching potato chips under a sign saying "Poetry Pit"; others are constructing mobiles, talking into tape recorders, arranging color slides against a window, and listening to music on a record player.

Almost every square foot of space from ceiling to floor seems to be filled with student work of some sort. Graffiti cover white shelf paper across one wall from one corner to another. Mobiles turn slowly from the ceiling. Two large movable partitions contain collages of magazine pictures and samples of student writing.

"Ms. Freem, I think we have visitors," someone calls.

"Ms. Freem, somebody's here," calls another.

A lively young teacher emerges from behind a collage-covered partition and deftly twists her way through students and movable furniture.

"I hope the noise doesn't bother you," she begins. "Students today seem to thrive on noise."

"What are you studying?" we ask.

"I was sure you'd ask that," she replies. "Most visitors seem to ask that question first. We're into poetry—all kinds. We find poetry, and we make some. Look around. We have poetry everywhere. Song lyrics, concrete poems, cinquains, haiku, diamentes, terse verse. Mostly, we're having fun with it."

"Ms. Freem."

"Ms. Freem."

"Excuse me," says Ms. Freem, and she disappears behind the same collage-covered partition.

We disappear unnoticed.

A blank sheet of theme paper covers the little window to A-103. As we enter and move along a chalkboard to the back of the room, all students' eyes follow.

A tired-looking woman sits behind a large oak desk and scans five rows. Behind her the chalkboard is empty. Fire drill instructions and a few notices from the office are the only items on the bulletin board. Two small boxes on the desk carry the notices "Papers In" and "Papers Out." Both are empty.

"Let's see, I think we left off yesterday on page 34, Act II, Scene II, line 115."

"No, Ms. Ignorem, it was page 32, line 65," says a neatly groomed girl who sits straight in her chair in the front row.

"Oh yes, let's see. It was third period that read up to line 155 last Friday."

"Do we have to do this stuff again?" asks a boy from somewhere by the windows.

"Tom, we have only four more pages in this scene. Then I'll let everyone read Scene III silently while I try to finish grading Friday's short-answer test.

"But we're wasting time. Who would like to be Romeo?"

No answer. No hands in the air.

"John, you wouldn't mind being Romeo, would you?"

John mumbles something and looks around under his chair.

"Ms. Ignorem, I don't have no book."

"Well, I guess you'll just have to sit and listen."

John grins, and everyone else quickly looks downward.

"Randy, *you* have a book. You be our Romeo."

Some laughter from girls, then quiet.

"Do we have a Juliet?"

No answer. No hands up.

"We can't get through this scene without a Juliet. Sara, you haven't read in some time. You be Juliet."

*Teacher.* (nods in Randy's direction) "Line 66, Randy."

*Romeo.* With love's light wings did I uh . . . perch these walls;
      For . . .

*Teacher.* "O'erperch, Randy."

*Romeo.* For stony limits cannot hold love out,
      And what love can do that dares love attempt.

*Students.* (laughter)

*Teacher.* "Go on, Randy."

*Romeo.* Therefore thy kindmen are no stop for me.

*Teacher.* "Kinsmen, Randy."

*Juliet.* If they do see thee, they will murder thee.

*A Student.* (mumbling) "It's about time."

*Teacher.* "Randy, it's your turn."

*Romeo.* Alack, there lies more peril in thine eye
>    Than twenty of their swords! Look thou but sweet,
>    And I am proof against their enemy.

*Teacher.* "Enmity, Randy."

Stifling our yawns, we edge toward the door. All eyes except Romeo's, Juliet's, and Ms. Ignorem's follow until the latchbolt clicks behind us.

After exercising our arms and legs a bit, we stand before A-104 and check the big white-faced clock high on the wall outside the door. Fifteen minutes left in the period. A mirror fills the little window. Well, in we go.

From the doorway, we can see only one group of 10 students, who seem to be closed off from the rest of the room by two movable partitions. A boy spots us and points his finger at another pair of partitions. The whole room is unrealistically quiet.

As we peer around the edge of a partition, a thirtyish dark-haired woman with sparkling dark eyes smiles, puts a finger to her lips, and motions for us to follow her out into the hall.

"I am Ms. Guidem," she begins. "I'm sorry about all the nonverbal directions, but our rule today is not to talk or make any kind of noise."

Getting no response, she goes on.

"We have read the first chapter of *Diary of a Young Girl* by Anne Frank. To experience something of the isolation felt by Anne and the other characters with her, we have borrowed these partitions so we can wall ourselves off into little groups. Students in each group will be allowed to move about, but they must not make any noise that others outside the group can hear. They are to imagine that any noise, no matter how slight, could mean their discovery and capture, and probably their death. We will be in isolation for at least two full class periods. Maybe we'll get on each other's nerves, but that will only make the experience more meaningful."

"Do you think this will help them to understand and appreciate Anne Frank's *Diary?*" we ask.

"Definitely! The assignment for each night will be to write a detailed diary entry of the experience in class that day. Students will write about their own feelings and will describe the effects of the situation on others in their group. Then we'll come together in discussions to sort out our own feelings and to see how they compare with observations Anne Frank has made about herself and her group."

The school bell was shattering!

Variety High School does not exist, and Mr. Loadem, Ms. Assignem, Mr.

Tellem, Ms. Freem, Ms. Ignorem, and Ms. Guidem are of course all stereotypes. It would not be fair or reasonable to assume that they represent high school English teachers. Yet the authors of this book, during visits to secondary school English classrooms all over the nation and in several foreign countries, have found some of these traits and tendencies in English teaching in almost every school. But, as we have said elsewhere in this book, no single teaching approach or style, however traditional, different, or bizarre it may seem to visitors, leads inevitably to good results or poor results. The teacher who is well informed, thinks and plans ahead, cares about students, and truly tries to help them learn, will probably succeed. Of all teachers described above, Ms. Ignorem is the only one who might be called hopeless. She simply doesn't care enough about the subject or her students to put any real effort into either. Mr. Tellem, who is suffocating students with his telling, is nevertheless fairly well organized and tells students what to expect in the course. And he appears to be working hard at what he does. Ms. Freem appears to be somewhat disorganized, and perhaps she could guide her students to read poetry that would be more challenging, but she works closely with students and motivates them to read and write. And her students seem to be enjoying doing both. Ms. Guidem is perhaps the most creative and most thoughtful teacher of all. Her visitors were at first so startled by her isolation of students and her insistence on complete silence that they almost drew a wrong conclusion. But Ms. Guidem has thought through her approach carefully, and she has designed it to provide personal experiences that students can carry to a literary work so its portrayal of the human experience will be more significant to them. By writing their own feelings and observations in their diaries, her students are brought closer to discussing Anne's observations, to discovering the feelings behind them, and to realizing what these observations reveal about Anne and the nine people who endured the anguish of isolation with her. Consequently, some important questions are now possible in class discussion. Take for example these suggested by Mrs. Charlene Tibbetts, University High School, University of Illinois, Urbana:

FIRST QUESTION: *Who does Anne write to in her diary?*

FIRST ANSWER: *(specific evidence): Anne writes to an imaginary girl named Kitty.*

SECOND QUESTION: *What does Anne tell Kitty?*

SECOND ANSWER *(specific evidence): Anne describes her loneliness.*

THIRD SPECIFIC EVIDENCE: *Anne comments on the other people in hiding.*

FOURTH SPECIFIC EVIDENCE: *Anne vents her anger and frustration.*

FIFTH SPECIFIC EVIDENCE: *Anne discusses her philosophy of life.*

THIRD QUESTION *(leading to conclusion no. 1): Why does Anne tell Kitty these things?*

*Inductive Leap no. 1*

CONCLUSION no. 1:    Anne needs someone to talk to because there is no one her age in the Secret Annex she feels close to when she first goes into hiding.

*FOURTH QUESTION (leading to conclusion no. 2): Why does Anne call her diary Kitty rather than James, Jim or Joe?*

*Inductive Leap no. 2*

CONCLUSION no. 2:    Anne makes up a girl's name to write to because she is the age when she would have a close girl friend to confide in if she were living a normal life.[1]

Regardless of whether you design an inductive lesson, as Mrs. Tibbetts has done, or a deductive lesson, you should take a hard look at goals, materials, and techniques. These questions may serve to start the process:

Am I too rigid in my selection of literature? in my structure of the class? in my methods?

Do my students learn *about* literature instead of having experiences *with* literature? Do my students really get involved in what they read?

Am I willing to try an unorthodox technique that could help students to approach literature creatively, even if I know that it will require far more effort and more time, and if I suspect that it could threaten my sense of security and stability as the director of their learning?

Surely, as an English teacher, you will want to create approach responses rather than avoidance responses. In other words, you will want students to enjoy literature and to read voluntarily, not to regard its reading as a task to be avoided if at all possible.

The remainder of this chapter and all of the next two chapters are written in this light, but with the assumption that there is no single way to attain students' interest and involvement.

## DEVELOPING A RATIONALE

### THREE REASONS FOR READING LITERATURE

Why do we teach what we teach? That question might be phrased differently as "Why should we teach what we should teach?" or "How can we determine what we should teach?" It is related, obviously, to the even more basic question, "Why read literature?"

Let us consider that question, "Why read literature?" and then see how our conclusions may guide us in selecting literature for high school teaching and also in determining what we do with that literature.

We read literature for three interrelated and overlapping reasons: for pleasure, for information of a kind not available in an encyclopedia, and for a means of sharing our cultural heritage. We cannot separate these three with definite partitions, but, nevertheless, we can try to look at each in turn.

## Pleasure

We get our pleasure from different things, and the most truly educated persons are probably those who are most versatile in their joys. Such persons may turn in succession to a book, an art museum, a science exhibit, a kitchen stove or a jigsaw, a fishing rod or a set of golf clubs, a baseball game, a lecture, and the late late show on television.

The person who knows how to read well enough can obtain a variety of pleasures vicariously. Though a baseball story by Ring Lardner should not be substituted for an afternoon in Yankee Stadium, the Lardner story may make the next baseball game a more vivid experience. The players on the field emerge as human beings; the Lardner reader is a better baseball fan because he or she realizes that baseball uniforms cover players who in background and temperament are themselves far from uniform.

Vicariously one could travel under the sea with Jules Verne decades before the first submarine was built. Vicariously one can visit lands that one may never see even with today's jet travel. Vicariously one can go back into the past and live as one's ancestors lived. Much of the pleasure of literature comes from such vicarious experiences. They help to create a versatility of pleasure.

Part of the pleasure for one who knows how to read well comes from a conscious recognition of artistry. We applaud what is done well, whether the act is one of juggling, painting a picture, playing the piano, or arranging words. The literary artist, though perhaps depicting "what oft was thought," chooses words so that we may add "but ne'er so well express'd." We derive pleasure from the artful simplicity of Housman or Frost or Hemingway, from the resonant voice of Milton, from the dilettante extravagances and metrical experimentation of Swinburne, from the barbed satirical mastery of Swift or the gentleness of the remonstrances of Addison. The musics of Poe and Lanier have their beauty, and so has Millay's cry of exultation, "Oh world, I cannot hold thee close enough!" and so has Robinson Jeffers' bitter anguish.

Some years ago an advertiser ran a series of ads using the slogan "It's fun to be fooled, but it's more fun to know." It is fun to read literature even though one does not recognize the writer's techniques, but it is more fun when we do know what the writer has done to move us. If we can note how a novelist has assembled the parts of a plot, how a poet has blended together rhythm and words to suit the purpose, how a playwright has characterized in only a few sentences, our appreciation is heightened. This does not mean that we have to count all the similes or scan all the lines, but it does mean that we analyze enough to identify the key aspects of the writer's craft.

Other parts of the pleasure can be identified. There is, for example, the pleasure of the puzzle, comparable to that of solving the Chinese box or ring puzzle; we attain this pleasure when we outguess the detective in a mystery story, or we attain it when we extract the essential kernel from a difficult lyric poem. There is also the pleasure of satisfying our curiosity about people, of comparing them with ourselves, of identifying ourselves with some of them, and of observing how they react when thrust into changed surroundings or faced with unaccustomed obstacles. This is related, no doubt, to the pleasure obtained from discovering how things turn out—the age-old love of a story, which has its incipience in curiosity. Then there is the pleasure of intellectual stimulation—the stimulation that comes from new ideas and insights, thinking about these insights, and forming one's own conclusions. ''The fundamental goals are that students should find personal satisfaction in reading literature/drama or in viewing drama by enjoying the mental/physical sights and sounds of literature. Yet, they should gain practical insights into life and develop critical thinking skills.''[2]

## Information

The pleasure of intellectual stimulation is related to the second reason for reading literature: It gives information of a kind not available in encyclopedias. If we want facts, we go to reference books. But, if we want insights different from those afforded by facts, we go to literature.

Dr. Sterling M. McMurrin, former U.S. Commissioner of Education, speaking on ''Education for Freedom in a Free Society,'' said,

*One of the major deficiencies in our national effort to meet the challenges before us is the almost complete failure of the American people to recognize that the strength of a nation lies in its art and music and literature, and in its philosophical sophistication and the quality of its social sciences, just as much as in its physics and chemistry or its electrical engineering. When we raise the question of the survival of our Nation it is a question of proximate range of statesmanship and machinery. But when we speak of the decline or rise of our culture and the strength of the Nation for the long haul ahead, it is a question of the full cultivation of our spiritual, artistic, moral, and intellectual resources. Those who suppose that great music or great poetry or a knowledge of classical literature is not essential to not only the quality but even the survival of a nation and its culture are quite unaware of the lessons of the past.*

The insights that are deeper than mere facts are so numerous and varied that they can only be illustrated. In Crane's *Red Badge of Courage* is a portrayal of fear and self-finding more revealing than any of the studies made by psychologists. In Jonathan Swift's satire is a revelation of human weakness; it is a warning, a sermon. We recognize that we are the Lilliputians who will go to war over which end of an egg should be cracked first; we recognize that we are sometimes the Yahoos, with their repulsive habits; we recognize some twentieth-century scientists in the eighteenth-century scientists ridiculed by Swift. In George Orwell's *Animal Farm* and in William Golding's *Lord of the Flies* are disclosures of weaknesses that allow tyranny and dictatorship to rise and flourish in a society. In *Death of a Salesman* are weaknesses that prevent an individual from distinguishing the difference between reality and illusion.

From the poetry of Robert Frost we learn once more the value of elemental things. The greatest accomplishment of the hired man in Frost's poem was his ability to load a hayrick tall and secure, every forkful in its place. The hired man reminds us of the bootmaker in John Galsworth's short story "Quality," who made such good shoes that it took years to wear them out. We contrast the work of the hired man and the bootmaker with the shoddy workmanship, the built-in obsolescence, of so many items we buy today, and we wonder why we have lost what we have lost, and what the consequences may be, and what we may do to regain integrity and the pride that was once ours in a job well done.

From books like Mark Twain's *Life on the Mississippi* or O. E. Rölvaag's *Giants in the Earth* we can learn more than the history books tell us about the lives our ancestors lived. These are not glamorized, sleek presentations. Mark Twain's Mississippi is not just a broad, beautiful river with picturesque scenery along both banks; it has sand bars and mud, rough and sometimes violent men, sweat and confusion. Rölvaag's pioneers are both brave and fearful; in Beret, the pioneer wife who lacked the strength and the balance needed in a new land, we have one of the most sensitive portraits in all literature. We can learn much about the early black experience in America from Margaret Walker's *Jubilee,* Ernest Gaines' *The Autobiography of Miss Jane Pittman,* and Alex Haley's *Roots.* We can learn about the American Indian presence from John G. Neihardt's *Black Elk Speaks.*

The humorous writers give us insights, too. Ogden Nash's famous four-line parody of "Trees," in which he laments that unless the billboards fall he'll never be able to see a tree, is more eloquent than most hour-long speakers on the polution of the natural environment. A drive along U.S. 1 in the East reveals the truth of Nash's lines.

"Literature is not a body of knowledge to be learned," insists James E. Miller, past president of the NCTE. Its function is to provide a "confrontation with life." Exploration of literature has lasting meaning "only if it leads to personal discovery."[3] Literature does contain information, Miller is saying, but that information should be experienced, thought about, and made a part of one's being—not just memorized for an examination.

## Cultural Heritage

History classes bring parts of our cultural heritage to students; so do classes in science, mathematics, art, music, and so on. Can we in English identify as basic to our common heritage a number of literary selections that every American should know? Once the colleges, through their entrance examinations, in effect determined such a canon, including works like "The Bunker Hill Oration," Burke's "Speech on Conciliation," "Evangeline," "Idylls of the King," *Hamlet,* and *Macbeth.* After the turn of the century such dictation was rightly opposed. But the net result has been that we Americans have so little reading in common—on any academic level—that the late Professor William R. Parker of Indiana University asserted that even among his graduate students in English he could not count upon all of them to know any given work of literature.

It seems unfortunate that television rather than literature provides a common bond among most Americans. Anyone from a bank president to a ditch digger can refer to any of a dozen currently popular TV programs with fair assurance that the others present will understand the reference. Next week new programs, new allusions; next year many or most of this year's programs will be off the air, supplanted by something else. Without being hostile to television one can justify the statement that it is ephemeral, it lacks roots, and it provides but a transitory bond. Neil Postman, a frequent critic of English teaching, makes this observation:

> *Too many school curriculums reflect the same discontinuity as television, and that is one of the things that needs to be corrected. There ought to be intellectual continuities and cohesions between one subject and another. By paying attention to the historical roots of different subjects, we can see that the great contributors to different fields didn't look upon things as fragmented.*[4]

Literature could provide a permanent bond for us. The NCTE's *National Interest and the Teaching of English* makes the case for literature in our cultural heritage this way:

> *The young who study our language and literature come into the best contact possible with the dreams, hopes, and aspirations, as well as with the roots of our culture. The rich texture of myth and folklore of lumbering, pioneering, and railroading stimulates the imagination and is a vehicle for the perpetual transmission of the American heritage. Only through the imagination do the complex natures of our various regions—Down East, the Old South, the prairie, the corn belt, and the mining town—become ingrained in our rising generations. Many of the books our youth read suggest the richness which we define as our heritage—Our Town, Huckleberry Finn, "The Devil and Daniel Webster," "The Death of the Hired Man," Abe Lincoln in Illinois,*

*The Scarlet Letter, Moby Dick. These stories are founded upon an older and wider tradition, but one still ours—David Copperfield, "The Ancient Mariner," "The Deserted Village," "Elegy Written in a Country Churchyard," Robinson Crusoe, Macbeth. And this literature depends upon and blends with an even older tradition—the temptations of Faust, the mystic Bluebird, the penetrating humor of Don Quixote, the wandering of Ulysses, the heroic figures of Greek and Roman myth, the just and overseeing God of the Bible. The base of the heritage is as broad as the humanistic tradition.*

## SELECTING THE LITERATURE

Valid reasons for reading and teaching literature suggest answers to some of the questions often asked about choosing the literature to be taught.

### SHOULD ONLY CLASSICS BE ASSIGNED?

College entrance examinations decades ago demanded familiarity with prescribed classics; even if they had not, the typical English teacher of 1910 would have cringed at the suggestion that the vulgar upstart Jack London be taught. William Lyon Phelps early in the century was regarded as dangerously radical when he encouraged his Yale students to read Stevenson.

But the old order changeth. London and Stevenson have attained respectability and have made the going easier for such of their descendants as Ernest Hemingway and C. S. Forester. Out the window have gone Burke's "Conciliation," Halleck's "Marco Bozzaris," and Landor's "Iphigenia and Agamemnon." Less attention is paid to Alexander Pope, and the name of Carlyle is never uttered in most classrooms. Most teachers today try to select for study only those pieces that have something clearly worth saying to today's young people and that say it well; these teachers realize that some of the old and some of the new meet this requirement.

Extremists exist on both sides, of course, though they are relatively few. Battling for an almost exclusive diet of classics are some teachers who argue that little contemporary literature is as good as what has stood the test of time; that the classics, because they are so well presented, can have even more appeal for adolescents than do materials whose chief virtue is contemporaneity; and that, if students are not exposed to the world's finest writing in high school, many of them will never read a line of it. On the other side are some teachers who assert that most classics are too difficult for teenagers, difficult not just in language but also in conception and scope; only mature minds, these teachers say, can grasp what Shakespeare is really talking about or what Milton is saying about the ways of God.

A middle ground seems to be best. We must face the fact that most of the reading our students do after graduation will be taken from contemporary materials—newspapers, magazines, books-of-the-month, and so on. As teachers we need to make our students' reading more discriminating than it would have been if we had never existed. We can teach discrimination only by introducing to our classes many varieties of reading and by helping students to understand the similarities and differences among these varieties. We need to present Homer, Chaucer, Hawthorne, and others, with sufficient skill that our students will not only see what has made these writers live but will also be able to use them as touchstones for the evaluation of other literature. The classics should be taught as samples of the best thinking and writing that humanity has yet achieved, and as expressions of the sensitivity of unusually perceptive human beings. Those children who are intellectually able to realize the mental and emotional penetration of great writers will have as a permanent possession the desire to find in other literature that which is no less evocative.

When considering a selection, a teacher should give it a high mark if it is readable by students and if it will introduce them to some of the personalities who ought to be known to almost everyone. Somewhere in their high school careers many students should become acquainted with such semilegendary figures as Horatius, King Arthur, Marco Polo, and William Tell; and with such literary immortals as Oedipus, Sinbad, Chaucer's Knight, Cervantes' Don Quixote, Swift's Gulliver, and Irving's Rip Van Winkle. Students in junior high school are usually ready for the myths of Greece, Rome, and Scandinavia, and for simple versions of the Round Table stories and other legends. But greater maturity—the near maturity of high school juniors and seniors, though it may vary with individuals, seems essential for an understanding of the Knight and other Chaucerian characters, and Oedipus or Antigone.

The contemporary has its virtues, too, if it is carefully chosen. Some of today's literature will be tomorrow's classics. The first teacher to introduce O'Neill, Wilder, Hemingway, Steinbeck, Faulkner, Dickinson, or Frost to students was departing from the classical canon, but today we realize that this teacher chose well. The important point to remember is that, although modern writers of first rank are worth including, little class time should be spent on the tenth raters—or even the third.

In espousing the cause of contemporary literature, Darwin Turner speaks about other problems:

*In the process of searching for new materials, many teachers expanded the canon of literature. Some, it is true, went to extremes to discover "relevant" literature. Introducing sociological, economic, political materials, they discussed those issues with never a glance to the literary quality. Self-conscious and perhaps insecure because of their fear that they had not been adequately trained to teach literature, some sought instead to teach sociology or political theory, disciplines in which they were even less competent.*[6]

Those selections with literary merit, both of the past and the present, Professor Turner says, deserve to be taught as effectively as possible. We assure the relevance of first-rate works "by teaching them as though they are something more than the pastime of dilettantes, fragile glassware to be admired from a distance, or Sunday sermons for the bored."

## HOW DIFFICULT SHOULD THE LITERATURE BE?

It is impossible to assess literary difficulty with exactitude. Formulas have been devised in the attempt, but because they involve counting polysyllables and measuring sentence length yet cannot provide a yardstick to measure the difficulty of conceptions, they are hardly satisfactory. Readability formulas show, for example, that *Tom Sawyer* and *Huckleberry Finn* are equally difficult books, but anyone who has read and understood both stories realizes that *Huckleberry Finn* is infinitely more complex, multilayered, harder to grasp. Edgar Dale illustrates clearly how simplicity of words may conceal depth of meaning:

> *In Dostoevsky's novel The Brothers Karamazov, Father Zossima asks: "What is hell?" and answers, "... it is the suffering of being unable to love." A fifth grader can pronounce these words, recognize them perceptually, but can he* **read** *them? He can't get the meaning because he is conceptually immature.*[7]

But how can a student's conceptions mature if the student is constantly exposed to immature conceptions? There is a way out of the apparent dilemma. The principle of pleasure that we have discussed implies that what we teach should be capable of bringing pleasure to our students at the intellectual or maturational level they have attained at that time. In other words, a selection should not be so far beyond the understanding of students that there is no possibility of pleasure. Yet often it should be slightly beyond their full comprehension. Robert Browning provides the justification:

> Ah, but a man's reach should exceed his grasp
> Or what's a heaven for?

As Edgar Dale has demonstrated, *The Brothers Karamazov* may very well be far beyond the reach of a fifth grader; on the other hand, it could provide a worthwhile aesthetic reading experience for many high school or college students. At the high school level, it will probably stretch many general readers into reaching a bit higher, but that could be the advantage in using it. Louise Rosenblatt, whose view is that "a text, once it leaves its author's hands, is simply paper and ink until a reader evokes from it a literary work—sometimes, even, a literary work of art,"[8] advocates some stretching:

THE TEACHING OF HIGH SCHOOL ENGLISH

*Concern with the quality of the literary transaction should not, however, be vulgarized into an assumption that "poorer" or "easier" texts are being prescribed for the general reader. It is possible that despite the reader's not assimilating some of the elements of The Brothers Karamozov, he might still be stirred to organize a more sensitive, more firmly structured evocation from that text than from one to which he could "do greater justice."*[9]*

A well-chosen literary selection should stretch the student slightly; it should make the student extend himself or herself. If it does not stretch, it provides no new challenges; the student might as well spend the time before the TV set. But if it is too far out of reach, the student will give up in despair. In addressing the question of suitability, Barrett John Mandel, a college literature teacher, says, "Literature is worth reading when it stimulates intense or lively or deep or inspired thought or feeling (better yet, thought and feeling) in the reader. When such activity is happening, education is going forward." A well-chosen selection, then, should stretch both thought and feeling, and in the transactional view of Rosenblatt, should provide a rich "lived-through" aesthetic reading experience.

## MUST ONLY LITERATURE WITH A CAPITAL L BE ASSIGNED?

Perhaps no one can define exactly the line a writer must cross in order to be an author of literature. It may be helpful, though, to recall Van Dyke's definition of "literature": "Literature consists of those writings which interpret the meanings of nature and life, in words of clearness and power, touched with the personality of the author, in artistic forms of permanent interest." A notice of sale seldom possesses any of these characteristics, nor does a news story about yesterday's murder or last night's basketball game. The purpose of the bill or the news story is utilitarian—to give information. But a nonutilitarian selection such as a story in a pulp magazine is not necessarily literature. In such a piece, a reader may be guided by little more than curiosity about how events will turn out.

Rosenblatt's definitions of "efferent" and aesthetic reading support the distinctions made above. In "efferent" reading, the reader's main concern is with what can be carried away, "toward concepts to be retained, ideas to be tested, actions to be performed after the reading."[10]* Obvious examples would be the reading of a science textbook, an automobile service manual, or a drivers' manual designed to prepare a prospective driver to pass a test and receive a license to drive.

*In aesthetic reading, in contrast, the reader's primary concern is with what happens **during** the actual reading event. Though, like the efferent reader of*

---

*From *The Reader, the Text, the Poem* by Louise M. Rosenblatt. Copyright © 1978 by the Southern Illinois University Press. Reprinted by permission of the Southern Illinois University Press.

*a law text, say, the reader of Frost's "Birches" must decipher the images or concepts or assertions that the words point to, he also pays attention to the associations, feelings, attitudes, and ideas that these words and their referents arouse within him. "Listening to" himself, he synthesizes these elements into a meaningful structure.* **In aesthetic reading, the reader's attention is centered directly on what he is living through during his relationship with that particular text.** *(Emphasis is Rosenblatt's)*[11]*

Somewhere on a continuum from efferent to aesthetic is reading such works as The Book of Isaiah, the Song of Songs, Emerson's essays, Lincoln's Gettysburg Address, and Gibbon's *Decline and Fall of the Roman Empire*. In Rosenblatt's words, "The usual definitions of literature-as-art have not provided a satisfactory basis for categorizing them." Thus, some utilitarian selections are on the borderline between "mere reading" and "literature."[12]* For example, some of Ruskin's prose dealing with art or with the dignity of labor is utilitarian in that it strives to inform, but it also possesses the characteristics of "literature."

For practical purposes, as a rough guide only, the line between "mere reading" and "literature" might be drawn thus:

| "Mere Reading" | "Literature" |
|---|---|
| 1. May be utilitarian or affective (emotional) | 1. Is always affective |
| 2. If utilitarian, has primary purpose of informing | 2. Gives an author's personalized interpretation of life |
| 3. If affective, lacks one or more of the last four qualities listed under "literature" | 3. Is clearly and strikingly written |
| | 4. Is in an artistic form of lasting interest |
| | 5. Invites aesthetic reading |

Briefly, the question to consider is this: Should any material that is not "literature" and does not always invite aesthetic reading be admitted to the high school English course?

The answer appears to be a qualified "yes." In their lives after graduation, many students will have more occasion to do utilitarian reading than affective. They will, for example, read sales ads and brochures; book, TV, and movie reviews; political campaign material; and newspaper and magazine articles to get information and form opinions. The English department has not done its duty if its students are graduated without knowing a great deal about how to read various kinds of utilitarian materials.

*From *The Reader, the Text, the Poem* by Louise M. Rosenblatt. Copyright © 1978 by the Southern Illinois University Press. Reprinted by permission of the Southern University Press.

But although the inclusion of some utilitarian reading is highly desirable in each year of the junior and senior high school, there is seldom a strong reason for including any affective material that lacks one or more of the qualities of literature. Outside the classroom, students will sometimes read comic strips and pulp magazines. In class, however, they may read with profit selections that are of no less interest but are of satisfactory quality. Eventually, through the teacher's guidance, most (but not all) will search in their reading for qualities the poorer comics and the trashy magazines do not possess. They will also, it is hoped, apply literary criteria to the many "junior novels" or "adolescent novels" found in community and school bookstores, in school libraries, and offered by national school paperback book clubs. As students seek higher levels of aesthetic reading in these books and recommend only the best, the literary quality of adolescent fiction should improve. These novels have improved since their rise to popularity in the 1950s, but many are still cliché-ridden and lack artistic quality.

Although not literary works of art, adolescent novels that possess some degree of literary quality can be useful in the junior high and in the lower grades of senior high as bridges or stepping stones toward more mature reading. This concept, made popular in the 1950s by Dwight Burton and other authorities on adolescent fiction, is still valid. Rosenblatt acknowledges that it is with some of these novels that "the freest, most honest, and most personal literary transactions" may occur. But, she reminds teachers, "the real problem is in the maintenance of that spontaneity and self-respect while at the same time fostering the capacity to undertake rewarding relationships with increasingly demanding texts."[13]*

## SHOULD THE WHOLE CLASS READ THE SAME LITERATURE?

The situation observed most often in an English classroom is that of the teacher commenting on a single piece of literature or conducting a discussion of it. David Bleich describes the climate of the traditional classroom this way: "In the classroom, the teacher's authority is an effigy of the author's authority in the reading experience."[14] Fortunately, not all English teachers are this narrow and restrictive as they teach a work to the whole class. They work very hard toward student interpretation "as a communal act." The aim: to conduct a discussion that will enable each member of the class to create " 'the truth' through his response to other responses."[15]

Observations by the teacher, as well as those by literary authorities outside the classroom, can heighten a student's awareness of a text, but the teacher should place the greatest emphasis on recognizing and guiding students' responses.

*From *The Reader, the Text, the Poem* by Louise M. Rosenblatt. Copyright © 1978 by the Southern Illinois University Press. Reprinted by permission of the Southern Illinois University Press.

Students want to talk about literature which interests and perplexes them, and they want to know how their classmates have reacted to it. The teacher's role is that of facilitator, skillful questioner, and guide.

Sometimes teachers control class discussions of a text too tightly because they fear that divergent responses may lead the discussion too far away from certain essentials to be found in the work. They may also be afraid of problems which divergence itself may present as any two student readers interact. Bruce Miller sees any one of three combinations as possible:

> *(1) both readers can be wrong, can misconstrue the work; (2) one of them can be right and the other wrong; (3) both can be right and yet differ from each other, as in the case of ambiguities of reference or layers of interpretation.*[16]

But Miller sees much value in such circumstances. In open discussions, he finds, readers can discover their errors and reject them, and they can be helped to understand more completely their individual experiences with the work. And many other advantages may accrue: some instruction in close reading, analysis of style, discussion of what to look for in literature, explanations of how each part contributes to the whole, and examination of the author's purpose. Whole class reading and discussion can also assist students in relating literature to life, in distinguishing one type of literature from another, in learning the special techniques to apply to each type, and sometimes in seeing how literature grows not only from the author's experiences but also from the age in which he or she lives. Thus, whole class reading and discussion can greatly widen and deepen a student's own relationship with a work.

Group reading, used especially in thematic units but possible also in other arrangements, may involve reading of the same or similar material by several students in a class. They discuss within the group, perhaps with the aid of questions or in a framework prepared by the teacher, and they usually find some way to share their reactions with the class, maybe through panel discussions, reports, or dramatizations. The material read by a group is teacher-approved, although students may assist in the choices and sometimes select their group on the basis of what is to be read in it. Groups may form to share common reading interests or to learn from other students with different interests. Sometimes groups will accomplish a very specific reading task, such as reading a book in common and presenting it as a candidate for reading and discussion by the whole class. In doing so, each group will compete with several other groups with books to nominate.

In individual reading, perhaps no two students in the class are reading the same book. Some of the choices may be perfectly free, as in Daniel Fader's program, described in *Hooked on Books: Program and Proof;*[17] some may be free within prescribed limits, such as those of a literary type or a list of books on similar or varied subjects; some may be chosen in conference between the teacher and the student. Often the teacher schedules individual conferences with students to ask questions and engage in a dialogue about each book. This procedure presupposes that the teacher has read each book, and that the quality of the dialogue will depend upon the kind of relationship the teacher and the student have had with the book. In some schools, supervised individual reading has become the heart of the reading program. It should never replace class and group reading, however, because those have values not otherwise attainable.

The question of whether the whole class should read the same literature is not as significant as those that deal with the quality of the student's experience with each work read. Each arrangement, whether it involves reading and discussion of the same work by the whole class, reading and discussion by a small group of students, or individualized reading with or without teacher conferences, should envision reading as an active process, one that includes many learning experiences designed to heighten the student's individual transaction with the work. In that process, the teacher becomes a key figure. And, in that process, the teacher chooses questions over statements much of the time. Barbara Stanford and Gene Stanford describe the teacher's role this way:

> . . . the teacher listens carefully to students' own honest responses to literature and builds from there. The teacher attempts to discover the level that the student is presently operating on, accepts and affirms that level, and then slowly introduces experiences to help develop more mature intellectual skills. If the student does not understand on a literal level, the teacher may be used as a guide in how to read a work of literature. If the student reacts negatively to a literary work, the teacher accepts that reaction and encourages the student to analyze the reasons for disliking the work. As much as possible, the students should be encouraged to read and enjoy the works they respond to at that age. Often young people will respond to romantic novels and poetry with an intensity that they will never feel in later life. If properly nurtured, this response can lead to enthusiasm for reading other forms of literature and a lifelong interest in reading.[18]

The following diagram shows a desirable reading plan for a class. As a plan on paper, it can appear static. The teacher, however, can make it into a dynamic process involving much student interaction and student-teacher interaction. Whole class reading and discussion can lead to group reading and individual reading. Individual reading can give students opportunities to respond in groups and before the whole class. In every situation and at every stage, the teacher serves as a guide.

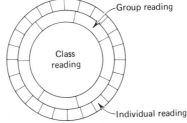

# HOW SHOULD ENGLISH TEACHERS DEAL WITH CENSORSHIP OF LITERATURE?

Censorship of high school literature usually occurs when school officials, but more often parents, decide that they must act to prevent children from reading something that threatens a concept or an attitude that they believe is essential to the moral, political, or social development of children in their community. International tension, wars, minority movements for or against social change, a fundamentalist or evangelical religious movement, or a conservative political movement can increase the incidence of censorship nationally. One school board member with a child in an English classroom, or for that matter any person with a strong conservative, fundamentalist, or even a liberal attitude, can start a local campaign to ban books. Unlike the school board member, the citizen at large may not have immediate access to the power structure that sets policy and directly or indirectly establishes curriculum. But this citizen may approach a local member of the clergy, write a letter to a local newspaper, call the principal, discuss the problem with sympathetic neighbors and friends, write a letter to the president of the school board, or contact a number of textbook watchdog groups around the nation. Unfortunately, the English teacher is often alerted by a letter in a newspaper or by a group of citizens in the principal's office. By that time, the movement to censor the identified materials may be well on its way.

Once a number of well-established citizens challenge materials publicly, the entire school system is carried into a kind of public arena where school board members, administrators, teachers, children, and parents will choose sides.

One approach that parents may use fairly early in the process is to have an attorney write a letter that may begin something like this: "You are hereby notified that (*name of student*) is not allowed by the undersigned to . . . ." And it may end: "If removal of this child from any class or meeting or assembly is necessary to meet the above requirements, any damage, emotional, physical, mental or otherwise caused by this separation or removal shall be deemed to be the personal and/or collective responsibilities of the parties to whom this notice is sent and/or listed above, resulting in possible appropriate action." The notice may seek to prevent the child from reading a specific book, or it may seek to prevent exposure to all literature containing such things as praise of humanity, one-worldism, mythology, intellectual inquiry, ethnic views, death, profanity, violence, mysticism, anti-Americanism, racism, sexism, women's liberation, pagan cultures, and sexual desire.

If teachers resist such pressure, harassed administrators and harassed teachers may refuse to communicate openly with each other; teachers' associations may enter the arena; and administrators may take action that will give teachers or a parent who sides with teachers cause for a lawsuit. Note the following excerpts from a complaint filed in a U.S. circuit court April 6, 1979:

*Ms. ( a teacher) was required to comply with defendants' directives by physically cutting a few pages containing such words as "hell" and "damn" from all class copies. . . .*

*Among the terminated courses were "Black Literature," "Gothic Literature," "Folklore and Legends," and "Science Fiction."*

*. . . defendants ordered that two additional courses be deleted from the high school English curriculum. These courses were "Shakespeare" and "Creative Writing."*

*On information and belief, defendants ordered the termination of the above-mentioned courses from the school's curriculum solely because the teaching methods and/or contents of the courses offended their social, political and moral beliefs.*

Eight months later, a judge found no violation of constitutionally protected rights and dismissed the case with the comment that "there is no way for school officials to make the determinations involved except on the basis of personal moral beliefs." The appeals court suggested redirecting the complaint to other issues and upheld the right of the school board to fire an English teacher on the grounds that the board, not the teacher, establishes standards for instruction.

This illustration should not suggest that English teachers and sympathetic parents back away from all legal confrontations. Not all cases defending students' right to read have encountered as much difficulty. But litigation may not be as fruitful as one might expect in a democracy. "Judges have been understandably reluctant to establish legal precedent in suits involving school censorship since no judge wishes to create precedent which may be reversed upon appeal."[19] Lawyers may not present the case effectively. Judges with heavy case loads may rely presumptively on case law which has little to do with the main issues presented by the plaintiffs. Teachers who choose to be plaintiffs are likely to find the process stressful, financially costly, lengthy, and professionally damaging.

Perhaps nothing is as exhilarating as winning a tough legal battle, but a court case can set professional relations and public relations back to the point where trust, respect, and confidence will be very difficult to reestablish. It is foolish to build defenses until a legal showdown is the only way to resolve the problem. Kenneth Donelson reminds us that "there is a chill in the air." But Robert Hogan suggests that we English teachers have added to the chill by becoming belligerent, pedantic, defensive, and aloof. He sees "an open door" as the "last line of defense under present circumstances."[20]

A comparison of two national surveys shows that the incidence of censorship initiated by parents has accelerated very significantly. The first, done in 1966, showed 48 percent initiated by parents and 42 percent by members of the school staff. The second, done in 1977, showed 73 percent initiated by parents, 23 percent by the school staff, and 4 percent by students.[21] Obviously, the most important task is gaining parents' respect and confidence. Given the rise of conservative thinking in the 1980s, the time is late, but perhaps not too late.

The first step is obviously self-examination. All English teachers, not just the English chairperson, should develop a written philosophy that the teachers truly believe in and will stick by. Doing this must involve considering the beliefs and aims of school officials and parents openly and honestly, never in a condescending way. Teachers must know the meanings and implications of every statement they make. If they speak about the importance of a student's personal relationship with literature, they cannot be thinking mainly of their own preferences for certain selections.

The next step is to write objectives that relate directly to the philosophy, making certain that every objective is relevant to everything said about subject, materials, and methods. Clarity is essential, so teachers should avoid professional jargon that parents and school officials might not understand.

With the philosophy and the objectives in mind, the department should launch a public relations campaign directed at students, school officials, parents, community groups, librarians, and the media. Personal contacts, not written explanations, will do the most good. The classroom should be open to visitors and all should be encouraged to come by for a discussion about anything they question. Frankness and sincerity will keep the door open; condescension will close it. English teachers must teach with the support of students, parents, and school officials. The plan is to win over as many as possible.

Teachers should develop procedures for selecting books and for handling complaints. They should invite to their planning sessions participants from all groups mentioned. Direct participation may not be possible in all cases, but teachers should keep informing everyone and keep inviting responses.

Teachers should also read every book completely and carefully before requiring it or recommending it and should write a rationale for every book that has caused controversy elsewhere, and for every other book that could cause it locally. They should be sure that every rationale is consistent with the stated philosophy and objectives. Finally, they should keep informed about censorship problems and procedures. The NCTE and the American Library Association are good sources.[22]

## TEXT, TEACHER, CRITIC, OR READER: WHO OR WHAT IS THE AUTHORITY?

Many English teachers who were schooled in the "New Criticism" during the 1960s taught as though only the literary text mattered, apart from all biographical, social, political, and personal concerns. As such, the text was defined as a language construct, to be studied closely and objectively. A decade later, confused and disturbed by transactional theorists, these teachers lamented the fact that subjectivity was rapidly becoming high fashion and that the integrity of the text as a literary entity was being threatened with extinction. Their disconcertedness is understandable. Teaching literature, like teaching any other area of English, can be frustrating for teachers who have built their goals and strategies around one school of thought.

It seems ludicrous to suggest that the text will be killed by those who say that it is not a poem, a short story, or a novel until the reader makes it so. A text still carries the authority that comes with generally recognized excellence as a work of art. It never deserved any kind of supreme authority before being read, nor did it deserve any immunity from subjective interpretation. The text will live; in fact, it may enjoy a more vigorous life. Aesthetic reading is a life-sharing process. The reader is life-giving, and the text is life-giving. No text is immortal; its readers keep it alive.

Some teachers of literature fear that attaching main importance to the reader's personal relationship with a text will make the teacher relatively unimportant. This anxiety is equally ludicrous. A student's relationship with a text is enhanced by whatever that student can carry to the text. A teacher can do much to prepare a student for the experience. Each reader must create his or her own meaning from the text, but the reader should be able to test the validity of that meaning by finding support for it in the text. As a fellow reader eager to discuss responses with a student, as an instructor and a resource person, and as an experienced guide, the teacher fills many essential roles.

Nor does increased attention to reader response deny the importance of scholars and critics. They enjoy the authority that comes with training and experience in their specialities as reader-responders. "Coming to the critic after one's own transaction with the text, one can be helped to realize more keenly the character of that experience."[23] One undeserved authority sometimes assigned to scholars and critics, though, is that of proxy readers. Sometimes it is as much the tone of their language as it is the substance of their comments that inhibits some readers and makes others believers. The reader must realize that it is his or her *own* experience that matters most.

If a behavioral goal for literature were appropriate, it might be this: "Given a text, the student will read it aesthetically and will create from it a meaning that is personally significant." Too often literature is treated as though it has little or nothing to do with aesthetics. The student reads the text for what he or she expects others will want to hear about it. Teachers often seem to be saying, "If you read such and such, you will find so and so"; even, "If you read such and such, you will find it relevant, truthful, beautiful, and personally rewarding." This is the kind of intrusive talk that can destroy the integrity of any student's attempt to discover whether a text can be any of these things. This is what keeps literature in the minds of scholars, critics, and teachers and often keeps it out of the minds of students.

## ARRANGING AND APPROACHING
### ARRANGING THE LITERATURE

Four principles of arrangement are widely used in planning reading in literature:

1. Chronological order
2. Types of literature
3. Central themes
4. Students' experiences

In addition, teachers occasionally employ various combinations of the above arrangements, or modifications of them. For instance, a variation of the chronological approach is the "culture epoch" plan, in which each unit is centered upon the literature and other cultural elements of the Colonial Period, the Revolutionary War Period, and so on. Less frequent is the organization of a course with a few authors or a few classics as centers of interest or points of departure. The "guided free reading" mentioned earlier might also be called a method of arrangement. Correlation with history or some other subject is a plan followed in some schools. A few teachers, it seems, follow no plan of arrangement but merely teach whatever they want to whenever they want to. Other teachers, especially in British schools, simply follow up on clues from the class—deciding on the basis of students' reactions whether to introduce another play or some lyric poetry, or a short story with a particular theme, or something else.

Special mention should be made of humanities courses, which still enjoy some popularity. There is no neat definition for such courses; apparently no two are alike. Some of them attempt to relate literature to movies, television, and other media. Others, usually called "interdisciplinary," combine literature with art, music, architecture, philosophy, history, or religion, or with any two or more of these. Some are separate or isolated courses, offered only as electives. Others are correlated with offerings in another field: for example, the decade of the 1920s is studied in U.S. History at the same time that music of the period is studied in Music Appreciation and the literature is studied in English III. Some humanities courses are team-taught by teachers from different departments; others are taught by English teachers with special interest in and knowledge of the related fields. The students are often grouped flexibly from large group to small seminar group, and they may work flexibly with time allotments, from 2-hour blocks to 15- or 30-minute modules. Independent study (self-instruction and inquiry) is encour-

THE TEACHING OF HIGH SCHOOL ENGLISH

aged, sometimes in special "resource rooms" equipped with a wide variety of materials in the humanities.[24]

Often these courses follow the "culture" epoch" plan, showing for instance the similarities in Romantic literature, art, and music and perhaps contrasting them with the more formalized cultural arts of the preceding century. A major virtue of humanities courses is that they take literature out of a vacuum by showing its often surprising close relationship with other arts. Drawbacks are that few teachers are adequately prepared to offer such instruction, plus the fact that all aspects of the course, including the literature, may be treated superficially. We can speak about these good qualities and drawbacks from some experience, but unfortunately we know very little from research about the success of such integrated or correlated approaches in teaching the humanities.[25] Most of the professional literature on the subject is description and exhortation.

Experience and common sense tell us that each of the four methods of arrangement has some good qualities and some drawbacks. The major pro's and con's of these arrangements appear to be as follows:

## Arrangement by Chronology

### Pro's

1. Chronology, because it follows the inexorable calendar, affords the most orderly plan of procedure.
2. Students learn the pattern of development of literature.
3. Students learn some of the relationships between literature and history.
4. Students do not stay with one type long enough to become bored with it.

### Con's

1. Learning to enjoy literature is much more important than learning who wrote what when.
2. The literature that students usually find least interesting is often presented first.
3. When time runs short, modern literature is likely to be neglected.
4. Sometimes the chronological course in literature degenerates into a course in literary history.

## Arrangement by Types

### Pro's

1. Students learn to distinguish literary forms.

2. They can easily compare works by different authors who used the same medium.

### Con's

1. It does students little real good to be able to identify a type of literature.

2. Too much stress is put upon distinctions that are not always clearcut (e.g., between short story, novelette, and novel.)

3. They learn how the writing of each type has changed.
4. They may be stimulated to further reading of the type being studied.
5. Teachers can easily combine this arrangement with some other.

3. Students acquire no idea of the whole pattern of development of literature.
4. Time devoted to a type that some dislike is a desert for them.
5. The selections often have no continuity or similarity other than being of the same type.

## Arrangement Around Themes

### Pro's

1. Students become aware that literature deals with essential questions about the human condition.
2. Interest in ideas can lead students to further reading.

3. Selections from different countries and different centuries may be introduced in the same unit.
4. Students usually do not stay with one type long enough to become bored with it.
5. Difference in authors' points of view may be studied.

### Con's

1. Controversial themes can lead to confrontations with parents and school officials.
2. Sociology, psychology, and history may be stressed too much, literature too little.
3. Sometimes selections are chosen not because of their quality but because of their themes.
4. Students may acquire no idea of the whole pattern of development of literature.
5. Some students may not be interested in the general theme of the entire unit.

## Arrangement Around Student Experiences

### Pro's

1. Students investigate and ponder problems that affect their own lives.

2. They are usually encouraged to create their own meanings from the reading selections.
3. They are urged to do wide, independent reading.

4. Teachers find it generally easier to discover and deal with individual differences in this arrangement than in others.

### Con's

1. Emphasis on value clarification can lead to confrontations with parents and school officials.
2. Material read may sometimes be of inferior quality.

3. Students may acquire no idea of the whole pattern of development of literature.
4. The subjective nature of the arrangement may make evaluating and reporting students' growth in learning more complex and difficult.

## Incomplete frames

### Sample 1 (Character analysis)

In the story _____ by _____ the major character is _____ who is _____. Another main character is _____ _____ who _____ is also important in the story.

The problem which the major character faces is that _____.

The problem is finally resolved when _____.

The story ends with _____.

The lesson I learned from reading this story was that _____
_____.

### Sample 2 (Essay: Time order)

At the end of _____ what happened was that _____.

Previous to this _____
_____.

Before this _____.
_____.

The entire chain of events had begun for a number of reasons including _____
_____.

Some prominent incidents which helped to trigger the conflict were _____
_____.

### Sample 3 (Essay: Comparison-contrast)

_____ are different from _____ in several ways. First of all _____

while _____.

Secondly, _____

while _____.

In addition, _____.

while _____.

Finally _____.

while _____.

So it should be evident that _____.
_____.

The fact that no one method of arrangement emerges as superior to all others should cause no particular surprise or alarm. There are no panaceas in teaching. If someone could find a plan of arrangement that has no weaknesses, . . . but that is only utopian dreaming. In some situations it is necessary to take what is available, improve it if possible, but use it effectively. In other situations, teachers may have more freedom to innovate. In all situations, though, teachers must think of students first in using existing arrangements and in developing different ones.

Arrangements around themes, topics, and student experiences have been found most satisfactory in the seventh, eighth, ninth, and tenth grades. Fine distinctions among types usually make little impression on students in those grades, especially in the junior high years. Similarly, younger students' sense of chronology is as a rule insufficiently developed to make a chronological organization meaningful; the year 1880 to most 12-to-14-year-olds sounds no nearer in time than 1680, and not much nearer than 1492. But the seventh-to-tenth graders can nonetheless profitably study a number of selections that will engage their interests and serve as stepping stones to literature of the highest quality. The teacher cannot only provide selections with literary value but encourage students to "explore why certain writing brings them pleasure, to attend to details that reveal setting, character traits, and other factors that are involved in analyzing a literary work."[26] However, emphasis is not on the work and not on external analysis; it is on developing a personal awareness of literature through personal experiences and personal responses.

Arrangements by types or chronology is better suited to the eleventh and twelfth grades, although even in these years long-continued exposure to lyrics or essays should probably be avoided. (Lyric poetry is so intense that few persons read much of it at one sitting. Lyrics are on the spice shelf of literature; none of us would make a meal of cloves.) The average 16-year-old, according to some psychologists, has reached or passed the average mental age of the whole population. If he or she will ever be able to learn about the types and the chronology of literature, and if these things are worth teaching, then the ages of 16 and 17 would seem to be the logical time to present them.

There are various ways of attaining a little variety in arrangement. Among possible variations of the above procedures are these:

1. Use the chronological order, but begin with modern literature. After a while, raise the question, "How did our literature get to be this way?" Then go back to early literature and work forward, keeping the question uppermost and drawing many comparisons between past and present writings.
2. Move quickly into the present, using representative selections from earlier periods as preparation for understanding ideas and points of view in modern literature. (One problem in doing this might be moving to what Ronald

LaConte calls "entrapment in the present," with its narrow view of literary heritage and its preoccupation with inferior literature.)

3. With an emphasis on heritage, use a thematic approach by presenting a "thematic polarity" such as *loyalty and treachery*. Examine these concepts in the literature of different periods from ancient Greece to modern America, even extrapolating into literature dealing with the future.

4. Take a comparative approach, teaching a classic such as Plato's *Apology* with Kafka's *The Trial*. Less demanding than this comparison of a classic and a modern work is Becky Johnson's unit "Voices for Justice," which brings together several types: Walter Van Tilburg Clark's *The Ox-Bow Incident*, Jerome Lawrence and Robert E. Lee's *The Night Thoreau Spent in Jail*, Lord Byron's "The Prisoner of Chillon," and other relevant works.[27]

5. Bring together various types from classic to modern in a unit called "The Hero as 'Super' Man."[28] An interesting contrast in points of view might come from *Beowulf* and John Gardner's *Grendel*.

6. Use the topic "Roots" as the focus for a multicultural approach. A study of family ancestries may lead to the reading of various types of literature from Western Europe, Eastern Europe, Africa, Near East, Far East, American Indian nations, and Mexico, from past to present.

A plan developed in 1965 by the English Curriculum Center of Carnegie-Mellon University for "able students" but modified by teachers for heterogeneous classes and still widely used is as follows:[29]

| 10th Grade | *U*niversal concerns of man | *M*---- | *L*---- |
|---|---|---|---|
| 11th Grade American Literature | *U*---- | *M*odification by culture pattern | *L*---- |
| 12th Grade English Literature | *U*---- | *M*---- | Literary art forms; genres; techniques |

*Thus the tenth-grade course gives primary emphasis to the universal concerns of man as they appear in world literature (in translation)—such concerns as love, heroism, human weakness, portraits of social conditions or practices, and the search for wisdom. The eleventh-grade course consists of American literature which demonstrates how universal concerns are modified by the American culture pattern from Puritan times to the present. The approach to the American literature chosen is roughly historical, but looks nothing like the traditional survey. Rather, the course focuses on important aspects of the*

146        

*American character as they are revealed in our literature—such aspects as American Puritanism, the American desire to get ahead in the world, American optimism, and the American social conscience. The twelfth-grade course is primarily made up of English literature, and it gives major attention to the most sophisticated perceptions of the nature of literature, those implied in our definition by the phrase "verbal art forms." Once again, the treatment of literature is roughly historical; but this time the focal points are the various literary art forms: tale, tragedy, epic, satire, novel, and drama of social criticism.*

This arrangement, it will be noted, combines the chronological, typological, and thematic approaches, and it may incorporate student experiences. Particularly noteworthy is its emphasis upon the universal concerns of man, as modified by different cultural patterns. Certainly that is what literature is mainly about. The criticism that this emphasis advocates secular humanism as a religious philosophy—a view expressed by some textbook censors—is pure nonsense.

In some schools, this arrangement is used much as it appears above; in others, though, it serves as a guide for short courses and electives, and articulation from grade to grade may not be the same. American literature, for example, is sometimes introduced at the tenth-grade level, and English literature is offered at the eleventh-grade level.

The emphasis given to competency based programs and mastery learning units at the beginning of the 1980s has forced some teachers to work small skill-focused units into their literature courses, and lessons on specific skills into their units. "In teaching a focused mastery lesson on noun clauses, for example, the English teachers simply break the flow of the thematic unit and say, 'Let's take a direct look at noun clauses today and maybe tomorrow. Then we'll get back to the theme of the unit.' In teaching an integrated lesson, they say, 'As you prepare to write your essay on the nature of contemporary heroes, we want to teach you some important skills in eliminating paragraph problems.' "[30] Skillful teachers should be able to work needed mastery lessons into a literature unit or course without doing serious damage to continuity. A greater threat to aesthetic reading development could be continued emphasis on subskills of reading, and on carefully restricted and controlled utilitarian reading, the kind that Rosenblatt calls "efferent." If this emphasis becomes predominant in competency based examinations, the development of aesthetic reading could suffer greatly.

## SIX BASIC APPROACHES

The six basic approaches—historical, sociopsychological, personal, value-seeking, cognitive, and analytical—outlined in the rest of this chapter and illustrated in greater detail in the next two chapters, appear to be in widest use at the present time. The historical approach seems to have moved somewhat from previous concern with biographical and historical facts to a study of literature as cultural heritage, rich in thematic possibilities. The sociopsychological approach, influenced by what has been called the "romantic radicalism"[31] of the 1960s and early 1970s, and kept alive by anxieties over social change, political corruption, war, technological advancements, and environmental damage, finds its expression in humanities courses and in short courses and units on such topics as Equality, Conformity, Justice, and One World. The personal approach has been influenced by advocates of personal growth and by research on personal response to literature. The value-seeking approach has become less moralistic and didactic, but it rather vigorously urges students to examine points of view and develop a sound personal code. The cognitive approach concentrates on meanings in literature. The analytical, influenced by so-called "New Critics" of the late 1950s and most of the 1960s, considers the text an object to be analyzed with informed, scholarly objectivity, so that the work itself can be appreciated and understood as a whole

## The Historical Approach
In its traditional sense, the historical approach emphasizes the biography of the writer and the literary and historical events of the age in which he or she lived. In some historical courses, apparently the aim is to parade great works. In survey courses, particularly those using anthologies of American, English, or World literature, it has been a bits-and-pieces overview, a disjointed, distorted, superficial introduction to authors, works, influences, ideas, and trends. Surveys can lead to some familiarity with many works and to some sense of the historical development of literature, but they rarely give the student the time or the encouragement to question and ponder human issues and relate them to present realities. It is out of this sense of inadequacy that teachers have moved from the narrow focus and the panoramic coverage to new interest in literary heritage. A confrontation with human issues in literature of the past can help students to grapple with human problems today. Reading, then, should be "a continuing dialog on the moral and philosophical questions central to the culture itself."[32] Put another way, "the study of literature enables us to discover the compulsions and discontents in civilization—with the benefit of perhaps gaining some control."[33]

## The Sociopsychological Approach
The purpose of the sociopsychological approach is threefold. The teacher attempts to help students increase their knowledge of people, add to their understanding of the age in which the literature was written, and apply this knowledge and understanding to current living. The sociopsychological approach of necessity overlaps the historical but differs in that flesh is restored to the bones exhumed by the archaeologist; it differs also in that an attempt is made to

compare the flesh and nerves of the there and then with the flesh and nerves of here and now. The chief weakness of the sociopsychological approach is that it may lead to neglect of some of the qualities considered especially "literary." Its compensating virtue is that it demonstrates that people were people in the fourteenth century, and that people are still people; it helps to define people. Because most students are interested in people and in their social interactions, they especially like this approach; it gives them considerable opportunity to respond to literature in the light of their own knowledge of human beings, themselves included.

## The Personal Approach

Personal growth, experience, discovery, engagement-involvement, personal response, openness, and transaction are terms used to describe the various points of view and emphases used in the personal approach. Sometimes the goals are expressed as twofold: "First, the teacher can attempt to encourage students' naturally developing literary interests and aesthetic sense. Second, literature can be used to teach the identity and interpersonal skills needed for mature adulthood."[34] The teacher tries to create a classroom atmosphere that encourages free, spontaneous reactions to literature chosen for its known interest to students. At its best, the approach draws students into personal transactions with texts that can provide aesthetic literary experiences, and it guides them to ask, "What temperamental leanings, what view of the world, what standards, made it less or more easy for me to animate the world symbolized by the text? What hithertountapped potentialities for feeling, thought, and perhaps action, have I discovered through this experience?"[35]* With increased experience under skillful guidance, the student will learn "to face the uniquely personal character of literary experience, and then to discover how in this situation critical discrimination and sound criteria of interpretation can be achieved." At its worst, the approach degenerates into aimless role-playing, pointless discussions, and shallow, insincere emotive responses by students who have learned only how to play a "fun" game with their teacher.

## The Value-Seeking Approach

The value-seeking approach overlaps the personal approach, especially in its emphasis on experience and personal growth. Its supporters believe that "English succeeds much of the time if it moves students to look at their own experiences, at the world of experience that they reconstruct through language, and at their values. Good teaching practice in English has always led to the examination of values."[36]

*From *The Reader, the Text, the Poem* by Louise M. Rosenblatt. Copyright © 1978 by the Southern Illinois University Press. Reprinted by permission of the Southern Illinois University Press.

It is certainly true that English teaching has emphasized values for a long time. McGuffey readers of the nineteenth century customarily attached a conveniently labeled "moral" at the end of each selection, and early spellers placed words in the context of sentences about virtuous conduct. Not many years ago, English teachers considered it appropriate practice to emphasize values that they believed were essential in building "upright" character and good citizenship. Wars, political scandals, rapid social change, and fears about ideological change have broadened the values studied. In a national publication addressed to English curriculum, we are told: "Teachers are looking again at their subject primarily for those aspects of it that are humane, that extend human experience and human sympathies. These aspects nurture thoughtful assessment of oneself and of one's values in relation to the larger society and its values as reflected in its literature and in its language, particularly its public language."[37]

At its best, the value-seeking approach allows students to do their own grappling with human values and problems in a wide variety of literature that in the judgment of teachers and students is interesting to students and well worth their time. At its worst it imposes views on students, gives students no real opportunity to confront problems that concern them most, and offers works that are poorly written and do nothing to stretch the student aesthetically, humanistically, or intellectually.

### The Cognitive Approach

This approach could very well be called the meaning-seeking approach. Ideally, its purpose is to uncover the exact meaning lurking behind each author's sentences, paragraphs, or stanzas. Some teachers are more willing than others to acknowledge the legitimacy of a student's interpretation when it varies sharply from that of the critics, even if the student can account for the whole of the meaning by using the text as support. Most teachers who advocate the cognitive approach view the text as literature—as a novel, a short story, or a poem—before the student encounters it. In other words, the teacher views it as a literary object, perhaps even one of great artistic importance, to be studied carefully for meaning. Formalistic teachers are interested in the meaning of the text itself. Those who acknowledge the author's intention search for it. Those who acknowledge other influences may welcome contributions from history, sociology, psychology, anthropology, philosophy, theology, linguistics, and other fields, and they may encourage students to discuss their own interpretations freely. Where this approach parts company with the personal approach, especially with transactional analysis, is that it concentrates more on the text as object than on the student as reader. The approach does not seek to evolve a personal response from the reader, but it does seek understanding. Understanding, obviously, is prerequisite to reaction.

### The Analytical Approach

The last approach may be called the analytical, although this term is too restricted. The analytical approach involves examining the ideas, the imagery, the mechanics, and the tone of writing in order to discover what each contributes to the total impression. It is thus the "lit crit" system deplored by many modern British teachers but beloved by followers of Brooks and Warren or John Crowe Ransom and other specialists in literary criticism. It contributes particularly to evaluative responses, but may support others. The constant aim, especially in the high school, is to help the student to see the selection as a whole, by assisting him or her to see the function of each part. For example, students discover that the repeated references to sleep in Macbeth serve purposes of characterization and assist in the development of the theme. In other words, the goal of the analytical approach is synthesis through analysis. The weakness of the approach is that in distorted form it becomes what students call "picking to pieces." Its value is that, through its use, students can discover that true literature does not just happen but results from careful planning, selection and rejection of details, and painstaking workmanship. An even greater value is that, if the teacher uses the analytical approach competently, the students improve in their reading ability by learning to distinguish tree from grove in whatever they read. In this approach, attention is definitely on the text. Of all six approaches mentioned here, this one gives least recognition and credit to students' personal responses.

These six approaches may not seem, on the surface, to be all-inclusive, but a little pondering will show either that other so-called approaches are subdivisions of these six or that they are not truly approaches at all. The use of audiovisual aids, for example, does not constitute an approach, for such aids are tools or vehicles that may be used in any of the six basic approaches. Some educators have identified a so-called "competency based" approach—often called a "mastery" approach—and have tried to relate it to teaching literature. Apparently it stems from a sense of urgency about teaching basic knowledge and skills that students will need to function in the society. To call it an approach to teaching literature, which involves mainly aesthetic reading, is to ignore the spirit and purpose of teaching students to respond personally to literature. Teachers who have used the six approaches outlined above, or any combination of them, would acknowledge that developing skills is a common goal to achieve with all approaches, but they would probably resist applying "systems efficiency" to aesthetic reading.

## CHOOSING THE APPROACHES

The constant use of any one of the six approaches is objectionable on at least two counts: loss of interest and failure to show the versatility of literature. Obviously, day-after-day repetition may lead to boredom for both students and teacher. If students are given the impression that authors write only that their works may be analyzed, or if they are led to believe that knowing literature means merely knowing that it has a heritage or that it addresses sociological and pyschological problems, they are likely to say, "Literature! Nobody cares about that stuff except English teachers, and they wouldn't either if they didn't get paid for it!" Not one "pure" approach but, rather, a multiple approach is best in the teaching of literature. English teachers are not extremists. Observations by the authors of this methods text support the following assessment:

> ... teachers have been prudently eclectic in their orientation to the curriculum. Rather than committing themselves completely to a single orientation, they have as far as can be determined, absorbed into their practice something of each orientation. They cling to their discipline, but without the fervor of the academic rationalists. They teach the cognitive processes, but not to the exclusion of all else. They consciously or unconsciously shape the curriculum in terms of shifting societal trends. They use bits and pieces of a technological approach where that seem appropriate. And, out of choice or necessity, they respond as best they can to the needs of the students before them.[38]

At the beginning of this chapter, we visited for a few minutes in classes taught by Mr. Tellem, Ms. Freem, Ms. Ignorem, and Ms. Guidem. You may recall that Mr. Tellem was getting ready to give a lecture on "motifs" in *Death of a Salesman*. Discussions of these could of course lead students into a socio-psychological approach to the play. Why does Willy feel that material success is so important? Why is he unable to face reality? What are his illusions? Who shares them? What does Willy's situation say about the work ethic in our society? About other aspects of the American Dream? If Mr. Tellem wished, he could ask students to do dramatic readings of parts of the play, perhaps in a kind of theater in the round or readers' theater with chairs placed in a circle to "experience" these parts and get more meaning from them.

Ms. Freem, you will remember, engaged her students in personally finding, sharing, and writing poems. She could extend this personal approach to dramatizations and oral readings, but she could also bring a poem into class and lead a discussion on its meaning. Students could follow with group discussions of some other poems about poverty, the natural environment, freedom, or other topics and themes.

Ms. Ignorem, whose approach is close to a nonapproach, could ask questions that will help students to discuss themes of love, hate, and honor. Can love survive in environments created by hate? What are the problems, even today, of being young and in love, knowing that parents on both sides could have serious conflicts over the situation? She could ask students why characters act as they do. She could help them to see that Shakespeare varies the rhythm of his poetry according to the character, the action, and the situation. If she continues to ask students only to read around the class throughout the play, they will dread going to class, and they will have little or no understanding of the play as a whole.

Ms. Guidem, as we know, led her students through playing roles and writing diaries as ways to help them to respond on a more personal level to tensions revealed at the beginning of *Diary of a Young Girl*. To continue with this kind of activity throughout their study of this work would probably bore students. However, these experiences could help prepare students for questions about point of view, characters, setting, events, tone, and other elements of the work. And it should help them to engage more actively and thoughtfully in discussions about fear, oppression, tolerance, consideration, prejudice, self-discovery, maturity, and other matters relating to a sociopsychological view of the work.

The examples given above should not suggest that the teachers mentioned should move from one approach to the other as described. The choice of approach should be made in light of the knowledge, ability, and interests of the students and the teacher, the characteristics of the literature, and the objectives of the study of literature.

## THE NEED FOR VARIETY IN TEACHING LITERATURE

A high school junior said, "I like English this year. Got a good teacher. Mr. Jones makes it interesting, doesn't kill it off the way some of 'em do."

"How does he make it interesting?" she was asked.

"Oh, I don't know. I never thought about how he does it. I imagine it's variety, though. We do lots of different things in class and read lots of different kinds of things. Other years we just repeated the same kind of thing over and over—for instance last year, when we had to pick all the literature to pieces. It got awful dry, like—well, like just practicing shooting free throws in basketball would be. I like basketball, and I know that free throws are important, but, if there wasn't anything to basketball except standing in the same spot and doing the same thing over and over, I'd quit."

---

**THE IDEA BOX**

TEACHERS APPROACH LITERATURE

From his studies of literature in the schools of New Zealand, Alan Purves makes these observations about teachers' approaches: "The personal development group shows a lesser interest in whether it is a proper subject for a story, metaphors and language, and a greater interest in whether the characters resemble people the

---

reader knows, whether the work reflects the world of the reader, the lesson to be learned from the work, the emotions raised by the work and its affective success. The complexity group tends to favor questions analysing metaphors, language, and part-whole relationship and evaluating the work on formal grounds. The heritage group is least concerned with formal analysis and evaluation and relating the work to the reader.''[39] Does some of this sound familiar?

## TEACHERS DO CHANGE

John Clifford of the University of North Carolina recalls going into high school teaching in the 1960s ''sure what was needed was an emphasis on literature as literature.'' He recalls: ''Instead of creating a climate of sharing, I was analyzing; instead of encouraging emerging insights, I was telling. So I started thinking more seriously about readers.'' But then, he recalls, ''I got stuck in another cul-de-sac: a deep subjectivity which holds that any response will do.'' Influenced largely by Rosenblatt's books, he now believes ''that each reading is an individual event, that the reader recreates a work of art through an active mingling of both reader and text.'' In transactional analysis, he finds a ''necessary basis for critical inquiry.''[40]

## HOW CAN KIDS DECIDE WHAT A ''GOOD'' BOOK IS?

Pearl Aldrich and her class devised a checklist to differentiate a serious from a superficial book. Among the points: The serious book presents a universal truth about life, but the purpose of the superficial book is to make the reader's dreams come true. In a serious book, personality changes are slow and often painful, but in a superficial book they are quick and easy.[41]

## CONTROVERSIES ABOUT CULTURE

The first chapter of a report on a national survey of humanities in the 1980s takes the view that ''the Western tradition includes popular culture and non-Western elements.'' Ideological separation of these, it claims, distorts the real issues in our culture. Traditional forms of cultural expression should not be separated from those of cultural pluralism. The humanities should not be seen as elitism or populism. It may be that some high school English teachers are too far on the side of ''high culture, which often refers to a finite list of works, authors, and standards. . . .''[42]

## MOTIVATION BY LOCAL ANALOGY

Often a local analogy will make a work more real to students. For example, Jerome Carlin has introduced Frost's ''Mending Wall'' by having his students suppose that a battered fence separates their house from a neighbor's. Should the fathers pay $150 to get it repaired, or tear it down to give children more room to play?[43]

## CONTENT IN AMERICAN LITERATURE

''Our courses in American literature and history must correct the imbalance in attitudes, point of view, knowledge, materials, emphases that has existed far too long. No longer can anyone justify offering pupils books, other materials, and assumptions representing almost entirely a white, middle class world. English courses should include points of view, materials representing a wide cross-section of artistic achievements by various groups comprising our pluralistic society." (From a convention speech by Alfred H. Grommon, past-president of NCTE.)

## SEXISM, A CULTURAL LEGACY

H. Lee Gershuny reviews archetypes and metaphors of man as artist-patriarch and woman as obedient wife and mother in Judeo-Christian literature, as well as classical images of "gods and goddesses who duplicated the social stereotypes and biological roles of males and females."[44] High school students might examine such stereotypes more closely in the heritage approach to literature, with the aim of discussing the images that literature should project today if it is to be an honest reflection of today's culture.

## THE RICH HERITAGE OF FOLKLORE

Folklore can open many approaches. Jill May of Purdue University points to the style of early tales from other lands, to the "sense of rhythm," the concise yet descriptive language, the overall meter that evokes mood and sets scene, and the vivid images. In American stories, she finds "an oral history of American political beliefs, of American social change, of American regionalism, and of American humor." "Older students," she adds, "can learn something about the creation of a political image by reading some of the legends concerning our great leaders and comparing these to well written biographies of the same people."[45] For collections of American folk stories, she recommends books by Richard Chase.

## WHAT IS A GOOD TEENAGE NOVEL?

Sylvia Engdahl, a writer of teenage novels, has offered her views on the "good" teenage novel. Here are some excerpts:

> First, few if any of the good ones are easier to read than the average adult novel considered suitable for younger high school students. Writers for teenagers do not limit vocabulary, nor do they use a less complex style than they would in fiction for adults (except in the case of stories specifically produced for 'slow readers,' which are not really 'novels' in the literary sense).
>
> Second, novels of quality for teenagers do not preach. A writer who approaches young people in a condescending way receives short shrift from today's editors and reviewers. One can use a story to reflect one's views, just as an author of adult fiction can—but they must be views about life, not about how young people, as distinguished from other people, ought to look at it.
>
> Third, teenage novels, if good, are not devoid of concepts worth pondering and worth discussing. Although fiction for the young ordinarily stays within the bounds of good taste, its themes are confined neither to traditional ideas nor to fashionable new ones. Thus it can hardly be called uncontroversial.
>
> A fourth thing novels for adolescents do not offer is shelter from the world as it is. Because of their honesty, such books cannot ignore the grimmer aspects of life any more than they can ignore aspects some adults consider shocking.

Finally, contemporary teenage novels are not mere vehicles to provide reluctant readers with a fictional reflection of their own lifestyle and their own specific problems.[46]

## TWO GOOD FIELD MANUALS ON CENSORSHIP

These books contain very practical information and suggestions on avoiding and handling censorship problems: Edward B. Jenkinson, *Censors in the Classroom: The Mind Benders,* Carbondale, Southern Illinois University Press, 1980; James E. Davis, ed., *Dealing with Censorship,* Urbana, NCTE, 1979.

## INCOMPETENCY BASED ENGLISH

Recently a school board refused to allow a high school teacher to add readings of Aristotle to his unit on *Julius Caesar,* even though the teacher said his aim was only to help students better understand the play as a tragedy. They claimed that this "added" reading went beyond what should be expected in the course. If school boards can lower ceilings in an effort to standardize competency, and thereby control it more efficiently, will English have to stoop through the 1980s and beyond?

## ON REACHING

Looking into the 1980s, the Commission on the Humanities makes this observation:

Some popular novels are more subtle than others, some Greek or Navajo myths are more profound than others, some Black autobiographies more enlightening than others, some of Shakespeare's plays more effective dramatically than others. It is in no way undemocratic to recognize these distinctions, and only confusion and bigotry gain by denying them. All people have the capacity to reach for high standards of expression, interpretation, and discrimination: these are not exclusive privileges of one class or culture.[47]

## HOW DOES A WRITER SURPRISE?

Thomas E. Gaston of Purdue University asserts, "Style consists of purposeful and patterned violations of expectations, violations that approach but never exceed predetermined limits."[48]

## LITERATURE ISN'T SCIENCE

We must never forget that literature belongs to the humanities and that "humanities" by definition refers to that which is *human*. If the study of literature is permitted to degenerate into analysis and classification, or even into mere explication of pattern and imagery, it becomes less human, more scientific, more mechanical.

## APPROACHING WORLD LITERATURE

A rich source of information and ideas is *Guide to World Literature,* NCTE. It is organized to help teachers approach world literature thematically, generically, historically, and comparatively. A short excerpt from the introduction should illustrate the kinds of approaches possible:

> Individual and cultural differences may be explored by examining time. Jay Gatsby in Scott Fitzgerald's *The Great Gatsby* believes he can recapture time, that time can be made to stand still. In contrast, Shingo, the hero in the Japanese work *The Sound of the Mountain* by Yasunari Kawabata, is keenly aware of the passing of time; however, the reader's response to Gatsby and Shingo is similar. The transience of time is explored by the French writer Colette in *My Mother's House* and in Sido, by the Japanese writer Murasaki in *The Tale of Genji*, and by the American writer Willa Cather in *Lucy Gayheart*. These three writers in the works mentioned may also be compared for their treatment of love.
> ... For example, the theme of war: the eighth-century satire on militarism by the Chinese poet Po Chu-i, "The Old Man with the Broken Arm"; Stephen Crane's novel *The Red Badge of Courage;* the sixteenth-century Vietnamese poems, "On War" by Phung Khac Khoan, "On the War-Scattered Refugees" by Pham Mguyen Du, and "Lament of a Warrior's wife" by Dang Tran Con, and the twentieth-century Vietnamese poem, "Who Am I?" by Tru Vu; Remarque's novel *All Quiet on the Western Front*—all these view war as an anti-human experience.[49]

## IF YOU WERE AN ARTIST

Sometimes ask students to imagine that they are artists employed by a magazine to illustrate stories and poems. Have them describe the picture they would draw or paint to illustrate an especially significant part of a literary work read by the class.

## HOW AUTHORS NAME THEIR CHARACTERS

Phyllis E. Nelson's students have enjoyed "The Name Game." In this method, students study original meanings of people's names, suitability or irony of names authors choose, famous people with this name, how the name aids understanding of the character, and how authors choose names for their characters. Example: Ichabod (which means "inglorious") won't win the girl.[50]

## LITERARY "TRIP"

"We begin our English literature course by taking a 'trip' to England. This involves writing letters to travel bureaus, keeping a diary, reading background materials, compiling a bibliography, using reference tools, listening to records such as 'White Cliffs of Dover,' making a scrapbook of pictures and articles from periodicals, and finally presenting a travel talk." (Hortense Finch, Davenport, Iowa.) Of course, this technique would work equally well with the literature of any country.

## LITERARY MAPS

1. Let students make their own. In American literature, a literary map of their own state or region is stimulating. Several state associations of English teachers have prepared printed maps. The 1980–1981 *NCTE Catalog* lists maps from Colorado, Illinois, Indiana, Maine, Minnesota, New Jersey, Pennsylvania, Virginia, and Wisconsin. Also listed by NCTE for sale are these maps to help

visualize literature: Odyssey, Iliad, Macbeth, Aeneid, and Julius Caesar. Maps such as these can serve as models for students. If no literary map of their state exists, they might make one similar to one of the other state maps. If a map showing settings and actions in a literary work would help them to visualize, they might make one as a class or group project.

2. If a literary map of your state exists, its chief value may be to dispel students' notion that famous authors have always lived far away. A literary map of the United States helps students to associate authors and their works with their locales. A literary map of the British Isles is valuable, since British names mean little to American students, many of whom do not even know whether London is in the northern or the southern part of England. Making literary maps of other countries is an excellent project for world literature. A collection of literary maps adds both color and informativeness to a classroom and may be referred to frequently for specific points.

## BUILDING AN INTEREST IN BOOKS

1. Encourage students to start their own personal libraries now. National school paperback book clubs, such as those by Scholastic and Xerox, provide books of high interest for individualized reading. Students may swap books until they finally decide on those they wish to keep. Students' clubs sometimes run book fairs or bookstores in the school. Students also collect books during the year from people in the community and sell them in an annual book sale. The proceeds could buy books for the classroom or the school library.

2. Encourage students to help select books for the library. They can write for publishers' catalogs or borrow some from the school librarian, read advertisements and reviews, and discuss the most suitable books to be bought with limited funds. This project could coincide with National Book Week.

## DEVICES FOR REVIEWING

Students often think of a review as "tell-us time"; they wait until the teacher "tells" them in one period what is significant about everything everyone has said, read, and done for the past few weeks. And students can become impatient if they feel that this is not happening. Nevertheless, it is not helpful for the teacher to conduct a review by "laying it out" for them to copy, memorize, and regurgitate. Students will learn more if they help prepare the review and participate actively in it in the following ways:

1. Try a "Stump the Experts" contest, with students asking questions of class "experts" who volunteer and prepare in study groups.
2. Let students make up questions involving recognition of stories they have read. For example, "In what story are combs, a watch chain, and a woman's beautiful hair significant?"
3. Try a variation of TV quiz contests. This should appeal especially to junior high students.
4. Original plays or skits may be used to review and clinch the subject matter of a

unit. For example, students might role-play situations in selections and then ask others to guess not just what the situation is, but who or what caused it, and how significant it is to the story, play, or novel.

5. Students may construct *who, what, when, where, why,* and *how* questions for their classmates' review, with each student responsible for one or two questions in each category. Caution the class to ask important questions, not minor ones such as ''When did Tennyson write 'Ulysses'?'' The teacher may indicate in advance that one or two of these student-made questions will actually appear on the test.

## TESTS ON LITERATURE

1. Try asking some questions that probe for facts, some that require interpretation, some that necessitate relating a selection to other literature or to life.
2. For variety, give occasionally a short open-book test.
3. Help your students to learn to organize their answers.
4. Make sure that all lead-ins or ''stems'' to short-answer questions are clear and contain sufficient information for decisions. Make sure that ''essay'' questions are stated clearly. ''Discuss the theme in *The Pearl*'' is confusing in several ways. Make sure that key words in ''essay'' questions mean what you want them to mean, so that students won't go off in directions you consider unfruitful.
5. On some occasions, let each student make out a set of final-examination questions that he or she thinks would be fair. Choose the questions from those submitted.
6. Before a short surprise test, allow two or three minutes for reviewing notes. This procedure encourages careful, methodical notetaking.

## THE HANDICAPPED IN ADOLESCENT FICTION

Janet Stroud of Purdue University notes that in early adolescent fiction handicapped characters were ''either idealized or vilified.'' She also finds that ''handicaps were vaguely described, symptoms didn't always fit the disability, and miraculous cures were much in evidence.'' In contrast, Ms. Stroud finds new objectivity and realism in the portrayal of handicapped characters in modern adolescent fiction. In addressing English teachers, Ms. Stroud stresses selecting books that are ''realistic, objective, sensitive, entertaining, and well-written.'' These are the books that ''have the potential to change attitudes.''[51]

# FOOTNOTES

1. ''Developing an Inductive Lesson Plan,'' in *Ideas for the Literature Class, 7–12,* Fred Preston, ed., Springfield: Illinois Office of Education, 1978, pp. 9–10.

2. *Basic Objectives in Language Arts K–12,* Indiana Department of Public Instruction, 1978, p. 41.

3. In *Professional Growth for Teachers,* Third Quarter, 1967–1968.

4. Frank McLaughlin, "The School as Thermostat: An Interview with Neil Postman, Part I," *Media & Methods,* Jan. 1980, p. 25.

5. P. 16.

6. "Teaching Contemporary Literature," *English Journal* 68, Sept. 1979, p. 49.

7. *Newsletter,* Oct. 1962, p. 2.

8. *The Reader, the Text, the Poem: The Transactional Theory of the Literary Work,* Carbondale: Southern Illinois University Press, 1978, ix.

9. Rosenblatt, p. 154.

10. Rosenblatt, p. 24.

11. Rosenblatt, pp. 24–25.

12. Rosenblatt, p. 35.

13. Rosenblatt, p. 140.

14. *Readings and Feelings: An Introduction to Subjective Criticism,* NCTE, 1975, p. 94.

15. Bleich, p. 95.

16. *Teaching the Art of Literature,* Urbana: NCTE, 1980, p. 22.

17. New York, Berkley Publishing Corporation, 1966.

18. "Process Curriculum for High School Students," in *Three Language-Arts Curriculum Models,* Barrett J. Mandel, ed., Urbana: NCTE, 1980, p. 151.

19. Kenneth L. Donelson, "Obscenity and the Chill Factor: Court Decisions about Obscenity and Their Relationships to School Censorship," in James E. Davis, ed., *Dealing with Censorship,* Urbana: NCTE, 1979, p. 74.

20. "Some Thoughts on Censorship in the Schools," in *Dealing with Censorship,* p. 95.

21. Lee Burress, "A Brief Report of the 1977 NCTE Censorship Survey," in *Dealing with Censorship,* pp. 14–47.

22. For many of the suggestions in this section, the authors are indebted to Professor Edward B. Jenkinson, Indiana University.

23. Rosenblatt, p. 148.

24. Allan A. Glatthorn, *A Guide for Developing an English Curriculum for the Eighties,* Urbana: NCTE, 1980, p. 86.

25. Glatthorn, p. 75.

26. Richard E. Hodges, "The English Program, Grades Six through Nine: A Heritage Model," in *Three Language-Arts Curriculum Models,* p. 87.

27. In *Thematic Units in Teaching English and the Humanities,* Second Supplement, Sylvia Spann and Mary Beth Culp, eds., Urbana: NCTE, 1980, pp. 155–161.

28. A unit by Betty Blanchard in *Thematic Units in Teaching English and the Humanities,* Sylvia Spann and Mary Beth Culp, eds., Urbana: NCTE, 1975, pp. 91–106.

THE TEACHING OF HIGH SCHOOL ENGLISH

29. *A Senior High School Curriculum in English for Able College-Bound Students,* Volume I: The Tenth Grade, (Carnegie-Mellon University, 1965), p. 3.
30. Glatthorn, p. 89.
31. Glatthorn, p. 1.
32. Arthur N. Applebee, *Tradition and Reform in the Teaching of English: A History,* Urbana: NCTE, 1974, p. 248.
33. Hamida Bosmajian, "Literary Tradition and the Talent of the Individual Student: A Heritage Paradigm," in *Three Language-Arts Curriculum Models,* p. 224.
34. "Process Curriculum for High School Students," p. 150.
35. Rosenblatt, pp. 145–146.
36. Helen C. Lodge, "Values in the English Classroom," in *The Teaching of English:* The Seventy-Sixth Yearbook of the National Society for the Study of Education, Part I, University of Chicago Press, 1977, p. 127.
37. Lodge, p. 131.
38. Glatthorn, p. 14.
39. *Achievement in Reading and Literature in the Secondary Schools: New Zealand in an International Perspective,* Wellington, New Zealand National Center, International Association for the Evaluation of Educational Achievement, 1979, p. 69.
40. "Transactional Teaching and the Literary Experience," *English Journal* 68, Dec. 1979, pp. 36–39.
41. "A New Method of Evaluating Fiction," *English Journal* 54, Nov. 1965, p. 744.
42. Commission on the Humanities, *The Humanities in American Life,* Berkeley: University of California Press, 1980, p. 9.
43. "A Pattern for Teaching Literature," *English Journal* 55, March 1966, p. 291.
44. "Sexism in the Language of Literature," in *Sexism and Language,* Alleen Pace Nilsen et al., eds., Urbana: NCTE, 1977, p. 115.
45. "Using Folklore in the Classroom," *English Education,* Feb. 1980, pp. 148–154.
46. "Do Teenage Novels Fill a Need?" *English Journal* 64, Feb. 1975: reprinted in *Young Adult Literature in the Seventies,* Jana Varlejs ed. Metuchen, N.J.: The Scarecrow Press, Inc., 1978, pp. 48–52.
47. *The Humanities in American Life,* p. 11.
48. *English Journal* 59, Jan. 1970, p. 65.
49. Warren Carrier and Kenneth Oliver, eds., *Guide to World Literature.* Urbana: NCTE, 1980, p. 4.
50. *English Journal* 56, March 1967, p. 439.
51. "Selecting Materials Which Promote Understanding and Acceptance of Handicapped Students," *English Journal* 70, Jan. 1981, pp. 49–52.

# 6

## TEACHING
## FICTION
## AND
## DRAMA

## WHY DO PEOPLE READ NOVELS, SHORT STORIES, AND PLAYS?

There are many ways to think of books as objects. A person browsing through a bookstore before a holiday or someone's birthday may see books as gifts. The appearance of the book—the design on its jacket and the fact that it is printed on glossy paper—may make it seem especially desirable. An interior decorator may choose books with the rich look of embossed leather to add a dignified tone to a library, or those with colorful paper jackets to add an informal tone to a family room or living room. A would-be scholar may like the feeling of security that walls of books seem to provide. The student may see books as required readings. A librarian may see them as objects to be cataloged, arranged, and kept track of. A literary scholar may see them as objects to analyze objectively, or as tools of scholarship. And, of course, other people see books as literary art objects. Those of us who are readers take another view.

> *We are much more inclined to forget, if we can, that a book is an object of art, and to treat it as a piece of life around us; we fashion for ourselves, we objectify, the elements in it that happen to strike us most keenly, such as an effective scene or a brilliant character. These things take shape in the mind of the reader; they are re-created and set up where the mind's eye can rest on them. They become works of art, no doubt, in their way, but they are not the book which the author offers us. That is a larger and more complex form, one that is much more difficult to think of as a rounded thing. A novel, as we say,*

*opens a new world to the imagination; and it is pleasant to discover that sometimes in a few novels, it is a world that "creates an illusion"—so pleasant that we are content to be lost in it. When that happens there is no chance of our finding, perceiving, recreating, the form of the book. So far from losing ourselves in the world of the novel, we must hold it away from us, see it all in detachment, and use the whole of it to make the image we seek, the book itself.*[1]

The text of a novel, a short story, a poem, or a play can be read with the kind of personal involvement that creates images of art, and it can be read with a detachment intent on seeing it as a whole. One way of reading doesn't necessarily preclude the other; the experienced, critical reader is not ruled by the text or ruled by personal thoughts and feelings. The best reader is a creative reader; "he is the maker of a book which may or may not please his taste when it is finished, but of a book for which he must take his own share of responsibility."[2]

Novels, short stories, and plays allow us to perceive images of life for moments in our minds, where we ask our own questions about images and create our own answers. Anyone who goes to fiction for the answers to the meaning of life forfeits the chance of finding them. Fiction provides partial answers to age-old questions. "Who am I?" "Why was I born?" "Is life purposeless?" "Are people merely accidental excrescences on a planet that is but an atom in the universe?" Because no author is omniscient, the reader knows that he or she will never find complete answers to the author's metaphysical queries. But the creative reader knows also that from a clue here and there it is possible to piece together a philosophy of life that will serve, or that it is possible to amend an existing philosophy.

The drama, of course, also reveals truths about life, but it is especially successful (at least on the stage, its intended habitat) in carrying us out of ourselves. Studying plays in schools is an artificial activity, taking them from their medium, the stage, and exposing them only to visual rather than both auditory and visual scrutiny. The best teachers, however, try to make play-reading more than just reading, in ways that we shall note in parts of this chapter, and they also emphasize the importance of reading plays creatively. Consider these questions that Louise Rosenblatt asks: "Does not the reader leaning above the page of Shakespeare's script have to respond to the symbols by hearing in his inner ear the sounds of the words and the rhythms of the verse? Does he not have to call up what these sounds point to, in idea and action, so that he may create the play? Does not the reader, like a director, have to supply the tempo, the gestures, the actions not only of Hamlet but of the whole cast?"[3]*

*From *The Reader, the Text, the Poem* by Louise M. Rosenblatt. Copyright © 1978 by the Southern Illinois University Press. Reprinted by permission of the Southern Illinois University Press.

# SOME OFTEN-ASKED QUESTIONS

The answers to these frequent questions are no doubt too arbitrary, but let's risk them; they may provoke worthwhile discussion.

*Q.* How should we select the novels we teach?

*A.* That depends on your students, your purposes, and the overall emphasis and plan for your unit or course. In general, choose relatively short and "easy" novels for junior high, longer and "harder" ones for senior high. But ruthlessly reject any novel that you cannot respect for its literary quality. Your time and students' time shouldn't be wasted on trash.

*Q.* Does this mean concentrating on *Pride and Prejudice* and *Tale of Two Cities?*

*A.* Of course not—even though some students will be able to read these two novels with interest and understanding. Many other novels of literary value are available. With a junior high class, Annixter's *Swiftwater,* Forbes' *Johnny Tremaine,* Stevenson's *Treasure Island,* Steinbeck's *The Pearl,* Richter's *The Light in the Forest,* Fast's *April Morning,* Marshall's *Walkabout,* or any of a number of other books is fine. With a senior high class, the choice is much wider. Golding's *Lord of the Flies,* Steinbeck's *Grapes of Wrath,* Hemingway's *Old Man and the Sea,* Zindel's *The Pigman,* Fitzgerald's *The Great Gatsby,* and many others have been successful in the classroom. See the Idea Box at the end of this chapter for many other titles and articles on teaching them. And look again at some of your favorites to see how suitable they may be for your students.

*Q.* Should all members of a class read the same novel?

*A.* Not necessarily, though some reading in common is desirable. Sometimes try having three or four groups reading different novels, perhaps relating to the same theme. Use panel discussions, along with class discussions on questions all novels can illuminate, to bring the class together. Sometimes each student may read a different book and report to the class on what it seems to say about certain important questions.

*Q.* How long should we spend on a novel?

*A.* Seldom more than three or four weeks, often less. Frequently, potential enjoyment has been killed by prolonged study.

*Q.* How much should be assigned at a time?

*A.* If the novel is not too difficult and if the students are fairly able, then read the whole novel (with the help of a few guiding questions) before discussing it in class. But with long or difficult novels, you may need to make perhaps 10 or 15 assignments. Reserve some time, though, for discussing the whole novel, so that students aren't left with the impression that the work is only a number of vaguely related episodes.

164

*Q.* What kinds of questions should we ask?

*A.* To lay the foundation for *why* and *how* questions, teachers need to ask some *who, what, when,* and *where* questions; however, good teachers keep these to a minimum. The most overused question among weaker teachers of fiction and drama is "What happened next?" Some examples of *why* and *how* questions are these: "Why is Huck usually afraid to approach strangers?" "How does Clemens employ irony in the chapter where Huck dresses as a girl?" "Why does Kino open the small oysters before opening the ancient oyster that contains the pearl?" "At the end of the novel, why does Kino suggest that Juana throw the pearl away?" "Why does Juana tell Kino to throw it away?" "How do the various songs in *The Pearl* help to establish changes of mood?" Some questions should establish details, some should converge on cause-and-effect relationships and main idea, and others should extend beyond the work to applications to characters and situations in other literature and to students' own lives.

*Q.* What plays should we teach?

*A.* Choose high-quality one-act plays for the junior high years. Move on, as your classes' abilities permit, to Maxwell Anderson, James M. Barrie, Tennessee Williams, John Galsworthy, Oliver Goldsmith, Kaufman and Hart, Arthur Miller, Eugene O'Neil, Edmond Rostand, Henrik Ibsen, William Shakespeare, George Bernard Shaw, Robert E. Sherwood, Edward Albee, and Thornton Wilder, or others that have been successful. With able students, Sophocles, Euripides, Aeschylus, and the like are possible.

*Q.* Which plays by Shakespeare?

*A.* You'll not confine yourself to Shakespeare, of course. Today the most popular choice by far, is *Macbeth.* Others frequently taught are *Julius Caesar, Romeo and Juliet* (both frequently with sophomores), and *Hamlet* and *Othello* (generally seniors). Other plays taught in high school include *The Tempest, As You Like It, Twelfth Night, Much Ado About Nothing, A Midsummer Night's Dream, King Lear,* and less often, but deserving, *Henry V* and *Henry IV,* Part I.

*Q.* How should we teach a play?

*A.* Remember that it is a play. Use much reading aloud in dramatizations of scenes, not in reading lines by turns around the room. British teachers tend to plunge students immediately into dramatizations, without any preliminaries about, for example, the Globe Theater or Shakespeare's biography. Help students to visualize the action as stage action—for example, to be aware of what other persons are doing while one is speaking. Stress characters and characterization. Discuss theme and underlying meanings, using *why* and *how* questions. Three weeks is often enough time for a full-length play, though the range may be from a few days to four or five weeks.

*Q.* To what extent should composition and the study of language be related to fiction and drama?

*A.* Increasingly, good schools are asking students to write on literature-oriented topics, especially in the junior and senior years. It would be unwise, however, to devote *all* compositions to literature, because students need to write on other topics also, to be successful in college and in various occupations. The study of language is often profitable in connection with literature. Such topics as these may be considered: How does Shakespeare's language differ from ours and from Chaucer's? What peculiarities of sentence structure and diction mark the stories of Hawthorne, Irving, Poe, Cooper, Hemingway, and so on? How does stage conversation differ from actual conversation?

*Q.* Which of the six basic approaches should be used with fiction and drama?

*A.* All, at different times. Often two, three, or more will be used with a single work. The choice depends upon the needs of the class, the purpose of the study, and the characteristics of the literature being studied. Teachers' beliefs and personalities will also affect choices. The ultimate goal is that *each* student will respond to a work in a way that is personally rewarding, both emotionally and intellectually. Some examples about the use of each approach follow.

## THE HISTORICAL APPROACH

The teacher's intentions in using this approach are to present authors as human beings and to clarify time relationships—to show that people for many years have been much like us, and to give the students some understanding of the continuity of literature and the relationship between history and literature. Adults who lack such understanding are likely to carry distorted mental pictures like those of a character in Dos Passos' *Manhattan Transfer:* "I always think of history as lithographs in a schoolbook, generals making proclamations, little tiny figures running across fields with their arms spread out, facsimiles of signatures."

Traditionally, the historical approach has meant study of the history of American and English literature. At its worst, this study has degenerated into the memorization of names and dates: "In what year did Dickens die?" "Give the titles and dates of three novels by Thackeray." "What happened in 1881?" At its best, it has brought recognition that each writer's characteristics were shaped by the time in which he or she lived. The historical approach disagrees with the theme of such a book as *Shakespeare Apart,* whose author declared that Shakespeare was apart from, different from, and superior to, everything else in his age; the historical approach says that Shakespeare and every other author is not *apart* but *a part.*

The historical approach may include a variety of goals for students. Note the following list from "American Literature, Chronologically Speaking," a course developed for use in San Diego City Schools:

## COURSE OBJECTIVES

Skills in reading, writing, and oral language will be further developed as the student becomes able to:

- *Analyze and define "American character" as it has developed through the literature of various periods.*
- *Analyze specific differences among literary works of different periods.*
- *Evaluate various types of literature in the context of the times in which the works were written.*
- *Discuss and identify specific historical influences in modern literature.*
- *Identify stylistic and idiomatic differences between various authors and periods.*
- *Recognize levels of spoken and written English and understand how their use and acceptability have changed in various periods.*
- *Trace the chronological development of one genre of American literature.*
- *Discuss literary works as means for self-expression and self-definition.*[4]

The above list is wide-ranging: it fosters a sense of cultural relationship that should help a student to better cope with current problems and with concerns about the future; it provides opportunities to develop a sense of development and continuity in literature; and it encourages personal responses to works.

As our culture changes, it is important for teachers to make adjustments in the historical approach. Robert P. Parker, Jr. says that we have stressed "the antiquarian and the critical" but have neglected the human aspects.[5] Ronald LaConte agrees and adds that our courses "tend to be concerned with the form, style, historical sequence, and even a bit with the content of the *works,* but seldom do students experience a genuine feeling of identification, of sharing with other humans a 'shock' of recognition." LaConte also points to our preoccupation with our British lineage and our "narrow ethnic focus."[6]

### Wide Reading Pertaining to the Period

If the historical approach is to help students relate the past to the present and to the potential of the future, both teacher and students must read widely, and they must read for connections and projections as they respond to literature. How one book may enrich another is obvious: Bret Harte and Edward Eggleston throw light on Mark Twain and his America; Ross Lockridge's *Raintree County* adds depth to understanding of Whitman's poetry or Crane's *Red Badge of Courage;* Jane Austen, Charlotte Brontë, George Eliot, and even Thomas Hardy make

Dickens' England seem more real; the writings of Defoe's contemporaries bring the early eighteenth century alive. The student may read about ancient Peru in Victor Von Hagen's *Highway to the Sun* before reading about more recent Peruvians in Thornton Wilder's *Bridge of San Luis Rey*. Books about the period of World War II help to recreate a time many of their parents can't remember and may assist in bridging the generation gap by acquainting students with the world their grandparents once knew. Books such as Frederick L. Allen's *Only Yesterday* and *Since Yesterday* and Mark Sullivan's *Our Times* interpret earlier years of twentieth century America, and *The Long Week-End, A Social History of Great Britain, 1918–1939*, by Robert Graves and Alan Hodge, describes entertainingly the period between wars.

The teacher and students should not wait until they are well into the course before making some of the connections described above. As Brooke Workman says in the introduction to *Teaching the Decades*, first they must lay a sound foundation so that connections sought later will be more meaningful:

> *Indeed, before the students even investigate a past decade, they must begin with their American value system, the theoretical basis for the "whys" that they will be asking throughout the course, if not throughout their lives. By examining American values, past and present, and how these values are transmitted, the students will better understand themselves and their friends and relatives. They will make that discovery as did one of our students: "I think more about everyday things." This thinking about everyday things is what we are after: the methodology of an American, both outsider and insider, exploring himself and his society.*[7]

### Clues from the Literature Itself

The best way to learn about a past age is to read the fiction and drama of that age. In Shakespeare one senses the exuberance of the Elizabethans but also becomes aware of their worries, their class distinctions, their independence combined with habitual obeisance to royalty and nobility. Fielding's *Tom Jones* paints a sprawling panorama filled with earthy, often bawdy men and women driven by desires as strong today as they were in the eighteenth century. The novels of Dickens show a grimily picturesque London with its multitudinous small shops, its streets and alleys, its one-of-a-kind English men and women. Mark Twain's writings show the nineteenth-century American small town, the robust Mississippi River men and those of farther west, and a concern with man's continuing inhumanity to man. O. Henry depicts the New York of the early twentieth century. Such writers as Chekhov and de Maupassant reveal that Russians, Frenchmen, and people from other nations are not basically different from Americans or Englishmen.

The forces that drove people, the roots of human conflict, and the ideas of

THE TEACHING OF HIGH SCHOOL ENGLISH

goodness, truth, and beauty are portrayed in the fiction and drama of the past. Those forces, those roots, and those ideas and ideals have changed superficially in this age of technology, but basically they are the same; fiction and drama dramatize both the superficial differences and the basic similarity. They help students to define what *human* means and what for centuries or millenniums it has meant.

### Clues from a Variety of Activities and Media

Students can also learn about a past age from maps, drawings, pictures, slides, filmstrips, videotapes, motion pictures, radio and TV programs, newspapers and magazines, and from various activities and projects. Ancient mapmakers reveal the mythology and superstition that affected their view of the world. Certain painters and illustrators show that they were keen observers of human nature. Old newspapers and magazines are filled with insights about people who lived decades ago. Some radio and TV programs, especially on educational stations and channels, dramatize famous historical events. Students should be encouraged to tune in on such broadcasts and to talk about them in class, especially when the programs are related in some way to literature the class has read or is reading. Television tapes are also available, as are historical motion pictures, and have the advantage that they can be shown when they are most appropriate.

Students can of course also draw maps and pictures to recreate and visualize a past age, and they can use these, as well as slides and other materials, to give reports on the backgrounds of authors and selections. Preparing a newspaper relating some of the events in a literary selection such as *Julius Caesar* or *A Tale of Two Cities* is an activity frequently used in classrooms. Making time charts; writing and presenting skits, video and radio programs, slide-tape shows; participating in book talks and debates; interviewing parents and grandparents; and taking field trips to theaters and museums and historical sites can also be worthwhile activities.

### Correlation and Integration

In some schools, history and literature are integrated in a two-period-a-day course which carries credit for both history and English. The theory is that the history throws light on the literature, and vice versa. American history and American literature are the courses most often combined in this way. The strengths of this procedure are that it does demonstrate that literature is inevitably an outgrowth of the social, economic, and political climate and that it does make history seem real—not merely "little tiny figures running across fields with their arms stretched out." One weakness is that it works well only for America, because courses in the history of England, or Europe, or the Orient are seldom included in high school offerings. A second weakness is that some important periods of history produced little literature of merit; in America the periods of exploration, colonization, and the Revolutionary War are of great significance to history but not to literature. (This weakness may be overcome, however, by choice of literature written later but descriptive of these periods.) A third possible weakness lies with teachers. The integrated course demands broad knowledge and wide interests, and some teachers are not well prepared. Teachers who contribute only their "thing" to the course may want to develop questions for tests and class discussions dealing with main issues and generalizations. A fourth possible weakness is the lack of instructional materials and other resources. The course will not have much potential if the English teacher comes to class with only a literature anthology, and the history teacher comes with only a history textbook.

## THE SOCIOPSYCHOLOGICAL APPROACH

The historical approach, as we have noted, can increase students' awareness of how people act and react in various circumstances, why they react as they do, and how they interact with other people. It does so by focusing on the humanness of the literature of past periods. The sociopsychological approach considers human relations and human understanding the main focus and may use the historical approach to reinforce it. The main belief is that through vicarious experiences with literature we can come to better know ourselves and others.

### METHODS OF EMPLOYING THIS APPROACH

Even without any conscious effort on the part of the teacher, students inevitably learn about human characteristics when they read. Shakespeare's *Julius Caesar* illustrates the strength of emotions and the constancy of human conflict; Goldsmith's *She Stoops to Conquer* shows that eighteenth-century ideas of what is funny differed little from our own; Poe's "Gold Bug" demonstrates human ingenuity; Garland's "Under the Lion's Paw" exemplifies the misuse of power; Wilder's *Our Town* shows how people take for granted the important things in their day-to-day living; Salinger's *Catcher in the Rye* presents a sensitive young person whose good instincts are thwarted both by society and his own shortcomings; Golding's *Lord of the Flies,* Knowles' *A Separate Peace,* and Kurt Vonnegut's *Slaughterhouse Five,* like most artistic novels, probe underlying human drives; the novels of Ellison, Baldwin, and Wright are among many of recent decades that have analyzed the problems and revealed the mental and emotional reactions of black people. Whether the teacher wills it or not, students learn many social and psychological truths from the mere act of reading.

But the teacher can and should expedite the learning of these truths. This is usually done through the point of view and emphasis in courses and units. Note the following introduction to a course called Modern Literature:

*Writers have often tried to answer the question: How does man face the stress and complications of living in today's world? In* **Modern Literature,** *you will discover many of the moral and social problems facing the individual and mankind. Through the reading and discussion of a number of books such as* Hiroshima, Fahrenheit 451, *and* When the Legends Die, *you will meet and analyze interesting characters struggling for meaning, identity, and happiness in life.*[8]

It should seem obvious to students reading the above introduction (and this is only a small excerpt) that the emphasis will be on the characters, on why they think, act, and react as they do. The rest of the material given to students very clearly explains what will be expected of students.

Discussions involving the sociopsychological approach can be especially lively, because they focus upon people—and most people would rather talk about people than about anything else. Here is a list of questions representative of the kinds that may profitably be considered by a class at various times. (Some of these may need simplification for some classes; examples are often helpful.)

## Understanding a Character

1. What kind of person is _____? What is your evidence?
2. If _____ were living today, what kind of clothes would he (she) choose?
3. What is there in _____'s character that makes him (her) disliked (or liked, feared, laughed at, etc.)?
4. What would _____ do if he (she) found himself (herself) in (a certain hypothetical situation)? How does this differ from what you would do?
5. Does _____ usually reason out what he (she) should do, or does he (she) merely react emotionally? Your evidence?
6. Is _____ actually true to life, or is he (she) only a stereotype? (Teaching the recognition of stereotyped characters is one of the best services that a teacher can perform, because too many persons think in terms of the "typical" Negro, Jew, Mexican, American Indian, Frenchman, Russian, etc.)
7. Are any of _____'s actions surprising to you? Can they be accounted for by anything in the story? Are there any inexplicable developments (such as an abrupt reformation, as in *As You Like It*)?
8. How and why does _____ change in the course of the story?

## Understanding the Character's Relation to Environment

1. Why do you suppose _____ is the kind of person he (she) is? What clues concerning his (her) background are included in the story? How has his (her) background contributed to making him (her) this kind of person?

2. What does the selection show about family relationships? About the way people get along in a neighborhood? About racial attitudes?
3. What is _____'s (a male) attitude toward women? What is _____'s (a female) attitude toward men?
4. Is it appropriate that _____ should be married to _____? What are some of the factors that determine whether a couple are well matched?
5. What is the real cause of the conflict between _____ and _____? Could it have been prevented? If so, how?
6. Why do _____ and _____ react toward one another as they do? How does _____ influence _____?

## Understanding General Principles of Human Behavior

1. What similar incidents have you experienced or heard or read about? What historical incidents are parallel?
2. Is the ending in harmony with the portrayal of the characters?
3. Ten years after the end, what has probably happened to the chief characters? What makes you think so?
4. What evidence is presented to show that a group of people who share a difficulty tend to cooperate better than they otherwise would? (This question is only a sample of many of the same kind to help the students understand the theme or social implications of a selection.)
5. Who are usually responsible for human progress—people who try to be exactly like everyone else or people who dare to be somewhat "different"? Your evidence? May "differentness" be carried too far? (These are examples of dozens of general thought questions that may bring stimulating discussion.)
6. What are some of the major problems faced by all human beings? What are some of the problems peculiar to people of the twentieth century? Of twentieth-century America?
7. What are some important concerns and motivations of all human beings? (For example, food, clothing, shelter, power, the need to be needed.) Which of these are prime concerns of _____? Your evidence?

This rather long list is by no means exhaustive, but is intended only to be representative of discussion questions using the sociopsychological approach. Examinations may often contain similar thought questions.

Ken Styles and Gray Cavanagh have illustrated differences between the kind of question that asks for factual recall and those that ask for thinking: *Factual recall*—"What honors did Duncan confer on Macbeth?" *Convergent thinking*—"How did Lady Macbeth strengthen her husband's will to kill Duncan?" *Divergent thinking*—"What might have happened if Lady Macbeth had not gone mad?" *Judgmental thinking*—"If they had come to power by natural and legal means, who do you think would have made the better king, and why—Claudius or Macbeth?''[9]

## THE PERSONAL APPROACH

Of all approaches discussed in this chapter, the personal approach places the greatest emphasis on the student. The teacher *must* think of the student first in planning, teaching, and evaluating. Everything is done in the interests of each student's personal growth. Literature is not considered something for the student to learn about; it is simply one of many resources that may provide worthwhile personal experiences that may help the students to answer old questions and raise new ones—in short, to explore life and grow personally. Consequently, the teacher frequently asks himself or herself questions like these: ''What are students interested in at the moment?'' ''What sort of experience in or out of class might raise questions about things of greatest concern to them?'' ''What selections might be most helpful as students seek answers?'' ''What selections could I take to class to motivate students to talk and write?'' ''As they talk, how can I guide discussions so that no student will be put down in the attempt to say something personally meaningful?'' ''How could role-playing this scene help the students to experience the play more effectively?'' ''How could blindfolding students help them to experience *The Miracle Worker* on a more personal level?'' ''What has happened to the feelings of students as a result of reading this novel or play?'' ''What kinds of questions should I ask to find out?'' ''How can they share their feelings about the work with other students and with me?'' ''How can I guide students to talk and write about what this reading experience has truly meant to them individually?'' ''How can I guide them without seeming to intrude?''

All of this may seem to place too much faith in the ability of students to grow emotionally and intellectually under their own power. Suzanne Howell, a teacher who has successfully guided students to express their feelings from reading experiences, describes a scenario that many teachers fear will occur often in their classrooms:[10]

*Teacher:* Howja like the story?
*Students:* Great. I really liked it.
*Teacher:* Yeah, I did too. (And on to some irrelevancy or other.)

As Ms. Howell points out, this is the kind of scene that could very well occur as ''the result of the teacher's lack of preparation or lack of awareness of what he/she is doing.'' Barbara and Gene Stanford add that this approach will probably fail if the teacher lacks empathy, is unable to show acceptance, is inconsistent and seems ''phony,'' is not well prepared, and is not able to work effectively as a facilitator.[11] And it can fail if the teacher isn't observant.

To guide the students through experiences and processes, because the program is process-oriented, the teacher must be an "incurable kid-watcher." Of course, one could say, all good teachers are. Yes, but the teacher using this approach must do it with special care and feeling and must have greater confidence in subjective evaluation. The teacher must also be a greater risk-taker. As Dorothy Watson points out, it is through risk-taking, hypothesizing, and miscuing that "learners make sense of their world." It is through risk-taking that the results "will be meaningful, important, and satisfying for both teacher and learner."[12]

## METHODS OF EMPLOYING THIS APPROACH

This approach will not work unless the class atmosphere is one of trust, openness, honesty, and sincere interest in the feelings and ideas of all. The important things about the setting of a classroom, as effective teachers know, are not time and place, but conditions that encourage students to do their best on their own. Knowing that the teacher is truly interested in one's personal feelings and ideas is more encouraging than seeing information on the board, receiving handouts, listening to lectures, or being told that a novel or play is one of the very best ever written.

There is a general belief among teachers who use the personal approach that creative dramatics helps encourage trust, responsiveness, and creativity. Knowing that their students may not be ready for such activity, teachers may take them through a number of "warming-up" exercises, including the mirror game (one student is the mirror reflecting another's actions), pantomimes, improvisations, and finally spontaneous skits. These experiences are good background for dramatizing scenes in (or related to) fiction and drama. Acting out parts of fiction and drama, can help students to visualize characters, situations, and actions, and can help them to have a personal relationship or transaction with selections read.

Other methods include asking students to write in "response journals"; to close their eyes and try to visualize a scene read orally by the teacher or a student; to write personal responses for duplication and class discussion; to encourage *all* students to listen to and acknowledge classmates' oral responses to literature without adverse criticism; to use readers theater to dramatize fiction and drama; to draw and paint pictures, or make mobiles or collages that convey personal feelings and ideas inspired by a selection; to hold brainstorming sessions, cracker-barrel sessions, or rap sessions about feelings experienced and ideas found; to ask a student to talk into the tape recorder about a selection; and to ask students to talk to each other about a selection that the teacher will say nothing about whatsoever.

Gene Stanford says, "I have had great success in a two- or three-week unit on short stories by making available to students a large number of stories to choose from and a long list of possible things to do with the stories.'' Below are a dozen abstracted from a list of 30 he has used with students:

*Write a T.V. script for one of the stories you have read. Either turn the script in or assemble a cast and read it to the class.*

*Imagine you are one of the characters in a story you read and write a diary about your thoughts and feelings and the events in your life.*

*Write a letter to a character in a story you have read, giving him advice.*

*Put a character from a story you have read into a totally new setting of your invention and tell how he would react in those circumstances.*

*Compose an imaginary encounter between two characters from different stories.*

*Don Wolfe has stated that ''a short story is a study of two parts of the same hero, one part of him at war with another.'' Demonstrate how this is true in stories you have read. OR: Describe a time in your own life when two parts of you were pulled in opposite directions.*

*Choose a character and tell what you would have done in his place, giving reasons for your decision.*

*After determining the theme of a particular story, attempt to prove that it is a valid or invalid way of viewing the world.*

*Write a new ending for a story you have read. Consider what other changes must be made in the story to make your ending logical and how your ending would alter the overall meaning of the story.*

*Is there a character in any story you have read who is similar to someone you know in real life? Describe this person, pointing out the similarities to the fictional character.*

*Explain which character* **you** *are most similar to.*

*Express the theme of a story through a dance you have devised yourself.*[13]

The strength in these assignments is that they fully acknowledge personal responses and find some way of asking the students to relate them to the text of the story.

Any activities genuinely in the spirit of the literature may be adopted, provided that they have intrinsic worth for the students. One teacher, whose class was reading *As You Like It,* asked each student to be responsible for a contribution that should grow out of the play and in no way violate its spirit. As a result, two girls made costumes and used them to act out scenes in the play; a boy with musical talent composed melodies for the lyrics and sang them; some students drew scenes on a long scroll, which they unrolled to present the story; several built model stages; some drew characters; and some wrote imaginary letters from Shakespeare, accounts of a visit to an Elizabethan theater, Elizabethan diaries, character sketches, or short plays of the same type. Did they learn anything about Shakespeare or drama? Probably, because they had enjoyed what they associated with Shakespeare and because they had to read carefully in order to make their contributions.

Plays, as has been remarked, were written to be acted, not to be studied. Because that is true, one of the best activities to employ when a play has been assigned is to act it out. Students will take most of the parts, but the teacher should not be simply a spectator. Before doing any acting, the class must understand the events and the chief characteristics of each role, just as professional actors must. In *Twelfth Night,* for instance, they must recognize that Orsino is lovesick; Maria, frisky; Andrew, cowardly; Toby, jolly and drunken; the singing fool, plaintive. Parts of the room, one teacher suggests, may be marked—Duke's throne, Olivia's palace, and so on; each of the players may be given a simple identifying token—Olivia, a veil; the clown, a dunce cap; Maria, an apron; Malvolio, a yellow cross-gartering made of crepe paper. Action must accompany reading the parts—students bow or curtsy to the Duke, crouch behind imaginary trees, and laugh at Malvolio. Undignified? Perhaps, though not unduly. Shakespeare was a great dramatist partially because he knew when to unbend. His serious scenes owe much of their effectiveness to the contrast with the hilarious ones. Shouldn't we teachers follow the lead of this author whom we revere?

Examples given above should support the contention that a teacher using the personal approach does not have to fall into the meaningless scenario of "Howja like the story?"... "Great."... "Yeah," and find nothing else to say or do. Neither does the teacher have to gush about the literature or do anything that would be embarrassing or foolish. Instead, by having students participate actively in dramatization, discussion, and writing, the teacher allows them to react emotionally as well as intellectually.

## THE VALUE-SEEKING APPROACH

As we have noted, the historical approach to literature can increase students' understanding of the problems, aspirations, successes, and failures of people in past generations, and it may make students a little wiser as they cope with today and plan for tomorrow. The sociopsychological approach can help them to understand why people, alone and with others, believe and act the way they do. The personal approach asks them to get into literature personally, respond freely to it, and come to some understanding of the personal significance of that experience. In these three approaches, students encounter values, but teachers do not teach expressly for values. In the value-seeking approach, though, teachers ask students to examine the values that characters in literature hold, to compare these points of view with their own, and from this examination to develop a personal code worth living by.

English teachers do not have to look far for a rationale for urging students to examine values in literature. Technology in the 1980s has raised a host of vital issues:

> *Urgent ethical and social questions are being raised in the behavioral sciences and in areas of biomedicine such as experimentation with human subjects, genetic engineering and behavioral control, human reproduction, and the termination of life. Technology has generated extraordinary demands on space, energy, and natural resources. The resulting questions about pollution and about constraints on growth are essentially ethical and aesthetic. Communications technology raises ethical and social issues such as the already visible tendency to model expectations for human behavior on the capacities of computers.*[14]

Racial violence, political corruption, and involvements in the internal affairs of other countries also raise moral and ethical questions. So do conflicts between religious and secular groups, and actions taken by certain religious groups to influence governmental institutions. Justice, truth, honor, freedom, respect for life, goodness, the respect for uniqueness among people, and many other issues have to do now with the survival of the world. Nothing is more relevant as we look at literature than the examination of values. Unique opportunities occur in English. "The literature class, after all, may be the only place where an open-ended discussion of values and concerns across the spectrum of personal and social living is possible."[15]

## METHODS OF EMPLOYING THIS APPROACH

This approach may be worked into the context of historical, sociopsychological, or personal growth approaches, or it may be applied more explicitly in thematic units dealing with such topics as justice, freedom, love of nature, and the search for truth. In applying this approach within other approaches, the teacher would make a special point of asking students to examine the codes and values held by characters. What does Plato's *Apology* say about goodness? How do your values conflict with life as depicted in Ray Bradbury's *Fahrenheit 451?* What does Thoreau seem to value most in "Where I Lived, and What I Lived For" (from *Walden*), and how does this compare with your view of nature? What values does Huck Finn struggle with most vigorously, and what does he learn about life in the process? What conflicts over values appear in *To Kill a Mockingbird?* Who are the "good people" in this novel, and what about them makes them "good"? What does the narrator, Jean Louise (Scout) Finch, finally reject and accept? As illustrated above, units frequently contain a mixture of fiction and nonfiction, but both offer opportunities for a closer look at values. Greater opportunities occur within units such as "Nature: A Rediscovery" by Sharon Gates of Mobile,

Alabama, which is concerned with love of nature; "Grow Old Along with Me" by Zora Rashkis of Chapel Hill, North Carolina, which concerns "values about growing old"; and "Utopia: Dream or Reality?" by Barbara Wise and Eleanor Walker of Mobile, Alabama, which asks students to consider "what is good in the society."

The trend in teaching values, though it will depend on the individual teacher, is generally not didactic but concerned with providing selections with different points of view and encouraging the student to develop a personal code. The teacher cannot ask the student to avoid ethical issues, because they are at the heart of literature and life, but neither should the teacher push personal values onto students. In many respects, the teachers' methods in this approach are similar to those in the personal approach. The teacher is guide and facilitator. Louise Rosenblatt describes the process that teachers should make possible for students:

*The reader draws on his own internalized culture in order to elicit from the text this world which may differ from his own in many respects. Moreover, the text may yield glimpses of the personality and codes of the author. The literary transaction may thus embody, and probably to some extent always embodies, an interplay between at least two sets of codes, two sets of values. Even when the author and reader share the same culture—that is, when they live in the same culture, their uniqueness as individual human beings would insure this interplay.[16]\**

The teacher's main contribution, then, is to help students to think between the lines; to encourage them to question and think as they read, so they will get into the stuff of which philosophies are made. An author seldom makes a bald statement of his or her purposes and beliefs; the student must put clues together to discover them, and often must attempt to differentiate between an author's point of view and those of his or her characters. So the student must read thoughtfully, attending not just to the events of the story or play, and he or she must relate what is read to other bits of knowledge. From wide reading and much thinking and discussion, the student formulates a philosophy that may serve well in the manifold events and decisions of the present and the future.

## THE COGNITIVE APPROACH

From time to time in describing other approaches, we have alluded to meaning. The growing interest in student response has focused attention on the reader as creator of meaning. This may or may not be the meaning that an author intended, but as Rosenblatt and other transactionalists believe, this fact doesn't necessarily make the student's interpretation invalid. Some teachers work mainly toward helping students to discover and understand the author's meaning—assuming of course that the teacher and the critics and scholars who indirectly support the teacher really know what the author's meaning truly is. Still another view is that the meaning to strive for is the "realized" meaning, the meaning that the text itself conveys, whether or not it is the same as that which the author claims it should be. To suggest that the only meaning worth considering resides with the student or the author or the text is not the purpose of this section of the chapter. Separating reader and author from text is a foolish endeavor anyway. One thing that English teachers seem to agree on is that it is more important for a student to be able to find meaning in the reading experience than to be able to recall later in life a certain number of predigested meanings, however scholarly they might be. A student who leaves a classroom believing that the only reliable meanings reside in the teacher's head, in lecture notes, or in *Cliff's Notes* has not learned how to read. A student who leaves a classroom believing that any personal interpretation is valid, even one that cannot be sensibly supported by the text, has not learned how to read.

## METHODS OF EMPLOYING THIS APPROACH

Methods vary from asking students to read a short story or a one-act play, for example, and then telling them that the teacher will wait as long as it takes for them to say something significant about it, to telling students what any "intelligent" reader ought to find there. Of course these are extremes. Somewhere between them the teacher tries to intervene in ways that will be instructive but will not inhibit the free discussion of works read or the free reading of works unread. Some teachers give students guide questions before reading and follow up on them in class discussion. One shortcoming of this method is that students may read for the meanings they think the teacher wants. Other teachers provide some background details and also go over difficult words in advance. Others concentrate on showing students how to read for meaning. They use selections for demonstration purposes, going through them with students carefully period after period, pointing out or asking questions about symbols, motifs, and other things.

Some even give students the plot outline of a Shakespeare play or a complex novel, assuming that now that the students know "what happens" they will pay more attention to how it happens and why. This technique may shift some attention from what to how and why, but it doesn't give students much-needed practice in finding details and sequences for themselves. And if the teacher is not careful to explain the purpose of such a handout, students may think that they already have all they need to know. Teachers have also asked students to role-play characters, discuss works with other readers, read critical reviews and commentaries, compare and contrast elements in novels or plays, report on background reading, and respond to questions sequenced to carry thinking to "higher levels of comprehension."

One method has been used so often with difficult selections that it should be described here in some detail. This is the paraphrastic method. It involves the translation of sentences, paragraphs, or longer passages into language that the student comprehends.

This approach has serious disadvantages but at times may be necessary. One disadvantage is that constant repetition of the question "What does this mean?" may lead to boredom. Another may be that the candle lighted by the explanation doesn't always reveal anything significant; the amount of understanding may not be worth the effort. In short, it could endanger the sensitivity of students to what is important in literature.

Nevertheless, at times brief use of the paraphrastic method may be essential to the understanding that must precede discussion of underlying significance. A passage from *The Merchant of Venice* may illustrate the procedure useful with a class not previously exposed to Shakespeare:

**Solanio.** *Believe me, sir, had I such venture forth, | The better part of my affections would | Be with my hopes abroad. I should be still | Plucking the grass, to know where sits the wind; | Peering in maps for ports, and piers, and roads; | And every object that might make me fear | Misfortune to my ventures, out of doubt, | Would make me sad.*

In this passage, students' difficulties arise chiefly from failure to understand the situation, the use of words in unfamiliar ways, peculiarities of sentence structure, and incomplete development of one or two thoughts. In other passages, the troubles might come from figures of speech or unknown words or allusions.

In the first place, the student must have a picture of the scene. Antonio, Salarino, and Solanio are standing talking on a street in Venice (not floating in a gondola as one student thought). Antonio has complained of being sad—he does not know why—and Salarino and Solanio are suggesting that the reason is that he is worried about his ships at sea. Therefore the "sir" in the first line refers to Antonio; it suggests also the respect that Solanio has for the merchant.

When the student comes to "had I such venture forth," he or she may be temporarily baffled. For one thing, the clause is not constructed as we usually would construct it today. Recall to the class that we do sometimes say "had I known" or "had I been there" instead of using the "if" construction. "Venture forth" may be misinterpreted for two reasons: The words have meanings strange to us, and "venture" is here a noun and not a verb. Solanio therefore means "if I had such an investment at stake" or, in other words, "if I had so much merchandise at sea."

"The better part of my affections would/Be with my hopes abroad" causes little trouble except for the word "affections," which here refers to thoughts rather than love. Solanio is saying, "Most of my thoughts would be about the ships carrying my fortune." Some students may need to be shown that the sentence does not end with "would." Many students, in both silent and oral reading of poetry, stop completely at the end of each line.

"I should be still/Plucking the grass, to know where sits the wind" contains two difficult words and one undeveloped thought. "Still" has the old meaning of "constantly" or "always"; yet a student may think that "be still" means "be quiet." "Sits" refers to the direction from which the wind blows. But why does Solanio say that he would be plucking grass? Someone will probably realize that he means he would toss blades of grass into the air in order to discover the direction of the wind.

"Peering in maps for ports, and piers, and roads" goes along with "I should be still." Solanio says that he would be constantly engaged in plucking grass and looking at maps. The word *roads* does not mean highways, but anchorages.

"And every object that might make me fear/Misfortune to my ventures, out of doubt, Would make me sad" needs a little elaboration and requires explanation of "out of doubt." Students may suggest objects that might appear to Solanio, who is on dry land, that could make him fear the loss of his ships. "Out of doubt" is misleading until it is translated as "beyond doubt" or "surely."

The entire passage, then, would be paraphrased in some such way as this: "Believe me, Antonio, if I had such a large investment at stake, most of my thoughts would be about the ships that carry my fortune. I should be constantly picking blades of grass and throwing them into the air in order to find the direction of the wind, or examining maps to locate ports, piers, and anchorages where my ships might be. Every sign I happened to observe that would make me fear the loss of my ships would surely make me sad."

This passage has been analyzed at some length because it exemplifies several of the difficulties that students often encounter. Students, because of limited experience, do make absurd misinterpretations. A classic example was given by the late C. H. Ward, who told of a boy's explanation of

> The stag at eve had drunk his fill
> Where danced the moon on Monan's rill . . .
> With one brave bound the copse he cleared.

To the boy, a stag is "when a fellow hasn't got any girl." This stag had been drinking one moonlight night at Monan's roadhouse (grill?) and, presumably when he was about to be arrested for intoxication, had jumped over the police-men (copse) and escaped. Impossible? Ward assured us that it was true, and any experienced teacher can cite instances of misconceptions equally absurd but perhaps less amusing.

Variations from normal wording or sentence structure often puzzle students.

An intelligent girl once pointed out what she called a "misprint" in a British story: The time was come"; to her, "was come" seemed an error. Hawthorne's "what with telling the news . . . Dominicus was delayed" baffles a student who has not previously encountered the "what with" construction. Some students may become lost in a sentence no more complicated than this from Bret Harte:

> *Of their married felicity but little is known, perhaps for the reason that Tennessee, then living with his partner, one day took occasion to say something to the bride on his own account, at which, it is said, she smiled not unkindly and chastely retreated—this time as far as Maryville, where Tennessee followed her.*

Often an entire passage does not need paraphrasing, but only a word or two requires explanation. It is best if a student can supply the information; otherwise the teacher should try to do so. If the teacher cannot (and there are numerous passages in Shakespeare and other authors about which scholars disagree), he or she, of course, should avoid bluffing. The teacher may hazard an intelligent guess; but guesses need not be numerous, if the teacher anticipates students' probable difficulties and decides how to attack them.

The paraphrastic method is not necessarily dull, although it is more susceptible to dullness than any other in the cognitive approach. If it is used only when needed, and if the presentation is enlivened with illustrations, this method may be as interesting as its results are valuable.

## THE ANALYTICAL APPROACH

In the late 1950s and much of the 1960s, the analytical approach to literature was probably the most widely used, often in combination with the sociopsychological. Most college English courses, strongly influenced by the unfortunately named "New Critics," concentrated on such things as literary structure, imagery, and symbolism, regarding each work as an entity isolated from history and from society, or else, influenced by other critical schools, sought energetically for archetypes or regarded each work as an opportunity for in-depth psychological searching. *Explication de texte* (which combined paraphrastic and analytical methods) was in vogue. High school teachers took such courses as undergraduates or graduates, and tended to use similar methodology in their high school classes.

Recently, however, antagonism toward preoccupation with the analytical approach has been growing. Among the identifiable reasons is the feeling that only the top fourth or fifth of students gain much from constant analysis, and that it tends to turn less able students away from literature rather than toward it. The widely publicized Dartmouth Conference, whose British participants were almost violently opposed to "lit crit," brought focus to this feeling.

So why consider this approach at all, given the currently growing antipathy for it? It does have value, we believe, if it is employed occasionally but not constantly, and if the stress is not upon abstruse literary terminology but rather upon broad description of the author's techniques. Such study may (1) increase the attainment of what we vaguely call "appreciation," (2) help the student to differentiate between inferior and superior pieces of literature, (3) better prepare the student for some college classes in which analysis is still stressed, and (4) sometimes help in personal writing.

Particularly important is investigation of the interrelationships among (1) setting, (2) style, (3) characterization, and (4) plot. Also involved is the study of the effect of each of these upon theme, and some consideration of other literary qualities such as imagery, symbolism, irony, paradox, and voice.

## SETTING

The setting of most modern fiction and drama usually is a determining factor in theme, characterization, and plot. This was not always true; in the "once upon a time" stories the setting is almost anywhere and anytime. Today's authors realize, as Clayton Hamilton reminded us, "that any given story can happen only in a given set of circumstances, and that if the setting be changed, the action must be altered and the characters be differently drawn." The stories of Kipling's *Plain Tales from the Hills,* for example, would be considerably different if the setting were not India in Queen Victoria's time; tales about China, or even tales about India as it was in Queen Anne's time, would of necessity differ markedly from those that Kipling has given us.

Setting is a matter not only of place but also of time and "moral environment," to use a phrase of Burges Johnson. A story about Chicago in 1980 differs from one about Chicago in 1920, and differs still more from a story about Fort Dearborn in 1820. Moral environment similarly varies with both place and time. For example, in some lands it is still immoral for a woman to leave her house without wearing a veil; in the United States the attitudes about such matters as divorce, dress, and the rights of ethnic and minority groups are considerably different from those of 100, 50, or even 20 years ago.

"Some stories or plots can take place only in certain settings. Events in *April Morning* stem from man-made conditions in Lexington and Boston; events in *The Scarlet Letter* follow conditions imposed upon characters by Puritan moral law in early New England." Traditions that go back for many generations, as symbolized recurrently by songs, affect what Kino does in *The Pearl.* "In *The Light in the Forest,* True Son behaves the way he does because he stands bewildered between two ways of life...."[17]

A writer of fiction may show the setting in either of two basic ways: cataloging and suggesting. Sir Walter Scott and many of his contemporaries illustrate the catalog method, writing long paragraphs of description, offering details and more details, describing almost every tree in the grove. As Robert Louis Stevenson puts it, "Some places speak distinctly. Certain dank gardens cry aloud for a murder; certain old houses demand to be haunted; certain coasts are set apart for shipwreck." In literature, certain settings "cry aloud" because authors have created a kind of atmospheric setting through suggestion. "In the very brief first chapter of *The Scarlet Letter* (hardly two pages in length), mood is suggested by such words and phrases as *sad-colored garments, gray, cemetery, prison, grave, sepulchers, jail, gloomy, ugly, black flower of civilized society.* Here the reader is also made to wonder about the incongruity of finding in this setting a wild rosebush because it is described by such words and phrases as *delicate gems, fragrance, fragile beauty,* and is immediately surrounded by such words as *condemned, doom, stern,* and *sorrow.*"[18] Modern writers sometimes use the catalog method, but more often choose only a few representative details that suggest the rest of the picture. They have adapted the poet's technique of selecting and pruning. Thus, in Marjorie Kinnan Rawling's short story "A Crop of Beans," in which the setting has importance as a motivation of the action, a few phrases and sentences like these set the stage: "live oaks and palmettos," "blinding blue of the Florida afternoon," "swaying palms, precise and formal against a turquoise sky," " 'Floridy don't make none o' her own troubles,' she grumbled. 'They all come in from some'eres else. Wind from the south an' cold from Texas,' " "a small melodeon . . . the sole ornament of the main room."

The dramatist's problem is different. Because plays are to be acted, not read, the spectators see the setting, or at least part of it, and do not need a description. Therefore, the dramatist merely gives some technical details concerning placement of exits and furnishings. Occasionally the dramatist may suggest or recall special attention to a detail, or to something not visible on the stage, but primarily confines comments to brief stage directions. It is largely through the uses of voice, music, lighting, and action, as interpreted by the director and actors, that moods and other conditions of setting play their part.

Teacher and class should now and then talk about points like those discussed. Students may note the method that an author employs to portray the setting, and discuss the reason for including some details and excluding others. Often elements of the setting are tied closely to the action and the characters. Because this is true, questions that may be asked frequently are "What does [a certain part of the setting] show about [a certain character]?" "What effect does [the setting or part of it] have upon [a character]?" "What different effects does [the setting or part of it] have upon [two characters]?" "What do these different reactions say about the characters?" "What do they say about the conflict between them?"

When the class is occupied with a play, diagrams or pictures of the stage are often helpful. In a presentation before the class, a few lettered labels and some suggestions of furnishings are useful. Settings of Shakespearean plays, with their many changes of scene, require more visualization than do most others, although Shakespeare helped by letting his characters comment upon their surroundings. Thus King Duncan, before Macbeth's castle, remarks about the "pleasant seat" and the "sweet" and "nimble" air, while Banquo observes the "jutty frieze, buttress [and] coign of vantage"; in *As You Like It,* much of Act II, Scene I serves to paint the Forest of Arden.

In summary, teacher and class will try to visualize the setting of each novel and play, and will try to decide why the author uses that setting, how he or she presents it, and what effect it has upon the characters or the action.

## STYLE

Matters of style should be touched rather lightly in the high school years. Unlike setting, style is elusive and abstract. Even scholars and critics have failed to reach agreement on its definition. Such ingredients as choice and arrangement of words, sentence structure and sentence length, and tricks of expression are commonly recognized, but over and above all these is the mysterious element of personality that led Buffon to state, *"Le style est de l'homme même."*

Some of the less subtle distinctions in authors' styles even fairly inexperienced readers can discover. They can quickly become aware that Hemingway does not write like Poe, that Somerset Maugham's quietly dramatic sentences have no resemblance to Dorothy Parker's barbs, that O'Neill's characters do not talk like Goldsmith's, that Barrie's stage directions are distinguishable from Maxwell Anderson's. Further, they can learn to identify some of the causes of disparity, such things as Hemingway's terse tough-man-to-tough-man sentences, Poe's love of polysyllables and his use of mood-creating words, and Barrie's amiable chitchat.

Students sometimes may profitably analyze the ways in which an author achieves a particular effect. They read, perhaps, Chekhov's "Grief," the account of the driver of a horsedrawn cab who can find no one to listen to his account of the death of his son. They read the concluding sentence: "Iona's feelings are too much for him, and he tells the little horse the whole story." They note the simplicity of that sentence, its shortness, its restraint; they see that a less competent author would have gone on and spoiled the effect. They wonder about the use of the present tense throughout the story, and comment upon how the use of that tense makes the action seem nearer and more real. Little things, they discover, make the difference between a good story and a great one—the selection of a word, the sound of a sentence, the emotional burden of a phrase, the color of a clause. A useful teaching device is to translate a "just right" sentence into a drab, feebly wandering one, or to substitute an abstract noun or a sickly verb for a vigorous word, and have the students note the loss; the power of the original is made apparent by the contrast.

Other students may be led further. These are the students who like to write or who want to know the "how" of everything. Their curiosity is high. Use them as leaders of class discussions on matters of style. Ask them pointed questions about why an author chooses a particular word or uses short sentences in one place and long ones in another, or why the author builds up a feeling of tension or hatred or longing. These students will welcome such questions and dig deep for the answers.

## CHARACTERIZATION

Now let us turn to the matter of characterization. When one has finished reading a story or a play, how does one know that a character is noble, cranky, whimsical, fickle, or something else? One has learned from the author's use of one or more of the nine basic methods of revealing a character:

1. Telling what kind of person the character is.
2. Describing the character (clothing, environment, etc.)
3. Showing the character's actions.
4. Letting the character talk.
5. Relating the character's thoughts.
6. Showing how other people talk to the character.
7. Showing what other people say about the character.
8. Showing how other people react because of the character.
9. Showing how the character reacts to others.

Most elementary of these methods is the first. An unskilled writer says, "Fred was a grouchy old man," but an experienced author knows that showing is superior to telling and therefore uses one of the other devices.[19] Dickens frequently employs the second method, taking his reader down the streets and alleys of London to a black old gateway, or into a vast hall with massive but cobweb-covered furniture; there he meets someone whose person and accountrements Dickens sweeps before the reader's eyes by giving a single impression and then filling in the details. Almost inevitably, authors employ the third and fourth methods to reveal character. For example, when Huck Finn disguises himself as a girl, Mrs. Judith Loftus readily penetrates his incognito but, thinking he is a runaway apprentice, aids rather than hinders his flight. These actions reveal both her quick intelligence and her kindliness. Further, almost every sentence that she speaks tells something about her. She says, "You do a girl tolerable poor, but you might fool men, maybe," and the reader knows from that one sentence that she is blunt, good-natured, not well educated, and slightly contemptuous of masculine acumen.

Because what a person thinks is often more significant than what he or she says, authors often take the reader inside characters' minds. A Shakespearean soliloquy does that, and so does O'Neill's device in *Strange Interlude,* where the characters not only talk to one another but also speak their true thoughts for the audience to hear. Novelists, of course, when they use the omniscient point of view, often recount what their characters are thinking. The last four methods of revealing character may be illustrated in almost any story or play.

Composition teachers have expressed much concern with the ''voice'' used by the writer. Gary Taylor, of Blytheville, Arkansas, argues that ''voice'' is important in the study of literature, too, and that students can learn about characters by observing how the author creates the voice of each. He says, ''An awareness of the possibilities of characterization through diction, word length, sentence-length, punctuation, stress, and syntax should bring to the student a keener appreciation of the craft of the fiction artist.''[20] Clearly, though, such study should be only a sometime thing: if every story were so anatomized, boredom would be inevitable.

In classroom consideration of characters, the analytical and the socio-psychological approach emphasizes human beings and their interrelationships, whereas the analytical stresses the author's technique. Very desirable is a combination of the approaches, founded upon two basic questions: ''What kind of person is _____?'' and ''How do we know that he (or she) is?''

## PLOT

In a story or play, the characters are usually involved in a series of events called the action or plot. (Some modern short stories, of course, are virtually plotless.) A plot is a more or less artificial tying together of incidents involving the same character or characters leading to a solution of a conflict. The artificiality arises from the fact that the loose ends, common in real life, are concealed in the story, and only those persons and events essential to bringing the story to a conclusion are retained. In life, much conversation and many actions are aimless, but in a play or story the author generally reports only conversation and incidents that have a bearing upon the outcome; thus Shakespeare time after time plunges into the heart of a scene, ignoring the ''Hello, nice weather we're having,'' and so on that would be typical of actuality. In life, dozens of big and little things happen every day, but, in a story, the author selects only those that move the narrative forward.

Many questions can explore relationships between events and other aspects. In Steinbeck's *The Pearl,* for example, we can ask questions like these: ''If Kino was so suspicious of the doctor, why did he allow him to treat Coyotito?'' ''How does Kino's refusal to sell the pearl affect other people in the novel?'' We can also explore the plausibility of events, and in doing so find relationships. ''Although the trackers were highly expert, they were not able to catch Kino and his family. Although the rifleman did not see Coyotito, he killed him. Even though

Kino knew that possession of the pearl was bringing about evil events, he kept it. After all they had endured, Kino and Juana threw the pearl away. Are any of these events or decisions so unlikely that they could not possibly take place in real life?"[21] Sometimes there is significance in something a character might be expected to do but does not do. Sometimes the "What if?" or the "Do you suppose?" kind of question is useful; it compares what is known with what must be guessed, and in so doing may reveal relationships, pull things together, and help clarify theme. In *The Pearl* we know that having a rifle meant a great deal to Kino. At the end of the novel, we know that Kino placed his rifle on the ground before he threw the pearl into the water. We don't know whether he took it with him later or not. This is not a point to belabor, but some conjecture might shed light on the theme.

Basic to plot is conflict. One force opposes another force. Generally a character has a goal, but there are obstacles (conflicting forces) that make it impossible for him or her to reach that goal. A story is usually an account of the battle between a character (or a group of characters) and the forces that make the goal hard to attain. Sometimes through skillful questioning a teacher can lead students to discover on their own some of these basic conflicts in literature: man vs. man, man vs. society, man vs. self, man vs. nature, and man vs. God (or conscience). In some stories more than one of these pairings may be present.

The easiest narrative structural unit to make clear to a class is the short story. Unaided, students will say only that the plot of a story tells what happens; prompted further, they will add that it involves moving forward in time. In your classes, you may try to show them that an author does more than move characters forward, that he or she presents a series of closely linked episodes. Each episode is related to each other episode. Thus, in the "boy meets girl" or "girl meets boy" story, the very first episode generally suggests why _____ may love _____, why _____ may lose _____, why _____ may win _____. The four episodes in such a story might be diagrammed as below. Each part of the story is related to every other part. Each incident grows naturally out of the preceding incidents. Each one, after the first, happens because of one or more of the others.

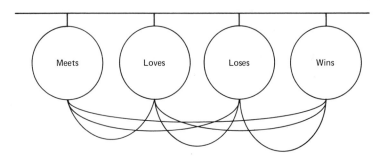

THE TEACHING OF HIGH SCHOOL ENGLISH

"We frequently speak of 'weaving' a plot," you remind the class. "By looking at the lower part of the diagram, you can begin to see what is meant by that expression; some of the lines cross one another, forming the beginning of a web. Naturally, the more episodes we have, the more interwoven the plot will be. That is, each episode introduces some complication and makes the plot more intricate, like this" (and you show the following diagram):

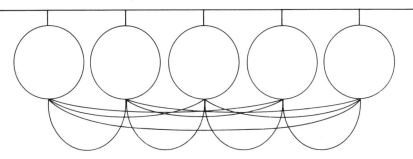

"The important thing to remember is that each part of the well-plotted story is related to every other part, is either the cause or the effect of one or more of the other parts. There are no unrelated segments. Each complication is present—at least potentially present—from the beginning, and each is usually solved at the end."

The diagrams of most stories are fairly easily evolved by a class (perhaps not by individuals) on the principles just explained. The value, of course, lies not in the diagramming but in the understanding of story technique and character relationships that results.

Nine short stories out of ten are constructed similarly. So are most novels and dramas, although in these the episodes, and hence the complications of the web, are more numerous, and digressions more frequent. Nevertheless, once the students have grasped the fundamental principles of plot, they have little difficulty in seeing how a novel or play, as well as a short story, is put together.

Understanding of principles of construction can add tremendously to anyone's enjoyment. Although the class should not be made to analyze painstakingly the plot of every story or play assigned, enough such analyses should be made to help the students see that stories do not "happen" but are built by an author who cleverly weaves together a number of essential and related episodes.

Setting, style, characterization, plot, and the relationship of each of these to the central idea—all of these are involved in the analytical approach. Like any of the other approaches, it is good if not overdone, if not allowed to degenerate into "picking to pieces." Just as a visit to an automotive assembly line gives one more complete knowledge of automobiles, and perhaps more interest in them, so an investigation of the assembly technique used by an author makes a story or a play more understandable and more enjoyable.

# COMBINING THE APPROACHES

Let us assume that you have decided to use the historical approach, and that you have selected American novels, short stories, and plays from the beginnings of the industrial revolution to the present to examine the effects of industry and technology on the values of Americans. Obviously, you hope your students will learn far more than the names of some American authors and the titles of some of their works, even more than some facts about the development of fiction and drama in American literature. You will be asking your students to read literature in which characters ask, "What does it mean to be an American human being?"[22] In fact, it will be difficult to find American literature that fits your topic and doesn't ask this question. You may hope that your students will not only recognize social and personal values but will examine them in terms of their own lives. Your course or unit will give them the opportunity to do so; you must decide how and to what extent you will help them to do it. There is nothing about the historical approach that will prevent you from using the personal approach, so you will be able to encourage them to respond to works personally. Activities designed to further personal growth do not have to conflict with a cognitive approach or an analytical approach. You may want to examine a work closely with them in an effort to help them improve the quality of their own relationships with literature. You will be able to work in any direction. You will be able to incorporate any one of these approaches within one or more of the others, or blend them in any number of ways. Only a very inexperienced, very naive, or very rigid teacher would try to stick to one of these approaches and completely ignore the others. Only a scatterbrained teacher would try to stuff all of these approaches into the same course on the chance that the six would somehow act like a net and catch all of the students. Common sense would argue against both extremes. As a serious-minded yet flexible teacher, you will have a sound rationale for combining, and you will have a plan for doing so.

---

**THE IDEA BOX**

AMERICAN VALUES

Dwight L. Burton suggests that the following "myths" might form a good framework for identifying what is American about American literature:

1. *The Puritan myth of the dangers of happiness.*
2. *The myth of the work ethic.*
3. *The frontier myth of unlimited possibilities for the individual who has strength, courage, and wit.*

---

THE TEACHING OF HIGH SCHOOL ENGLISH

*4. The myth of the significance of the individual's everyday life.*
*5. The myth of the importance of material success.*
*6. The myth of cultural pluralism.*
*7. The myth of youth's alienation from the adult establishment.*
*8. The myth of the inevitability of progress or improvement.*[23]

## "SOCIAL CRITICISM AS THEME"

Kitty O. Locker of the University of Illinois writes in the *Illinois English Bulletin* about social issues in Victorian novels: the meaning of money, and its relationship to happiness; the definition of a "gentleman"; the viability of religion in a scientific age; human ties and creativity amid technology; governmental regulation of private enterprise; vocational versus liberal education; roles appropriate for women. Especially interesting is her examination of Dickens' novels *Hard Times* and *Great Expectations* in view of official British reports on child labor.[24]

## TRY A READATHON

Do you believe that anyone would pay your students to read books? People pay children to walk and ride bikes. The NCTE has published a "Readathon: Sponsor Sheet" to establish a contract between each reader and a sponsor. The money could go to the student, to the school, or to a worthwhile cause in the community. And, of course, students could be motivated to read more books.[25]

## AUTHORS HAVE THEIR SAY

It can be enlightening to read what authors have to say about their own works or about literature in general. Jack Schaefer and Roald Dahl have their say in Stephen Dunning's *Teaching Literature to Adolescents: Short Stories;*[26] Arthur Miller and Rod Serling speak in Alan Howes' *Teaching Literature to Adolescents: Plays;*[27] 11 famous authors comment in William West's *On Writing By Writers;*[28] over 30 authors of novels for adolescents comment in Kenneth Donelson and Alleen Nilsen's *Literature for Today's Young Adults;*[29] and over 100 "great poets" comment on their own poems in Paul Engle and Joseph Langland's *Poet's Choice.*

## CHOOSING A NOVEL FOR CLASS READING

If enough copies are available, you may use the "loaded deck" method. Name several worthy novels, tell a little about each, and let the class choose the one they would like to read.

## OPPOSING FORCES

In the study of a play or novel, analysis of the forces working for or against the protagonist—perhaps writing them in parallel columns—adds to the understanding. (Norman, Okla., High School)

## CALL AN AUTHOR

This is one of "thirty-four alternatives to book reports" included in a publication from NCTE: "In *The Catcher in the Rye*, Holden Caulfield describes a good book as one that 'when you're done reading it, you wish the author that wrote was a terrific friend of yours and you could call him up on the phone whenever you felt like it.' Imagine that the author of the book you read is a terrific friend of yours. Write out an imaginary telephone conversation between the two of you in which you discuss the book you read and other things as well."[30]

## INTRODUCING A BOOK

A class that has studied a novel or play may prepare an interesting short program to introduce the book to next year's (semester's) class.

## IF YOU TEACH HUCKLEBERRY FINN

Despite the thousands of pages of commentary, the best statement made about *Huckleberry Finn* is still Mark Twain's own: "A book of mine in which a sound mind and a deformed conscience come into conflict and conscience loses." The novel may well be taught from that point of view, with emphasis upon Huck's "sound mind" and the way that his upbringing ("deformed conscience") has affected his thinking.

## UNDERSTANDING FLASHBACKS

In dealing with a story using flashbacks, ask the students to rearrange the events, putting them into strict chronological order. Then discuss what was probably the author's reason for altering this sequence and what the story gained or lost as a result.

## MULTICULTURAL LITERATURE

These sources should be helpful as you choose multicultural literature for your classes: Barbara Dodds Stanford and Karima Amin, *Black Literature for High School Students*, NCTE, 1978; Anna Lee Stensland, *Literature by and about the American Indian*, NCTE, 1979; Philip D. Ortego, ed. (articles on Mexican American literature) *English in Texas*, Summer 1976, Texas Joint Council of Teachers of English; see also *English Journal*, March 1977.

## TESTING COMPREHENSION

Basing many of his examples on Conrad Richter's *The Light in the Forest*, George Hillocks of the University of Chicago suggests questions on these levels: *Literal Level of Comprehension*—(1) Basic Stated Information, (2) Key Detail, (3) Stated Relationship; *Inferential Level of Comprehension*—(4) Simple Implied Relationships, (5) Complex Implied Relationships, (6) Author's Generalization, (7) Structural Generalizations. His article in the May 1980 *English Journal* should be an excellent guide for developing questions for discussions and written tests.[31]

6. Imagine that you have been given the task of conducting a tour of the town in which the book you read is set. Make a tape describing the homes of the characters and the places where important events in the book took place. You may use a musical background for your tape.

7. Make a time line of the major events in the book you read. Be sure the divisions on the time line reflect the time periods of the plot. Use drawings or magazine cutouts to illustrate events along the time line.

8. Change the setting of the book you read. Tell how this change of setting would alter events and affect characters.

9. Pick a national issue. Compose a speech to be given on that topic by one of the major characters in the book you read. Be sure the contents of the speech reflect the character's personality and beliefs.

10. Write a scene that could have happened in the book you read but didn't. After you have written the scene, explain how it would have changed the outcome of the book.[36]

## SOME DON'TS IN TEACHING SHAKESPEARE

Avoid: (1) "too much time on unrelated art and history projects," (2) "overexhaustive study of a single play," (3) "too much attention to footnotes, criticism, emendations," (4) "too much rapture," (5) too much teacher explication, too little student reading, (6) use of comic book or other cheapened versions, (7) "pushing Shakespeare on students who are too immature to handle it or are incapable."[37]

## SHAKESPEARE ISN'T DEAD

Teacher and class may gather from current magazines and newspapers allusions to Shakespeare or his characters.

## WHEN STUDENTS READ DIFFERENT PLAYS

John Sweet suggests topics such as these for essays when students have not all read the same play. Each student relates his or her play to the topic. "In a good play, the ending follows naturally and inevitably from the beginning." "At the heart of every drama is the success or the failure of an attitude towards life." "In every drama we see an individual at the end of his tether."[38]

## WHAT IS SCIENCE FICTION?

The following observations are from Lester Del Rey's *The World of Science Fiction:*

> Science fiction is an attempt to deal rationally with alternate possibilities in a manner which will be entertaining.
>
> All the common rules of fiction apply to science fiction; in fact, they apply even more strongly, since the writer must create acceptance, rather than find it in an already common background.
>
> In a sense, the writer has made a promise to the reader: accept the premise which I have tried to justify and I will then follow through as logically as I can.

Perhaps the most important element in distinguishing science fiction from other literature is that it should deal with something alternate to our reality.

Science fiction accepts change as the major basis for stories.

... the entertainment of science fiction comes less from vicarious emotions and more from the enjoyment of ideas than is true for other fiction.[39]

## INTERDISCIPLINARY SCIENCE FICTION

Janet Kafka points to some "interdisciplinary possibilities" with science fiction. Biology students might find Ursula K. LeGuin's story "Nine Lives" interesting because it deals with cloning. Edwin Addott's *Flatland* should interest geometry students. Those interested in computers and information technology should enjoy Stanislaw Lem's *The Cyberiad*. Arthur C. Clarke's "Jupiter Five" uses applied mathematics. L. Sprague de Camp's *Lest Darkness Fall* should appeal to students interested in history; in it, an archaeologist is transported back in time to 6th-century Rome.[40]

## TWO GOOD LISTS OF RESOURCE MATERIALS IN SF

In the January 1979, *English Journal,* Marshall B. Tymn of Eastern Michigan University lists, and annotates, books about SF authors, bibliographies, an anthology index, magazine indices, surveys and histories of SF, magazine surveys, book reviews, films, periodicals, and other kinds of sources. In the May 1975, *English Journal,* Janet Kafka lists novels, anthologies, short stories, fantasy, critical studies, journals, magazines, and other useful materials.

## USEFUL ARTICLES ON SPECIFIC NOVELS, SHORT STORIES, AND PLAYS

The following articles offer helpful teaching suggestions or literary analyses useful in the classroom. Except for those marked CE (*College English*), all are in the *English Journal.*

*All the King's Men* (Warren), Nov. 1969, 1169; May 1973, 704.

*April Morning* (Fast), Nov. 1969, 1186.

*Black Boy* (Wright), Nov. 1968, 1140.

"A Bottle of Milk for Mother" (Algren), Sept. 1971, 724.

*Brave New World* (Huxley), Sept. 1968, 820.

"The Bride Comes to Yellow Sky" (Crane), April 1965, 314.

"The Cask of Amontillado" (Poe), March 1967, 461.

*Catcher in the Rye* (Salinger), Oct. 1968, 977.

*The Crucible* (Miller), March 1961, 183.

*Cry the Beloved Country* (Paton), Dec. 1962, 609; Dec. 1964, 658.

*Darkness at Noon* (Koestler), Sept. 1961, 416.

*David Copperfield* (Dickens), Dec. 1965, 789.

*The Education of* H*Y*M*A*N*K*A*P*L*A*N (Ross), March 1968, 334.

*An Enemy of the People* (Ibsen), Dec. 1965, 626.

*Ethan Frome* (Warton), Sept. 1968, 818; Feb. 1970, 201.

*Fahrenheit 451* (Bradbury), Feb. 1970, 201.

*A Farewell to Arms* (Hemingway), Nov. 1962, 527.

Gilbert and Sullivan, March 1962, 203.

"First Confession" (O'Connor), Jan. 1970, 48.

*The Glass Menagerie* (Williams), Feb. 1968, 109; Jan. 1981, 34.

*Great Expectations* (Dickens), CE, Nov. 1961, 118; CE, Nov. 1961, 122.

*The Great Gatsby* (Fitzgerald), Oct. 1966, 853.

*Hard Times* (Dickens), Feb. 1969, 212; Jan. 1972, 23.

*The Hobbit* (Tolkien), Nov. 1969, 1175.

*Huckleberry Finn* (Twain), Jan. 1961, 1; CE, Dec. 1960, 178; CE, Dec. 1960, 172.

*The Invisible Man* (Ellison), Nov. 1966, 1019; Sept. 1969, 833.

*Julius Caesar* (Shakespeare), Oct. 1961, 451; Dec. 1960, 632; Sept. 1963, 411.

*The King Must Die* (Renault), Dec. 1969, 1335.

*The Light in the Forest* (Richter), March 1966, 298.

*Lord Jim* (Conrad), Oct. 1960, 447; Nov. 1966, 1039.

*Lord of the Flies* (Golding), Nov. 1964, 569; Nov. 1964, 575; March 1969, 408; Dec. 1969, 1316.

*The Lord of the Rings* (Tolkien), Oct. 1966, 841.

*Main Street* (Lewis), Oct. 1968, 985.

*A Man for All Seasons* (Bolt), Nov. 1966, 1006.

*The Martian Chronicles* (Bradbury), Dec. 1970, 1239.

*My Antonia* (Cather), Sept. 1970, 774.

*The Nigger of the Narcissus* (Conrad), Jan. 1967, 45.

*1984* (Orwell), CE, Jan. 1961, 235.

*The Old Man and the Sea* (Hemingway), Oct. 1962, 459.

*One Flew Over the Cuckoo's Nest* (Kesey), Jan. 1972, 28.

*The Ox-Bow Incident* (Clark), Dec. 1970, 1245.

*Portrait of the Artist as a Young Man* (Joyce), Feb. 1968, 200.

*The Pigman* (Zindel), Nov. 1972, 1163.

*Pygmalion* (Shaw), Dec. 1970, 1234.

*The Red Badge of Courage* (Crane), Nov. 1961, 534; Jan. 1968, 24.

*The Red Pony* (Steinbeck), Dec. 1970, 1252.

*Richard III* (Shakespeare), Dec. 1971, 1214.

"Rip Van Winkle" (Irving), Dec. 1964, 643.

*Romeo and Juliet* (Shakespeare), Oct. 1962, 484; Jan. 1981, 34.

"The Secret Life of Walter Mitty" (Thurber), April 1965, 310.

*The Secret Sharer* (Conrad), Jan. 1967, 49.

*A Separate Peace* (Knowles), Dec. 1965, 795; Dec. 1969, 1322.

"The Short Happy Life of Francis Macomber" (Hemingway), Jan. 1971, 31.

*Siddhartha* (Hesse), March 1973, 379.

*Slaughterhouse Five* (Vonnegut), Oct. 1975, 25.

*Tom Sawyer* (Twain), Jan. 1962, 51.

*True Grit* (Portis), March 1970, 367.

*Victory* (Conrad), Jan. 1969, 40.

"The Witch" (Jackson), Dec. 1971, 1204.

*The Zoo Story* (Albee), Jan. 1968, 21.

# FOOTNOTES

1. Percy Lubbock, *The Craft of Fiction,* New York: The Viking Press, 1957, p. 6.
2. Lubbock, p. 17.
3. Louise Rosenblatt, *The Reader, the Text, the Poem: The Transactional Theory of the Literary Work,* Carbondale: Southern Illinois University Press, 1978, p. 13.
4. From "Teaching Strategies for American Literature 1, 2 and Advanced American Literature 1, 2," Prepared by Mary A. Barr and Maria E. Theodore, 1974.
5. "The Uses of Literary History," *English Education,* Oct./Nov. 1975, p. 14.
6. "A Literary Heritage Paradigm for Secondary English," in *Three Language-Arts Curriculum Models,* ed. Barrett J. Mandel. Urbana, Ill.: NCTE, 1980, p. 126.
7. Urbana, Ill.: NCTE, 1975, p. 1.
8. *Apex: Evaluated and Revised,* Trenton, Mich.: Trenton Public Schools, 1975, pp. 188–189.
9. "Language Across the Curriculum: The Art of Questioning and Responding," *English Journal* 69, Feb. 1980, p. 26.
10. "An Experiment in Literary Response," *English Journal* 66, Feb. 1977, p. 42.

11. "Process Curriculum for High School Students," in *Three Language-Arts Curriculum Models,* Urbana: NCTE, 1980, pp. 140–141.

12. Dorothy Watson, "Process Paradigm: Grades Six through Nine," in *Three Language-Arts Curriculum Models,* p. 93.

13. "Individualized Response to the Short Story," in *Humanizing English: Do Not Fold, Spindle, or Mutilate,* eds. Edward R. Fagan and Jean Vandell. Urbana, Ill.: NCTE, 1970, pp. 26–28.

14. Commission on the Humanities, *The Humanities in American Life.* Berkeley: University of California Press, 1980, p. 16.

15. Dwight L. Burton, "Literature Study Today: An Attempt to be Objective," *English Journal* 69, May 1980, p. 32.

16. Rosenblatt, p. 56.

17. William H. Evans, "On Teaching Setting," in *The Structure of Literature,* ed. R. F. Beauchamp, Middletown, Conn.: American Education Publications, 1969, p. 53.

18. Evans, p. 54.

19. For a detailed treatment of authors' methods of presenting characters and point of view, see Wayne Booth's *The Rhetoric of Fiction* (University of Chicago Press, 1961), one of the most scholarly treatments of the role of the author in the writing of fiction. In this work, Booth defends "telling" more vigorously than do most fiction theorists.

20. *English Journal* 57, Oct. 1968.

21. William H. Evans, "Teaching John Steinbeck's *The Pearl,*" in *The Creative Teacher: The Literary Experience,* ed. William H. Evans. New York: Bantam Books, Inc., 1971, p. 127.

22. Brooke Workman, *Teaching the Decades,* Urbana: NCTE, 1975, p. 3.

23. Burton, p. 33.

24. "Social Criticism as Theme: A Strategy for Teaching *Hard Times and Great Expectations,*" *Illinois English Bulletin,* Fall 1979, pp. 35–43.

25. Candy Carter and Zora M. Rashkis, eds., *Ideas for Teaching English in the Junior High and Middle School,* Urbana: NCTE, 1980, p. 207.

26. Glenview, Ill.: Scott, Foresman and Company, 1968.

27. Glenview, Ill.: Scott, Foresman and Company, 1968.

28. Boston: Ginn and Company, 1966.

29. Glenview, Ill.: Scott, Foresman and Company, 1980.

30. *Ideas for Teaching English,* p. 214.

31. "Toward a Hierarchy of Skills in the Comprehension of Literature," *English Journal* 69, March 1980, pp. 54–59.

32. "Drama as Literature," in *Ideas for the Literature Class, 7–12,* ed. Fred Preston. Springfield: Illinois Office of Education, 1978, pp. 23–26.

33. In *Thematic Units in Teaching English and the Humanities,* eds. Sylvia Spann and Mary Beth Culp. Urbana: NCTE, 1975, pp. 169–178.

34. Rochelle Park, N.J.: Hayden Book Company, Inc., 1979, pp. 158–162.
35. *English Journal* 59, Jan. 1970, p. 52.
36. *Ideas for Teaching English,* pp. 212–214.
37. Gladys Veidemanis, ''Shakespeare in the High School Classroom,'' *English Journal* 53, April 1964, p. 240.
38. *English Journal* 53, Nov. 1964, p. 589.
39. New York: Ballantine Books, 1979, pp. 5–10.
40. ''Why Science Fiction?'' *English Journal* 64, May 1975, pp. 51–52.

THE TEACHING OF HIGH SCHOOL ENGLISH

# 7

## TEACHING
## POETRY
## AND
## NONFICTION

Possibly the two most compelling reasons that poets give for writing poetry are that it gives them pleasure and it helps them to deal with human experience. The pleasure is obvious. Shelley finds in poetry life's ''best and happiest moments''; Frost speaks of ''playing the words'' in ''Choose Something Like a Star''; Mark Van Doren remembers his ''formal pleasure'' in writing ''Undersong.'' Sometimes a poet encounters ''a period of nervosity of illumination,'' an experience that unless written down immediately would have no chance of becoming a poem. Other poets, on reflection, agree with X. J. Kennedy who says, ''Poems leave me grateful to them only if while in the making they are slow to let me in on their ultimate purposes.''

However long poems take to write, part of the pleasure seems to come from the clearer insights into life that such word-working makes possible. Lawrence Ferlinghetti says, '' 'New York—Albany' is a favorite poem of mine because it fills a central moment in the middle of the journey of my life when I came to myself in a dark wood. . . .''[1] John Ciardi remembers ''Bridal Photo, 1906'' as an experience that ''brought to life in me an awareness that existed only as a seed before I entered the experience.'' Phyllis McGinley calls the effort ''an attempt to express the inexpressible.''[2] But that, too, gives pleasure. William E. Stafford reflects on his effort to write ''The Farm on the Great Plains'' this way: ''There are emergences of consciousness in the poem, and some outlandish lunges at communication; but I can stand quite a bit of this sort of thing if a total poem gives evidence of locating itself.''[3]

What does all of this have to do with reading poetry? Mainly that the two most compelling reasons for reading poetry are that it gives pleasure and helps to make some sense of life. And like writing it, reading it is not easy to define. In speaking to students, Ciardi makes this observation: "In one everlasting sense, a poem is itself, and no 'explanation' will do for it. For a poem is not something said about something; it is something happening. A poem is an experience, and how can one 'explain' an experience? He may look back, he may describe, he may say this or that was central to what happened; still the experience remains itself."[4] Louise Rosenblatt defines the reader's experience this way:

> *The poem, then, must be thought of as an event in time. It is not an object or an ideal entity. It happens during a coming-together, a compenetration, of a reader and a text. The reader brings to the text his past experience and present personality. Under the magnetism of the ordered symbols of the text, he marshals his resources and crystallizes out from the stuff of memory, thought, and feeling a new order, a new experience, which he sees as the poem. This becomes part of the on-going stream of his life experience, to be reflected on from any angle important to him as a human being.[5]\**

Rosenblatt by no means describes the event as an accident. It is an informed event. The more one knows about music, ballet, or painting, the greater may be one's pleasure. The more one knows about poetry, the more one may enjoy it. But many students are reluctant to do what is necessary to increase enjoyment. They claim (and rightly) that poetry is artificial, that people don't really talk like that. Some feel that, once they understand a poem, the result is not worth the effort. Some have become antagonistic because teachers have gushed too much about poetic beauties or have dismembered every line. Most of the objections, though, are to the difficulties of reading poetry. A poem is by its nature highly compressed; a single reading will seldom reveal many of its secrets.

The objections to poetry may best be met in terms of the main purpose for reading poetry: pleasure. Enjoying rhythm, treating the comprehension of compressed language as the solving of a puzzle, and discussing the broadly applicable human truths of the individual insights and emotions—these are representative of the kinds of pleasure we shall discuss in connection with the six fundamental approaches.

Two complicating factors are that not all students are ready for the same kind of pleasure at the same time, and that students acquire misconceptions and negative attitudes in the elementary grades and only confirm them in the high school. A national study by Ann Terry (1972) of the poetry preferences of students in upper elementary grades supports many findings of earlier studies and reveals interesting new information. Children like humor, stories, and rhythm and sound in poems. They dislike free verse, and, interestingly, have more success writing haiku than in reading it. Interest in poetry apparently peaks in the

---

*From *The Reader, the Text, the Poem* by Louise M. Rosenblatt. Copyright © 1978 by the Southern Illinois University Press. Reprinted by permission of the Southern Illinois University Press.

THE TEACHING OF HIGH SCHOOL ENGLISH

fourth grade and declines steadily. Inner-city students show the greatest interest in poetry, rural next, and suburban the least. Terry's study also shows that half the poems that are "teachers' favorites to read to their classes" are disliked by "a significant number of participating students." Among the reasons for disliking poems are that they don't rhyme, are too short, don't make any sense, don't speak about familiar things, are not funny, have no story, and speak about things students can't do or dislike doing.[6]

By the time students get into high school, some dislikes turn into hatreds. Robert Burroughs (1977), a teacher at San Luis Obispo, California, High School, conducted an informal study and concluded that some students really hate poetry. This finding is not new to teachers; neither is Burroughs' assertion that students have been induced to hate it. This study also confirms the fact that students believe only teachers know what a poem means.[7]

Part of the problem lies in this statement by Josh, one of Mr. Burroughs' students: "If I think trees in the poem symbolize death and the teacher doesn't, why can't she deal with the fact that it means death to me?" If Josh sincerely believes this but the teacher believes the idea is ludicrous, the teacher should give the interpretation a fair hearing, should really listen, should ask for personal reasons and for support in the text, should ask students (if this is a class discussion) to listen and ask questions, and should ask the kinds of questions and offer the kinds of information that invite Josh to consider other evidence. Questions, whether asked by the teacher or by students, must stem from a sincere interest in what Josh is saying; they must not, even by implication, intimidate or belittle him in any way. This procedure should not lead Josh to assume that anything he says is right, though. If skillfully handled by the teacher, it can encourage Josh and other students to engage in an intelligent pursuit of the best possible response, but one that is still one's own.

## THE HISTORICAL APPROACH

Some teachers believe that taking the historical approach with poetry diverts too much attention from reading poetry aesthetically. The approach certainly may be abused; it may, for example, become largely a matter of emphasizing unimportant biographical facts, dates, and the like. But the historical approach is justified in high school teaching when knowledge of the circumstances of writing will help to clarify the poem, when the poem sheds light upon the age in which it was written or which it describes, or when the poem relates to a historical subject.

No true poem, of course, has ever been written that did not grow from the author's current thinking and feeling. Some poems, however, illustrate the author's thoughts and emotions better than others. Here are three examples.

Bryant's "To a Waterfowl" developed from a personal experience. Twenty-one years old—not the gray-bearded, bald-headed old man pictured in the anthologies—Bryant was walking the seven miles from his home to Plainfield, Massachusetts. He was worried, uncertain. Because of lack of money, he had not been able to complete his college work. He wanted to write and had written, but he knew that his writing could not yet support him. He had passed his bar examination but had no law office, no chance to practice. On this day, a chilly one in December 1815, he was going to explore the possibility of opening a law office in Plainfield. But the future was doubtful and dreary. The sun seemed to be setting on his bright youthful hopes just as it had already disappeared in the west. Then, also in the west, Bryant saw a lone wild duck, flying rapidly southward. The young man noted the assurance of the bird, the straightness of its course. Certainly a higher Being was guiding it. And if that Being cared for this wild creature, need he, the poet, fear anything?

> He who, from zone to zone,
> Guides through the boundless sky thy certain flight,
> In the long way that I must tread alone,
> Will lead my steps aright.

Without an explanation like this, "To a Waterfowl" could seem to be just another poem. With the background, however, the reader could find in it new significance.

Poe's "Annabel Lee" has a less specific story attached to it than has "To a Waterfowl," but to appreciate it a class must be familiar with the story of Poe's tender love for his child-wife, Virginia, who had died three years before. They must know of her delicate loveliness, her singing ability, her lingering illness that often threatened death before it actually arrived. They should know that she had already inspired some of Poe's best work, such as "Ulalume" and "The Raven." They should also know that there is at least figurative truth in the line "She was a child and I was a child," because Poe never "grew up" to the conservatism and subdued emotionality that usually accompany adulthood. And the class should know, too, that "Annabel Lee" was probably the last poem that Poe wrote—that memory of his dead wife remained sharp within him up to the time he died.

Quite different is the background of Siegfried Sassoon's "Suicide in the Trenches" or any other of his bitter antiwar poems:

> In winter trenches, cowed and glum,
> With crumps and lice and lack of rum,
> He put a bullet through his brain.
> No one spoke of him again.

At 28, Sassoon himself had gone to war. He knew its filth, its heartlessness, its blood. Twice wounded, he was awarded the Military Cross for rescuing injured soldiers under fire, and he threw the decoration into the sea. Later he declined the D.S.O. because he had come to believe that war is completely futile. In his poem—indeed in his whole life after World War I—his chief aim was to fight war:

> You smug-faced crowds with kindling eye
> Who cheer when soldier lads march by,
> Sneak home and pray you'll never know
> The hell where youth and laughter go.

These illustrations should make it plain how knowledge of the poet may clarify some poems and make them vivid experiences, not dull words. Similarly, knowledge of the age in which a poet lived may often remove a poem from the realm of the abstract.

Chaucer's "Prologue" may serve as the example here. To those who know medieval history and are familiar with H. O. Taylor's *Medieval Mind,* R. L. Poole's *Medieval Thought and Learning,* and G. G. Coulton's *Medieval Panorama,* the knights, squires, yeomen, monks, friars, franklins, clerks, reeves, summoners, and manciples seem at least as distinct as next-door neighbors on a foggy day. But between our students and these characters is a brick wall, one in which we must make at least a few chinks if we cannot tear it down.

Consider, for instance, the Clerk:

> A Clerk ther was of Oxenford also,
> That unto Logyk hadde longe ygo.
> As leene was his hors as is a rake,
> And he nas nat right fat, I undertake,
> But loked holwe, and therto soberly.
> Full thredbare was his overeste courtepy,
> For he hadde geten him yet no benefice,
> Ne was so worldly for to have office.
> For him was levere have at his beddes heed
> Twenty bokes, clad in blak or reed,
> Of Aristotle and his philosophye,
> Than robes riche, or fithele, or gay sautrye.

A combination of the paraphrastic and the historical approaches seems essential here: the paraphrastic to clarify word meanings and sentence structure, and the historical to add facts essential to understanding and appreciation. Unaided, some students will assume that the clerk sold groceries; Oxenford and Oxford they will suppose to be two different places; "nas nat" will be meaningless; and so on. The second line opens the way to a little discussion of medieval education. The line does not mean "Who'd turned to getting knowledge long ago" (as translated in one modern version) but means rather, that the clerk had long since been familiarized with the "trivium" (grammar, rhetoric, and logic) and was probably studying the "quadrivium" (arithmetic, geometry, astronomy, and music); in other words, he was an advanced student. Line 6 offers opportunity to show some pictures of medieval costumes. Lines 7 and 8 point out that a more worldly scholar than the clerk might abandon his desire to become a priest in order to accept a position as secretary to some rich man or government official. Line 10 provides an opening for a discussion of what books were like before the invention of printing, and how costly 20 books would be. Line 11 might well be passed over quickly with only a mention of Aristotle's doctrine of the "golden mean" for the few students who might be interested. Pictures of medieval musical instruments would illustrate line 12, and a musically inclined student might find here a good subject for a report.

Not all the "Prologue," of course, is crammed with so many reflections of the fourteenth century as these lines are, but, nevertheless, this poem and many others have sufficient historical connections to make such study worthwhile and interesting. The poetry suggests the social history, and the social history enlightens the poetry.

Political history also has often been tied closely to poetry. Obvious examples are Emerson's "Concord Hymn" and Whitman's "O Captain! My Captain!" To teach these without reference to their historical background would be not only pointless but almost impossible. Somewhat less obvious examples are Longfellow's "Skeleton in Armor," which might be related to the puzzle of who really discovered the New World; ballads, both English and American, some of which have a historical foundation; "London, 1802," which demands an understanding of the England that Wordsworth described as a "fen of stagnant waters"; and Tennyson's "Locksley Hall," published in 1842 but foreseeing aviation, gigantic aerial wars, the steady advance of science, and a "Federation of the world" that has yet to be attained.

As a final and somewhat different example of the usefulness of the historical approach, consider Keats' "Ode on a Grecian Urn." Obviously, in teaching this poem one needs to comment upon Greek art and pagan religious rituals. But why does Keats say that the urn carries two quite different scenes, the one depicting love and pursuit and near frenzy, the other a sedate procession of pious persons on their way to perform an act of worship? The dichotomy is not characteristic of classical Greek art. As Gilbert Highet says, "The sculptor or painter who decorated a vase would not think of mingling half-naked bacchantes with decently dressed churchgoers, any more than we should put voodoo drums into a Bach choral prelude and fugue." But Keats knew that the Greeks were somewhat schizophrenic persons, in constant conflict within themselves. To quote Professor Highet again, "The conflict was a struggle between the life of reason, for which they were uniquely gifted, and the dark forces of the passions, to which

206

they were terribly sensitive.'' Apollo, the god of reason, and Bacchus, lord of revelry, warred within them. Keats was sufficiently informed about the Greeks to recognize this conflict and to dramatize it in his poem.

When one of these close connections exists:

poem ← → the poet's life
poem ← → the poet's time
poem ← → the time depicted in the poem

the historical approach is justified. It removes the poem from the pages of a book and places it in its proper historical context—in physical surroundings that may be made familiar, and among real people with fears, tears, joys, and aspirations not unlike our own.

## THE SOCIOPSYCHOLOGICAL APPROACH

In their preoccupation with those elements of poetry that are supposed to make a text a literary work of art, critics and scholars have tended to separate a poem from its personal, social, and political message. Poets themselves sometimes object to this, saying that criticism has placed the emphasis where they never intended it to be. This does little good of course if the critic also takes the position that the poet is a very poor judge of the worth of his or her own poem. Artistry generally ranks above content. To some extent this is the way it should be; many bad poems have been written as emotional responses to sensed wrongs in the society. But a poem that does speak powerfully about a personal, social, or political concern also demands to be read for its message.

Societies certainly haven't ignored the social and political messages in poetry. Many of the world's best poets have been branded heretics, dangerous radicals, and enemies of the state. They have been jailed, executed, or banished, and their works have been burned. Many others have had to flee their countries in order to continue their work. Poets have also been honored by the state. England has had its poet laureates, and twentieth-century America has paid great tribute to Sandburg and Frost.

English teachers should not disguise the fact that occasionally they choose poetry to raise personal and social consciousness. No one would argue with the idea that the purpose of poetry as art is to please. We supported that position at the beginning of this chapter. But we also said that poetry, like fiction and drama, can instruct. Kay Boyle, a contemporary fiction writer and poet, has this to say about the writer's social responsibility. In her comment are parallels to what could be called the teacher's social responsibility: ''The writer does not offer solutions. This is not his role. But he offers men courage by revealing to them dimensions they had not known were theirs. The writer—and the poet and fiction writer above all—has taken on the responsibility of presenting the predicament of man, and this presentation is what the cautious and the uneasy in any society have always feared."[8]

Poetry offers endless opportunity for adding to knowledge of human beings. It offers, too, tentative conclusions—guesses to be weighed and modified. Shelley called the poet the legislator of mankind, but this does not mean that the poet knows all the answers. But a poet does raise many questions and does supply clues to help answer them.

In the following paragraphs we shall consider some familiar poems to illustrate the use of the sociopsychological approach. In the first group are poems about individuals; those in the second are about the relationships between two or more persons; those in the third refer to large groups.

## POEMS ABOUT INDIVIDUALS

In considering Edwin Arlington Robinson's poem "Richard Cory," the class would discuss the kind of man that Cory was—rich, regal, handsome, courteous, and envied by all. But why did such a man commit suicide? What may have been lacking in his life? What really are the ingredients of a rich, full life? Other of Robinson's characters, such as "Miniver Cheevy" and "Mr. Flood's Party," offer equally good portrayals for consideration of the individual.

In "Lucinda Matlock," Edgar Lee Masters has portrayed a woman who possessed the secret that Richard Cory apparently lacked: "It takes life to love life." Was Cory all superficiality? "He glittered when he walked." But Lucinda did not glitter; there was a depth in her that possibly Cory could never have. She worked hard, gave birth to 12 children of whom eight died young, nursed the sick, wandered through the fields,

> Shouting to the wooded hills, singing to the green valleys.
> At ninety-six I had lived enough, that is all—
> And passed to a sweet repose.

The teacher might ask the class why Lucinda was happy, whom they have known comparable to her, what the ingredients of happiness are. Masters' *Spoon River Anthology* and *New Spoon River* are filled with additional sketches, many of them suitable for class discussion.

Poe's "The Haunted Palace" is not about a palace but about "a mind haunted by phantoms—a distorted brain," as he himself explained. In dealing with this poem, the teacher would probably combine the paraphrastic and sociopsychological approaches, having the class explain first what the poem says about the palace and then translating it into what it implies about a human mind. The class would also supply its own illustrations. What, for instance, may have been the "evil things, in robes of sorrow, [that] assailed the monarch's high estate"?

In "Ozymandias," what did Ozymandias look like? What did his appearance show about his character? What does the inscription on the pedestal show about him? Would you have liked to be one of his subjects? Can you think of two or three modern men who were like Ozymandias and shared his fate? If being a "king of kings" will not enable a person to be long remembered, what will? By asking such questions, the teacher will do more than clarify the character of the king in Shelley's poem; the teacher will help the class to see that mere possessions and power do not insure immortality in the hearts of human beings.

Some individuals in poems are nameless, but names are not essential when observations about these individuals apply to people the world over. In other poems, we suspect that the poet alone is the person under scrutiny, but this fact isn't as important as one's personal experience with the poem. One might want to know that the poet is speaking about someone who meant a great deal to him or to her, but to internalize the thoughts is of far greater importance. "Saint Judas" by James Wright begins "When I went out to kill myself" and ends "I held the man for nothing in my arms." Between these lines is much that could apply to Richard Cory. "The Room" by C. Day Lewis describes a place deep within the palace where the king could be by himself and reassure himself that "he was real." In speaking about this poem, the poet refers to "solitude and integrity—for any man or woman." It speaks to adolescents, too. Students can speak about the importance of having a room to themselves at home, or, if not, at least a place to go to be alone. A fireplace, Herbert Clark Johnson suggests in "A Boy's Need," can be a place to dream. "My father moved through dooms of love" by E. E. Cummings might be compared with Masters' "Lucinda Matlock." Cummings says his poem is "not only a portrait of a particular person (one erect generous whole human unique being) but a celebration of the miracle of individuality—by contrast with everything knowable and collective, common and corrupting, cowardly and truthless.'"[9] In the poem and in Cummings' statement about it, there are many questions a teacher could ask. The human qualities celebrated by Cummings might also be contrasted with those celebrated by the state in W. H. Auden's poem "The Unknown Citizen."

## POEMS ABOUT TWO OR MORE PERSONS

Poetry that clarifies family relationships has especial value in this age, when some persons fear that the family unit is disintegrating. A poem like Burns' "The Cotter's Saturday Night" affords a splendid opportunity to consider what family life was formerly like, how and why it has changed, whether the changes have resulted in improvement or loss, and what the future of the family unit seems to be. Involved in such a discussion would be a consideration of how much authority parents should exert; what assistance, advice, and cooperation a child has a right to expect from parents; whether parents should interfere in their children's choice of friends; what parents have a right to expect of their children; whether grown children should contribute to meeting the household expenses; and so on. Phyllis McGinley's very short poem "The Adversary" opens some interesting questions, too. Why is a mother "hardest to forgive"? In what sense could a mother's understanding be called relentless? Is the title surprising? McGinley's poems "The Doll House" and "Ballade of Lost Objects" also concern family life.

In "Forbearance," Emerson names only one quality for which he would value a friend, but suggests several others. As students enjoy talking about friendship, a teacher may use a poem such as this as an entrance to a free discussion of the qualities that a genuine friend should possess. For contrast, the teacher might have students read William Blake's "A Poison Tree" and discuss what grows from anger and wrath.

Consider also such selections as *Sonnets from the Portuguese,* "Maud Muller," "My Last Duchess," and so on. We ignore the steadily increasing number of teenage marriages in the United States; we conveniently ignore the fact that tens of thousands of girls now in American classrooms will mother illegitimate children. What has this to do with literature? Only that young people need to know more about human relationships, and that literature helps to clarify these relationships.

Selections like some of Mrs. Browning's *Sonnets from the Portuguese* portray the beauty of married love and strongly imply that such love between a well-matched couple is worth waiting for. Whittier's "Maud Muller," read superficially, suggests that the Judge and the rustic Maud would have been happy if they had married; but closer reading leads one to ask whether this is true—whether they were suited for one another, what qualities a well-matched couple hold in common. (Bret Harte's pointed parody "Mrs. Judge Jenkins" mercilessly reveals Whittier's sentimentality.) Browning's "My Last Duchess" indicates how the pride and the jealousy of one of the partners may bring a marriage to a tragic end. Abundant are other poems, as well as short stories, novels, and plays, pertaining to different aspects of married life.

## POEMS ABOUT GROUPS

Much poetry enlightens the relationships not of a few people but of vast groups of people. Whitman's "I Hear America Singing" should lead to a discussion of means of earning a livelihood, of ways of enjoying one's work, and of methods of choosing a lifework; it might lead to a discussion of other selections pertaining to the building of skyscrapers, the life of a doctor or nurse, the work of a pilot, and so on. Other points of view worth examining can be found in "Florida Road Workers" by Langston Hughes and "The Misery of Mechanics" by Philip Roth. What songs are these workers singing? Do different groups in the society from bank president to road worker have anything in common? What fruits of labor might be examined in ''A Valedictory to Standard Oil of Indiana'' by David Wagoner? Poetry can provide many insights into the dreams as well as the realities.

Wars and hunger, according to historian Carl Becker, are man's two greatest enemies, and either may extinguish the human race. Wars are the most unthinkable acts of violence between groups. No side really wins; to call any war a ''popular war'' or a ''good war'' is inane. America's use of the atom bomb in World War II and its involvement in Vietnam have done much to caution us against using such phrases to describe wars remembered by most adults. The scars run deeper now, and with every international incident the fear of annihilation grows stronger. Today most of us look upon war as something hateful, a childish way of settling disputes that could destroy the world. Poems like Whitman's ''Come Up from the Fields, Father,'' depicting a family which receives the news that its son and brother has been killed; and Joseph Langland's ''War,'' which also describes the effects of such loss, emphasize the pain that reaches beyond the battlefield. Hardy's ''The Man He Killed'' suggests that the enemy is human also. Of course, often much is done in basic training to convince soldiers otherwise. ''An Airstrip in Essex'' by Don Hall begins saying farewell to the ''white fogs of the invasion winter'' of World War II, but ends alluding to mist rising from a ''jagged wall'' in Poland. No one dares turn completely away from war, even an ''old ruined'' one.

The worst victims of poverty are children. The social origins and the political implications of it mean nothing to them; as Gwendolyn Brooks says in ''From The Children of the Poor,'' ''plentitude of pain shall not suffice/Nor grief nor love shall be enough alone'' to ease their suffering. Is anything *enough?* What can a society do to correct this wrong? Have we ever tried? For an earlier comparison, students might read ''To an Unborn Pauper Child'' by Thomas Hardy.

City life has been a product of our development as a nation. In our increasingly urbanized life, writers frequently emphasize the problems inherent in dwelling within congested areas. In ''Chicago,'' ''Mamie,'' and ''Clean Curtains,'' Sandburg sees both the glory and the gloom of city life; he hears Chicago laugh ''the stormy, husky, brawling laughter of youth,'' but he knows, too, that in Chicago is Mamie, from a little Indiana town, underpaid Mamie, who has always dreamed and still dreams of ''romance and big things off somewhere.'' In the city also are the new neighbors who put up clean curtains, only to lose them to the ''dust and the thundering trucks.'' The modern meaning of the term *inner city* is reinforced by the contrast between the shadows among ''huddled and ugly walls'' and the sunlit ''blue burst of lake'' in Sandburg's ''The Harbor.'' Modern visitors to the inner city have become familiar with ''the place losing itself, unnamed''; the isolated, gutted place waiting for ''the high-rise blocks,'' as described in Thom Gunn's poem "The Produce District." Writers, it seems, tend to stress the undeniable squalor of the cities and to ignore the equally undeniable advantages of urban life. A good class discussion will consider both sides—what is good and what should and can be bettered.

As a rule, poems by members of minority groups should not be singled out for special comment. That a Jew should write a poem is no more remarkable than that a Methodist or a Catholic should; that a Negro or Japanese or Mexican can write beautifully should excite no more surprise than the fact that an Englishman can. In general literature units or poetry units, one should take each poem for whatever it happens to offer, regardless of who wrote it. Yet at the same time one must recognize the right of students who belong to ethnic and cultural minority groups to learn more about their roots and to value this identity. We also know that Americans who do not belong to such groups should better understand minority points of view. Minority literature can be gathered to meet these needs. And, in a more general poetry course or unit, one without such focus, a poem by or about members of minority groups should be discussed as frankly as a poem about war or city life or country life or anything else. The students in today's classes are tomorrow's lawmakers, tomorrow's citizens who must live together. The teacher who can do anything to build in them a respect for equal rights and opportunity should be more than pleased.

Many students still like poems of patriotism, even though they may occasionally question decisions made by the nation's leaders. The greatness of one's own land is a topic that most people never tire of extolling.

> Breathes there a man with soul so dead
> Who never to himself hath said
> "This is my own, my native land"?

The teaching of patriotism, however, is no longer of a chauvinistic variety but of a broader type, one that is concerned with the possible contributions of a nation to world peace and world advancement. A poem like Longfellow's "Building of the Ship" and especially a more modern poem like Russell Davenport's "Old Glory" may illustrate what has been called "the higher patriotism":

> Old Glory! Guard the hopeful and the good,
> And lead us onward, unconfusedly,
> That in our freedom others may be free!

For an interesting contrast, ask students to evaluate the kind of patriotism shown by the speaker in E. E. Cummings' poem "next to of course God America i."

Wordsworth's sonnet "The World Is Too Much With Us," may serve to illustrate many poems that help students ponder some of the big and possibly abstract questions concerning human conduct and human relationships. Do we devote too much of our time to "getting and spending"? What else does life offer? Wordsworth advocates paying more attention to nature. Is he right? What could we gain from following his advice? What besides nature may make our lives truly rich?

For many more poems like those mentioned—poems that shed light upon individuals, upon the interrelationships among a few individuals, or upon the possibilities of rapport within large groups—the sociopsychological approach is invaluable if not indispensable.

## THE PERSONAL APPROACH

The personal approach stresses pleasure and personal growth. This pleasure is inherent in the language, rhythm, story, emotional intensity, and pictorial qualities of poems. It may come also from oral reading or other activities associated with teaching poetry, activities that can stimulate personal growth. We teachers have experienced that pleasure, but how can we get our students to experience it?

The solution seems to lie in doing many things with poetry—not just one thing again and again. One of the attractions of sports is that there are many types of plays in each game, not the same play repeated ad infinitum. Poetry can have the same appeal. Teacher and class can (1) read aloud, (2) dramatize, (3) present choral readings, (4) sing, (5) discuss, (6) compare, (7) write about, (8) emulate or imitate, (9) illustrate with words, (10) illustrate with pictures, (11) listen to recordings, (12) laugh about, (13) memorize (voluntarily), (14) collect favorite poems or passages, and (15) serve as cocreator. These methods of employing the personal approach are discussed in the following paragraphs.

### ORAL READING

That a teacher should read aloud with effectiveness is obvious. Constant application of only one rule leads to good oral reading: The voice should "do the thing shall breed the thought." That implies, of course, that the reader must understand the selection—its mood as well as its ideas. The reader conveys the mood and the listener perceives the thought. With a serious passage, the voice suggests the seriousness; for a light passage, the voice is lilting; in an exciting passage, the voice becomes tense and breathing more rapid. This may sound difficult, but if one really understands and *feels* a poem, the voice tends to adjust itself with little conscious effort by the reader. It is easy because it is natural; when one talks, it is natural to adjust delivery to what one is saying. Good poetry is natural enough that one can read it without becoming pompous, oratorical, silky smooth, or sickeningly sweet. Natural delivery has the advantages of placing pauses where they belong (not necessarily at the end of each line) and of avoiding excessive stress upon the accent and rhyme. Practice is essential, of course, but if a college senior preparing to teach English devotes 10 minutes a day through the school year to oral reading of various kinds of poetry and keeps the above rule constantly in mind, his or her reading at the end of the year should be satisfactory. This is almost certain to be true if the future teacher uses a recorder to listen to and improve upon the use of stress and pauses.

Most of the reading aloud should not be done by the teacher, though. Some teachers unwisely distrust students' reading, saying that poor reading will spoil the poem for others. But how can students ever learn to read aloud well if they have no chance to practice? They do not have to read before the entire class. In fact, more students will get this practice if they read within small groups at a voice level no higher than that they would use in carrying on group discussion. (Some high schools have listening booths or listening stations in or near classrooms where students can go to record their oral reading in practice sessions.) The teacher can listen to students reading in their groups and perhaps record samples to go with written notes and oral tips to be given the student later in an individual conference. The classroom atmosphere should be friendly and informal. If some students will be more comfortable sitting on the floor in groups, the teacher should allow them to do so.

## DRAMATIZING

Classes enjoy dramatization of poetry. A ballad such as "Get Up and Bar the Door" may be dramatized with little time-consuming preparation, as it falls readily into dramatic form. Another approach is to encourage students to try different versions or to try to do parts of one from memory after hearing it two or three times. The teacher can read or play different versions of an old ballad to emphasize the point that many details changed as ballads were passed on through song. Reading of parts in such a poem as Poe's "Raven"—with a narrator, a speaker, and a hoarse raven—assists visualization and understanding. Informal staging of Readers' Theater in the classroom or on stage in the auditorium can also encourage dramatization. Excerpts from *John Brown's Body* or *Western Star* are especially appropriate.

## CHORAL READING

No one should worry about producing professional results, but students will need to work out an arrangement and practice it. Tone, pace, and rhythm will be important. Deciding who will do what in solo and in unison, deciding whether to use any background music or humming or bodily movements, going through the entire selection, and making changes will be the basic steps. Students should be encouraged to play with the poetry—that is, to try out pitch levels, intonation, facial expressions or whatever they believe will help clarify the meaning they want to convey through their interpretation of the selection. Among the many possible selections are "Jazz Fantasia" by Whitman, "The Creation" by Johnson, "We Real Cool" by Brooks, "April Rain Dance" by Hughes, and the ballad "Lord Randal." Students who have tried choral reading say it is not only a lot of fun but an aid to understanding the meaning of the poetry.

## SINGING

Much poetry was written to be sung. Then why not sing it? If the teacher cannot lead the singing, there is usually a student who can. Ballads, perhaps one or two of the boisterous American folk ballads or cowboy songs such as "The Old Chisholm Trail," make a good entering wedge. Later, lyrics by Shakespeare, Jonson, Burns, and others may be sung. Ballads should be "sung, acted, danced to, made up jointly," says Rachel Potter of Sheffield, England.[10]

## DISCUSSING AND COMPARING

Discussions of poems should be lively and interesting. A good discussion inevitably involves more than one of the approaches. Comparisons of poems or between poets (e.g., Frost and Wordsworth, the rhythm of Chesterton's "Lepanto" and the rhythm of Lindsay's "The Congo") are invaluable. Alan Purves points to the advantage of asking students to sit in a group without the teacher and talk about a poem before a video-recorder. This procedure gives students a chance to see how effectively they have listened to others and to themselves.[11]

## WRITING

Analytical writing in connection with poetry seldom adds to the enjoyment. Sometimes, though, the members of a class, or a few students, become sufficiently excited over something they have found in a poem to want to express their enthusiasm on paper. This effect is unlikely to occur often, but when it does, it should not be stifled. Also, a few students like to write verse of their own, verse possibly inspired by or modeled on something they have read. To get all students to engage in such an activity, some teachers use the group poem technique and find that classes which have written group poems tend to be more appreciative of the efforts of professional poets. The teacher may take a class for a walk around a city block or past part of a lake, asking them to be perfectly silent and to keep their sensory organs alert. After returning, the students write on the board words and phrases indicating what they have seen, heard, smelled, and felt. (Young people tend to express themselves much more picturesquely than older ones; with a class of adults, the phrases obtained are generally trite ones like "rippling water," "swaying grass," etc.) They then find some element that seems to tie most of the phrases together—usually a dominant impression. The last step is assembling the pertinent phrases in coherent order and applying a little polish to make the result reasonably like free verse.

Many schools have had great success with poetry writing through the efforts of poets who come into the classrooms to teach under a Poetry-in-the-Schools Program. Ardis Kimzey has written a delightful book, *To Defend a Form,* about her experiences at all grade levels.[12] The fresh ideas and the enthusiasm and spirit generated by poets in the classroom are all very contagious. By reputation, poets are generally very lively teachers, especially when they are in rooms filled with young people.

## ILLUSTRATING

Because a poem is highly compressed, a class often profits from expanding its meaning through illustration. The illustrations may be in words: examples of what the poet was saying, or experiences or scenes comparable to those the poet presented. Or they may be pictorial: photographs, drawings, or paintings supplied by both teacher and the class to assist visualization. Collages of pictures from magazines, sometimes with the poem as part of the collage, aid visualization. Mobiles also aid visualization because they can illustrate the meaning of a poem through concrete arrangement, motion, and location. Words and phrases can be arranged much as they are in some concrete poems, and parts of the mobile can also be shaped to contribute to a total impression. A poem about wind can be placed by an open window or by a fan where it will move; a poem about sunlight can be placed by a window where it will reflect light. Sometimes taking a poem out of its usual arrangement, making a ''visual'' poem of it by giving it a concrete form to illustrate its meaning, and then returning it to its original arrangement can help clarify meaning.

## PLAYING RECORDINGS

Numerous recordings of favorite poems are available, some of them made by the poets themselves. A recording may be played before or after the class has read a poem, both before and after, or during silent reading of the lines. Some research shows that following along with a good reading can help clarify meaning. Several commercial publishing houses have worthwhile recordings and will send descriptive literature.

## ENJOYING HUMOR

Shared laughter means shared enjoyment. A fairly large proportion of the poetry read should be light and amusing. Limericks, parodies, folk ballads, and some poems by Holmes, Field, Lear, Gilbert, Daly, and Nash are examples of appropriate light verse. Earlier in this chapter, we cited research indicating how much students in the upper elementary grades enjoy humorous poems. As students become older, their tastes will change somewhat, but the poem that makes them laugh will still rank very high in popularity.

## MEMORIZING

Memorization should be encouraged but not required. Memorization that is forced, as a requirement or as punishment, or is tied to "extra credit" is counterproductive. It works against all of the defensible reasons for reading poetry. Three observations on memorization: (1) If poetry is taught effectively, students will *want* to tuck away certain lines and brief passages. (2) Choral reading and dramatization tend to fix certain lines without the student's conscious effort. (3) If the teacher occasionally quotes a few lines pertinent to the topic being discussed, some students may be motivated to memorize some lines on their own.

## COLLECTING

Adolescents enjoy collecting stamps, coins, matchbooks, records—almost anything. Why not encourage them to collect poems? As individuals or as a class they may make notebooks of favorite poems. If they wish, they can make the notebook into a kind of private diary where they also write personal reactions to the poems or write down anything significant that the poetry brings to mind. In one small school, each senior class prepares a book of its favorites for presentation to the library; the books prepared by earlier classes are read and compared with what the present class is doing. In other schools, classes have collected poems on topics of particular interest to them: nature, city life, poetry to be sung, poems about America, heroism, problems especially crucial to adolescents, and so on. Collections kept in the school from year to year can also give teachers a better idea of students' changing tastes.

## CREATIVE READING

All reading is creative, but aesthetic reading, and especially that which involves poetry, demands high levels of creative response. Students who have understandably concluded that the only way to get meaning from a poem is to pick it apart in the classroom and then write an analytical paper about *the* meaning should be heartened by the fact that much modern poetry defies the search for a single meaning. Modern poets tend to think of their readers as cocreators, not simply as consumers. Also attractive to some students should be the fact that many modern poets avoid traditional form. In referring to modern poetry, one teacher has used the term *expressive form*. The only rule (a kind of nonrule) is that "the form of any work of art is not pre-established or pre-existent, but individual and unique, a function of the particular expressive needs of the content of the work."[13] Thus, Cummings can arrange his words and lines—and the spaces between and among them—in any way that allows the poem itself to emerge. If he wishes, as in "Buffalo Bill's defunct," he can place one word on a line or telescope several into one unbroken line of writing or print. The acid-sharp image conveyed by the "exact" word has taken the place of didacticism and generalization. The poet also exercises the freedom to surprise or shock the reader purposely by violating conventions of left-to-right progression, spacing, rhyme, rhythm, topic, capitalization, punctuation, metaphor, and so on.

But such apparent radicalism in poetry should not imply that "anything goes" when students respond to a poem. Each unexpected thing about a poem should be examined in light of what it contributes to understanding the poem as a whole. To do this with some modern poems, a reader does indeed have to be a cocreator.

Some of these methods of employing the personal approach will work better than others in your classes. You may wish to give each of them a brief trial and thereafter emphasize the ones that bring the best results. The last one, creative reading, is enhanced by all of the others.

## THE VALUE-SEEKING APPROACH

With the value-seeking approach, teacher and class find and discuss the viewpoint toward life in the poem. They may or may not accept that viewpoint. "Poetry does not demand our belief; it invites us to experience," as Miller and Slote say. The students examine the viewpoint from several sides, compare it with other viewpoints, and evaluate it in light of their own experience. Several poems will be discussed to exemplify this approach.

In "Miracles," Whitman calls all commonplace things "miracles"—houses, bees, fish, rocks, food, companionship, the new moon. Is he right? A "miracle" is defined as a wonderful thing. What is wonderful about a honeybee? About a rock? How does Whitman's definition of "miracles" differ from yours? What are some things that you consider miracles?

"Growing Up" by Keith Wilson concerns a boy who, while hunting with his father, intentionally misses a jackrabbit and encounters silence from the father "who counted misses as weaknesses" and "who would've been shamed by a son who couldn't kill." The situation is told in the first person from the boy's point of view. Whether students in the class hunt or not, this poem presents opportunities to share points of view. It also raises questions about respect for life. In "Traveling Through the Dark" by William Stafford, a motorist came upon a dead deer by the side of the road and discovered that "her side was warm; her fawn lay there waiting, alive, still, never to be born." The motorist "hesitated" and "thought hard for us all" before pushing the deer over an embankment. What thought made the motorist hesitate before rolling the deer into the canyon? What would your thought be? Are these deaths simply unfortunate? In "Death of a Dog" by Babette Deutsch, why does the poet say "A dog's death is a death men do not praise"? In "The Grey Squirrel" by Humbert Wolfe, of what significance is the fact that the squirrel was shot by a Christian? In "Hurt Hawks," why does Robinson Jeffers say, "I'd sooner, except the penalties, kill a man than a hawk"? What "gift" did he give the hawk in killing him? Would you take the same action? Would you do it for the same reason?

Frost's "Mending Wall" has been taught as an argument between an internationalist and an isolationist, with the latter having the last word. Such an interpretation is not necessarily farfetched, because one of the pleasures of poetry is that it can be given wide application. There is danger, however, in saying that Frost *intended* to convey any such idea, a danger of reading into a poem something that was not written into it. To apply the thought of a poem to something outside is one thing, but to say that the "something outside" is really inside is perverting the poem. Frost merely says that two neighbors, of unlike temperaments, each spring mend the stone wall between their fields; one is opposed to the mending because he sees no need for walls; but the other, moving in the darkness of time-worn beliefs, insists that "Good fences make good neighbors."

Without referring to international implications at all, a class can ponder the questions of why the two men were different, whether it is true that good fences make good neighbors, what kinds of fences we put up between ourselves besides physical ones, and whether people still tend to repeat the ideas learned in their childhood. Then, if someone sees that fences between neighbors are like fences between nations, good, but it should not be said that the fences-between-nations idea is in the poem itself.

Stephen Crane's short poem "I Saw a Man" is a good introduction to symbolism:

> I saw a man pursuing the horizon;
> Round and round they sped.
> I was disturbed at this;
> I accosted the man.
> "It is futile," I said,
> "You can never"—
> "You lie," he cried,
> And ran on.

A hint from the teacher will give the key that the horizon symbolizes ideals. The discussion then may center upon whether it is futile and senseless to pursue ideals that can never be reached. Who is right, the speaker or the pursuer of the horizon? What have people gained from seeking the ideal means of transportation, the ideal means of communication, the ideal form of government? Who is more likely to leave "footprints on the sands of time"—the one who says "You can't" or the one who says "I can try"?

The mother in Langston Hughes's "Mother to Son" tells her son,

> Life for me ain't been no crystal stair . . .
> But all the time
> I'se been a-climbin' on.

One boy, catching the significance at once, remarked, "My dad was climbing up the ladder of success but came to a place where a couple of rungs were missing, and he fell through and had to start all over." Class discussion may profitably expand the metaphors. What are the tacks, splinters, boards torn up, and bare places in life's stairway? Does everybody find them? Is life for anyone a crystal stair? Would crystal stairs become tiresome after a while?

Some teachers believe that a frontal attack in teaching values is necessary. Helen C. Lodge gives some reasons for this stance:

> *A theory of teaching explicitly for values, focusing on clarification of values, is receiving increasing attention because it focuses thinking on a central need of the decades ahead—the need to involve students in a study of their values as guides to action through examining dilemmas that all individuals face, making choices, and looking at moral consequences. Students coping with these dilemmas and their consequences must commit themselves, must look at consequences of choices made, and thus must look at themselves.*[14]

Use of the value-seeking approach, then, gives opportunity to explore authors' opinions, to elaborate upon them, and to agree or take issue with them. It is an approach useful in teaching students to think clearly and in developing their philosophies of life.

## THE COGNITIVE APPROACH

A teacher once pointed out some of the vocabulary difficulties that students encounter in Milton's minor poems. *Cloister* they confuse with *cluster, furrow* with *furrier* or *burrow, dame* with *Dane* or *dam, hamlet* with *hammock,* and *haycock* with "a bird that lives in the hay." Such students may read "The upland hamlets will invite" and get a mental picture of someone being lured by a slanting hammock; "the tanned haycock" is a sunburned bird; and "the studious cloister's pale" is a cluster of pale, overworked students. It is almost beyond the imagination to guess how students may interpret "sable stole of cypress lawn," "daisies pied," "country messes," and "Jonson's learned sock."

Some of the word substitutions may have something to do with the student's expectations while moving ahead in reading. The student anticipates the meaning correctly or incorrectly and substitutes a word to fit into what is anticipated. Rosenblatt ponders this possibility but points out that research on miscue analysis by Kenneth S. Goodman and Yetta Goodman applies to informative material, not to poetry, and that with respect to aesthetic reading "The notion of 'comprehension' changes."[15] Obviously, here is an interesting area for research.

Beside the traps of vocabulary lie the pits of allusion. In the first 20 lines of "L'Allegro" are at least 10 allusions that will mean little or nothing to the average high school senior—words like *Cerberus, Stygian,* and so on.

Morasses of sentence structure also abound. One example will suffice:

Straight mine eye hath caught new pleasures,
Whilst the landskip round it measures.

Even though a student knows that *straight* means "straightway" or "at once," *whilst* means "while," *landskip* means "landscape," and *measures* means "examines," the couplet is still unintelligible unless the student also knows that *it* refers to "eye" and is the subject of the clause. The student who does not realize this interprets the second line to mean that the landscape is examining something; the one who does realize it can see that the couplet means, "Immediately my eye has seen new pleasures while it examines the surrounding landscape."

Although Milton's poems set more toils for the unwary than do most others taught in high school, similar perils lurk in many non-Miltonic poems. Sometimes textbook annotations suffice to clear the way; textbook editors have become more and more helpful during the twentieth century. But, even with the annotations, some students will continue to misinterpret unless the class is guided by a capable and conscientious teacher.

You will recall that in describing the cognitive approach to fiction and drama we described the paraphrastic method in some detail. With poetry, as with fiction and drama, the paraphrastic method is employed to prevent gross misinterpretations. It is not a lively method, but it does have value in clarifying meaning. Often it may be used as a preliminary to some other approach. Students must understand the words and the sentences in "My Last Duchess," for instance, before they can discuss it as a social document.

Miller and Slote in *The Dimensions of Poetry* point out that a poem may be summarized, paraphrased, or explicated, while they emphasize that the result of any one of these processes is by no means the same as the poem itself. A summary "captures and preserves only the bare substance of what is said in the poem, its non-poetic part." They illustrate with a summary of this poem by Emily Dickinson:

The Bustle in a House
The Morning after Death

Is solemnest of industries
Enacted upon Earth,—

The Sweeping up the Heart,
And putting Love away
We shall not want to use again
Until Eternity.[16]

Their summary, "One of the most difficult of all tasks in life is the emotional adjustment following the loss through death of someone close," is, they say, 'like the bruised rind of an orange from which all the golden juices have been squeezed." A paraphrase, in contrast, is longer, follows the original closely, and attempts to convey the full meaning: "On the day after the death of a beloved relative, the soberest activity in the home (the soberest, in fact, in the world) is the disposition of the affections which have lost their object and which will be superfluous until a spiritual reunion outside time is effected." Such a paraphrase is "like a black-and-white photograph of a brilliant masterpiece of art."

An explication, however, is less inclusive than either a summary or a paraphrase. It attempts to answer the hard questions about meaning, to show relationships among parts not obviously related. In the Dickinson poem, for example, why is the word *industries* used? Why *enacted*? How does one sweep up the heart? How can love be put away?

A series of penetrating questions, requiring close reading and close thinking, may bring the same results as a paraphrase. Sister Mary de Lourdes Muench, R.D.C., illustrates such questions in her article "Taking the Duchess off the Wall."[17]

The point of all this, the point that the teacher must always remember in paraphrasing, summarizing, or explicating, is that the poem is an entity that cannot be replaced by something else. The paraphrastic method (broadly enough defined to include summary and explication) may help to make clear, but the result must not be said to equal the poem itself.


## THE ANALYTICAL APPROACH

Just how much knowledge of poetic theory and terminology should be taught to high school students has long been a moot question. Is the architecture of the poem the important thing, or is it only incidental to something more important— the meaning and implications? Can meaning and implications be adequately taught if there is no understanding of the architecture? Some teachers expose students to every literary term that they themselves know, hoping that at least a few will stick; at the other extreme are a smaller number of teachers who call a poem a "story" and point out none of its distinguishing characteristics. And, in

THE TEACHING OF HIGH SCHOOL ENGLISH

the middle, the majority of teachers introduce students to the poetical theory and terminology that seem most valuable to them.

Here the majority is probably right. The student must know something about poetic architecture in order to understand and appreciate, just as anyone who knows something about naves, transepts, arches, and keystones can better appreciate the beauty of a cathedral. But minute metrical analysis is more the province of the professional poet or scholar than it is of the high school student who may soon be driving a truck or working in a laundry.

It is the whole poem that demands attention. Diction, figures of speech and other devices, sentence structure, and verse form are of significance only because of what they contribute to the whole. A "good" poem represents a happy blend of the thought and the poetic devices. The wrong device—inappropriate verse form, for instance, or an unwisely chosen simile—may spoil a poem. If Homer sometimes nodded, his descendants often do. Shelley, for example, wrote a serious poem about death, beginning,

> Death is here and death is there;
> Death is busy everywhere.

It is a bad poem because the meter does not fit the thought; if the subject were a rambling wreck from Georgia Tech, the verse form would be more appropriate and the poem might be better. Wordsworth's occasional infelicities are notorious. In a poem about the curse laid upon a young man by a poverty-stricken old woman—a theme that Coleridge might have handled with consummate skill—Wordsworth begins,

> Oh! what's the matter? what's the matter?
> What is't that ails young Harry Gill?
> That evermore his teeth they chatter,
> Chatter, chatter, chatter still!

The prosaic "what's the matter?" is hardly fitting in a serious poem about a curse; the feminine rhyme, as in *matter* and *chatter,* gives a humorous effect of the sort that Byron often intentionally attained and that we associate with Ogden Nash in our day; the repetition of *chatter* belongs to Tennyson's "Brook" but is out of place here; and the verse form no more fits the subject than does that of Shelley's poem on death.

The point of these negative observations is that a teacher ought to teach that good poets sometimes write bad poems and that a good poem is a unit in which all elements are in harmony. The metrical form, the similes, and so on, are not merely surface decoration; they are intrinsic. A poet does not write a rough draft of a poem and then say, "I'll add a few similes to increase the attractiveness."

The similes are, instead, natural outgrowths of the idea or emotion that the poet is expressing. Neither does a true poet choose a particular word because it is euphonious or because it is the first one that comes to mind; the poet selects it because it is the one that best reveals the meaning and best conveys the mood. This observation is not limited to traditional poetry. A modern poem, one that treats form as a part of creative expression, has a central purpose if it is a good poem, and everything about its framework, no matter how surprising, should be examined in light of how effectively it contributes to that purpose. It may not find its artistic balance in traditional structure, but it will have artistic tension, and it will play parts against parts, words against words, to express itself as an artistic whole.

In using the analytical approach, then, one does not pick to pieces, but one notes the contribution of each piece to the whole pattern. Students learn definitions of technical terms almost incidentally through class discussions. A student who has memorized the words ''A metaphor is a figure of speech in which a term is applied to something to which it is not literally applicable'' does not necessarily know what a metaphor is, but the student who has often talked about such expressions as ''The wind was a torrent of darkness'' and ''The fog comes on little cat feet'' probably does. This latter student has examined the contribution of metaphors to individual poems, has understood the work that they do, and has recognized that they are implied comparisons. As a result, the student's experience with poetry has probably been much happier than that of another who was told to memorize dry definitions, or the one who was told to find and copy 50 metaphors from *Julius Caesar,* or the one who was left with the impression that poets sprinkle metaphors over their poems as an employee at Dairy Queen sprinkles nuts over a sundae.

In a book that for decades has been read by British teachers of English, *English for the English,*[18] George Sampson warns against breaking into the mood of a poem by analyzing its parts:

> *What pleasure should we get from a performance of the C minor symphony if the conductor stopped the orchestra at every occurrence of the main theme to expatiate upon the wonderful significance with which Beethoven can invest a simple rhythmic phrase, or from a performance of the B minor mass if a choir were silenced while someone explained the harmonic effects that make the hushed close of the* Crucifixus *such a wonderful moment? It is delightful to have these beauties of musical language pointed out to us; but not while we are on the emotional plane of the performance.*

If Sampson is right, a three-stage study of many poems would seem desirable. The first stage would involve one or two readings (at least one aloud) for the pleasure the poem can afford. Then would come any necessary paraphrasing, possibly a discussion of historical background, possibly some discussion of the author's purpose or point of view, and some analysis of the poetic techniques employed. After that, through one or two additional readings, the poem would be reassembled, so to speak; these new readings, with the light added by the second stage, should result in greater enjoyment than the first ones.

Comparing of authors' techniques is also often useful in analysis. For example, Linda J. Clifton tells of her success in having her students compare the Simon and Garfunkel song ''Richard Cory'' with E. A. Robinson's poem.[19]

To further clarify the importance of studying the architecture of a poem, in the second stage of the process just described, let us briefly consider several aspects of the ''Rime of the Ancient Mariner.''

In the first place, the basic verse form used by Coleridge is the ballad stanza. For this poem, the ballad stanza is appropriate because the subject matter is akin to that of the Middle English ballads, which often stressed the supernatural. (It is probable that this stanza was widely used in the late medieval times because it is versatile and because it is an easy form to compose, to learn, and to sing.) Sometimes, though, Coleridge departed from the pattern and included stanzas of five, six, or seven lines. The reason is that the longer stanzas prevent the monotony which might result from constant employment of the ballad stanza in a lengthy poem.

The archaic diction of Coleridge's poem also contributes to the total effect. The ship leaves an unnamed country; the story takes place at an indefinite, unknown time. The language, therefore, should not suggest the here and now, but instead a vague ''there'' and an indefinite ''then.'' Words such as *stoppeth, eftsoons, swound,* and *gramercy* remove the poem from 1798 and carry the reader backward two centuries, three centuries, or more.

The frequent repetition is deliberate and appropriate. You recall that when the ship was becalmed,

> There passed a weary time. Each throat
> Was parched, and glazed each eye.
> A weary time! a weary time!
> How glazed each weary eye.

Coleridge wanted to stress the weariness. How could it be better stressed than by repeating the word *weary?* Or how could the Mariner's loneliness be better emphasized than in

> Alone, alone, all, all alone,
> Alone on a wide wide sea!

Coleridge used alliteration for an equally specific purpose. As the south wind pushed the ship rapidly along,

TEACHING POETRY AND NONFICTION

225

The fair breeze blew, the white foam flew,
The furrow followed free.

The alliteration is more than "pretty"; it serves to hasten the line, to accentuate the speed of the ship. Consonantal alliteration often does this, whereas vocal alliteration (as in "Alone, alone, all all alone") tends to make a line move more slowly.

Personification—the sun as *he,* the moon as *she,* the storm blast as *tyrannous,* Death and Life-in-Death, the articulate spirits of the sea, and so on—is more appropriate in this poem than in most. The setting is a vague period reminiscent of the Dark Ages, when many people believed that the physical forces of the world were conscious beings, often hostile to humans. Moreover, it is human nature to employ a sort of reverse empathy and transfer our feelings to inanimate things; without thinking, we employ figurative expressions like "biting wind," "cruel sea," and "relentless sun." Shipwrecked persons have been known to curse the sea as if it had plotted against them; travelers on a desert have looked upon the sun as a personal and implacable enemy. Coleridge's use of personification, then, is intrinsic in the situation he describes.

The similes and metaphors serve to clarify, to picture, to make real the unreal. "Mast-high" and "as green as emerald" show us the ice; the seamen's hailing of the albatross "as if it had been a Christian soul" demonstrates how happy the men were to see any living thing but suggests also the mysterious power of the albatross and the cruelty of killing it; "as idle as a painted ship upon a painted ocean" dramatizes the ship's complete lack of movement. Hardly can a more ghastly picture than that of Life-in-Death be imagined; yet the picture is composed largely of figures of speech:

Her lips were red, her looks were free,
Her locks were yellow as gold:
Her skin was white as leprosy,
The Night-mare Life-in-Death was she,
Who thicks man's blood with cold.

In teaching "The Ancient Mariner," then, or any other poem in which it seems desirable to refer to poetic devices, one should help students understand the appropriateness of the meter, diction, and figures. Sometimes it is wise to discuss the organization of the whole poem, how each part fits, why each part is where it is. If students can be led to regard a poem as a unit to which each part contributes, their appreciation will be considerably increased.

In an extraordinarily useful article,[20] Howard Creed says, "The framework is significant: the guest, next of kin to the bridegroom, is on his way to celebrate a ceremony that fuses two people into one; but he is stopped to be taught that there is a more universal unity than that of an isolated marriage, that all the world is one." In discussing imagery, Creed states,

> *I see no reason why an alert class, after being reminded that the Romantic imagination works best by moonlight, shouldn't be able to discover for itself which events in the poem happen under the moon, which under the sun, and whether or not any particular pattern of moon-sun imagery seems to be used. A simpler analysis, and one easily fitted into the fusion of the natural and the supernatural, can be made of the sequence of the vivid images as the voyage progresses: the natural images of the harbour (kirk, hill, lighthouse) giving way to the supernatural images of the polar sea (the skeleton ship, for instance) and then returning (lighthouse, hill, kirk).*

Perhaps no two teachers would completely agree concerning which technical terms ought to be introduced during the study of poetry. It would seem, though, that any technical term that is innate to the poem being discussed is appropriate, but that no term should be dragged in simply because the teacher happens to know it. Further, it seems reasonable to assume that a simile or an anapaestic foot is not important in itself, but attains significance only because of the part it plays in the structure of the poem.

In other words, no teacher should do what one teacher actually did: She could never remember the distinction between metonymy and synecdoche but knew that both were figures of speech. Therefore, once each year she relearned their definitions and required her class to memorize them!

The analytical approach (which could as well be named the synthesizing approach) has merit when it is used to help students understand clearly how a poem is constructed, and what function each constituent part performs. But if it becomes merely a process of disassembly, it is almost valueless. As a participant in the Dartmouth Conference said, "The dryness of schematic analysis of imagery, symbols, myth, structural relation, *et al.*, should be avoided passionately at school and often in college. It is literature, not literary criticism, which is the subject. It is vividly plain that it is much easier to teach literary criticism than to teach literature, just as it is much easier to teach children to write according to abstract model of correctness than it is to teach them to use their own voices."[21]

## NONFICTION

Traditionally, nonfiction has played a very weak role in high-school English programs. Anthologies for the ninth and tenth grades have sometimes included biographies and essays as part of a general introduction to various genres, but for many students this has been their only study of nonfiction. With the increasing interest in elective courses in the 1960s, especially ones centering on socio-psychological issues, nonfiction increased in popularity and use. A point made by Robert Carlsen and others is that knowledge is exploding so rapidly in our time that English teachers can no longer ignore students' demands to be informed through nonfiction.[22] Another observation is that teachers seem not to be making such sharp distinctions between fiction and nonfiction, possibly because some of the traditional distinctions are disappearing anyway. In *Literature for Young Adults,* Kenneth L. Donelson and Alleen Pace Nilsen report that in a survey asking 300 teachers to recommend novels, 20 books listed are nonfiction. Included were Peter Mass' *Serpico,* Maya Angelou's *I Know Why the Caged Bird Sings,* Dee Brown's *Bury My Heart at Wounded Knee,* Claude Brown's *Manchild in the Promised Land,* Vincent Bugliosi and Curt Gentry's *Helter Skelter,* and even Henry David Thoreau's *Walden* and Lorrain Hansberry's *A Raisin in the Sun.*

It is difficult to understand why Thoreau's *Walden* and Hansberry's play found their way into the list. Donelson and Nilsen suppose, perhaps somewhat charitably, that the "emotional appeal" of the 20 books caused the teachers to think of them as fiction.

Fictional biographies, autobiographies, chronicles, memoirs, diaries, and letters are not new to literature, but recent books have caused authors and critics to invent such terms as "nonfiction novel," "creative nonfiction," "literary journalism," and "journalistic fiction." Truman Capote's *In Cold Blood* is just one book among many that have inspired this terminology. In commenting on this recent trend to blend fiction and nonfiction, Donelson and Nilsen recall that in his acceptance speech for the best novel of 1975 before the National Book Critics Circle, E. L. Doctorow said, "There is no more fiction or nonfiction—only narrative."[23]

Writing in the *English Journal,* Deborah Rosen describes a course in nonfiction that she has taught at Pompano Beach Senior High School in Florida. She does make distinctions between fiction and nonfiction, as her objectives indicate: "To study writing techniques used in nonfiction and compare and contrast those techniques to those used in fiction; to explore author's point of view and objectivity toward his subject; to discuss and read different subgenres in nonfiction (such as the biography, the autobiography, social criticism); and to examine current nonfiction to familiarize the student with American culture as prominent writers perceive it."[24]

This course also opens the way for all six approaches discussed earlier in this chapter. Studying writing techniques would seem to involve the analytical approach to some extent; exploring the author's point of view gets into the cognitive; reading books as social criticism involves the sociopsychological; considering aspects of American culture could draw upon the historical approach, especially if changes in attitudes are discussed; examining values obviously involves culture and social criticism. By using some of the activities mentioned

228                                      THE TEACHING OF HIGH SCHOOL ENGLISH

earlier with the personal approach, any teacher could encourage personal responses and further personal growth.

The following breakdown of subgenres and representative selections illustrates the wide scope of the course and its possible appeal: Political nonfiction—*Boss, All The President's Men, The Selling of the President, 1960;* Biographical nonfiction—*Death Be Not Proud, Serpico, Zelda;* Autobiographical nonfiction—*Alive, Black Boy, Cavett, Up the Down Staircase, The Water Is Wide;* Social criticism—*The American Way of Death, Future Shock, Silent Spring;* Documentary—*Black Like Me, Hiroshima, In Cold Blood.* Obviously other nonfiction books would be good substitutes under any of these categories.

In addition to using modern works such as those just mentioned, teachers should expose students to a number of the classics. In the first place, the classics often have historical significance and thus help us to understand ourselves by clarifying our backgrounds. Second, they usually possess high literary merit. Third (to adduce an old argument), everyone should have an opportunity to share knowledge of our common cultural heritage—to know something about the best that has been thought and said. Fourth, superior students, at least, may use the classics as Matthew Arnold advised: as "touchstones" by means of which other pieces of writing may be judged.

Biographies from earlier periods clearly lend themselves to the historical approach, as do certain essays such as the *Tatler* and *Spectator* papers. Steele and Addison also provide splendid material for the sociopsychological approach, because they along with Goldsmith, humanize the eighteenth century perhaps more than do any other writers. Essays such as Lamb's "Dissertation upon Roast Pig," and travel accounts such as Stevenson's *Travels with a Donkey* or some of Harry Franck's *Vagabonding* stories lend themselves to the personal approach. Almost any personal essay or biography may justify occasional use of the value-seeking approach. Frances Bacon, Benjamin Franklin, and possibly Thomas Huxley and a few others whose writings are sometimes taught in high school need to have their essays partially paraphrased before students can do much else with them. The analytical approach may be employed in the comparison of styles and techniques of various early nonfiction writers; the personal essay, for example, may be used to demonstrate that the typical pattern is the reporting of observation and then the reporting of speculation upon what was observed.

Nonfiction selections, both new and old, make useful contributions to many units and courses. A review of high school English curriculum guides from school systems in many states will reveal that nonfiction plays a strong supporting role. It provides useful historical and mythological backgrounds, as well as information about authors and their works. Humanities units are strengthened by numerous books about art, music, science, theology, anthropology, and other fields. Units taking a sociopsychological approach rely upon books on government, law, energy, psychology, as well as upon newspapers, magazines, and government documents and reports. Units with special topics such as Sports in Literature, Women in Literature, and Black Literature frequently use biography, journalism, and social criticism. A unit on Literature of the American West could draw upon "a number of magazines that focus on the history of the American West: *Pioneer West, Frontier Times, True West, Real West, True Frontier, Western Frontier,* and *Old West,* with articles ranging from the history of the shootout at the OK corral to a listing of Indian treaties broken by U.S. soldiers."[25] Units and courses taking other historical approaches can find support in materials from historical societies, museums, nearby colleges and universities, local libraries (microfilm copies of old newspapers), records in city halls and county and state buildings, state historical publications, the U.S. Government Printing Office, and many other resources that are free or inexpensive. Some units on science fiction make liberal use of science materials for verification and comparison. It is through such electives, short courses, and units that most students are studying nonfiction in high schools today.

The daily newspaper, easily the most readily available nonfiction reading material, is overlooked by many English teachers. Units on newspaper reading are not new to high school English, but their scope has been fairly narrow. Generally the aim is to acquaint students with the different types of reading that a newspaper requires, and then to use newspapers as a high-interest, low-difficulty source for building basic reading skills. In some cases, teachers have used the variety in newspapers and among newspapers to teach students how to discriminate between acceptable journalism and trash.

The possibilities are almost unlimited. Stephen Judy of Michigan State University speaks about constructing "an entire curriculum based on little more than the Sunday *New York Times,* with its near-universal interest in news, travel, anthropology, books, the fine arts, music, sports, gardening, history, hobbies, and world issues."[26] Ronald E. Dehnke and Ann W. Ely recommend using the newspaper to help "bridge the gap between schoolwork and life." For example, in dealing with the concept of reality, they suggest an interesting way of studying literature and newspapers together. Their procedure is as follows:

1. *To "hook" the kids (the personal realm), ask them:*
   *—What section of the newspaper do you look at first?*
   *—Is that section about today's events? The here and now?*
   *—Does the newspaper deal with reality?*
2. *To collect and* **analyze** *data the class would have to consider first whether the newspaper and literature deal with the same events. Thus: Have you ever read a poem, short story, or novel about any of the events found in today's paper? At this point, group the class by interest or topic and have each group read a given piece of literature. It could be something like this:*

THE TEACHING OF HIGH SCHOOL ENGLISH

*A. The busing controversy and racial prejudice—read* To Kill a Mockingbird.

*B. Any traffic fatality—read Karl Shapiro's poem, "Auto Wreck."*

*C. War, and protest—read* Sons *by Evan Hunter.*

3. *Pursuing this "reality" theme the class then compares the reality in litera-ture selections with that in the newspaper. By so doing students handle the* **categorizing** *step.*

*—How does the treatment of reality in your novel, poem or play compare with the treatment of reality in the newspaper?*

*—Is one more real than the other?*

*—What are newspaper concerns?*

*—What are literature concerns?*

4. *From these conclusions* **generalize:**

*—The newspaper handles reality in the following ways:*

*—Literature handles reality in the following ways:*

*—They compare and contrast in the following ways:*

5. *Now to* **verify** *the generalizations, each student may independently choose a novel, poem, short story, etc., and find a matching issue or event in the newspaper. Does each deal with reality in any of the ways you have generalized? Or is it a new way? And off they go on a brand new inquiry.*[27]

Drawing upon their experience with the Newspaper-in-the-Classroom project sponsored by the *Indianapolis Star* and *Indianapolis News,* Dehnke and Ely offer many other useful ideas, including comparing newspapers and literature in their treatments of politics and social institutions (family, church, law). These ideas and some outlined in their approach to the theme of reality suggest the usefulness of newspapers with almost every approach to literature discussed in this methods book.

To a large degree, the success of newspaper programs in English classes is due to support by the American Newspaper Publishers Association Foundation and cooperating newspapers around the country. If your local newspaper has no consultant to work with classroom programs, you can at least subscribe to ANPA newsletters and inquire about other publications. One recent issue of the newslet-ter "Teaching with Newspapers" contains suggestions on studying the style and organization of news stories; identifying symbolism in editorial cartoons and relating them to symbolism in literature; studying unfamiliar words found in art, music, and so on (helpful in humanities courses); studying stereotyping by loaded words and slanted context; and acquainting students with the cultural, aesthetic, environmental, and tourist attractions of their own community. The ANPA Foundation Bibliography, *Newspaper in Education Publications* (1980), contains these sources: "Newspaper in the Classroom—High School English Teacher's Guide (1974), Evansville Printing Corporation, Evansville, Indiana;

"The Newspaper in Secondary English and Language Arts" (1977), *Minneapolis Star and Tribune;* "The Newspaper in the Classroom: Teaching Aids for Secondary Schools/English" (1970), Copley Newspapers, La Jolla, California.

A 1977 study has revealed that media and reading specialists are not the best judges of why many students show little or no interest in reading newspapers. The specialists blamed TV and other visual media, as well as deficient reading skills, for this lack of interest. The students ranked the visual media toward the bottom of their list, however, and didn't mention reading problems at all. The young people ranked adult bias as their greatest reason for loss of interest. The 150 young people involved in this study apparently viewed newspapers as written by middle-aged writers for middle-aged readers, as too rational, and as a steady diet of "establishment-oriented" thinking.[28]

English teachers may not be able to do much to change the middle-aged bias that some adolescents detect in their local newspapers, but they can help students to see that newspapers vary widely in stance. Students who may tend to think that all newspapers are the same can be helped to see that some are ultrasensational, others ultraconservative, and the majority in-between. We may or may not be able to agree precisely on the dividing line between good and bad periodicals, but the places where we draw our respective lines will probably not be far apart. Our students, however, may not have that critical knowledge unless we instill it in them. Because adults—somebody's former students—do not know or do not care, the sensationalizing newspapers and the most lurid of the cheap magazines flourish.

A partial solution is the teaching of a unit on newspapers and another unit, perhaps in a different year, on magazines. For this the sophomore and junior years appear most satisfactory, because students on these levels are better able to read a large variety of materials and judge them with more discrimination than are younger students. Some teachers, though, have successfully taught such units in the junior high school.

The usual procedure is to provide a number of newspapers or magazines, varying in quality from worst to best. By reading and by making detailed comparisons, students learn the strengths and the weaknesses of the various periodicals. It is unrealistic to expect to convert an entire class to a sincere respect for *The New York Times* and *Harper's,* but it is not unrealistic to expect to bring each student to a place somewhat above his or her original level. A student who comes to recognize distortion of facts, emphasis upon the trivial, and omission of significant news in an inferior newspaper, is more likely as an adult to purchase a fairly good newspaper. Similarly, a student who has come to realize that the lurid magazines are repetitious and inaccurate is likely to buy something a little better at the newsstand.

In one unit, the teacher asked each student to bring to class his or her favorite

THE TEACHING OF HIGH SCHOOL ENGLISH

newspaper. The class discussed the points that they believed intelligent people ought to know about newspapers and made notes from the "Canons of Journalism" as named in Edgar Dale's *How to Read a Newspaper:* responsibility, freedom of the press, independence, sincerity, truthfulness, accuracy, impartiality, fair play, and decency. The students evaluated the various newspapers in the light of these canons and compared them with *The New York Times* and *Christian Science Monitor.* They noted and deplored the dearth of "pitchers" and "jokes" and sports news in the latter two, but were impressed by the number of important national and international news stories that were omitted from the papers they usually read. The teacher says that, although she has no proof that any of the students became confirmed in wise newspaper reading habits, she does know that they began to have a new conception of the meaning of a newspaper and to consider newspapers critically.

Roberta Monteith recommends these objectives for newspaper study: (1) To show how language can be used to sway people. (2) To gain an understanding of the scope of a newspaper. (3) To learn to compare the treatment of news. (4) To become aware of slanted news. (5) To differentiate between lurid, limited, objective, and general news. (6) To judge the logic of editorials. (7) To read newspapers that have national recognition. (8) To interest students in reading some newspapers daily.[29]

A magazine unit may be handled in a similar manner. A creative variation, which brought satisfactory results when an Illinois teacher tried it with a group of sophomores, involves emphasis upon the advertising. Students are shown that most magazines are simply media for advertisers and that each advertiser aims at the estimated mental level and the interests of the readers. Nothing more clearly demonstrates the low caliber of some magazines than their advertisements; just as a person is known by the company he or she keeps, so a magazine is known by the advertisements it keeps. These sophomores quickly saw how gullible people would believe that they could "have a physique like mine in 90 days," "learn to throw your voice into a trunk," "play the piano in one month," "get a high school education in three months," "solve this easy puzzle and win $1,000." Because the sophomores did not want to be classified on such a low mental level, they agreed that these magazines were not for them.

Some teachers have planned units on travel books and modern biography as parallels to units on newspapers and magazines. "Round-the-world trips," with each student responsible for one of the countries on the itinerary, have proved popular, as have units on "The Lands of Our Ancestors," "Europe Today," "Europe Yesterday," "From Here to There in Fourteen Days," and so on. A Missouri class studied biographies of nineteenth- and twentieth-century personages; separate committees specialized on scientists and national leaders; each student prepared an interesting report on some one person; there was a "Guess Who" program with five carefully prepared clues concerning each biography;

students presented radio skits to dramatize highlights; and the class tried to find concerning these great men and women—"the source of their dynamic living" and "what they have discovered about life."

Some teachers, interested in the value-seeking approach, employ biographies in hopes that students will examine the ideas and values of people who have contributed significantly to humanity, and in the process will be helped to develop their own moral codes. Lois Taylor says that she emphasizes questions such as these: "What qualities have these people that make their lives remarkable? In what ways did they go along with the pattern of life set by their society? In what ways did they break away? Were they just different, or did they actually and actively oppose the society in which they lived? What difficulties and discouragements did they surmount? What goals did they set and how did they achieve them or change them? What standards do they reveal in their relationships to others?"[30]

No extended discussion of the use of the six approaches with nonfiction is necessary; as indicated in several places above, the teacher need only observe the principles already illustrated in considering fiction, drama, and poetry.

---

### IDEA BOX

SOME (POETIC?) TERMS

The 10 terms below are from a list of 34 created by Dick Calisch and his English staff at Elk Grove, Illinois, High School:

*Allegory.* A poem about crime and violence in the back streets.

*Denotation.* An explosive poem.

*Epistle.* Poem written on wall above latrine (see onomatapoeia)

*Free verse.* A book of poetry issued by teacher with no deposit required.

*Haiku.* A poem about a stoned dove.

*Idyll.* Poem written when one has nothing else to do.

*Ode.* A plagiarized poem that you intend to pay back.

*Pastoral.* Poem containing a sermon.

*Rhyme scheme.* A secret plot among poets to sell their works.

*Trochee.* Poem recited to ease a sore throat.[31]

"POETRY IN PERFORMANCE"

Jim Nagle of Danville, Illinois, Junior College begins with recordings by Randy Newman and Paul Simon, shows the similarity in structure between Bob Dylan's "A Hard Rain's a Gonna Fall" and the ballad "Lord Randal," and plays Judy

---

Collins singing Will Holt's musical rendering of William Butler Yeats' "The Song of Wandering Aengus." Oral presentations by two teachers from the college, and use of the readers theater approach with his students add interest. At the end of his article, Nagle lists the titles of 42 selections that he and two colleagues recommend for song and oral interpretation.[32]

## DRAMATIZING "RICHARD CORY"

Janie B. Yates describes several successful approaches to "Richard Cory" through oral interpretation and dramatization. After reading the poem the "wrong way" (monotone, distracting mannerisms, etc.), she said it from memory "to one of the students as if I were her very old grandmother. To a boy . . . as if I were his little daughter. To the whole class . . . as if I were a citizen of the town talking to a group of strangers." Next, she divided the class into four groups with these results: "Group one improvised the first lines of the poem by portraying Richard Cory walking proudly down the street smiling and nodding to the three townspeople who discussed, as they watched him, what a fine, rich, successful man he was. In group two, two boys improvised a scene in which Richard Cory confided to his friend a tragedy which had struck him. Group three showed Richard Cory walking home alone with his head down and his body sagging. In group four, three students portrayed townspeople the next morning discussing Richard Cory's suicide. At the end of the hour, I divided the students into groups of three, and I gave each group a poem to interpret as it saw fit."[33]

## "SELL-A-POET"

"In addition to the more formal approaches to poetry structure, figures of speech, and poets considered in group study," Nan Clausen's seventh and eighth grade classes "sell" poets. Each student selects a poet, memorizes two poems, and presents them to the class. "For visual appeals, they have produced films, animations, slides, photographs, posters, costumes, props, light machines, strobe lights, and more. For audio—tapes, cassettes, recorders, live choruses, and video tapes have been used. For tactile—live models such as pets or little brothers, three-dimensional models, flannel boards, etc. For olfactory—the spray scents have ranged from perfume to pine to Raid (for "Archie and Mehitabel"), and the food smells have been mouth watering."[34]

## SHOULD A POEM BE ANALYZED OR READ ALOUD?

Michael True, professor of English, Assumption College, and former chair of the NCTE Committee on Poets in the Schools, believes it necessary to read poems aloud. He says that all discussions of poetry are preparations for oral reading. "I have come to think, in fact, that time spent reading a poem aloud is much more important than 'analyzing' it, if there isn't time for both. I say that on the assumption that one of our goals as teachers of English is to have students love poetry. In conveying our own fascination for the sound and rhythm of language, we say over and over again, in every way we can, 'Never outgrow your appreciation and delight in the essential humanity of language.' "[35]

## "CHARACTER POEMS AND SHORT STORIES"

Aware of students' interest in characters in short stories, Stephen Graff of Monticello, New York, High School works character poems such as "Walter Simmons," "Elliott Hawkins," "Maud Muller," "Lochinvar," "The Ballad of William Sycamore," "The Highwayman," and "Richard Cory" into a story unit. Interest in short story characters carries over to characters in poems, even to their writing character poems of their own.[36]

## STATING THEMES

A comparison of two or more statements of the theme of a work may lead to understanding. One statement is accurate; the others flawed. For example, for Browning's "My Last Duchess," "Fra Pandolf captured the grace and beauty of my last Duchess; although I regret her death, I shall now be honored to have the Count's daughter marry me." "My last Duchess showed too little respect for me and was not formal enough with others; now, if the dowry is sufficient, I shall honor the Count's daughter with my hand."

## UNDERSTANDING METAPHOR

If you say, "He has two strikes against him" when you are not talking about baseball, or when you call a person a skunk, you are using metaphors and symbols in essentially the way that a poet does. Building on this idea, with several sports and several animals, Edward Hubert shows his students that they themselves use metaphors frequently.[37]

## PICTURES IN POETRY

Read to your junior high school students a short descriptive poem, and ask them to draw something that they "see" in it. If some of them say that they can't draw, let them write a word picture. A haiku or a poem by an "imagist" should provide good examples.

## POETS STRUGGLE FOR DEFINITIONS

Often poets attempt to sharpen our awareness of a word's meaning. Students may study some poems from this point of view. For example, how do Donne, Wordsworth, Millay, and Ransom define death differently? Students may also attempt their own metaphoric definitions.

## "ANALYZING A POEM FOR ORAL INTERPRETATION"

A student should go through several steps in preparing for oral interpretation. (1) Read the poem at least once to get a personal reaction to it (emotional appeal and meaning). (2) Read the poem aloud several times, listening for sound, tone color, harmony, etc. (3) Take notes as you classify the poem by type (narrative, lyric, etc.), determine its speaker and the poet's attitude, see figurative language, become aware of its sensory appeals, encounter unfamiliar words, see connotative and denotative values in key words, find motifs (words and ideas), and recognize the overall structure of the poem. (4) Explain in a few sentences how your analysis will aid oral interpretation. This process of discovering, reacting, anticipating, and organizing is a very beneficial prereading experience, and, if used regularly, should lead to significant improvement.[38]

## MORE ON POETRY AND MUSIC

1. You might devote an hour to a ballad party, with records or cassette tapes, class singing, and possibly the presentation of an original ballad or two.
2. Anna Haig, Bronxville, New York, recommends having students find music and a painting that express the same mood as some poem. The student names the mood, describes the painting briefly, copies a few bars of the music, and quotes from the poem. In Cheraw, South Carolina, students keep a ''poetry-picture'' scrapbook, with appropriate pictures to accompany poems or excerpts from poems.
3. ''I use the theory that the first poetry was sung and that great poetry has the same elements as great music. I show how poetry is set to music and what patterns of rhythm are most readily adapted to music. I show how parodies are written. I read 'Boots' by Kipling to show the accented syllables. I read a few lines that I have written.'' (Elizabeth B. Barton, Clanton, Ala.)
4. Harold P. Simonson, in Puyallup, Washington, spends a week playing records and reading related poetry. Some of his pairings include Tschaikovsky's ''None but the Lonely Heart'' with Wilde's ''Requiescat,'' Debussy's ''La Mer'' with Byron's apostrophe to the ocean in *Childe Harold*, Debussy's ''Clair de Lune'' with De la Mare's ''Silver,'' Grofé's ''Sunrise'' from the *Grand Canyon Suite* and Grieg's ''Sunrise'' from Peer Gynt with Dickinson's ''I'll Tell You How the Sun Rose'' and G. B. Hoover's ''Mountain Dawn.''[39]
5. Use a drum in the classroom to show the beat in poems with a marked rhythm. (Marguerite Chamberlain, Franklin, N.H.)

## JUNIOR HIGH STUDENTS DISCOVER POETRY

Eric W. Johnson's junior high students, in Germantown Friends School, arrive at these characteristics of poetry: (1) rhyme (not always) (2) rhythm (almost always)—meter (3) form—verses; rhyme and meter a part of form (4) emotion—expresses feeling usually (5) concentration—says a lot in a few words (6) figurative language—comparison.'' Johnson finds Robert Nathan's ''Dunkirk'' a good opener, follows it with W. R. Benét's ''Skater of Ghost Lake,'' then a group of poems with students assigned to discuss meaning, form, sound, feelings created, and memorable lines. Students also write limericks, couplets, and a poem each, and learn principles of oral reading.[40]

## ''POETRY FOR NINTH-GRADERS''

August Franza and his ninth graders asked these basic questions about poems studied: ''First of all, what is the 'sense' of a poem? What does the poem say? What does it tell us about? Secondly, what is the 'feeling' of the poem? What moods and emotions are conveyed to the reader? Thirdly, what is the 'theme' of the poem (if one can be determined)? What idea is the author trying to get across? What is the significance of the poem? Finally, what is the 'form' of the poem?... Then we asked general questions. Does the poem make us aware of something we did not know before? Does it make us 'see' more clearly commonplace things we have taken for granted? Does it help us understand the complexities of human behavior? Has it introduced a new thought, idea, or vision we have never before considered?''[41]

## POETRY AND CAREER EDUCATION

''Poets on Work,'' a thematic unit by Kay Kimbrough, includes these poems: William Blake, ''The Sword''; Robert Frost, ''Two Tramps in Mud Time,'' and ''The Tuft of Flowers''; Khalil Gibran, ''On Work''; Langston Hughes, ''Alabama Earth''; Fenton Johnson, ''Rulers: Philadelphia''; Carl Sandburg, ''God Is No Gentleman''; Walt Whitman, ''I Hear America Singing.'' While increasing their understanding of poetry, students discuss and write about points of view toward work found in the poems.[42]

## HAIKU FOR SCIENCE STUDENTS

''Haiku: Touching Nature Through Poetry'' is representative of the interest among some science teachers in using poetry to '' 'feel' the importance of issues'' in science. Robert L. Rowsey, a science teacher, invites students to share poems, sits outdoors with them while they ''read, sing, or recite the poems or songs they have chosen,'' introduces the haiku form, and encourages students to write original poems. What does this have to do with English teachers? Sometimes we wonder if some science students can be encouraged to read and write poems. Apparently they can when they can see the relationship between poetry and their major interests.[43]

## INTRODUCING POETRY

Maxine Crawford of Baker High School in Mobile, Alabama, has much variety in her 14 day poetry unit. First, she creates an atmosphere of excitement in her classroom with signs indicating ''The Poet's Corner,'' ''The Poetry Table,'' and the ''Poetry Wall.'' ''Macavity is coming'' and ''Have you been vaccinated against onomatopoeia?'' also catch attention. The schedule: *Day One*—Introduction (wall is for writing, table for browsing; read ''How to Eat a Poem'' by Eve Merriam, etc.); *Day Two*—Continue introduction; read sample narrative verse, ballad, lyric; Continue introductions with sonnet, light or humorous verse, limerick, modern verse (teacher and students read aloud); *Day Four*—Discuss some characteristics of poetry; *Day Five*—ballad day (sing, play guitar, use recordings); *Day Six*—Discuss figurative language in sample poems; *Day Seven*—Show filmstrip *Come to Your Senses* (Scholastic) and discuss imagery; *Day Eight*—Rhyme and Rhythm, with Eliot's ''Macavity: The Mystery Cat'' for choral reading; *Day Nine*—Nonsense day, with recordings and oral readings of poems by Carroll, Lear,

Lindsay, Nash, and Richards; *Day Ten*—Writing day (students write "one-liners" as contributions to class poem, and write unrhymed lyrics beginning with "I wish," "I would like," etc.); *Day Eleven*—Record and play back students' original poems, and explain haiku; *Day Twelve*—Write haiku from travel posters; *Day Thirteen*—Have a "poetry party" with students' poetry booklets, collages, oral readings, recordings, etc.; *Day Fourteen*—Rap day (students discuss their feelings about poetry, about the class, etc.). Evaluation is based upon poetry booklets (collected notes and examples), oral reading, participation in discussions and choral reading, and writing assignments (original verse and an essay on some aspect of poetry).[44]

## HELPS IN TEACHING SPECIFIC POETS

These articles (in the *English Journal* except where the designation CE for *College English* appears) provide insights useful in teaching some important poets:

*Matthew Arnold.* Friedrich, Gerhard, "A Teaching Approach to Poetry," Feb. 1960, 75. (Especially on "Dover Beach.")

*William Blake.* Cleckner, Robert, " 'The Lamb' and 'The Tiger': How Far with Blake?" Nov. 1962, 536.

*Robert Burns.* Fisher, Mary C., "Ayr Lines, Ceiling Unlimited," Jan. 1960, 39.

*John Ciardi.* Southworth, J. G., "The Poetry of John Ciardi," Dec. 1961, 583.

*S. T. Coleridge.* Owen, C. A., "Structure in 'The Ancient Mariner,' " Jan. 1962, 261.

*E. E. Cummings.* Ray, David, "The Irony of E. E. Cummings," CE, Jan. 1962, 282.

*T. S. Eliot.* Smith, Grover. Jr., "Getting Used to T. S. Eliot," Jan. 1960, 1.

*Lawrence Ferlinghetti.* Kent, Brother Edward, "Dare-Devil Poetics: Ferlinghetti's Definition of a Poet," Dec. 1970, 1243.

*John Keats.* Slote, Bernice, "Of Chapman's Homer and Other Books," CE, Jan. 1962, 256.

*Wilfred Owen.* Bartel, Roland, "Teaching Wilfred Owen's War Poems and the Bible," Jan. 1972, 36.

*Karl Shapiro.* Southworth, J. C., "The Poetry of Karl Shapiro," March 1962, 159.

## ANALYSES OF SPECIFIC POEMS

Published in the *English Journal,* all of the following articles except one appeared during the 1960s, a period when explication was popular:

Matthew Arnold, "Dover Beach," May 1965, 446.

W. H. Auden, "O What Is That Sound?" Dec. 1962, 656.

Elizabeth Bishop, "Jeronimo's Horse." March 1963, 221.

E. E. Cummings, "what if a much of a which of a wind," March 1966, 352.

Emily Dickinson, "If you were coming in the Fall," Sept. 1970, 771.

Richard Eberhart, "The Groundhog," April 1963, 229.

Robert Frost, "Carpe Diem," Feb. 1965, 135; "Neither Out Far Nor in Deep," March 1969, 214; "Nothing Gold Can Stay" and "Stopping by Woods," May 1966, 621 and 624.

W. W. Gibson, "The Ice-Cart," Jan. 1966, 98.

G. M. Hopkins, "God's Grandeur," April 1964, 285; "Spring and Fall," Nov. 1962, 584.

Robinson Jeffers, "Hurt Hawks," Sept. 1962, 439.

James W. Johnson, "The Creation," Nov. 1963, 643.

Marianne Moore, "The Monkeys," Jan. 1963, 65.

Wilfred Owen, "Disabled," Oct. 1962.

William Shakespeare, Sonnet 90, Sept. 1964, 459.

Karl Shapiro, "Auto Wreck," Nov. 1964, 630.

Wallace Stevens, "The Poems of Our Climate," Nov. 1965, 762.

May Swenson, "Cat and the Weather," Feb. 1966, 221.

Edward Thomas, "The Sign-Post," Sept. 1965, 568.

Richard Wilbur, "The Juggler," Dec. 1965, 879; "To an American Poet Just Dead," May 1963, 376.

W. B. Yeats, "Red Hanrahan's Song about Ireland," May 1965, 448.


THE NEW JOURNALISM: A UNIT APPROACH

John Hollowell of the University of Arizona describes a unit he has taught on the new journalism. Including reading nonfiction and criticism of it, and writing short pieces and a research paper, this unit uses these works as texts: Truman Capote, *In Cold Blood;* Norman Mailer, *St. George and the Godfather;* Tom Wolfe, *The Electric Kool-Acid Test;* Tom Wolfe and E. W. Johnson, eds. *The New Journalism.* Students also read excerpts from Mailer's *The Armies of the Night,* George Plimpton's *Paper Lion,* and McGinniss's *The Selling of the President,* as well as several short pieces. Students study techniques used by these modern writers in writing the personality sketch, presentation of self (writer becomes a character in the nonfiction novel), realism, political pieces, and selections on subcults in the society. Interesting comparisons are made between *The New York Times* story "Wealthy Farmer, 3 of Family Slain" and Capote's nonfiction novel *In Cold Blood,* and between the films *Crime and the Criminal* and *The Novel—The Nonfiction Novel: A Visit with Truman Capote* (both relating to *In Cold Blood*). One of the research paper assignments also seeks comparisons: "Write an extended comparison of a nonfiction novel and a traditional novel about the same subject." Mailer's *Armies of the Night* or *Miami and the Seige of Chicago* or Thompson's *Fear and Loathing on the Campaign Trail '72* may be compared with Robert Penn Warren's *All the*

*King's Men* or Tom Wicker's *Facing the Lions. In Cold Blood* may be compared with Dostoevski's *Crime and Punishment* or Dreiser's *An American Tragedy.*[45]

## WHY TEACH NONFICTION?

Non-fiction is real. As a stimulus and a model, it can help our composing assignments avoid academic insularity and be more in touch with contemporary writing. And a non-fiction text can be stretched over a whole semester's work, as the class pauses to consider theme, structure, syntax and character. Distinctive books . . . can be treated as contemporary literature, as applied rhetoric, or as provocative catalysts for discussions. They should also remind us that essay writing can be a powerful, creative force, capable of ennobling, interpreting and re-creating a panoply of experiences.[46]

## MYTHOLOGY IN MODERN LIFE

Mercury automobiles, Atlas tires, Jupiter and Thor missles, Venus pencils, and the like may help students to see that remains of Greek and Roman mythology still exist.

## WORKING NONFICTION INTO UNITS

Several recent units published by NCTE illustrate the possibilities of combining nonfiction with fiction, drama, and poetry to strengthen assignments and class activities. Velez H. Wilson's unit ''The Exodus Theme in Black American Literature'' includes Bob Gibson and Phil Pepe's ''No Way Out'' from *Ghetto to Glory* and Alex Haley's *Roots.*[47] Judy Mednick's unit ''Male⇄Female in Literature and the Media'' makes liberal use of biography and autobiography, as well as books like Julius Fast's *The Incompatibility of Men and Women and How to Overcome It,* Elizabeth Janeway's *Man's World,* and Margaret Mead's *Male and Female.* Also included is an activity asking students in male-female pairs to discuss the sex-role stereotyping in cartoons.[48] Helen Wood's unit ''A Moral Dilemma: Individual Conscience Versus Established Authority'' uses John F. Kennedy's *Profiles in Courage,* George Reason and Sam Patrick's *They Had a Dream,* Dickerson G. Lowes' *The Greek View of Life,* and William Harlan Hale's *Horizon Book of Ancient Greece* (both as background for *Antigone* and other selections).[49]

## NONFICTION SURVIVAL KITS

*Reading for Survival in Today's Society,* a publication in two volumes, contains directions and selections to help students develop competency in reading labels, printed directions, schedules, magazine facts, current events, newspaper classified information, weather reports, driver's handbook, signs, maps, travel information, dictionary, telephone directory, job application forms, bank information, city information, state government information, national government information, advertised specials, magazine consumer information, newspaper consumer information, job-related information, recreational information, apartment leases, home furnishings, automobile purchase information, insurance, bills, credit cards, coupons, order forms, postal service forms, food purchase, food preparation, and instruction manuals.[50] In light of the emphasis on basic competency in the 1980s, English teachers may be asked to work more informational material of this kind into their programs.

BIOGRAPHICAL PROFILE GUIDE

Although the following is from a list used in the social studies classroom, it can help students reading biography to prepare reports:

1. *Describe the person's physical appearance and tell how it influenced her/his self concept; furthermore, relate how others reacted to the person. . . .*
2. *Evaluate the formative years, three to twenty-one years of age, to ascertain if a particular person, group, or event was a determining factor in her/his personality. Explain what the influence was and the effect it had.*
3. *Characterize her/his temperament, attitudes, values, beliefs, and interests. These will add substance to the personality.*
4. *Look for habits, since they will provide clues to behavior patterns.*
5. *Report on any special talents or abilities the person had which made her/him outstanding.*
6. *Recount any unusual problems the individual faced and be sure to portray how the person handled the problems.*
7. *Evaluate any decisions rendered by the person which may have influenced her/his role in shaping the world.*
8. *Conclude . . . with a personal evaluation of that person's place in history based on her/his achievements.*[51]

# FOOTNOTES

1. Comments by Frost, Van Doren, Kennedy, and Ferlinghetti are from *Poet's Choice*, eds., Paul Engle and Joseph Langland. New York: Dell Publishing Co., Inc., 1962.
2. "Inside a Poem with the Poet," in *On Writing by Writers*, William West. Boston: Ginn and Company, 1966, p. 145.
3. In *Poet's Choice*.
4. "Inside a Poem with the Poet," p. 143.
5. *The Reader, the Text, the Poem: The Transactional Theory of the Literary Work*, Carbondale: Southern Illinois University Press, 1978, p. 12.
6. *Children's Poetry Preferences*, Urbana: NCTE, 1974, pp. 47–53.
7. "On Teaching Poetry," *English Journal* 66, Feb. 1977, p. 49.
8. "The Writer's Social Responsibility," in *On Writing by Writers*, p. 2.
9. In *Poet's Choice*.
10. *English Journal* 57, Oct. 1968.

11. "Inside Every Poem, There Is a Human Being Trying to Get Out," *English Education,* Spring 1971, p. 124.
12. New York: Teachers & Writers, 1977.
13. Richard Damashek, *Teaching Modern Literature: Poetry and Fiction,* Springfield: Illinois Office of Education, 1978, p. 1.
14. "Values in the English Curriculum," in *The Teaching of English:* The Seventy-Sixth Yearbook of the Society for the Study of Education, Part I, Chicago: University of Chicago Press, 1977, p. 126.
15. *The Reader, the Text, the Poem,* p. 63. See also footnote 8, p. 183.
16. Reprinted by permission of the publishers from Thomas H. Johnson, ed., *The Poems of Emily Dickinson,* Cambridge Mass.: The Belknap Press of Harvard University Press, copyright, 1955, by the President and Fellows of Harvard College.
17. *English Journal* 58, Feb. 1969.
18. London: Cambridge University Press, 1921.
19. "The Two Corys: A Sample of Inductive Teaching," *English Journal* 58, March 1969.
20. "The 'Rime of the Ancient Mariner': A Rereading," *English Journal* 49, Jan. 1960, p. 215.
21. Quoted in John Dixon, *Growth Through English,* Reading, England: National Association for the Teaching of English, 1967, p. 60.
22. G. Robert Carlsen, *Books and the Teenage Reader,* New York: Harper & Row, Publishers, 1980, p. 203.
23. Glenview, Illinois: Scott, Foresman and Company, 1980, p. 342.
24. "American Nonfiction," April 1976, p. 61.
25. Stephen N. Judy, *The ABCs of Literacy,* New York: Oxford University Press, 1980, p. 250.
26. Judy, p. 249.
27. "The Newspaper; Medium Rare," *English Journal* 64, May 1975, p. 45.
28. "Up-date NIE," Washington, D.C.: American Newspaper Publishers Association Foundation, Jan. 1978.
29. "Newspapers Aid in Teaching Logical Thinking," *English Journal* 55, March 1966, p. 348.
30. *Reading Improvement,* Spring 1965.
31. "A Glossary of Poetic Terms," *English Journal* 68, May 1979, pp. 45–46.
32. "Poetry in Performance: The Value of Song and Oral Interpretation in Teaching Literature," *Illinois English Bulletin* 67, Fall 1979, pp. 18–22.
33. "Oral Interpretation of Literature: A Success Story," *English Journal* Jan. 1980, p. 93.
34. "Sell-A-Poet," *English Journal* 67, Nov. 1978, p. 70.
35. "Teaching Poetry: Many Teachers Don't," *English Journal* 69, May 1980, p. 43.

36. In *Humanizing English: Do Not Fold, Spindle, or Mutilate,* Edward R. Fagan and Jean Vandell, eds., Urbana: NCTE, 1970, pp. 52–54.

37. "On the Teaching of Poetry," *English Journal* 54, April 1965, p. 334.

38. Excerpted from *Ideas for Teaching English in the Junior High and Middle School,* Candy Carter and Zora M. Rashkis, eds., Urbana: NCTE, 1980, p. 182.

39. "Music as an Approach to Poetry," *English Journal* 43, Jan. 1954, p. 19.

40. *English Journal* 50, Nov. 1961, p. 546.

41. *English Journal* 47, Dec. 1958, p. 575.

42. In *Thematic Units in Teaching English and the Humanities,* Sylvia Spann and Mary Beth Culp, eds., Urbana: NCTE, 1975, pp. 15–24.

43. Robert E. Rowsey, *The Science Teacher,* Nov. 1979, p. 36.

44. "How to Eat a Poem: An Introduction to Poetry," in *Thematic Units in Teaching English and the Humanities,* pp. 3–12.

45. "The New Journalism and the Student Voice," in *Thematic Units in Teaching English and the Humanities,* First Supplement, 1977, pp. 3–1.

46. John Clifford, "Distinctive Non-Fiction to Teach By," *English Journal* Dec. 1979, p. 73.

47. In *Thematic Units,* First Supplement, pp. 59–65.

48. In *Thematic Units,* First Supplement, pp. 45–53.

49. In *Thematic Units,* pp. 109–118.

50. Anne H. Adams, Anne Flowers, and Elsa E. Woods, Santa Monica, Cal.: Goodyear Publishing Company, Inc., 1978.

51. Walter G. Debrowski, "Character and Personality Profiles in the Classroom," *Social Education,* Oct. 1978, p. 533.

# 8

## AN ENGLISH LANGUAGE PROGRAM: PART 1

## HISTORICAL BACKGROUND

### THE THINNESS OF MUCH LANGUAGE TEACHING

Until 1950 or so, comparatively few persons had any clear vision of English-language teaching as anything more than grammar and usage, and even those two components of language study have always been confused. Only rarely would an *English Journal* article say something about the desirability of studying history of the English language or the use of the dictionary. After S. I. Hayakawa's *Language in Action* (1941) became a book club selection, an occasional teacher developed a unit or even a semester-long course in semantics. Almost no one mentioned dialects except to deplore them. Too many teachers thought of a dialect as "any language different from my own."

Before the 1950s most people had assumed that grammar was grammar, and did not imagine any kind of linguistic description that would differ markedly from the Latin-based one they had learned as children. Some scholars, however, had not been satisfied with that grammar and as early as the 1920s had been working on alternate descriptions. In the 1950s a flood of books and articles appeared extolling "structural linguistics," which emphasized the spoken rather than the written language, separated form from meaning in sentence analysis (e.g., by examining "sentences" such as "The wolders adeled a tadful poggy"), showed that English sentences follow only a few basic patterns (illustrated, for instance, in a highly successful textbook, *Patterns of English,* by Paul Roberts, in 1956), and argued that the function of grammar and grammarians is only to describe the language as they find it, not to attempt to correct it.

Structural linguistics converted many teachers, was ignored by more, and

245

simply confused some experienced teachers not flexible enough to shift from old concepts and terminology.

The confusion became greater when articles began to appear about still another kind of grammar, generative-transformational, which had been brought to linguists' attention by studies reported by Zellig Harris and in a small book, *Syntactic Structures,* by Noam Chomsky of MIT, in 1957.[1] T-G grammar, also called generative grammar or transformational grammar, was concerned with the ways that our minds generate new sentences. Early transformationalists said that we employ a limited number of "kernel" sentences, which are in the active voice, are positive rather than negative, are declarative, and are very simple in structure. By means of various kinds of transformations these kernels can be changed to passive voice, to negatives, or to interrogatives, modifiers may be added, and by a combining transformation a simple sentence may be made compound or complex.

As an example of the transformation from active to passive, Chomsky used a formula for changing a sentence like "John admires sincerity" to "Sincerity is admired by John": $NP_1$—V—$NP_2 \Rightarrow NP_2$—is—$V_{en}$—by—$NP_1$.[1] Essentially this says that to form the passive we move the nominal *sincerity* ($NP_2$) to the front of the sentence, use *is* and the past participle *admired* ($V_{en}$), and put *by* and the nominal *John* ($NP_1$) at the end of the sentence. This formula will account for almost any passive voice structure.

Chomsky's followers greatly complicated his theory, pointed out considerable differences between the "surface structure" and the "deep structure" of sentences, and prepared huge, page-filling "sentence trees" to illustrate their points. High school English teachers looked on in dismay, sometimes despair. They took college courses or went to summer institutes devoted to T-G grammar, but with a few exceptions went away convinced that T-G grammatical theory appeared to be sound but not teachable to the majority of high school students.

And the end was not yet. Here and there they heard of still other grammars: tagmemic, stratificational, sectoral, and who knows how many more. Why, they wondered, should they teach any grammar at all when even the linguists couldn't agree on how to describe the language? Furthermore, the structuralists had told them that five- or six-year-olds already know the basic principles of grammar even though they have never heard of a noun.[2] And there were echoes of old, old voices which said that knowledge of formal grammar doesn't really help a person to speak and write.

So why teach grammar, these teachers continued to ask. They thought (mistakenly, perhaps) that it is more fun to teach literature anyway. So in the 1960s and 1970s the amount of attention to grammatical study in American high schools declined precipitously, almost to the point of disappearance in some schools.

Unfortunately, both teachers and the general public define *grammar* too broadly, using the term to refer to anything having to do with language study. So when teachers threw out grammar (description of language forms), they also threw out most of what they had been teaching about usage (e.g., the verb or pronoun needed in a particular context). And other, also very important aspects of language study—semantics, dialectology, history of the language—had never been very firmly entrenched, so they too tended to be eliminated in many schools.

In the 1960s there had been considerable emphasis, especially in curriculum study centers sponsored by Project English in the U.S. Office of Education, on the need for a balanced program in the English language. Such centers, particularly those in Minnesota and Nebraska, had advocated only modest attention to formal or descriptive grammar, granting that in the past too much time had been spent on sentence analysis and the like. They also advocated teaching up-to-date usage, ignoring for the most part the old *who-whom, shall-will,* and *the data is* (or *are*) controversies but still trying to shoot down *you was* and *Him and me seen it.* They argued persuasively that students' sensitivity to language and consequently their ability to use it effectively can be enhanced by the study of semantics (which includes the effects and not just the meanings of the words we choose), of dialectology (which shows that some variations are normal, historically explainable, and even interesting), and of the history of the language (which builds the important concept that there are no eternal rights and wrongs in language, a constantly changing thing). Some schools even paid a little attention to onomastics, the study of names, which fascinated many of their students.

But when, in many schools, grammar went out the window, these other valuable aspects of language study flew with it. Students in many American high schools were doomed to even greater linguistic ignorance than their predecessors. Some English teachers seemed to believe that composition, too, was part of grammar, so they also reduced their attention to that, hurting their students still more.


## AN APPARENT DECLINE IN VERBAL ABILITY

In the 1970s some news magazines called attention to an important development in American education. The scores made by students in college entrance examinations were steadily moving downward, year by year. Although the decline in mathematics scores was considerable, that in verbal scores was even greater. The reasons were many and complex. They included the changing nature of the college-bound population, the frustrations with the war in Vietnam, the omnipresent television set, and heavy teaching loads. In many schools, too, little attention was paid to the English language.

The same news magazines, many commentators, and unhappy parents sought, as usual, a simple solution. "Back to the basics!" they cried, and although the definition of *basics* varied from person to person, it was usually thought to consist of much grammatical analysis and endless drills on usage, even though the results of such analysis and drills had never proved very satisfactory in the past. The most reactionary of the would-be saviors would have virtually eliminated literary study in favor of sentence diagramming.

Clearly something needed and still needs to be done, not just to improve entrance examination scores, but to prepare graduates to face a world that increasingly demands and requires as much precision in language as it does in its machines. But the answer is not to go back to what has never been very successful. Rather, it is to plan and teach a language program that will interest students in the language, that will not overemphasize trivia, that will tell students truths instead of the linguistic half-truths that have sometimes infected our teaching, and that will develop in them a greater linguistic sensitivity.

This chapter and the next are intended to outline in broad strokes one such program and to offer suggestions for teaching it. No doubt variations from it, even large variations, are possible. The present chapter will consider the teaching of grammar and history of the language. The following chapter will be especially concerned with the word: usage and dialectology, vocabulary building and use, semantics, and lexicography.

## TEACHING GRAMMAR

### THE NEED FOR PEDAGOGICAL GRAMMAR

Remember that *grammar,* as the word is used by linguists, refers only to a description of the language. Grammar is subdivided into *phonology* (the sound-system of a language, which is never exactly the same as that of another language), *morphology* (the forms of words, generally with special reference to such things as affixes and internal changes), *syntax* (the structure of connected segments such as phrases, clauses, and sentences), and *lexicon* (the vocabulary, the total body of morphemes, like *woman, -ly, usual,* or *un-,* that the user of the language may draw upon).

How much grammar—especially how much syntax—should be taught to junior high and senior high school students who are native speakers of English?

Not much.

Older teachers, who spent class hour after class hour having students underline subjects and encircle verbs, or comment on the grammatical characteristics of every word in Burke's "Speech on Conciliation," or draw sentence diagrams that looked like something from a geometry book—such teachers did not produce many students who loved and respected the language and used it effectively. Neither did those younger teachers whose students drew vast sentence trees and

248

struggled painfully with the construction of phrase structure rules that resembled equations in advanced algebra.

But it is as great a mistake to abandon grammatical study altogether as it would be to go back to 1916, when 42 percent of New York State's English class time was given to parsing and the like. *The basic reason for offering some instruction in grammar is that it shows how the English sentence works*—how the parts cooperate with each other to assist us in the expression of meaning.

For this purpose we need not traditional, structural, transformational, or some other conventionally recognized grammar, but a pedagogical grammar. This is one that selects from the welter of theories and terms just those few that will help ordinary students (few of whom will become linguists) to understand the basic characteristics of the most powerful tool they are likely to own, their language.

What this pedagogical grammar ought to do is to stress and clarify the systematic nature of the English sentence. A sentence is not a random collection of words. If the preceding sentence had been phrased *Not words sentence a a collection of random is,* you would not have understood what we were saying. Small children learn the language—any language—as quickly as they do because every language is systematic and patterned. Children learn the basic patterns, together with the less advanced transformations, at a very early age. They also learn, and continue to learn throughout their lives, words and more words and groups of words that can fit into the various slots of a sentence. If there were no patterns, no slots, the learning of a language would be much more difficult or even impossible; in fact, any communication except the simplest probably could not be made.

But why should students be taught the description of a system that most of them already follow capably enough to be understood by their peers? One reason is just to help them see that it *is* a system. Students often feel that they live in a chaotic, unpredictable world, a world without system. That which is regular may comfort them, whether it be the constant and predictable orbiting of the planets around the sun, the constant presence of a mountain on the horizon, or something so seemingly unimportant as the methodical working of the English sentence. Another reason for teaching about the system of the sentence is that many students gain self-confidence when they realize that in large degree they have already mastered the operation; it takes a reasonable amount of intelligence to follow the system for putting a sentence together, but most of them do it (at least in speaking) hundreds of times a day, so therefore they are reasonably intelligent. Further, as numerous studies have revealed, an understanding of the basic system may lead to more extensive use of sentence combinations, a decrease in babyish sentences, a growing maturity in sentence construction.

Twentieth-century grammarians, diverse though they are, have done much to clarify the syntactic system of English—to help us all to understand how the

English sentence works. Even though no one of the descriptions may be completely satisfactory for schoolroom use, a grasp of the central features of these descriptions enables a teacher to select pieces that fit together as a reasonably coherent whole. The following highly condensed explanation concentrates on syntax and draws freely on several schools of grammatical thought; it includes some concepts, such as that of the kernel sentence, that appear to have pedagogical value even though professional linguists have abandoned them in their own modern abstruse speculations.

The use of language consists of employing increasingly complex sets of symbols revealing associations and differentiations. It is thus a reflection of the thought-process, which basically is composed of associating and differentiating.

## THE BASIC PATTERNS OF THE ENGLISH SENTENCE

When any one of us puts a sentence together, basically what we are doing is assembling two or more symbols of concepts, assembling them in a form that shows a relationship. For example, if we say "Water evaporates," we are saying in effect, "The thing that is composed of hydrogen and oxygen and that is designated in the English language by the symbol *water* [Concept 1] performs either now or as a characteristic mode of behavior the action designated in English by the symbol *evaporates* [Concept 2]." More elaborate sentences may bring together a substantial number of concepts. The words used in each sentence (except possibly for a few "function words" such as *of* or *the*) are in effect shorthand symbols that may stand for either a single person or thing or for huge abstractions with many ramifications, such as *love* or *democracy*. If they were not assembled in a systematic fashion, not even an approximation of the speaker's or writer's meaning could be conveyed to the mind of another.

The systematic arrangement accomplishes two purposes: It clarifies the relationship for the speaker or writer (or restates a previous clarification), and it conveys to the listener or reader what the speaker or writer believes the relationship to be.

The number of basic relationships is small, although no complete agreement exists about how many there are; it may be 3 or 4 or 9 or 17 or some other number, but certainly not a large number.

For teaching purposes it may be enough to talk about three basic relationships that language expresses. Consequently there are three corresponding basic patterns. In describing the patterns we will use these abbreviations:

NP—noun phrase (a noun or its equivalent, one word or more)
*be*—any form of *be*, and in some sentences *seem, become, remain,* or equivalents
Vi—intransitive verb (does not take an object)

THE TEACHING OF HIGH SCHOOL ENGLISH

Vt—transitive verb (takes an object)
ADJ—adjective
ADVp—adverb of place

The Pattern 1 formula is NP + *be* + (NP or ADJ or ADVp). A child uses this pattern when she says "Baw pwetty" (Ball pretty) although she hasn't yet learned the mysteries of *be*. Her hidden formula is NP + *be* + ADJ. Other examples of Pattern 1:

Mary seems beautiful. Melons taste delicious. NP + *be* + ADJ
 (Linking verbs like *seem* and the verbs of the senses are semantically different from *be* but function similarly.)
George is a fireman. My sisters were actresses. Spinach is a vegetable. NP[1] + *be* + NP[1]
 (The raised [1] indicates that both NP's refer to the same person or thing.)
Jeff became a policemen. Henry remained a student. The boy grew tall. The weather turned cold. Either NP[1] + *be* + NP[1] or NP + *be* + ADJ
 (The verbs *become, remain,* and their semantic equivalents function like *be.*)
Visitors are downstairs. The children are here. NP + *be* + ADVp

Note that in the various examples of this pattern the verb *be* or something much like it is a constant. The number of verbs usable in this pattern is quite limited.

About a fourth of modern American kernel sentences may be classed as Pattern 1.

The Pattern 2 formula is NP + Vi. A child's "Dah bweak" (Doll break) follows this pattern, which is characterized by an intransitive verb, of which there are thousands. Unlike *be,* they indicate actions, but unlike the transitive verb, they do not refer to a "carrying across" of the action to an object. Other examples:

Louise hurries.
Fish swim.
Water evaporates.

About 30 percent of modern American kernel sentences may be classed as Pattern 2.

The Pattern 3 formula is NP[1] + Vt + NP[2]. (The 2 shows that the second NP names a person or thing different from NP[1]. An exception is a sentence like *Joe hurt himself.*) A child's "Daddy bweak bwoon" (Daddy break balloon) follows the pattern. The distinguishing features of Pattern 3 are the transitive verbs (very numerous) and the direct object, which is acted upon by the subject. Examples:

Marge invited Helen.
Charles burned his fingers.
A landslide demolished the house.

Sometimes a Pattern 3 sentence is complicated by the insertion of another NP, especially after verbs carrying a meaning similar to "give" or "make." These additions are called, in traditional grammar, indirect objects and objective complements.

## Examples:

I gave her a dollar. $NP^1$ + Vt—*give* + $NP^2$ + $NP^3$
Robert told his son a story. $NP^1$ + Vt—*give* + $NP^2$ + $NP^3$
Cary sold Ralph his car. $NP^1$ + Vt—*give* + $NP^2$ + $NP^3$
Hunger made him a savage. $NP^1$ + Vt—*make* + $NP^2$ + $NP^3$
The voters elected Reagan President. $NP^1$ + Vt—*make* + $NP^2$ + $NP^3$
We consider Reginald an upstart. $NP^1$ + Vt—*make* + $NP^2$ + $NP^3$

There is also a variation with an adjective at the end:

The victory made Walter famous. $NP^1$ + Vt—*make* + $NP^2$ + ADJ

About 40 to 45 percent of modern American kernel sentences may be classed as Pattern 3, making it the most numerous.

Note that Pattern 1 does not indicate an action. Rather it tells something else about the NP—usually defining, classifying, describing, or locating.

Pattern 2 indicates that the NP performs an action, as we have seen, but the action is not one that is said to affect anyone or anything else. When *fish swim*, they are not swimming anyone or anything.

Pattern 3 also indicates that the NP performs an action, but this time the action does affect someone or something else. The landslide obviously affects the house.

Actually, we say a very limited number of things in English. We say, over and over, that somebody or something can be defined, classified, described, or located in a certain way, or that somebody or something performs an action, or that somebody or something performs an action affecting somebody or something else. By putting different symbols (words or groups of words) into the sentence slots, we can play infinite variations on just these three central themes.

## TEACHING THE BASIC PATTERNS

The odds are that your language textbook does not classify sentences in a way similar to that just described. That's all right; don't throw it away. You can teach inductively the three basic patterns without the use of the book, and then you can look at some of its sentences as examples of the patterns and observe other things about what goes into the slots.

One way to teach the patterns is to show a simple picture that depicts action— say a dog encountering a cat. Ask the students to tell in three words (not counting *the*) something about the appearance of each animal: "The dog is brown." "The cat looks afraid." Then ask them to tell in two words what the animals are doing: "The dog growls." "The cat bristles." Finally ask them to tell in three words what one animal does or may do to the other: "The dog chases the cat." "The cat scratches the dog." Write several of the sentences suggested, and then look at them and note the simple structure. Repeat with a different picture.

Another way, more suitable for older students, is to use a preselected para-graph or so of simple prose. Make sure that all three patterns are represented and that the sentences are relatively unencumbered with dependent clauses or other distractors. Again note that the basic parts of each sentence almost without exception follow one of the three patterns.

## SINGLE-BASED TRANSFORMATIONS

Even this small amount of study will demonstrate the systematic nature of the language. A few minutes or an hour or so may be spent in looking at what some grammarians call single-based transformations. These are changes made in a single sentence to affect its meaning or to make it conform to present conven-tions. Most common are the following:

1. Addition of words such as *the, a, an, this, that, these, those, some, his* (determiners): *The* dog growls.
2. Addition of adverbs (especially indicating manner or time): The dog growls *angrily. Then* the cat hisses.
3. Addition of negatives: The dog is *not* brown. The dog does *not* growl. (Comment on the usefulness of *do* in modern English.)
4. Formation of questions: Is the dog brown? Does the dog chase the cat? Where is the cat? Why does the cat run? The cat is afraid, isn't it?
5. Formation of commands or requests: Speak! Hurry! Chase the cat. Please chase the cat. (Note that the NP[1] is dropped here.)
6. Formation of the passive (This is possible only with Pattern 3.): The cat is chased by the dog.
7. Changes in verb form to signify tense or other aspects: The dog *is growling*. The cat *bristled*. The cat *may be* afraid. The cat *must have been* hungry.

Notice with the class the systematic nature of these changes, too. Determiners, for instance, cannot be placed randomly, nor can negatives. Most questions and passives follow established patterns. Commands and requests routinely omit the NP[1]. Verb forms, determined mainly by meaning, may not be arbitrarily changed; for instance, we always say *must have been* rather than *have must been* or *been have must*. Only adverbs are somewhat flexible in their placement.

If your students are not native speakers, much drill in some of these transformations is necessary to make them habitual—drill in *use,* not in theory. The use of determiners, which native speakers employ without thinking, is especially difficult for many non-native speakers. For your home-grown Americans, however, the point of the exercise is quickly made: that these changes are further illustrations of the basic orderliness of the English language. Most English-speaking students already use these pattern variations, and all can understand them on TV or in the classroom. (In a discussion of usage in the next chapter, we'll consider what should or should not be done for those students who diverge from the patterns. Decisions about whether to use *he* or *him,* for instance, can most often be made on the basis of whether or not an NP[1] slot is being filled.)

## DOUBLE-BASED TRANSFORMATIONS

More time should be spent on the double-based transformation, which is now better known as sentence combining.

As early as 1966 Donald Bateman and Frank Zidonis of Ohio State described a degree of success in improving sentence structure in this way,[3] and John Mellon, using different tactics, got somewhat the same results in an experiment described in a Harvard dissertation.[4] In 1973 Frank O'Hare described successful sentence combining that involved a minimal use of grammatical terminology.[5] O'Hare's little book should be consulted both for its theoretical foundations and its examples of specific techniques.

Studies reported in *Research in the Teaching of English* generally confirmed the usefulness of sentence combining. They tended to show that the practice can lead to fewer excessively short sentences, to a reduction in the number of *and . . . and* sentences, and, perhaps most importantly, to a clearer indication of how ideas are related.

A simple example of combining involves the switch of an adjective from one sentence to another and the deletion of unnecessary words:

> Mike is a boy + Mike is strong = Mike is a strong boy.

This kind of transformation most of your students make without thinking.

A little more complex is this:

> Matilda straightened the picture + Matilda is a meticulous girl = Matilda, who is a meticulous girl, straightened the picture.

Or this:

THE TEACHING OF HIGH SCHOOL ENGLISH

Matilda straightened the picture + Matilda is a meticulous girl + The picture was on the wall = Matilda, who is a meticulous girl, straightened the picture on the wall.

The appositive remains unclear to many students. They may easily be shown that it requires deletion of *who is* or *which is* in sentences like the above:

Matilda, a meticulous girl, straightened the picture on the wall.

What grammarians call adverbial clauses also result from double-based transformations.

Matilda saw a crooked picture + She straightened it = Whenever (When, If) Matilda saw a crooked picture, she straightened it.

Those same basic sentences could also be combined as a compound sentence:

Matilda saw a crooked picture, and (so) she straightened it.

That combination is of course quite legitimate, but often the use of a connective such as *when, whenever, after, before, if, because, although,* or *so that* shows more explicitly the relationship between ideas than does the overworked *and* or *so*.

Participles may be introduced as other useful tools in combining:

*Seeing* a crooked picture, Matilda straightened it.

So may gerunds:

Matilda's meticulousness is illustrated by her *straightening* of crooked pictures.

Most of the work in sentence combining should require construction rather than analysis. It is indeed true that people learn by doing. The mistake made by many teachers of grammar in the past was to rely on someone else's sentences, usually those in a textbook, almost exclusively. The rewards are much greater if students work with the expression of their own ideas.

For example, at the Air Force Academy a class of first-year cadets spent half a class period talking about possible combinations of a pair of sentences written by one of them: "The Air Force is the nation's first line of defense. It must cooperate with other branches." The cadets realized that some way must be found to show the relationship between the ideas. They experimented with *though* at the end; with connectives such as *although, even though, but, however, nevertheless;* with a *which*-clause; with an appositive; with putting the burden of cooperation on the other branches. Each time, the cadets discussed the changes in meaning or emphasis and tried to relate the revision to its context. Nobody was bored. The instruction was some of the most effective that the observer (one of the authors of this book) has ever seen.

Whatever grammar you teach, and however much or little of it you teach, you will get best results by encouraging students to think rather than to memorize. Basically you are asking them to take a look at the processes that they themselves use in constructing sentences, and gradually to add to those processes by writing sentences of kinds they do not ordinarily write—particularly those they can achieve by sentence combining. You and they will place little emphasis on defining and classifying, but will spend most of the time on illustrating and building.

Almost always you will find, here and elsewhere, that the inductive approach is superior to the deductive. In the former you build up an understanding of the principle. In the latter you start with the rule or principle and then continue with dissection of illustrative sentences. More than two decades ago the authors of *The English Language Arts in the Secondary School* contrasted the approaches:

> *The inductive method (discovery of a generalization through the study of many specific illustrations) should for the most part be used in introducing a new grammatical point. Although there is nothing wrong with stating a grammatical point first and then illustrating it, a more effective procedure, usually, is to have the student find for himself from the analysis of a number of carefully prepared sentences the principle for which he has need. The important point here and elsewhere in the teaching of grammar is that the student should not be tempted to memorize a statement instead of developing a clear concept.* [6]

## PROBLEMS IN SYNTAX

### TALKING ABOUT SENTENCES

Study of grammar somewhat like that just described will enable students to understand the system of the English sentence and will perhaps add a few structures to their syntacticon (their repertoire of syntactic structures).

Much talking about sentences and their structure is useful. Sometimes, for instance, a group of words may be found that does not resemble any of the usual sentence patterns. Suppose that Frances, a girl in your class, encounters "Along the highway sped the black Cadillac." Frances observes that something seems wrong, or at least different, about the structure. You say a word of praise, and with the class take a closer look at the sentence, noting that word order has been shifted from the conventional "The black Cadillac sped along the highway." Instead of NP + Vi (+ Adv), Frances' sentence uses inverted order: (Adv) + Vi + NP. The class notes that this is an optional kind of transformation; writers sometimes use it for special effects. Students may construct other examples: *Next came the band* or *To this goal were all his efforts directed.* Then or later they may look at other kinds of inverted sentences, such as those starting with *nor* (e.g., *Nor did his injury keep him out of the game*) or with an adjective (e.g., the palindrome *Able was I ere I saw Elba*). Many questions, they will have noted, are inversions of statements: *Is he?* is the inverted form of *He is.*

Suppose that at another time Larry finds a sentence fragment such as "Never again" or "On the contrary." These represent a different kind of transformation, one in which deletions have occurred. Usually the context will suggest at least approximately what has been chopped out. For instance, Larry's "On the contrary" may occur in this context: "You may suppose that the twins learned their lesson. On the contrary. The next day they were once more climbing the same tree." The fragment is shortened from something longer such as "On the contrary, the twins did not learn their lesson." The short form was used to prevent unneeded and perhaps boring repetition.

The class notes that fragments are frequent in conversation:

"Where to?"

"Gym."

"Why?"

"Big game today."

The class observes that such fragments (actually deletion transformations) are a kind of shorthand. In the rush of conversation, more than in writing, we often leave out parts of sentences that our listeners can readily supply for themselves. Without the deletion transformations the conversation above might have gone like this:

"Where are you off to?"

"I am going to the gymnasium."

"Why are you going to the gymnasium?"

"A big game is being played today."

Fragments, if the deleted elements are easily recoverable, are useful in speeding up conversation. And if the listener does not understand, he or she can ask for clarification. When something is written or printed, though, there is usually no opportunity to ask questions. For that reason—to assure clear communication—fragments are relatively rare in writing.

The point of all this is that much talking about sentences is beneficial. It can shed light on rather rare constructions, such as inversions after an adverb, and on the virtues and limitations of other structures such as the fragment. Such open discussion gets much better results than, say, a flat, unreasoned, and unrealistic demand that students never use fragments.


## DIAGRAMMING

The beloved Columbia professor Allan Abbott used to tell his classes that he had learned so well in secondary school how to diagram sentences that he could construct a diagram of the 16-line opening sentence of *Paradise Lost*. "But," he said, "the chief adverse criticism of the themes I wrote in college freshman English was 'faulty sentence structure.'" Although some teachers and textbooks still use their own variations of the nineteenth-century Reed-Kellogg system, there is hardly an iota of evidence that such instruction leads to improved student-written sentences. Students who already "know their grammar" may enjoy diagramming as a mental activity, but few students who do not already understand descriptions of syntax learn much about it through their attempts at schematic picturing.

Very simple diagrams such as an arrow or a brace to show what goes with what, may be helpful. But complicated diagrams, such as those that Professor Abbott learned as a boy, have little value.

The sentence trees of the transformationalists are another kind of diagram. Tall sentence trees with a multitude of branches appear to be no more useful as pedagogical tools than Reed-Kellogg diagrams were. The teacher or even a student may occasionally draw a compact little tree or one branch of a tree, to illustrate a particular point, but when branches and twigs and leaves spread all over the chalkboard, students often can't see the sentence because of the trees.

## PROGRAMMED AND COMPUTERIZED INSTRUCTION

A number of programs have been published, intended to teach principles of sentence structure or to combat specific structural weaknesses in students' sentences. With such programs, students work independently, at their own speed, on series of "frames" that build toward mastery of a concept. Linear programs move methodically, frame by frame, from something like "Birds fly" to much more difficult structures. Branching programs, rarer and much more complicated than linear ones, send the student to elementary explanatory frames when he or she makes a mistake.

Computer-assisted instruction, which relies heavily on programmed materials, has been advocated by some educational technologists. In a form that some proponents consider ideal it consists of these elements: (1) detailed diagnostic tests, with results marked and recorded by computers; (2) a varied wealth of teaching materials, including programmed offerings, slides, transparencies, films, recordings, microform readers, individual small-screen television sets, and the like; (3) a system by which the computer makes individual assignments in these materials, on the basis of the diagnostic tests; (4) continuous evaluation by means of frequent computer-analyzed mastery tests; (5) further assignments (or repetition of assignments when needed), based on results of mastery tests.

Some teachers of English look with horror on such mechanization as a forerunner of a dehumanized "brave new world." School, they fear, may become a place where socialized learning would be confined largely to the gymnasium.

But without going to extremes, a teacher can make some use of programmed

258

or computer-assisted instruction for purposes of supplementation and gap-filling. If, for instance, only a few students in a class need help with a particular syntactic problem, repeating this material wastes time. Instead, the students needing this instruction can be assigned appropriate programmed material, whereas others work on things that they as individuals need, or engage in reading or other humanistic activities.

Not all programs are equally good, however, just as all textbooks are not equally good. Some of the first programs devised for English stressed mere identification and were not superior to the conventional workbook. Now, though, some programs do stress sentence building or attacks upon particular sentence weaknesses. The choice must be made with care, and assignments made in accordance with what will most profit each student.

## THE HONEST APPROACH TO SENTENCE IMPROVEMENT

Improvement in sentence structure and a closer approach to standard usage (about which more will be said in the next chapter) will come only if the student *wants* to improve. As Professor Allan F. Hubbell once said,

> *An individual's linguistic usage is among other things the outward sign of his most deep-seated group loyalties. If the usage of the group or groups with which he identifies himself is not that of Standard English, the schools are not likely to have much effect on his practice. For the blunt fact is that only if his loyalties shift will his grammar change. In a democratic society, the schools have an obligation to make a knowledge of the standard language available to everyone. And teachers have an obligation to make the instruction as interesting and meaningful as possible. They should not be surprised, however, if the nonstandard forms of English continue to flourish. They are hardy growths and will be with us for a long time to come.*[7]

The time-dishonored method of having students memorize rules may as well be forgotten. No more successful has been the constant use of the labels "wrong" or "incorrect" or the admonition "Watch your grammar."

Some classes and some students are eager to bring their sentence forms and their usage into conformity with Standard. These are usually the students with cultured parents or with parents who wish they were cultured. Less frequently they are intelligent students who are eager to surmount what they have come to recognize as handicaps of their environment.

But thousands of students have never been convinced, and perhaps can't be, that the language a teacher encourages them to practice is a language they should learn. They will not be convinced by such essentially dishonest statements as "This is the only right way to say it" and "Successful people are always careful of their language."

The honest approach to a don't-care class takes some such form as this:

*I'm not going to pretend that using "good English" will make you rich and successful. Maybe it will help; maybe it won't. I know a hundred persons whose English seems worse to me than my own does but who have a lot more money than I'll ever have. And I'm not going to pretend to you that one way of saying something is always right and that other ways are always wrong. We'll look a little at history of the language and discover that ideas of right and wrong in English have changed from century to century. And I can't tell you that people won't know what you mean if you say "I ain't got nothin'."*

*But I can say this to you: Sometimes it will be important to you to make your meaning so clear that nobody can possibly misunderstand you. Sometimes you will write letters that will affect your future. Sometimes you will talk with people who will be sizing you up for a job that is important to you. Some of you will want to go to a college where it is simply taken for granted that you use language in the ways that happen to be socially approved in this century; if you don't, out you may go, even though these colleges may be using a poor reason for getting rid of you.*

*So what we're doing here is learning about the language that many of today's leaders, in all kinds of work, consider most clear and most acceptable. It is something that will be useful to know and that* **may** *make a difference in your future, though I can't say for sure. I'll not say that "haven't any" is better than "ain't got none," but many important people today* **think** *it is better, and for that reason I'll say maybe you'll want to have it available.*

## INDIVIDUALIZING INSTRUCTION

One method of individualizing instruction in syntax, as well as other elements of language, has already been mentioned: the use of carefully chosen programmed or computerized learning materials. Another exists in relation to marking of compositions. If Ellen writes too many *and . . . and* sentences, give her some appropriate work. If Ron has a penchant for dangling modifiers, try having him make up some intentional danglers that produce a ludicrous effect; he may learn more from this than from correcting a workbook exercise.

The small-group plan may also be used. Four or five students have the same kind of problem in sentence structure. Let them meet with Beverly, for whom the problem does not exist, so that she can provide the necessary help. Simultaneously other groups may work on other problems.

Sometimes a large part of a class, but not all, needs work on a stumbling block. Instead of wasting time of students who you know do not need this instruction, allow them to read or do some other constructive work.

Individual conferences are extremely valuable and are possible for those teachers whose course load is not too heavy. Often a little personal encouragement and individual help bring big returns.

## COMBATING THE MOST PERSISTENT ERRORS IN SYNTAX

When the word *error* is used with regard to language, it is usually defined in this book as a construction or usage that results in a reduction of clarity, and occasionally as a construction or usage that deviates enough from Standard English that in some situations its user may be penalized.

Some teachers have argued that errors should be largely ignored save for an occasional question like "Would it be clearer if you . . . ?" It is certainly true that Americans (more than the British) have overemphasized, often pettily, the attack on errors. But until American society becomes as permissive about sentences as it has about sex, teachers will have to continue their attempts to overcome student use of sentences that are unclear or well outside the pale of standard practice.

Among the sentence errors that are most difficult to eradicate are the undesirable fragment, the comma fault, excessive coordination, faulty subordination, dangling modifiers, faulty word order, faulty parallelism, and pronounced incoherence or lack of logic. Each of these will be discussed briefly.

### The Undesirable Sentence Fragment

Some fragments, as mentioned earlier, are useful and may be employed by professional writers. The undesirable fragment is one that is unintentional and that results from confusion with a complete sentence.

The best way to prevent fragments is to teach what a sentence is. A class that has mastered sentence patterns realizes that every kernel sentence has at least two slots, one for the subject (the NP[1]) and one for the verb. The two most common kinds of unacceptable sentence fragments are (1) the dependent clause punctuated as a sentence, and (2) a group of words with a participle instead of a finite verb. For example:

**1.** Because the water in the canteen was almost gone.
**2.** The sand stretching endlessly before us.

In some contexts, even such fragments can be defended, but ordinarily they cannot. A student who has learned that such constructions are the result of transformations used in sentence combining is more likely than not to combine them with other sentences or to change them so that combination is not necessary. For example:

**1.** Because the water in the canteen was almost gone, we realized that thirst might become a real danger. (*or*) The water in the canteen was almost gone. That made us realize . . .

**2.** The sand stretching endlessly before us was beautiful but terrifying. (*or*) The sand stretched endlessly before us. It was . . .

Students can be shown, repeatedly if necessary, how a clause or a phrase can be attached to a related sentence. A reminder that a participle needs a helping verb is also pertinent. Ask the class, "Would you write, 'I running'?"

In an article filled with specific suggestions, Kellogg W. Hunt advocated substituting nonsense words to make clear that a fragment is a fragment:

> **In years later after the foons wamped it** *can stand as the answer to a question or the beginning of a statement, but students quickly see that it is only a fragment. Whether or not it is a complete thought, it is an incomplete structure. The student's original was* **In years later when the Italians conquered it.**[8]

Some rather bright student will probably ask the old question "Why can't we use sentence fragments? Professional writers do." You may give the old answer that professional writers sometimes consciously use sentence fragments for special effects. It is the unconscious use that is to be condemned. If a student, or a whole class, has consistently demonstrated mature ability in sentence construction, encouragement may indeed be given to stylistic experimentation, including use of fragments.

### The Run-on Sentence and the Comma Fault

The run-on sentence consists of two or more sentences run together without punctuation, for example, "I arrived home late the door was locked." The comma fault or comma splice is the same, except that a feeble comma tries in vain to hold the sentences apart: "I arrived home late, the door was locked." These mistakes, like the undesirable sentence fragment, may be attacked through instruction in sentence patterns, through occasional review of legitimate ways to combine sentences, and through much practice in building sentences with proper terminal punctuation. It is also useful to show that a reader's task may be increased when sentences are run together, for example, "I found the ring on the floor beside it was a note." (The comma fault is discussed further in Chapter 11.)

### Excessive Coordination

This is the *and . . . and* or the *so . . . so* sentence, in which ideas are strung together as if they were beads of equal size: "I talked with Sam, and he is my older brother, and he is very smart, and he advised me to call the police, so I did." Instruction and practice in sentence combining can help a student to write more sentences like "I talked with Sam, my very smart older brother, who advised me to call the police. I did so at once."

## Faulty Subordination

The complex sentence has pitfalls of its own. Used effectively, it can make writing precise. When in a given context one idea is clearly more important than another, the less important one should be subordinated structurally. Suppose that a student wants to say that lightning struck his house and that the time was about eight o'clock. In all likelihood, unless there is a special reason for stressing the time, it would be unwise to combine the two ideas as "It was about eight o'clock when lightning struck our house." Ordinarily "Lightning struck our house about eight o'clock" is a stronger statement, or "About eight o'clock" may come first.

A second pitfall is the "house-that-Jack-built" construction. This usually consists of a string of adjective clauses each modifying a noun in the preceding clause: "This is the dog that worried the cat that killed the rat that . . ." It may also consist of a string of loosely related adverbial clauses: "Dad agreed because he wanted me to go because he thought I needed the experience because . . ." The name "house-that-Jack-built" may help both to clarify the problem and to laugh it out of existence. Assisting the student to see the underlying relationships of the parts may lead to a satisfactory revision. Sometimes a long sentence of this kind may need to be divided into two or three sentences.

Student-written sentences illustrating either excessive coordination or faulty subordination may afford excellent material for class discussion and for the sentence manipulation that is often highly productive. Duplicate the sentences, write them on the chalkboard, or show them with an overhead projector.

## Dangling Modifiers

Sometimes the dangling modifier is a "howler," as the British may call it: "After failing in geometry, the principal had a talk with Stuart." "Standing on the peak and looking into the valley below, his heart pounded at the beauty of the scene." Usually, though, it is more prosaic: "By getting tickets early, good seats will be available."

When you find a dangling modifier in student writing, remark that it reminds you of a sentence you once read. On the board write a howler. (Maybe this: "Cooing softly under the bridge, we could hear pigeons.") Show the class why the howler does not make sense, and then show them that the sentence under discussion follows a similar unorthodox pattern, even though it may not be funny. Get the class to make corrections. Show them that there is often more than one way to place modifiers for clarity but that sometimes, for reasons of logic, a modifier can be in only one place in a particular sentence. Write down some more howlers or look at some examples in the textbook. The class corrects these. To clinch the point, write a few verbal phrases like these:

Upsetting the bucket,
While living in Spokane,
To make a kite,

Ask the students to finish each of these sentences. Have them test each sentence by noting whether the modifier has something that it can logically modify. Someone is almost sure to write, "While living in Spokane, it was very rainy." Let the class help the writer of that sentence to see that "it" was not living in Spokane.

Kellogg W. Hunt, in the article previously cited, made this suggestion:

*I can give them* **Puffing and panting, the wamble was woobled at last.** *In place of the first nonsense word, students will substitute words for people, for animals, for a number of things that can puff and pant. But when I substitute what a student wrote, they reject it with a laugh. I write on the blackboard,* **Puffing and panting, the top of the hill was reached at last.** *They see that tops of hills don't really puff and pant even when they are being reached. They see this far more clearly when I substitute nonsense syllables than when I lecture to them on dangling modifiers.*

*The class may also practice different clear ways to make combinations. For example they combine "The play delighted the audience" and "The audience was laughing uproariously" as "The play delighted the audience, which was laughing uproariously," "Laughing uproariously, the audience was obviously delighted by the play," but not "Laughing uproariously, the play delighted the audience."*


## Faulty Word Order

In English, more than in most other languages, word order is important. The reason is that English words no longer have distinctive endings to show how they are used in a sentence. Consider, for example, "The girl saw the soldier." In some other languages, Latin for instance, the word order in that sentence could be changed considerably without affecting the meaning. But in English, if we say "The soldier saw the girl," the meaning is different, or if we say "Saw the girl the soldier," there is no meaning.

Most problems in word order arise in the placement of modifiers. One needs to admit to the class that some sentences are very difficult to write. For example, try straightening these out: "Seated in front of her were several men whose heads only she could see." "Carol is the girl in the hallway with blue shorts." When one happens upon such a sentence, often the best solution is to start the sentence in an entirely different way.

Students, however, often write sentences in which only a shift in word order is needed for clarity. As always, stress the fact that in writing and speaking we are trying to express our thoughts clearly so that others can understand us. Perhaps students have written sentences such as these: "I pulled the heavy fishing line up on the bank on which I found only a tin can filled with mud." "Ted was arrested before his intended crime was committed by the police chief." Although you could talk technically and at length about the systematic placement of modifiers, the results will probably be better if you have the class apply simple logic: "Where was the tin can that was filled with mud?... How can we make the sentence say that?"

## Faulty Parallelism

Grammatically equivalent elements should normally be stated in equivalent grammatical forms. But you may have students who write, "The dictionary shows us how to pronounce a word, its meaning, and where it originated." Maybe that sentence can be overlooked in the writing of many students, but good juniors and seniors should do better.

There are four main situations in which parallelism is needed: (1) in a series, (2) in comparisons, (3) with *be* and linking verbs like *seem,* and (4) with correlative conjunctions. The last two cause little difficulty and may be ignored with most classes. But a faulty series, like the illustration above, and a faulty comparison such as "I like baseball better than to run races" may demand attention.

Concentrate first on the series. Write, "The dictionary shows us the _____ of a word." Ask, "What does the dictionary show us about a word?" Someone says "Pronunciation." The class tests that in the blank and sees that it will fit. But the next person says "How to spell it." Testing that, the class sees that "The dictionary shows us the how to spell it of a word" does not make sense, and changes the insert to "spelling." Other inserts will be other nouns, like "meaning," "history," or "part of speech." Get the class to construct sentences with other series of nouns, then with series of adjectives, clauses, gerunds, and infinitives.

At another time, consider parallelism in comparisons. Write, "I like *baseball* better than *track.*" "I like *to play baseball* better than *to run races.*" "I like *playing baseball* better than *running races.*" Help the students to see that the italicized parts are the things being compared and that within the same sentence they are stated in the same form. From the class get other comparisons requiring parallel construction.

Able students will enjoy observing how masters of the crafts employ parallelism for special effects. The novels of Alan Paton offer especially good examples.

## Pronounced Incoherence and Lack of Logic

The varieties are myriad and not always classifiable, and often are accompanied by spelling or punctuation errors. Here is an example from an examination paper of a sophomore: "Juluis Cesar went forum and soothsayer sayed be wear of Idies of March but didnt and died (got killed." This student needs much help, but he reveals enough about the content to show that his is not a hopeless case.

But with as poor a student as this (unless there is a foreign background), you may as well face the fact that sentence polish for him or her is eternally impossible. Indeed, you may feel like adopting the traditional tactics of a coach whose team loses most of its games—work on building character. (Not a bad idea, really.) Your goal is to bring such a student up to a sixth-grader's level. Praise even a five-word sentence that is clear. Let pairs of students sometimes work together in writing and revising their papers; this student and others will profit from the experience. Help the student to see that careless omission of words is like careless omission of clothing or careless assembly of a bicycle brake. Show how easy it is to misread something like "Julius Caesar went forum."

You will have succeeded with such a student if he or she becomes a respectable adult citizen who can write sentences like these: "Please send me one claw hammer. The catalog No. is X1905. I enclose a check for $8.00."

## TEACHING THE HISTORY OF THE ENGLISH LANGUAGE

### WHY TEACH LANGUAGE HISTORY?

For a number of years some of the leading American high schools have been incorporating instruction in the English language. Sometimes the instruction is only casual and incidental, as for example when the teacher and the class note differences between Shakespeare's language and that of today, or when they discover the meaning of an unfamiliar word. Sometimes it is more methodical, in the form of a planned unit or two. There is room for both kinds: the casual instruction can create an appetite for the more formal and has the advantage of relating language history to other parts of the program; a well-developed unit, however, provides a coherent view of language growth over the span of centuries.

Why teach the history of the language? Here are a few of the reasons:

- Such study builds an awareness that language is not a fixed thing, but that it changes in relation to historical events and social and economic developments, that it responds to the needs and interests of people. The language is changing steadily even today, and will continue to change as long as anyone uses it.
- Knowledge of the characteristics of language of a bygone day makes it easier for students to read the literature of that period. The language barriers to Chaucer, Shakespeare, Milton, Swift, and even to some nineteenth-century writers, are considerable, but can be reduced by a modest amount of historical study.
- In the history of the language are found explanations of why people speak in different dialects. Patterns of settlement reveal, for instance, why New England, the Midlands, and the South have different dialects.
- Similarly, historical study explains many of the differences in usage, often

showing that forms currently in bad repute (e.g., *have wrote, ain't*) were once widely accepted.

- Knowledge of language history also clarifies many oddities of the English language, such as the spellings of *doubt* and *colonel* or the use of the plural *were* with the singular subject *you*.
- Historical knowledge makes clear how words enter a language, how the huge English vocabulary developed, and what may happen to a word after it is entrenched in the language. Thus it may increase students' interest in words.
- Study of language history shows how English is related to many other languages of the world.

## THE DRAMA IN THE HISTORY

English has changed so much in the past 1000 years that only after special training can we read what King Alfred wrote. But this vast change is actually only the combined results of countless small changes.

Most of these small changes involve conflict. One form or one word or one pronunciation or one spelling does battle with another. The battle may be short or long, bitter or quiet and almost unnoticed, widespread or localized.

We can find many examples in our own century. Just a few are listed below:

When the automobile was invented, it had to be called something.

*Automobile* was only one of the candidates. It did battle with *autogen, autogo, autopher, autovic, autokinet, electromobil, ipsometer, molectros, motorcycle, self-motor, trundle,* and perhaps other words. *Automobile's* victory was fairly apparent by 1910 in the United States, later in England. Today, however, *automobile* steadily loses ground to *car,* which used to mean mainly "railroad car."

The verbs *reminisce* and *contact* have been vigorously attacked as barbarisms. *Reminisce* has clearly won and is now unquestioned. *Contact* (as in "I'll contact you") is winning because it is shorter than *get in touch with.*

*Data is* now is ahead of *data are,* but the struggle has been fierce. Conservatives argue that *data* is a Latin plural, but others say that it means a unified set of material and is therefore singular.

*Ms.,* with a push from the women's rights movement, has acquired wide but not universal acceptance. The battle goes on. *Ms.* will win, because the language needs a title to designate a woman without reference to her marital status.

Plurals of many compound nouns are in doubt: *notary publics* vs. *notaries public, attorney generals* vs. *attorneys general, time outs* vs. *times out.*

*Into* may be usurping certain functions of *in:* "She is *into* basket-weaving." "A snowstorm will be *into* the Midwest" (an expression used often by a former NBC weatherman).

*Everyone . . . they* seems to have many more users than *everyone . . . he or she.* Its users include several recent American Presidents. But the battle continues.

Few persons now question such slightly simplified spellings as *plow, catalog, sulfur, quartet, esthetic,* but attempts at more thorough modifications attract little support.

Similar confrontations have gone on for centuries. You need not examine many of them with high school students, but a few examples will help to show how very different our language would be had the fights not turned out as they did. Details of the battles may be found in almost any history of the English language.[9]

Old English had many inflectional endings. Successive groups of invaders, and the Anglo-Saxons themselves, began reducing or omitting them, thus finally eliminating all noun endings except the plural and the possessive, and reducing verb forms to four or five. To make up for the loss of the endings, word order in sentences became relatively fixed.

Speakers of Old English, like speakers of most modern Continental languages, had to learn whether each noun was masculine, feminine, or neuter. After many battles and several centuries, natural gender ousted this system of grammatical gender and greatly simplified the learning of the language.

Large numbers of Old English verbs shifted from "strong" (which many persons now call "irregular") to "weak." Those few dozen that did not, such as *see, do, write, take,* are now the most generally troublesome.

After the Norman Conquest hundreds of English words battled with Norman French words. Sometimes English won, sometimes French.[10]

Renaissance scholars and Dutch printers are responsible for such spelling oddities as *doubt* and *ghost.*

Most students can readily be interested in accounts of such battles and can become alert to some of those going on today. They should be helped to see that, more often than not, the simpler or more useful of two opposing forms will win, but that there are limits beyond which simplification cannot go without reducing clarity.

## SHOWING THE RELATION OF ENGLISH TO OTHER LANGUAGES

You may want to work out with the class a chart tracing the languages descended from the Indo-European spoken several millenniums ago, probably in northwestern Europe but gradually spreading to almost all of Europe and to parts of Asia. The chart will show that English has a sibling relationship to other Germanic languages (High and Low German, Dutch, Flemish, and the Scandinavian languages), has a first-cousin relationship to Latin-descended languages (Spanish, Portuguese, Romanian, French, and Italian), and a similar relationship to Greek, Scots Gaelic, and Irish Gaelic, and has a second-cousin relationship to Balto-Slavic languages (Lettish, Lithuanian, Bulgarian, Slovenian, Serbo-Croatian, Polish, Czecho-Slovak, and Russian), and a similar relationship to Iranic and Indic languages (Persian, Hindi, Bengali, Romany).[11]

One way to illustrate the closeness of relationship of English to other Germanic languages is to show students how to count to ten in several of those languages. In contrast, a less closely related language such as French shows fewer similarities, and an unrelated language like Japanese shows none except through coincidence.

| English | Dutch | German | Danish | French | Japanese |
|---------|-------|--------|--------|--------|----------|
| one | een | eins | en | un | ichi |
| two | twee | zwei | to | deux | ni |
| three | drie | drei | tre | trois | san |
| four | vier | vier | fire | quatre | shi |
| five | vijf | fünf | fem | cinq | go |
| six | zes | sechs | seks | six | roku |
| seven | zeven | sieben | syv | sept | shichi |
| eight | acht | acht | otte | huit | hachi |
| nine | negen | neun | ni | neuf | ku |
| ten | tien | zehn | ti | dix | ju |

## THE HISTORY OF AMERICAN ENGLISH

A unit on American English is especially suitable in conjunction with the study of American literature. It may be presented either all at one time or scattered appropriately throughout the year. Among topics suitable for inclusion are these:

The languages of American Indians; Indian words surviving in Modern English
How early settlers named unfamiliar things (e.g., *skunk, catbird, Jack-in-the-pulpit*)
French and Spanish influences on American English; the influence of other languages
How American places got their names
Sources of people's surnames (e.g., names chosen by blacks after emancipation; changes of name)
Similarities and differences between British and American English; criticisms of American English by British writers
The influence of independence on American English
Syntactic and stylistic changes in American English from 1600 to the present; the

trend toward shorter sentences; language experimentation in American writing (e.g., Whitman, Cummings)

Changes in American pronunciation

American spelling

Historical reasons for dialects; dialects in literature; American dialects today. (See the next chapter)

Growth of the American vocabulary; sources of new words; some recent coinages; words for the spage age

American slang; rapidity of change in slang; up-to-date slang in your school[12]

## THE HISTORY OF BRITISH ENGLISH

In the study of British English, once more either a chronological unit or a tie-in with British writings of various periods is possible. A glimpse of Old English may be offered through a passage such as this Old English version of the Lord's Prayer:

*Father our, thou that art in heaven,     be thy name hallowed.*
Fæder ure, ðu   ðe   eart on heofonum, si  ðin nama gehalgod.

*Come       thy kingdom. Be done  thy will  on earth*
To becume ðin rice.      Gewurðe ðin willa on eorðan

*as       in heaven.   Our  daily           bread give us*
swa swa on heofonum. Urne gedæghwamlican hlaf   syle us

*today.   And forgive us our debts  as       we forgive our*
to dæg. And forgyf  us ure gyltas swa swa we forgyfa urum

*debtors      And not lead   thou us into temptation, but deliver*
gyltendum. And ne  gelæd ðu   us on  costnunge, ac  alys

*us from evil.   Amen.*
us of     yfele. Soðlice.

The purpose of study of such a passage is not to teach students to read Old English (graduate English courses in universities do that), but only to give them some familiarity with an older form of the language and thereby to gain a better understanding of its modern development. Among the points that can be observed in the example are these:

1. Although there have been changes in pronunciation, some Mod E words have the same written form as in OE (*on, and, we, us*).
2. Other words, though they have changed in spelling and pronunciation, are still similar to their OE forms (*fæder, ure, eart, heofonum*, etc.)

3. Some Mod E words are derived from OE words that look very different (e.g., *daily* represents a considerable shortening of *gedæghwamlican, loaf* comes from *hlaf*).
4. Some words have been lost from the language and replaced by others (*gewurðe, costnunge, alys*). In some instances a form related to an OE word survives in German (as *rice* is a cognate of German *Reich*).
5. OE words more often have inflectional endings than do Mod E words (e.g., *ure, urne,* and *urum* for *our, forgyf* and *forgyfa* for *forgive,* inflectional endings on *heofonum* and *eorðan*).
6. OE word order often differs from that of Mod E (e.g., *fæder ure, To becume ðin rice, urne gedæghwamlican hlaf syle us*).

Similarly, passages in Chaucer and later writers may be examined to compare them with Mod E. (Incidentally, Chaucer, who lived in the fourteenth century, did *not* write Old English. The language of his time is called Middle English.)

Here are some other suggestions for activities in connection with the study of older forms of the language:

1. To show the contributions of other languages to English, the class draws a river with Anglo-Saxon as the source. Into this river flow tributaries as follows: Celtic (small), early Latin borrowings (small), Danish (small), Norman French (large), Latin in Renaissance times (large), Greek in Renaissance times (medium), later French (large), Italian (medium), Spanish (medium), and then a number of small, medium, or large tributaries that in the last few centuries have contributed to English, including German, Greek and Latin again, French again, Chinese, Japanese, African languages, American Indian languages, Indian, Russian, etc.
2. Choose a somewhat longer OE passage than the Lord's Prayer. A selection from the writings of King Alfred, such as his account of the voyage of Ohthere, is suitable. With the class, scrutinize it carefully, as we did the Lord's Prayer.
3. Trace the spelling of a few words from OE to the present (e.g., *all, home, it, few, summer, how, sail* (verb), *might* (verb), *they*. Note that spelling did not become very systematized until after the invention of printing; discuss why this was so. (The *Oxford English Dictionary* is the best source for this exercise.)
4. Devote a little attention to the pronunciation of older forms of the language, noting especially how several vowel sounds changed in a regular pattern, as illustrated by *ham→home, hus→house, swete→sweet, ridan→ride.* A student might report on the Great Vowel Shift, which gave to English vowels values different from those in Continental languages.
5. Compare some forms of OE nouns, verbs, and adjectives with their modern

equivalents, noting the numerous inflectional endings on the former and the comparatively few such endings in Mod E. How does Mod E get along with so few inflections?

6. Study the Norman Conquest and its influence on the language: class distinctions, contributions to vocabulary, expediting of the loss of inflections, gradual merging of English and Norman French (with English predominant).

7. Besides looking at the language of Chaucer, examine some other short passages in Middle English. Parts of Layamon's *Brut* (c. 1205) may illustrate the transition from OE to ME. Students will also find interesting some passages from *The Travels of Sir John Mandeville* (translated into English c. 1377). Verses from Wycliffe's Bible, translated in Chaucer's time, may be compared with later versions.

8. As an example of the language just before Shakespeare flourished, the class may look at a scene from *Gammer Gurton's Needle,* which uses a southwestern dialect instead of the London dialect that was soon to become preeminent. Then, in looking at the language of Shakespeare, the class may observe not only vocabulary differences from Mod E but also word order, the manner of phrasing questions and negatives, forms of verbs and nouns and adjectives (e.g., *most unkindest*). The *do*-transformation, now used in questions like *Did he respond?* and in negatives like *He did not respond,* was just coming into being. Shakespeare used both it and older forms like *Responded he?* and *He responded not.*

9. Compare sentence length in the prose of Milton, Swift's and Johnson's essays, and nineteenth-century prose with sentence length today. Discuss any advantages or disadvantages that today's relatively short sentences may have.

10. Compare conversational style as reflected in one of Sheridan's or Goldsmith's eighteenth-century comedies with modern conversational style.

11. Find and give examples of how words may enter the language (by borrowing, compounding, use of affixes, functional shift, onomatopoeia, backformation, acronyms, blending). Find and give examples of what may happen to words once they are in (degeneration, elevation, generalization, specialization, radiation, shortening, lengthening, metathesis, shifts in pronunciation and spelling).

12. In light of the historical study, list some of the outstanding characteristics of Mod E, such as huge vocabulary, few inflections, tendency toward short sentences, existence of various dialects, rather fixed sentence patterns, extensive use of transformations, single accepted spellings for most words.[13]

# THE IDEA BOX

## NONVERBAL DIFFERENCES

According to Phyllis Roehm of LaSalle College, "The Puerto Rican student with bowed head and downcast eyes listening to his teacher is expressing the good manners of his culture, not defying the teacher."

Whites, according to Mrs. Roehm, usually look away from the person they are speaking to but look at the person they are listening to. Blacks usually do just the opposite. The result can be misunderstanding or even breakdown of communication in a conversation between a white and a black if either or both are unfamiliar with this cultural pattern and misinterpret the signal systems.

Such cues, always present in interpersonal relations, may carry as much as 90 percent of the "message."[14]

## MORE ON NONVERBAL COMMUNICATION

Books like Julius Fast's *Body Language* have familiarized us with the idea that much communication is nonverbal. A good, brief introduction to the subject is Charles R. Duke's "Nonverbal Behavior and the Communication Process," *College Composition and Communication,* December 1974, p. 397.

A now somewhat dated but still useful book, Edward T. Hall's *The Silent Language,* discusses such things as time, space, gestures, and facial expressions as devices of communication. Because these differ from culture to culture (e.g., clapping hands is not universally a symbol of approval), this kind of knowledge is of value to a traveler. Moreover, it may help students to understand more clearly that spoken language too is tied to the mores of a people.

## NEW "ELEMENTS" IN ENGLISH

"Chemistry teachers are not loath to add another element to their charts, and physics teachers do not resent acknowledging an alternative theory about the structure of matter. What is it about a changing language and changing tastes in language that English teachers generally find so threatening?"[15]

## THE LANGUAGES OF OTHER WORLDS

Imagine meeting a being from another world who uses (not necessarily speaks or writes) a language entirely different from any on earth. Describe that language. How might we learn to communicate with the stranger?

A fascinating article that describes a dozen or more such beings as portrayed in science fiction is "Strange Bedfellows: Science Fiction, Linguistics, and Education," by Beverly Friend, *English Journal,* October 1973, 98. Reading it will put you a step or two ahead of your most imaginative students.

## SEVEN CATEGORIES OF LANGUAGE INSTRUCTION

John Bushman recommends attention to these seven categories of language study: (1) Exploring the Nature of Language. (2) Exploring the Structure of Language. (3) Exploring Usage in Language. (4) Exploring Language Heritage. (5) Exploring Geographical and Social Dialects. (6) Exploring Semantics. (7) Exploring the "Silent Language."[16]

## THE EVANSTON LANGUAGE PLAN

Evanston, Illinois, Township High School has organized its language work like this: "for the ninth-graders, a fairly long, linguistically-oriented language unit which gives them some exposure to lexicology-lexicography, dialectology, and the history of the language, all of which, excepting the grammar, they will study in more detail as they go through school. The sophomores have a two-week unit in lexicology-lexicography; the juniors concentrate on dialectology, and the seniors study the history of the language."[17]

## WHAT A SPEAKER REVEALS

In "Language-Learning Objectives: A Checklist," Arnold Lazarus includes this item: "To understand that whenever a speaker in literature or life makes an utterance, he always reveals one of more of the following: his historical era, his geographical stance (country, region, locality), his age (infancy, childhood, adolescence, adulthood, senility), his sex (male, female, effeminate, tomboyish), the age and sex of his audience, the size of his audience (from intimate to public), his formal education (lack of education, half-education, 'prestige' dialects), his socioeconomic status . . . , his cultural milieu's values, sports, and pastimes."[18]

## "A LANGUAGE UNIT IN THE JUNIOR HIGH SCHOOL"

Among 15 assignments suggested by Thomas E. Melchior are examination of the language of advertising, building a scrapbook of affective language, using highly connotative words, examining fictional language of teen-agers, and noting variations in TV language according to sex, age, education, and so on.[19]

## ENGLISH AROUND THE WORLD

An interesting project for a group of able students is to examine the extent and the variety of use of English around the world—not just in English-speaking countries but in Mexico, Scandinavia, Russia, Japan, Malaysia, Africa, South America, and so on.

## A DAY'S ENGLISH

To provide motivation, some teachers have students list all the uses they make of language in one day, from hearing Mother's "Time to get up" to the last "Good night.'' Presence of both formal and informal English may be noted; speaking, listening, reading, and writing should all be noted.

## THE ROLE OF GRAMMAR IN THE CLASSROOM

Robert C. Pooley presented an exceptionally clear history of the teaching of grammar in his *Teaching English Grammar* (in 1957), along with a specific discussion of grammar's present and potential role in the English classroom; even though several schools of grammar have developed since that time, Pooley's treatment is useful for perspective. So is his *Teaching English Usage,* second edition, 1974.

## WHAT A SENTENCE IS

According to William Reynolds, ''The overriding concern must be—does the sentence move the reader from here to there so that he can follow what the writer wants to say? 'Real life,' says Saul Bellow, 'is a relationship between *here* and *there.'* We could do worse than suggest that showing the relationship between here and there is a working definition of a sentence.''[20]

## CONSCIOUSNESS OF THE RECEIVER

The explanation of much unclear language is that speakers or writers incorrectly or unthinkingly assume that the listener or reader has the same knowledge as they themselves have. As a result they leave out information necessary for the stranger to understand. They say, ''Just keep on down this street,'' failing to tell the stranger that the street turns and then changes its name.

Repetitive exercises involving role-playing as strangers and informants can increase clarity of communication. *Stranger* means anyone not familiar with the locale, history, biography, customs, ethnic background, or any other characteristics of an area or a group of people.

## SENTENCE VARIATION

Thomas Wilcox finds it useful to ask students to write the ''same'' sentence in five different ways. For example, (1) Joan awakened at seven o'clock, and she went downstairs to breakfast. (2) Since it was already seven o'clock when Joan awakened, she jumped out of bed and ran downstairs to breakfast. (3) Joan knew that breakfast was always at seven o'clock, so she hurried out of bed and downstairs. (4) ''Oh, my goodness! It's seven o'clock. I must hurry downstairs for breakfast,'' Joan said upon awakening. (5) When Joan awakened at seven o'clock, the thought of breakfast increased her speed downstairs.[21]

## ''AN OUTLINE FOR WRITING SENTENCE-COMBINING PROBLEMS''

Charles R. Cooper of SUNY at Buffalo offers a useful although incomplete outline to guide teachers who want to develop sentence-combining exercises. The main headings are ''Noun Modifiers'' and ''Noun Substitutes.'' *English Journal,* Jan. 1973, p. 96.

## SENTENCE-COMBINING DEBATE

For a debate about the merits of sentence combining, see articles by William Strong (pro) and Robert J. Marzano (con) in the February 1976, *English Journal*. Letters supporting and opposing sentence combining are printed in the December 1976, *English Journal*.

## WHY DIAGRAMMING DOESN'T WORK

[Critics say] that much of our trouble [with language and writing] can be traced straight to the decline in the teaching of How to Diagram Sentences. The problem with traditional diagramming was that it didn't accurately reflect the structure of the sentences. The usual example (Chomsky's) is this pair of sentences:

(a) John is easy to please.
(b) John is eager to please.

These two sentences, in traditional sentence diagrams, are exactly alike in structure. Yet any native speaker of English knows that in "John is easy to please" John is the object of the action, while in "John is eager to please" he is the subject.[22]

## "DO WE NEED TO TEACH A GRAMMAR TERMINOLOGY?"

Emphasize language use more than grammatical terminology, and your students will probably do all right on college entrance tests. Gary A. Sutton studied and gives examples of test questions on which he based this conclusion.[23]

In general it is accurate to say that neither College Entrance Examination Board tests nor the tests given by individual institutions place emphasis on the ability to classify grammatical constructions. What they *do* stress is ability to distinguish poor constructions from good ones; those institutions that require compositions also emphasize the ability to compose coherent sentences in thoughtful, coherent paragraphs.

Students should, however, have a clear awareness of a few basic grammatical terms, such as *noun, verb, adjective, adverb, clause, phrase*. These are convenient shortcut terms that enable them to discuss sentence structure without being verbose.

## MOTIVATION FOR CHANGE

... "When students really feel that language is a means of social mobility, they make astonishingly fast progress in acquiring standard English through aural-oral [pattern practice] methods. In the language laboratory at Dillard University in New Orleans, for example, college freshmen with a clear sense of a need for standard English in their future professional lives have shown great skill in acquiring a second dialect and in shifting from one dialect to the other as the situation demands. There are many individual students in junior and senior high school with this kind of self-direction, but they are by no means in the majority."[24]

## BUILD YOUR OWN PREPOSITION BOX

Rebecca Ann Dick, of Somerset, N.J., makes a large box with no top or bottom, decorates it with 23 doodled prepositions, and prepares a card for each preposition. One student, "It," acts out a preposition of his choice (e.g., crawls *through* the box, puts something *on* it), and calls on a classmate to identify the preposition. Great fun for junior high school [or middle school] wigglers, says Ms. Dick.[25]

## THE USEFUL DOUBLE NEGATIVE

Not all double negatives are undesirable. There's one in the preceding sentence. For another example, this bakery commercial: "Everybody doesn't like something, but nobody doesn't like Sara Lee." Or this: "I didn't want to not wear them," which isn't quite the same as "I wanted to wear them."

## "SHOW 'EM AND LET 'EM COPY"

In wartime an ververbal instructor was trying to tell a recruit the principles for adjusting the barrel of a machine gun. No success. A combat veteran took over. "Look, Mac, this way," he demonstrated. The recruit understood at once. Said the combat veteran to the instructor, "If we tried to explain *how* everything works, we'd never win a war. Show 'em and let 'em copy." A group of New England teachers points out that people learn most of their grammar and usage by imitation, too.[26]

## GRAMMAR IS A MAP

... "The professional grammarian is the mapmaker who charts all the known roads of the English language; grammar is the map; the teacher is the driving instructor who chooses the most useful roads recorded on the map and teaches them to his students. Ultimately the students develop their own judgment and read the map for themselves. The mapmaker does not say ... , 'You must use this road and no other.' He says, 'Here is the map of the roads,' and he may, by the red and black lines on his map, indicate which are most used and which are in best condition. . . ."[27]

## SENTENCE PATTERNS

After unscrambling a number of sentences such as "crawls baby a" or "eats elephant daisies the," junior high students determine what the usual sentence patterns are. Later they enjoy a "pattern hunt" to find examples of these patterns in newspaper or magazine articles. (Grace Ashenfelter, Urbana, Ill.)

## GAMES FOR JUNIOR HIGH

1. The baseball game is a favorite. Have two teams. A right answer to a question on grammar (or something else) is a single; a wrong answer is an out.
2. In the old game of adverbs, one student (It) is sent out of the room. Others decide on an adverb to act out. When It returns, class members help It to find Its identity by doing what It asks, for example, "Go to the chalkboard in the manner of the adverb," "Make a face that suggests the adverb."

## MAD-LIBS

Mad-Libs is a commercial game for which a classroom version can be improvised. A group of students makes up a "story" of a few sentences but leaves out, say, eight nouns, three verbs, two adjectives, two prepositions, and an adverb. Without hearing the story the class makes a random list of eight nouns, and so on, and then everybody tries to fit the class list into the blanks. A painless way to teach parts of speech.

## TENSE STUDY

Ellen Newman takes a sentence like "Yesterday I washed my sweater" and substitutes *tomorrow* for *yesterday*. Students realize that another change is then needed. They try again with *today* and other time words.[28]

## "WRITTEN ENGLISH IS A 'SECOND LANGUAGE'"

Robert L. Allen points to differences between spoken and written English—for example, in possessives, spelling, written substitutes for intonation, indicators of paragraphing—and suggests the need for a grammar truly descriptive of written language.[29]

## USEFUL STRUCTURES IN WRITTEN ENGLISH

Andrew MacLeish analyzes eight structures fairly common in written English but not in spoken: (1) Pre-junctural adjective or participle (*Confused,* he sat down.); (2) Pre-junctural infinitive (*To make the team,* he practiced every day); (3) Pre-junctural absolute (*His friends* having left, John went to bed); (4) Nominal *that*-clause as subject (*That they would not come* was the problem); (5) Infinitive and infinitive phrase as subject (*To see* his father was his greatest wish); (6) Nonrestrictive relative clause (She has a large hat, *which is red and woolly*); (7) Nonrestrictive appositive (Joe, *the star of the team,* made the touchdown); (8) Conjunction *for* (She closed the door, *for* it was raining).[30]

## MOVABLE MODIFIERS

Dorothy Dakin, writing in the Puget Sound *English Notes,* suggested using cards on a flannel board. Print on the cards the parts of a sentence such as *The leaves of the trees rustle/ when the wind blows/ in the forest.* Move the parts around to note possible positions of modifiers and resulting changes in meaning or emphasis.

## BUT MAY I START A SENTENCE WITH BUT?

Professional writers often start sentences with *and* or *but*. There is no reason for teaching students that the practice is illegal.[31]

## DEPARTMENT OF SLIGHT CONFUSION

Students may enjoy collecting slightly confusing sentences from ads, newspaper stories, or other sources, and posting them. For example, an announcement by an airline steward, "When the seat belt sign is turned off, we suggest that you still keep it loosely fastened."

## WHICH SENTENCE IS BETTER?

"School spirit is when somebody gives up something he wants to do to cheer at an unimportant football game." "School spirit is loyalty to the highest ideals of the institution." Louis Zahner, a distinguished New England teacher, preferred the first, because "The content is the precious cargo; start with it, find and teach its appropriate form. . . . Our job is to wed form and content." So, said Zahner, we praise the fullness of an idea, condemn the empty words of a platitude, and thus we build the desire to say well what is worth saying.

## PARALLEL CONSTRUCTION

Margaret Lamon, of Siena High School, Chicago, demonstrated parallel construction and introduced students to this useful grammatical and rhetorical device by writing a speech of Brutus (*Julius Caesar*) in this way:

Romans,
  countrymen
and lovers!
    hear me
      for my cause,
    believe me
      for my honor,
    censure me
      in your wisdom.

## "A TEACHER'S ADVENTURES IN PROGRAMLAND"

One teacher's evaluation: "Programming by itself is no panacea. It is one more teaching device to be used when and where it does the job best. For teaching grammar and rhetoric, a well-conceived and well-taught program has proved to be the most effective device I have ever used."[32]

## APPLYING LINGUISTICS TO LITERATURE

E. E. Cummings often dropped verbs into noun slots ("sowed their isn't," "went their came"). D. H. Lawrence used different syntactic structures for expressing different moods. These are two of the discoveries made by Sallie Isaacs' classes when they applied linguistics to literature.[33]

## A CASE FOR ONOMASTICS

Students make up imaginary accounts of how a town got its name and then check against George R. Stewart's *Dictionary of American Place-Names* (Oxford University Press, 1970) for the real explanation. For example, Wounded Knee, S.D., Braintree, Mass., Tell City, Ind., Sleepy Eye, Minn.[34]

    Actually, the study of personal and place names can interest many students. They like, for instance, to trace the origin, and perhaps variant spellings, of their own names. A good source of information is Elsdon Smith's *New Dictionary of American Family Names* (Harper and Row, 1973).

## "AMERICAN TRADITIONS OF LANGUAGE USE"

Michael G. Crowell traces the history of American attitudes toward language from the neoclassical (prescriptive) through the romantic (like Whitman's) to the present scientific.[35] Also informative for a teacher is Patricia Moody's "The American Grammatical Revolution," which describes a number of early grammar books.[35]

## WHERE DO WORDS COME FROM, TEACH?

R. C. Simonini, Jr., described 15 sources of new words, as distinguished from native or borrowed words: (1) Idiomatic compounds (*egghead, Iron Curtain*); (2) Greek and Latin combining forms (*astronaut, demography*); (3) Derivatives (*belittle, bizonal*); (4) Semantic change (*bologna, bug* for *microphone*); (5) Self-explaining compounds (*supermarket, ballpoint pen*); (6) Acronyms (*Texaco, NASA*); (7) Blends (*chortle, cinemonster*); (8) Functional change words (*knowhow,* the plane was *missiled*); (9) pure root creations (*kodak, dacron*); (10) Shortening (*bus, bra*); (11) Reduplication (*wishy-washy, hush-hush*); (12) Echoism (*ack-ack, zipper*); (13) Back formation (*baby sit, fact find*); (14) Sound symbolism (*sweetie, sneeze*); (15) Mistaken *-s* singulars (*specie, pea*).[36]

## "DOWN GIANTWIFE: THE USES OF ETYMOLOGY"

Charlton Laird discusses (fascinatingly) how students' vocabularies may be enriched as they become increasingly aware of word etymologies and interrelationships. For example, did you know that all these words have a common source: *much, mickle, megaton* (and a number of other *mega-* words), *maharajah, mahatma, magistrate, master, magnitude* (and other *magn-* words), *maximum, maxim, major, majority, mayor, majesty?*[37]

## THE USES OF LANGUAGE HISTORY

Edwain A. Hoey suggests a few of the rich insights that students may attain through study of language history: understanding of language change, the impossibility of purism, the interactions of language and society, the development of dialects, and the ways that "rules" were formulated.[38]

## GRAMMAR VERSUS USAGE

This distinction between grammar and usage may help to clarify your students' understanding: "Grammar is a list of *possible* ways to assemble sentences; usage is a smaller list of *socially preferred* ways within a dialect. Usage is trendy, arbitrary, and above all, constantly changing, like all other fashions in clothing, music, or automobiles. Grammar is the rationale of a language; usage is its etiquette."[39]

EMULATING SYNTACTIC PATTERNS

One of the productive devices used by Gary Sloan of Louisiana Tech to teach effectiveness in writing sentences is to imitate the syntactic patterns of professionals. For example, Bertrand Russell's "Philosophy begins when someone asks a question, and so does science" leads to "Lions heel when trainers crack the long whip, and so do students" and "Joy enters when one becomes a proud parent, and so does sorrow."[40]

# FOOTNOTES

1. *Syntactic Structures,* The Hague: Mouton & Co., 1957, p. 43.
2. See Walter Loban's *Language Development: Kindergarten Through Grade Twelve,* NCTE, Urbana, Illinois, 1976, for a detailed scholarly account of the growth of sentence structures in those 13 years.
3. *The Effect of a Study of Transformational Grammar on the Writing of Ninth and Tenth Graders,* Champaign: NCTE, 1966.
4. *Transformational Sentence-Combining: A Method for Enhancing the Development of Syntactic Fluency in English Composition,* Cambridge: Harvard University, 1967.
5. *Sentence-Combining,* Urbana, NCTE, 1973.
6. New York: Appleton-Century-Crofts, 1956, pp. 376–377.
7. "Multiple Negation," *Inside the ACD,* Oct. 1957, p. 3.
8. "Improving Sentence Structure," *English Journal* 47, April 1958, p. 209.
9. These histories may prove especially useful:
   A. C. Baugh, *A History of the English Language,* Second edition, New York: Appleton-Century-Crofts, 1957.
   J. N. Hook, *History of the English Language,* New York: The Ronald Press Company, 1975.
   _____, *The Story of British English,* Glenview: Scott, Foresman and Company, 1974. (A high school textbook.)
   L. M. Myers, *The Roots of Modern English,* Boston: Little, Brown and Company, 1966.
   Thomas Pyles, *The Origins and Development of the English Language,* Second edition, New York: Harcourt Brace Jovanovich, 1971.
10. Baugh, cited in the note above, has a long list of words we use that were once Norman French.
11. Most of the histories listed above will provide basic material for such charts. For concise descriptions and examples of all major languages of the world,

see Kenneth Katzner, *The Languages of the World,* New York: Funk and Wagnalls, 1975.

12. Useful in the study of American English are these books: J. N. Hook, *The Story of American English,* New York: Harcourt Brace Jovanovich, 1972 (a high school textbook); Thomas Pyles, *Words and Ways of American English,* New York: Random House, 1952.

13. Many helpful teaching hints may be found in Joseph Milosh's *Teaching the History of the English Language,* Urbana, NCTE, 1972.

14. NCTE *Council-Grams,* March 1977, p. 59.

15. Mary Virginia Taylor, "The Folklore of Usage," *College English* 35, April 1974, p. 756.

16. "The Power of Language," *English Journal* 59, Nov. 1970, p. 1091.

17. Dorothy M. Griffin, "Dialects and Democracy," *English Journal* 59, April 1970, p. 551.

18. *Word Study,* Feb. 1965.

19. *English Journal* 56, Sept. 1967, p. 858.

20. "Some Thoughts on Writing," *English Journal* 65, May 1976, p. 12.

21. In *Writing Exercises from* Exercise Exchange, Littleton Long, ed., Urbana, NCTE, 1976, p. 37.

22. Suzette H. Elgin, "Why *Newsweek* Can't Tell Us Why Johnny Can't Write," *English Journal* 65, Nov. 1976, p. 34.

23. *English Journal* 65, Nov. 1976, p. 37.

24. Charles Suhor, "Pattern Practice," *English Journal* 60, Dec. 1971, p. 1223.

25. *English Journal* 66, April 1977, p. 75.

26. E. J. Gordon and E. S. Noyes, eds., "What About Grammar?" in *Essays on the Teaching of English,* New York: Appleton-Century-Crofts, 1960, p. 35.

27. Gordon and Noyes, pp. 44–45.

28. "An Experiment in Oral Language," in *The Disadvantaged Learner,* S. W. Webster, ed., San Francisco: Chandler Publishing Co., 1966, p. 513.

29. *English Journal* 65, p. 739.

30. "Some Structures for Written English," *English Journal* 58, Sept. 1969, p. 877.

31. For two discussions that offer perspective, see Herman R. Struck, "The Myth about Initial Conjunctions," *English Journal* 54, Jan. 1965, p. 42, and Paul C. Rodgers, "The Two Hundred Years' War," *English Journal* 55, Jan. 1966, p. 69.

32. Grace L. Graham, *English Journal* 58, Feb. 1969, p. 261.

33. "From Language to Linguistic Criticism," *English Journal* 57, Jan. 1968, p. 47.

34. Trudy Nunn, of Nevada, California, in *Potpourri,* Spring 1976.

35. *English Journal* 65, Dec. 1976, p. 33.
36. "Word-making in Present-day English," *English Journal* 65, Sept. 1976, p. 752.
37. *English Journal* 59, Nov. 1970, p. 1106.
38. "History Might Help," *English Journal* 57, Oct. 1968, p. 1041.
39. Ian S. Fraser and Lynda M. Hodson, "Twenty-one Kicks at the Grammar Horse," *English Journal* 67, Dec. 1978, p. 52.
40. "Writing as Games," *English Journal* 67, Nov. 1978, p. 44.

# 9

## AN ENGLISH LANGUAGE PROGRAM: PART 2

## DIALECTS AND USAGE

### SOME DEFINITIONS

No two persons speak their language exactly alike. There are always at least minor variations in enunciation, pronunciation, and intonation. The speech peculiar to an individual is called an idiolect. Everybody (including you) speaks an idiolect.

A group of similar idiolects, even though they differ somewhat from one another, is called a dialect. Everybody (including you) speaks a dialect. Dialects may differ in vocabulary, pronunciation, and grammar. What is a *tonic* in New England may be a *soft drink, soda, pop, soda pop, dope,* or something else in another part of the country. What is a *thing* to most other Americans is a *thang* to many Texans. Most people say *hair is* but some say *hair are.*

Dialect geographers broadly distinguish American dialects as Northern, Midland, and Southern, and then subdivide them in various ways, for example as East and West Texas, or Northeastern United States, or upstate and downstate Illinois. In some places they have found small "pockets" or "islands" in which there are distinct dialectal differences from the surrounding areas. The West coast, particularly California, is a mélange of dialects as it is of people.

But dialects are not exclusively a matter of geography. Many Mexican-Americans have speech characteristics not shared by the majority of Americans. So do many Polish-Americans, Italian-Americans, Pennsylvania German-Americans, black Americans, and other national or ethnic groups.

In England there are still class distinctions as well as the others. Almost

284

everyone in what is considered the upper class speaks Received Standard, the English heard on most BBC broadcasts and in most lectures at Oxford or Cambridge; some people from the lower class learn Received Standard, but most do not and often speak dialects that vary considerably from one another. In America, class distinctions are less obvious and are likely to be based on education or wealth or both, rather than birth.

There are also language distinctions, called dialectal by some linguists, in sex and age. The vocabularies and the intonation patterns of women and of men are not precisely the same. Children, teen-agers, young adults, mature adults, and old people do not talk quite alike.

## INFORMATION, NOT ERADICATION

To attempt to eradicate dialectal differences is ridiculous. They start in infancy and soon become well established. They are not innate, though. The child of illiterate black parents, for instance, if brought up by educated foster-parents in a highly literate community, will speak like his or her foster-parents and associates, not like the natural parents.

In general, Americans are tolerant of modest degrees of dialectal differences, if comprehension is not seriously affected. They elected as President a New Yorker who said "nîther" instead of the more common American "nēther," a New Englander who talked about "Cuber," a Texan who said "thang," and a Georgian who said "hep" for *help*.

Before much was known about dialectology, many teachers assumed that people shouldn't speak a dialect. Everybody should speak "correct English," and these teachers believed that they knew what correct English was. Usually it was the language that they themselves spoke natively or that they had laboriously learned in school and college. A dialect, they thought, used wrong pronunciations, wrong words, wrong grammatical forms. It was a bad thing that should be extirpated.

The constant attack on dialectal differences sometimes had a blighting effect on students. They were made to feel that their language and that of their parents and friends was inferior, something to be ashamed of. Some of them did their best to eliminate the variations between their speech and that which teacher and textbook said was correct. Others merely did the exercises and emerged unaffected. Still others—the ones adversely affected—concluded that here was only one more piece of evidence showing the unreality and the uselessness of school; they were penalized because they didn't learn to "talk like a book," and often these penalties, along with others imposed by the school, made them decide to drop out at the earliest possible time.

Lack of knowledge about dialectology had another harmful effect. Say that a Southern boy moved into a Northern community, or vice versa. He talked differently than the natives, so they ridiculed and imitated his speech derisively. Many children are less tolerant of language differences than adult voters are. Unless the boy was strong and agile enough to beat up his tormentors, or unless he had skill in football or some other activity prized by the school, the torture might last a long time. But if the children had known some of the facts about language variation—for instance, that they themselves spoke dialects—they might have accepted him a little more readily.

## THE PRESENT ATTITUDE

Today enlightened English teachers try to avoid the errors of their predecessors. For one thing, they build understanding that everyone speaks a dialect and that dialectal variations are interesting. Life would be monotonous if every human being were blonde, blue-eyed, and five feet eight inches tall, and also if every human being possessed the same skills and the same temperament. We don't expect all people to be exactly alike, and we'd be bored if they were. Language variation can add its own spice to living and to our appreciation and enjoyment of our fellows. This attitude of interest in and acceptance of mutually comprehensible dialects is easier to inculcate than it would have been 50 years ago, for radio and television have exposed today's students to many dialects, people now travel more than they once did, and Americans move to other communities more often than was once true. Therefore, there is ever-increasing opportunity to hear many different dialects, to realize that people who speak differently may nevertheless be worthwhile.

One step in teaching about dialects lies in familiarizing students with the chief reasons for the existence of dialects. Geographical dialects exist mainly because of patterns of settlement. Thus, French influence is evident in parts of Canada and Louisiana, German in parts of Pennsylvania, Elizabethan English in pockets in the South or the Midlands, Spanish in the Southwest. Within a given community the speech patterns of today may still reflect the influence of Finns, Norwegians, Italians, Irish, or some other group who settled a century ago.

Another reason for the existence of geographical dialects is physical barriers—mountains, rivers, large lakes, and so on. Even though settlers on the two sides of a barrier may have similar language backgrounds, they gradually diverge in language if they do not communicate steadily. Perhaps the most dramatic example of this is the growth of the Romance languages from the parental Latin. Because there was little mingling across the Pyrenees or the Alps, the Latin in what we call Spain, France, and Italy became more and more divergent until eventually what started out as only small dialectal differences became different languages.

The influence of a leader may also sometimes affect the language of an area. For example, it is said that the lisped Castilian *c*, as in *Barcelona,* exists because a Spanish king lisped. He said "Bar*the*lona," for example, his courtiers who

THE TEACHING OF HIGH SCHOOL ENGLISH

wanted to be like him said the word in the same way, and the common people later imitated the courtiers. Today the influence of a leader may be less potent, but historically it was probably the cause of a number of variations.

It is more difficult to locate the ultimate sources of social dialects. Certainly differences in speech have for thousands of years gone along with differences in social rank. There are hints of this in ancient drama, and anthropologists have described tribes in which use of one set of language forms was the prerogative of chiefs only, or in which men and women spoke essentially different languages. The language of medieval serfs was apparently highly unlike that of their masters. Shakespeare reflected the difference a few centuries later by the artifice of having his "inferior" characters speak in prose (the Porter in *Macbeth*, Bottom and his fellows in *MND*), whereas his dukes and kings spoke a blank verse that in reality would have been far beyond their powers.

If we could explain with assurance why social dialects exist, we would no doubt have to draw on such historical bases. In countries where class distinctions have been openly made, the lower classes were uneducated and were restricted to menial tasks. Though many lower class individuals were unquestionably as intelligent as their social superiors, their lack of advantages usually left them less articulate, more repetitive in their speech, less able to use abstractions, and less concerned with "refinements" of their speech because refinement of any sort had little relevance in their lives.

In America's supposedly classless society, millions of people still receive poor education, live in ghettos or rural shacks, and speak a language that the snobbish regard as inferior and incorrect. Others, especially those climbing out of poverty, still employ the language of their childhood or modify it by trying to use some of the forms they hear in the school, office, factory, or on television. Each person, in fact, generally tries to use a language appropriate to his or her surroundings. The change to a different type of language, however, sometimes results in problems when the person returns to the former environment.

Teachers know (society being what it is) that users of a nonstandard dialect may in some circumstances be penalized for its use; some doors are open and good jobs are available to the speaker of a standard dialect, but the doors may close and a "No Vacancy" sign may go up when a nonstandard speaker appears.

So teachers have a dilemma. They know that there is nothing inherently inferior in expressions like "I's heah" or "She don' wan' none," and that the users of such expressions may be as capable as other persons. But they know also that influential segments of society value "I'm here" and "She doesn't want any" and have their own ways of rewarding persons who use them, their own ways of penalizing those who do not.

Faced with this dilemma, modern teachers spend quite a bit of time teaching facts and attitudes about dialects. They may start with recordings illustrating geographical variants, about which people are less sensitive. When they come to social variants, they make it clear that nobody's language is wrong or inferior.

One kind of language, called standard, is however more highly regarded by many influential people of all races. This prestige dialect is thus introduced to students as one of the variants. Children are given opportunity to learn about it, to practice it, and to decide eventually for themselves whether they want to use it when it seems appropriate to do so. In other words, there is no condemnation of the children's present language and that of their parents, nor is there forced use of the prestige dialect. But the instruction is there, and the students can decide for themselves how much use they want to make of it.

## SOME USEFUL MATERIALS

Thirty-two maps from linguistic atlases are reproduced in Carroll E. Reed's *Dialects of American English*.[1] Through their use, students may learn about dialect areas, isoglosses, and dialect geographers' methods of indicating frequency of use of such synonyms as *cottage cheese, Dutch cheese,* and *smearcase*. The small book also has useful information about colonial English and regional variations.

Roger Shuy's *Discovering American Dialects*,[2] in addition to providing many examples of geographical differences, makes suggestions for dialect "fieldwork" that students can do. For example: study local history to find out where early settlers came from and what kinds of changes in population have since occurred; find the origins of local place names; conduct a questionnaire study to discover local residents' names for various things. Shuy also recommends study of dialects in various literary works, such as *The Yearling, I Remember Mama, Giants in the Earth, Papa Is All, My Antonia, The Education of Hyman Kaplan, Mr. Dooley Says, In the Tennessee Mountains, Huckleberry Finn,* and *Gentle Persuasion*.

*People Say Things Different Ways*,[3] by J. N. Hook, which has an accompanying *Teacher's Resource Book,* has as its setting a high school that serves a military base and consequently draws students from many backgrounds. In the book students from various parts of the United States, as well as England, Australia, Canada, and Taiwan, discuss the dialects of the areas where they grew up. Some of the students are black, Puerto Rican, and Mexican-American; one or two of them are militantly opposed to making any modifications at all in the language habits they formed at home. The book, written with a light touch, gives scores of examples of dialectal variations and provides a glossary of basic terms used in dialectology.

## SOME ADDITIONAL CONSIDERATIONS

Some teachers argue that no attempt at all should be made to teach standard English, the dialect which at the present time is the one preferred by the majority of editors, teachers, and employers of skilled and semiskilled workers. Even to describe it as an alternative, they say, may make children feel that their own language is inferior.

In 1974, after long debate, NCTE's Conference on College Composition and Communication approved a resolution almost to that effect and published it with an elaborate and useful supporting statement.[4] The parent NCTE accepted the resolution with some modifications which suggested that every student should have an *opportunity* to learn Edited American English (the written form of standard English). The CCCC resolution is as follows:

> *We affirm the students' right to their own patterns and varieties of language—the dialects of their nurture or whatever dialects in which they find their own identity and style. Language scholars long ago denied that the myth of a standard American dialect has any validity. The claim that any one dialect is unacceptable amounts to an attempt of one social group to exert its dominance over another. Such a claim leads to false advice for speakers and writers, and immoral advice for humans. A nation proud of its diverse heritage and its cultural and racial variety will preserve its heritage of dialects. We affirm strongly that teachers must have the experiences and training that will enable them to respect diversity and uphold the right of students to their own language.*

In support of the leave-their-language-alone position, Joan Isenbarger and Veta Smith of Kalamazoo have told of requiring their white students (prospective teachers) to undergo a session in which they were told that their English was wrong and that they had to master a black dialect.[5] "The responses indicated that more than three-fourths of the students felt threatened by the teacher, probably because of the extreme difficulty in acquiring a 'new' dialect and the teacher's general lack of sympathy with the problem." (After the session, 85 percent of the students said, "I would like to learn more about dialects.")

Geneva Smitherman, while a lecturer in Harvard's Afro-American Studies Department, wrote: "I denounce as futile, time-wasting, and perhaps even racist the current attempts to move Black students from saying 'He tired' to 'He is tired,' from 'He do' to 'He does,' etc. Such goals involve only lateral moves and Black students need (upward) vertical moves."[6]

But spokesmen in favor of exposure to standard English have been no less vehement. Said Jessie M. Wright:

> *The foreign student who comes to us to learn English as a second language is taught "his hat" and not "he hat." No corruption of the phrase is acceptable to the teacher. How drugged must be the conscience of the teacher who accepts "he hat" from the black American in his class and further anesthetizes himself with his pious concern that he will injure the black spirit if he*

*makes the poor fellow change his speech pattern and learn "white English."*
*What if that same black says that two plus two equals five? Must that be*
*accepted as black arithmetic?*[7]

Others with Wright's point of view argue that it is insulting to treat blacks as if they are incapable of learning what millions of American immigrants from all over the world have learned and learned well.

Joe Black, one-time pitcher for the Brooklyn Dodgers, was the first black man to win a World Series game. Later he became a vice-president of the Greyhound Corporation. Roger Kahn tells about him in *The Boys of Summer,* a book about the old Dodgers:

*He makes one point to everyone. It is bigotry to exalt the so-called special language of the blacks. "What is our language?" he asks. " 'Foteen' for 'fourteen.' 'Pohleeze' for 'police.' 'Raht back' for 'right back.' 'We is going.' To me any man, white or black, who says whites must learn our language is insulting. What he's saying is that every other ethnic group can migrate to America and master English, but we, who were born here and whose families have all lived here for more than a century, don't have the ability to speak proper English. Wear a dashiki or an African hairdo, but in the name of common sense, learn the English language. It is your own."*[8]

Suzette H. Elgin says that the issue is not "goodness" or "correctness" but "appropriateness":

*I try very hard to get straight in the minds of my students the distinction between "good" and "appropriate." My native Ozark dialect is not "appropriate" for conducting diplomacy at the United Nations. . . . The speech a teenager from Harlem uses on the street is not considered appropriate for participating in a job interview. GOODNESS has nothing to do with it. . . .*

Linguists have nothing against Standard English. They have nothing against teaching Standard English so long as the socioeconomic system of the country requires that a student be equipped with the prestige dialect to have a fair shake in life, and so long as a way can be found to do that teaching without destroying the child's self-respect and that of his family and his people.[9] She adds a comment by Leonard Newmark, a California professor of linguistics, who tells students that using some dialects for certain purposes is like trying to eat tomato soup with a fork. "There's nothing 'bad' about it at all, it just doesn't work *for those purposes.*"

Caroline E. Eckhardt of The Pennsylvania State University concurs, saying that students who do not learn generally accepted usages are, rightly or wrongly, often denied social mobility. Employers, she says, often reject applicants because of applications that do not adhere to standards.[10] This is true even when the employer is completely unaware of the race of the applicant.

290                

Smithie Henry, who describes herself as "a black teacher of predominantly black children" in Oakland, California, says that her children "tend to enjoy adding another dialect to their own." Her procedures commend themselves to many thoughtful teachers:

*We do not attempt to substitute standard English for the students' dialect, but rather to build up their knowledge of the way things are said in school and business. Acceptance and reshaping keep children from feeling insecure. No one says or suggests that they "talk wrong."*

*Since a child's language is so deeply connected with his attitudes toward himself and his world, he must develop a positive attitude toward the school and business communication tool—standard English.*[11]

One important point only occasionally made is that some dialects—not just some black dialects—are difficult for users of standard English to understand, and therefore the users of those dialects find it difficult to obtain jobs in which they must communicate with customers or others. Prejudice is not always the reason why some workers can get only menial work or none at all; the incomprehensibility of their language (to those outside their own group) is sometimes the cause. In the nineteenth and early twentieth centuries many Irish, German, Italian, Jewish, Hungarian, and other immigrants faced the same problem. Many of them continued using their most comfortable language in their own homes and neighborhoods, but kept trying in their occupations to use forms of the language that others could understand without difficulty. Most succeeded, or if they did not, their children did.

To summarize the point of view of the authors of this book: Dialects, except when they represent extreme variations from what the majority of educated Americans speak, are enjoyable and should not occasion worry to anyone. No dialects are "wrong." When they are difficult for the majority of Americans to understand, however, the law of self-preservation suggests that their users should know how, in public places, to move closer to conformity with the language that happens to be more widely understood. It is the schools' responsibility to make instruction available, whether or not the students choose to accept it.

## USAGE

Some syntactic usages have been discussed in the preceding chapter. Here we shall be concerned with the forms of individual words.

*Usage* refers to the choice between one form and another: *you was* vs. *you were, I seen* vs. *I saw, played well* vs. *played good, haven't any* vs. *ain't got none.*

Once more there are no absolute and permanent rights and wrongs. *Ain't,* for instance, was once much more respectable than it is now; at least two of our first

Presidents used it in their conversations. The double negative, as in *ain't got none,* was for centuries accepted without question, as it still is in some dialects. But, just as table manners change (we no longer throw bones under the table to the dogs), so does language etiquette. Some forms that used to be "in" are now "out," and vice versa. And use of the form that is out, trivial though the matter may be, disturbs many people whom we may not want to disturb. The user of *ain't got none* is simply not accepted in some social circles and in some kinds of work; he or she is not likely to be elected to the corporate board. Justly or unjustly, as we saw in the discussion of dialects, penalties and rewards are determined in part by one's usages.

The high school class in a previously mentioned book, *People Say Things Different Ways,* discussed what "good English" is and decided that it has these characteristics:

**1.** Good English is clear to the listener or reader.
**2.** Good English is effective; it is language that has a good chance to get results.
**3.** Good English is often colorful.
**4.** Good English does not offend the people you are with.

Usage is involved mainly in the fourth of these qualities. The statement is perhaps just another way to say that "Good English is appropriate."

Most people, says Dr. Jack Cameron of the University of Calgary, "object only to the few items of clearly nonstandard English; to breezy slang expressions in inappropriate situations; to chronically slurry enunciation; to a paucity of vocabulary; and to a lack of general fluency (i.e., the ability to maintain a flow of relaxed, intelligent speech.)"[12]

The number of usage items is relatively small. The most basic and probably the most important are these:

**1.** Verb agreement in number (chiefly the forms of *be* and *have*)
**2.** Past tense and past participle forms (about 40 pairs like *saw-seen* and *took-taken*)
**3.** Nominative case pronouns as subjects (trouble seldom occurs except when another pronoun or a noun is present: *She and I were, He and Judy were*)
**4.** Objective case pronouns as objects of verbs, prepositions, and verbals (same comment as for 3; *saw Lois and him, for her and me*)
**5.** Adverb as a modifier of an action verb (*engine runs well*)
**6.** Double subject and double negatives (not *Alice she didn't want none*)

The instructional task certainly does not seem insuperable when the list of major offenders is so small.

But the offenders are stubborn. A child who has grown up hearing and saying *He run* and *Me and him was almost froze* is not likely to shake the habit after one or two mentions that *He ran* and *He and I were almost frozen* are standard.

For some students (usually the faster learners) clarification of principles will help. For example, that certain pronouns (*I, he, she, we, they*) are used in the first slot of sentences, even when other words are present: therefore *she and I were*. Other pronouns (*me, him, her, us, them*) are the usual ones in the third or fourth slot: therefore *I saw Lois and him*. The principle of singularity and plurality will help these students to distinguish between *was* and *were*. Another useful principle is that some verb forms (*saw, took,* etc.) are used without a helping verb like *have,* and that others (*seen, taken,* etc.) require such a verb.

But other students have trouble in applying principles. Drill—usually simple, repetitious oral and written drill—will help some of them. Others—is it defeatist to say this?—don't want to change their language or add alternate versions and probably will not do so; they are satisfied with their environment and the language of that environment.


## SLANG

Webster's unabridged defines *slang* as "nonstandard vocabulary composed of words and senses characterized primarily by connotations of extreme informality and usu. a currency not limited to a particular region and composed typically of coinages or arbitrarily changed words, clipped or shortened forms, extravagant, forced, or facetious figures of speech, or verbal novelties usu. experiencing quick popularity and relatively rapid decline into disuse."

A half-century ago a poll of teachers of English showed that they considered slang so undesirable that its elimination was a major goal of their teaching. Today's teachers, more realistic, regard slang as playful language of a type that has existed for centuries and that changes in details from year to year. Except when overused or used in inappropriate places, it is not a great cause of worry. Teachers may echo the thought of William Lyon Phelps, a once-famous Yale professor of English:

> Our slang's piquant as catsup. I decry it
> Not as a condiment, but as an entire diet.

Teachers may talk with their classes about slang and its characteristics. Some classes make dictionaries of current slang (and learn a little about lexicography and the writing of definitions while doing so). Others analyze slang expressions, perhaps finding some of the characteristics noted in the Webster definition above. One class, after noting the color and raciness and figurativeness of much slang, also made a list of occasions on which it should not be used:

—*whenever any written record is meant to endure* [*because slang is almost always transitory*];

*—whenever exact definition is necessary [because slang is usually imprecise— suggestive rather than definitive];*

*—whenever communication is with an adult, person in authority, or non-member of the group [because outsiders may not understand];*

*—whenever one wishes to use language that will command respect*[13]

One very serious high school student worried that constant repetition of slang may be mentally debilitating. "Over and over," he complained, "I hear the same people saying 'Like you know man I gotta get my head together about this like you know man.' They're only phonograph records, repeating mindlessly. Or they're vegetables with voices." Perhaps the boy was saying in his own way what Professor Phelps had said much earlier: An "entire diet" of slang is certainly undesirable.

# VOCABULARY: ACQUISITION AND EFFECTIVE USE

## EXPERIENCES AS THE BASIS OF VOCABULARY BUILDING

All available evidence points to the belief that vocabulary grows as alert children and adults encounter new experiences. Words do not exist in a vacuum and are not learned in a vacuum. The weekly list of 20 randomly selected words is almost a vacuum; tests made several months later will usually reveal that only a small proportion of previously unfamiliar words from such a list will be remembered. Words learned in a meaningful context are much more likely to stick in the memory.

Despite its shortcomings, television brings our students experiences and consequent knowledge that they otherwise might never attain. A fad for westerns brings information about mesas, buttes, and saguaros; a fad for courtroom drama clarifies the meanings of *plaintiff, defendant, habeas corpus;* a fad for doctor stories dramatizes a score or two of medical terms. More offbeat programs add information on a wide range of subjects, such as space travel, and with the information comes the relevant vocabulary. Radios, newspapers, and magazines, accessible now in almost every home, provide still more information.

Within the schoolroom, films, filmstrips, and recordings are rich resources. English field trips to libraries, colleges, newspaper plants, museums, theaters, government buildings, and places related to literature may directly broaden experience. Pictures, maps, bulletin boards, and chalkboards may supplement experiences.

In short, more opportunities exist now than ever before for students to step outside the boundaries of home and school and to participate at least vicariously in the varied experiences of the human race. From these experiences are derived the words to describe them.

Alert teachers use such opportunities. Television, filmstrips, and the like are part of their teaching arsenal. So is a constant attempt to associate words with ideas, and ideas with things. Straight thinking involves accurate use of words. Through class discussions, students can have stimulating experience with ideas, particularly when the ideas are translated in terms of tangibles. Few students—indeed, few adults—can think in abstractions. Teachers can assist students to associate words, even abstract words, with things. In fact, if students do not make such associations, words will lack meaning. The child who can glibly quote the dictionary definition of *democracy* as "government by the people" knows less about the word than the one who has examined a specimen ballot, attended a town meeting, taken part in a mock political meeting, and participated in student government. If you tell a child that a symphony is "an instrumental composition in sonata form for a full orchestra," the child's understanding will be less than if he or she hears a symphony.

Alert teachers stress the rich experiences afforded by literature. Although no one lives long enough to participate personally in even one-millionth of the experiences that life offers, each, through books, can participate vicariously in multitudinous activities—sharing in the acts, observations, thoughts, and emotions of thousands of other people near or remote in time and place. Literature, chosen wisely and read well, opens the floodgate of experience.

## INCREASING INTEREST IN WORDS

"Here is your list of useful words for this week. Look each one up in the dictionary, copy its definition, and write a sentence containing the word. We'll have a test on Friday." This is the traditional method of vocabulary building, which still has its practitioners. It is not valueless, particularly if the words listed are useful. But it has its weaknesses. One is its puny motivation. Another is that a word out of context may be misunderstood. For instance, one youngster looked up *quaver* and found that it means "shake"; she had trouble in understanding why it is incorrect to say, "I quavered the tablecloth." Still another weakness is that most of the words are soon forgotten.

Better than the list approach or any other single approach is maintaining an on-going interest in words. This means that there is some talk about words in almost every class period—oblique references in discussions of literature, direct comment in study of composition, remarks about the language of a TV newscaster or news special, and so on. It means that the teacher uses variety in the attack on the problem.

The trouble with much vocabulary building is that it is spasmodic, whereas it should be part of every day's work. It need not be labeled "vocabulary drill"; in fact, often no drill will be involved. The teacher must be interested in, and well informed about, words. When questions arise that the teacher cannot answer, the class should search together for answers. In a story, a class found a woman characterized as a *mimosa*. Neither teacher nor class knew the word. Upon looking it up, they found that it is another name for the "sensitive plant," which shrinks away when it is touched. When someone noticed that it is derived from the same word as *mimic* and *pantomime*, the class tried to guess at the connection. They returned to the story to find why the author had used this word and uncovered examples of the character's sensitiveness. Had the teacher said merely, "Look up the word," the class would have missed a wealth of associations. *Mimosa* itself is not a particularly valuable word, but the class discussion that arose from it threw light on the story, added the useful words *mimic* and *pantomime* to several students' vocabularies, and increased interest in words. In this teacher's class, such study of words is common, yet it does not smack of drill.

## SOME DEVICES

### Expansion of Meaning
It has been said that it is not more words that make an educated man or woman, but more meanings. With this in mind, classes have explored all the meanings of common words like *light, name, go, tie, fast, start, lie, dream,* ard *beat*. The result is at least a better understanding of the versatility of words.

### Learning from Words Previously Known
Sometimes it is possible to determine word meanings by associating them with other words. Thus the word *micrometer* is composed of elements already familiar in *microscope* and *meter*. A bright student may be able to put the parts together and decide that a micrometer is something to measure small objects. A valid criticism of this technique, though, is that guesses may often be erroneous; the student may decide mistakenly that *micrometer* means a small measurement. The chief value of association is that meanings once learned may be more easily retained because of an awareness of similarities.

At the heart of Frank C. Flowers' method for building understanding of words and dictionary use is the study of words in groups. For example, *organic, organically, organicism, organist, organizable, organization, organizational, organizationally, organize,* and *organizer*. The contributions of base meaning and affixes are studied in detail.[14]

### Learning from Context
Six-year-old children may have a vocabulary of several thousand words, even though they have never touched a dictionary; they learned the words by hearing them in context. The dictionary is valuable to verify a guess about a word or to define it when the meaning cannot be obtained from the context. But anyone should attempt first to determine the meaning by noting the surroundings of the

THE TEACHING OF HIGH SCHOOL ENGLISH

word. For example, if a student does not know the meaning of *tractable* in the sentence "The children were more tractable than she had anticipated; in fact, only Joel was at all stubborn," he or she should follow the contextual clues before referring to the dictionary.

Here are some types of clues that students may use in ferreting out meanings. Some teachers compose sentences employing such clues:

1. The experience clue, which enables students to draw on their own experience; e.g., their experience with crows enables them to define *raucously* in "A pair of crows called raucously."
2. The comparison or contrast clue, as in the example of *tractable*.
3. The synonym clue, in which the sentence contains a near-synonym.
4. The summary clue: "He was completely *disheveled*. His hair was mussed, his shirttail was out, . . ."
5. The association clue: "He was out of it in an instant with the *agility* of a pickpocket."
6. The reflection of a mood or situation clue, as with the word *melancholy* in the first sentence of "The Fall of the House of Usher."
7. The previous contact clue, which helps students familiar with the Emancipation Proclamation to understand *emancipate*.

## Notebooks

A favorite device is to have students record, define, and copy in context the new words they have learned. One teacher of middle school students suggests that only one new word be put on a page; below the word the student pastes or draws a picture illustrating or suggested by the word; under the picture go a definition and a sentence using the word. *Relaxation,* for instance, may have a picture of a cat stretching lazily. The value of the device is in the association of the word with something tangible. Caution: older classes may consider the procedure too babyish.

## Word Diaries

Some students may be encouraged to keep for a few weeks a word diary in which they record useful new words they hear or read, together with the context and an original sentence.

## Synonyms and Antonyms

Able students enjoy discovering the fine distinctions that exist among near synonyms. *Distant, far,* and *remote,* they discover, do not mean exactly the same thing, nor do *decadence, deterioration,* and *degeneration,* or *dominant, domineering,* and *dominating.* Less able students will often fail to see the distinguishing points in such words, but even they can profit from discussion of the numerous specific synonyms for *go* and *say*. In French schools, teachers spend time in having students find the exact antonyms of given words, the theory being that one does not actually know a word unless one also knows its opposite.[15]

## Games

Word games are fun and, with junior high school students, may be played as rewards. Some classes have vocabulary bees, comparable to spelling bees. The teacher keeps a list of interesting, useful words encountered in literature or employed rather incidentally in class. Students use these words in sentences or define them, as they wish. The teacher or an elected student is the judge, and three students, equipped with dictionaries, may be a court of appeal. Possible variations of this game are endless.

In teaching slow learners, Nancy J. Doemel sometimes let them play "Scrabble" or "hangman," or create trees showing families of words. Her students also discussed what they called "funny" words, and helped one another with word choice in their compositions.[16] In other classes students have brought words they have encountered in their reading, and challenged their classmates to define them; archaic, technical, and foreign words were barred.

In the game of "hanky-panky" a player says, for instance, "Large swine. Hank-pank." The response is "big pig" (one-syllable words). Or a player says "Humorous cottontail. Hanky-panky." The "hanky-panky" shows that the responses are rhyming two-syllable words: "funny bunny." ("Hankety-pankety" is used for three syllables. One teacher said that the game taught his students useful things about rhyme, definitions, and spelling variations for the same sound.

## Language Play in Advertising

Don L. F. Nilsen of Arizona State teaches his students vocabulary and some characteristics of the English language by having them search for playful language used by some advertisers.[17] For example, phonological relationships: "Our stockings cover a multitude of shins." Parody: "Den of Antiquity" (antique shop) or "Blessed Sellers" (religious books). Pun: "People who knead people" (massage parlor). Adverbs in the form of "Tom Swifties": "I would like another pancake," she said flippantly. Unorthodox breaking of a word: "Plan a head" (hairdresser). The *New Yorker* magazine is one good source for clever advertisements.

## Units

Short units, closely related to other work in oral and written composition, may stress words. A teacher in a vocational high school taught one unit based on the origins of the last names of his students, another on geographical slang, and others on military slang, baseball slang, and Hebrew derivatives. (In a school

THE TEACHING OF HIGH SCHOOL ENGLISH

with, say, many Italian students, classes may be interested in words that English has borrowed from Italian.) Especially enlightening was a unit called "One Word Led to Another." Starting with the word *kilometer*, the vocational students thought of two other words based on either *kilo* or *meter*, then two words based on each of the two new words, and so on. They thus learned much about root words and families of words.

Another teacher asked students to check on words they thought might describe them or their personalities: *burly, ruddy, prim, prepossessing, swarthy, punctual, tactful, veracious, energetic,* and so on. In other units students had fun with malapropisms or puns, studied the diction in advertising and in headlines, and made collections of picturesque speech.

## Derivations
Many words have fascinating histories. A few examples are *lunatic, salary, supercilious, curfew, pecuniary, kindergarten, familiar,* and *boycott.* Students enjoy discovering that *lunatic* comes from the Latin word for "moon" and that it was once believed that lunacy arose from being in the moonlight too much. When they know the derivation of *salary,* they can see a connection with the expression "He's not worth his salt."

## World Words
The English language has borrowed from dozens of other languages. A teacher stimulated the interest of one sophomore class by placing a large map of the world on the bulletin board. The students tried to find English words taken from the languages of as many countries as possible. The words were typed and fastened to the map in appropriate places. At the end of the month, some of the world's land areas were no longer visible.

## Roots and Affixes
Knowledge of the meanings of 40 or 50 Latin and Greek roots and affixes will enable some students to add hundreds of words to their vocabularies. More important, it will show them relationships between words and help them to use words with greater accuracy. From the Latin *audire* "to hear" come such words as *audibility, audible, audience, audile, audiometer, audition, auditive, auditor, auditorium,* and *auditory.* From the Greek *chronos* "time" are derived such words as *chronic, chronicle, chronogram, chronological, chronologist, chronology, chronometer,* and *synchronize.* Other especially useful roots are listed in the Idea Box.

## Programmed Instruction
A few experimental programs for individual learning have been developed. They make it possible for each student to concentrate on a group of words least familiar

to him or her. In the program, a student may be given brief information about a root such as *spect* "look at." Then come a number of multiple-choice questions such as "*Retrospection* means (*a*) preparing for the future, (*b*) becoming worse, or (*c*) a survey of past time." Following that the student faces a number of frames devoted to words he or she missed. The frame for *retrospection* explains the derivation of the word and requires the student to do some sort of little follow-up exercise on it.

### History of the Language

One of the best ways to build an interest in words is to refer frequently to details of the fascinating history of the English language. Let students know that the English language is alive, has long been alive, and is still changing. Let them know that words are being born as old ones are dying. One of the services that teachers of English can render is to instill in students a wholesome, creative attitude toward language—the kind of attitude that existed in Elizabethan times.

Information about how words enter the language can be interesting. The routes of entry, with an example or two of each, are these:

1. Sheer invention (rare): *Kodak*
2. Compounding: *railroad, out-of-date, barn*
3. Addition of affixes or combining forms to existing words: *unknown, newness, cigarette*
4. Functional shift (use of a word as another part of speech): to *ink* a contract
5. Back formation: *editor → edit*
6. Extension of meaning: the fifth *power* of a number
7. Figurative language: *lady's slipper* (flower), *Red* (for Russian)
8. Use of initials (acronyms): *CORE, Nabisco*
9. Conversion of proper nouns to common: *sandwich, volt*
10. Onomatopoeia: *fizz, pop, meow*
11. Telescoping: *brunch, electrocute*
12. Borrowing from other languages: *betatron, blitzkrieg*

The yearbooks of some encyclopedias contain lists and definitions of selected new words, and publishers of some dictionaries occasionally prepare supplements of recent additions to the language.

Study of what may happen to a word after it enters the language also deserves some time. Among a number of changes that may be considered are those in the following list:

1. Shortening: *taximeter cabriolet* became *taxicab* or *taxi* or *cab*.
2. Metathesis: *bird* was once spelled *brid; wasp* was *wæps*.
3. Generalization (broadening of meaning): *cupboard* was a board to hold cups.
4. Specialization: although *liquor* may still mean any liquid, it is usually specialized to refer to alcoholic beverages.

**5.** Elevation: *pastor* was once a shepherd.

**6.** Degeneration: *knave* (cf. German *Knabe* "boy") once meant "boy"; *hussy* was once any housewife.[18]

Students also like to learn how places and people get their names. Over half of our states have Indian names. Other places are named for persons (*Lincoln, Jonesboro*), are descriptive (*Mapleton, Wolf Point*), or are humorous (*Rabbit Hash, Git-Up-and-'Git*). Persons' names often indicate physical characteristics (*Longfellow, Brown*), are names of occupations (*Miller, Smith*), are derived from places (*York, Lake*), or are patronymics (*Johnson, Fitzgerald, O'Brien*). George R. Stewart's *American Place-Names* and Elsdon D. Smith's *New Dictionary of American Family Names* are excellent sources of information.

### Dialect Study

Dialects often involve the use of different words for the same thing. Examples: *bag, poke, sack, toot; faucet, spigot, hydrant, tap; canteloupe, mushmelon, muskmelon; green beans, sallet beans, snap beans, snaps, string beans.*

# LEXICOGRAPHY AND SEMANTICS

## LEXICOGRAPHY

Many students need help in learning to use the dictionary efficiently. From unhappy experiences, some students have come to regard dictionaries as foes rather than friends. The chief trouble is that numerous students have not learned to find a word quickly. Using a desk dictionary, a student in the senior high school should be able to locate in 15 or 20 seconds any word that he or she can spell. (You, the teacher, should need no more than 12 seconds.) Teach students to know the alphabet thoroughly (including immediate recognition of which comes first, *sp* or *sm*, etc.), to open the dictionary in about the right place, and to use the guide words at the top of each page. Help them to analyze dictionary entries to see what a wealth of information each contains. (Some publishers of dictionaries furnish free or inexpensive pamphlets containing dictionary exercises.) Spend a little time with them in noting the special sections that some dictionaries offer. Contrast a good dictionary with an inferior one.

Here are a few examples of worthwhile dictionary problems. Each student may make up one or two others for classmates to answer.

**1.** Why do Londoners sometimes call their policemen "bobbies"?

**2.** What three different kinds of animals are called "gophers"?

**3.** What is a corollary? How do the British pronounce the word?

**4.** Find definitions of *scale* referring to zoology, botany, metallurgy, and music. Use *scale* in sentences that will illustrate each definition.

**5.** How does the Gregorian calendar differ from the Julian?

**6.** What might you expect to see if you heard someone shout "Hoicks!" or "Yoicks!"?

**7.** Does your dictionary suggest that some meanings of *fix* are less formal than others?

Some of your students will be interested in the history of dictionaries. A good introduction is the 10-page article in the *Encyclopaedia Britannica*. Reports on Noah Webster and Samuel Johnson may also be of interest, as may a brief study of how modern lexicographers work. Some dictionary publishers can supply leaflets of information if you or a member of your class writes for it.

Especially valuable is the construction of a class dictionary pertaining to some topic of interest to most of the students: school slang, technical terms in football or another sport, current musical lingo, or the jargon of coal mining or some other occupation prominent in the community.

## CONNOTATION AND DENOTATION

Words often convey more than their dictionary definitions. Robert C. Pooley illustrated the point in this often-reprinted example:

**1.** *I think I'll hit the hay.*
**2.** *It's time for me to turn in.*
**3.** *I believe I'll go to bed.*
**4.** *I think it is time to retire.*
**5.** *I shall withdraw to seek repose.*

> ... *Sentence 1 is intentionally slangy, appropriate only to intimate circumstances when humor is the intent. Sentence 2 is still intimate, but less slangy; it would pass as appropriate usage in the close family circle. Sentence 3 is the simplest and most direct of the five forms; it is acceptable usage in almost any circumstances. Sentence 4 implies less intimate circumstances; the word* **retire** *is a polite substitute for the blunt "go to bed." This form would be appropriate to a guest in the home of relative strangers. Sentence 5 is stilted and artificial. The simple act of going to bed makes such elaborate wording slightly ridiculous. Yet there are people with a mistaken idea of elegance who would prefer sentence 5.* [19]

From the choice of words in sentences we infer not only a factual meaning but also some of the attendant circumstances and even the mood and character of the speaker.

Because words do carry connotation as well as denotation, they may cause emotional reaction. By changing a single word, one may subtly move someone else to favor or oppose an action or idea. Suppose that a bill is before Congress. A person neutral toward the bill says, "Congress intends to pass it." One who favors it says, "Congress promises to pass it." An opponent says, "Congress threatens to pass it." Likewise, if one favors something new, it is an improvement, but if one dislikes it, it is a hastily conceived innovation. A judge who is one's friend sometimes receives gifts, but a judge whom one detests takes bribes. A statesman whom one likes is conservative, but a politician whom one dislikes may be reactionary. Consciously or unconsciously, one allows the emotional overtones of words to affect choice; usually unconsciously, listeners or readers are affected by these emotional overtones.

Students seldom think much about the connotations of their language. Most, however, can be brought to see that it may make a difference whether one calls a girl "slim" or "skinny" or "svelte." Most can learn that the majority of our communications are intended to be factual and therefore should be stated in neutral words. But when we are trying to create a favorable impression, words with favorable connotations—"purr" words—are appropriate. If we want something to be disliked, words with unfavorable connotations—"snarl" words—are suitable. In a news story, for instance, we should use uncolored, neutral words, but in subjective writing such as poetry, we should seek words that will move the reader.

## THE IMPORTANCE OF SEMANTIC STUDY

Professor Charles Weingartner would make semantics central to the English curriculum. He asserts that "the study of semantics can do more to help students become more perceptive and sophisticated users of language than can any other form of language study."[20]

Whether or not we accept a position of centrality for semantics, we must grant its value. All of us are engulfed daily, hourly, in a sea of words. According to *Common Sense in Advertising,* by Charles Adams, the average adult American reads 10,000 to 20,000 words a day (mostly in newspapers), is exposed to 11,000 radio and TV words, and sees 560 advertisements (of which he or she actually takes note of only 76). Someone somewhere is constantly trying to convince us to do something, try something, believe something, accept certain information, behave in a certain way. Each of these someones steadily uses words (sometimes along with pictorial, musical, or other reinforcements) to convince and persuade. Many of the motives are or should be suspect: The persuader often has some sort of personal gain as the hidden reason for the attempt. Semantic analysis often reveals or at least hints at the hidden reason, and the reader's or listener's response may be changed when that reason becomes apparent.

The persuaders often do not agree with one another. "Buy *my* product," says one. "*My* product is best," says another. "Elect *my* superb candidate," one person pleads. "The country will be in trouble unless *this* man is elected," another person threatens. The study of semantics can help people to weigh evidence, to make up their minds, to recognize the ''crap'' that Weingartner says fills so many utterances. The success of democracy depends in large measure on citizens' ability to do these things—to choose the stronger candidate, to detect the ''crap'' in the statements of each candidate and to place more trust in the one who uses less of it, to decide the relative degrees of desirability in the two or more sides of a controversial question.

Even in relatively small personal decisions an awareness of semantics can be helpful. What does the guarantee of a new refrigerator actually guarantee? Who is our strongest candidate for Student Council representative? What was the minister actually driving at in his sermon? How shall I react to Tom when he again says, ''If you really love me, you'll let me''? (What is Tom's definition of *love?* Is it the same as mine?)

To some extent children have been denied the opportunity to take a close look at the process of language, to examine truths, untruths, and half-truths and to distinguish one from another, to understand the use of language as both a tool and a weapon, to see how words divorced from reality have often shaped the destiny of a person or a nation or a large part of the world. (Hitler used semantics masterfully.) Grammar stresses basic form, usage stresses current linguistic etiquette, but semantics gets into content, gets in fact into the minds of the senders and the receivers of content.

## METHODS

Semantics digs into connotations. One starting point in its study is with pairs of related sentences. For instance:

He is one of the homeless unemployed. (This creates a feeling of pity and possibly a desire to help the poor unfortunate.)
He is a tramp. (The word *tramp* suggests dirt, shiftlessness, and a possible tendency toward criminality.)
She is generous. (Generosity is considered a virtue.)
She is a spendthrift. (I wouldn't want to marry a person like that.)
He is a holder of uncommon views. (This suggests that he may be praiseworthy because of his presumably independent thinking.)
He is a crackpot. (He holds uncommon views that we don't like.)
She sauntered down the lane. (She is pleasant and carefree.)
She sneaked down the lane. (She is a deceitful person, afraid to be seen.)

Study of headlines may also be valuable, especially when two or more newspapers are available for comparison. One paper may head a story DEMOCRATS BLOCK TAX CUT; another, DEMOCRATS SUCCEED IN HOLDING TAX LINE; another, CONGRESS DEFEATS TAX SLASH.

An enjoyable little 5- or 10-minute game is that attributed to Bertrand Russell, involving comparisons such as this: "I am firm. You are stubborn. He is a pig-headed fool." Other starters: "I am a genius." "I am intelligent." "I am relaxed." "I have a good time at parties." "I am athletic."

A key concept of semantics is that language is symbolic. "The map is not the country." To teach the concept of such symbolism, you may want to use a conversation similar to the following. Begin by printing the word APPLE.

"What is that?"
"Apple."
"Can you take a bite out of it?"
"No."
"Why not?"
"It isn't a real apple."
"Then what is it?"
"It's a word that means a kind of fruit."
"A symbol?"
"Yes."
"What if everybody called it a 'glag' instead?"
"Then 'glag' would be the symbol for the kind of fruit."
"What if I called it a 'glag' and you called it an 'apple'?"
"Then we'd have trouble understanding each other, because we'd not be using the same symbols."
"What if I think that all apples are red and you know that some are yellow or green? Do we then understand the symbol 'apple' in the same way?"
"No."
"Can you think of any words that you and your parents don't always understand in the same way?"
"Get home *early.*" "Be *good.*" "Do you really *need* the car?" "It's a *free* country."
"Let's look at the word 'free' a little more. Do you think that words like *freedom* and *democracy* mean the same thing to everybody, both here and in other parts of the world?"

Students need to become familiar with various questionable tactics that unscrupulous speakers and writers use as they manipulate symbols. (1) *Name-calling:* using a bad label in order to make us oppose something or someone. "He is incompetent." "He is unprogressive." "He is a radical." "The plan is undemocratic." "He was involved in an shady political deal." (2) *Glittering generality:* the reverse of name-calling. "He fought bravely for his country." "She is a superior cook." "She was a ravishing beauty." "Old Dominion Virginia-cured ham is tops" (although it's processed in Kansas City). (3) *Transfer* or *testimonial:* connecting a person, idea, action, or thing with something or someone highly regarded: "In the well-run home, Nomar is as necessary as soap and water." "Doctors use Antamine." "Strike for Harry and for England!" "Hollywood endorses Glamour Hour." (The *u* in *Glamour* adds prestige, too.) "The soap that lovely women prefer." (4) *Plain folks:* using the theory that what is "common" is best. Using the plain-folks approach, office-seekers sometimes plow corn, sing hillbilly songs, and repeat the commonplaces that "plain folks" supposedly like to hear. (5) *Band wagon:* urging others to follow the crowd. "More people smoke Dromedary cigarettes than any other brand." "Be sure that your vote is included in the landslide of ballots for Adams." "Most thinking people prefer the *Herald.*" "The magazine that business people believe."

The chief tests to apply to statements like these are two: Is there any evidence to support the statement? If the statement is true, does it matter? For example, consider a magazine advertisement, "TV stars prefer Purple Night perfume." Perhaps the ad names five actresses who have sold testimonials of the perfume's efficacy in doing whatever perfume is supposed to do. Does this really mean that in general "TV stars prefer" the perfume? And even if it does, is the endorsement by these five actresses a sufficient reason why Janet should use Purple Night? Is another brand actually more suited to her and more within her budget?

Another teaching technique leading to straight thinking and to a correspondingly apt use of words is to make conscious attacks upon generalizations. "All generalizations are false—including this one" is more than an academic wisecrack; it points at the widespread tendency to generalize, to oversimplify. The validity of generalizations ("Women are fickle by nature." "All men are beasts.") can be weighed. Most students will unthinkingly accept some such statements simply because they have heard them frequently. It is both provocative and wholesome, therefore, to have the class point out numerous exceptions which show that a generalization has only limited applicability. Once a pattern of attack has been established, students become less and less gullible in accepting statements of "allness." They begin to question whether all cowboys are noble and fun-loving, all gangsters ride in black sedans, all private detectives are smarter than policemen, all Southern sheriffs are despicable, all Swedes are big, blond, and stupid, all Jews are avaricious, all Poles lack intelligence, all Italians are musical, and so on. They may pursue the attack further to the point of definition. What is a black? If a man is one-thirty-second African in ancestry, is he a black? In Sinclair Lewis's *Kingsblood Royal,* is Kingsblood, whose great-great-great-grandfather was black, a black? Is Kingsblood's daughter? In the light of recent studies concerning the races of humanity, is any narrow definition of race permissible? A highly desirable broadmindedness may grow from such analysis. "Never accept statements using *never* or *always;* always reject them."

A variation of the approach is to analyze proverbs, which of course are generalizations. The purpose is not to prove that the proverbs are wrong but to show that exceptions do exist and that proverbs sometimes contradict one another. For example, "A stitch in time saves nine" is antithetical to "Don't cross the bridge before you come to it." Some teachers place two familiar proverbs side by side and have students decide whether they are similar in meaning, opposite, or unrelated.

## DOUBLESPEAK

In the early 1970s NCTE formed a committee on public doublespeak. The occasion was an NCTE recognition that "language is often used as an instrument of social control" and a resolution to "keep track of, publicize, and control semantic distortion by public officials, . . . , commentators, and all those who transmit through the mass media." The word *doublespeak,* originated by George Orwell, refers most often to the use of euphemisms in an attempt to deceive. Not all euphemisms are undesirable; for instance, the motivation to use *passed away* instead of *die* is kindliness. But the NCTE committee and others who have written on the subject have found countless examples of deceptive euphemisms in the language of public officials and others. One well-known example was the use of the word *inoperative* to mean "false" during the Watergate investigations. A Presidential press secretary used the word as a bland way of saying "We lied."

Edmund Farrell found that military public relations personnel in the Vietnamese war used doublespeak blatantly:

*waterborne guard posts (naval ambushes)*
*armed reconnaissance (bombing)*
*limited duration protective reaction strikes (air raids)*
*incontinent ordnance (bomb that went astray)*
*new life hamlet (refugee camp)*
*termination with extreme prejudice (murder)*[21]

*Select out* may mean "discharge, fire," a *short fall* is a mistake, *acceptable rates* (of crime, unemployment, military losses) are low enough not to cause a revolution, a *cost overrun* means "Somebody's robbing us," and a *credibility gap* exists when "we are getting caught in our lies."[22]

Other examples:

**over-zealous** *(doing normally commendable things that the administration or the boss doesn't want brought out into the open)*
**open classroom** *(arranging chairs in a circle or in small groups instead of in straight lines)*
**voluntarily** *recalling the hairspray at the* **request** *of the Federal Drug Administration. [Boldface added] (withdrawing it before somebody goes to jail.)*[23]

Even dentists get into the act. What used to be a filling is now a *restoration,* dentists who used to grind a tooth now *prepare* it for the restoration, they *recommend* where they formerly suggested, they talk about your *investment* rather than the cost, and you find that the *fee* (formerly bill) will keep you from taking a vacation.[24] Doublespeak follows us to the grave, where there are no longer such things as undertakers, hearses, and corpses, but more expensive and expensive-sounding *funeral directors* or *morticians, professional cars,* and *floral tributes,* and our *loved ones* slumber in *reposing rooms.*

The NCTE published two collections of articles on the subject. One is *Language and Public Policy,* edited by Hugh Rank in 1974. The second, replete with teaching suggestions, is *Teaching about Doublespeak,* edited in 1976 by Daniel Dieterich. It includes not only political language but also the language of advertising and the role of language in sex stereotyping.

The basic way to attack doublespeak is to ask repeatedly, "What does this really mean? What is insinuated that is not said? When the actual meaning is revealed, how do you react to it?" With practice, some students become adept at recognizing doublespeak and appropriately discounting statements made in that distorted variety of language.

## OBJECTIVE AND SUBJECTIVE WRITING

A factual explanation of how to change a tire should normally employ uncolored, unfigurative words. So should an objective statement of a candidate's qualifications for public office. But a poem, play, short story, or personal essay may—indeed, must—be subjective, because it offers an interpretation of a facet of life, not a photograph. Shelley's "To a Skylark" is not a scientific, unbiased description of a bird but a frankly personal statement of admiration.

Failure or unwillingness to recognize a difference between the two types of writing leads to a confusion between factual and persuasive or emotional presentations and may reveal itself in such things as editorialized news stories or prosy imaginative writing. When a teacher fails to see the difference, he or she is likely to praise only vivid writing, even when straightforward prose is more suitable for the purpose. Vivid writing has its place, but so has quiet presentation of facts. Both teacher and student should keep in mind the purpose of the writing, and choose accordingly.

Objective writing presents verifiable facts: "Dr. Ladd's car is parked in front of the Jackson house." Subjective writing, in contrast, makes judgments, which may or may not be accurate and verifiable: "Someone in the Jackson house is sick." That judgment is not necessarily true. Maybe Mrs. Ladd drove the car, or maybe the doctor is making just a friendly visit, or maybe he entered the house across the street. Exercises to help students distinguish facts from judgments can be useful throughout their lives.

In subjective as well as in objective writing, one needs to choose appropriate words. In addition, because subjective writing is often figurative, one needs to select fitting figures of speech. Characteristically, a poor or untrained writer uses figures that are either trite, far-fetched, or mixed: "The burning sun was hot as fire." "She tripped downstairs like a feather in a breeze." "That snake in the grass is barking up the wrong tree." Once a student combined all the figurative vices by writing, "The sky was as black as pitch, and it was raining pitchforks." It takes a creative mind (not necessarily an "educated" one) to originate an effective simile or metaphor, but even an ordinary mind can borrow somebody else's tropes and use them effectively. The test of a figure of speech is always its appropriateness in the particular situation.

Students frequently have the impression that figures of speech are things that only authors employ, perhaps to vex and confuse readers. A teacher should help them see that tropes, especially metaphors, abound and that there is good reason for their existence. When we refer to the arm or leg of a chair, the eyes of a potato, or the hands of a clock, we are speaking metaphorically. "A hangdog expression," "leaden sky," "carefree laughter," "raining cats and dogs"— hundreds of more or less common expressions are figurative. "Wheel" for "bicycle," "Washington says" for "government officials say," and "a volume of Wordsworth" are other examples of tropes in daily use. Slang is composed largely of figurative language.

Why use tropes? Primarily for picturesqueness, for persuasion, and for clarification. "The moon was a glistening white balloon, released by a careless child" is picturesque, but it also portrays clearly the appearance of the moon on a particular night. "He is like Hitler in his lust for power" tends to persuade us to detest the person described. Thoreau's comparison of the shape of Cape Cod to "a bended arm" enables us to visualize the Cape. Students may enjoy finding illustrations of tropes used for all three of these purposes. One class, divided into committees, concentrated on metaphorical language in slang, advertising, cartoons and caricatures, songs, editorials, and sports writing. They learned that figurative language is not used by poets alone.

## A UNIT IN SEMANTICS

In an article worth reading in its entirety, a Utah teacher, Solveig Torvik, several years ago described an unusually fine unit in semantics.[25] Torvik used it with seniors, but it can be simplified for younger students. The following paragraphs offer only brief examples of the sort suggested by Torvik.

1. Symbol-thing confusion. A girl becomes ill when she sees a picture of a spider; another faints when she sees the word *snake*. These girls are confusing symbol with reality. An *A* on a report card is in inadequate symbol of the

knowledge and skill it supposedly represents. A swastika or an American flag is only a geometrical figure, but each is invested with emotional overtones that vary from person to person. "You think you think, but words structure your thinking for you."

2. Generalizations. Generalizations, says Torvik, are acceptable if one can find 100 percent proof to support them; but one seldom can. In this part of the unit students learn to question words like *all, never, always, everybody.*

3. Inferences, judgments, reports. Students examine groups of statements like these:

(Report) Mary Smith didn't get in until two o'clock last night
(Inference) I bet she was out tearing around.
(Judgment) She's a worthless hussy. I never did like her looks.

Inferences and judgments, students learn, are often confused with reports (statements of fact).

4. Classification. Mother 1 is not Mother 2. Puerto Rican 1 is not Puerto Rican 2. Mary today is not Mary yesterday. American democracy 1976 was not American democracy 1776. Democracy in Russia is not democracy in the United States. Classifications shift, and differ with individuals, times, places, and other circumstances. What's "good" for A may be "bad" for B.

5. Abstractions. "The students can then be led to see that specific referents for such words as *justice, love, evil, patriotism, good,* and *moral* are essential in actually communicating what one means to say *in this instance.* 'For example' becomes a key phrase in writing and discussion."

6. Directive, affective, informative uses of language. Language is often used to direct or influence actions of other human beings. A directive may be defined as expected behavior rather than a report of facts or a universal truth: "Mothers love their children."

7. Two-valued and multivalued orientation. The best answer to a question like "Do you love school or hate school?" is often "Sometimes one, sometimes the other." Two-valued thinking is either-or-thinking: either this or that must be true. In reality a number of choices may exist. The search for *the* answer is often futile, for there may be several answers or many shades of a "right" answer.

Students exposed to imaginative, many-exampled study of semantics, such as that used by Torvik, are less likely than others to accept statements uncritically. They learn much about the power of language to influence others and about their own need to examine language to see where it may be taking them.

# THE IDEA BOX

## IF YOU TEACH MEXICAN-AMERICANS

When anyone is learning a second language, characteristics of his or her native language interfere. For instance, Spanish has only 5 vowel phonemes, but English has 11. Most problems in Chicanos' pronunciation (and that of other Spanish speakers) exist because they have not yet mastered the additional six phonemes of of English. For example, they may say "Hees" for *his* because there is no /I/ in Spanish.

Another example of interference is that Spanish *en* may mean either "in" or "on." Some students have trouble remembering which English preposition they should use in a construction like "walking _____ the forest."

Ricardo L. Garcia offers a brief, nontechnical analysis of the problems that many Mexican-American children face in phonology, morphology, syntax, and semantics in "Toward a Grammar of Chicano English," *English Journal,* March 1974, p. 34.

Earlier, Kenneth Johnson, in *Teaching the Culturally Disadvantaged,* Palo Alto: Science Research Associates, 1970, listed these problems shared by many Mexican learners of English:

1. Difficulty with English sounds contained in these words: miss, brother, share, very, cap, rice.
2. Accent on wrong syllable: perfectly, office.
3. Final consonant clusters dropped: strength.
4. Syllable added in pronouncing -ed: jumpted, talk-ed.
5. Double negative.
6. Past tense and past participle: have went.
7. Omission of needed -s in verbs: he talk.
8. Double subject.
9. Addition of s to already plural nouns: the mens, the childrens
10. Combining English and Spanish: marketo, watcho.

## COMPARING DIALECTS

"A Checklist of School Language" is presented in "The Analysis of Student Talk," by Hugh Agee of the University of Georgia. It includes some rather unusual dialectal items such as "USED TO FASTEN PAPERS TOGETHER: stapler, staple machine, stapling machine, staple gun, stamp gun." Agee also says, ". . . for the sake of comparisons, students may wish to correspond with a school in another community, and possibly even in another state, to check their findings. Findings may also be compared against usages of older speakers in the community."[26]

## MORE ABOUT DIALECTS IN LITERATURE

Jesse Colquit of Belcher, Louisiana, recommends the use of regional literature in the teaching of dialect. For example, Jesse Stuart's "The Split Cherry Tree"

(Kentucky); J. R. Lowell's "The Courtin'" (New England over a century ago); Robert Frost's "Mending Wall" (New England); Mark Twain's *Huckleberry Finn* (Missouri and the South over 100 years ago); Richard Chase's *The Jake Tales* (Appalachia); "Git Along, Little Dogie" (the old West); Jessamyn West's *The Friendly Persuasion* (Quakers of the past century); Bob Dylan's songs (contemporary); poems by Langston Hughes or James Weldon Johnson (black).[27]

## IS NONSTANDARD ENGLISH ILLOGICAL?

No, answers William Labov. "They mine" for "They are mine" may be different but is not illogical, since such languages as Hebrew, Hungarian, and Russian also lack a present copula. Labov's *The Study of Nonstandard English* (NCTE, 1970) dispels a number of misconceptions concerning variant speech.

## SECOND DIALECT

At St. Mary's Dominican College, New Orleans, "Business Speech" is the title given to a course for those who need to master a second dialect for use in business or a profession. This term avoids the pejorative connotations of other titles, such as "Remedial English," and does not suggest that this variety of speech need be used in the home.

## REGIONAL DIALECTS

Evelyn Gott's "Teaching Regional Dialects in Junior High School" concerns regional pronunciations, dialect areas, and British vs. American English.[28]

## "OLD ENGLISH SURVIVAL IN MOUNTAIN SPEECH"

In Ozark speech Jewell K. Fitzhugh found not only color but also many survivals from Old or Middle English. Excellent for use in a unit on dialects.[29] In your own community, perhaps students can also find such remnants or, alternatively, note traces of foreign speech patterns.

## "EFFECTING DIALECT CHANGES THROUGH ORAL DRILL"

William R. Slager gives detailed suggestions for oral drills involving repetition of the same sentence, substitutions in parts of a sentence, completion of sentences, transformations to questions, combining two sentences.[30]

## IMAGINATIVE WAYS TO TEACH USAGE

Richard L. Graves says that the study of usage should rely not just on textbooks and other conventional sources but also on current magazines, television scripts, lyrics of ballads and popular songs, underground newspapers, films, posters, news stories, and advertising (which may be "the most carefully constructed writing going on in America today.")[31]

## "WHADDYA MEAN 'GOT'?"

The teacher prepares a large number of sentences in which *got* is used in different senses, and asks students to supply alternative verbs. Sample sentences: He *got* his own breakfast. He *got* molasses on his vest. He *got back* to work. He couldn't *get along* on his present pay. The point, of course, is not that forms of *get* are wrong but that sometimes other verbs may be more precise.

## ON THE OVERUSE OF *BE*

Randall Shutt of Northern Arizona University argues that *be*-less writing is often stronger and more accurate than that sprinkled with forms of *be*. So, instead of writing *She is a bad driver*, his students are required to be specific: *She ran six stop signs last week. She doesn't use her turn signals. I saw her make a U-turn on a hill. She hit a fire hydrant yesterday.*[32]

## DO BLACKS AND WHITES HAVE THE SAME SYNTACTIC PROBLEMS?

A doctoral dissertation by Marilyn S. Sternglass showed that in the writing of black and white college remedial writing classes there were "no *qualitative* differences in the nonstandard features . . . but there was a *quantitative* difference. That is, the black and white students produced the same kinds of nonstandard forms, but the black students produced them more often."[33] Note that the study was of written, not spoken, forms.

## *FROM THE* EXERCISE EXCHANGE

*Writing Exercises from* Exercise Exchange, NCTE, 1976, is a fine collection of tested classroom procedures, especially for use with able students. Among suggested exercises on words are these:

"Invigorating Vocabulary Building," by Harry P. Kroitor. Students rewrite a sentence like *A man went into the building* by substituting synonyms, antonyms, or other equivalents for most of the words.

"Eliminating Wordiness," by Laurence Perrine. Teacher rewrites a passage, padding it with unneeded words and repetitiousness of ideas. Students are asked to "wring it out."

"Recognizing Prefabricated Phrases," by Patrick E. Kilburn. Students are alerted to such empty expressions as "The basic fundamental truth is that . . . ," "This brings us to the essence of the question of . . ."

"Making New Metaphors," by Howard C. Brashers. At two different places students make two different lists of twenty-five nouns, verbs, adjectives suggested by their surroundings. Then each student "combines words or concepts from the two lists to make original images or metaphors."

## "STUDENT-CENTERED VOCABULARY"

Eighth-graders in Toledo, Ohio, chose for themselves the words to add to their vocabularies. Every two weeks each student brought in a word for the class.

Criteria: probably unfamiliar to the class; previously unfamiliar to the student; found outside of school; useful; not too technical or scientific; English.

Each word was presented to the class on a mimeographed form listing the correctly spelled word, a student-written definition, an example sentence, a synonym and an antonym (if possible), source. The teacher selected from four to ten of the words, and all studied them, were quizzed on them, and were encouraged to use them in writing assignments. Some students made posters for their words.[34]

## OTHER VOCABULARY-BUILDING DEVICES

Teacher writes a word like *signal* (all different letters) on the board. Students (slow junior high) choose a category (e.g., music, education, or food) and write down all the words they can think of in that category for each letter in the word *signal*. They profit from the exchange of words and discussion of the meanings. A good way to spend that left-over 10 minutes. Synonym and antonym contests are also useful, says Grace Ashenfelter of Urbana, Illinois; in teams, students write as many synonyms or antonyms as they can discover for a given word.

## SYNONYMS IN BLANKS

Give a definition and the first and last letters of a synonym; for example, *unfriendly:* h _ _ _ _ _ e.

## STUDENTS AS WORD COINERS

Know what *geobios* is? Earth life, of course. How about *megamaniac?* Big nut. Jean L. Campbell's junior high students had fun coining words based on roots and affixes she helped them to define. They tried their hands at writing things like "One day as a decigenarian was autoporting himself to school, he was stopped by multimicroorganisms."[35]

## PLAYBOOKS NEEDED

Our vocabulary textbooks (and language books in general) are overly serious, Edgar Dale of Ohio State once said in a lecture. We need more "playbooks," with puns, anagrams, word games of various sorts. If no such books are available, teacher and students can still do much playing with words in class. Dale's *Techniques of Teaching Vocabulary* (Field Educational Publications, 1971) contains hundreds of useful exercises.

## "AMELIA BEDELIA"

Peggy Parish's poem about a maid calls students' attention to facets of our confusing language; students enjoy adding other examples. For example, told to dust the furniture, the maid put dust on it. "Draw the drapes." (She drew a picture.) "Put the lights out." (She hung the bulbs on a clothesline.) "Dress the chicken." (As a boy or as a girl?)

## MANIPULATING NEW WORDS

For a word to become an active part of a student's vocabulary, it must be used. Among useful manipulative activities: (1) give the antonym of the word; (2) ask a question using the word (e.g., "Is it *inevitable* that the Yankees will win the pennant this year?"); (3) compare the meanings of words (e.g., "Is a person who is *vigilant* ever *cowardly?*"); supply another form of the word (e.g., *imply, implication*); name contexts suitable for use of the word (e.g., *marauders* could be used for pillaging soldiers, for pirates swooping down on a coastal village, for some of the Danish invaders of medieval England).

## THE EVIL OF OVERWRITING

A study of nonfiction such as the best of Winston Churchill or of Rachel Carson or of Annie Dillard may help both a teacher and the students to realize that the best prose is not flashy, not decorated with gingerbread, not cryptic, not flowery, and never—never—wordy.

## THE EXACT WORD

1. Says Budd Schulberg of F. Scott Fitzgerald's revising of *The Great Gatsby:* "Throughout the manuscript (and on through the galley revisions) one follows Fitzgerald's tireless quest for the *mot juste* as he changes *shadow* to *silhouette, quickly* to *vigorously, he interrupted* to *he suggested, a sort of joy* to *a joyous exaltation, looked* to *glanced, My house was on the tip of West Egg* to the more direct *I lived on West Egg.*"[36]
2. Remind students that other noted authors have often had to struggle to find the precise word; for example, Elizabeth Browning used to put pyramids of words in the margin while she wrote, and then would select the most appropriate one. Conrad and Flaubert sometimes sought the right word for hours. Mark Twain said that the difference between the right word and the almost-right word is as great as the difference between the lightning and the lightning bug.
3. Tell students of trouble sometimes caused by failure to choose the right word; for example, the ambiguous sign "Fine for fishing."
4. Write a paragraph with numbered blanks replacing certain words. Below, write the numbers, with four or five suggested words for each. Students are to pick the word that best fits the context. (A paragraph from a contemporary professional writer may be chosen. Students try to select the word(s) that he or she used.)
5. Discuss with students the shades of difference in words usually considered synonymous, such as *wages, salary, fee, stipend, remuneration, emolument, honorarium, dole.* It is wise to have Webster's *Dictionary of Synonyms* available to check questionable distinctions.
6. Try a "Find a Better Word" exercise. Sentences illustrating misconceptions of words may be accumulated for the exercise, especially from students' writing. Examples: "We should *mimic* noble men and women." "He *administers* a restaurant."

## RELATED WORDS

Mabel Lindner, in Latrobe, Pennsylvania, had her classes study groups of words related to such things as menus, medicine, and plays and ballets that the class saw. Frederic Baxter's West Bend, Wisconsin, students improved their vocabularies through newspaper study, finding that words in headlines are often defined in the news stories and that even the comics and the advertisements may lead them to new words and new meanings. Edgar Logan's sports-minded Detroit students were interested in colorful words pertaining to boxing and other sports and were encouraged to get away from more abstract terms by using these "physical" words in their writing.

## SOPHOMORES VERSUS SAID

Martha Pence's sophomores in Kittanning, Pennsylvania, found in their reading 567 substitutes for *said*. Perhaps their reading benefited as much as their vocabularies. (A student-made list of substitutes for *nice* or other excessively used adjectives may sometimes prove usable.)

## MALAPROPISMS

Students will enjoy some of the malapropisms available in various book-length collections of "bloopers." A few examples: "One of the most controversial subjects of our time is mercy killing, also known as youth in Asia." "A posthumous work is something written by an author after his death." "The vessel was engulped by the ocean."[37]

## AN IDIOM EXERCISE

The class discusses the literal and common meanings of familiar idioms. For example, Pick me up at four. She turned the corner. It was a busy day. He flew in on a jet. The ocean liner set sail at noon. (Students may think of others for analysis.)

## METAPHORS

1. Talk about the difference between a "*gloomy* night" (literal) and a "*gloomy* look" (figurative). Other examples: "warm hands," "warm heart"; "roaring lion," "roaring fire"; "break my leg," "break my heart," "break my word." Have students use words like these both literally and figuratively: *sea, root, anchor, hound, crown, tower, mountain, river.*
2. Talk about favorable and unfavorable metaphors applied to people. For example, a girl may be a peach, a lemon, the apple of someone's eye; a man may be a fox, a pig, a snake in the grass, a mule, a sheep, a lion in battle, a jackal, or a sly dog.

## MRS. CLAY'S FRECKLES

"Mrs. Clay had freckles, and a projecting tooth," Jane Austen wrote. In eight words (or two brush strokes) she painted a portrait. Let your students try their hands at two-stroke portraiture.

## IN DEFENSE OF CLICHÉS

Charles Suhor has found that writers as reputable as E. B. White, James Baldwin, Norman Mailer, and William Buckley (as well as countless media newspersons) are not above using an occasional cliché like *not above, woefully inadequate,* or *when I first laid eyes on it.* Clichés are "part of our 'cultural heritage," and without them our language would "have a cold, alien, antiseptic quality." "They are language inventions that people share, scarely noticing that they do so, in every phase of life from lovemaking to addressing the MLA." Suhor does not plead for "a cliché in every sentence," but urges that teachers recognize that an occasional one is not shameful.[38]

## A FEW WORDS WITH INTERESTING HISTORIES

abundance, accost, aftermath, aggravate, agony, ambition, assassin, astonish, ballot, bonfire, candidate, capital, congregation, curfew, deliberate, easel, enthrall, extravagant, fool, garret, halcyon, inaugurate, intoxicate, journey, milliner, panic, pedigree, prevaricate, remorse, tantalize, taxicab

## WORD ORIGINS

In a study of word origins, try giving students a short list of English words of Anglo-Saxon origin for which they are to find English synonyms derived from Greek or Latin, and another list reversing the procedure. Among many possible pairs: *tongue, language; heavenly, celestial; red, vermilion; forgiveness, pardon.*

## USEFUL ROOT WORDS

Besides knowing the meanings of the most common affixes, students will find it helpful to know the meanings of these roots: *aqua, audio, bene, corpus, credo, dominus, ego, facio, frater, jungo, locus, loquor, mater, mitto, multus, omnis, pater, pes, primus, pugno, scribo, socius, solus, totus, utilis, verto, video; aer, arche, autos, bios, chronos, cratos, grapho, homos, hydro, logos, metron, micro, orthos, pan, pathos, penta, philos, phone, polis, poly, pseudos, psyche, sophos, tele, theos.*

## TAUTOLOGY

Give students practice in reducing the verbiage in sentences like these (preferably their own):
[Our candidate] is frank, candid, honest.

When it comes to budget-cutting to deal with the deficit, here is a place where we can look toward saving the taxpayers some money.

Men aren't the only ones who become violent, because some women do.

... accused of allegedly defrauding ...
... increasingly dwindling ...[39]

## OUR WORD

A class invents a word, for example, *flib,* meaning "needing a haircut." Class members try unostentatiously to get the word used around school—by slipping it (always in a self-defining context) into a school newspaper story, a PA announcement, casual conversations. They thus learn how and perhaps why words do or do not catch on.[40] The author also suggests class-made specialty dictionaries, for example, of automotive terms, words about the sea, and of course current teen-age slang.

## ENCOURAGE USE OF THE DICTIONARY

"I stimulate use of the dictionary by frequently using it myself, in class." (Elizabeth Barton, Clanton, Alabama)

## CB IN THE CLASSROOM

Harvey A. Daniels suggests that students may analyze the linguistic characteristics of citizens' band radio, such as "We stopping for coffee," that a glossary of CB terms be compiled, that CB users be interviewed, and that the CB dialect be compared with others.[41]

## HIDDEN ASSUMPTIONS

Students may examine advertisements to try to discover hidden assumptions. For example, one partner in a marriage (usually the husband) is stupid; woman's place of glory is the home; little children are always cute; teen-agers are interested only in fun.

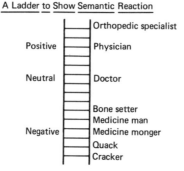

A Ladder to Show Semantic Reaction

Elaine Smith, who devised this particular ladder, also has students describe three times what they see in a picture that each selects from a magazine. One description should be positive, one neutral, one negative.[42]

## COURSES IN DOUBLESPEAK

Les Patton of Castle Rock, Colorado, briefly describes two 9-week courses in doublespeak, based on its use in advertising, media, politics, racist and sexist oppression, the military, and religion. The class used newspapers, magazines, TV ads, and textbooks called *How Words Change Our Lives* and *Making Sense*.[43]

## SEXIST LANGUAGE

Available from NCTE is a leaflet suggesting than *man* can be written *humanity* or *people,* that *he* can be recast in the plural, reworded, or replaced, that *lady lawyer* should be *lawyer,* and so on. NCTE also has a book by Alleen Pace Nilsen and others, *Sexism and Language,* 1977, that goes into considerably more detail about the ways that language has been and is used to discriminate or apparently discriminate against women. On the other side, arguing that most such discrimination is only imaginary, see an article by Lance Alter in the December 1976, *English Journal.* Also note the awkwardness that results in some sentences when *he or she* and *his and her* replace *he* and *his,* and the laughable quality of words like *statespersonlike.*

## STYLISTIC PARODIES

Able students may sharpen their observation of style by attempting to imitate the sentence structure, typical word choice, and point of view of various authors. Let them try, for example, to write such a story as "Little Red Riding Hood" in the styles of Hemingway, Faulkner, Dickens, Addison.

## SHOW; DON'T TELL

Provide a number of sentences that simply tell something, for example, "Rollie made a fine catch in deep center field." Ask students to rewrite, *showing* what happened: "At the crack of the bat, Rollie turned his back to the infield and raced toward the center field wall. As he reached it, he spun around and sprang high into the air. The ball struck the fingers of his glove and plopped into his bare hand as he fell to the ground."

## THE IMPORTANCE OF CONTEXT

1. To dramatize for students the need for considering the meanings of words in context, have them compose sentences in which the context requires a specialized meaning; for example, "A goose is one bird from which you can get *down.*" Other words to suggest to the students who stare uncomprehendingly: *runner, fly, well, corn, boxer, ring, diamond, gridiron, flat, light, type, base.*
2. Discuss the prime meaning of certain words to various persons; for example, *pipe* to piper, plumber, organist, oil worker, Dad; *court* to a king, judge, tennis player, suitor; *log* to mathematician, sailor, woodsman.

## A JOURNALIST'S ADVICE

Sally Winfrey got good results from her Englewood, New Jersey, students by urging these rules of a journalist: (1) Make your sentences short. (2) Use the right word, especially the verb, to picture what you are telling. (3) Avoid weak words. (4) Avoid trite expressions as you would a puff adder.

## HOW MEDIA SLANT NEWS

Students can have fun noting examples of slanting in news magazines or in broadcasts. For example, "*Unhappily* this occurred." "He was *understandably* reluctant." "He said it was a debacle. *So it was.*" "The President, *of course,* will run again." (Two months after this last quote President L. B. Johnson announced that he would not be a candidate.)

## SEMANTIC EXERCISES

1. Have students write paragraphs in which they explain the connotations that given words have for them; for example, *football, television, Saturday, court room, crash, mathematics, April.* Or ask for both the connotations and denotations of words: *date, average, childish, antique, tenement.*
2. Use semanticists' subscripts (e.g., democracy$_{USA}$, democracy$_{USSR}$, automobiles$_{1935}$, automobiles$_{1982}$). Ask students to point out common elements (if any) in the things being discussed, and also the differences.
3. Think of a specific house or piece of real estate. Write an advertisement intended to interest possible buyers. Then write what an unscrupulous real estate dealer might tell the prospects if the dealer thought he or she could persuade them to buy a different, more expensive property.

## WHO ARE THE CONSERVATIVES IN USAGE?

In a doctoral dissertation at the University of Illinois, Raymond D. Crisp found that in judging matters of usage, language specialists are most liberal or persuasive, followed in order by members of the American Dialect Society, elementary section members of NCTE, college section members of NCTE, members of the Conference on English Education, secondary section members of NCTE (high school teachers), editors of publishing houses, members of the Journalism Education Association, representatives of the news media, contemporary authors, members of MLA, leading businessmen, editors of newspapers, and (most conservative) editors of magazines.

## THE SPEECH OF NEW YORK CITY

We don't know why some New Yorkers say "Doily boid gets da woim," says Ann L. Sen, but historical linguistics can tell us much about the speech of America's largest city.[44]

## ONE THING AT A TIME

Faced with students who wrote "black English," James L. Collins of Springfield, Massachusetts, learned two especially useful things: (1) Concentrate more on content than on the language, especially in the early stages. (2) Concentrate on one thing at a time: e.g., the *s* plural, then the *s* on verbs where it is needed.[45]

320

## "YOU KNOW . . . YOU KNOW . . ."

For a delightful, light, but helpful article about overuse of "you know," as well as many other amusing, insightful comments about language, see children's book author Natalie Babbitt's "Profile: Learning the Language," *Language Arts* 54, November/December 1977, p. 953.

## "GRAFFITI VERSUS DOUBLESPEAK"

For 100 or so examples of doublespeak and graffiti, useful in comparing the two, see Don Nilsen's article. For example, "Dial soap 'does it all' " is doublespeak. A graffito: "You were never lovelier, and I think it's a shame."[46]

## A BARRED GRUNT BY ANY OTHER NAME

"The National Oceanic and Atmospheric Administration is seeking sweet-sounding names for dogfish, ratfish, cancer crab, barred grunt, wolffish, jack, and saucer-eye porgy. The agency's goal is to boost sales to housewives and to establish a standardization of fish names."[47]

## "SOLILOQUY ON A GLITCH"

You have to read this! Peggy J. Browning of Great Falls, Montana, loves words and teaches her seventh graders to love them, too. They play rhyming games, play with *gn* and *pn* and *mn*, get curious about words that come from people's names, imagine some inventions and name them, change *hate* to *love* (hate, late, lave, love), and . . .[48]

# FOOTNOTES

1. World, 1967.
2. NCTE, 1967.
3. Scott, Foresman, 1974. See also a fine, specific unit by Charles R. Duke, "Discovering Dialects," *English Journal* 62, March 1973, p. 432.
4. *Students' Right to Their Own Language,* Urbana, 1974. A helpful 12-page bibliography on dialects and usage is appended.
5. "How Would You Feel If You Had to Change *Your* Dialect?" *English Journal* 62, Oct. 1973, p. 994.
6. "Grammar and Goodness," *English Journal* 62, May 1973, p. 771.
7. "The Hegelian Principle," *English Journal* 62, Oct. 1973, p. 964.
8. Quoted in *College Composition and Communication* 24, May 1973, p. 372.
9. "Why *Newsweek* Can't Tell Us Johnny Can't Write," *English Journal* 65, Nov. 1976, p. 29.

10. "In Defense of Trivia," *English Journal* 63, April 1974, p. 11.
11. "Motivating Black Children," in *Through a Glass Darkly,* ed. Edward Fagan and Jean Vandell, Urbana: NCTE, 1971, p. 9.
12. "Language Testing," *English Journal* 63, Feb. 1974, p. 82.
13. Dennis R. Dean, "Slang Is Language Too!" *English Journal* 51, May 1962, p. 324.
14. "Discovering Truth about Words," *English Journal* 39, Feb. 1970, p. 159.
15. In learning a word one first puts it into the class to which it belongs and later distinguishes it from other members of the same class. The word *erudite* was included in a multiple-choice test administered to 87 recent high school graduates. Ten defined it as "rude," five as "rough," eleven as "polite," 31 as "well-educated," and 30 as "ignorant." The last figure is the significant one, because these 30 students realized that the word referred to knowledge but did not yet know whether it pertained to much knowledge or little. Even though they gave the opposite of the true meaning, they knew more about the word than did those who defined it as "rude," "rough," or "polite."
16. "Vocabulary for Slow Learners," *English Journal* 59, Jan. 1970. p. 78.
17. "Teaching English through the Language of Advertising," *English Journal* 65, Feb. 1976, p. 29.
18. Details concerning word invention and the histories of many words are available in numerous books on language history, including J. N. Hook's *History of the English Language,* Ronald Press, 1975.
19. Robert Pooley, *Teaching English Usage,* New York: Appleton-Century-Crofts, 1946, p. 29. (Second edition, 1974).
20. "Semantics: What and Why," *English Journal* 58, Nov. 1969, p. 1214.
21. "Where's the Good Word?" *English Journal* 62, Oct. 1973, p. 977.
22. Richard Gambino, "A Glossary of Evasive Language in Government," *English Journal* 63, Nov. 1974, p. 24.
23. Based on Howard Livingston, "Language and Meaning," *English Journal* 63, Sept. 1974, p. 18.
24. Terence P. Morgan, "Public Doublespeak," *College English* 36, Oct. 1974, p. 190.
25. "Teaching Semantics in High School," *English Journal* 58, Dec. 1969, p. 1341.
26. *English Journal* 61, Sept. 1972, p. 878.
27. "Oral Language Activities," *English Journal* 63, Dec. 1974, p. 79.
28. *English Journal* 53, May 1964, p. 342.
29. *English Journal* 58, Nov. 1969, p. 1224.
30. *English Journal* 56, Nov. 1967, p. 1166.
31. *High School Journal,* May 1972.
32. In *On Righting Writing,* ed., Ouida H. Clapp, Urbana: NCTE, 1975, p. 78.

33. "Dialect Features in the Composition of Black and White College Students," *College Composition and Communication* 25, Oct. 1974, p. 259.

34. Donald H. Kahle, *English Journal* 61, Feb. 1972, p. 286.

35. "Hydrozoology in the Microcosm," *English Journal* 54, Dec. 1965, p. 861.

36. Quoted in *English Journal* 65, Nov. 1976, p. 51.

37. Michael Borkoff, "The Almost Right Word," *College Composition and Communication* 27, Dec. 1976, p. 408.

38. *College Composition and Communication* 26, May 1975, p. 159.

39. Examples from Stewart Justman, "Mass Communications and Tautology," *College English* 38, March 1977, p. 633.

40. Donald Small, "Doing Things with Language," *English Journal* 65, April 1976, p. 86.

41. "Breaker, Break, Broke," *English Journal* 65, Dec. 1976, p. 86.

42. *English Newsletter* (Youngstown State University), Spring 1977.

43. *English Journal* 65, April 1976, p. 63.

44. "English in the Big Apple," *English Journal* 68, Nov. 1979, p. 52.

45. "Dialect Variation and Writing," *English Journal* 69, March 1980, p. 48.

46. *English Journal* 67, Feb. 1978, p. 20.

47. Quoted in Alan Dittmer, "Language Is Alive," *English Journal* 67, Dec. 1978, p. 21.

48. *English Journal* 69, March, 1980, p. 46.

# 10

## GROWTH IN WRITING ABILITY

Although this chapter focuses on writing, many of its principles apply equally well to oral composition. The choice and development of a topic, for instance, are significant in both types of composing.

We (the authors of this book) believe that the process of composing is too frequently confused with mere searching for "correctness" in syntax, diction, spelling, and punctuation. For that reason we have paid little attention to those considerations here, although we treat them in detail in other chapters. Students are usually more willing to learn and follow matters of linguistic etiquette when they are genuinely interested in what they are writing. So this chapter concentrates on a rationale for composition, the selection and development of topics, and the evaluation of results.

## WHY TEACH COMPOSITION?

### AN ANSWER FROM NCTE

The National Council of Teachers of English has several commissions which deal with broad instructional matters (in contrast with the relatively focused concerns of NCTE's numerous committees). One of those commissions, that on composition, has issued an 18-point position statement. The first six points all have relevance to the question "Why teach composition?"

*1. Life in Language. In many senses, anyone's world is his language. Through language we understand, interpret, enjoy, control, and in part create our worlds. The teacher of English, in awakening students to the possibilities of* language, can help students to expand and enlarge their worlds, to live more fully.

2. **Need for Writing.** *Writing is an important medium for self-expression, for communication, and for the discovery of meaning—its need increased rather than decreased by the development of new media for mass communication. Practice and study of writing therefore remain significant parts of the school curriculum and central parts of the English course.*

3. **Positive Instruction.** *Since a major value of writing is self-expression and self-realization, instruction in writing should be positive. Students should be encouraged to use language clearly, vividly, and honestly; they should not be discouraged by negative correction and proscription. They should be freed from fear and restriction so that their sensitivity and their abilities can develop.*

4. **Learning by Writing.** *Learning to write requires writing; writing practice should be a major emphasis of the course. Workbook exercises, drill on usage, and analysis of existing prose are not adequate substitutes for writing.*

5. **Required Writing.** *No formula dictates the amount of writing that should be required in a course—a paper a day or a paper a week. Ideally students should be allowed to write when they want to, as much as they want to, and at their own speed. Practically, however, students need class discipline and class discussion as well as freedom, and they should be frequently encouraged and at times required to write.*

6. **Classroom Writing.** *Inexperienced writers especially should have an opportunity to compose in school, with help during the actual writing process in clarifying ideas, in choosing phrasing, and sometimes in dealing with mechanical problems. Writing outside the classroom, of course, should be encouraged and sometimes required.*[1]

## OTHER ANSWERS

As a college student, Roosevelt Brown (later to become a superstar on the New York Giants football team) managed to flunk freshman composition for three whole years. As a senior, with the help of a dedicated tutor, he finally reached C level. His instructor has written:

> *Later, one day, Rosy showed me a letter from his "Mom" in New York City—especially the lines where she thanked his English teacher and complimented her son. "For the first time," she wrote, "I can just about understand everything you're trying to say."*[2]

Maybe that's a good reason for teaching writing—so that Mom, Dad, and others can just about understand everything somebody is trying to say.

Donald M. Murray, a professional writer and a University of New Hampshire professor, has listed seven reasons for teaching writing:

1. Writing is a skill that is important in school and after school.
2. Writing, for many students, is the skill which can unlock the language arts.
3. Writing is thinking.
4. Writing is an ethical act, because the single most important quality in writing is honesty.
5. Writing is a process of self-discovery.
6. Writing satisfies man's primitive hunger to communicate.
7. Writing is an art, and art is profound play.

As a teacher Professor Murray admits "the extraordinary pleasure of reading a page which is honest, specific, and clean." He claims a "secret eagerness to read each batch of weekly papers."[3]

Much black oral English is informal, lightly structured, personal, and stylized; it is known as "rapping." In contrast, "running it down" emphasizes content and is much more methodical. Michael D. Linn, of Virginia Commonwealth University, recommends "beginning a writing course with themes based upon the oral tradition with which the student is already familiar," and moving gradually to the stage where "the student knows he is *running it down,* seeking literal truth." Useful in the transition, Linn says, is the preparation of a few compositions by groups of four or five students, who can assist and criticize one another and arrive at some sort of organizational pattern.[4]

Novelist Barbara Wersba (*Tunes for a Small Harmonica, The Dream Watcher*) has elaborated on Murray's notion of writing as self-discovery. She told an interviewer that writing is a process of "unlearning all of the prejudices and conventional ideas that we're taught when we're young.... Writing is a process of self-discovery. Many writers, if you read what they say about themselves, say they write a book to find out what they think. I write a book to find out who I am." She adds a warning to the many persons, young and not-so-young, who think they would like to be writers: "I've discovered that most people who want to write really want to have written, because the labor involved is tremendous."[5]

In an unusual assignment, Sister Angelica Miller perhaps expedited the self-discovery. She asked each student in her all-boy class to write a long, thoughtful letter to himself, "Dear Me... ," as he expected to be when he was 45 or 50 years old. "Remind that future unknown self of all [your] hopes for him—of [your] ideals, [your] present hang-ups about adults, [your] fears for the unforeseeable future." She says, "It was to be a letter they could put away somewhere and read years from now." Most of the boys did write seriously, although a few "floundered in superficialities of allowing their own children long hair, flashy clothes...." Most wrote about their ideals; "they spoke to their future selves with a friendliness that was born of optimism and faith in themselves; they spoke with a clarity that was born of sincerity and truth."[6]

To teachers who think that the only important writing deals with literary topics, anthropologist Robbins Burling of the University of Michigan had this to say at an NCTE convention:

*Possibly you would not regard the content of* Dairy Herd Management *magazine as important. But the anthropologist in me rebels against such a value-laden judgment. . . . I dislike the elitism implied by presuming that some kinds of writing are more important than other kinds. I believe that cat fanciers, . . . business people, . . . deserve to have good writing in their own areas of interest. They deserve to have the skills that will allow them to produce their own sound prose.*

Leroy Haley of Hartland, Wisconsin, pleads that writing is important in the student's present tense:

*We teach writing because it is a form of linguistic expression, because linguistic expression is a basically and peculiarly human activity associated with that most important of human activities, the making of symbols. And we teach writing because all men need to be as human as possible, and as teachers our greatest role is to help as many people as we can [to] find tools to help them best realize their human potential. That is why we teach writing at any level.*[7]

Some persons, however, without necessarily disagreeing with Haley's main thrust, argue that students' later careers are often affected by their writing skill or lack of it. Research by John A. Daly of the University of Texas at Austin and Michael D. Miller of Florida shows that people who are fearful of writing tend to choose "such occupations they view as requiring little writing, and if, unexpectedly, they find themselves placed in positions where writing is demanded, will report they are unhappy." In other words, students' attitudes toward writing may influence their entire lives.[8]

A Louisiana bulletin devoted to career education refers to composition as "a journey into our inner being" and "a process of self-discovery, self recognition or understanding," as well as "an act of clarifying, arranging, and relating facts and ideas into larger meaning, and . . . a vital part of the thinking process." It continues with a quotation from K. Thomas Finley:

*If a person cannot express himself in writing, he may never even get an interview for the job he wants. And on his present job—if it requires any writing at all—he will throw promotional opportunities to the winds if he can't "talk" on paper. No amount of personal charm can overcome this handicap.*[9]

John H. Fisher, formerly executive secretary of the Modern Language Association and more recently head of the Department of English at the University of

Tennessee, has written eloquently about the need for teachers of writing and of English in general to avoid setting their sights too low:

*My growing conviction is that English departments have a grave responsibility to become centers for the discussion of integrity in speaking and writing, of censorship both overt and covert, of control of the media, of the psychological impact of the arts, of propaganda on every level from toothpaste to political campaigns, and of every other aspect of the way in which language knits together or divides our society. These seem to me more pressing problems for English departments than biographical and critical interpretation of poems and plays. And I think that it is our reluctance to address ourselves to these pressing problems that has led to the disenchantment of our colleagues in other departments and of the public at large with the humanities in general and with English departments in particular.[10]*

These numerous quotations—which could be multiplied—have demonstrated that the reasons for teaching writing are many and strong. But unfortunately there is evidence that inadequate practice in writing is provided in many high school classrooms. Countless freshmen tell their college instructors, "I've never written a theme" or "The only writing we did in English last year was a paper on *Hamlet*."

Certainly literary and visual studies are important. But writing deserves no less time and attention. Teaching writing is not easy, but it can be fascinating, especially as one watches students grow in their ability to find themselves, to think, to organize their thoughts, and to guide their lives by intelligence and not just raw emotion and impulse. It is doubtful that a teacher of English can find any greater reward.

## SOME OF THE POSSIBLE STARTING POINTS

Alarmed by the poor writing of many California high school graduates, faculty members at the University of California (Berkeley) began working regularly with high school English teachers in the Bay Area Writing Project, and later with representatives or surrogates throughout the nation. Within three years the results became significantly apparent in the writing of entering University freshmen.[11] Perhaps the very best starting point in attaining effective student writing lies in hiring teachers who are interested in writing, informed about compositional processes, and eager to develop students' expressional potentials.

### CHARACTERISTICS OF A GOOD ASSIGNMENT

Most instruction in writing, says Norman L. Frey of Winnetka, Illinois, takes place *after* the composition is written, when students are told "how, why, and

THE TEACHING OF HIGH SCHOOL ENGLISH

where they went wrong (or, in some cases, right).''[12] Frey, like many other good teachers, prefers to give each assignment in detail, and then as a class or in small groups "have the students begin the process of thinking and composing." They discuss possible things to include, various approaches to the assignment, possible organizational plans, and perhaps even some sample introductory sentences or paragraphs.

Frey thus uses a modern adaptation of what a distinguished French teacher, Julien Bezard of Versailles, did during the first quarter of this century:

> *We seldom give out a subject without adding some advice as to how to treat it; preferring, as far as possible, to discuss the home-work with the pupil before he does it rather than after. We try to encourage him, to show him what he would have little chance of discovering for himself, and, without rousing his suspicions, to turn him toward sources abundant in material. Yet care must be taken not to check his initiative, not to accustom him to read too much in his teacher's face, to lean continually on another's foresight.*[13]

Gilbert Tierney and Stephen Judy have suggested these criteria for the writing assignment:

1. *Motivation and stimulation: Are the directions adequate but not too restrictive? Is the topic basically interesting?*
2. *Appropriateness: Is the topic suitable for these students?*
3. *Open-endedness: Are options available in form and complexity?*
4. *Language play: Is there opportunity for linguistic or other experimentation?*
5. *The writer's function: Are students aware of possible approaches to the topic?*
6. *Voice: Is the voice or persona a natural one for the student?*
7. *Readers: Will there be a real audience and do the students know what it is?*
8. *Reactions: Will there be opportunity for the readers to react?*[14]

Sister Agnes Pastva of Elyria, Ohio, recommends that lessons requiring "tough, logical disciplines" be alternated with "spontaneous, intuitive, personal writing." Thus a student who excels in one variety has a chance to practice his or her specialty but also broadens scope by working on others.[15]

All the quoted advice is good. Even more basic, however, is building students' awareness that whatever they write should be a statement of "This I believe." If what the student writes about is as simple as an explanation of how a ball-point pen works, he or she is saying "I believe that a ball-point pen works like this." Or if he or she is writing a comparison of two books, the underlying statement is "I believe that these two books have these similarities and these differences."

Each composition, then, is today's statement by and about a developing human being. It is an attempt on the student's part to define one segment—tiny or large—of what the student believes about life, about humanity, about inanimate objects, about himself or herself. It is no mere exercise in copying or in mechanically making squiggles on paper; it is no mere exercise in well-formed sentences or in punctuation.

But not enough students have been taught to regard writing as a credo. Too often a student paper is only a rather random amalgamation of facts or observations, and it is bad writing because it is unfocused. Some years ago Professor Bertrand Evans of Berkeley described an all-too-typical theme by an entering freshman.[16] The student is writing about "My Home Town." Systematic and dutiful, he outlines his composition: I. Introduction—Name, Location, Size; II. Recreational facilities: Skiing, Swimming, Fishing, Hunting; III. Educational facilities: Grade schools, High school, Libraries; IV. Sources of income: Farming, Industry, Business; V. Conclusion. He writes the paper, with a sentence or two on each of the subtopics, and hands it in.

So what's wrong? The student had a *topic,* said Professor Evans, but he did not have a *subject*. A topic is the name of something, anything: hobbies, my hobby, atomic energy, bricklaying, my home town. A subject, in contrast, says something, states a belief: Hobbies are overrated; Aunt Sara is a miser; atomic energy offers only a small chance of solving the world's energy problems; bricklaying requires skills that I do not possess; my home town is an exciting place in which to live.

The teacher, giving an assignment, usually indicates a topic, not wanting to tell students what they should believe about it. The good teacher, though, helps the students to see some of the ways in which the topic may be made into a subject. One way to do that is to say: "Ask yourself, 'What do I believe about this topic? What do I want to prove about it?' Put your belief in the form of a short sentence. Include in the sentence one or more expressions that will allow differences of opinion. For example, in 'Aunt Sara is a miser,' not everyone's ideas of miserliness are identical. It is this ambiguous expression that you will concentrate on. You will show us what your idea of a miser is and show us how Aunt Sara fits it.''

Compositions written about subjects rather than about topics are inevitably idea-centered and thought-provoking. The teacher and classmates may disagree with what a student attempts to prove and may not share the writer's belief because their own experiences have been different. Sometimes the evidence presented may be demonstrably incorrect; sometimes there may be flaws in reasoning. If frank discussion of students' writing is customary in the classroom (as it should be—frank but kind and constructive), there will be statements of appreciation of good illustrations and strong arguments as well as suggestions about possible better illustrations and attacks on weak arguments.

Students *do* have something to say. They *do* have beliefs, even though those will and should change as they grow older. Each student has had experiences, has read a little, has heard and seen much, and has formed opinions worthy of

330

expression and sympathetic scrutiny. But many students have never learned that they can find something to say that will interest someone else, and hence their compositions too frequently have been pointless exercises that bore their writers. Well-conceived, well-made assignments can result in compositions at least a notch above those typically handed in today.

## REPRESENTATIVE ASSIGNMENTS FOR JUNIOR HIGH

The ingenuity of students is matched only by that of teachers. Here are a few of the many assignments that teachers have considered successful.

1. Often I begin by asking them to simply record as best they can what they see me do. Then I will make a series of motions (raise right hand, turn around, wink one eye, put book on head, etc.) waiting between motions for them to record. Then they read to the class what they wrote and are praised for their accuracy in recording.... Eventually we extend this recording to writing descriptive paragraphs, usually a "mystery person" paragraph describing in accurate detail a person in the class on that particular day. Sometimes we write "mystery food" paragraphs.[17]
2. For kids who exhaust their ideas on any subject in one vague paragraph, the daily journal works.... Writing at least a page a day for a semester will loose most kids out of the rut of listing 'What I Did and When.' They will begin to identify meanings in their lives and feelings, or at least words to identify them.[18]

Carol Mitchell of Thousand Oaks, California, has her "Standard" (below-average) students write in their journals three times a week. She announces topics, but they may choose something different. Sample topics: What traits of mine would I like to pass on to a child? The first time I ever stole something. If I inherited a million dollars, would I quit school? If I could change one thing about myself. Why I envy _____ . The teacher reads all entries, writes comments, but does not correct. What they write is confidential, and should be honest. The writing may be stories, poems, accounts of personal experiences, or anything else. Ms. Mitchell says that her procedure is effective with 85 per cent of these students, but not with those with whom there is little rapport.[19]

Marilyn Dixon of Mt. Airy, North Carolina, extends journal writing to the sophomore year. Although many teachers do not read student journals unless invited, she requires and reads at least two entries a week in the first term, and comments constructively on the content and style of each entry. In the second term she requires only one weekly entry and *suggests* topics, such as a protest statement or an analysis of a quotation or proverb in which the writer believes. There is no journal writing in the third term, and one weekly entry in the fourth.[20]

3. With her junior high students in San Diego, Patricia Phelan uses these and other motivations:
   (a) She writes along with the class.
   (b) Each youngster forms a "monster" out of a smidgen of plastic clay. The next day all are told, "Your creature came alive last night. Tell us what happened."
   (c) She cuts captions from newspapers or magazines.
   Students use them somewhere in a story.
   (d) She cuts out photographs or drawings showing two or three people. Students write conversations to fit the pictures.[21]

4. Students may prepare a four- or six-page newspaper related to *Johnny Tremain* or other historical novel the class has read. Suggested contents: major news stories of the day, articles of local interest to the people of the time, a map, an editorial, a letter to the editor, a political cartoon, classified ads, a fashion article, wedding or birth or obituary notices related to the book, recipes, letters of advice, feature articles on book characters.[22]

5. Harvey S. Wiener of City University of New York suggests starters like these for brief narratives:
   When I played hooky, I . . .
   We always got in trouble when . . .
   My teacher lost her temper when . . .
   I was embarrassed at school when . . .[23]

6. In "What Am I" compositions, each student writes a description of an object without naming it. Clues to its identity build up, and in the last sentence the writer gives a particularly obvious clue. All papers are read to the class, whose members try to guess what the object is.[24]

Other suggestions are in the Idea Box. To generalize concerning the qualities of successful writing assignments for the junior high, we see that basically they are lively and imaginative; they give each child an opportunity to treat the topic individually, personally. They tend to be fun. They are (with the exception of many of the journal entries) suitable for sharing with the whole class or a group within the class. Although the quality of results will vary widely, they are topics that almost every student can write about. Finally, most of them by their very nature make it relatively easy for each student to convert topic to subject.

## RABUN GAP AND BEYOND

One of the greatest success stories of English teaching in recent years is that of Eliot Wigginton, a teacher in the Rabun Gap, Georgia, high school. Wigginton's 140 students in 1966 began to produce a quarterly magazine, *Foxfire*, "that preserves the skills and traditions of the local community while teaching required language arts skill.'' The students interviewed older residents of the area, finding out how people formerly lived, and they wrote up the interviews. From the magazine, as years passed, grew several commercially published *Foxfire* books.

*What's more, the Foxfire idea has become a focal point for numerous other student projects. In Foxfire Video, students are using an entire television production studio, and Foxfire Records is producing a series of albums, again with students doing all the work. Foxfire Press is publishing its own books (independently of the four Foxfire volumes published nationally, compiling articles from the magazine). Students in Foxfire Furniture are working to create a local industry that will produce historically authentic furnishings— and where students may be employed after graduation.*[25]

For a while, Wigginton says, people believed that "*Foxfire* was a fluke that could exist only in Rabun Gap. But in the last five years, I have watched the light of Foxfire (the term refers to a lichen that glows in the dark) spread, through similar projects in scores of high schools from Alaska and Hawaii to Maine.'' Even though the teacher and students do not attempt to develop a major enterprise like that at Rabun Gap, they can adapt the plan, on a smaller scale, to local conditions. In large high schools, maybe students at only one grade level—the eleventh grade, perhaps—should be involved, or students in certain arbitrarily designated classes.

Interviews are basic parts of the procedure. (The teacher should consult an appropriate administrator to present information about the project and to make sure about school policies concerning such unusual activities. And partly for safety, interviewers should normally work in pairs or trios.) Unlike the residents of Rabun Gap, many of the interviewees will not know about making split-bottom chairs or planting in the light of the moon, but most of them will have other areas of expertise, such as these:

*history of the neighborhood or the community*
*details about work activities in local factories, etc.*
*schools of a bygone day*
*living through the Great Depression*
*recipes for ethnic dishes*
*songs of yesteryear*
*entertainment before television*
*working on a Model-T Ford*
*dating customs*
*practices in rearing children*
*survivals of immigrant traditions*
*names of people and places*
*holiday observances*
*language(s) of the community*[26]

Among the values of a Foxfire-like experience are the practice of interviewing people of different ages and thus perhaps broadening human sympathies and increasing courtesy, practice in writing (including such mechanics as the use of quotation marks), practice in weighing the relative importance of content items while deciding what to include and delete, practice in organizing, and practice in reporting and explaining accurately (an inaccurate recipe, for instance, may result in failure). Wigginton reports what may be even a greater value:

> *As older people share their experiences, the great human themes emerge to bring to life the literature the students may be reading: 92-year-old Aunt Arie Carpenter, for example, saying with a great, warm smile to several of my kids, "I'm too old to do most of the things I used to enjoy doing. Can't spin anymore, can't crochet or quilt anymore, can't raise a big garden anymore. But I can still love." Or Charlie Ross Hartley, who survived a logging accident in which he lost a leg, and then strapped a two-by-six onto the stump as a substitute for the missing limb and became one of the finest builders in the Southern Appalachians.*

The end-product may be only a sharing by the students of their experiences, but a simple little duplicated magazine or a small book may have more readily apparent significance. And if the interviewees and their families can be given copies, rapport between school and community may be substantially increased.

## REPRESENTATIVE ASSIGNMENTS FOR SENIOR HIGH

1. John C. Martin, Hazel Crest, Illinois, gets good response from his reluctant writers by asking each to write one or more paragraphs about "something in your life that you would like to get rid of or change."[27]
2. A successful book and a very successful Broadway play, *The Me Nobody Knows,* is largely in the unedited language of ghetto youngsters. The teacher responsible for the remarkable work, Stephen M. Joseph, urged but did not force each child to write a page frequently, with the option of signing it, not signing it, or writing it but not handing it in.[28]
3. Cut out from old newspapers some letters to Ann Landers, Dear Abby, or other advice-giver. Keep the replies from the students, but use a number system to match them with the questions. Students choose letters to answer. Later, they may want to compare their answers with the original.
4. Alfred L. Crabb, Jr., of the University of Kentucky, recommends showing (preferably projecting) the face on a *Time* cover. Ignoring whatever they may know about the person, the students talk about the face as a face. "Such problems as how to describe the eyes: the eyebrows, the eyelashes, the eyelids, the whites, the irises, the pupils, the over-all eye shape, the placement on the head, the width, the size, the shadows, the wrinkles and creases,

all these emphasize the necessity for accuracy, clarity, and completeness. . . . Soon similes and parallels will be suggested, and different ways of describing a single feature will permit discussion of which is the most effective. Problems in organization arise. . . . After this open discussion, the class is asked to write the description. . . ." Next, each student is given a different *Time* cover and asked to repeat the process by himself or herself. In discussion, each cover is projected while the student's description is read. The class comments on the accuracy, completeness, vividness, etc.[29]

5. Students in Kay Sanders' Los Angeles classes are asked to write a letter or a journal entry about the London stage c. 1600. Ms. Sanders suggests questions like these: "You are on your way to the Globe Theatre and a performance of *Julius Caesar* [or another play]. Is it possible that you are an actor and a member of the repertory company? What part will you play today? . . . What problems face you on stage? Or, . . . are you a groundling or a member of the wealthy class? How are you dressed? Where will you sit? Why are you drawn to the Globe?"[30]

6. To learn about differences in point of view, student groups write about the same incident in different personae. For example, for an ad about a pet for sale: the advertiser, a prospective buyer, the mother or father of the prospective buyer, the pet itself. Or, for an auto crash, with a boy and girl in each car: one driver, the other driver, one passenger, the other passenger, the police officer who investigated, an observant witness.

7. Some writing in the senior high school should be of "practical" sorts, the amount perhaps varying from one class or community to another. Among the obvious kinds are form-filling, business letters of various kinds, job or college applications and resumés, instructions on how to make or do certain things, explanations of how something works, answers to examination questions.

8. In many high schools a large part of the writing concerns literature. The topics vary according to the literary sophistication of the class. In general, the topics that most students can handle are those pertaining to characters in the literature; to "iffy" questions such as "In *Julius Caesar,* what might have happened if Brutus had stayed for Antony's oration?"; to follow-up questions such as "What happened after the book ended?"; to parallel experiences and emotions of the students themselves; to relating the literature to the life the student knows. Harder for many students are topics involving the ideas and the controversies implied in the literature, or the comparison of one work with another. Usually only the fairly able or very able students are equipped to deal in detail with matters of literary technique and form. "Literature is people" may well be the teacher's slogan, at least until he or she finds that at least some members of a class are capable of dealing with literature on a more abstract basis.

One way to accommodate individual differences in a class is illustrated by a tactic used by Mary C. Sommers of Lincoln, Nebraska. What she does with *Hamlet* may be adapted to any substantial literary work. She prepares about 40 "thesis statements" on the play. Each student draws one and may trade for a different one or make an alteration in the statement. The purpose of the writing is to prove or deny the truth of the thesis statement by specific references to the play. Sample theses: Gertrude is weak-willed. *Hamlet* resembles modern murder mysteries [or a specific one]. Horatio is a skeptical stoic. Hamlet faces a hostile world. Hamlet possesses great sensitivity. *Hamlet* contains images of disease and decay. (Note that various theses refer to characters, ideas, and literary characteristics. The opportunity to trade or modify leads each student to a reasonably suitable subject.)

9. Jonathan Kozol, one of the angry critics of modern schools, believes passionately that students should write about matters of social concern, that they should become young reformers: "The language that we learn in public school is one of ethical antisepsis and of political decontamination. It is the language of an intellectual cease-fire while the victims are still dying. It is also a language which, by failing to concede *real* oppositions, denies a child or adult right or power to make strong, risk-taking choices. The student learns to step back and to steer away from moral confrontations. He learns to ascertain the quickest highway and the best approach to middle places of inert comparison and dysfunctional concern: places where choice does not reside and anger does not threaten."[31]

Richard Larson, a past chair of the Conference on College Composition and Communication, has offered some significant advice (paraphrased here) concerning assignments.

1. Analyze each prospective assignment before you give it. Specifically, what do you hope students will accomplish? Is the material needed for it readily available?
2. Consider what students will need to know in order to do well on the assignment. Is it within their present range?
3. Decide what you must teach now in order to assure students a fair chance to do the assignment well.
4. Word the assignment carefully. Try to make it stimulating and specific, not vague and indefinite.
5. Determine in advance what your standards of evaluation will be.
6. Explain the assignment fully to the students. Issue reminders or review as necessary the techniques and procedures needed. Suggest sources of information (if appropriate). Let the students know what you decided in 5.
7. In evaluation, make special note of where the student has and has not succeeded in reaching the objectives of the assignment.

**8.** Discuss the assignment with the students when you return the papers. Read papers that do well what was assigned, and point out changes that would have made other papers better.

## HELPING STUDENTS TO DEVELOP THEIR IDEAS
### A TYPICAL SUCCESSFUL PROCEDURE

Each student needs to find the writing process that can most generally be successful for him or her. Professional writers themselves have diverse work habits. Some work very methodically, planning and outlining in considerable detail before they write, but others improvise upon the bare, unassembled bones of an idea to see what may fit together. Some do their revising as they go along, but others may go through several drafts plus a final revision. Many do their best work in certain surroundings: H. L. Mencken, for example, could write in Baltimore but not in New York.

Nevertheless, it is possible to describe and illustrate several steps that work well for many people. Students may need to experiment by omitting some steps, combining steps, or adding steps as needed. The teacher ordinarily ought not to insist that every student try to follow exactly the same process.

After a topic has been assigned or chosen, the writer needs to decide what he or she believes about the topic—in other words, translate the topic into a subject. Sometimes the subject is apparent at once, but many people find it only after they start to put words on paper.

So the student—let's call him *Tom*—looks at this topic, starts making some jottings and doodlings. Say that the topic is "Lady Macbeth." Tom writes *cruel, greedy, ambitious, heartless,* and a few other words. He thinks then about the pathos of the hand-washing scene and feels a surge of sympathy for the woman whose conscience was troubling her, whose husband had outstripped her in cruelty and now paid little attention to her, a woman haunted by a dark night in her past, perhaps a woman whose reason was tottering. He wonders, "Was she really such an evil person?"

Can any excuse be found for her inciting her husband to commit murder? Did she do so because of her love for him, her wish to help him succeed? Tom tries to phrase his belief: "Lady Macbeth wasn't quite as bad as she seems," and perhaps a tentative title emerges, such as "A Defense of Lady Macbeth."

Note that in arriving at his subject, Tom is also narrowing it. He is not going to write everything possible about Lady Macbeth; he will consider only those things relevant to a defense of her.

Next he adds to his evidence. Already he knows that he can build sympathy for Lady Macbeth through the sleepwalking scene, but what else is available? He rereads the pertinent passages in Act I. Obviously there's nothing there that makes her appear very lovable. He wouldn't like to have her as his mother, he decides. But she loved her husband, was ambitious for him. She does not think of the jewels and the fine clothes that she might have as queen, but only of "the golden round" for his head. She is kind to the messenger: "Give him tending." She is shrewd: "Look like the innocent flower / But be the serpent under 't." She is strong in determination: "But screw your courage to the sticking-place / And we'll not fail." In Act II a softer part of her nature is revealed: "Had he not resembled / My father as he slept, I had done 't." And she is bold: "Give me the daggers. . . . If he do bleed, / I'll gild the faces of the grooms withal."

Tom thinks some more about his evidence. Lady Macbeth has many qualities generally praised, even though she misuses them: love of her mate, ambition, kindness, shrewdness, strength, tenderness toward those she loves, boldness. If there is a chance, Tom talks with classmates or the teacher about his idea, which he is still willing to modify. He clearly can't present Lady Macbeth as an ideal woman. He plays again on an earlier idea. Maybe that should be his focus: "I Wouldn't Want Lady Macbeth for My Mother, But . . ."

Tom's teacher has often stressed the need to think in terms of the prospective readers, and has suggested that ordinarily her students should address their classmates and try to use illustrations and a tone suitable for the other students. Tone is related to "voice," a term now used in many classrooms, and to "persona," the person as whom one writes. Tom is not writing as a Shakespearean scholar or as a psychologist, for he is neither of these. He is not here writing as an older brother, telling a child an exciting story. He is writing as a student, as a careful reader of *Macbeth,* as someone who has become interested in a puzzling character in the play. And he is writing for classmates who have read the play but who perhaps have not thought much about the enigmatic lady.

With these considerations in mind, Tom decides to adopt a semiserious tone. He cannot honestly support with complete seriousness the idea that Lady Macbeth was an admirable woman. He may use a bit of irony: "Mothers should be strong, affectionate, tender, self-sacrificing, resourceful. Lady Macbeth was all of these. What more could anyone want?"

How should the parts be arranged? Being a fairly methodical student, Tom jots down a few words to suggest each of the parts that he may include, and afterward puts in a number or a notation after each part to indicate where it may fit. His list looks like this:

| | |
|---|---|
| What good mothers are like | (1—introduction) |
| Why I wouldn't want LM as my mother, though I admire her | (3) |
| Her good qualities | (2—several paragraphs) |
| strength | (2-b) |

| | |
|---|---|
| deep love | (2-a) |
| resourcefulness, shrewdness | (2-d—relate to strength) |
| ambition | (2-c—relate to strength) |
| tenderness | (2-a—combine with love) |
| conscience | (2-f—sleepwalking scene) |
| self-sacrifice | (2-e—tie back to deep love) |
| Misdirection of her excellent qualities | (tie in with 3—use as conclusion) |

Tom has really written a simple, informal outline, good enough for most purposes. Usually only a long research paper or something similar needs a meticulous outline—unless the writer is one who works most happily without one. (Some teachers do argue in favor of an elaborate outline, saying that it shows clearly the relative importance of each point. In general, though, most students detest formal outlines, and if they are required to hand one in with a composition, many admit that they prepare it *after* the composition is written—somewhat like preparing a floor plan after the house is built.)

By following his informal outline, Tom finds the writing rather easy. He does not need to stare at blank paper, nor does he make a number of ineffectual starts.

As he writes, with his copy of *Macbeth* before him, he refers to the play for specific examples; often he copies brief passages as evidence. More methodical writers would have made notations in the rough outline to show which passages to use as references, but few students and certainly not all professionals are quite so methodical as that.

Tom, unlike many writers, is a reviser-as you-go-along. So he scratches out a word here or there, writes substituted words between lines, modifies his punctuation, checks a spelling, draws an arrow to show a transposition, sticks in a *however* or other desirable transition, and so on.

When he finishes, he rereads and makes a few more changes. If time permits, he sets the composition aside for a day or two so that he can reread it again, with a fresh mind, and perhaps make a few more changes.

Finally, he makes a clean copy to submit to his classmates and teacher.

## VARIATIONS

Tom's procedure won't work equally well for everyone, but it is basically sound and has proved successful often enough to warrant such a detailed description.

James Thurber didn't write that way. He once asserted that he never knew what any of his characters would say until they said it. Nevertheless, he thought endlessly about whatever he was writing, even though he did not plan very methodically. At cocktail parties, when his wife saw him standing abstracted, she would sometimes whisper, "James, you're composing again!"

Through improvisation, through one word or idea leading to another, the Thurbers write best. They feel chained if they must prepare and follow an outline; it makes their writing mechanical and often dull.

Other writers know their main headings—and hence the general pattern—but no more.

Some writers, including many students, whet their minds by discussing with their friends whatever they are writing. Often ideas or examples from such discussion find their way into the product. Other writers, though, especially many young professionals, find that talking much about their books hinders their writing, dulls their pen, reduces their imagination; if they "talk out" a book or a story, they may never get it down on paper.

Practices in revision, too, vary. Some professionals write draft after draft, but in contrast Jack Kerouac simply put a long roll of paper into his typewriter and typed and typed and typed, folded up the resulting manuscript, and sent it off to a publisher. Shakespeare, to the displeasure of Ben Jonson, who was an inveterate reviser, is reported never to have "blotted a line."

Circumstances also necessarily influence procedures. If Tom had had only an hour of class time to do his paper, or if he had been faced in an examination with a 10-minute question, "Characterize Lady Macbeth," he obviously would have had to modify the process drastically by some short-circuiting. Or if he had been writing his paper for a group that had not read *Macbeth,* he would have had to fill in enough about the story to make his explanation comprehensible.

To summarize, although all students need some practice in following a procedure like that which Tom used in "I Wouldn't Like Lady Macbeth as a Mother, But . . . ," no teacher should insist that this is the only "correct" way to write. There is no correct way, but many possible ways, and each writer needs to discover the way or ways that best fit his or her temperament.


## PARAGRAPH STRUCTURE

Some of the writing that students are asked to do may well be a single paragraph in length; some of it, obviously, may be longer, consisting of several paragraphs assembled in some sort of orderly fashion.

Students may be shown that there are both typical and atypical paragraphs. The typical textbook-recommended paragraph begins with a general statement—a *topic sentence,* as it is usually called. Following the topic sentence, one or more additional sentences provide examples, details, evidence, or other information that develops the opening sentence. (The paragraph you are now reading is typical. Note that the first sentence introduces and to a slight extent summarizes what the rest of the paragraph develops.) The atypical paragraph exists in many forms but is no less legitimate. Sometimes the topic or subject of a paragraph is so apparent that no topic sentence is needed. At other times, atypical structure is demanded by the context.

Students need to be taught both kinds of paragraphs. They can be shown that in the typical paragraph, the presence of the topic sentence serves as a guide to both writer and reader. It helps the writer to avoid extraneous, irrelevant material, and it helps the reader to grasp quickly what each paragraph concerns. The series of topic sentences in a long composition may provide an abbreviated version of the whole thing. The atypical paragraph has no topic sentence, or if it does, that sentence comes in the middle or at the end. Here is a list of some of the characteristics that may be present in atypical paragraphs:

1. Topic sentence not at the beginning.
2. No topic sentence, or implied topic sentence.
3. One sentence instead of several sentences (sometimes just a phrase or a word, such as *On the contrary* or *No*).
4. An introduction or summary that covers several paragraphs rather than just one.
5. Treatment of more than a single topic.
6. In descriptive writing, often only a quick, highly selective glimpse rather than a detailed photograph.
7. In conversation, an accurate but selective reproduction of what was said. (People don't regularly employ topic sentences while conversing.)

The narrative paragraph is almost always atypical. Students should be helped to understand that a new narrative paragraph is usually required in these circumstances:

1. With each change of speaker.
2. At the end of each significant bit of action.
3. When attention is switched from one character to another.
4. When an important new character, setting, or emphasis is introduced.
5. If the material differs in some way from its context (e.g., several sentences of description inserted in a story).
6. If the type of reader being addressed may need the psychological relief of a break on the page (e.g., a young reader needs more breaks than a sophisticated adult).
7. If dramatic effect will be heightened (i.e., short paragraphs, if not used excessively, tend to be more dramatic than long ones).

Whatever the variety of paragraph, it should hang together as a unit and (as part of a longer piece) should contribute its bit to the development of the whole. A paragraph is less often faulty because it is short or lacks a topic sentence than because some of the parts do not belong or are strung together without adequate attention to continuity.

## STRUCTURE OF THE LONGER COMPOSITION

When Tom developed his paper on Lady Macbeth, he was exemplifying (consciously or not) three much-emphasized qualities of most pieces of writing: unity, coherence, and emphasis. His paper had unity; all parts of it contributed to explaining why Tom believed that Lady Macbeth had praiseworthy but misdirected characteristics. It had coherence; that is, the parts were arranged in orderly fashion. And it had emphasis: of necessity Tom stressed Lady Macbeth's good qualities, devoting the long central section of his composition to that topic.

How should the principles of unity, coherence, and emphasis be taught? Unity is perhaps the easiest to teach, although the lesson may need reiteration in different forms. A good starting point with young students is realia—say five pencils and a pen, or three apples and an orange. Ask "Which doesn't belong?" Unity basically means belongingness. Groups of words may also be used: subway, museum, silo, theater; the silo probably wouldn't fit into a composition on city life. For students who have studied mathematical sets, the concept of unity may be related to the set; it is difficult to think of a set as comprising, say, three rocks and a dog. The next step up is to show that in the "set" called a composition, each part should belong. If a student starts with an irrelevant joke or if an example doesn't exemplify the topic or if a fact or an idea does not contribute to what the writer is trying to do, unity is violated. And the reader is distracted in his or her attempt to grasp what the writer was driving at.

Emphasis, at least the underlying principles of it, is also rather easy to teach. Common sense dictates that we should emphasize what we consider most important. Usually the best way to do so is to give more space and attention to what needs stressing. Students often violate this principle—say in a composition about a trip to Yellowstone Park. Some of them devote so much space to trip-preparation and details of the journey that they are reduced to only a few sentences for such things as the mud pots, the Yellowstone river, the beautiful winding mountain roads, and the elk and bear—all of which they should probably have described in considerable detail. The most advanced students may be shown other techniques for emphasis—such as heightened style—but for the majority, emphasis is mainly a matter of proportion.

Coherence is the most difficult of the three major principles to teach. It results mainly from using a pattern of organization. Simplest is the chronological: this happened first, then that, and then something else; or do this first, then that, then that, and you'll get a delicious butterscotch pie. Spatial order, useful in description, is a systematic presentation of the physical features of a room, house, museum, or whatever. Deductive order starts with an explanation of a principle or an idea and then moves into definitions, examples, arguments, comparisons, or anything needed to develop the main point. Inductive order, which is the order followed by scientists in most of their research, starts with specific facts or examples and then draws a conclusion about what they show. Large-to-small organization is exemplified in many newspaper stories, in which the lead gives the gist of the story and succeeding paragraphs provide details. Small-to-large involves building to a climax. Other types of organization include easy-to-difficult (as in a chapter in a mathematics or science textbook) and the development of a comparison or a contrast. In a long piece of writing, two or more patterns of organization may be blended.

Simple examples may be presented for most of these patterns. Chronological, for instance, can be illustrated by a list of what a student does before reaching school in the morning, or a list of events (hour by hour) in a typical or specific school day. For teaching inductive order, a chemistry student may be asked to describe briefly a series of tests used in identifying an unknown substance. When a student composition clearly follows any certain order of presentation, the class may look at it and decide what the order is. For the visual-minded, a few simple line drawings are helpful: the flight of an arrow for chronological, a series of boxes of increasing size for small-to-large, and so on.

## WHAT GOES INTO THE CONTAINERS?

So far we have discussed mainly the structures, the containers that will hold the students' information, ideas, or imaginative flights. But students are often unaware of how much they know that can be put into the containers. Part of the teacher's job is to bring them to that awareness.

The use of small groups to talk over inchoate compositions is especially helpful. Allan Glatthorn of the University of Pennsylvania makes this interesting point:

*Having watched more than 15,000 hours of television [students] are inclined to be passive in their learning. Reared in a competitive society, they have not learned to work cooperatively for the common good. We need to emphasize cooperative learning. Having been rewarded for obedience and dependence, they are reluctant to assume responsibility for their own learning. We need to encourage more student-directed learning. All these observations suggest that the English classrooms need to make extensive use of student-directed small groups, working cooperatively on common learning tasks.* [32]

Margaret Labby's students at Lincoln High School, in Portland, Oregon, prepare a quick first draft of a composition and then read it to a small group, asking basically, "What questions haven't I answered? What parts would you like to know more about?" Other questions may concern clarity, organization, or improvement of the beginning and ending. The students usually find that their peers have many legitimate suggestions for enriching the content, and they revise accordingly.[33]

Lack of specificity is a major weakness of much student writing. The peer groups can and should insist that pat and dull and basically uninformative phrases such as *a beautiful sight, a good time, exciting game, interesting story,* or *walked some distance* be expanded, made concrete and specific. Saul Pett, Associated Press feature writer, offers advice most students need:

> *Don't tease me unless you can deliver, baby. Don't tell me the situation was dramatic and expect me to take your word for it. Show me how it was dramatic and I'll supply the adjective. You say this character is unpredictable? When, where, how? Give me the evidence, not just the chapter headings.*[34]

James McCrimmon illustrates the point in this way: On a transparency, he shows a student's composition: '' 'The Secret Life of Walter Mitty' tells about a man's daydreams. His wife nags him and he begins to dream. In his dreams he is a hero who has many adventures, such as a pilot and a doctor. In real life he is a very ordinary person. . . .'' McCrimmon gets from students answers to the questions "What isn't specific enough? How can it be made more so?"[35]

In some classrooms, posters or clever little student-made drawings are put up under such a heading as "Don't Have Anything to Say?" The posters illustrate various methods of development: examples, details, comparison, contrast, classification, definition, reason, inferences, causes, effects, descriptions, appropriate anecdotes. They serve as reminders to students having trouble in finding ways to turn their topic sentences into full-blown paragraphs.

## TRANSITIONS

"A transition," you say to your students, "is like a bridge. It helps your reader to follow you from here to there." Start with time-transitions: "Yesterday I flunked a history test. *Today* I made an A in English." Let the students list a dozen or two such transitions: *later, soon, then, next, after a month, when spring came, before the concert was over,* and so on. Go on to words showing simple addition: *and, in addition, besides, furthermore, moreover,* and so on. Spend a few minutes on contrast: *but, on the other hand, unlike his brother.* Introduce other transitions such as *for instance, because she was unhappy after her father's death, on the other side of the road, who meanwhile was eating raw eggs.*

Offer a rather dramatic example of the need for transitions: "Jess is a star football player. He scored five baskets last night." With transitional elements added: "Jess is a star football player. However, he must be versatile, for he scored five baskets in the basketball game last night." Supply a number of pairs of unclearly related sentences, and let the students experiment with various transitions to show somewhat different relationships.

THE TEACHING OF HIGH SCHOOL ENGLISH

## ON THE PRACTICE OF PARTS

Music teachers give their pupils scales and finger exercises, sometimes disguising them as little songs and melodies. Some teachers of beginning swimming give arm and leg and breathing exercises on dry land, and expert swimmers often practice separate movements and then coordinate the parts. Football coaches drill their charges in separate fundamentals of blocking, tackling, ball-carrying, and so on. Examples of the practice of parts can be multiplied.

Applications of the principle of "divide and conquer" certainly belong in the English classroom. Not every piece of writing need be a full-blown composition. There can and should be dozens, scores, of little exercises—not all to be graded—that will give students practice in the bits and pieces that can be assembled into a larger whole. Practice in grouping things, then in grouping ideas. Practice in differentiating relevant from irrelevant details. Practice in listing examples. Practice in writing paragraphs—typical and atypical. Practice in organizing a moderately complex subject without actually writing about it. Practice in supplying transitions. Practice in writing many small compositions that put some of the bits and pieces together. And, because of shortness of time, necessarily limited practice in the larger endeavors.

# IMAGINATIVE WRITING

That almost any kind of writing can be imaginative is illustrated by the success of such cookbooks as *The Joy of Cooking,* which is replete with whimsy and quips, as when a ham is defined as "two people and eternity." However, English departments sometimes offer courses—usually called Creative Writing—that stress the writing of stories, poems, and plays rather than the expository modes we have been considering so far. We'll make only a few suggestions for teachers of such courses, in which students are especially encouraged to engage their inventiveness and their "literary" inclinations.

Don't assume that only the brightest students can write creatively. As long as a quarter-century ago one teacher observed that her good creative writers often had IQ's of 95 to 106, were not proficient in spelling and punctuation, daydreamed a lot, and were sometimes called "dumb" by other teachers.[36] The situation probably hasn't changed very much.

## SOME PROCEDURES THAT WORK

A speaker at an NCTE convention, Myra Cohn Livingston, said that no one can teach creative writing. "One can only make children aware of their sensitivities, and help children learn of the forms, the basic tools of poetry, into which they can put their voices."

And, we may add, one can provide a receptive, enthusiastic environment. One can furnish information about how professional writers work. One can suggest unusual topics or unusual ways of looking at our little slice of the world, but still give all students great freedom to choose their own topics, their own ways of looking, their own slices. One can offer a pat on the back and a shoulder to cry on. Sometimes the best thing one can do is get out of a student's way.

Here is what some teachers do.

Karen Boyer, of Springfield, Illinois, gets greatest success with her creative writing classes by having them write stories for young children. These stories permit their own imaginations to roam, yet they must keep in mind the age-limitations and probable interests of their potential readers. The results range from poetic fantasies like John Ciardi's to gangling humor like that of Dr. Seuss.

Alvin Alley, of Auburn University, recommends five-sentence sensory descriptions. For instance, students are asked to describe the feel of what is probably a dog under the table when you can touch but not see it, or to describe their fears after falling into a large trunk when alone in an attic and the lid falls down and locks.[37]

Students may make notes or keep a journal in which they write about family members, funny or happy or sad days, friends, school events, conflicts in school, places that would be good settings, types of work, emotional experiences. They select one that could be a take-off point for a short story. Then they choose a conflict (often growing naturally out of differences in the people who were observed); the conflict becomes a basis of a plot. They choose a point of view from which the story will be told, and the theme (which is comparable to the "This I Believe" discussed earlier). Then they develop the story.

In Stuttgart, Arkansas, Diane Henton's students are given a mythical thousand dollars to "buy" one or more characters. Ms. Henton has prepared a list of characters, with an interest-grabbing thumbnail sketch of each. A student serves as auctioneer. Each student writes a narrative in which the character(s) he or she purchased figure prominently.[38]

Students invent six characters (or nine) and ascribe certain characteristics (different for each) to them. The teacher suggests a situation involving all the characters, and students as individuals work out the stories. For instance, you (as one of the characters) prepare your will. To which of the others do you leave your $100,000? Or, you are on a space journey with eight others, and only five of you can get back to Earth. Which five?[39]

A California teacher asks students to describe a novel means of transportation for use in a fantasy world—for instance, roller skates that can fly; or to describe, as an inhabitant of another planet, odd things and customs found on Earth; or to come up with a fantastic explanation of why it rains, why the sun rises, why the tides rise and fall, and so on. Another California teacher, Jane Waxenburg of Piedmont, has her classes read and discuss stories and articles about imaginary worlds and then invent a world of their own. The students then write short essays about their world's schools, government, war or peace, flowers, animals, food, transportation, climate and weather, "odd" customs, and so on.[40]

Edgar Lee Masters' *Spoon River Anthology* serves as a take-off for some poetry writing by Dorothy L. Ivey's students in South Holland, Illinois. Ms. Ivey clips obituaries from newspapers, and each student selects one to write "a poem in the style of Masters." "Students have produced some beautiful contemporary poems during the twenty years I have taught. Most memorable have been the poems resulting from reading about Ralph Bunche; about the Marshall University coach who died with his team crossing the mountains in Colorado; about President Eisenhower; and about a high school girl who had run away from home and died in a rooming house fire." She usually avoids obituaries of local people.[41]

A teacher in Mount Forest, Ontario, suggests:

*A poem composed of one or two words repeated, or up to five words, say, patterned in different ways, alliterated or jarring, words of movement or words relying on sense impressions such as smell or taste or touch, can surprise students with its evocative power. Something like:*

> *sand sliding slowy,*
> *snow slowly,*
> *sand slowly sliding,*
> *sliding,*
> *snowly sliding*
> *sand.*

*connects sound and sight impressions, even the sense of touch intrudes, and the simplicity and limited number of the words makes the power of each individual word self-evident.*[42]

Another teacher's students enjoy "grammar poems" and "diamond poems."

| 1 noun | beach |
|---|---|
| 2 adjectives | sandy, bright |
| 3 verbs | swim, dry, doze |
| 1 phrase | with the crowd |
| 1 synonym | seashore |

(The designated grammatical components may be altered.)

|  | 1 |  | *Saturday* |  |  |
|---|---|---|---|---|---|
| 1 |  | 2 | *no* | *school* |  |
| 1 | 2 | 3 | *play* | *all* | *day* |
| 1 |  | 2 | *up* | *late* |  |
|  | 1 |  | *great*[43] |  |  |

R. Baird Shuman, working with Virginia juniors and seniors, found this a useful procedure after the students had been introduced to writing poetry. Each wrote a short poem "about something you have seen, felt, or heard. Emphasize the feeling." Then each wrote a short poem "about something you would hate to lose." Finally each wrote a poem "in which you combine the two items you have written about above." One result:

The wind howls,
Bending trees;
And suddenly, with a crashing blow,
Plunges my TV set
Into dark
Silence.[44]

"As a part of a creative writing class or unit in creative writing, have each student bring in some item that moves them," Jack Welch recommends.

*The item may be an heirloom, a gift, a piece of sculpture, or a poem. The students will quickly become people both for the teacher and for the other students because personalities will emerge. But, be prepared for the appearance of what Benjamin DeMott calls the "humanness" of the students. . . . The teacher, after the showing, may go on to discuss ways that these items can be used in developing stories, essays, and poems.[45]*

"If you could not be yourself, *what* would you be and why?" "What is inside the secret chest that you have just found in your backyard?" "You have X-ray vision. What do you see when you look out the window?" Students in Beth Dakelman's creative writing classes in Martinsville, New Jersey, write on such topics for 10 minutes a day for several weeks.[46] Obviously, one of the most important assets to creative writing students is a creative teacher.

## EVALUATION AS A TEACHING DEVICE

The teacher faces a stack of compositions. What should be the goal in evaluating them?

Not just to attach a grade, certainly. Not to locate mistakes.

Rather, the goal should be to find something to say that will help each writer to move from his or her stage of development, whatever that may be, toward the next higher stage. Sometimes a suggestion on technique. Sometimes only a word of encouragement or praise. Sometimes a hint about improving organization. Sometimes a plea for going deeper into the subject. Usually more emphasis on content than on mechanics. In other words, as the teacher sits with marking pen or pencil in hand, he or she has a fine opportunity to provide for individual differences. Each paper is part of a growing mind. The teacher wants to help each mind to grow as straight and as strong as it can. The marking instrument can be an excellent tool in teaching.

In 1845, in a book called *Aids to English Composition,* Richard Green Parker suggested to teachers how they should evaluate writing:

> *Merits for composition should be predicated on their neatness, correctness, length, style, etc.; but the highest merits should be given for the production of ideas, and original sentiments and forms of expression.*[47]

Many modern teachers agree with Parker in his emphasis on content.

But not all evaluators have identical predilections. Paul Diederich asked 53 "informed readers" (both teachers and other educated people) to grade 300 essays by separating them into nine piles. Of the 300, "101 received every grade from 1 to 9; 94 percent received either seven, eight, or nine different grades; and no essay received less than five different grades from the 53 readers."[48] Further analysis showed five basic types of evaluators, according to what they emphasize: (1) ideas, content; (2) usage, sentence structure, punctuation, spelling; (3) organization and analysis; (4) wording and phrasing; (5) writers' personal qualities as revealed by the writing.[49] Because few students' compositions are likely to be excellent in all these categories, all them will probably be marked low by some evaluators.

The preventive of eccentric marking should be department-wide agreement on principles. Paul Diederich's own rating scale gives top priority to ideas and organization:

|  | Low |  | Middle |  | High |
| --- | --- | --- | --- | --- | --- |
| Ideas | 2 | 4 | 6 | 8 | 10 |
| Organization | 2 | 4 | 6 | 8 | 10 |
| Wording | 1 | 2 | 3 | 4 | 5 |
| Flavor | 1 | 2 | 3 | 4 | 5 |
| Usage | 1 | 2 | 3 | 4 | 5 |
| Punctuation | 1 | 2 | 3 | 4 | 5 |
| Spelling | 1 | 2 | 3 | 4 | 5 |
| Handwriting | 1 | 2 | 3 | 4 | 5 |

A college teacher, Glenn Matott of Colorado State (Fort Collins) says that in evaluating students' "factual/ideative" writing he looks at each piece from three perspectives:

*1. Content.   Is the factual matter accurate? Is there enough of it to adequately support the line of thought [the "This I Believe"]? Does the line of thought make sense? Is it logically valid? Are there identifiable fallacies?*

*2. Form [organization].   Has the subject matter of the paper been broken down effectively into units? Are these units (e.g., sections, paragraphs, sentences) presented in the most effective sequence? Are the connections between these units clear? In short, does the paper have a discernible "architecture," or is the content presented in a helter-skelter fashion?*

3. *Expression. Even though the content is clear, has it been expressed as well as it could be? Are there wrong word choices, awkward sentences, lumbering rhythms? Would some rhetorical strategy—an analogy, for instance—help to make a point more clearly or elegantly?*[50]

Matott adds this comment:

*So far as evaluation is concerned, I rank content, form, and expression in that order of importance and grade accordingly, tossing in the amount of proofreading I have to do for the student as an increasingly negative factor. However, the main point of my analysis is not to arrive at a grade, but to allow me to identify for the student where his strengths and weaknesses lie, and to suggest in specific terms what he might try in order to work toward improvement.*

A rating scale developed in the Cleveland, Ohio, schools is summarized in the Idea Box.

For writing other than "factual/ideative"—poems, short stories, and the like—different principles may well be applied. Ideally, no grades at all should be placed on such pieces. They should be read by students and teacher, savored, appreciated, commented on, maybe posted or "published" in some other way, possibly revised by the author, but sometimes just enjoyed. When grades must be given, perhaps criteria can be agreed upon by the class and the teacher, with the teacher leaning toward generosity.

Evaluation is time-consuming—a substantial part of the workload of an English teacher who is truly conscientious. Many persons have written suggestions for saving some of that time. Here is part of what Thomas N. Walters of North Carolina State suggests: (1) Read selectively, not all papers, except those marked "Please read." (2) Ask students to select pieces of their writing that they especially want appraised. (3) Have some papers prepared by pairs or teams of students, thus reducing the number. (4) Let groups of students evaluate one another's compositions.[51]

In "How to Avoid Grading Compositions," Eileen Wagner of Chester, Virginia, suggests:

1. *comprehensive commentary (takes much time)*
2. *selective criteria (concentrating on elements emphasized in the assignment)*
3. *random comment (commenting on part of the papers this week, other students' papers next time)*
4. *peer comment (Wagner prefers one-on-one rather than group)*
5. *self comment (student self-evaluation)*

**6.** tape-recorded comment

**7.** "leave it alone" (for it's the practice that matters)[52]

Concerning evaluation by students—a practice recommended by many teachers for some papers—Alan McLeod of Virgina Commonwealth University has written:

*One former student recently wrote that she had not "graded" a student theme/composition in two years.*

*The students in her classes in an inner-city middle school evaluate each other's work, rework their writings in terms of comments by their peers, and do not submit any written work to the teacher until at least one classmate agrees that the composition is readable. The teacher in turn makes encouraging comments on the papers submitted and discusses the student's writing with him.[53]*

Early in the school year, David Hill, of Charlottesville, Virginia, duplicates a one-page composition of each student in a class. Copies (names withheld) are distributed to all class members, who have a couple of days to read them and prepare positive and negative comments. Then for two or three days the students discuss the papers one by one. "The goal is helping each other. . . . By offering suggestions and alternatives for others, they usually make applications to their own writings. The student learns how others, his friends, view his writing. They often reveal things he does not realize. The skill he used in [evaluating] others' papers can now be applied to his own writing."[54]

Note especially "The goal is helping each other." If the teacher insists that help, rather than nit-picking criticism, is what is wanted, the class atmosphere will be much more pleasant and the results are likely to be better. Even when the group wants to comment on relatively small points, such as the structure of a sentence, it can use a positive approach. And—an incidental but important point—peers are sometimes more effective as teachers than teachers are. One teacher illustrates:

*When everyone in a group agrees that your sentence is not a sentence but a fragment, it is hard to reach for the salve of "teacher is against me." When a fellow student can explain how to make a fragment into a sentence it begins to seem that the writing of English is not an affectation or a plot.[55]*

There is a big difference between evaluating to *help* and evaluating to *correct.* Henry Maloney of Detroit has expressed the point like this:

*It has always intrigued me that teachers would "correct papers." That automatically assumes that something is wrong with them. Right? . . I see today's English teacher . . . as more of a "helper" than a "corrector."[56]*

Part of the help comes from judicious praise. It is generally assumed that praise is more desirable than negative criticism. Thomas C. Gee of Texas Tech verified this assumption experimentally with eleventh-graders. Two of his findings:

*Negative criticism and no feedback caused students to write less than students who were praised.*

*Praised students had more positive attitudes toward writing than students who were criticized or students who received no comment.*[57]

Perhaps the following quotation comes close to summarizing the main thrust of this section and this chapter. It comes from John Illo of Shippensburg, Pennsylvania, State College:

*The most frequent complaints by students [college freshmen] are that the high school theme, though it may be competently graded, receives little constructive comment, and that theme instruction concerns errors rather than methods of composing, with not enough attention to the content and logic of the paper.*[58]

A positive framing of the same statement might read:

*What students especially appreciate is constructive comment on their compositions, and what they especially profit from is instruction in content, logic, and methods of composing.*

---

**THE IDEA BOX**

DO CHEMISTS COMMUNICATE?

E. T. Klemmer and F. W. Snyder reported a study of what 1500 chemists in 42 industrial companies do in their working day. From 50 to 80 percent of their time is given to communication.[59]

FRUSTRATION

Carl Wonnberger, on the basis of 32 years of secondary teaching, said that even slow students can learn to write:

The trouble . . . is that too many students are frustrated in their English study and begin to think of English as a formal discipline instead of a functional tool for man and the aspirations of man, that they get lost in verbal calisthenics, identification of ''speech parts,'' the memorization of definitions that do not define, the filling in of blanks in workbooks, diagraming, and doing all manner of things that have no possible justification in the study of language and the development of sound language habits.[60]

THE TEACHING OF HIGH SCHOOL ENGLISH

## WHY DO SOME STUDENTS WRITE BADLY?

We believe that much of the bad writing in the schools is a result of the student's failure to understand what is expected of him when he is asked to write and his lack of a basic knowledge of language that goes beyond syntax and usage. Therefore, we attempt to help the student understand exactly what he is to do, how he goes about achieving his purpose, and how he asks questions to help him gather information, find precise words to communicate that information, and put it all together for a designated reader.[61]

## MISAPPLIED ENERGY

"The pupils could parse and construe sentences and point out the various parts of speech with great facility, repeating the rules of grammar in each case, yet they were utterly unable to put this theoretical knowledge to any practical use, as they showed when called upon to write an ordinary business letter." (From a report to the Quincy, Massachusetts, school board in 1873.)

## FREEDOM AND DISCIPLINE

"Freedom is vital to release a student author into integrity of expression, into provocative, fresh response in both idea and design. Discipline is vital to equip him with the skills and devices necessary to will, order, and effectively communicate the raw response unleashed by the uninhibited experience."[62]

## TOPICS FOR JUNIOR HIGH

1. Two New Orleans teachers of seventh grades in different schools, Carole Berlin and Nancy Miller, arranged for their students to write to one another. The first letter, a "profile" of the writer, was required; follow-ups were optional. The profiles were shared orally with classmates, who suggested additions or other changes. The receiving school displayed the incoming profiles (which had been mailed). As the exchange continued, proofreading one's letters suddenly became very important, and each child usually wrote to five or six others.[63]

2. "Students write one-paragraph themes, each student describing some other member of the class. When themes are read, everyone tries to guess which student is being described."[64]

3. For an autobiography, encourage a central point of view, limited coverage, and enrichment by one or more appropriate anecdotes.

4. "Write about that special something that you know better than anyone in this room and that we, in some way or other, might benefit from or simply enjoy." That's what Jeanne W. Halpern of Ann Arbor, Michigan, asks her junior high school students to do, and she likes the results, which are on such subjects as "How It Feels to Grow Up in a Family with Fourteen Children," "What Living with a Mentally Retarded Child Means in Our Family," and "How to Be Successful at Lockpicking."[65]

5. For brief compositions, often followed by sharing and discussion, give students a situation to which they will respond by telling what they would do or how they think they would feel. For example, an auto accident in front of your house.

What would you do? A newspaper story about an injury to a friend. How would you feel? A TV program about a young drug addict. How would you react? Your house is on fire at midnight. What do you do?

6. Have students clip out the headline and first paragraph of one or more human interest news stories in a newspaper. In class distribute the clippings at random to the students. Ask each to develop a longer, more detailed version of the story, based on the limited information in the clipping.

7. Have students describe in 100 words or so a red foreign sports car (a) as police would describe it if it were stolen, (b) as a car salesman would, (c) as a hopeful teen-ager would to his or her overprotective wealthy grandmother, (d) as a conservative older brother would.[66]

8. In connection with reading "Rip Van Winkle," students describe, for a person who has been asleep 50 years, a convenience that did not exist before his nap. For example, color TV, microwave ovens.[67]

## THE IMPORTANCE OF DRAFTS

The early goal . . . is to churn out rough drafts. Emphasis is clearly not on quality but on finding one's own voice, finding out what one wants to say. Drafts are incomplete, tentative, just barely legible enough for someone else to read. They are not graded. Periodically . . we invoke the delightful strategy offered by Don Murray. The student selects a few of his papers that *he* thinks are most promising and polishes them for a grade. Between the drafts and the hand-ins comes the nitty-gritty of revision.[68]

## TOPICS FOR SENIOR HIGH

1. Each student writes a letter of complaint, praise, inquiry, attack, or what-have-you to the newspaper, TV, Aretha Franklin, the Rolling Stones, Ralph Nader, Silas Marner, Julius Caesar, Gloria Steinem, John or Robert Kennedy, Martin Luther King, Satan, or God. Because not all of these are likely to reply, a classmate acts as surrogate and answers the letter as the supposed recipient might.[69]

2. Persuasive writing, on topics selected by students themselves, brings good results to David Osgood in Summit, Illinois. The teacher suggests current issues—pollution, abortion, strikes, any current headline topic that transcends personalities—and students gather materials, not relying just on their present knowledge. Each student conducts a "campaign" to convince others of his rightness. Not just ordinary speaking and writing are involved but also bumper stickers, buttons, films, advertising, letters to the editor, taped messages, etc.[70]

3. Jayne Karsten of McLean, Virginia, has her class "brainstorm a list of various abstractions," defining such concepts as *self-reliance, justice,* and *time* through examples, analogies, or anecdotes. Then "I ask students to define a particular abstraction in any genre they wish: vignette, poem, brief expository essay, dramatic sketch, etc." *Circumscribe* has brought especially good results. Introduced by E. A. Robinson's poem "I Drew a Circle," the word is shown to refer to "closing out" as well as "closing in." "Manuscripts have come in reflecting how blacks are circumscribed by their color, closing themselves off from society, being closed off by society; how modern man is circumscribed by time and

a distorted value system; youth by lack of purposiveness or by too much purposiveness; a young girl by blindness; a boy by going steady; another boy by his passion for a particular sport."[71]

4. For practice in avoiding slanting, give students the raw data of a news story and ask them to write the first paragraph. Compare the results, watching especially for slanting.[72]

5. Peter Schiff's juniors in Syosset, New York, wrote for application forms to colleges they might want to attend or business firms they might like to work for. All these forms asked for autobiographical statements. The students wrote 200 to 400 word autobiographies meeting the requirements, and leaving out date of birth and other items covered elsewhere in the forms.[73]

6. Students are asked to attack or defend one of these ways of arriving at a moral decision:
   (a) Aristotle: Avoid extremes; in all actions, strive for the golden mean.
   (b) Moses: Just follow these commandments.
   (c) Bentham: Do what is best for most people.
   (d) Thoreau: Obey your own conscience.
   (e) Emerson: Act in accordance with Nature's Grand Plan.
   (f) Heffner: Do anything that doesn't hurt others or yourself.
   (g) Ferlinghetti: Whatever turns you on, Baby.
   (h) Fletcher: Make love your guiding principle.[74]

7. Each student chooses any art work: painting, song, story, sculpture, play. He or she establishes standards for judging a work in that genre, states them, and then applies them to the specific work.[75]

8. The Advanced Placement students of Betty B. Cornaby of Seattle, after reading *Jude the Obscure,* wrote open letters to the author on "any topic, concern, or response they had in relationship to the novel which they would like to discuss with Hardy, had they such an opportunity."[76]

"PRACTICE WITHOUT PAIN: THE IN-CLASS JOURNAL"

Linda W. Wagner reads a controversial or at least topically interesting paragraph or two to her students, who then write a paragraph or two of reaction in their journals. They also do some journal writing on their own time. In her classes, journals are looked at but not graded by the teacher; a good one can raise a student's composition mark.[77]

"GENERATING A COMPOSITION"

Oscar Bouise of Southern University has described a three-step process in writing: a parent idea, which is a general topic like *parents* or *dogs* or *people;* a topic idea, like *people with problems;* and a theme statement, like *People with seemingly insoluble problems need more than sympathy; they need help.*[78]

UNFINISHED STORIES

Grace Ashenfelter of Urbana, Illinois, read stories t , junior high school children, stopping at the climax. Students individually wrote their own conclusion and the class compared their versions. A very effective story for the purpose, this teacher said, is Shirley Jackson's "Charles."[79]

## STORY STARTERS

To generate somewhat unconventional personal narratives, Fred E. H. Schroeder suggests use of *New Yorker* covers, stop-action pictures, the writers' various "careers" as high-heel wearers or trout-fly tiers, etc., and looking back at one's sixth birthday or other remote personal event. Roland Osterweis tells how he used pictures from Edward Steichen's *The Family of Man* to inspire mainly black classes. As story seeds, Janet M. Thorpe advocates catchy phrases: "worth $575," "he threatened," "if I were," "Loneliness is," and so on.[80]

## "SLOW LEARNERS: STOP, LOOK, AND LISTEN"

After describing simple classroom incidents (dropping a book, turning out the lights, etc.) slow learners are asked to observe as carefully when they walk to class along the corridor. They are provided the opening sentence, "I stop in the middle of the corridor to look and listen."[81]

## COMPOSITION AS PROCESS

As an example of class preparation for writing, Milton A. Kaplan tells of reading Christopher Morley's "On Unanswering Letters," then having students discuss how they procrastinate about doing homework, and then assigning "a composition in the same [light] tone as the Morley essay, in which you excuse yourself for not doing something you really know you should do."[82]

## "'MAKE A TOWN' MAKES BETTER THEMES"

An unusual plan for a long series of single-focus themes is described by George Reinfeld. Students create an imaginary town, write descriptions of parts of it and of its citizens, explain its government and its problems, publish an edition of its newspaper, design its educational system and a recreational program, print a public relations brochure, and so on.[83]

## THE CONCEPT THEME

"Each student is to select one concept (such as distance, height, intelligence, love) and illustrate how his view of the concept has changed." Such themes, says Carol B. Yoakley of Oak Ridge, Tennessee, have unusual vitality, and "can evoke tears of laughter, tears of compassion and empathy, tears of catharsis. . . . We have had deep, searching papers on views of God and religion; philosophical comments on death, goodness, and education; and tender, humorous definitions of love."[84]

## "WRITING FROM THE MIND OUT"

In an NCTE convention talk, Bertrand F. Richards suggested that during the week students may be encouraged to write a great deal, without worrying about spelling, punctuation, or even coherence. Then on Friday they select one item and revise it to make it clear, effective, and correct.

## "WHO SAYS JOHNNY CAN'T WRITE?"

Students should on some occasions be allowed to choose the types of writing they do, according to Robert P. Parker, Jr., and Leslie Meskin. Each Thursday their students bring to class "a piece of writing as formal or informal as they wish, in whatever mode they choose, and, ostensibly, for a peer audience." These pieces are not read by the teacher except on request, but are read, responded to in writing, and discussed by another student in the class. (The response is due on Friday.) The authors illustrate with pieces showing considerable growth in fluency, sentence mastery, and especially in forthrightness and genuine interest in self-expression.[85]

## THE BREAKTHROUGH

After five unhappy years of reading dull, impersonal compositions, John H. Bennett of Kalamazoo, Michigan, tried this:

> I want you to write as fast as you can for twelve minutes. . . . Spell all the words wrong if you like, but don't . . . stop writing.
> You can write anything you like, so long as it is important to you and the truth as you see it. If your mind is a blank, remember that your mind is never a blank. From the moment you are born to the moment you die, your mind is always producing pictures. Just record the truth and write what is important to you.

After a few false starts the students caught on and started writing truth instead of fakery.[86]

## AN EXPERIENCE PORTFOLIO

Johanna Sweet, of Wolfeboro, New Hampshire, at the beginning of the year has each student check an "Experience Portfolio," a list of 120 items that *some* students might like to write about: scuba diving, home-made ice cream, pinball machines, coins, and astronomy. Each student checks each item: *A*. Haven't the faintest idea about this one. *B*. Yeah, I could fill you in a little. *C*. You're getting warm—I know quite a bit. *D*. This is really down my alley. *E*. I'd like to know more about this one. The sheet is stapled into each student's writing folder or notebook for reference throughout the year when the student complains, "I don't have anything to write about."[87]

## IMPROMPTU THEMES

In college most students may have to do considerable writing in class, under pressure. It is kind to give them some practice in the upper high school years.

## PRÉCIS WRITING

In some schools, especially in the upper forms of British schools, précis writing is used to help teach organization. The theory is that a careful précis will not only aid students to understand difficult material but will also show them how the author organized it. Then they may employ similar organizational patterns.

## DEVELOPING THE FIVE SENSES

Mary Ann Eichenberg has described many activities to encourage students to use their senses in their writing. For example, finding words to describe an ocean, finding substitutes for *walk* in specific situations, describing a food, describing an object such as a hair roller or a snippet of silk, writing about a bakery or a barber shop.[88]

## DRAWINGS BASED ON DESCRIPTIONS

Students in one class describe a real object that is before them (e.g., a wheel puller for a Model-T or the sounding tubes of a xylophone). Students in another class make drawings based on these descriptions, and write criticisms of what is unclear. Then the roles are reversed.[89]

## SPEAKING PRECEDES WRITING

Sometimes the best way to improve students' writing may be to give them many opportunities to talk, argue, discuss, describe, and so on. As Ruth Strickland, a past president of NCTE, has said, "If the ideas a child expresses orally are meager, immature, and lacking in clarity, his writing will exhibit all these problems in even greater measure."

## *THE* WHY-BECAUSE *APPROACH*

"Why do you believe such and such?" Vivian Buchan asks her Iowa students. Their "becauses" pour out. "Write them down, a paragraph for each *because,* and you'll have a composition," she tells them.[90]

## FRIENDLY AND BUSINESS LETTERS

1. Classes may enjoy writing Christmas letters of appreciation to their parents or other adults important in their lives—possibly *before* Christmas.
2. Some teachers have students write letters to parents, telling what they have learned during the semester.
3. Students in Natchez, Mississippi, wrote to students in other towns along the river. This plan may be varied according to local conditions. For instance, Danville, Virginia, may write to Danville, Illinois, or students in mountainous territory may write to students on the plains.
4. To teach mechanics of the letter, one teacher writes an error-filled letter to the class.
5. One teacher collects advertisements about free or inexpensive materials. Students write for any that they really want. (Caution: One whole class answered an ad concerning a free demonstration of pianos.)

THE TEACHING OF HIGH SCHOOL ENGLISH

6. Many teachers have students write letters to television stations or networks, praising good programs, criticizing poor ones.
7. A Massachusetts teacher prepares slips outlining situations for letters. Boys draw slips from one pile; girls, from another. Each student writes the letter called for. For example, "Ernest Nash, your good friend, has just received permission to invite you for a week's visit to the family camp in the White Mountains."[91]
8. Letters of appreciation to prominent persons (national, state, or local) make a good assignment. For reluctant writers, fan letters to current musical idols may stimulate action. Each letter should be specific, not just "I like you."
9. The five C's of business letters: Clear, Courteous, Concise, Complete, and Correct.
10. NCTE and the U.S. Postal Service have collaborated in an engaging 64-page book, *All About Letters* (1979), intended for students in grades 6 to 12. Reduced prices for orders of 20 or more.

EXERCISES IN THINKING

1. Because composition should stem from clear thinking, many teachers give their students various exercises in logic. One such is "balancing the books." Propose such a problem as that of the student who wonders whether he or she should take a job after school hours; have the class members make needed assumptions; line up in parallel columns the arguments pro and con, weigh the importance of each, and reach a conclusion.
2. Help students to differentiate opinion from fact. For this purpose, discuss statements like these: (a) Our basketball team lost 20 games and won 5 this season. (b) Our basketball team had a poor season. (c) Our coach is not a good coach. (d) Lack of student support cost us several victories.
3. Statements of opinion may be accepted if agreement is reached on the meaning of key terms and if those terms are measurable. For instance, in (b) above, if everyone agrees that *poor* refers to losing over half the games, the opinion may be accepted. But what if pre-season predictions were that the team would win no games at all? Help students see that some statements of opinion cannot be proved, for example, "Chocolate cake tastes better than any other kind."
4. Have students distinguish between hypothesis and reality. If an engine stops, the hypothesis may be that it is out of gas. But the flat statement "The engine is out of gas" does not necessarily represent reality; the engine may have stopped for another reason.
5. Discuss inductive thinking: reaching a conclusion on the basis of a number of bits of evidence. The classic example: Came home at night. Flipped switch—no light. Another—no light. Clock is not running. Other houses dark. What has happened?
6. Discuss deductive thinking: applying a generalization to a specific instance and reaching a conclusion. For example, test "He's an Italian, so he must like spaghetti" by the syllogism "All Italians like spaghetti. He is an Italian. He likes spaghetti." (The first statement, the major premise, is probably not true.)

7. Discuss with students such hasty generalizations as "I knew I couldn't pass algebra. I failed in the very first test." "Plane travel is unsafe. Every few days you hear about a crash." "Let's pick some mushrooms. The Smiths pick them every spring and never get sick from them."

## FOR CLARITY OF EXPOSITION

1. Have each student write a paragraph explaining to a "greenhorn" how to perform a simple task that can be demonstrated in class—for example, how to tie a shoelace or how to put on lipstick. The student reads his or her paper slowly while a volunteer greenhorn attempts to follow instructions, being careful not to do anything not included in the paragraph. If the instructions are inadequate, they must be revised.
2. As a variation, students prepare instructions for drawing a simple, unnamed object such as a fork, spoon, table, or chair. While one student reads, others, at the board, try to draw according to the directions. (A simple abstract linear design may also be the item to be drawn.)
3. Have students explain, as to a complete stranger, how to get from the school to various places in the community. The class may object to inaccuracies or to anything that would puzzle the stranger.

## IDEAS CONCERNING RESEARCH PAPERS

The question of whether to require students to write research (library, investigative, term) papers is hotly debated. If your school favors them, you might try some of the following ideas:

1. Kurt M. Jordan, in Fort Wayne, Indiana, has his college-bound seniors do a "community documentary." Each chooses a topic of local concern: racial integration in city police or fire departments, Fort Wayne's future mass transit needs, urban renewal, the city's recreational facilities, and so on. Research includes interviews, reading in back issues of the newspaper, or use of any other available types of information. The paper may take any form, such as a movie or slide production, but usually is a 1500 to 2000 word composition, with documentation as needed.[92]
2. The Oregon Curriculum Study Center recommended as the focus of junior research papers "The American High School Student Today." Students might choose, for instance, to write about causes of dropouts, rebelliousness, drugs, pregnancies, college plans, attitudes toward this or that.
3. Sister M. Christina of Rochester, New York, gets better results with several short papers rather than one long one. Some are based on research-within-the-book, perhaps a novel or a play that the class is reading and for which each student chooses a topic. If the book or play is historical, a student may examine part of the period depicted. Other papers, on nonliterary topics, may be in the form of magazine articles.[93]
4. As a variation of 3, a Chicago teacher has recommended "The Historical Basis for Characterization of _____ in _____." His example is charac-

360                                     THE TEACHING OF HIGH SCHOOL ENGLISH

terization in *Abe Lincoln in Illinois,* but the topic can fit other literary works based on history.[94]

5. The choice of subject is of major importance. A subject is good if it interests the student, material from at least four or five sources is available, and it is not too large and general and vague. ''Aviation'' is a poor topic; ''Before the Wright Brothers Flew'' is better.'' Help students to limit topics. Emphasize that an encyclopedia is no more than a starting point, and thereby forestall copying two pages from the *World Book.* Teach note-taking. Require handing in of notes or a rough draft before the finished paper. Stress the content, not fancy covers and clipped illustrations.

6. To reduce plagiarism, discuss and illustrate proper use of sources and quotations.

## ''LEARNING TO THINK AND TO WRITE''

Says S. I. Hayakawa (who later became a U.S. senator), ''The way to get students to think is to treat them as if they were capable of independent thought. The self-fulfilling prophecy will operate, and the students will start thinking.'' Hayakawa also recommends frequent periods in which students write rapidly and continuously, for 15 or 20 minutes, ''without pausing, without taking thought, without taking pen from paper. If the student runs out of things to say, he is to write the last words he wrote over and over again over and over again over and over again until he can find other things to say. The paper is to be turned in unsigned—unless the student feels like signing it. . . . [There] will be tremendous improvement with about the third or fourth exercise.''[95]

## MORE SUBJECTS FOR WRITTEN WORK

1. Usually, the closer the subject, the better the result. But there should be room for imaginative writing, too, even though the students will never see Xanadu.
2. Have students jot down their writing ideas in a part of their notebook.
3. Occasionally have students write explanations of how a story made them change their minds, how environment made the characters what they were, how a fictional portrayal helped them to gain an understanding of a living person, or how a personal problem may be solved by a parallel in fiction.
4. Albuquerque, New Mexico, High School has used subject matter of other departments for theme subjects in English, when practicable.
5. After juniors in Charles Reich's class in Port Washington, New York, read the four stories in Steinbeck's *The Red Pony,* in which the unifying theme is Jody's learning of basic, universal things, they were given this writing assignment: ''Look back into your earlier years to discover an incident or moment when you first became aware of some basic truth—the more staggering, the better. The discovery may be of a factual or a philosophical nature. Emulate the Steinbeck style in a composition by using as much vivid, sensory, connotative detail as possible to describe your discovery.''[96]

## CHANGE OF FOCUS

Eighth-graders in Oak Harbor, Washington, were asked to watch a dramatic TV program to notice the numerous changes in camera focus in a single scene. Then each child chose a scene from a short story read in class and described the camera focuses, angles, and emphases he or she would use in a TV dramatization. "Students seemed to see the point of the activity and wanted to have this sort of assignment again," say Lee Odell and Joanne Cohick.[97]

## "PUBLISHING" WHAT YOUR STUDENTS WRITE

Students gain confidence and exert more care when some of their writing reaches readership other than the teacher. Stephen N. Judy suggests these means of "publishing":

1. Read the paper aloud to the class.
2. Record it "for the class library of recorded literature." [But will anybody ever really listen to it?]
3. Post it on the bulletin board.
4. Submit it to the school newspaper or magazine.
5. Ditto it for the class.
6. Circulate it in manuscript form.
7. (For a play) Arrange for a readers' theater presentation.[98]

## THE ORGANIZATION OF A TV COMMERCIAL

Most TV commercials, says Richard L. Smith, consist of three parts: a "grabber" (attention-getter), a "demo" (the sales message, which is clear, graphic, well-organized), and the "pay-off" (the conclusion, which completes the little story introduced by the grabber). The same organization is one that can often be used in student writing. At least, becoming aware of it shows students the importance of organization.[99]

## HELP STUDENTS IN FIVE WAYS

Robert Blake believes that teachers can help young writers in five chief areas: (1) the composing process, including prewriting, planning, first draft, rewriting and editing; (2) varieties of writing (giving practice in various varieties); (3) skills of writing, such as developing good beginnings, using forceful and accurate verbs; (4) better sentences, with emphasis on sentence combining; and (5) discussion of students' writing, praising a great deal, commenting on style, and helping each student to find the writing voice best for him or her.[100]

## BASIC SKILLS

Teachers in the Tonawanda, New York, middle school say, "The basic skills in the complex act of writing are (1) awareness of audience and purpose, (2) choice of voice or persona appropriate for the audience and purpose, (3) the ability to adjust language and sentences to make them appropriate to the voice-audience-purpose, (4) the ability to give shape and pattern to a whole piece of writing, and (5) the ability to choose appropriately from among a full repertoire of writing strategies and syntactic skills. Spelling and punctuating consistently are secondary skills which are best treated informally when an individual student makes a mistake, never by whole-class instruction. Naming parts of speech or diagraming sentences is a form of linguistic study that has no relation to writing performance."[101]

## DOESN'T NEAT
## IT ~~DONT~~ HAVE TO BE ~~NEET~~

Timothy L. Bergen, Jr., of Columbia, South Carolina, argues that too many teachers insist on excessive speed in writing, but that: "Speed is not the only demon. Neatness is often valued above style. A composition paper full of corrections and crossed-out lines may be far more valuable to the teacher in appraising a student's awareness of the preciseness of the right word or phrase than an immaculately typed essay. Writing is one subject in which the student ought to be encouraged to ramble around and even be messy, if need be, in search of the answers."[102]

## TRANSITIONS

Duplicate a piece of well-written expository prose, but eliminate as many as possible of the transitional links between sentences and between paragraphs. In small groups, students try to find the now-unexpressed relationships and suitable words to express them. Groups compare their recommendations, and finally the teacher lets them see the original.

## DESCRIPTIVE WRITING: A PLANNED SEQUENCE

In the *Wisconsin English Journal* a number of years ago Sister David Marie suggested the following sequence for description:

1. Informative description, an objective report (e.g., describing for the cleaners a dress for which the claim check has been lost)
2. Somewhat more imaginative description, written from a single physical point of view (e.g., a flower garden or the inside of a room)
3. Description requiring change of physical point of view (e.g., outside and inside of a house, or going around on a Ferris wheel)
4. Description with a dominant impression (e.g., loneliness, peace, drabness, gaiety, fear, or disorder)
5. Description of the physical appearance of a person
6. Development of one basic character trait
7. Blending of external and internal characteristics of a person ("A loud, brazen individual and a reserved, retiring person would probably not dress alike.")
8. Suggesting character rather than stating it (may be combined with 7)
9. Using setting to reveal character (e.g., a girl's room or even a looseleaf notebook)

10. Describing from several mental points of view (e.g., "Describe the prom from the point of view of a girl who is going, of one who hasn't been asked, of the mother of a girl who hasn't been asked, of a faculty member, of the janitor.")

## ON PARAGRAPHS

Richard A. Meade and Geiger Ellis studied the paragraphing in *Saturday Review, English Journal,* and letters to the editor. Fifty-six percent of the paragraphs did not follow procedures prescribed in standard textbooks (like those described as "typical" in this book). Of the 44 percent that did, development by examples ranked first, with development by reasons, chronology, contrast, repetition, cause-effect, definition, and description trailing far behind. Of the nontextbook methods, a combination of procedures ranked first, followed by "additional comment," "two themes," "one-sentence paragraphs," "opposition," and "question."[103]

## DEVELOPING A PARAGRAPH

1. In Pittsburgh's Schenley High School some teachers follow the practice of taking a couple of student-written paragraphs that are unnecessarily general and then rewriting them with enough detail to make them vivid. The students then examine the contrasting paragraphs to see how they can expand and brighten a generalized, dull statement.
2. Useful in teaching paragraph development are exercises in which students merely list all the details they might include if they were writing a paragraph. Give them such topic sentences as these: "Christmas morning is a hectic time at our house." "No cats are better than one cat." "Washing a car is easy if one prepares for the job."

A second step may consist of deleting the items that do not harmonize with the others.

## TEN SUGGESTIONS FOR THEME BEGINNINGS

(1) Definition of a key word or phrase, (2) brief, vivid history of the subject, (3) direct statement of the writer's position on an issue, (4) statement of major divisions of the paper, (5) description of topic without naming it, (6) a relevant anecdote, (7) general statistics relevant to the reader's interests, (8) contrast of two opposing views, (9) question or questions to be answered, (10) brief narrative.[104]

## A BEGINNING IN TEACHING STRUCTURE

The basis of organization is the kind of sorting that even a small child can do. Thus

can readily be grouped as

THE TEACHING OF HIGH SCHOOL ENGLISH

□ □ □ □ △ △ ○ ○ ○ ○

## WHY AVOID I?

Emerson, Franklin, Thoreau, Jefferson, Montaigne, and Gandhi often used first person in their essays. Why, then, do some teachers insist that students avoid *I?*

## A CONTRAST OF STYLES

Able students may enjoy writing the same thing in contrasting diction, says Priscilla Tyler of the University of Missouri at Kansas City. For example, Latinate and Anglo-Saxon: "Will the cosmonauts of tomorrow traverse interstellar space in solitary crews—audacious, infinitely peripatetic?" "Tomorrow will skyfarers sail from star to star in lonely crews—fearless, boundless wanderers?"

## SIX LESSONS IN EXPOSITION

In the tenth grade, Anna Lou Klein gets results with this series of compositions: (1) Explaining by writing a concrete illustration. (2) Describing by using detail. (3) Achieving unity by choosing important details. (4) Making a point by comparing or contrasting. (5) Convincing by employing logical arguments. (6) Using imagination to explain, delight, convince, embroider, or lengthen the paper without wordiness.[105]

## NO KINESICS

"The trouble with the written word is that it comes to us without kinesics—no voicebox, no eyebrows. And the writer's task is to surround his words with other words on the paper so that his reader may infer the quality of the desired speaking voice. That is an art at all levels of writing." A useful concept for both literary study and composition work.[106]

## ORGANIZATION

1. Ask students to write single sentences explaining what their purpose might be if they were writing on specific topics. For example, Advice to a Practical Joker: "My purpose would be, through presenting an account of a joke that caused an injury, to discourage practical jokes that may be harmful."
2. To keep students reminded of the need for a plan, some teachers ask them to indicate at the end of a composition what type(s) of organization they have used.
3. "We can clarify thinking on the relationship of sub-topics and main topics if we insist on a more specific statement than 'The sub-topic is *related* to the main topic.' Pupils should understand that the sub-topic is *part* of the main topic. When they have had many illustrations of this relationship they can see why a certain sub-topic is illogical and correct the error."[107]
4. Help students to see that a good topic sentence does not merely name the topic but also may suggest approximately how the topic is developed. Poor: Pinochle

is the game I want to discuss. Better: Pinochle is an easy game to learn but a difficult one to play well.

5. Duplicate pairs of paragraphs. One in each pair will be notably deficient in unity, coherence, or emphasis; the other, on the same or a similar subject, will be especially strong. Ask students to compare the two and to analyze the weaknesses and strengths.

## GUIDE TO REVISION

Perhaps you or you and a class can develop a guide for students' use in revision. One such guide asks first for a look at the arrangement of ideas, and follows with questions about sentence structure, diction and style, and mechanics, with a number of specific questions under each heading.

## REVISION BY A CLASS

Duplicate a composition that needs extensive revision. Turn the class loose on it. At first they may concentrate on spelling, punctuation, and usage, but they should be led to question basic elements such as truth, convincingness, number and effectiveness of examples, and organization.

## PLAGIARISM

Clues to possible plagiarism, but not definite proof, are these, said Richard Braddock: (1) Much better than usual writing; (2) smooth writing with careless spelling, punctuation, or omissions; (3) content with which the writer would probably not be familiar; (4) writing that does not match the assignment.

To forestall plagiarism, Braddock recommended (1) making frequent writing assignments, with about half done in class; (2) requiring submission of a rough draft of an out-of-class paper; (3) avoiding assignment of the same topics year after year; (4) clarifying what plagiarism is and why independent writing is important.[108] (Be sure to teach students how to give credit for bits they copy or summarize to strengthen their writing.)

## "THE STUDENT-CENTERED CONFERENCE"

Conferences about writing are of two kinds, directive and nondirective, says Charles R. Duke. He favors the latter, which is positive and avoids intimidation and fear of failure. It should be conducted during the writing process rather than at the end, he says.[109]

## "THE WRITING PROCESS AND THE TAPE RECORDER"

Seniors read *Death of a Salesman* and listened to a recording of it. Then, with tape recorders, small groups discussed study questions, played back their discussions, and exchanged tapes with other groups. Finally, each student chose a topic and wrote a critical paper. "The papers were the best products that the senior literature teachers had ever received,'' said Patrick F. Berger of West Senior High School, Baldwin, Missouri.[110]

## "WRITING PARAGRAPHS ABOUT PARAGRAPHS"

James L. Allen, Jr., of the University of Hawaii at Hilo, finds it useful to ask older students to write a paragraph analyzing the paragraph structure of a given article or essay. They may, for instance, classify the types of development used, comment on the presence or absence of topic sentences, note transitional devices and perhaps inadequacies in development or clarity.[111]

## HOW TO TREAT THE "ENEMIES LIST"

1. *Dullness.* Take the dullest subject you can imagine—for example, the subject assigned on a patriotic essay contest—and discuss how even it may be brought to life.
2. *Vagueness.* Change "a vehicle" to "a newly waxed Volkswagen with rain beads on the hood." And limit subjects drastically.
3. *Deadwood.* Have students examine your collection of old horrible examples, and then have them look at their own writing to chop out redundancy, gobbledygook.[112]

## CREATING CHARACTERS

According to novelist James Yaffe, the central part of writing fiction is the creating of characters. Construction, language, and all other elements are important only in terms of their success in bringing characters to life. A student naturally begins by making himself or herself the main character, but can gradually learn to get inside other people's skins.

## LITERARY WRITING

1. What the child writes is less important than what writing does for the child.
2. In the teacher's file should be a gradually growing accumulation of the best writing done by students. A student who is asked to make a copy for the file is motivated to do still better work. The teacher may choose appropriate material to read to classes or may keep the file open for their browsing.
3. During the year, each student may make a "magazine" of his or her various writings.
4. Let your class, if it wishes, prepare an anthology of original verse or fiction.
5. In a unit involving *King Arthur and His Knights, The Once and Future King,* and *A Connecticut Yankee,* eighth-graders each chose one Arthurian character and wrote an adventure for him consistent with the sort of person he was.[113]
6. In writing poetry, start with the image or the emotion or the idea, then search for the form that will best express it. A poem is often a picture; the form is the canvas and the paint, the medium for transmitting the picture.

7. Youngsters can handle some forms easily and well. Euclid Junior High School in Ohio has had a schoolwide haiku contest each year; in the seventh grade the haiku has been used to introduce the idea of form in literature. In the eighth grade, teachers have taught a "blues form," and able students have experimented with tankas, cinquains, triolets, and free verse, as well.
8. Paintings have sometimes inspired students' short stories. Students tell the imaginary story behind the painting, or the story of one of the persons or objects portrayed.
9. Popular ballads and country music may also serve as starting points for stories. The students develop character traits and events barely hinted or referred to in the lyrics.
10. Students may be asked to clip a news story concerning a large number of people, for example, "Thousand Homeless as Floods Strike." The assignment: Pick out one person involved, and build a story on what happened to him or her.

## "CREATIVE WRITING IN THE READING CLASS"

Sub-par junior high readers wrote and bound their own individual "books" (a dozen pages or so) and presented them to their parents. (Good motivation for both reading and writing.) The teacher suggested both routine and imaginative topics, but allowed freedom of choice.[114]

## A POEM FROM A NAME

Sue Holt's junior high students in Zanesville, Ohio, write their names letter by letter vertically in the left margin. Then for each letter, each student writes a word descriptive of himself or herself. Later, each word is extended into a full line, and the sequence of lines becomes a poem.[115]

## "CONCRETE POETRY: CREATIVE WRITING FOR ALL STUDENTS"

Concrete poetry may be classified as general, found, and a-b-c. The first consists of typographical artistry, the second of miscellany from advertising or other sources, and the third of words in a-b-c order. Such poetry, says Lavonne Mueller, is "consistent with the visual world of the adolescent."[116]

## WORD CINQUAINS

*Line 1*—one word names topic. *Line 2*—two words define or describe topic. *Line 3*—three words express action. *Line 4*—four words express personal attitude. *Line 5*—one word gives synonym for the topic. For example, this verse by a seventh-grade class:

Halloween
  Inky, gripping
    Deceiving, terrifying, haunting
      Dancing spirits roaming freely
        Mystery

Sister Junette Morgan moves from word cinquains to syllable cinquains, haiku, tanka, Korean sijo, and rhymed poetry.[117]

## "PRELUDE TO THE MAKING OF A POEM: FINGER EXERCISES"

Charles Rathbone suggests dozens of finger exercises: for example, lists of onomatopoeic words, alliterative brand names, a sentence catching the sound of a subway train coming into a station, a rhythmical monologue for a circus barker, a plain and a fancy menu, "animal metaphors" like "Anticipation is a twitching poodle."[118]

## TRIAL SCENES

Students may enjoy converting into trial scenes some appropriate episodes from literature. For example, suppose that Macbeth had been brought to trial shortly after Duncan's death. The defense could contend that there were no witnesses, and of course a wife need not testify against her husband.[119]

## STUDENT REACTIONS TO WRITING

Some years ago West Virginia high school students were polled to get their reactions to the way theme writing was taught them. They advocated more writing (!), definite directions, choice of topics, information about grading system, use of models, much writing in class, help in writing poetry, chance to read classmates' themes. Among their dislikes: lack of explanation of a grade, failure to recognize plagiarism, overemphasis on serious subjects, lack of discussion of what makes a good theme.[120]

## GIMMICKS IN GRADING

1. Sometimes, try for a month or so to mark only good things in students' writing, ignoring all errors or weaknesses.
2. Suggest that groups evaluate by listing their reactions under the heads "Strong Points" and "Weak Points."
3. As a once-a-year device, have "state's attorneys" and "defense lawyers" analyze papers.
4. Don't be afraid of using humor in written comments, but beware of satire, irony, sarcasm. Don't be afraid to praise, but avoid overuse of that colorless word *interesting*.
5. Bar or line graphs may show students' progress in selected phases of writing. Time-consuming to construct, though, unless you teach students to keep their own graphs up to date.

## GRADING TRADING

In 1902 Gardiner, Kittredge, and Arnold recommended trading of sets of papers between classes "of equal rank" in different schools, with all papers written on the same subject. Each class evaluates the other's compositions in detail. About eight decades later the idea still seems good.

### A GRADE OF Q

Max S. Marshall suggests that instead of E or F for a composition a teacher should use a Q, which means, in effect, "There is a serious question about the quality of this paper. Let's examine the question together and see what we can do about eliminating the problem."[121]

### "PEER EVALUATION AND PEER GRADING"

Perhaps it is better to ask students to comment constructively on each other's compositions rather than to have them assign grades, suggests Neil Ellman of Rahway, New Jersey.[122]

### CLEVELAND COMPOSITION RATING SCALE

**A.** Content—50%

| | |
|---|---|
| Convincing | Unconvincing |
| Organized | Jumbled |

| | |
|---|---|
| Thoughtful | Superficial |
| Broad | Limited |
| Specific | Vague |

**B.** Style—30%

| | |
|---|---|
| Fluent | Restricted |
| Cultivated | Awkward |
| Strong | Weak |

**C.** Conventions—20%

| | |
|---|---|
| Correct Writing Form | Incorrect Form |
| Conventional Usage | Substandard |

### "THE PERILS OF PAPER GRADING"

Three kinds of especially odious paper-markers, says Gary B. Sloan of Louisiana Tech, are the Nit-Picker, who is "seized with an irrational, demonic urge to red-pencil the putative solecism"; the Compulsive Revisionist, who rewrites "Holden was sick of dirty-minded people" as "Holden had developed a pronounced aversion for individuals enamored of subject matter less than spotless"; and the Partisan, whose "volcanic pen," when the Partisan finds an idea with which he disagrees, "erupts and fills every nook and cranny of the paper with scalding criticism."[123]

### HOW NEAT IS YOUR OWN HANDWRITING?

If your own handwriting is neat, you tend to give low grades to students whose writing is messy. If your own penmanship is messy, you are not influenced one way or the other. Schuyler W. Huck and William G. Bounds reported those findings.[124]

## CAREFUL EDITING INFLUENCES STUDENT GRADERS

An Ohio teacher occasionally has her students anonymously evaluate stories written by classmates, using a 5-4-3-2-1 scale. Sometimes there will be a bimodal distribution of scores, for example, many 4's and 2's, few 3's. The teacher reproduces these stories, but corrects punctuation and other mechanical errors. The 2's vanish, and most of the ratings are 4's and 5's (high scores). "I hope this shows them that careful editing, as a final step in writing a paper, can have a tremendous effect on the audience."[125]

## LET'S PLAY EDITOR

Gordon R. Wood has pointed out that, though it is the students who need practice in editing their writing, in actuality it is the teacher who gets this practice. Instruction in what an editor looks at and how he or she works may help students to edit their own work. A copy editor from a local newspaper may be willing to talk to the class.

## HOW MANY THEMES?

Research at Florida State suggests that writing ability is not related directly to the number of compositions written. Nevertheless, teachers at Murray State University found that the majority of students placed in remedial classes had done little writing in high school. Although there is nothing sacred about a theme a week, considerable practice in writing (like considerable practice at the piano) seems essential for success.

## COMMENTS DO HELP

In a controlled experiment, Dr. Ellis B. Page found that greatest average improvement was made by students whose teachers commented rather specifically on test papers; next largest improvement, by students whose papers carried such comments as "Excellent!" or "Let's raise this grade!"; and smallest improvement by students who received only a grade with no comment.

## A CONFESSION ABOUT GRADING

David Tabakow admits that his grades go down as he moves through a stack of papers, because the sixteenth paper doesn't show any insights he hasn't found in the first 15. He finds that he seldom gives a low grade to a long paper, or a very high grade to a short one. A paper that he doesn't understand gets a B unless it is very badly or very well written. "The task of grading, *judging* someone else, is very anxiety producing."[126]

## "MEASURING GROWTH IN WRITING"

Read Charles Cooper's article in the *English Journal* for March 1975, if you are interested in finding out whether your students (after a year or more) are really learning to write. He recommends measurement of six categories: (1) standard usage, (2) syntactic fluency, (3) writing quality, (4) willingness to write, (5) valuing of writing, (6) contributions to group effort. Cooper suggests fairly specific ways to measure each of the six.

## "STIMULATING WRITING THROUGH JOB AWARENESS"

Alan McLeod of Richmond, Virginia, lists 34 writing exercises related to getting and keeping a job.[127] And Thomas N. Turner of the University of Tennessee, in "A Stylish Wedding," lists 49 ideas for "informing career education with creative writing and composition."[128]

## "EVERYONE DOES NOT THINK ALIKE"

Mexican-American and black students typically think holistically, reacting to "the environment as a whole." Many other American students (and apparently most teachers) think analytically, focusing on "part of a field as discrete from its surroundings." So says Grace L. Cooper of the District of Columbia, who asserts that teaching methods need to be related to students' cognitive modes. (Much research is needed on what may be an important group of differences, if the theory is correct.)[129]

## "A UNIT FOR WRITING CHILDREN'S STORIES"

Nell Wiseman of Charleston, Illinois, describes a six-week unit in which high school students enjoyed writing stories for young children. The unit culminated in reading the stories to real, live kindergarten and primary classes.[130]

## EXPLAINING TECHNICAL TERMS

"The doll blows on the cubes for luck, and I promptly crap out." "Gel the lights in the upstage right portal!" Jay Amberg's students in Highland Park, Illinois, have fun explaining the technical terms they've encountered at work or in other places.[131]

## A WRITING PLACE

At East High in Buffalo there is The Writing Place, where "The student walks into the airy, bright room, and is greeted by an English teacher who sits down with the student at one of the tables. They begin talking about the student's writing." The article "One-to-One to Write" describes procedures for establishing such a place.[132]

## HOW TO HANDLE THE PAPER LOAD

Gene Stanford and a committee edited for NCTE a 135-page booklet, *How to Handle the Paper Load*, in which 27 teachers discuss their varied ways of coping with considerable amounts of student writing. Free writing, journals, students as editors, peer evaluation, and focused grading are among the techniques described.[133]

## HOW STUDENTS AND EXPERIENCED WRITERS REVISE

Nancy Sommers, New York University, studied revision procedures of college freshmen and experienced writers. Students "scratched out" and "cut out." To experienced writers, some of them professionals, revision typically "means taking apart what I have written and putting it back together again." Perhaps, though, going through the student phase is a prerequisite to development of the more mature procedure.[134]

## MORE ABOUT REVISION

Dan R. Kirby and Tom Liner of the University of Georgia discuss three sorts of revision: in-process (while the writing is being drafted), editing (after a draft is completed), and proofreading ("eliminating surface errors").[135]

## PEER EVALUATION

Irvin Peckham, who worked with the Bay Area Writing Project of California, describes a semester in which students only read and wrote. What they wrote was commented on, orally and in writing, by classmates. "Kids do learn from each other," he says.[136]

## LETTING STUDENTS KNOW HOW YOU EVALUATE

Thomas Carnicelli, University of New Hampshire, hands out a one-page "Guide for Evaluating Essays," covering content, point of view, organization, style, mechanics, and degree of difficulty, with a key question or two under each heading. The last is "How ambitious is this paper? Has the writer attempted something difficult, or played it safe?"[137]

# FOOTNOTES

1. "Teaching Composition: A Position Statement," *College English* 36, Oct. 1974, p. 219.
2. Harry Lee Faggett, "Instructional Assurance," *College Composition and Communication* 24, Oct. 1973, p. 295.
3. "Why Teach Writing—and How," *English Journal* 62, Dec. 1973, p. 123.
4. *College Composition and Communication* 26, May 1975, p. 149.
5. From an interview with Paul Janezko, *English Journal* 65, Nov. 1976, p. 20.
6. *English Journal* 61, May 1972, p. 694.
7. *Wisconsin English Journal*, Oct. 1976, as quoted in *Council-grams*, March 1977, p. 61.

8. *Research in the Teaching of English,* Winter 1975, pp. 242, 250.

9. *English Resource Guide with Emphasis on Career Education,* Bulletin No. 1337, Louisiana State Department of Education, 1974, p. 1.

10. "Truth vs. Beauty," *English Journal* 62, Feb. 1973, p. 212.

11. Shirley Boes Neill, "How to Improve Student Writing," *American Education,* Oct. 1976, p. 6.

12. "Teaching Before the Composition Is Written," in *They Really Taught Us How to Write,* Urbana: NCTE, 1974, p. 6.

13. *My Class in Composition,* Harvard University Press, 1925, p. xxv.

14. Based on "The Assignment Makers," *English Journal* 61, Feb. 1972, p. 269.

15. "Teaching for Success," *English Journal* 12, Dec. 1973, p. 1276.

16. "Writing and Composing," *English Journal* 48, Jan. 1959, p. 12.

17. Patricia Gray, "That Awful Age!" *English Journal* 66, April 1977, p. 30.

18. Mary Lou Jellen, in *They Really Taught Us How to Write,* Urbana: NCTE, 1974, p. 31.

19. "Standard Problems," *English Journal* 62, Feb. 1973, p. 263.

20. "Why Johnny Can't Write: A Reply," *North Carolina English Teacher,* Winter 1976, p. 10.

21. "How to Get Kids to Write," *English Journal* 62, April 1973, p. 63.

22. Adapted from Marilyn Burghdorf and Jeanne Wright, La Crescenta, California, in *Potpourri,* Spring 1976.

23. In *Ideas for English 101,* ed. by R. Ohmann and W. B. Coley, Urbana: NCTE, 1975, p. 176.

24. William J. Hunter, in *Through a Glass Darkly,* ed. by Edward Fagan and Jean Vandell, Urbana: NCTE, 1973, p. 84.

25. This quotation, like others in these paragraphs, is from *The Education Digest,* Jan. 1978, p. 42. It is based on Eliot Wigginton's article in *Media and Methods,* Nov. 1977, p. 49.

26. The last six of these suggestions come from Raymond J. Rodrigues of the University of Utah, a Foxfire enthusiast. In *On Righting Writing,* ed. by Ouida M. Clapp, Urbana: NCTE, 1975, p. 37.

27. *English Journal* 65, April 1976, p. 81.

28. Suggested by R. Baird Shuman, University of Illinois.

29. "Describing a Face," in *Writing Exercises from* Exercise Exchange, ed. by Littleton Long, Urbana: NCTE, 1976, p. 100.

30. *Potpourri,* Spring 1976.

31. "The Politics of Syntax," *English Journal* 64, Dec. 1975, p. 27.

32. "Cooperate and Create: Teaching Writing Through Small Groups," *English Journal* 62, Dec. 1973, p. 1274.

33. "Personal Growth and the Teaching of Writing," in *On Righting Writing,* ed. by Ouida M. Clapp, Urbana: NCTE, 1975, p. 101.

34. *Illinois English Bulletin,* Nov. 1960.
35. "A Cumulative Sequence in Composition," *English Journal* 65, April 1966, p. 425.
36. Selma Bishop, "What I've Learned about Creative Writers," *Clearing House,* Oct. 1950, p. 89.
37. *College Composition and Communication* 23, Dec. 1974, p. 377.
38. *English Journal 65,* Sept. 1976, p. 74.
39. Alan D. Engelsman, "A Piece of the Action," *English Journal* 61, Feb. 1972, p. 252.
40. *Potpourri,* Spring 1976.
41. "Writing from Obituaries," *English Journal* 64, Oct. 1975, p. 51.
42. Antony Christie, "Making with Words," *English Journal 61,* Feb. 1972, p. 247.
43. Suggested by William J. Albright, in *I, Image, Imagery, Imagine,* and reported in *English Journal* 64, Oct. 1975, pp. 64–65.
44. *English Journal* 62, Dec. 1973, p. 1267.
45. "On the Importance of Cohesiveness in Writing Classes," *College Composition and Communication* 24, Oct. 1973, p. 294.
46. *English Journal* 62, Dec. 1973, p. 1272.
47. Quoted in Stephen N. Judy, "Writing for the Here and Now," *English Journal* 62, Jan. 1973, p. 69.
48. *Measuring Growth in English,* Urbana: NCTE, 1974, p. 6.
49. Diederich, pp. 6–8.
50. *College Composition and Communication* 27, Dec. 1976, p. 357.
51. "Alternative Activities . . . ," *North Carolina English Teacher,* Winter 1976, p. 14.
52. *English Journal* 64, March 1975, p. 76.
53. In *Measure for Measure,* ed. by Allen Berger and Blanche Hope Smith, Urbana: NCTE, 1972–73, p. 37. (This 119-page booklet is devoted entirely to evaluation in English and contains many practical and thought-provoking short articles.)
54. "Awareness," in *They Really Taught Us How to Write,* Urbana: NCTE, 1974, p. 113.
55. Michael Platt, "Correcting Papers in Public and in Private," *College English* 37, Sept. 1975, p. 24.
56. David Sohn, "A Talk with Henry Maloney," *English Journal* 65, Feb. 1976, p. 9.
57. *Research in the Teaching of English,* Fall 1972, p. 212.
58. "From Senior to Freshman," *Research in the Teaching of English,* Feb. 1976, p. 134.
59. *Journal of Communication,* June 1977.
60. *Michigan English Teacher,* March 1961.

61. From the Introduction to Edward B. Jenkinson and Donald A. Seybold, *Writing as a Process of Discovery,* Bloomington: Indiana University Press, 1970.

62. Jayne Karsten, "Technique and Tactics," in *They Really Taught Us How to Write,* Urbana: NCTE, 1974, p. 68.

63. The whole story is told in "Help! I'm a Prisoner in a Letter Factory," in *On Righting Writing,* ed. by Ouida M. Clapp, Urbana: NCTE, 1975, p. 48.

64. Suggested by Elaine Clark, Central High School, Grand Rapids, Michigan.

65. *English Journal* 66, March 1977, p. 76.

66. Susan Latter, Newhall, California, in *Potpourri,* Spring 1976.

67. Cathy Bisson, Lampoc, California, in *Potpourri,* Spring 1976.

68. William A. Clark, "How to Completely Individualize a Writing Program," *English Journal* 64, April 1975, p. 66.

69. Arthur Daigon, "English: A Three-Ringed Circus," *English Journal* 6, Oct. 1973, p. 1115.

70. David Osgood, "The Campaign," *English Journal* 61, Oct. 1972, p. 102.

71. "Technique and Tactics," in *They Really Taught Us How to Write,* Urbana: NCTE, 1974, p. 68.

72. Betsy Kaufman, "EJ Workshop," *English Journal* 63, Sept. 1974, p. 77.

73. "Autobiography Meets the English Class," *English Journal* 62, May 1973, p. 784.

74. Lemley, College of Redwoods, in *Potpourri,* Spring 1976.

75. Ron Martin, Newhall, California, in *Potpourri,* Spring 1976.

76. In *They Really Taught Us How to Write,* Urbana: NCTE, 1974, p. 29.

77. *English Journal* 57, Feb. 1968, p. 221.

78. *English Journal* 56, Oct. 1967, p. 1011.

79. Any story that has a quick, decisive ending may be suitable.

80. All three of these suggestions are in the January 1968, *English Journal 57,* pp. 79, 93, 113.

81. *English Journal* 57, Sept. 1968, p. 866.

82. "Compositions: Assigned or Developed?" *English Journal* 58, Nov. 1969, p. 1194.

83. *English Journal* 54, March 1965, p. 214.

84. In *They Really Taught Us How to Write,* Urbana: NCTE, 1974, p. 49.

85. *English Journal* 65, Nov. 1976, p. 42.

86. "Writing and 'my own little postage stamp of native soil,'" *English Journal* 62, April 1973, p. 579.

87. *English Journal* 65, Sept. 1976, p. 50.

88. "Bringing a Class to Its Senses," *English Journal* 54, Sept. 1965, p. 515.

89. *English Journal* 55, March 1966, p. 328.

90. "Priming the Pump and Controlling the Flow," *English Journal* 56, Jan. 1967, p. 109.

91. Betty Leach, "Assignment—Social Letter," *English Journal* 48, Sept. 1959, p. 336.

92. Glen Love and Michael Payne, "The Research Paper," *English Journal* 56, May 1967, p. 739.

93. "Training for Research Writing," *English Journal* 53, Nov. 1964, p. 610.

94. Carlisle L. Rast, "The Beginning Research Paper," *English Journal* 50, Oct. 1961, p. 469.

95. *College Composition and Communication* 13, Feb. 1962, pp. 6, 8.

96. "Study Questions for *The Red Pony*," *Exercise Exchange*, April 1962, p. 4.

97. In *On Righting Writing*, ed. by Ouida M. Clapp, Urbana: NCTE, 1975, p. 42.

98. "Writing for the Here and Now," *English Journal* 62, Jan. 1973, p. 75.

99. "Try TV Commercials," *Clearing House*, Dec. 1972, p. 223.

100. "How to Talk to a Writer," *English Journal* 65, Nov. 1976, p. 49.

101. Charles R. Cooper, et al., "Tonawanda Middle School's New Writing Program," *English Journal* 65, Nov. 1976, p. 56.

102. "Why Can't Johnny Write?" *English Journal* 65, Nov. 1976, p. 36.

103. "Paragraph Development in the Modern Age of Rhetoric," *English Journal* 59, Feb. 1970, p. 219.

104. Lawrence E. Nelson, "In the Beginning," *English Journal* 55, March 1966, p. 342.

105. "Expository Writing for Amateurs," *English Journal* 53, Jan. 1964, p. 16.

106. Walker Gibson, "The Speaking Voice and the Teaching of Composition," *English Leaflet*, Winter 1963.

107. Suggested by Margaret Mosher, Roosevelt High School, Chicago.

108. Lee Odell and Joanne Cohick, "You Mean, Write It Down in Ink?" *English Journal* 64, Feb. 1975, p. 48.

109. *English Journal* 64, Dec. 1975, p. 44.

110. In *On Righting Writing*, ed. by Ouida Clapp, Urbana: NCTE, 1975, p. 18.

111. In *Through a Glass Darkly*, ed. by Edward Fagan and Jean Vandell, Urbana: NCTE, 1971, p. 82.

112. Gloria C. Crum, in *They Really Taught Us How to Write*, Urbana: NCTE, 1974, p. 130.

113. Eleanor K. Friedman, "Studying King Arthur in the Eighth Grade," *English Journal* 51, March 1962, p. 200.

114. Anne B. Edelman, *English Journal* 64, Jan. 1975, p. 60.

115. *English Journal* 65, Sept. 1976, p. 52.

116. *English Journal* 58, Oct. 1969, p. 1053.

117. "Writing Poetry in Junior High," *English Journal* 57, Oct. 1968, p. 1009.

118. *English Journal* 54, Dec. 1965, p. 851.

119. Ted Gordon edits one such scene in *Clearing House*, Feb. 1968.

120. Lorena A. Anderson, "Ways and Means in the Teaching of Writing," *English Journal* 51, Dec. 1962, p. 621.

121. *Intellect,* Oct. 1973.
122. *English Journal* 64, March 1975, p. 79.
123. "The Perils of Paper Grading," *English Journal* 66, May 1977, p. 33.
124. *American Educational Research Journal,* Spring 1972.
125. This report by an anonymous teacher is taken from the *English Newsletter* of Youngstown State University, Spring 1977.
126. *This Magazine Is About Schools,* Summer 1972.
127. *English Journal* 67, Nov. 1978, p. 42.
128. *English Journal* 68, Oct. 1979, p. 59.
129. *English Journal* 69, April 1980, p. 45.
130. *English Journal* 68, May 1979, p. 47.
131. "Around the World in Eighty Grips," *English Journal* 67, Dec. 1978, p. 43.
132. Nina Luban, et al. *English Journal* 67, Nov. 1978, p. 30.
133. Urbana: NCTE, 1979.
134. "Revision Strategies of Student Writers and Experienced Adult Writers," *College Composition and Communication* 31, Dec. 1980, p. 378.
135. "Revision," *English Journal* 69, March 1980, p. 41.
136. *English Journal* 67, Oct. 1978, p. 61.
137. *English Journal* 69, March 1980, p. 67.

# 11

## IMPORTANT
## DOTS
## AND
## CURLS

## FIVE AXIOMS CONCERNING PUNCTUATION

To teach punctuation intelligently, a teacher should understand five things about it.

*Axiom 1. The purpose of punctuation is to help a reader understand a writer's meaning.* When writer and reader both understand that ! shows strong feeling (almost a shout), writer uses the mark to help to indicate the feeling, and reader sees it and says to himself, in effect, "Aha! Strong feeling! This is almost a shout!" Similarly with the other marks. "Men work together," said Robert Frost, "Whether they work together or apart." Writer and reader work together even though miles and years separate them.

You may recall that, when Bottom and his fellows present "Pyramus and Thisbe" in *Midsummer Night's Dream*, Quince mangles the prologue by putting vocal periods ("stops," as the British call them) in the wrong places:

> . . . All for your delight
> We are not here. That you should here repent you,
> The actors are at hand. . . .

Theseus comments, "This fellow doth not stand upon points." Lysander elaborates, "He hath rid his prologue like a rough colt; he knows not the stop. A good moral, my lord: it is not enough to speak, but to speak true."

Quinces are not merely sixteenth-century phenomena. Joe Quince and Marjorie Quince may be in every American high school classroom. They know not the stops, and as result they often do not speak or write true.

### 379

To help them, lead them to see what happens if punctuation is lacking or is out of harmony with the principles generally accepted in our age. Have them imagine, for instance, that no punctuation marks or capital letters exist. (Capitals have a signaling function similar to that of punctuation marks.) Give them a little paragraph like the following, and ask them to time themselves to find how long it takes each of them to understand it thoroughly:

*i am enjoying my stay in st petersburg where i have a room one with a glorious view of the bay in the grandvilla hotel where did you tell me that you stayed when you were here in the manor house was it that is where louella and i ate dinner friday morning and noon meals we usually take in our own hotel*

After the students have timed themselves, have them insert the needed capitals and punctuation and time themselves again. Most students' time will be cut at least in half.

Then raise the question "Suppose each of us punctuated to suit himself or herself. What would the effect be?" Hand out another paragraph without capitals or punctuation, and ask each to punctuate it, not according to rules already learned, but letting the imagination roam. The student may use X's, for instance, or circles, or check marks, or anything else, and may capitalize at will. Let the completed papers circulate for a few minutes, so that students can see what would happen if we had no common agreements about what punctuation to use where.

***Axiom 2. Most punctuation marks are written substitutes for intonation.*** When we speak, the things we do with the voice tell a listener a great deal. He or she hears that one group of words is a statement, another an exclamation, another a question; that a phrase is attached to a preceding part of a sentence rather than to a following part; that the White House is meant and not just any white house. The listener has unknowingly learned in childhood the principles of juncture and intonation that linguists have described scientifically, and he or she uses these principles in interpreting the spoken word.

The reader, however, does not hear a speaking voice. Hence the reader must rely upon the visual symbols that have been developed as substitutes. The symbols are less than perfect, but if they were sufficiently complete to reflect all that the voice does, they would be too numerous and cumbersome to learn with ease.

Some teachers recommend study of the oral stress-patterns described by structural grammarians, so that students may become aware of the relationship between the ways we say things and the ways we punctuate them. For example, natural oral reading of "a short, jolly, chubby young man" shows that two commas but not three are needed.

Not all marks are substitutes for intonation. Some, such as the punctuation in the formal parts of a letter, are simple matters of convention.

*Axiom 3. Variations in the punctuation of a sentence may result in difference in meaning, lack of meaning, or difference in emphasis.* Here are examples of difference of meaning:

> Henry said his teacher was ill.
> Henry, said his teacher, was ill.

> She brought thirty-five dollar bills.
> She brought thirty five-dollar bills.

Too much punctuation, too little punctuation, or misplaced marks may make a sentence almost meaningless. Examples: "When, after the first, snowfall—of the season, he brought out his, old, pair of skis; his lovely, worshipful, bride, was lost (in admiration), because, he could move, at all, on those, clumsy things." (Only two marks are needed.) "Old elephants like old men, cherish memories, and relive their days of glory." (Insert a comma after *elephants* and delete the comma after *memories*.)

Differences in emphasis are revealed in these sentences: "The candidate spoke well, but he carefully avoided local issues." "The candidate spoke well. But he carefully avoided local issues." (The second version puts more stress on the second idea.)

*Axiom 4. A rule of punctuation is only a statement about what at present is customary practice.* "Right" or "wrong," then, means only that a mark in a particular context is or is not used in accordance with current custom, or that it aids or reduces clarity and the smooth flow of a sentence.

The misuse of a mark, therefore, is sometimes only a social blunder such as using the wrong spoon. Yet, like other social blunders, it may have both social and economic consequences. No one can say how many carelessly written social letters have caused misunderstanding, heartache, and the cooling of friendship. No one can say how many persons have failed to get or keep positions they wanted, or to gain advancement in their chosen professions, because their writing was sloppy in spelling, punctuation, or other mechanics. No one knows how many legal cases have depended on the interpretation of a clause that would have meant something quite different if a comma had been inserted or omitted.

Nor can anyone estimate the dollars-and-cents cost of faulty punctuation. The story is told of a father who wired what he intended as a refusal of his daughter's request for a fur coat: NO AMOUNT IS TOO MUCH. The lack of a stop after NO cost him several hundred dollars. The federal government once passed a bill saying that "all foreign fruit, plants" should be admitted duty-free. The intention was to say "all foreign fruit-plants." Before the error could be corrected, $2 million in duty had been lost. In the early days of our space ventures, NASA sent its first probe toward Venus. It failed, at a cost of $18 million. The reason for failure: a hyphen missing in an equation.

In summary, a writer's and a reader's mutual understanding of current conventions of punctuation may lead to clear communication and sometimes may help to keep friends and save money.

*Axiom 5. Punctuation cannot make a bad sentence good.* Some students seem to believe that they can correct almost any writing fault by slipping in an extra comma or two. Thus one student wrote, "Flying just beneath the low-hanging clouds I saw a V of wild geese." She tried, unsuccessfully of course, to remedy the dangling modifier by placing a comma after *clouds*. The only cure possible for that sentence was redrafting.

## OBLIGATORY AND OPTIONAL PUNCTUATION

### OBLIGATORY PUNCTUATION

Some principles of punctuation afford virtually no choice in ordinary writing. (Advertising writers intentionally indulge in eccentricities.) The obligatory uses should be taught as established conventions followed by all careful modern writers. The following list includes the chief of these, exclusive of certain formularized practices in letters, footnotes, bibliographies, and other writing not involving complete sentences.

#### Terminal Punctuation

1. Period after a sentence making a statement
2. Period after a command or a request, even though phrased as a question ("Will you please close the door.")
3. Question mark after a direct question
4. Exclamation mark after a sentence (especially if short) expressing strong feeling
5. Comma after a sentence quoted within a sentence, unless a question mark or an exclamation mark is required ("That is all," she said. "Is that all?" she asked.)

#### Divisional Punctuation

1. Semicolon to separate complete statements within a sentence when *and, but, for, or, nor, yet,* or *so* is not used
2. Colon to separate a formal list from the rest of the sentence
3. Quotation marks around quoted sentences or parts of sentences; comma after *he said,* or colon if the statement is very formal
4. Single quotation marks around a quotation within a quotation
5. Comma to prevent momentary confusion ("Whatever is, is right.")
6. Comma to separate consecutive modifiers of the same type ("The angry, snarling dog pursued him relentlessly, endlessly.")

7. Comma to separate pairs of items ("His meal consisted only of bread and milk, and tea and lemon.")
8. Comma to separate items in a sequence ("Refer to Act I, scene i, line 14.")
9. Comma or dash used to separate words used for effect ("Long, long ago he should have decided—decided to make the climb.")
10. Dash to signal an abrupt change in structure ("When he was—Don't drive so fast!")

### Parenthetical Punctuation

1. Comma to enclose nonessential clauses ("Grassy Blue, who played left tackle, was injured.")
2. Commas to enclose nonessential phrases if clarity will be enhanced ("A bookcase, laid flat on the floor, occupied one corner.")
3. Commas to enclose nonessential appositives (Her first novel, *Martin,* was a best-seller.")
4. Dashes or parentheses to enclose strongly interruptive elements
5. Brackets to enclose interpolations in quoted material

## OPTIONAL PUNCTUATION

The University of Chicago's *A Manual of Style* says of the comma, "There are a few rules governing its use that have become almost obligatory. Aside from these, the use of the comma is mainly a matter of good judgment, with ease in reading as the end in view." What is true of the comma is true in varying degree of the other marks also. Punctuation is an art and not a science.

In a number of situations, of which the most important are listed below, a writer may choose between one mark and another or between one mark and none. Sometimes clarity will dictate one choice or the other, or sometimes the emphasis will be changed by the presence or absence of marks, but occasionally the choice is completely free. It seems wise to indicate and permit this freedom to students; if they follow the obligatory uses, they should not be criticized if they depart from the teacher's or the textbook writer's preferences in the optional ones, although they should be reasonably consistent in their own choices. (Some preferences of the authors of this book are indicated later; your own may be different.)

1. Comma optional before *and* in an *a, b,* and *c* series ("The flag is red, white, and blue." Or ". . . red, white and blue.")
2. Commas optional in an *a and b and c* series ("The ground was hard and cracked and sun-parched." Perhaps more emphatic: ". . . hard, and cracked, and sun-parched.")
3. Commas or question marks in separating two or more parallel questions in the

same sentence ("When will she have time for shopping, for cooking, for keeping house?" Or "... for shopping? for cooking?...")

**4.** Comma optional before *and, but, for, or, nor, yet,* or *so* in a compound sentence (usually present in a long sentence)

**5.** Comma optional to set off an introductory word, phrase, or adverbial clause unless demanded for clarity

**6.** Commas, dashes, parentheses, or sometimes no marks with interpolated phrases ("He may, or may not, win the election." "He may—or may not— win the election." "He may (or may not) win the election." "He may or may not win the election.")

**8.** Comma optional to indicate omission of one or more words ("Hyperbole refers to exaggeration; litotes, to the opposite." Or "... litotes to the opposite.")

## MODES OF PRESENTATION

A common method of teaching punctuation is to devote some lessons to terminal punctuation, some to the comma, one or two to the semicolon, and so on, according to the needs of a class. This procedure has the advantage of affording a systematic overview of the specific uses of each mark.

A second method is to teach punctuation together with sentence structure. When the class is studying the compound sentence, for example, the teacher helps students to learn the ways in which varying forms of the sentence may be punctuated. This instruction is timely and useful; it has the special merit of permitting the class members to practice the usage as they compose sentences requiring it.

A third procedure is to devote bits of class time to a certain type of punctuation only when a large portion of the class needs it, and when individuals want help with specific problems in their writing. Motivationally this procedure is especially good, but it does create the risk that some students will not encounter certain punctuation usages that they may eventually need.

All three of these procedures have something to commend them, and they are not mutually exclusive. One may reinforce the others. The first helps to tie up loose ends. The second should be followed when a kind of sentence structure is being introduced or reviewed. The third affords special help to individuals.

The remainder of this discussion will consider the major marks one by one, concentrating on chief uses and major trouble spots, along with hints for teaching.

### THE PERIOD

The most important of punctuation marks is the period. High school students seldom omit a period except through carelessness, but many of them substitute a comma for it. Thus is born the hated comma splice, also called the comma fault and the run-on sentence. This error often persists through the senior high years and appears in thousands of papers written by college freshmen and even in those by upperclassmen.

Juliet to the contrary, there is something in a name. As long as one teacher called the error a comma fault or comma splice, he could not eradicate it. In the hazy way that all of us sometimes think, students apparently believed that a "comma fault" was a failure to use enough commas; as a result commas and comma faults both increased remarkably, despite the teacher's hours of work. When he began to use the term "run-on sentence" for the same error, its frequency decreased somewhat. "Run-together sentences" helped a little more. And "Siamese sentences," suggesting the unnatural linking of Siamese twins, proved especially effective.

A teacher in a Champaign, Illinois, junior high school used a different device to help students determine whether a comma, semicolon, or period is the right mark. She told them, "When you are writing a sentence, pretend that you are a sign-maker and that the reader is driving a car. You put up a comma sign to tell him to slow down, a semicolon sign to say that here is a spot where he must almost stop, and a period sign to represent a stop." This device is obviously only an inadequate rule of thumb, but it has the positive merit of reminding the writer that he or she is always responsible for helping the reader.

Some students use not too few periods but too many. They write, "Silas was very lonely. Although he enjoyed counting his gold every night." Correcting the habit of punctuating sentence fragments as sentences is not easy. Here, punctuation and knowledge of sentence structure are especially closely linked. The student who knows what a sentence is does not write graceless, unintentional fragments. The cure for this error is not to preach punctuation but to teach sentence structure.

Structural linguistics, although now seldom mentioned in schools, suggested one useful way to differentiate the need for a comma from the need for a semicolon or period. The structuralists pointed out that a slight rise in pitch, as in two places in *My uncle, who lived in Nebraska, was a bachelor.* usually requires a comma, but that a fall in pitch (as at the end of that sentence) generally requires a stronger stop.

## THE QUESTION MARK

In high school most omissions of needed question marks arise from carelessness. Sometimes, though, a student will use unnecessary question marks as in "I wondered whether I should run?" or "After our warm (?) trek through Maine last December . . ." The first error is caused by unawareness that an indirect question is actually a statement and should be punctuated with a period. The second is perhaps written by the same student who writes "Ha ha" or "Laugh now" after a joke; he is trying to make sure that his irony or humor is not overlooked. Tell him that, although the question mark is sometimes used to indicate uncertainty (Chaucer, Geoffrey, b. 1340?), punctuation should not be necessary to show that the writer is trying to be funny.

## THE EXCLAMATION POINT

One of the least troublesome of punctuation marks is that denoting exclamation. Two cautions, though, must sometimes be given individual students: (1) Despite the practice of comic-strip artists, one exclamation point is sufficient. Two or more of them shout deafeningly in the reader's ear. (2) Like any other device for securing emphasis, exclamation points should not be overused. A long series of exclamatory statements tires the reader; besides, the third or fourth exclamation usually seems less emphatic than the first.

## THE COMMA

The text that the senior class used had a section of 35 or 40 pages devoted to comma uses. Most of the section consisted of rules, exceptions, and illustrations. The volumes used by the other classes contained the same section in abridged and slightly varied form. The then-inexperienced teacher (one of the authors of this book) tried to get his students to master all the rules, but it seemed that when they learned to set off nonrestrictive appositives they forgot transitional words, and when they remembered transitional words they forgot names in direct address. They did not learn much about using commas, even though they did fairly well on a test of the rules (quite unwisely administered). One sophomore wrote, "Use commas to separate members of a series and use them also to set off nonrestrictive elements because those are not really needed and use them between clauses in a compound sentence."

The fault was the teacher's. He did two things that were entirely wrong. In the first place, he falsely assumed that knowing the rules and being able to apply them were synonymous. The result was mere verbalism: the students could parrot the rules but could not punctuate a sentence. In the second place, he taught each rule as an entity. He pointed out no similarities among the rules; indeed, he may not have seen any. Each rule was there in its own little shell.

After that first painfully inadequate teaching, he began to emphasize understanding and using, not parroting. And he gradually learned that most of the multitudinous comma rules may be reduced to three, which can be taught inductively.

What do the following sentences have in common?

Just opposite a tall building was in flames.
To cope with these people must be energetic.

THE TEACHING OF HIGH SCHOOL ENGLISH

Mary Howard was here, but he has gone.
Her crying spell over the girl went home.
If James is sure there can be no mistake.

In each of those sentences, a comma is needed to prevent momentary misreading. Insert commas after *opposite, these, Mary, over,* and *sure.*

*Comma rule number 1:*  *A comma may be used to prevent a possible misreading.* If a sentence is poorly constructed, of course, punctuation alone cannot make it clear.

Now to develop the second comma rule. What characteristic do all these conventionally punctuated sentences share?

Oh, I didn't know that.
The lesson being finished, Sandra was happy.
He insists, I should warn you, that his employees be punctual.
Yes, I agree. No, I don't think so. Well, you may be right.
After that, Mother, we went to a concert.
Helen, above all, is meticulous.
In March, 1982, he announced his candidacy.
Portland, Oregon, has a splendid school system.
"You see," he said, "I was once wealthy."
Dorothy, who is my sister, was at the station.
Dorothy, my sister, was at the station.
These five answers, however, are only partly correct.

In each of those sentences is one element that is not essential. The element may add interesting or relevant information, but it is not really needed. If you read any of the sentences without the part set off by commas, the meaning may be reduced, but it is not changed. For example, *I agree* means the same as *Yes, I agree. Dorothy was at the station* means basically the same thing as *Dorothy, my sister, was at the station.*

*Thus comma rule number 2:*  *A nonessential part of a sentence should be set off with one comma if it comes first or last in the sentence and with two commas if it comes anywhere else.*

You notice that this rule does not make a separate issue of restrictive and nonrestrictive clauses. The term *restrictive* seems never completely clarified for any except the brighter students. Therefore, nonrestrictive clauses may simply be called nonessential clauses. They thus fall into the same category as *however, oh,* words in address, and other nonessential elements. When students write a sentence such as "Henry, who is two years older than I am, led the way," they recognize that the clause is not essential and set it off with commas. When they write a sentence such as "People who lack loyalty are traitors," they see that the clause is needed and, therefore, omit commas. *Needed* is an easier word than *restrictive*.

Now to develop comma rule number 3. What do the following sentences have in common?

The tall, straight soldier entered.

The soldier was tall, straight, and young.

We hunted pheasants in the cornfields, in the patches of long grass, and near the pond.

The old man asked who we were, what we wanted, and why we had knocked on his door.

Helena started to answer the question, but Hermia interrupted her.

Each comma in those sentences separates adjoining ideas that are stated in the same form and that serve the same kind of purpose. In sentence 1, *tall* and *straight* are both adjectives describing the soldier. In 2, *tall, straight,* and *young* are adjectives again modifying *soldier*. Sentence 3 has three adjacent prepositional phrases used as adverbs modifying *hunted*. Sentence 4 contains three noun clauses used as objects of the verb. The last sentence consists of two equal clauses.

**Comma rule 3 might be stated thus:**  *When two or more words or groups of words are similar in form and function, they should be separated by commas.* If students are sufficiently advanced to understand the expression *coordinate elements,* the rule might be stated like this: *Use commas to separate coordinate elements within the sentence.*

There are two corollaries to this rule. One is that, in an *a, b,* and *c* series, the comma before *and* is optional. It seems preferable to have it there, but because many reputable publications omit it, one cannot insist upon it. The chief reason for preferring the comma before *and* is that some sentences may be misread if it is left out. For example, in "Charlotte, Lucille and Alice called today," it is difficult to say whether the sentence means that two persons called or three. A comma after *Lucille* would make it clear that three persons called. A second reason for the preference is that the comma distinguishes a true series from a false one:

That tall, ugly, and unpainted house is my home. (True series; comma before *and.*)

That tall, green and white house is my home. (False series; no comma before *and.*)

The teacher's personal preference, however, should not carry much weight. If students still omit the comma before *and* in a series, they are in the company of many professional editors.

The second corollary is that sometimes words appear to be the same in form and function when they actually are not. For instance, consider *four tall trees.*

THE TEACHING OF HIGH SCHOOL ENGLISH

*Tall* modifies trees, but *four* modifies *tall trees;* it does not tell how many trees there were, but how many tall trees. Similar expressions not requiring commas are *large brick building, the first heavy snowfall,* and *blue silk dress.* Show students two tests to find out whether a comma is needed between modifiers. One is to insert *and* between the modifiers. *Four and tall trees* is almost nonsense; no comma. *Tall and straight soldier* makes sense; therefore a comma. The second test is to invert the order of modifiers. *Brick large building* is un-English; no comma. But *straight, tall soldier* is as good as *tall, straight soldier;* a comma is desirable. Modern linguists, by classing words such as *four* and *first* as determiners, *tall, large, heavy,* and *blue* as adjectives, and *brick* and *silk* as nouns or noun adjuncts, show an accurate grammatical reason for the needed punctuation. Coordinate adjectives (*tall, straight soldier*) are separated by commas, but determiners and adjectives (*four tall trees*) or adjectives and noun adjuncts (*large brick house*) are not.

These three comma rules summarize the multitudinous rules sometimes found in textbooks, except for those dealing with such formalized matters as the punctuation of parts of a letter. They are statements of general principle; they use no difficult terminology. A student need not know 40 definitions or memorize 20 rules.

If the textbook you use does not reduce or group rules similarly, you may still point out that the basic principles apply and that the text shows subdivisions of the big three. So when your sophomores read the rule that a nonrestrictive appositive should be set off by commas, help them to see that in "The Mississippi, the Father of Waters, flows past St. Louis," *the Father of Waters* is just one of the nonessential elements they have been looking at. Students may study the other examples of the nonrestrictive appositive and see that they fall into the same category. They contrast these nonessential words or phrases with "Mark Twain's novel *Huckleberry Finn* is more profound that his *Tom Sawyer*" and note that *Huckleberry Finn* is not set off, because it is essential rather than nonessential; the sentence would lose its meaning without those two words.

The uses of commas and all other punctuation marks may be taught most effectively if the teacher emphasizes (1) that a writer, always having a reader in mind, should ask himself or herself, "How can I punctuate this so that even a stupid or willfully stubborn reader will understand?" (2) that a small number of rules, thoroughly mastered, will be enough to guide the writer to punctuate almost any sentence, and (3) that where legitimate options exist, students are permitted at least the degree of freedom that the editor of a reputable modern magazine would grant them.

## QUOTATION MARKS

Junior high school students readily grasp the fundamentals of using quotation marks but seldom are mature enough to understand and remember the intricacies.

As with any other mark of punctuation, the first step in teaching is to let the students see why quotation marks are used. Trick sentences may be employed to advantage:

The author said the reader was an ignoramus.

"The author," said the reader, "was an ignoramus."

Paragraphs that are confusing until quotation marks are inserted will also be valuable.

Most junior high school students can learn to use a separate paragraph for each speaker, put quotation marks around what each speaker actually says, and indicate the break around such inserted elements as *he said*.

The intricacies such as the punctuation of several paragraphs spoken by the same person and the punctuation of a quotation inside a quotation may best be left until the sophomore year or later, except when a class or some bright students ask questions about such intricacies or show that they have mastered the more fundamental processes. Always it is best to teach technicalities in response to a need felt by the students themselves. For example, the students may be preparing to write a composition that is almost certain to contain considerable dialogue. Before they write, they may be shown what is standard practice in using quotation marks in various situations.

Let your students know that the relative placement of closing quotation marks and other marks of punctuation is simply a matter of convention. Americans have adopted one set of conventions; the British, a different set—just as Americans refer to *truck, hood,* and *gasoline,* whereas the British say *lorry, bonnet,* and *petrol.* We Americans place periods and commas inside closing quotation marks, and colons and semicolons outside. But we let logic, not an arbitrary rule, determine whether the question mark and the exclamation point go inside or outside. The British usually let logic determine all the placements. Examples of American usage follow.

"I agree," she said.

Steinbeck wrote "The Red Pony"; he did not write "The White Rabbit."

He recited a couple of lines from "To a Mouse": "The best laid plans of mice and men / Gang aft agley."

"Who's there?" he asked.

Did he say, "Five more"?

"Watch out!" she shouted.

"What a "conbobberation"!

## THE SEMICOLON

Although many youngsters in junior high school may master the chief use of the semicolon—to separate two rather closely related ideas each expressed in sentence form—usually the tenth grade is the best time to put emphasis on this useful mark, with review and practice as needed in the eleventh and twelfth grades.

Here is an excellent inductive procedure used by one teacher. She asks her students to bring to class six sentences containing semicolons. The sentences are to be taken from contemporary printed material, but not from advertising, poetry, headlines, and the like. Each sentence is to be written or pasted on a 3- by 5-inch card. In class she tells the students that a semicolon is like a "weak period" or a "strong comma." The students examine their sentences to see how the semicolons are employed, discussing them in groups, and copying some of them on the board or the overhead to clarify various points. As a class, they try to formulate their own rules. One class came up with these:

**A.** Use a semicolon when the ideas in sentences are so closely related that a period would make too distinct a break between them. Sometimes the second sentence may contain a word that states the relationship between the two ideas. Typical relationship words: *besides, nevertheless, similarly, also, then, furthermore, instead, however.*

**B.** Use a semicolon between items in a series if the items contain commas, or if they are long and complicated.

**C.** Use a semicolon before the conjunctions *and, but, for, nor,* in a compound sentence if the sentence is long and involved, or if there are other punctuation marks within the sentence, or if you wish to give special emphasis to the last part.

The students' examples on the cards are tacked under A, B, and C on the bulletin board. When one of the students comes up with a sentence that does not appear to follow one of these rules, such as "Broadway has its musical comedies; London its dramas," the class and teacher examine it. They find, for the example given, that the second half is a complete sentence with the verb implied and that it fits under rule A.

The advantage of such a procedure is that it shows students that semicolons are not just things that are studied in school. Their "research" and their active thinking enable them to remember much more than if they just listen to a lecture by the teacher or study a textbook discussion. Textbook practice exercises, or some homemade ones, may clinch the understanding.

One caution is necessary. Some college freshmen who have half-learned the use of the semicolon write, "Although it was raining hard, we decided to leave; since we were already late." Pressed for an explanation, these students say, "In high school, the teacher said that when there was some other punctuation, we should use a semicolon between clauses." The caution, then, is this: Stress the fact that the basic use of the semicolon is to separate clauses that could stand alone as sentences. The clause *since we were already late* cannot. If a sentence has a long and involved series, especially if the elements in the series contain commas, then a semicolon is justified between the elements, as in this example: "We spent spring weekends at Aunt Jane's, either in her town house or at the lake; long summer days with Uncle Judd, who owned a small farm; fall Saturdays, which seemed much less pleasant, at home.'' The semicolon is primarily a mark to be used in compound or complex sentences; simple or complex sentences almost never need it unless a series is involved.

## THE COLON

The colon is not a troublesome mark. In junior high school, its use after the salutation of a business letter should be taught. Mention that this use is only a matter of etiquette; everyone expects it of us. Ninth graders may also learn that a colon is used before a formal list. Tenth graders may learn miscellaneous uses of the colon: before a formal quotation, between biblical chapter and verse, and between hours and minutes (8:24 A.M.). Your brightest seniors can understand how a colon may introduce a follow-up statement for which a preceding independent clause has made the preparation: ''A novelette is not a small novel: it is an art form with characteristics of its own.''

You may want to tell students that the colon is a formal mark of punctuation, that you associate him with white tie and tails, and that he is seldom found in boisterous surroundings. And when someone asks why a semicolon is not half a colon, since *semi-* means half, you may answer that the word *semicolon* is now a misnomer and that in present American usage there is no relationship between the colon and the semicolon, although originally the semicolon was intended to indicate a shorter pause than that shown by the colon.

## THE APOSTROPHE

Perhaps the apostrophe and the hyphen should be treated in our chapter on spelling, because both are spelling devices, used in single words, rather than punctuation marks, which separate parts of sentences. Convention, however, places these marks with punctuation.

After reading a few reams of student themes, you may come to the conclusion that the number of times the apostrophe is omitted just about balances the number of times it is used unnecessarily. If students would only put apostrophes in the right places . . .

Here is what some of them do. They omit apostrophes in possessives, misplace them in contractions, insert them to form possessives of personal pronouns (especially *it's* for *its*), and insert them to form all sorts of plurals. Many of the errors are due to students' carelessness; some may be caused by poor teaching.

The first step is to let students see that apostrophes are too important to be neglected. Have them pronounce these words:

shed   were   wed   shell   well   hell   as   is

Then insert an apostrophe in each word, and have someone pronounce them again:

she'd   we're   we'd   she'll   we'll   he'll   a's   i's

Motivation, all-important motivation, consists often only of letting them see why!

With the students' help, build on the board a rather long list of words in which apostrophes are used to show omission of letters. The words above (except *a's* and *i's*) will be included, and also words like *o'clock* and numbers like *'83* (meaning 1983). Be sure to stress that the apostrophe always goes into the place where the letter or letters were taken out. By such emphasis, you can prevent monstrosities like *were'nt* and *ar'ent*.

Tell your students that the second use of the apostrophe is related to the first. Several hundred years ago some people believed that the proper way to show possession was to use the noun with the pronoun *his*. Instead of writing *Henry's shoes* these people wrote *Henry his shoes;* similarly, they wrote *the king his crown,* and so on. When they pronounced *Henry his shoes* rapidly, however, the *hi* could hardly be heard (let the class try it); the result sounded like *Henrys shoes. The king his crown* sounded like *the kings crown.* Here they ran into difficulty, because *kings* might mean two kings, or it might indicate possession. Someone then got the idea of using a little mark to show that the *hi* had (supposedly) been left out. In that way our form for the possessive originated.

It seems best to teach possessives by having students write the words in phrases—*a king's crown, a woman's hat, Edward's watch,* and so on. Doing so may prevent the tendency to use the apostrophe in such a sentence as "Two kings fought for the crown." It is also best to be sure that students master singular possessives before they go on to plural possessives. Many a ninth grader has been confused because he was told about *kings' subjects* before he had really learned *king's subjects.*

In teaching plural possessives, teachers have found the following procedure successful. Start with simple plurals. Ask the students to spell the plurals of such words as *dog, raven, lady.* Put these in one column, and for a second column have students spell the plurals of irregular nouns such as *man, woman, ox.* (With advanced classes, words such as *sister-in-law* and *alumnus* may be included.) Then, after each plural noun write, with class help, the name of something that noun might possess, as *dogs tails.* Ask the students how the possession could be made clear. Someone in the class will say that an apostrophe should be used after the *s* in *dogs.* Go down the first column, inserting an apostrophe after each final *s.* Have the students copy the list of phrases in their notebooks, because the act of writing will tend to make the principle stick.

Then turn to the second column. The problem is different here, because these plurals (*men,* etc.) do not end in *s.* Show the students that these irregular plural possessives are formed by adding an apostrophe and *s*. Have them copy the second list.

The next day, dictate a number of phrases from both lists, and add a few others for additional practice. Repeat a few days later, and repeat after that until perfection has been attained. Vary the phrases sufficiently that rote memory will not suffice; it is the application of the principle, not memory of a few phrases, that you want. Students who make two perfect scores in succession may be excused from later drills.

Possessives of words like *Jones* cause particular trouble. Unless a student asks the question, probably Mr. Jones should be ignored until you are confident most of the class can handle him. When he finally demands your attention, tell the class that *Jones* (*Dickens, Burns*) is a regular noun; let them use *Jones's* as the singular possessive, just as they would write *Smith's*. (Actually either *Jones'* or *Jones's* is standard; what you want to avoid is *Jone's*.) The plural may also be taught as a regular plural, like *churches*. If your students learn to write *the Joneses' automobiles*, you have done a good job of teaching this matter.

Many students write *her's, your's, our's, their's*, by analogy with *dog's*, etc. Some teachers, after their students have made such an error, review the forms of personal pronouns, stressing that *hers, yours, ours*, and *theirs* are personal pronouns. "No personal pronoun," they say, "ever takes an apostrophe. Nobody would write *m'y* for *my*, or *hi's* for *his*. There is no more reason for apostrophes in any other personal pronoun." The same reasoning applies to the possessive *its*, although that word is used as a possessive adjective rather than as a pronoun. A simple injunction: "Never write *it's* unless you can substitute *it is* or *it has;* the possessive form is always *its*."

## THE HYPHEN

Show your students that the hyphen at the end of a line prevents misreading in such a sentence as this:

> . . . He climbed up the flag
staff.

Let them also see that there is a reason for the hyphen in compound numbers. Call their attention to the sentence already cited: "She brought thirty five dollar bills." Help them to see that the placement of the hyphen makes a difference of $115.

Encourage the use of the dictionary when students must divide a word at the end of the line, but teach a few basic principles of syllabication to reduce the need for the dictionary. Show students that failure to divide between syllables sometimes leads to impossible or ridiculous pronunciations: flagst-aff, packthread, thoro-ugh. Show them that ordinarily their own ears can tell them where the division should be.

Concerning the hyphenation of compound adjectives and nouns, you will need to explain that the practice changes with time. When Dr. Naismith invented his game, he called it *basket ball* because players threw a ball into a peach basket. As the game became better known, the two words were felt to be closely associated, and were written with a hyphen. Today we consider the words as a unit—*basketball*. The same thing has happened to *football* and *baseball*. That is, a word may be written as two words in one period of time and with a hyphen in another; it may be written with a hyphen in one decade and solid in another. Advise students to refer to the dictionary when they are in doubt about whether a compound noun should be hyphenated (although dictionaries sometimes do not agree).

Let them see that words linked together to form single adjectives need to be hyphenated except when the dictionary indicates that they are written solid. Call to their attention the difference between *the strange looking glass* (a mirror) and *the strange-looking glass,* between *the man made mistakes* and *the man-made mistakes,* and between *the woman eating tiger* and *the woman-eating tiger.* Dictate a few expressions such as *a never-to-be-forgotten moment, an old-time dance, a quick-as-a-flash retort.*

## PARENTHESES

Parentheses are used, especially in rather formal writing, to show the insertion of material that has no structural relation to the rest of the sentence. Teach inductively, using numerous examples. For instance,

I am enclosing a check for five dollars and twenty-seven cents ($5.27).
These questions (page 47) remain unanswered.
William Shakespeare (1564–1616)
His reply (it was delivered in a speech in New Haven) aroused much controversy.

College teachers are sometimes rightfully distressed because somebody, somewhere, has taught students to enclose in parentheses words or groups of words that are to be disregarded. Material in parentheses is *not* disregarded. If a student wants to show that something should be omitted, he or she should neatly draw a line through it.

## THE DASH

Dashes are useful in writing that is not very formal and are occasionally found even in formal writing. The teacher must not advocate frequent use of dashes, though, or some student may become a dashomaniac. The dash is not an all-purpose mark.

Its chief use is to indicate an abrupt break in thought or construction. For example,

When I was—there's a skunk, George!
This machine—another one like it is over there—is a router.

It may be used to indicate hesitation:

I—I doubt it.

Finally, the dash may set off an introductory appositive or an appositive loosely attached at the end of a sentence:

Sympathy and willingness to make haste slowly—these are two requisites for any teacher.
He did possess something that was superior—his teeth.

Have students use two short marks or one rather long mark for a dash, to distinguish it from a hyphen. In typing they may use two hyphens, because the standard typewriter keyboard has no dash. (Some commercial schools, however, teach the use of space-hyphen-space for a dash.)

The dash is not a very important mark of punctuation. If most of your students do not know the more useful marks, do not spend time on the dash, except possibly to explain its use to your more capable students.

## BRACKETS

If your seniors write a research paper, they may need to know about brackets. These marks have a very limited use. They are not alternative forms of parentheses. Brackets are used primarily to enclose one's personal comments or corrections when one is quoting from someone else:

The senator continued: "Our state is now a national leader in the production of coal. [Applause] We now . . ."
"When Rhodes died in 1901 [actually 1902], he left six million pounds to the public."

A second use, very rare, is to represent parentheses within parentheses:

The new state (the boundaries of which [see map, p. 647] had recently been ratified) still had no constitution.

## ITALICS (UNDERLINING)

It is conventional to underline titles of books, magazines, newspapers, plays, and motion pictures, and to place quotation marks around titles of short stories, poems, and other short pieces. Nearly all your students can learn this convention quickly.

The other uses of underlining (italics) are less important; some, indeed, such

THE TEACHING OF HIGH SCHOOL ENGLISH

as underlining the names of ships, trains, airplanes, and the almost defunct pullman cars, seem on the way to the discard pile.

The use of underlining to indicate a word referred to as a word or a letter or number referred to as a letter or number is still common and useful. "She left an o out of sophomore" may be slightly more clear than "She left an o out of sophomore." "He said that the when was misplaced" is easier to read than "He said that the when was misplaced." (An alternative is to put quotation marks around the word, letter, or number, but this practice sometimes leads to rather cluttered-looking pages.)

Caution is necessary in teaching the use of underlining for emphasis. Too many students make a vice of underlining. Some seem to reason that if one underscore creates emphasis, two should create more. In the paper of one student some words were underlined five times, and an applicant for a secretarial position once double-lined every sentence in her letter of application because she wanted the letter to be emphatic. (She did not get the job.)

Some students like to know the relationship between underlining and typesetting. When a printer sets copy, he or she will set in italic type anything underlined once, in small caps anything underlined twice, in capitals anything underlined three times, and in boldface anything underlined with a wavy line.

## CAPITALIZATION

As remarked earlier, capitalization is closely related to punctuation. It is a signal to the reader, just as a punctuation mark is. It tells the reader, "Here is the beginning of a new sentence, or here is a proper noun or something comparable to a proper noun, or here is some kind of title."

The seventh grader will usually know that he or she needs a capital to start a sentence, to indicate the pronoun *I,* and to designate names of persons and places. Beyond these things, his or her knowledge of capitals will probably be sketchy. Many children use too many capitals rather than too few: some high school compositions have a slightly German look because so many nouns are capitalized.

A week spent on capitalization in any grade is likely to be three days wasted. A few of the principles will stick, but because there are 20 or more capitalization rules, many will be forgotten. A better technique is to take up individual questions as they arise and spend class time only on common problems.

For example, suppose that the students are going to write papers dealing with athletics in their school. The teacher will anticipate the kinds of capitalization they will need and discuss the matter with the class. The composition will have a title. Which words do we capitalize in titles? There will be a reference to this high school and perhaps to other schools. When do we write *High School* and when *high school?* Teacher and class will provide illustrations, and the principles are more likely to be remembered because they are presented when the students feel a need for them.

Similarly, when one writes a letter, one usually refers to one's relatives. So, before the students write letters, they talk over the question of when we capitalize *Mother, Aunt,* and so on, and when we do not.

The capitalization errors most frequently made by students are in names of relatives, seasons, directions, and school subjects. To the young student, capitalization looks hit and miss (and, to be truthful, it is not completely standardized). Sometimes people do capitalize *Uncle, South,* and *Algebra,* and sometimes they do not; but whichever students choose, they are wrong, it seems. Poets get by with capitalizing *Winter,* but Miss Demeanor tells students not to do so. The apparent contradictions do not make sense.

Why are *Uncle, South,* and *Algebra* capitalized part of the time? There is the key: Why? Consider these sentences:

But I haven't any money, James.
But I haven't any money, Uncle.

He lives in Alabama.
He lives in the South.

I am taking Algebra 1.
My brother took two years of algebra.

In the first pair of sentences, *Uncle* is used as a proper noun, the equivalent of *James.* In the second, *South* is a proper name, including Alabama and other states. In the last pair, *Algebra 1* is also a proper name; it does not refer to algebra in general but to this particular algebra course.

But sometimes these words are not used as proper names:

My uncle came for a visit.
We walked south two blocks.
He enjoys studying algebra.

In these sentences *uncle, south,* and *algebra* are not the names of specific people or things. That can be proved, at least in the first two, by trying to substitute a proper name. Most persons would not write:

My James came for a visit.
We walked Alabama two blocks.

Let them see why! If one teaching technique is of greater importance than any other, it is probably that one—let them see why.

# THE IDEA BOX

IMPORTANCE OF PUNCTUATION

1. Legend has it that the Czarina of Russia saw on the desk of Alexander III a note: "Pardon impossible; to be sent to Siberia." She changed the punctuation: "Pardon; impossible to be sent to Siberia."

2. As a motivating device, occasionally write a tricky sentence for students to punctuate. For example, write without punctuation or capitals, "Bill, where Henry had had 'had,' had had 'had had,' 'Had had' had had the examiner's approval." Or, "That that is, is; that that is not, is not. Is not that it? It is."

3. Here are some favorite examples and a few new ones, showing how punctuation may affect meaning:

Woman! Without her, man would be a savage.
Woman without her man would be a savage.

Louise thinks her employer is attractive.
Louise, thinks her employer, is attractive.

Mr. Rice, the superintendent came in.
Mr. Rice, the superintendent, came in.

"Bill," called Ralph, "Come here!"
Bill called, "Ralph, come here!"

The tight-rope walker almost fell.
The tight rope-walker almost fell.

The net was made of four wire cables.
The net was made of four-wire cables.

She is there now.
She is there now!
She is there now?

No man can be happy.
No. Man can be happy.

... this long, powerful snake ...
... this long-powerful snake ...

The following make sense if properly punctuated:
The Indian Toti went off by himself to eat the rattlesnakes and the lizards squirming uneasily in the fragile box at my elbow spoiled my appetite.
Lord Wellington entered on his head a helmet on his feet a pair of well polished boots on his brow a cloud in his hand his favorite walking stick in his eye fire
The fight over the boys came home
While I was dressing my little brother came in

**4.** In *Ralph Roister Doister* (*ca.* 1553) Ralph had a scrivener pen this epistle to the wealthy woman he was courting:

> Sweete mistresse, where as I love you, nothing at all
> Regarding your substance and richnesse; chiefe of all
> For your personage, beautie, demeanour, and wit
> I commende me unto you: Never a whitte
> Sorie to heare reporte of your good welfare.

His false friend, Merygreek, transmitted the message like this:

> Sweete mistresse, where as I love you nothing at all,
> Regarding your substance and richnesse chiefe of all,
> For your personage, beautie, demeanour, and wit,
> I commende me unto you never a whitte.
> Sorie to heare reporte of your good welfare.

**5.** Encourage your students to collect sentences in which mispunctuation would cause comic misreading.

## IT WORKS IN CASA ROBLE

Teachers in Casa Roble High School, Orangeville, California, use catchy titles for the Learning Packages (short individualized units) they have developed to teach various concepts. For example,

> I'll Make Him Belong to You (apostrophe)
> Make Me Make Sense (comma)
> How to Make Words Talk (quotation marks)
> Using Stop Signs in Writing
> Speling Right Maks Better Sence

## "PUNCTUATION FOR THE READER—A TEACHING APPROACH"

Paula Backschneider of Purdue recommends an inductive approach in which students analyze the uses of the various marks and, as a class, formulate in their own words a set of punctuation rules. (Different classes, obviously, may not group or express the rules in exactly the same way.)[1]

## THE TEACHER VERSUS THE PRO

"If [a] student reads very much today, he knows that writers seem to commit [the comma splice]. What is he to think? Who is right? His teacher, who very likely writes less than he does himself? Or this guy who has a book on the market? I just finished reading C. P. Snow's *Last Things*. Some English teachers I know would have 'failed' that book for its comma splices alone."[2]

## "PUNCTUATING THE COMPOUND SENTENCE"

J. C. Gray teaches this formula: ; = (, + cc). (The cc means coordinating conjunction.)[3]

## INTELLIGENCE AND PUNCTUATION

Although it can hardly be argued that poor punctuation and poor capitalization are signs of intelligence, mere eyeballing will show that many bright students attempt structures (such as complicated sentences or long conversations) that leave them open to more likelihood of error than do simple statements such as "I saw a woodpecker." Perhaps this fact suggests the folly of simply counting errors in determining a grade. A student cannot fairly be penalized for a mistake in a construction not yet studied or one that he or she attempts while trying to stretch beyond present capacity.

## BULLETIN BOARD REMINDERS

In some classes, part of the bulletin board or chalkboard is reserved for reference purposes. Principles of punctuation or other frequently needed principles may be posted there as convenient reminders to students.

## DISTRIBUTING PUNCTUATION MARKS

Some teachers in junior high school occasionally pass out sentences with all necessary punctuation marks at the end. Students put the marks where they belong.

## ELIMINATING "SIAMESE SENTENCES"

Experienced teachers know that the comma splice is often caused by a student's failure to supply the word necessary to relate the meanings of the two clauses. For example, "He breathed rapidly, he was nervous" needs a *because*. Spend some time in examining such connectives in various contexts. Not only punctuation but also sentence structure may benefit.

## PUNCTUATION IN BUSINESS LETTERS

Madeleine Sparks, in Westbury, New York, had her business seniors study punctuation in real business letters, analyzing the reason for each mark and checking their analyses against textbook rules. In groups of five, the students presented their findings to the class.[4]

## PUNCTUATION CHART

Here is a convenient summary of the most widely followed punctuation practices. You may want to prepare and post a chart based on it or to duplicate copies for individuals to refer to. (Permission is hereby granted.) The amount of grammatical terminology has purposely been kept small.

# A Simple Guide to Basic Punctuation

| Pattern | Usual Punctuation | Example |
|---|---|---|
| 1. A statement | Period at end | He went home. |
| 2. A question | Question mark at end | Did he go home? |
| 3. An exclamation | Exclamation mark at end | Run for your lives! |
| 4. Any construction that may be misread without punctuation | Usually a comma | To overcome this, work is essential. |
| 5. A series of grammatically equal items | Usually a comma or commas | (a) She writes novels, plays, and poems. (b) ... a scrawny, underfed kitten |
| 6. Two complete statements connected by *and, but, for, or, nor, yet, so* | Usually a comma, sometimes a semicolon if there is much other internal punctuation | (a) Man proposes, but God disposes. (b) Although the day was cold, she felt warm, cheerful, and optimistic; but Harvey, who walked with her, was grouchy. |
| 7. Two complete statements not connected by *and, but, for, or, nor, yet, so* | If written as one sentence, a semicolon between the statements | The squirrel scurried along the ice-coated wire; beneath it ran a dog, barking hopefully. |
| 8. Introductory clause (not used as the subject) followed by a complete statement | Usually a comma after the clause; now tending increasingly to be omitted | While she played the organ, he washed the dishes. |
| 9. At beginning of a sentence, words not necessary to basic meaning | Usually followed by a comma | Well, I can find time if I must. |
| 10. Within a sentence, words not necessary to basic meaning | Usually a comma on each side; less often dashes, parentheses, or brackets | My father, who objected to cigar smoke, thought that a bit of snuff was all right. |
| 11. At end of a sentence, words not necessary to basic meaning | Usually preceded by a comma | He made a poor impression on my father, who objected to cigar smoke. |

THE TEACHING OF HIGH SCHOOL ENGLISH

| 12. | After such words as *as follows* | Usually a colon | He ordered the following merchandise: two condensers, three dozen spark plugs . . . |
| 13. | With quoted words | Double quotation marks around the exact words quoted | Helen exclaimed, "He was never in Ithaca!" |
| 14. | Preceding a quotation | Usually a comma | (See 13 and 15.) |
| 15. | Quotation within a quotation | Single quotation marks | Bert asked, "Who said, 'Whatever is, is right'?" |
| 16. | Titles of short literary works, etc. | Quotation marks | Poe's "The Raven" |
| 17. | Titles of books, plays; names of magazines, newspapers | Underlining | *Roots; Newsweek; The Chicago Tribune* |

## FOOTNOTES

1. English 1. *English Journal* 61, Sept. 1972, p. 874.
2. Don Stoen, "Stuttering Pencils," *English Journal* 65, Nov. 1976, p. 40.
3. *English Journal* 51, Nov. 1962, p. 573.
4. "A Practical Approach to Punctuation," *English Journal* 42, March 1953, p. 158.

# 12

## SPELLING

## MOTIVATION FOR SPELLING

You have heard the saying that one should be careful in deciding what one wants, because one is likely to get it. If students decide that they really want to learn to spell, they are likely to learn to spell, unless there are severe mental, emotional, or physical problems.

Here are several suggestions for motivation. None is infallible, but one will work with some students, another with others. A combination of the six should effect a wholesome desire to improve and to continue improving.

## BUILDING AN INTEREST IN WORDS

Help students to see that words are like people. Words have personalities—drab, shy, colorful, scary.... Like people, too, they often belong to families: the Ables and the Ibles, the Pres and the Pers, the Graphs, the Meters, and so on. The English language has been a melting pot for words as America has been a melting pot for people; just as it is sometimes interesting to find out a person's ancestry, so it is often interesting and informative to discover the ancestry of a word.

An explanation of some of our odd-looking spellings can itself be motivational. For example, *colonel* goes back to an Italian *colonello* ''a column of soldiers'' such as the officer might lead, but the French, from whom we borrowed the word, stuck an /r/ into the pronunciation, at least for a time, and at one time spelled the word *coronel*. Our *aisle* was sensibly spelled *ile* in Middle English, but scholars traced it back to French *aile* and Latin *ala* and recommended that it be spelled with an *a* to show its heritage; the *s* got in by confusion with *isle*.

See Chapter 9 for further discussion of building interest in words.

## DEMONSTRATING WHY SPELLING HAS BECOME LARGELY STANDARDIZED

Have each of your students write three or four sentences on any subject. Tell them to spell all the words in any way they wish—no holds barred. The more original the spelling the better. Write something like this as an example:

Hwenn thuh Inngglissh lannggwidge wuzz jungrr, itt wuzz vehree dyfruhnt phrumn thuh lannggwidge ovv 2da.

Have students exchange papers and try to read what their classmates have written. The time will not be wasted, for they will prove to their own satisfaction that, if each person spelled to suit himself or herself, confusion and loss of effort would result.

## EMPLOYERS' ATTITUDES TOWARD SPELLING

Ask your classes why, in their opinion, employers prefer employees who can spell. If you can collect (or, better, have your students collect) a few testimonials from local businesses and industries, your hand can be further strengthened.

## MAKING CORRECT SPELLING A CHALLENGE

Unless students are determined to learn to spell, they will not do so. For some students the greatest challenge may come from awareness that bad spelling may cause failure at a job or in college. (Some evidence suggests that the greatest weakness of students placed in remedial English is poor spelling; at least it is generally the most noticeable.) For other students the challenge may be to pride: "You aren't going to let 26 little letters get you down, are you?" One teacher made a friendly wager with a class, betting that the class could not make an average score of 95 percent on a semester test. At stake were some special (and legitimate) privileges that the class wanted. The poor spellers were so much hounded and helped by their classmates that the average was 98 percent.

## CONTINUING MOTIVATION BY PRAISING IMPROVEMENT

Graphs or charts to show individual improvement are often motivational. Praise of the student who has just overcome the habit of confusing *their, there,* and *they're* is pedagogically sound, even though he or she still misspells a dozen words in one paper. To tell a class that it is improving in its spelling brings better results than to say, "Your spelling is worse than that of any other class I've ever taught."

## "THEIR OWN ACTUAL SPELLING PROBLEMS"

R. Baird Shuman reported an unusual technique followed by one of his student teachers in a writing class:

> *My intern declared a moratorium on penalties for misspelling. He told his students that they should never fail to use a word simply because they were not sure how to spell it, nor should they interrupt the flow of their writing to go to the dictionary and look the word up. Rather, they should circle any words which they were unsure of. If they had spelled the word correctly, the teacher put a check mark above it. If they had spelled it incorrectly, he wrote in the correct spelling and urged the student to learn the spelling.*
>
> *The result of this experiment was that students began to concentrate on their own very actual spelling problems rather than on hypothetical ones, and soon their spelling improved. Also, their vocabulary range increased because the students now had no reason to avoid using a word which they could not spell with any assurance.*[1]

## SELECTING THE WORDS TO BE TAUGHT

Word counts have revealed that about 1000 words constitute the basic vocabulary of English. Many of these are used over and over: *a, an, the, you, of, with,* and so on. If one were to take random passages of English writing totaling 100,000 words, one would find that about 90,000 of the words were these basic 1000 employed again and again. Some 4000 words account for about 95 percent of everything written in English.

Common sense, then, dictates that these relatively few words are the ones everyone should know how to spell. The spelling bee of great grandfather's day placed stress instead upon long, difficult, and seldom-used words. Sometimes students learned the orthography of words they could not define or use. Today we emphasize spelling for use. Because few students will ever have occasion to write *dysgenic,* that word is not taught, but because all will probably need to write *coming, certain,* and *choose,* these are taught.

However, of the 1000 to 4000 most common words, not all cause spelling problems, at least for most high school students. Words such as *with, sand, window,* and *understand* are not misspelled by many students except through rank carelessness. It is wasteful to spend time on words already mastered. Some of the frequently employed words, though, do cause trouble. These are the "demon" words, such as *than, forty, existence,* and *recommend.* For instance, a group of 25 students who had just graduated from high school, in writing that totaled about 110,000 words, misspelled 291. The only words misspelled by more than one student were *already* (2), *believe* (2), *convenience* (2), *doesn't* (3), *evidently* (2), *immensely* (2), *incidentally* (2), *indispensable* (2), *its* (5), *it's* (3), *nuisance* (2), *occasionally* (2), *preceding* (2), *receive* (3), *review* (2), *similar* (2), *strenuous* (2), *than* (4), *their* (4), *then* (2), *there* (3), *too* (9), *truly* (2), *woman* (2), and *writing* (2). For this particular group, then, 25 words accounted for almost a fourth of the errors. Mastery of a relatively small number of demons—100 or 200—may reasonably be expected to reduce spelling mistakes by a third to a half.

No two lists of demons are exactly alike. The 417 words in one list, compiled by Thomas C. Pollock, were found to account for 52.4 percent of spelling errors of college students.[2] Another list, prepared by Fred C. Ayer, is a composite based on 12 spelling books.[3]

Instead of dividing any list randomly or alphabetically, a wise teacher may select only the words actually misspelled by his or her own students, or, with a class that needs considerable help, will teach together groups of words that have something in common. Here are some of the possible groups:

1. Words with two pairs of double letters: *accommodate, address, aggressive, balloon, commission, committed, committee* (a rare three-pair word), *embarrass,* etc.
2. *ie* and *ei* words: *achieve, conceit, belief,* etc.
3. Words ending with *-ance, -ant: attendance, attendant, significance, significant,* etc.
4. Words in which a consonant is doubled before a suffix: *beginner, preferred, occurred,* etc.
5. Words in which silent *e* is retained before a suffix: *arrangement, changeable, careful,* etc.
6. Words ending with *-ence, -ent: adolescence, adolescent,* etc.
7. Words in which *a* is used in an unaccented syllable (representing the sound of schwa): *boundary, separate,* etc. (Other words, in which e, i, o, u, or *y* is used in such a syllable, would be treated in other lessons.)
8. Plurals of *-ey* words: *alleys, monkeys, volleys,* etc.
9. Homonyms or near-homonyms: *complement, compliment; advice, advise;* etc.
10. Words ending in *-ar: calendar, grammar, dollar,* etc.
11. Words in which *y* is changed to *ie: allies, ladies, babies,* etc.
12. Words in which a nonstandard pronunciation may cause a spelling problem: *amount, athlete, especially,* etc.
13. Keeping a *y* before an *-ing: carrying, studying, hurrying,* etc.
14. Words in which a silent *e* is dropped before a suffix: *arousing, giving, losing,* etc.
15. Words ending in *-or: author, actor, doctor,* etc.

The theory behind grouping is that the speller learns to associate words that belong together. Thus, most -*ance* words also have forms in -*ant,* and if a group of such words is learned at one time, one is more likely to remember them because of the association. But (and this is important) the -*ence* and -*ent* words should not be taught in the same lesson as the -*ance* and -*ant* words or even soon afterward, because doing so will completely confuse and defeat the association. Similarly, if *ar* words are taught this week, the *or* and *er* endings should be deferred to other times.

Perhaps the biggest single problem in English spelling involves the vowel in an unaccented syllable. There is nothing in the sound to show, for instance, what the fourth letter of *separate* is, or the fifth letter of *specimen.* The vowels *a, e, i, o,* and *u,* and sometimes *y* and various combinations such as *ia* or *ai* are all used in such places, and no workable rule exists to tell us which we need. Several hundred common words pose this problem. Grouping is the best solution, although not a foolproof one. Teach the *a* words in September, say, the *e* words in November, and so on. An occasional mnemonic device (e.g., there's *a rat* in *separate*) may help some students, but one can hardly concoct and remember a different device for each such word.

The doubling or not doubling of consonants causes other problems. Note that in some words (*commission, possess*) there are two doublets; in some (*occasion, imminent*) a doublet occurs early in the word and nowhere else; and in some (*necessary, parallel*) the only doublet occurs farther on in the word. Words in these three categories may be taught as separate groups.

Some words are not readily groupable. They are unique or almost so in the difficulties they offer: *psychology, pneumonia,* and *ecstasy,* for example. Students should be told frankly that these words must be learned individually, although an occasional student may note a resemblance to a less common word, such as *pneumatic.*

## CLASS PROCEDURES

Although learning the spelling of a word is in the last analysis the result of individual effort, some group instruction may make that effort easier. In this section we shall look at what the teacher and class can do together; in the next, at what the student needs to be encouraged to do alone.

### PHONETICS

You may have some students who do not know the usual sounds of letters. Although today's reading instruction in the elementary schools typically combines phonic and other approaches, there are still some schools in which students never learn to "sound out" words. A study made in Indiana revealed that students who have never learned phonetics have about a 50 percent greater chance of being retarded in spelling than those who have received such instruction. Students who lack knowledge of common sounds are likely to write some such curiosities as *brapoly* for *probably* or *furtst* for *forest*.

If your students need such training, spend a few minutes a day for several weeks with simple one-syllable words, grouping them as the "at" family (*bat, cat, scat,* etc.), the "it" family, the "and" family, and so on. Give additional drill on the usual sounds of consonants, employing both real and nonsense words such as *bib, bob, bab, beb, bub.* Move on to simple combinations such as *batboy, hotrod,* and so on. Teach the blends: *sl, sp, st, ch, sh,* and the like. Next may come some clarification of the effects of a final *e* or of a doubled letter, as in *fad* and *fade, hug* and *huge, hoping* and *hopping.* All this is elementary work and is not very helpful with unphonetic spellings such as *thought* and *sergeant,* but it does prevent some of the more ridiculous misspellings.

One huge study conducted at Stanford University (the final report is 1716 pages long!) has elaborated greatly on what has just been said, and is resulting in improved practices in teaching spelling. The researchers summarize their results in this way:

> *A modern spelling program is possible today as a result of new research both in linguistics and in teaching-learning theories. Such a modern spelling program will (1) start from the child's possession of a large aural-oral vocabulary; (2) teach him how to break these words into component sounds; (3) lead him to discover the correspondences between the phonemes and the alphabetical letters that have come to represent these sounds in standard American-English spelling; (4) help him to discover the influences that position, stress, and environment have in the choice of grapheme from among the several options; (5) guide him to go beyond the phonological analysis to examine the morphological elements such as compounding, affixation, or word families; (6) teach him how to use all his sensorimotor equipment of ear-voice-eye-hand to reinforce each other in fixing the standard spelling in his neural system; and (7) help him to build a cognitive-based spelling power that should make possible a writing vocabulary "unlimited" or limited only by the size of his spoken vocabulary.*[4]

## PRONUNCIATION

Slovenly or otherwise inaccurate pronunciation may lead to misspelling. Class drill on frequently mispronounced words such as those in the following list may eliminate a few spelling errors:

accidentally (Note AL)
Arctic (two C's)

athlete (two syllables)
attacked (two syllables)
barbarous (No I)
cavalry (CAV)
diphtheria (note PH)
diphthong (note PH)
drowned (one syllable)
February (two R's)
film (one syllable)
government (GoverN)
jewelry (not joolery)
laboratory (LABOR)
mischievous (three syllables)
perform (PER)
perspiration (PER)
probably (three syllables)
relevant (REL)
remembrance (lost E)
sacrilegious (Cf. sacrilege)
surprise (two R's)
temperature (TempER)
tragedy (not tradegy)

## GROUPING OF WORDS

Grouping was discussed earlier in the chapter. Here are some added examples:

| | | | | |
|---|---|---|---|---|
| define | imagine | sincerely | perform | smooth |
| definite | imaginable | merely | perforate | booth |
| definition | imaginary | severely | perspective | loose |
| definitive | imagination | | pertinent | |
| | imaginative | prove | | |
| | image | move | already | |
| | | lose | altogether | |
| | | | almost | |

## MNEMONIC DEVICES AND GAMES

Associational devices in limited numbers may be helpful, but too many of them create more confusion than they dispel. The teacher may suggest to Tommy, who can never remember how to spell *grammar,* that *Ma* is in the last syllable. The school *principal* is one's *pal,* but a princi*ple* is a ru*le.* Do you *believe* that there is a *lie* in *believe?*

Games may occasionally be used for teaching spelling, but when they are, they should be regarded just as educational fun and not as serious competition for grades. The old-fashioned spelling bee has little value except for good spellers, for the others do not participate after a word or two. One variation of it, which partially overcomes objection, is to have two teams standing. As soon as a player spells a word (or two words) correctly, he or she may sit down. When one team has only three (or five) standing, it wins. Another variation is to have everyone remain in the game, a point being given a team for each correct spelling. Words that someone has missed may be reintroduced later in the session, with two points awarded for the right spelling.

## PREFIXES AND SUFFIXES

The spelling of words to which affixes are attached puzzles students rather often, giving them trouble especially in deciding whether or not to double a letter. Exercises like this are valuable:

| | | |
|---|---|---|
| *diS* | + *agree* | = *diSagree* |
| *diS* | + *appoint* | = *diSappoint* |
| *diS* | + *Satisfied* | = *diSSatisfied* |
| *smooth* | + *Ness* | = *smoothNess* |
| *drunkeN* | + *Ness* | = *drunkeNNess* |
| *suddeN* | + *Ness* | = *suddeNNess* |
| *finaL* | + *Ly* | = *finaLLy* |
| *principaL* | + *Ly* | = *principaLLy* |

## INDUCTIVE TEACHING OF RULES

The value of spelling rules has been warmly denied and hotly defended. In the nineteenth century, some textbooks contained dozens of rules with hundreds of illustrations and scores of exceptions. At present, the consensus is that only a few rules are worth teaching and that those should be taught inductively.

Here is an illustration of teaching a rule inductively. The teacher writes on the board *hate, name, arrange, fate,* and *like.* He or she asks what all of these words have in common and gets the answer that each ends in silent *e.* Then the students are asked to spell *hateful, namely, arrangement, fateful,* and *likeness.* The teacher writes these words opposite the first list, underlining the suffixes. "What would happen if we didn't keep the *e* in *hateful?*" The students explain that the *e* prevents confusion between *hateful* and *hatful* and between *fateful* and *fatful* and that one would tend to mispronounce *arrangement* if the *e* were not there. The teacher wonders aloud whether the suffixes have anything in common and is told that each begins with a consonant. He or she calls for other words ending in silent *e;* the students find suffixes to add to words like *state, late, white,* and so on, but notice that other words such as *dice, while,* and *please* do not take suffixes beginning with consonants.

At this point the teacher may pause to have the class formulate a rule which says that, when a suffix beginning with a consonant is added to a word ending in silent *e,* the *e* is retained. He or she, however, may first go back to the original list and ask the class to spell *hating, naming, arranging, fatal,* and *likable,* writing these words in a third column. Here is something new, because the *e* has been dropped. A little judicious questioning reveals that the distinction between these words and the ones in the second column exists because here the suffix begins with a vowel. The teacher comments that there is a good reason for dropping the *e,* for if one saw such a word as *fateal,* one might have trouble pronouncing it. More illustrations and then on to the formulation of a rule something like this: In adding a suffix to a word ending in silent *e,* retain the *e* if the suffix begins with a consonant, but drop the *e* if the suffix begins with a vowel. (Any testing, however, should be on actually spelling words, not on restating a memorized rule.)

One more step remains—mentioning the most important exceptions. On the board the teacher writes *singe* and tells the class that, for a good reason, this word is an exception. He or she writes *singeing* and lets the class see that the *e* is retained here before a vowel. "Why?" Immediately someone sees that *singing* would be confusing. The teacher refers to *shoeing* and *hoeing,* commenting that *shoing* and *hoing* would look like names of Chinese provinces. He or she may mention a few other exceptions, such as *dyeing, courageous, noticeable,* and *judgment* (although *judgement* is a common variant).

Later practice does not involve the restating of the rule except to verify a spelling. At subsequent class meetings, though, the teacher does give much practice in adding suffixes to many words ending in silent *e.* Without such practice, the rule will have little value.

Four other rules are of particular worth. They may be taught inductively, several weeks apart, by following procedures similar to the one just described. These are the rules:

**1.** Words of one syllable ending in a single consonant preceded by a single vowel double the final consonant before a suffix beginning with a vowel (*lag, lagging; plan, planned*).

**2.** Words of more than one syllable ending in a final consonant preceded by a single vowel double the final consonant before a suffix beginning with a vowel, if the syllable preceding the suffix is accented (*occur, occurred; prefer, preferring; repel, repellent;* but *travel, traveled, traveling; preference*).

**3.** Final *y* preceded by a consonant changes to *ie* before an *s* or a *d* (*army,* armies; *fly, flies; ally, allies, allied;* but *turkey, turkeys; attorney, attorneys*—because a vowel precedes the *y*).

4. In the *ei, ie* combinations pronounced *e* as in *feel, i* comes before *e* except after *c* (*believe, receive*). The most common exceptions are contained in this sentence: "Neither leisurely financier seized either weird species."

## TEACHING FROM LISTS

In the junior high years some teachers devote part of each class period to spelling. The most common pattern involves a weekly list of about 20 words. On Monday a pretest is given, and students immediately study the words they missed. (If they miss none, they are excused from spelling for the week.) On Tuesday they once more study for a few minutes the words they missed; Wednesday brings another test and more study; Thursday, more study; and Friday, a final test and study of any words still missed. The strong points of this procedure are that the test-study plan has been proved efficient and that each student works on only the words that he or she misses. Its weaknesses are those inherent in any plan in which the teacher uses the list approach; particularly, the words may not be the ones that these students need.

Ideally, each student should work on his or her own individualized list, but no teacher has time to draw up 100 or 150 tailor-made lists every few days. Here are some possible compromises:

1. Have each student keep a record of all words he or she misspells in any class. Each week the student adds these (up to a limit of say five words) to the list assigned the whole class. He or she studies these and at test time a spelling partner pronounces the words as an individualized part of the spelling test.
2. Divide the class into two or three groups on the basis of spelling ability, and prepare separate lists. The poorest spellers, for instance, may concentrate on the customary demons; the others, on other useful words encountered in their reading.
3. Sometimes have each student draw up his or her own list of "Words I Should Learn to Spell." In testing sessions, use spelling partners.

Able classes in the senior high school may need no work with lists, although some students may need help. Bright students may be made to feel completely responsible for the correctness of their spelling.

# INDIVIDUALIZED PROCEDURES

## DISCOVERING ONE'S OWN ROAD TO SUCCESS

Individual differences exist in methods of learning. What works well for one person does not necessarily work well for another. Let your students know that a person may recall a spelling mainly by motor, auditory, or visual means. Some persons, in a sense, have spelling at their fingertips; once they have written a word, say *existence,* a few times, they can write it automatically, without thinking. Others remember with their ears: "ex-is-tence," they say, perhaps exaggerating the pronunciation to remind themselves of the *e* after *t*. Still others have camera vision; when they encounter a new word, they take a "snapshot" of it, and when they need the word again, it flashes on a "screen" inside their heads: They say that they actually see the word. And some persons combine two or all three of the methods. Having students think about their own techniques for remembering may assist them in making best use of their strongest assets without ignoring other means of remembering.

Harry Shefter, in a popular paperbound book, *Six Minutes a Day to Perfect Spelling*[5], advocates a five-step procedure in learning a word. His steps include the three techniques just described as well as some others: "SEE THE WORD" (i.e., look at it carefully, spotting its peculiarities and possible trouble spots); "THINK THE WORD" (i.e., associate the word with something that may help you to remember it: "She screamed 'EEE!' as she passed the cEmEtEry."); "FEEL THE WORD" (i.e., pronounce it carefully); "BUILD THE WORD" (i.e., relate it to other forms or to similar words: *beauty, beautiful, beautify, beautifully, beautification*). Lawrence P. Shehan[6] varies Shefter's formula a little, emphasizing these six steps: See it! Say it! Hear it! Check it! Write it! Use it!

To increase independence in studying spelling among children in upper elementary grades, Howard Blake recommends giving them individual copies of questions they may find useful to answer.[7] Blake's list consists of 43 questions under the headings of phonetic analysis, structural analysis, meaning, and usage. Representative questions: "What other words can I write that begin like this word?" "What story, poem, announcement, report, letter, or instruction can I write using this word and others on the list?" Blake emphasizes that each child should select from the 43 questions the ones that seem to him or her most useful in studying.

An NCTE committee long ago recommended this still-useful procedure:

> *In studying a word, a good procedure for a learner is, (1) to say each syllable distinctly and look at the syllable as he says it, (2) with eyes closed to think how the word looks, (3) to look at the word again to check his impression, (4) to write the word and check with the book, (5) to repeat twice the writing and checking. If on any one of these five trials he misspells the word, he should copy it in his spelling notebook. Finally, he should write the group of words studied as a parent, brother, sister, or friend pronounces them for him.*[8]

Harold Blau suggests the use of a tape recorder, with earphones. The student pronounces a word into the microphone and then copies it, pronounces another, and copies it, and so on; later, he or she writes (rather than copies) each word as his or her own tape-recorded voice pronounces. Blau also suggests writing with "magic markers" on white cards, perhaps with a different color for each syllable. "Changing the medium seems to help to change the mind set. Also, poor spellers seem to learn more easily from the words 'writ large.' "[9]

From an assortment of suggestions such as these, a student should find, through a little experimenting, what works best for him or her. Do not be surprised to find that few students are likely to agree on exactly the same formula.

## CHARACTERISTICS OF GOOD SPELLERS

Good spelling is not necessarily a mark of high intelligence. Rather, it is likely to be the result of certain attitudes and habits described by E. W. Dolch:

> ... the "good speller" (1) checks his guesses, (2) proofreads for spelling, and (3) studies the spelling of new words, which means (a) he gets the exact pronunciation of each new word, (b) he asks if this sounding tells the letters, and (c) where it does not, he finds a means of remembering the exact letters at the difficult spot. He makes this rapid check in all subjects, in English, in history, in science, or what not. He habitually makes this check, and does it in a few seconds only.[10]

## THE SUSPICION QUOTIENT

Students should be taught "to become wary of seldom used words and sensitive to the possible problems with commonly used ones," says James Conely of Troy State University (Alabama). Their "suspicion quotient" should send them frequently to the dictionary.[11]

## PROOFREADING

Many of the spelling mistakes in composition result from hasty writing followed by careless proofreading. Hurried writing is not necessarily to be condemned, for one's pen must often race to keep up with one's thoughts. It often results, however, in misspellings that one knows how to avoid, such as *then* for *than,* or the confusion of *their, there,* and *they're,* or a careless transposition of letters. Proofreading should catch all such obvious errors, and in a student with a developed suspicion quotient should result in occasional consultation of the dictionary.

## SUMMARY

Improvement in spelling most often results from proceeding in these ways:

1. Motivate spelling.
2. Teach the words that most students will need.

3. Encourage students to find and master their own demons.
4. Consistently group spelling words that have some characteristics in common, and call these characteristics to students' attention.
5. Suggest a variety of attacks on spelling problems.
6. Encourage visualization.
7. Teach correct pronunciation.
8. Teach phonetics, if necessary.
9. Encourage tracing, writing in air, etc., to build the "feel" of a word.
10. Use a very few mnemonic devices, but do not discourage students who like to develop their own.
11. Teach the addition of prefixes and suffixes.
12. Teach only a few rules, always inductively, and recall them often, through examples.
13. When teaching a list, use the test-study procedure.
14. Use a few spelling games, especially with younger students.
15. Give individual help when needed.
16. Encourage the dictionary habit (the "suspicion quotient") for checking guesses.
17. Give plenty of practice in writing; remember always that spelling is a writing, not a speaking, skill.

---

### THE IDEA BOX

POSITIVE ATTITUDE

Students' attitudes toward spelling are likely to be most favorable, says Hal Funk, when the following conditions exist:

> (1) The teacher's positive attitude toward spelling; (2) Spelling being properly emphasized in the total curriculum; (3) Provision for a strong dictionary program; (4) Specific standards set for proofreading [and] neatness . . . (should be developed with students); (5) Spelling kept in proper perspective in the total composition program, especially in the creative writing experience; and (6) Provision made for daily spelling instruction.[12]

"A COMMON-SENSE APPROACH TO TEACHING SPELLING"

This pamphlet, written at Ball State University, Muncie, Indiana, compares results of teaching spelling through the individualized approach, with each student concentrating on the words that trouble him or her the most, and through a conventional use of word lists. Students following the individualized approach seemed to spell somewhat better at the end.

THE TEACHING OF HIGH SCHOOL ENGLISH

## SPELLING FOR YOUR JOB

Students, sometimes working in pairs, construct and learn to spell lists of words they may need to know in their own future occupations. This procedure may improve motivation for learning to spell other words, too.

## FOUR MAIN REASONS FOR SPELLING PROBLEMS

1. The language itself (e.g., the various ways in which /o/ may be spelled, or the different pronunciations of the same letter or group of letters).
2. Mispronunciation (e.g., saying ''nucular,'' ''excape,'' ''enviorment,'' ''sacreligious'').
3. Confusion of similar words (e.g., sim*ilar,* fami*liar;* l*ead,* l*ed; a*ffect, *e*ffect; *ac*cept, *ex*cept.
4. Confusion of root words: ''explanation'' ← *explain;* ''miniscule'' ← *mini-.*[13]

## A HARD LOOK AT THE WORD

One of the spelling techniques recommended by Sister Josephina, C.S.J., is having students observe anything noteworthy in the meaning, root, prefix, or early history of each troublesome word.[14]

## LOGICAL ANALYSIS

Often a moment's thought will clarify a spelling. For example, why are there two *k*'s in *bookkeeper?*

## HOW CAN I LOOK IT UP IF I CAN'T SPELL IT?

In a thesaurus, look up a synonym, or even a word in the same category, advises G. Howard Poteet. It will probably show you the word you want. It may even suggest a more precise word.[15]

## A TAPE RECORDER AS A TIME-SAVER

Dictate groups of words into a tape recorder, being sure to enunciate clearly and, when necessary, to use illustrative sentences or phrases. A class or individual students may play the recording for practice or test purposes.

## HELP FOR THE NONSPELLER

Occasionally a student reaches junior or even senior high school with almost no knowledge of spelling. Unless he or she is very severely deficient mentally or physiologically (and there *are* several million learning-disabled children), the nonspelling child can learn the most common way that each sound is written. Misspellings may still abound, but at least what the child then writes can be comprehended. He or she may still write *bate* for *bait* or *hert* for *hurt,* but these spellings, unlike *prd* or *kalum,* can be interpreted.

Much practice is needed in copying accurately words that use the most common spelling, and then in writing the same words from dictation. For example, /i/ is usually spelled *i*, so the child practices *him, sip,* and so on; /e/ is usually *e*, as in *set* and *hem*. The consonant symbols are relatively uniform.

One excellent list of "Regular Graphemic Representations of English Phonemes" is in Robert A. Hall's *Sound and Spelling in English*.[16] Another is in C. C. Fries's *Linguistics and Reading*.[17] Or with a little thought you can make your own.

## SIMPLIFIED SPELLING

Minor simplification of spelling will do little good, but a new alphabet such as George Bernard Shaw and others have advocated would necessitate scrapping all our typewriters and compositors' equipment, retraining their operators, and re-teaching (to some extent) reading and writing to everyone. We need a system in which each English sound will always be represented graphemically in the same way. With such a system, no teaching of spelling would be needed after the second grade, as is true in Finland even now. One workable (but not flawless) system was almost adopted in England in the late 1940s. Its characteristics are suggested in this verse from *The New York Times:*

> Mai hart iz sad fer litel wunz
> Hw uend dher uei tw skwl
> Tw lern dhe Inglish langgwidj
> Uith its totel lak ov rwl.

Futurist Edmund Farrell says that increased use of computers may force upon us a considerable simplification of spelling.

## SPELLING PARTNERS

Frank Dunn, Sayville, N.Y., Junior High School, has students work in pairs on their spelling chores. Dunn has three levels of spelling words for each grade, assigning to each student words on the level list for which he or she is ready.[18]

## HOMONYM DOWN

To increase sensitivity to homonyms, Louise Swinney's tenth graders in Elsinore, California, have enjoyed an occasional spelldown with homonyms. The teacher pronounces a homonym; a member of one team spells it; and then a member of the next team must spell another version of it. The student may be asked to use in a sentence the homonym he or she has spelled.

## TROUBLE SPOTS

Because usually a word has only one trouble spot (e.g., the *b* in *subtle*), it is often useful to focus students' attention on that spot. For an extensive list, see an old but still useful book, Arthur I. Gates's *A List of Spelling Difficulties in 3876 Words*.[19]

THE TEACHING OF HIGH SCHOOL ENGLISH

### COMPETITION

Robert L. Coard of Minot, North Dakota, lists for lowerclassmen the words his seniors misspell and issues the challenge "Can you outspell our seniors?"[20]

### EXCUSING GOOD SPELLERS

Some of the best spellers may be excused from spelling work, with the proviso that they may at any time, through their compositions for instance, be called on to demonstrate that they are maintaining their ability.

### SPELLING "MUST" LIST

Let a class agree upon a short list of words that must never be misspelled. The list may gradually be enlarged.

### ANECDOTE FOR MOTIVATION

A motorist was arrested for parking beside a sign that said "No stoping." He was freed when he proved that he had not been "stoping," that is, digging for ore.

### IF YOU NEED A LAUGH

Read Mike Holmes's "A Spelling Lessen [sic]" and enjoy her [sic] account of a fifth-grade spelling lesson in which children struggle (sort of) with *boat* and *note, bite* and *right* (so why not *quight?*) and other joy-filled oddities of the English language. (Would you believe *qieut* as a spelling for *quiet?*)[21]

Or read "Our Spelling is a Muess," a student poem with rhymes like *tright* and *fright*.[22]

### "SPELLING INSTRUCTION THROUGH THE NINETEENTH CENTURY"

Gene M. Towery, University of South Florida, says that the spelling book was once the "single most important resource in the American educational system," teaching geography, grammar, and other subjects as well as spelling. Although this claim may be too high, the article offers a valuable historical survey.[23]

# FOOTNOTES

1. "25 to 1," in *Through a Glass, Darkly,* eds. Edward Fagan and Jean Vandell. Urbana, Illinois: NCTE, 1971, pp. 32–33.
2. "Spelling Report," *College English* 16, Nov. 1954.
3. *A Study of High School Spelling Vocabulary,* Austin, Texas: The Steck Co., 1945.

4. Paul R. Hanna, et al., *Phoneme-Grapheme Correspondences as Cues to Spelling Improvement*. Washington, D.C.: U.S. Government Printing Office, 1966, p. 116.
5. New York: Pocket Books, 1975.
6. *English Journal* 53, March 1964.
7. "Studying Spelling Independently," *Elementary English* 37, Jan. 1960, pp. 29–32.
8. *An Experience Curriculum in English,* p. 259.
9. "First Aid for Extremely Poor Spellers," *English Journal* 55, May 1966, pp. 583–584.
10. "Teaching Spelling," *Illinois English Bulletin,* March 1943, p. 5.
11. *College Composition and Communication* 25, Oct. 1974, p. 243.
12. *Peabody Journal of Education,* July 1972.
13. James Conely, "Speling," *College Composition and Communication* 25, Oct. 1974, p. 243.
14. "Spelling: The Responsibility of Every Teacher," *Clearing House,* March 1958, p. 393.
15. "A Brief Note on Spelling," *English Journal* 62, Oct. 1973, p. 1029.
16. Philadelphia: Chilton Press, 1961, pp. 43–44.
17. New York: Holt, Rinehart and Winston, 1963, pp. 171 ff.
18. "Multi-Level Spelling Program," *New York State Education,* May 1960, p. 22.
19. New York: Teachers College, Columbia University Bureau of Publications, 1937.
20. "Spelling-Game Time," *Clearing House,* Sept. 1955, p. 9.
21. *English Journal* 64, Dec. 1975, p. 8.
22. *College Composition and Communication* 26, May 1975, p. 211.
23. *English Journal* 69, Dec. 1980, p. 76.

# 13

## SPEECH
## COMMUNICATION
## IN
## THE
## ENGLISH
## CLASSROOM

## SOME GROUP PROCEDURES

Professional educators do not take lightly the act of giving themselves, their organizations, or their journals different titles. They do it only after considerable debate, and they try to do it as a majority. The act signals a major change in professional philosophy and thrust. We have seen librarians call themselves media resource persons or media specialists, and we have seen one of the organizations in educational media change from the Department of Audio-Visual Instruction to the Association for Educational Communications and Technology. In the field of English teaching, we have seen the journal *Elementary English* change to *Language Arts*. In the Speech field, we have seen the Speech Association of America become the Speech Communication Association and its journal, *The Speech Teacher*, become *Communication Education*. The following editorial extract from a recent speech text reveals the changing philosophy in that field:

> *Speech is no longer limited exclusively to the act of speaking. Instead, it is now regarded as central to a process that is paramount to all of us, that is, the process of communication. Once the role of speech is so accepted, then the various modes of speech can be studied with real effect and meaning.*[1]

The English teaching profession must also offer a more comprehensive approach to oral communication. In schools where all students take Speech courses, not everything described in this chapter need be offered in English courses. But because many schools have no required work at all in Speech, the English Department must take up the slack and incorporate in its program many of the activities described below. Because high school students must speak effectively in many circumstances and settings, English teachers should help them to develop the skills to do so. All too often, speech in the English classroom seems bent on preparing students only for speech in the English classroom. This seems to be narrow training in view of the many oral language skills needed by students in society today.

A comparison of two surveys indicates that English teachers today may not be giving any more attention to speech development than they did almost two decades ago. For two years during the early 1960s, a research team made on-site evaluations of the English programs in 158 high schools in 45 different states, making 306 visits in all. After analyzing data from thousands of questionnaires from both students and teachers, they included in their recommendations these remarks about speech:

*Speech and oral language skills are . . . neglected in the meager 4.9 percent of class time they receive, although teachers agree that they should stress these even at the expense of other activities. One re-emerging pattern is the semester of required speech, usually introduced at the tenth grade level, but in the long run proficiency in oral language cannot be developed through only one semester of work. It requires the continuing attention of the teacher of English at all levels of the high school program and a conscious emphasis on oral activities during other phases of English instruction.*[2]

An English Journal Readership Survey (1977), which produced responses from 585 junior and senior high school English teachers, revealed that English teachers expected students to speak and write clearly and logically, but then limited their students' speaking activities mainly to discussing literature and giving oral reports. The researchers found that in the senior highs today, "listening to the teacher talk about literature, doing textual analysis and writing interpretations are as important as free talk and discussion." Apparently, too, the teacher is still the principal audience for speaking and writing. One particularly disappointing conclusion from the 1977 survey is that "oral activities were done less often by lower ability students, who did more structured writing activities, such as writing answers to study guide questions, completing grammar exercises, and making vocabulary lists from literature."

The purposes, subjects, and data from these two studies are so different that generalizing from both cannot be easily defended, but a casual comparison does make one wonder whether speech in English classrooms today isn't very similar to speech in the English classrooms during the early 1960s. Particularly disturbing is this comment about the situation in 1977: "The goal emphasized by the fewest teachers was *to acquire the ability to adjust one's language for different audiences and occasions.*"[3]

## OBJECTIVES

The intention in oral English is not to produce platform speakers but to develop citizens who can participate satisfactorily in the everyday situations that demand spoken English. These situations may be grouped roughly according to their frequency in adult life, as follows:

*Group I,* often needed. Conversing and discussing in large and small groups, speaking to and conversing with one person, giving directions, telling stories and relating events, and reading aloud.

*Group II,* important but less frequently needed. Interviewing or being interviewed, making announcements, making introductions, giving reports, following parliamentary procedure, defining, and participating in panel discussions.

*Group III,* important but limited to special occasions. Giving book reviews, dramatizing, debating, platform speaking, after-dinner speaking, choral reading, reciting of memorized passages, and participating in radio or television programs.

*Group IV,* needed for professional work. Speaking to sell a product, speaking to law clients and juries, and giving professional dramatic performances on stage or for television.

All students should be given enough practice to become reasonably proficient in the situations named in Groups I and II. Less emphasis need be placed on Group III, and none at all on Group IV, except when a particular student wants assistance or when the oral work in English is designed to support an emphasis on career education.


## ORGANIZING ORAL WORK

Most oral communication should grow naturally out of other class activities. From the study of literature, language, and composition arise many opportunities for oral work. Short concentrated units, workshops, or extended lessons that relate to the work of larger units, can provide special instruction. Oral reading, class and panel discussions, reports, definitions, dramatizations, story telling, choral reading, and recitation are natural outgrowths of the "regular" study. A good class discussion is actually a conversation with much interaction taking place among students as they share different points of view, seek consensus, and try to reach a decision. Diffident students may be given more chance to converse if the class is occasionally divided into small groups, each of which is to talk about one aspect of the work. Short units or extended lessons may be devoted to the interview, parliamentary procedure, and additional speech activities that do not grow readily out of work in literature, language, and written composition.

## THE ROLE OF THE TEACHER

To develop students who can speak well, the teacher must be a reasonably competent speaker. That does not mean that a teacher should be an orator or a lecturer—few teachers could make a living on the lecture platform—but the teacher should have a satisfactory voice and the ability to express thoughts clearly and pleasingly. Occasionally hearing sound tapes of one's speech and trying to correct whatever deficiencies one discovers is helpful. Also helpful is feedback from videotapes, because then the teacher is aware of the total impact of communicating both verbally and nonverbally.

## SOME TEACHING TECHNIQUES

Some techniques that have been employed successfully in teaching each of the oral activities listed on page 423 are the following:

### Group I

### *Informal Discussions*

The combination of lecture and discussion remains the most frequent form of oral activity in the English classroom. A short, effective lecture can and should provoke class discussion, but often it does not. Sometimes the teacher confuses recitation with discussion. The fault may lie in asking questions that students can answer with one or two words. Such questions are dead-ended. Often a teacher teaches deductively—that is, uses the lecture to lay out rules, definitions, explanations, and generalizations—and then uses the time remaining to elicit examples from individual students. This technique has value, but it does little to encourage real class discussion. Discussion depends on the active flow of oral communication in the classroom and on continuing interactions among all participants, including the teacher. Traditionally, students expect the teacher to have the first and last words, to direct the flow of speech, make the most provocative remarks, decide whether students' remarks really contribute or not, settle all arguments with cogent observations, put into clearer language what students have said, and even determine what students meant to say. These expectations are totally unrealistic, but students can become too numbed or conditioned to see how presumptuous they are.

How can we break students out of the all-eyes-front syndrome? One simple method is to rearrange chairs in a circle or semicircle. In some long and narrow classrooms, an oval arrangement seems best. This method by no means guarantees that better discussions will take place, but at least students who sat near the back of the room are no longer looking at the backs of 30 or more heads. (Many who sit that far back of course do so to avoid class involvements.)

To improve class discussions, the teacher can also redirect students' comments and questions. The questions, "Do you all agree with George?" or "Does anyone have any questions?" leave openings for only "Yes" or "No." When a teacher senses that agreements and disagreements exist among students, a question should be more direct and more provocative. "Mary, are you going to let George speak for you?" "Paul, how does Mary's comment support (or change) your point of view?" Sometimes two or three students who disagree and need to speak to each other will still look to the teacher as though the teacher is supposed to tell the rest of the class what they need to say to each other. A teacher who faces this situation might say to a student, "Jim, don't look at me. Paul made the comment, I didn't. I suggest that you ask him the question you are about to ask me. You'll get a much better idea of what he means."

Getting all students to take part is sometimes a problem. If teachers remember the particular strong points of each student, however, they may occasionally supply a lead or a question that will bring in one of the silent ones. Sometimes a student who is hanging back can be brought into a discussion with a comment such as "Bill, you made a comment in your last paper about the way a character's whole attitude can be affected by a setting. I think we could find your point useful now in our discussion. Please tell us what you said." The attitude that each person has something worthwhile to offer usually brings results, and a few words of recognition or praise can transform a retiring student into one of the most active participants.

Occasionally teachers like to have a discussion topic determined in advance, with each student responsible for preparing and being ready to present three reasons for believing as she or he does. This is a valuable technique; however, some students may act as though they are responsible for only what they have prepared and may just wait for the chance to say it in an artificial way. Discussions can sometimes be more honest when students direct them. They can also be learning experiences of the highest order. A student discussion leader may realize for the first time that the role takes both preparation and finesse, and classmates may feel a greater responsibility for interacting with each other.

Before such discussions, the class might come to agreement on the characteristics of good conversation in small groups: alertness of each speaker and listener, tactfulness, courtesy, avoidance of showing off or talking too much, avoidance of interrupting, and so on. A teacher and students might through class discussions develop a more complete list of guidelines like those below:

1. Students should have a clear reason for small-group discussions. If the group is to discuss a subject, that subject should be fairly clear.
2. The group should be of manageable size. Usually a group of five or six is large enough for good interaction and small enough for efficient management.
3. If the group is to be organized with definite roles and responsibilities, these

roles should be clear to all members, whether the teacher or students make the assignments.

4. The group should soon have a sense of how to conduct its business most efficiently. It should establish both procedure and degree of formality.

5. All members should work for the good of the group in the interests of accomplishing the task *as a group*.

6. The group should have some sense of how long it will hold its discussion and what it will do with its accomplishments.

Group work can contribute to students' learning as it develops their oral skills, and it can also assist the teacher in a number of ways. The following list represents only a small number of the benefits of grouping for oral activities:

1. Students have more opportunities to communicate orally. All have the chance to participate.

2. Students can draw subjects, problems, and tasks into sharper focus.

3. Students can more easily pool their talents and more satisfactorily understand and appreciate the diversity among themselves.

4. Students who are reluctant to express themselves orally in larger groups may feel more at ease.

5. Students can acquire a better sense of what can be accomplished by group effort.

6. Students are more likely to assume individual responsibilities and to carry them through when working for each other.

7. Students gain a better sense of their peers as "audience" for oral expression. (Too often the teacher is the person addressed.)

8. Students have more opportunities to teach each other.

9. The teacher has unique opportunities to teach. For example, the workshop or laboratory atmosphere, as well as the physical arrangement of groups in the room, permits a teacher to interact more closely and more frequently with students.

10. Students will discover that group work often saves valuable time and improves the quality of their work. For example, the number of ideas exchanged in small groups could take many days to present individually before the class. Students have only to remember a solid week of oral book reports to realize this fact. Ideas presented to the class as a result of small-group discussion will probably be better defined. They will also have survived the test of student opinion, so they could carry more weight and hold greater interest.

### Speaking Person-to-Person

People most often speak to and converse with one person at a time. Speech may be very formal, even ceremonial, or it may be very informal and chatty; the purpose may be serious or frivolous; and of course communication can be effective or ineffective. The most common person-to-person communication in the English classroom takes place between the teacher and one student in a conference about work done or to be done, or between two students who are paired off to help each other. Aside from these experiences, dialogue is largely ignored. James Moffett and Betty Wagner lament this situation by saying, ''Actual dialogue is such a common, natural, and pleasurable experience, we often discount its value, especially as a classroom activity.''[4]

Both actual and invented dialogue can be used frequently in the classroom, and both can include a wide range of oral experiences. Students can converse informally, interview each other, even brainstorm. They can try to inform, define, direct, persuade, entertain; and in the process, they can learn to adjust their speech to accomplish these different purposes with different individuals. Dialogues can be held face to face or over a telephone, walkie-talkie, or citizen's band radio.

### Giving Directions

Almost any student can relate instances in which he or she was given unclear directions concerning the location of the post office, subway entrance, or some other place. If not, perhaps the student can remember trying to follow poor directions in getting around during the first week in a new school. The reason for the lack of clarity may have been the director's ignorance, inability to visualize, or poor speech habits. Junior high school students, working in pairs or small groups, may take turns giving and receiving directions in different ways under different circumstances. Explaining how to go from one place to another in the city or in the school building is not the same when the listener is a friend or a stranger, a person of the same age, or a very young child.

Clever teachers can dramatize the importance of clear oral instructions for doing things. In one case, the teacher could ask a student to use words alone (no gestures or motions in the air) to direct another student to reproduce a design on the chalkboard. The design, which could look like a circle overlapping a triangle within a parallelogram, is not shown to the listener. The speaker must decide which words are best at every step. The speaker must also think carefully about the listener's experience and knowledge of words. Will terms used in geometry help? If the speaker has been told at the beginning (and in private) that the listener is not supposed to know the language of geometry, the speaker must find other words. In any case, both speaker and listener realize that they must not assume too much or too little. Through not being allowed to use nonverbal signals, they also appreciate the extent to which these signals enrich and reinforce oral communication. Another technique could include giving directions to a student who is walking about or assembling something while blindfolded. Still another could be ''talking someone through'' an unfamiliar procedure. We are familiar with the scene sometimes enacted on television in which a pilot on the ground "talks" a passenger through a safe landing after something has happened to the pilot of the aircraft.

### Telling Stories and Relating Events

Although everyone enjoys stories, most persons unfortunately do not tell them well. They do one or another of the following: bring in irrelevant statements, add unnecessary *see's* and *you know's* and *like's*, relate events in illogical order, laugh before the hearers know what is funny, leave out important details, or spoil the climax. Three factors can help students to weave better tales: discussion of the characteristics of effective storytelling, plenty of opportunity to practice, and a teacher's encouragement. A teacher should encourage students to include pointed anecdotes in their reports on authors, to relate to the class stories or parts of stories that they have found interesting, and to bring into class discussion pertinent illustrative stories, funny or otherwise.

Storytelling belongs to many areas of English study: a story may be told by one person as a dramatic monologue, tall tale, parable, fable, or ballad; it may be told to one listener, to a small group, or to an entire class. A story can be told firsthand, or it can be retold after interviewing the original storyteller or simply listening to the tale. It can be the "real" story of something that has happened to a student, or it can be the fictional story of what happened or could have happened to a character in literature. It can be a story that Odysseus might have told at any point in his journey, a story that Beowulf might have told after returning from his encounter with Grendel, or a story that Huck Finn might have told to free himself or save face if presented with a situation not in the book. A story can be started by one student and unfold as other students add to it until it seems finished.

Students should learn that a good storyteller adjusts a story to suit the listener(s). For a high school student, an interesting exercise in "audience" might be telling a story to a class or a small group of children in first or second grade.

### Reading Aloud

Unfortunately, most oral reading in English classes is done by "turns" around the class or as an impromptu act by students asked to do it "on the spot" to support discussion or recitation. Nothing is more deadly than dull, monotonous reading around a class. A play is not even worth an autopsy after being killed this way. Impromptu reading can be good experience, but it should be balanced by frequent reading that is carefully prepared. Students who cannot read well, do not want to read, are not interested in what they are asked to read, and have no time to prepare, punish their listeners. If literature is read, they make it suffer also.

The understanding and appreciation of literature should be among the major goals of reading aloud. The preface to a current book on oral interpretation states this fact clearly: "The older view of interpretation as a performing act has been complemented—and, in some cases, replaced—by the view of interpretation as an instrument of understanding in literary study."[5] A teacher should be alert for opportunities to reinforce this view. Classes may discuss how a dramatic speech or poem should be interpreted. Perhaps the most famous example is Lady Macbeth's "We fail" (Act I, scene vii). Does Lady Macbeth say matter-of-factly, "We fail," or does she pause after "We" and say "fail" in a tone of disbelief, as if failure is impossible? In poetry, a class may discuss, and then demonstrate, how the short lines in "What Happens to a Dream Deferred?" by Langston Hughes should be read to convey most accurately the tension expressed by the poem.

Paul Hunsinger has developed some very useful principles that can guide students as they select literature, analyze the audience, and read a selection. These principles, somewhat abridged, appear below:

*Principles relating to the literature:*
1. *The literature selected must be of high literary merit.*
2. *The literature selected should be adaptable to oral reading.*
3. *The literary unities should be preserved in literature which is cut or adapted for oral reading.*

*Principles concerning the audience:*
1. *Analysis of the audience and adaptation to it are as important to the oral reader as they are to the public speaker.*
2. *The audience for whom the literature was prepared and the particular circumstances involved must be made clear to the reader's audience.*
3. *The audience must be persuaded that the oral reader is competent and effective in interpreting the literature.*

*Principles of presentation:*
1. *Techniques of presentation should come from the literature itself.*
2. *Eliminate techniques of presentation that draw attention to themselves and detract from the communication of the author's intention.*
3. *Use techniques of suggestion and restraint to maintain aesthetic distance and to establish the author's perspective.*[6]

Not all oral reading should be confined to literature; students should be able to read clearly and appropriately whether they are reading newspaper items, announcements, letters, prepared papers, or reports. During the conduct of a business or club meeting, a student may be asked to read a number of materials aloud. It is common practice to read minutes from the previous meeting, a letter from a member or nonmember, a resolution, a motion, and a list of recommendations, findings, or conclusions.

Oral reading, then, provides much opportunity for developing flexibility—a flexibility that may be carried over into other speech activities. It permits both a study of meaning and the clarification of meaning through effective use of the voice.

In recent years the use of Readers' Theater (also called Interpreters' Theater or Theater of the Mind) has become increasingly popular, first because it is fun and second because it may contribute substantially to improved oral reading. Readers' Theater is a blend of acting, public speaking, critical reaction, and sympathetic sharing. It differs from a play in that the performers do not ordinarily memorize their parts (though they should, if possible, practice before a performance); it differs also in that the audience through its imagination must furnish the scenery, action, costumes, make-up, and the physical appearance of the characters. Readers' Theater centers attention upon the author's text, which is brought to life by two or more performers who are usually seated behind lecterns (music racks are good), and each of whom may read two or more roles, one of which may be that of narrator. The action happens in the minds of the audience (hence the alternative name Theater of the Mind), although the readers are not necessarily completely invisible and may sometimes move away from their lecterns.

An Illinois teacher, Mrs. Regina Foehr, has described how moving an effective Readers' Theater performance may be. One of the student readers was describing a hole in the back of a cave: "His description and expression were so vivid that members of the class turned around to look toward the back of the room where his eyes were focused. The literature had come alive. Their 'mental image' had made them forget that they were in a classroom and not in a cave at all."

Student-written plays and stories can sometimes be adopted by students for Readers' Theater production in the classroom. Some of the best of these may find wider audiences in other classrooms, at PTA meetings, or in student assemblies.

Readers' Theater can be made more interesting through the use of some staging, but such things as scenery, lighting, costuming, and make-up should be added cautiously. If overdone, they can detract from the literature itself. Roy A. Beck points out that if scenery is used, it is usually only a "cyclorama curtain," which may vary in color to suggest different literary tones. Lighting, he says, can do much to establish mood, especially if dimmers are used. Costuming, if used at all, should be limited to a few accessories suggesting characterizations or a historical period. Mood music is best employed between segments of a reading or during transitions.[7]

Choral reading is often enjoyable. William H. Cullen recommends starting with unsophisticated material like rhythmic folksongs, moving then to poems like Sandburg's "Fog," "Chicago," and "Jazz Fantasia," and on to longer poems like James Weldon Johnson's "God's Trombones." The teacher-director, Cullen stresses, must be uninhibited and must stress student initiative.[8]

## Group II

### Interviewing

Although most students will take part in only a few interviews during their lifetimes, those few may be of major importance. Their chances of employment in their chosen work will sometimes depend upon the success of one interview. Some colleges also require interviews with their prospective students. Yet many employers and college interviewers complain that young people are often careless in appearance and manners, that they slouch and sprawl, that their answers to questions are delivered in a slovenly fashion, and that they have nothing positive to contribute. These complaints suggest that a valuable project for the junior and senior year is a short study of techniques of the interview, and dramatizations of good and bad techniques. Then the small-group plan can be employed to allow each student practice in interviewing and being interviewed for imagined positions. Students who have had such training, artificial though the situations are, are often loud in its praise.

Students can also conduct interviews to gather and convey practical information. Through interviews they can gather information for the school newspaper, a class project, or an investigative paper. They can also gather information from a visitor before introducing that person as a speaker in class or in the school auditorium. And they can experiment with the interview as a device for presenting information in person or over the school's public address system. For example, a student running for a class office can be interviewed or can hold a "press conference" to tell fellow students about her or his qualifications.

Students will soon learn that conducting an interview is more demanding than they realized. Procedures depend on the interviewer's purpose and on many other factors, but students discover quickly that they cannot escape all of the following problems and responsibilities: deciding on the best way to approach the subject; doing enough research on the subject to be able to ask good questions; making the best impression; deciding which question would make the best opener, and which ones should follow; persisting politely to get needed information; taking good notes while listening. And, as if this isn't enough, John Brady adds another problem:

> *Bringing the interview to an artful close is an art in itself. You want to leave your interviewee with the impression that* **he** *is doing the closing. And even after the last good-bye, you must still verify the facts in the interview, un-*

*tangle conflicting stories, get your source's approval of the transcript (if you* **really** *need it), and cultivate him with an eye toward future stories.*[9]

## Making Announcements

The good announcement is not unlike the lead of a news story, in that it usually answers the questions of who, what, where, and when, and sometimes why and how. In school many announcements must be made, and conscientious teachers see to it that each student occasionally has such responsibility. Committees in charge of bulletin boards, the classroom library, special occasions, and the like must make announcements. Homerooms and assembly programs also frequently necessitate announcements. Because in adult life almost everyone is occasionally expected to announce something to a group, practice in giving announcements based on the "five W's" is desirable.

## Introducing a Speaker

Although opportunities for introducing outside speakers are rather rare, one student may sometimes present another to a school group. The chairman of a discussion panel, for instance, may remind her classmates of some pertinent qualification of the next speaker. Or, in those schools where students sometimes appear before other classes to talk about their specialties, someone, preferably a student, must introduce them.

## Giving Reports

Reports in English and other classes are frequent and may be valuable. Too often, though, a report is dull and almost worthless because the student chooses too broad a subject (e.g., The Computer Business), fails to narrow it, takes notes on only an encyclopedia article, and simply summarizes what the encyclopedia says. Guided, the same student will cut the subject down to workable size, consult more than one source, and employ his or her own plan of organization for the material.

The report subjects should grow from the classwork and should not be chosen merely for the sake of having reports. Second, students should usually be given some degree of freedom in choosing the subjects of their reports, because they are more likely to make interesting whatever they themselves find interesting. Third, ordinarily not many reports should be given on the same day.

As an illustration, suppose that a senior class is studying eighteenth-century English literature. The teacher suggests that certain reports will enlighten and enliven much of the study. He or she invites the students to be on the alert for subjects that they would like to investigate, and in addition lists a rather large number of topics including such subjects as Whigs vs. Tories, eighteenth-century etiquette or dress or amusements, Fielding's *Tom Jones,* the story of Johnson's dictionary, and so on. Each student should choose the topic that interests him or her most and should talk with the teacher concerning sources of information and the most appropriate time for the report. The subject of etiquette should probably be discussed when the class is reading Addison and Steele, Johnson's dictionary when the class is reading from the *Rambler* essays, and so on. In other words, the reports are interspersed within the rest of the work, and each student makes his or her contribution when it is most meaningful.

The principles of organization—chronological or inductive, for example—are as important in oral as in written English. Time should be taken occasionally to refresh students' memories concerning the possible types of organization and how to employ them. The usefulness of outlines—at least topic outlines—can be more easily demonstrated for oral work than for written compositions.

Some shy students are extremely hesitant about giving reports; the thought of standing before the class terrifies them so much that they will even feign illness to escape. Sympathy for these students is better than scorn. Also, a gradual building up to reports is better than a sudden assignment. If teachers are aware that some students are excessively shy, they may first encourage participation while the students are seated, later have them place written work on the board and explain it, and then allow them to use notes freely in their reports. A friendly, cooperative atmosphere within the classroom is desirable and may be encouraged by the teachers' frequent praise of the student audience.

Sometimes a teacher may reveal a personal struggle to overcome stage fright, and may refer to famous stage actors and actresses who feel or felt frightened or even nauseated before each performance (as even the great Ethel Barrymore did).

In evaluating reports, as John B. Newman advises,[10] teachers should not overemphasize mechanics of delivery. Newman says that content, semantics, and general effectiveness are all more important than mechanics.

### Following Parliamentary Procedure

Because parliamentary procedure is of marked importance in our life (business, church, and club meetings, as well as local, state, and federal government), students should become familiar with the order of business and should be able to trace a motion, with amendments, from origin to disposal. In addition, they should know such technicalities as the procedure in electing officers, the method of addressing the chair, and the order of precedence of motions.

Class following of parliamentary procedure, however, need not be mere routine. In some classes, discussion of controversial issues is a more or less regular practice. A chairman and a secretary are elected, the topic is explained and then discussed, and the opposing points of view are summarized at the end of the hour. Students must be recognized by the chair before speaking. Discussion must be kept free of personalities. Courtesy should be the rule, with frequent use of such remarks as ''Mr. Chairman, I believe that Jim is partly right, but I would like to disagree with one statement.'' Opinion should be supported by as much factual evidence as is available.

A value inherent in such a plan of discussion is that it helps students to think about issues of importance to them. All students should develop the ability:

1. To employ a reflective and analytical technique rather than the argumentative technique in approach to controversial problems.
2. To display competence in, and inclination toward, defining key words and phrases used in discussion.
3. To display competence in reinforcing general or abstract concepts with appropriate concrete details.
4. To master and to apply the principle that the truth of a solution depends upon the degree to which it corresponds with the basic assumptions.

The types of subjects that may be considered in parliamentary discussions vary widely. Some teachers prefer national and international issues. Others advocate consideration of problems nearer the students: home difficulties, cheating, athletics, courtesy, movies, and so on. Community issues (generally nonpolitical ones) may be discussed; class consideration of such an issue as school-district reorganization has even been known to affect a community's decision on an important problem. One should begin with subjects in which students have an immediate personal interest and gradually branch out into topics with wider implications.

### Defining

Perhaps defining should not be listed as a special speech activity, because it is needed frequently in reports and discussions. But it provides enough pitfalls to warrant separate treatment. Much disagreement or confusion may be avoided if terms are carefully defined. Therefore, when Ray is talking about a "good football team," he should be expected to define "good"; when Katherine is talking about the education of Indians, both "education" and "Indians" need definition; when any student uses a technical term that may be unfamiliar to the class, he or she should pause to explain it.

Every good definition, students should learn, does two things: it places the thing being defined in a general category and then distinguishes that thing from others in the same category. For instance, if one is defining *psychiatry*, one says first that it is a science (the general category), then distinguishes it from other sciences by saying that it involves the treatment of mental diseases.

### Participating in Panel Discussions

In many ways the panel discussion is preferable to debate. It is less formal and more natural; it permits audience participation; and unlike debate it searches for truth rather than victory.

Careful preparation is essential to success in panel discussion. Students must be made familiar with the usual pattern: opening remarks by the chairman;

introduction of speakers; rather formal presentation of differing points of view by members of the panel; informal exchange of comments, additions, and rebuttals; and audience participation. (There are, of course, many possible variations of this pattern; in a less formal panel, there may be no set order for the speakers.) If the topic is a controversial one, care must be taken to have approximately an equal number of speakers for each side. The members of the panel must know exactly what issue or issues are involved, and who is to present which points of view. Material must be sought and organized as carefully as it would be for a debate.

Loren Reid suggests an ingenious method for appraising individuals' contributions to discussions of almost any type. He suggests that the teacher mark a tally each time a student speaks, even only a sentence or two. A *plus* indicates a helpful contribution, a *zero* a neutral one, and a *minus* a contribution that is "digressing, sidetracking, blocking or overly aggressive." Thus, some students may be marked like this:

Crews 0++0000000000
Goold ++++
Mutti 00-0-00-0-0
Page 0000+0[11]

It should be useful, too, for students to employ this device occasionally in evaluating their classmates' contributions. It should lead to careful listening and to critical thinking.

## Group III

The types of speaking listed under Group III—book reviews, dramatizing, debating, platform speaking, after-dinner speaking, choral reading, reciting memorized passages, and participating in radio and television programs—are of varying value as class activities. Dramatization, debates, and choral reading are not approached in the English classroom as performing arts; they are used mainly to further the understanding and appreciation of literature. Dramatization often stimulates visualization of situations involving conflict; debates help to clarify points of view and bring themes into sharper focus; choral reading can develop better understanding and appreciation in literature in the oral tradition. Class discussion about a piece of literature might lead to a debate, one that could be carried by the best "debaters" to another class studying the same selection. Concerning choral reading, Lawana Trout suggests "chant poems" which high school students can perform while studying literature by the American Indian. She acknowledges the point "that most oral tradition literature can stand free of its culture and be understood," but she finds that through participating in "chant poems," students experience the power of the oral words and are less likely to distort the true meaning in Indian literature.[12]

**Group IV**

Teaching the types of speaking needed for professional work is primarily the responsibility of the college or vocational school, not of the high school. The foundation for the specialized speech required of a salesperson or minister are laid in the elementary and high schools, but detailed work is possible only later, when one enters his or her vocation.

# THE IMPROVEMENT OF THE INDIVIDUAL'S SPEECH

The class activities that have been described should lead to improvement of speech habits by giving class members practice in numerous situations requiring speech. But there is still something more that the teacher can do to help individuals better their oral English. This is corrective and developmental work aimed at reduction or elimination of faults in speech.

## ENCOUNTERING SERIOUS SPEECH PROBLEMS

The teacher who is not a trained speech correctionist should never try to remedy faults that may be organic. Some persons have serious nervous maladjustments or malformed speech organs; anyone but a specialist who attempts to apply treatment for these persons may do irreparable harm.

The English teacher cannot assume, however, that students who have speech defects will be kept out of English classes. In fact, as "mainstreaming" becomes common, more handicapped students will be moved from special classes into regular ones. The goal of providing "least restrictive environments" is intended to help as many handicapped students as possible to move through school *with* the student body rather than segregated from it. As we pointed out in the chapter on reading, this goal broadens the English teacher's responsibilities.

Three main responsibilities should occur immediately. First, a teacher who encounters a student with a serious speech handicap should consult a speech therapist as soon as possible. If one is not available in the school or school system, the teacher should contact the State Department of Education or a nearby college or university. Secondly, the teacher must acquire a broader knowledge of the nature of speech disabilities and be willing to work with the student in the classroom (as time permits) in whatever way the therapist suggests. The third responsibility is to build within the classroom an atmosphere of "group," which honestly accepts and includes all of the students in the room. A student whose speech is different needs to be encouraged to do as well as possible. A disabled speaker can easily feel totally unworthy. Donald Ecroyd offers this sensible advice about working with such a student:

> *You can help him also by giving him some true perception of himself. Do not praise his speech if it is bad—he knows if you are being dishonest, and he*

*probably does not want your pity. But if what he says is understandable, tell him so, and commend his efforts. Call on him as you do the others, perhaps varying his task if the speech pathologist suggests it. But you will not help him feel that speaking is pleasurable, nor will you help him to learn to speak understandably if you take away from him all opportunity to speak. When he does speak, do not set your sights too high, and do not in any way give him the impression that you disapprove of what he does or are impatient with him.*[13]

## IMPROVING VOCAL QUALITY

Almost certainly among your students there will be a fairly large number whose vocal quality is poor. The three defects you will usually find are throatiness, thinness, and either nasality or denasality.

The throaty voice is unpleasantly deep and husky; the sound seems lost in the throat or even in the chest. The prevalence of throatiness, which results in making words hard to understand, accounts in large part for the fact that "Whadja say?" is the sentence most frequently spoken in the United States.[14]

Exercises in throat relaxation and in clear articulation may be recommended to throaty voiced students. A good exercise for throat relaxation is to sit upright, drop the head forward until the chin touches the chest, turn the head slowly to the right until the chin touches the right shoulder, then turn to the left, and repeat several times. Another is to take an imaginary drink of water and say "Oh" as the throat is open, a second drink and "Ah," and other imaginary drinks for the other vowel sounds. Still another exercise is to open the jaws wide and say the vowel sounds, to be followed later by words in which each vowel sound appears.

The thin voice lacks resonance, is usually high in pitch, and sometimes degenerates into an unpleasant whine. Humming is often mentioned to students as a means of increasing resonance. Long practice in sustaining the *m, n,* and *ng* sounds is also beneficial; these sounds may later be combined with vowels, as *am, em,* and so on, and, still later, sentences with many *m's, n's,* and *ng's* may be used.

Only the sounds of *m, n,* and *ng* should be allowed to pass through the nose. If any others do so, speech is described as nasal. The reverse of nasality, called denasality, occurs when the sounds of *m, n,* and *ng* do not pass through the nose.

Students may test their nasality by placing a finger beside the nose as, with the mouth open, they prolong the sounds of *m, n,* and *ng,* and then of other consonants and the vowels. If they can feel distinct vibration for the *m, n,* and *ng* sounds, and not for the others, their nasal resonance is normal. If, however, they feel much vibration when they pronounce vowel sounds, they should practice making the sound issue from the mouth instead of the nose; unless there is something organically wrong, they should be able to overcome their difficulties.

Denasality, though, is often due to stoppages and perhaps can be corrected only be a speech pathologist.

## IMPROVING PITCH

Most persons are unaware of their own vocal shortcomings because they have never actually heard themselves speak. If your school has a tape recorder, let your students hear themselves. More than likely each will say, or at least think, "Do I really sound that bad?"

One of the causes of "sounding that bad" is defective pitch. Very high-pitched voices are offensive, and very low-pitched ones are often monotonous. Frequently the only step needed for a cure is a conscious attempt to vary the pitch—for the low-pitched near-monotone to reach toward higher levels and for the person with high pitch to bring the voice down. The vocal apparatus in most persons can be used flexibly if it is given a chance, but nearly everyone uses it in the easiest way, regardless of whether that way is pleasant to hearers. Throat-relaxation exercises, like those described on page 437, are helpful, but primarily the treatment for most students is simply to make them aware of the deficiency and to suggest reasons for doing something about it.

## IMPROVING ENUNCIATION

As one-time British actor George Arliss declared, the chief defect of British speech is snippiness, and the chief defect of American speech is sloppiness. As a result of our lazy habits, we say "Uh, dunno," "Whurya gawn?" "Whuh timezut?" and so on. Although overprecise articulation seems affected, a happy medium exists for enunciation as for all things else.

Unless there is something wrong physiologically, anyone can improve his or her own enunciation. That fact implies that the teacher, or someone else, must supply motivation if enunciation is to be improved.

Poor enunciators tend to mumble, to insert extra syllables into words, or to omit syllables. The mumblers habitually speak indistinctly. Mouthers say "abaout" for "about," "baud" for "bad." The omitters tend to ignore middle syllables: "telscope" for "telescope," "connent" for "continent." All three defects, unless they are cured early, seem to increase with age. So, if you can motivate your students to struggle effectually against them, you can save many people hundreds of hours of unpleasant listening.

## IMPROVING PRONUNCIATION

It is not a criminal offense to mispronounce a word; in fact, if one could go back far enough into the past, one might find a time when the "mispronunciation"

438

was "correct." Pronunciations do change; Alexander Pope and his contemporaries, for instance, said "tay" for "tea" and "jine" for "join."

Right there is one entering wedge for correcting errors in pronunciation. Your students are modern—aggressively so. They want to do almost everything the way it is done today—none of this old-fashioned stuff for them. Encourage them to be as modern in their pronunciations as they are in their clothes or their music. Certainly, Grandpa said "crick," but we say "creek" today; Mark Twain's friends said, "genuwine," but we don't.

Let them know, too, on what basis dictionary makers establish what is correct pronunciation. The diacritical marks do not reflect someone's opinion; rather, they are determined by a careful study of how each word is pronounced by the majority of the educated people who use it.

If you use pronunciation drills, be sure to concentrate on words that you have heard a student mispronounce. Such drills are usually better than stopping a student who mispronounces a word; you should make a mental note of the error and include the word later in a list. You will thus save your students from embarrassment and antipathy toward speaking. Your list will probably consist mostly of common words: *asked, column, get, idea, just, library,* and so on.

One caution: Be sure that the pronunciations you attack are actually unaccepted. Some teachers have been surprised to learn that their favorite pronunciations of such words as *bouquet, gratis, isolated, menu,* and *panorama* are not the only ones listed in reputable dictionaries. Some dictionaries list li-ber-y and guv-er-ment as accepted alternatives.


## IMPROVING BODY CONTROL

Bernard shuffles up to the front of the class, glances in final desperation at the teacher, sways a little, puts both feet close together and sways some more, fidgets with his hands, and focuses his gaze on his toes as he begins to mumble at the floor. Bernard, or variants thereof, is in almost all classes. What can be done for him and his sister?

The importance of having a friendly class atmosphere has already been emphasized. That in itself will help Bernard and Bernardine, will give them confidence that their efforts will be received cordially, will contribute to the knowledge that they are before the class because they have something to offer and not because Teacher wants to criticize them. But there is something more that the teacher can do, something too rarely done in English classes. The teacher can give all the students practice in walking, in pantomiming, and in using the hands.

Here is how one teacher accomplishes this. In connection with vocabulary work, she and the class list as many synonyms as possible for *say* and *walk*. The ostensible purpose is to add words like *orate* and *saunter* to students' vocabularies. Then she asks for volunteers to act out some of the words in front of the class: Doris shouts, Jimmy strolls, and so forth. When the volunteers have performed, words are still left; the teacher asks the nonvolunteers, in pairs, to act out some of the words in order to demonstrate the contrast: Bernard skips while Roy totters. Having the shy ones work in pairs makes each less self-conscious.

Then, when all the words have been pantomimed, the teacher temporarily abandons vocabulary work and casually inquires about the characteristics of an attractive style of walking. "How do movie stars usually walk?" Gradually she elicits the information that graceful walkers carry their weight on the balls of their feet, keep their abdomens flat, have their shoulders relaxed, and lead with their chests.

She makes more use of pantomime on other occasions. (The British often do so, frequently having groups pantomime simple everyday acts such as brushing the teeth, applying make-up, or making tea. They sometimes also incorporate dance routines into classwork, on the theory that dance is itself a form of expression and that anything that helps to liberate the body can aid in communication.) She also has her students make many explanations at the chalkboard and give a chalk talk now and then. In the students' minds, the purpose is only to explain something to the class, but the teacher knows that when people use their hands in public, they worry less about them.

## IMPROVING CONTENT AND ORGANIZATION

In most speech activities, class and teacher should focus attention upon what is said. The delivery is, after all, only the vehicle for conveying thought; the thought itself is most important.

In class discussions the teacher may do much to encourage attention to facts. When George glibly condemns Congress as incompetent, he should be pinned down to specific accusations and asked for definite evidence to prove his statements. When Margaret says, "All French people are frivolous. I knew a French girl and she . . . ," there is the opportunity to demonstrate that an assuredly valid conclusion cannot be drawn from only one or two instances. When Clarence, whose family has voted Republican for 75 years, remarks bitterly that wars usually start during Democratic administrations, he not only is revealing personal prejudice but also is guilty of *post hoc, ergo propter hoc*. Whenever a student shifts from issues to personalities (a favorite trick of politicians), he is ignoring the question. Louise's remark, "Everybody's wearing whozits now, so we ought to get some," has the hidden premise that we should do what "everybody" is doing. Examples could be multiplied, but the point is simply that teachers should be constantly alert for weaknesses in reasoning and lack of evidence; they should encourage the class to challenge demonstrable fallacies. The intent is not to make a class argumentative but, rather, to make it mentally awake, one that thinks about what it hears.

The teacher should also remove some of the snags of content and organization before the students come to them. Unaided, most students will find little material for reports and discussions, and will not organize what they do find. With the teacher's help, however, they will uncover information in addition to that offered by the old standby, the encyclopedia. They will see how examples add to interest and clarity. The teacher also is responsible for showing the students how they can apply to their more formal talks the principles of organization they use in written composition. They learn that a good plan for a report is to have an interest-rousing opening, a body with not more than four well-illustrated main points (the most important usually last), and an ending that summarizes or restates in memorable fashion what has previously been said.

On the matter of permitting notes for rather long presentations, opinions differ. Students seem usually to do their best work if they are allowed to have notes on small cards—notes that will remind them of the steps in their talks. These notes should consist only of words or phrases, not complete sentences, because students tend merely to read anything written in sentence form. The little cards provide comfort, if nothing else; the students know that they cannot become completely lost when they have a few scribblings to which they may refer. There is nothing disgraceful about consulting notes; college professors who have given the same lecture a dozen or more times make extensive use of them. And one cannot help wondering how teachers can conscientiously forbid their students to use any notes when they themselves refer frequently to bundles of cards as they address the PTA.

In the follow-up evaluation of a rather formal talk, most remarks should concern content and organization. Although the class must be kept constantly aware of the importance of good enunciation, accepted pronunciation, and so on, comments should be more thoughtful than ''He said 'and uh' '' or ''He mispronounced 'Italian.' '' Judicious praise of what was said is superior to random criticism of the method of saying it. Additions to the content are in order, as are questions addressed to the speaker to elicit further information. Sometimes the teacher may speak favorably of the careful way in which Sally or Pete organized a presentation or may pause to comment approvingly on an especially happy illustration. Adverse criticisms should, as a rule, be given only after a number of presentations, and ought to refer to weaknesses observed in several of the talks. A unique fault in content or organization may be mentioned to a speaker in privacy, unless some questions and comments bring it out incidentally.

# THE IDEA BOX

## THE TALK-WRITE METHOD

In adapting Robert Zoellner's "Talk-Write" method of prompting college writing, Vincent Wixon and Pat Stone of McNary High School, Salem, Oregon, group students into small teams. One student of each team acts as writer, and another as questioner. By asking questions, one student encourages the other to "talk" out a theme while writing it on a large sheet of brown paper or on a section of the chalkboard. "When the composition is complete, it may have many sentences crossed out and changes in spelling, punctuation, or sentence and paragraph sequence, but it will say what the student intended."[15]

## "TEACHING CONFERENCE METHODS"

Fern Johnson and Barbara Sharf have found that helping students to plan a class meeting, convention, or workshop is an excellent exercise in group discussion techniques. Students in small groups plan an introduction, a keynote presentation, small group sessions, a large group session, a conclusion, and means for evaluating the conference. The "convention" can also encourage students to study a problem in which they have a mutual concern.[16]

## INTERVIEWING SENIOR CITIZENS

"The results have far exceeded the expectations of the assignment," says David L. Serres in describing interviews which his students in Seminole Junior College (Oklahoma) have held with older people who have lived in the community a long time. Each student selects a person who is known to him or her personally and then reports the highlights of the interview to the class. Included in the process are the techniques of interviewing, reporting, and often story-telling.[17]

## GUIDING CLASS DISCUSSIONS

Examples of questions and remarks that can improve discussions.

"Did this happen just by accident? If not, who or what caused it?"

"Why did this happen in the way it did rather than in some other way?"

"Which character in this story has the biggest problem? What is the problem?"

"Who in this story seems to need to learn the most?"

"Has this character changed? Become a different person in some way?"

"Does the way in which the character has changed have anything to do with the idea of the story? What is the idea, then?"

"What evidence is there for this belief?"

"I don't understand. Can you think of an example?"

"Is a middle-of-the-road position more sensible than either position?"

"Can anyone think of a circumstance in which this suggestion would work?"

"Can anyone think of a circumstance in which this suggestion would not work?"

"What points have we agreed on so far?"

"Have you ever had to . . . ?"

"What are some things you could do to . . . ?"

"What would you do if . . . ?"

## USES OF VIDEOTAPE

Videotape equipment can be very helpful in oral activities. If it is not available for regular use in English classes, sometimes it can be borrowed (tactfully) from the athletic department. This equipment enables individual students to watch themselves giving prepared speeches, groups to observe their conduct during group discussions, a teacher and the class to evaluate the success of a class discussion, and students to evaluate various kinds of skits (TV commercials, dramatic scenes, talk shows, etc.).

## MORE IMAGINATIVE CHORAL READING

At Macalester College, Mary Gwen Owens' students serve as directors of choral reading. The groups make their own selections and arrangements, and sometimes use music or props for special effects—even doing some square dancing at times.[18]

## OVERCOMING SPEECH FRIGHT

A survey reported by Charles Gruner shows that 101 of 121 students said that practice is the best way to overcome speech fright; 75 said that increased understanding of speech techniques helps; and 62 said that attitudes of the teacher and classmates are determining factors; better understanding of self was named by 53, and understanding of the nature and cause of speech fright was cited by 52.[19]

## IMPROMPTU SPEECHES

Students draw a topic from a box, take a minute or two to think, and then talk briefly on it. In another approach, the teacher passes around expressions and sayings (possibly taken from magazines, newspaper headlines, and pasted on squares of construction paper). In still another method, students draw an object from a box or bag (paper clip, clothes pin, hairpin), tell an interesting story in which it plays a major part, or describe an unusual use for it.

## "A SPEAKING APPROACH TO COMPOSITION"

A student gives the teacher a written thesis sentence for a talk. When the student finishes, each classmate writes what he or she thinks this sentence is—or should be. Discussion follows. Good practice in listening, and useful for providing focus in written composition, too, says R. W. Higbee.[20]

## CORRELATING SPEECH AND LITERATURE

Before studying short stories, students may relate anecdotes and expand upon them; later, stories may be read interpretively. Before studying essays, students may give informal talks on essay-like topics. Before studying lyric poetry, they may discuss and illustrate an emotion that poets often treat, such as feelings about death; later, they may interpret. And drama, of course, should be performed. These are among suggestions by William J. Reynolds.[21]

## COMBATING STAGE FRIGHT: MORE SUGGESTIONS

1. Advise fearful students to start a talk with something funny. Doing so may relax them and the audience too.
2. Help students select topics that they are genuinely interested in, even concerned about. Thinking about the subject will leave less time to think about the self.
3. Advise rehearsing the talk but not memorizing it. Fear of forgetting contributes to fright.

## OVERCOMING SHYNESS

1. "A good device for overcoming initial reticence is to introduce a subject which contains much controversial matter. As soon as the teacher sees that the subject matter has caught the fancy of the class, he allows students to select a chairperson and plan their own talks." (Arigo La Tanzi, Braintree, Mass.)
2. Another teacher begins by having students make an announcement of a real or imaginary event, including time, place, purpose, cost, and any other needed information. Generally, the more imaginary the event, the livelier the announcement. Second step: a prepared (but not memorized) 3-minute oral reading of anything the student likes.
3. A useful device for overcoming shyness and teaching thinking on one's feet is a modification of the old *commedia dell'arte*. The teacher or a student briefly summarizes a simple story with few characters. Students then act it out, improvising the dialogue. Once the students have become accustomed to making it up as they go along, they may be given a story with the ending omitted; the actors must then work out a reasonable solution by themselves *while* they are acting.

## THE SPEECH CONSULTANT

West Canada Valley High School, Middleville, N.Y., employs for 80 half-days a year a speech consultant from a nearby college. He has worked out a specific schedule of speech teaching and gives instruction beyond the scope of most English teachers.[22]

## A SIMPLE SPEECH PLAN

Wilmer Lamar describes a highly successful program for teaching speech in the English classroom. One of the many techniques he suggests is the following of a simple five-division outline for a speech: (1) awakener (question, striking statement, narration, arousing of suspense, quotation, personal incident), (2) point (statement of what the speaker is driving at), (3) reason (why the point is important), (4) examples (the body of the talk), (5) conclusion (restatement, quotation, relevant question, or call to action).[23]

## MEASURING CHANGE OF OPINION

Before an argumentative or persuasive presentation or discussion, ask class members to indicate on slips of paper whether they favor or oppose the proposition or are undecided. After the presentation, have them indicate "more strongly favor," "favor to about same degree," "more strongly oppose," "oppose to about same degree," "still undecided," "shifted from favor to undecided," "shifted from opposed to undecided," and so on. Have a pair of students tally the number and direction of opinion shifts. Later students should be invited to discuss reasons for these shifts.

## AUDIOVISUAL AIDS AND DEMONSTRATIONS

Encourage use of maps, charts, pictures, diagrams, and the like in talks and reports. These may be especially useful in how-it-works or how-to-do-it explanations.

Demonstrations, with actual objects, may help shy students forget themselves. For example, a basic dance step, artificial respiration, tuning a musical instrument.

## BRAINSTORMING

As a problem-solving technique (to be used only in the face of a *genuine* problem) try a brief brainstorming session. The rules: (1) Allow no adverse criticism, even if a suggestion seems utterly ridiculous. (2) Welcome imaginative ideas. (3) Try for many and diverse ideas. (4) Combine and improve ideas (called "hitchhiking").

A recorder notes all suggestions. A day later, the group appraises the ideas to see whether any of them or any combination of them may afford a solution.

## IMPROVING REPORTS

A West Virginia ninth grade class taught by Anna Brochick made these decisions about ways to improve its reports: (1) Every oral report must show that the reporter tried to make it good. (2) The beginning and ending should show some originality. (3) The reporter must try to use acceptable speech. (4) Material should be well organized. (5) The reporter should be easily heard. (6) Each report should be subject to group evaluation and to evaluation by the reporter.

## ORAL ENGLISH IN COMMUNITY AFFAIRS

The Speech Department of Reno, Nevada, recommends: "The speech program can help to promote community affairs such as Red Cross and Community Chest campaigns. Student participants become more civic conscious. Presenting such programs before adults makes for excellent public relations because the citizens of the community have an opportunity to see one thing that the schools are doing." This department also recommends inviting guests to class periods when there are special oral presentations.

## SPEAKER'S BUREAU

In Roosevelt High School, Chicago, a "Speaker's Bureau," with a faculty sponsor, was in charge of publicizing school activities. Members made announcements in homerooms, and sometimes were sent to speak before civic organizations such as Kiwanis or Union League Club. (Lynne Harford)

## BREATHING

"To obtain clear, distinct speech, the most valuable technique is the regular practice of diaphragmatic breathing and vowel sounding in class, in chorus. This need only be done enough to educate pupils to the idea that speech is always more clear and forceful when supported by well-controlled breath." (John Ferrett, Braintree, Mass.)

## CAPTURING COMMUNICATION ON CASSETTES

Alice Hibbard describes some excellent uses of the inexpensive audio cassette tape recorder in developing oral skills. Among uses in interviewing, she mentions obtaining oral histories of communities from long-term residents, seeking opinions from people on given topics, and conducting the personal interview. Even the book report can be brought back to life with cassettes. Students may use relevant background music or sound effects if they wish. Students are less likely to leave out information because of nervousness. Taped reports can be stored and used later by students.[24]

## THE MOCK TRIAL

Ron L. Fadley of Bowling Green State University reports success in using the mock trial in junior high to stimulate debate. As many students as possible should be used in the trial itself; if not as prosecuting attorneys, defense attorneys, witnesses, jury members, bailiff, and judge, at least as courtroom spectators. Fadley illustrates his teaching method by drawing upon a trial used in a law school; however, English can find selections of literature which raise many interesting questions about innocence and guilt.[25]

## THE STAGED SITUATION TO ENCOURAGE DEBATE

The staged situation is a well-known method in psychology classes. Students witness in the classroom a situation which they have reason to believe was not staged and are interviewed individually as to what happened and who was to blame. Vigorous debate usually follows such an experience before or after students find out that it is not "real." An impostor can also come into the classroom to present a point of view that stirs debate. For example, suppose an unknown adult were to ask

446                                          THE TEACHING OF HIGH SCHOOL ENGLISH

all students interested in cleaner air to raise their hands, and then tell them that he or she is glad to see the hands because they indicate that students will go along with a plan discussed with the administration to eliminate or severely cut the practice of allowing them to drive to school in their private cars. The speaker then outlines various ways in which students who are not bussed will travel in groups to not only help clean up the air, but save gasoline as well. After the speaker leaves, the teacher invites students to express their views. A word of caution: When in doubt, clear such things in advance with school administrators and department chairpersons.

## ON CONVERSING WITH COMPUTERS

Have you ever conversed with a computer? Nancy Thompson mentions microcomputers, a toy car, and a wheelchair that already respond to verbal directions. ''With the computer, all input—voice, image, or printed verbal or numerical data—can be transformed into the same kind of signals . . . Thus, the computer becomes the SUPER integrator of language . . . .''[26]

## ORAL ENGLISH IN CAREER EDUCATION

For some time English teachers have suggested that students write to vocational schools or colleges, and then in class present prepared talks on entrance requirements, courses, and training offered. The growing emphasis on career education has now broadened activities. Examples may be found in *Speech Resource Guide with Emphasis on Career Education* (1974), published by the Louisiana State Department of Education.

## THE TEACHER'S ROLE IN SMALL-GROUP DISCUSSIONS

A weak teacher will see small-group discussions as an opportunity to sit behind the desk or off in a corner to plan lessons or grade papers, but a strong teacher will see these discussions as a unique opportunity to teach. This does not mean that a teacher should move in on discussions; to do this would only inhibit oral communication. Robert Graham of the Oakland Schools, Pontiac, Michigan, suggests that the teacher sit ''on the periphery of a group and follow its talk,'' and then ask ''noncommitment type questions to refocus the task'' of the group. One technique is to make statements such as, ''John, I don't believe that you understand Mary.''[27]

## PROMPTING THROUGH PARAPHRASING

Julia Hurley Goelz, who teaches English at Claremont High School, Belmont, California, finds that students can be encouraged to talk in conversations and in small-group discussions if the listener occasionally paraphrases the main idea of a student's statement in a way that also echoes the tone which the student intended. This is interpreted by the student as meaning that the listener is listening, is really interested, and is trying to understand not only the message but its feeling. A speaker who is not sure that he has been understood should be able to ask the listener to repeat or rephrase what was said. Thus, repetition becomes a very important device in oral communication.[28]

## USING SMALL-GROUPS TO TEST SPEECH TOPICS

Charles M. Rossiter, Jr. of the University of Wisconsin-Milwaukee suggests that students might go into small group discussions with two or three possible speech topics. Group members give the student feedback which is useful in helping the student to choose the best topic. Group members help the speaker to determine whether a topic "(1) is sufficiently substantive to speak about to his audience; (2) is sufficiently delimited to be handled adequately within the time limitation of the assignment; (3) is of interest to the speaker and is something about which he has sufficient expertise to speak; and (4) is of interest to his audience."[29]

## READING ALOUD TO STUDENTS

One of the authors of this methods text recalls the strong interest generated in a high school class by a teacher who would occasionally perch on a tall wooden stool near the front of the room and read an interesting story, poem, or prose selection to the class. No one is too old to enjoy listening to oral reading when it is done well. A teacher who follows this practice (and does a good job) can inspire students to read aloud to each other.

## A TEACHER'S SPEECH SETS AN EXAMPLE

The teacher's speech should set the best possible example for everything discussed in this chapter. The teacher speaks in almost every circumstance and setting encountered by students. Teachers, too, must be able to speak effectively in one-to-one conversations, small groups, and large groups; they, too must be able to adjust to informal and formal occasions. Every rule and principle given to students applies to the teacher as well.[30]

## WILL COMPUTERS DO ALL OF OUR INTERVIEWING? PROBABLY NOT

John Brady ends his book, *The Craft of Interviewing,* with these interesting observations:

> Today, the interview is so widely accepted that it has even been mechanized. In Chicago, a group of lawyers recently turned some of the interviewer's task over to a computer. The machine poses some 300 to 400 questions to a prospective plaintiff, instantly summarizes the answers, and rattles off a ready-to-file lawsuit. The computer is designed to base questions on previous answers. With further programming, according to the *New York Times,* "the computer would as readily prepare a will, draft a bankruptcy petition, put together a consumer complaint, and help with other standard chores."
>
> While the computer may be a time- and moneysaver for attorneys, the writer's profession remains a cottage industry in comparison. Even Walter Rugaber, the *Times* reporter, had to use a telephone interview to get the story on computer interviews.[31]

THE TEACHING OF HIGH SCHOOL ENGLISH

# FOOTNOTES

1. Mary Frances Hopkins, Beverly Whitaker, and Bernard Brommel (eds.), *Contemporary Speech: A Comprehensive Approach to Communication,* Skokie: National Textbook Company, 1976, p. ix.
2. James R. Squire and Roger K. Applebee, *High School English Instruction Today,* New York: Appleton-Century-Crofts, 1968, pp. 257–258.
3. Candida Gillis, "The English Classroom 1977: A Report on the EJ Readership Survey," *English Journal* 66, Sept. 1977, pp. 20–26.
4. *Student-Centered Language Arts and Reading, K-13,* Second Edition, Boston: Houghton Mifflin Company, 1976, p. 275.
5. Joanna H. Maclay and Thomas O. Sloan, *Interpretation: An Approach to the Study of Literature,* New York: Random House, 1972, p. xi.
6. *Oral Prose & Oral Poetry,* Skokie: National Textbook Corporation, 1965, pp. 4–7.
7. *Group Reading: Readers Theatre,* Skokie: National Textbook Company, 1967, pp. 19–21.
8. "The First Thirty Minutes in Choral Reading," *English Journal* 57, March 1968, p. 395.
9. *The Craft of Interviewing,* New York: Vintage Books, 1977, p. xii.
10. "Semantics and the Study of Speech," *Speech Teacher,* March 1967, pp. 98–102.
11. *Teaching Speech,* Columbia, Mo.: Artcraft Press, 1960, p. 188.
12. "Experimental Approaches to Oral Traditional Literature," *English Journal* 64, April 1975, pp. 94–97.
13. *Speech in the Classroom,* Second Edition, Englewood Cliffs, N.J.: Prentice-Hall, Inc., p. 148.
14. Some years ago researchers for Funk and Wagnalls made this interesting but disconcerting discovery.
15. "Getting it Out, Getting it Down: Adapting Zoellner's Talk-Write," *English Journal* 66, Sept. 1977, p. 71.
16. *Speech Teacher,* Jan. 1975, pp. 74–75.
17. "Black Gold and Wildcats," *Communication Education,* Sept. 1976, pp. 255–258.
18. Marilyn E. Stassen, "Choral Reading and the English Teacher," *English Journal* 58, March 1969, p. 436.
19. "A Further Note on Speech Fright," *Speech Teacher,* Sept. 1964, pp. 223–224.
20. *English Journal* 53, Jan. 1964, p. 50.
21. "Let's Talk Speech," *English Journal* 57, Jan. 1968, p. 105.
22. "The Speech Consultant Teaches Speech in the English Classroom," *English Record,* XIII, No. 2, 1962, p. 30.

23. "Let Any Student Speak," *Illinois English Bulletin*, Feb. 1961.
24. "Tape Recorder in the Classroom," *English Journal* 65, May 1976, pp. 65–68.
25. "The Mock Trial as a Motivational Device for Junior High Debate," *Speech Teacher*, Nov. 1975, pp. 374–378.
26. "Computers: The *Super* Multi-Media Resource," *English Journal* 67, Jan. 1978, pp. 98–102.
27. "Talk-Drama as an Alternative to the Lecture," in *Lecture Alternatives in Teaching English*, Stephen Judy (ed.), Ann Arbor, Campus Publishers, 1971, p. 26.
28. "Repetition and Frustration," *English Journal* 63, Dec. 1974, pp. 45–49.
29. "Helping Students Choose Classroom Speech Topics More Realistically," *Speech Teacher*, March 1973, pp. 159–160.
30. See Karl F. Robinson and Albert B. Becker, *Effective Speech for the Teacher*, New York: McGraw-Hill Book Company, 1970.
31. *The Craft of Interviewing*, p. 231.

# 14

## LISTENING—REALLY

## IN THE CLASSROOM

### IS ANYONE LISTENING?

Have you ever looked around an English classroom and tried to guess who is really listening? Let's assume that you are observing a tenth grade class where the teacher is giving a short lecture to prepare students for class discussion of a short story. Mary in the front row is looking directly into the teacher's eyes and has a smile on her face. Is she listening to the teacher? Thoughts behind that smile may have nothing to do with what the teacher has said. In fact, Mary may not be able to repeat very much of the lecture, let alone comment on its meaning. John divides his time between looking at the teacher and writing in his notebook. Is he taking English notes, or is he doing his history homework? Paul is picking at his fingers and rarely looks up. He may be definitely listening, but only he knows. Larry in the back row has his head down on his desk and has closed his eyes. Is he asleep? Possibly. Dave has his literature anthology open to the story. Is he looking for passages relevant to the teacher's comments, or is he trying to read the story (yesterday's assignment) in case the teacher should call on him? Rita and Juanita, who sit several seats apart, have for several minutes engaged in creative nonverbal communication with each other. Occasionally they glance furtively at the teacher. Can you assume that they are definitely not listening?

It is also difficult to determine whether some high school students are listening to each other. Some never ask each other questions in class or in group discussions. Are they soaking up knowledge silently, or are they preoccupied with irrelevant thoughts? Others look up at every sound or movement outside their discussion group. A student from another group who walks to the pencil sharpener might get more attention than an immediate group member who is trying to say something important. The slouchers, the doodlers, the whisperers, the exiles, the know-it-alls, the squirmers, whether in a class discussion or a group discussion, may be listening, but a visitor might be uncertain. In many classrooms, listening seems to be taken for granted. And maybe that is the problem. Possibly no one, not even the teacher, is sure what can be done to improve listening. Worse yet, the assumption may be that anyone who can hear knows how to listen.

## LISTENING IS NOT JUST HEARING

All of the students described above might be hearing sounds that the teacher or other students are making; at least they might be able to say that someone is talking about something. But listening is not just hearing. Sara Lundsteen has defined listening to speech (sometimes called *auding*) as "the process by which spoken language is converted to meaning in the mind."[1] Listening to language, then, the kind of listening that students do most often in a classroom, requires conscious mental effort; it results in comprehension and extends to some kind of activity related to that comprehension. Lundsteen has broken the auding process down into these ten steps: (1) hear, (2) hold in memory, (3) attend, (4) form images, (5) search the past store of ideas, (6) compare, (7) test the cues, (8) recode, (9) get meaning, and (10) intellectualize beyond the listening moment."[2] The first two she identifies as physiological activity, three through eight as attention and concentration, and the last two as highly intellectual activity.

In a broad sense, people listen appreciatively, discriminatingly, pragmatically, and critically. Unlike the reader, the listener cannot vary at will the speed of receiving the message; but like the reader, the listener can choose the "message" which suits a purpose. Accordingly, the listener sets different goals for listening to music or poetry (both appreciative); engine noises, heartbeats, dialects, vocal stress (discriminative); requests, directions (pragmatic); lectures (pragmatic and critical); and campaign speeches (critical).[3] To accomplish a particular goal, the listener thinks about the sounds and translates these thoughts into feelings and actions.

## LISTENING CRITICALLY

Although all areas of listening defined briefly above are relevant and important subjects for study and practice in a high school English classroom, critical listening deserves special attention. If for no other reason, critical listening is important in a democracy because it can help students think clearly about the issues that constantly arise in a democratic nation. Essential to democracy is intellectual choice. We have to distinguish between the weighed words of the scientific pleader and the weighted words of the spellbinder. Constantly we are faced with the necessity of evaluating and choosing—between two or more candidates, isms, methods, or proposed solutions. There is no royal road to utopia—there may be no utopia—but we have to weigh the merits of each trail through the swamps and choose the least undesirable one.

## LISTENING—THE SILENT SUBJECT

It is ironic that listening, an extremely important school subject, has been surrounded by so much silence. Most secondary English curriculum guides and individual plans of study give little if any attention to teaching listening skills. Patricia and James Cunningham of the University of North Carolina, Chapel Hill, give these reasons for lack of instruction:

1. Listening is seen as a maturation process that just naturally gets better as the child gets older.
2. There are few guides, manuals, or other structured programs to direct listening instruction.
3. Improving listening is everyone's job and consequently is attempted by no one.[4]

## DEVELOPING A LISTENING PROGRAM

The two lists below (suggested by Lundsteen) could be very useful to an English teacher who is attempting to establish goals for a listening program:

### General Listening

1. *Remembering significant details accurately (knowledge of specifics)*
2. *Remembering simple sequences or words and ideas*
3. *Following oral directions*
4. *Paraphrasing a spoken message (comprehension by translation)*
5. *Following a sequence in (a) plot development, (b) character development, (c) speaker's argument*
6. *Understanding denotative (literal) meanings of words*
7. *Understanding connotative meanings of words (comprehension by interpretation)*
8. *Understanding meanings of words from spoken context (comprehension by translation and interpretation)*
9. *Listening for implications of significant details (analysis and interpretation)*
10. *Listening for implications of main ideas*
11. *Answering and formulating questions (interactive listening)*

12. *Identifying main ideas and summarizing (combining and synthesizing the who, what, when, where, and why)*
13. *Understanding relationships among ideas and the organizational pattern well enough to predict what may come next (comprehension by extrapolation)*
14. *Connecting the spoken material with previous experience and planning action (application)*
15. *Listening to imagine and to extend for enjoyment and emotional response (affective-toned synthesizing)*

### Critical Listening

1. *Distinguishing fact from fancy, according to criteria*
2. *Judging validity and adequacy of main ideas, arguments, and hypotheses*
3. *Distinguishing well-supported statements from opinion and judgment and evaluating them*
4. *Distinguishing well-supported statements from irrelevant ones and evaluating them*
5. *Inspecting, comparing, and contrasting ideas and arriving at a conclusion about statements, such as the appropriateness and appeal of one descriptive word over another*
6. *Evaluating the use of fallacies, such as: (a) self-contradictions, (b) avoiding the question at issue, (c) hasty or false generalization, (d) false analogy, (e) failure to present all choices, (f) appealing to ignorance*
7. *Recognizing and judging the effects of various devices the speaker may use to influence the listener, such as (a) music, (b) "loaded" words, (c) voice intonation, (d) play on emotional and controversial issues, (e) propaganda, sales pressure—that is, identifying affective loading in communication and evaluating it*
8. *Detecting and evaluating the bias and prejudice of a speaker or of a point of view*
9. *Evaluating the qualifications of a speaker*
10. *Planning to evaluate the ways in which a speaker's ideas might be applied in a new situation[5]*

However detailed they may be, goals do not make a program. Obviously programs also need strategies for helping students to reach the goals. A long-range strategy is the first consideration. Listening should be taught systematically throughout the entire scope and sequence of education in any school system. The Palm Beach County Schools describe this kind of articulation in *Language Arts Continuum K-12: Resource Guide—Secondary* (1974). This guide not only details advanced listening goals for grades 9 through 12, but less advanced ones for K-2, 3-5, and 6-8. Thus, the senior high English teacher can plan units and lessons that take into consideration knowledge and skills taught in primary, intermediate, and middle school/junior high grades; the middle school/junior high English teacher can plan in view of everything taught earlier and later.

Within a well-articulated program, teachers should have models to direct student learning. One model which certainly deserves more attention from high school English teachers was developed by Ralph E. Kellogg. It assumes four levels of comprehension: (1) recall of data or details, a stage during which the listener relies on memory and mentally asks questions such as "What?" "When?" "Where?" and "Who?"; (2) analysis, during which the listener searches for cause and effect relationships and asks "How?" or "Why?"; (3) synthesis, during which the listener pulls together everything from the first two levels and asks, "So what is the main idea, so what does all of this mean?"; (4) application, during which the listener wonders how the meaning applies personally to his or her life and could result in personal actions. Questions on this, the highest, level might be, "So how can I apply that main idea to a new situation?" and "So how can I apply that idea to me?"[6]

Uses of the Kellogg Listening Model in English classes seem promising. Students who are asked to formulate mental questions on these levels as they listen to oral presentations can develop a process for listening creatively and critically. Applications can go as far as imagination and effort will allow. As students listen to TV commercials prepared for the general public or to videotapes made by other students, they can be asked to listen to important details about the product, for evidence that the product works in ways guaranteed or implied, and for general assumptions made by the advertiser. Final questions would lead to inferences and to personal action: "So how can I use that product? "What will using that product mean to me or do for me?"

The four levels of the Kellogg model convert easily to listening charts or schedules that students can complete after listening to a speech or to a story, poem, or essay. Using key questions appropriate on each level, students would supply answers gained only through listening. An interesting application would be completing such a chart as a first step in learning how to take notes.

Richard Castallo, a reading resource teacher for Westhill Central Schools, Syracuse, New York, has developed a written guide for listeners who are learning note-taking. Given to students before a lecture, the guide begins with a one-paragraph prospectus of the lecture and includes a topical outline with blanks for students to fill in as they listen.[7]

An English teacher does not have to be unusually creative to think of such strategies and models for the classroom. Many techniques used in teaching other areas of English, especially reading, may be worth adapting for listening. In a way, the procedure is like using the Kellogg model. The teacher hears other teachers talk about procedures or reads articles and books such as this one and then asks questions such as these: "What are the details of this technique?"

"When, where, and by whom has it been used?" "How and why did it work?" "What is its main significance for the students?" "So how can I apply it in teaching listening to my students?"

## MORE TECHNIQUES FOR IMPROVING LISTENING

Here are some practical suggestions concerning ways in which students may become effective listeners. Adaptations of course are possible.

### The Teacher as Model

The teacher who is a good listener will help students develop their own expectations and procedures for listening. John Sweet writes of one teacher, "Basic to his skill is the fact that he is first and foremost a listener. He is a whole course in how to listen. Magically, he mixes relaxation with intensity. Formal and yet warm, he respects his students as persons. The attention of the class is focused on their truths, not his own."[8]

### Saying It Once

Repetition can be helpful, even quite necessary at times, but students should not expect to rely on it as people speak. Occasionally the teacher should tell students that something will be said or read orally only once and then should test the students on it. The kinds of things said might include simple directions for assignments to be done individually and turned in at the end of the period, helpful comments just before a major test in class, or a quotation or short poem read orally for class discussion. In such situations, one rule of course should be that students are not to ask anyone else what was said or read.

### Discussion of Listening

Students are usually amenable to reason, especially when they supply the reason. Therefore a class discussion on the why and how of listening may be valuable. The class may stress courtesy ("Listen to others as you would have them listen to you"), purposefulness, accuracy, and responsiveness. Young classes may need to talk about physical requirements for listening—such as having desks clear of irrelevant materials, not whispering or making other noises—and about the courtesy of showing interest by posture and facial expression, and of being patient when a speaker has difficulty. Discussions may be followed by having a volunteer committee construct a poster naming and illustrating the qualities of a good listener; this poster may be left for some time in a conspicuous spot as a reminder. If a student is adept at cartoons or caricatures, he or she may construct a special poster in order to laugh out of existence some of the faulty listening habits.

THE TEACHING OF HIGH SCHOOL ENGLISH

## Suggestions on What to Listen For

Before playing a record in a music-appreciation course, the teacher generally suggests that the students listen for something in particular—the function of a certain instrument or the repetition of a theme. This technique may be borrowed by the English teacher, who usually knows what to expect in an oral presentation. Once, for instance, when several ninth-grade students were explaining how to make things, the teacher simply asked the class members to try to follow each explanation and be ready to ask questions if there was something they did not understand. When an eleventh grade student was talking about the life of Walt Whitman, the teacher asked the class to listen for what they thought was the most interesting episode in the poet's life. Very little guidance will increase the intensity of listening; also, the understanding of the entire presentation seems to be increased when the students are supposedly concentrating on one item.

A variation of this might be to ask students to listen despite distractions. Most listeners cannot demand that all distracting sounds cease. To train students to focus on what is relevant to a particular purpose, Richard Halley of the University of New Hampshire suggests reading a story with irrelevant music in the background, also reading a story to one group while someone else is reading another story aloud to another group. Students then take tests on the verbal or nonverbal sounds they have been asked to listen for.[9]

The focuses in listening activities may be varied greatly. Students might listen for examples of similes, metaphors or onomatopoeia in poetry. They might be asked to close their eyes and listen only for noises outside the window or in the hall, and to describe their characteristics and sequences, even to guess their origins. They might also listen to a recording of a scene in a play, paying particular attention to clues as to why a certain character is so angry or so pleased.

## Quizzes

One should not allow students to assume that they will be held responsible only for the material in the textbook. If class periods have any value, much of what is said in class is worth remembering. Examinations, therefore, may cover content presented in class in addition to that in the textbook.

## Recording Class Sessions

Teachers as well as students are often unaware of how frequently they discourage others from listening. Speakers who talk constantly do not give listeners a chance to respond to them or, as in the case of a class discussion, to each other. Listening to recordings of actual class periods or just to short segments could help teachers and students judge how effectively they listened to each other.

LISTENING—REALLY

## Creating Sound Stories

Allen Berger and Anne Werdmann of the University of Pittsburgh have suggested that students might use noises in predetermined sequences to create a nonverbal story.[10] Sounds carefully created or found and sequenced can suggest moods, actions, suspense, climax, and so on, to listeners. The creators may explain their sound stories or choose not to do so, leaving interpretations up to listeners.

A variation sometimes used by teachers is the sequence of sounds to stimulate creative writing. Shuffling feet, a key rattling in a lock, a door opening and closing on squeaking hinges, a dog barking, glass breaking, and so forth, may suggest many different stories to students.

## Understanding Organization

Let us assume that you have been unable to attend a lecture and that you want to find out what the speaker had to say. If you ask an acquaintance to tell you about it, the person may say "It was good," "It was dull," "He speaks well," or "He talked about———," but chances are he or she will be unable to summarize the lecture for you. Why? Because listeners are often unaware of the organization of a talk, and, having no mental outline to follow, they are unable to reconstruct it. They may have listened to every word, but if they have not understood the organization, they will be unable to generalize or to refer to a point here and there.

Of double value to your students is listening to a speech or report in an attempt to understand its organization. The first value is that they can learn to give intelligent summaries of what they hear; the second, that they become conscious of the need for organization in order to assure clarity in their own speaking and writing. A procedure that may be employed is to review the possible methods of organization and to discuss ways of identifying the chief supporting points. A few comments on the use of transitions are apropos here. Then the students listen to the next assembly speaker, or to presentations by their classmates, and make analyses. Students who have been taught to listen for the organization of a talk usually comprehend it rather well; they also criticize more severely any rambling discourse.

## Selecting Main Ideas

A natural outgrowth, indeed a part of the study of organization, is the selection of main ideas. One procedure is to have students write papers of 150 to 200 words (the exact count isn't important) on such a topic as "What Our School Needs Most," "How to Improve the Job Market for Teenagers," or "What Our City Should Do for Bored Teenagers." After each paper is read, the members of the class try to reduce the main idea to one terse sentence. If the writer has not been clear, the listeners will not hesitate to say so.

A follow-up can be the oral reading of carefully selected passages from a current magazine, a newspaper editorial, or the work of a major nonfiction writer. Once more the students try to reduce the material to a single sentence. After this activity, the students should be able to supply a title as well.

### Listening for Contradictions and Faulty Reasoning

In a discussion or an argumentative presentation, a speaker will sometimes contradict himself or herself, although the contradiction may be well hidden. The classic example is that of the politician who comes out in favor of lower prices, higher wages, and larger profits.

Even more common than contradictions are flaws in reasoning and the use of propaganda techniques. High school students may be taught to identify fallacies and devices like these:

1. Begging and ignoring the question: talking about a related subject instead of the point at issue; talking about a person's strong or weak points instead of the facts or ideas actually involved; arguing in a circle (e.g., ''The Koran is the word of God. We know that, because it says so, and the word of God cannot lie.''); appealing to the emotions instead of to reason; stating as a fact something that remains to be proved
2. False analogy: inadequate resemblance between two things being compared
3. Hasty generalization: drawing a conclusion from too few examples
4. Faulty dilemma: submitting only two choices when more actually exist
5. *Post hoc, ergo propter hoc:* (after this, therefore because of this) assuming that, because one thing follows another in time, the later is based on the earlier (e.g., because the French Revolution was later than the one in America, the French people were necessarily inspired by the Americans)
6. Hidden major premise: failure to state the generalization upon which a conclusion is based (e.g., ''Giuseppe sings well because he is an Italian'' has the hidden premise that all Italians sing well)
7. Incompetent authority: using the opinion of someone who is not an expert in the field being discussed (e.g., ''_____ _____ the movie star believes that we should declare war at once'')

The purpose of keeping students alert for flaws in reasoning is not, of course, to make them hypercritical or one another. Rather, it is to help them as speakers to reason logically, and as listeners to be aware of types of faulty reasoning against which they should be on guard.

### Bringing in One's Own Knowledge

To listen creatively, one must relate what one hears to what one already knows. That means that a listener should classify it, compare it with related information or ideas, reject it if it seems worthless or false, and keep it if it appears valuable and true. The person with a well-ordered mind apparently files away information so that it can be quickly found. For example, he or she will file knowledge about nuclear power plants with previously filed knowledge about nuclear energy until a stimulus calls for it. The well-ordered listener/thinker will retrieve it and may draw another fact from another part of the file to form a thought—actually a creative response. In contrast with this possessor of a well-regulated mind is the person with a haphazard mind. This person does not regularly relate newly acquired bits of information to anything else; as a result, they drop quickly from memory or else become so badly scattered that they cannot be readily recalled. This listener also has a mental filing system but files too much under the heading "Miscellaneous."

Teaching students to relate new knowledge to previously acquired knowledge is one of the biggest jobs in education. In a sense it is the topic of most of this book and hundreds of other educational writings. Below are a few suggestions concerning ways of helping students to relate what they learn to what they already know.

The "post-mortem" is a very useful device. A challenging assembly speaker should not be ignored in the English class that follows the assembly program. Talk about what the speaker said; question statements of opinion and possibly facts: let the class amplify some remarks, and seek parallel incidents from life or literature. When a student has made an oral presentation, follow the same procedure. The oral work will probably improve when the class knows that more comes from its efforts than a mark in a gradebook; student attention will be heightened; and the processes of thinking will be accelerated.

The search for parallels is particularly stimulating. Suppose that a class has heard a report on James Russell Lowell in which the emphasis was upon his versatility—poet, critic, humorist, essayist, editor, professor, speaker, and international diplomat. Questions like these should be raised: "What other writers have held high government positions?" "Who is the most versatile person you have ever heard of?" "What versatile people do you know?" Parallels to almost anything are endless—history does repeat itself infinitely—and recognizing parallels seems to help in the improvement of mental filing systems and in subsequent thoughtful uses of such systems.

Similar to searching for parallels is supplying examples. The following illustration refers to a printed selection, but the same technique may be used after a talk. Van Loon, in his *Geography,* refers to prehistoric animals that "went about their daily affairs clad in the armor of a medieval knight." What were some of these animals? Other creatures, he says, have gone into "domestic service." For example? Man, van Loon goes on, has taken possession of the earth "by right of his superior brain and by the strength of his foresight and his shot-guns." What has man conquered by his brain? By foresight? By shot-guns? This searching for examples helps students to listen more attentively, to straighten up their mental files, and possibly to include more examples in their own writing.

Three more devices may be mentioned briefly. (1) Supplying contrasts is desirable. Suppose, for instance, that a student has been explaining to a senior class how plays were staged in ancient Greece. Pointing out the contrasts between Greek and modern or between Greek and Elizabethan staging will be valuable. (2) Sometimes a statement by a speaker will recall a proverb or a famous quotation. Let the students think of it. (3) When a talk has been about a person—fictional or otherwise—a clever teacher may construct certain hypothetical situations and ask what that person would do in each situation. As illustrations: "What would Hamlet do if an enemy army invaded Denmark?" "What would Thoreau do if he were living today and were told that he had to spend the rest of his life in New York City?" Questions like these lead students to bring together what they have learned about a person and what they already know about life.

Of all the aspects of creative listening, this relating of the known to the previously unknown is most important. It leads to minds that are awake, to critical response, and to retention of what has been heard.

## Evaluation

Evaluation of listening might very well begin with self-evaluation. Because listening is the area of English taken most for granted and given least attention, students may have no idea of how well they listen. A method of self-evaluation was developed by Lyman K. Steil for the listening training program for employees at Sperry Corporation. Students take three very brief quizzes. First they rate themselves as listeners on a seven-point scale from *superior* to *terrible;* then they identify the kind of person (multiple choice of five offered) who would rate them high as listeners; finally they rate themselves from *almost always* to *almost never* on a checklist of ten bad listening habits. After taking the quizzes, they compare their answers with statistics gathered from people who responded to the same questions in earlier testings. Sperry employees learn, for example, that 85 percent of previous test-takers rated themselves as average or lower, and that fewer than 5 percent considered themselves as superior or excellent. Listeners questioned identified best friend over boss, business colleague, job subordinate, and spouse as the person who would rate them high as listeners.[11] You might give students such categories as best friend, mother, father, teacher, and boss—even *other* for an open-ended response. Although "best friends" would probably win again, a discussion of lower ratings for other choices might start students thinking about the need to listen more carefully to everyone.

Other types of informal teacher-made listening tests might include short exercises to evaluate appreciative, discriminative, pragmatic, and critical listening.

Following individual testing, the teacher could underline or circle the places in the printed text where the student missed an important detail, confused one word for another, or failed to use an important contextual clue to the main idea. Students could make these notations individually as well after the teacher has read a passage to the entire class or to a small group. Interest inventories might also reveal some useful information, because listeners often listen only to what truly interests them. Improvement made in listening to subjects of interest might motivate students to test their skills on subjects that do not hold their attention as well. Teachers might also develop some effective tests using student skits, excerpts from drama on television, or taped class discussions. In using such tests, the teacher may ask, "What did Mary say to Frank that caused him to say what he did to Jim?" "Was John too critical?" "Did Mary offer any proof to back up her claim?" Segments from talk shows or from roundtable discussions of important ideas or news events, also include possibilities for this kind of testing. The value of the experience is that the students must listen to several people and think about what they are all saying and why, just as they often must do in life.

These and other informal tests could comprise a listening inventory, much in the way that collections of teacher-made reading tests make up reading inventories.

Published tests, if they are well done and are used wisely, can be useful complements to teacher-made tests. One problem in teaching listening at the secondary level seems to be a scarcity of published tests. Three tests designed for this level are: *Brown-Carlsen Listening Comprehension Test* (grades 9 through 13); *STEP Listening Test*, Level 2 (grades 10, 11, 12), and Level 3 (grades 7, 8, 9); *Durrell Listening-Reading Series* (grades 7, 8, 9). In addition to examining commercially developed tests, English teachers might consider those which departments of public instruction in some states have developed and printed for local use.

Tests developed by publishers, state agencies, researchers, and other teachers should be examined closely and used cautiously. Commercial tests are often limited in scope (students listen to only one person speaking or reading); they shift the focus of attention away from individual achievement to group achievement; and they may contain irrelevant or inappropriate subject matter. A teacher would be wise to at least check the reviews in *Buros Mental Measurements Yearbook*. Tests developed by teachers and testmakers in other school systems may also contain irrelevant and inappropriate content.

Teachers working in their own classrooms or collaborating with colleagues in the same school have a much better opportunity to develop listening tests that will effectively test the abilities of their students. Examining the work of other testmakers can be helpful, especially if teachers focus on techniques rather than on content, but English teachers should not rely heavily on such outside products. Each teacher is able to gather information continually throughout the year, so teachers in the same department are in the best position to evaluate a student's development from year to year. Observations, listening diaries and logs and journals, questionnaires, individual conferences, together with informal teacher-made tests, will provide the most valid and most reliable assessment of progress.

# LISTENING TO RADIO, TELEVISION, AND OTHER MEDIA
## AN ELECTROMEDIA ENVIRONMENT

Recently one of the authors of this book witnessed an informal inventory taken by an English teacher to determine which of the following media her high school students listened to most often: television, radio, or cinema. The teacher had hoped the answer would be television, because the new unit was on the language of television advertising; however, she discovered that radio was far ahead. At home while studying, in cars (where they spent much time "cruising" at night), in eating places, the students apparently listened constantly to stations that played music that "kids like." Admittedly they listened to the hype of disc jockeys, who often determine the success of record sales in the stores; admittedly they were influenced by the personality and persuasive techniques of these AM and FM hustlers.

Television, which may or may not fall somewhat behind radio in popularity, undoubtedly has a great influence on adolescents, just as it does on the general population. Most teenagers can recite several leading TV commercials word for word, are ready to talk about their favorite TV personalities and programs, and can remember a recent movie made for TV.

Together radio and television obviously play major roles in the informal education of teenagers. Today's expression is not likely to be "I know only what I read in the newspapers," but rather "I know only what I hear on radio and television." Knowing only what one sees and hears via the electronic media can be no more enlightening than knowing only what one reads from newspaper headlines, ads for commercial products, sports pages, and comic strips. This observation should disturb English teachers. The situation calls for a new focus on literacy and a new sense of what is worth listening to.

Listening simultaneously to diverse media is now commonplace to teenagers, who may listen to radio or stereo, listen to and watch television, listen to a friend on the telephone, and try to do a homework assignment all at the same time. Stereo music appears to complement rather than compete with the conversations teenagers have in eating places and teen centers. All in all, it appears that listening is likely to become even more complex as the electromedia revolution progresses.

## EDUCATIONAL PROGRAMS

Some educators once worried about the possible spread and influence of educational television, fearing a monolithic educational system in which, for example, every ninth grade English class in the nation would tune in on the same lesson: "A million students on one end of a coaxial cable and Mark Hopkins on the other." Not only would such a system fail to provide for individual differences, but it could also encourage indoctrination and thought control out of harmony with American ideals of democracy. The role of the teacher would be reduced to policing, supervising written work and physical activities, and giving grades. Fortunately, the likelihood that education will become so monolithic appears slight, but the danger does exist. Arguments for lock-step educational use on the grounds of economy and effectiveness will perhaps be heard increasingly. Such arguments have been offered to support computer-assisted instruction, a development that could also support standardization.

Commercial television is also being used for educational purposes, though few programs suited to those purposes are available during school hours. However, video recording equipment is available for home and school use, and advances in technology are likely to bring prices well within reach of many school systems. Using portable equipment, which in the future is likely to be smaller and lighter, the teacher will be able to tape many segments from programs and commercials, as well as plays, movies, and documentaries. In such cases, though, it would be very wise to ask the TV station whether permission is necessary. Asking to copy a segment to be used only in the classroom and then to be erased seems to be a reasonable request. Broadcasting companies may in some cases permit rather liberal use for educational purposes, and may rent or sell some very useful tapes. The teacher who makes tapes without permission and then stores them for future use is most likely to run into trouble.

## TEACHING DISCRIMINATION

Many English teachers have negative attitudes about the value of TV broadcasting. "The TV is out to get your mind, so this course will be devoted to surviving the dangers of the idiot box" is an introduction that hardly invites critical thinking. Instead, students should be taught to think critically and presented with a wide range of TV broadcasting. Discuss with them the endless retellings of the same tales in pseudowesterns, the sagas of suds, the annual changing fads or programs about detectives or sheriffs or lawyers or doctors, the silly audience-participation and quiz shows; hence the depictions of life as it never was nor can be; hence, perhaps worst of all, the shallow stereotypes of characters. But also show or discuss Shakespearean plays and other classics; specials such as "Holocaust" "Roots"; reports on at least the level of "60 Minutes"; TV adaptations of famous Broadway musicals; and science programs such as "Wild Kingdom" and "Nova." Some students have a very restricted view of what is available on television. Others in the family may have constantly watched game shows, inferior dramas, and sports spectaculars on the only set in the house.

Here, sketched very briefly, are a number of devices for helping students toward higher standards for listening and viewing. Some of these ideas may be combined in a unit titled an "On the Tube" or "On the Air," or some may be used between units. Probably each school system should agree to pay some systematic attention to television and radio throughout a student's formal education, with emphases differing according to the ages of the students.

### Analyzing the Amount of Time Spent

To help both teacher and class discover how large a share of the 168-hour week is devoted to broadcasts, students and teacher may prepare a simple questionnaire on listening and viewing habits. The number of hours spent each week on different kinds of programs should be included. Students are often impressed when they realize that as much as a seventh or a sixth of their 168 hours may be devoted to broadcasts, as much as a fourth of their waking hours. The questionnaire may be supplemented by another, on the listening time of other members of the family and other adults.

Daniel Lindley of the Chicago Circle Campus, University of Illinois, extends the questionnaire to include movies and other categories (live music, dance, theater, etc.) to take in the full range of viewing and listening for entertainment. Students analyze their viewing/listening charts and ask themselves whether they think the media productions are designed for them and are therefore important in terms of their own beliefs and their sense of identity. The students also ask whether programs are designed to make money from them, whether as viewers and listeners they have freedom of choice, and whether these media have contributed to adolescent culture which "owes nothing to either past or present 'adult' culture."[12]

A logical follow-up of the TV (and other media) questionnaire is a discussion of how large a role broadcasts *should* have in one's life. What does one sacrifice by staying glued to a set? What other activities are worthwhile? Why is time often called the most priceless possession? What would be a sensible amount of time per week for broadcasts? We often hear about getting our money's worth. How can we decide whether we are getting our time's worth?

### Preparing a Listening Guide

Students may be asked to keep up to date a section of the bulletin board called "Worthwhile Programs." The membership of the responsible committee should change frequently. Students may obtain information about future programs by writing to the networks and by reading *TV Guide* and other sources.

## Writing Letters

Individuals and classes may be encouraged to write throughtful letters to both sponsors and networks. Some of these letters may be critical of programs that seem too shallow, too improbable, too stereotyped. Perhaps more should be letters of reasoned praise for good programs. Dozens of such programs have been taken off the air because the audience response was disappointingly small.

## Reading and Writing Reviews

Some of the best newspapers have excellent review columns (which should be sharply distinguished from uncritical puffs). Weekly news magazines and some other magazines contain columns of penetrating analysis. Some of these reviews will appeal only to your brighter or more mature students, but other students will often enjoy reading someone else's reactions to programs with which they are familiar. A natural sequel to the reading of reviews is the writing of them.

## Summarizing Plots

A good exercise in writing and in criticism is to have students summarize, in the fewest words possible, radio or TV dramas. A frequent summary may be: "Good guys beat bad guys." A virtue of this device is that it shows up the monotony of plot of many programs, especially those in a series. In contrast, although plots of good plays may be similarly capsuled, these summaries less often are repetitive.

## Estimating Probability and Truth to Life

With a little training, students in both junior and senior high school can learn to pick out at least the glaring improbabilities in dramatic broadcasts. For instance, they can realize how unlikely it is that one man can be shot at week after week, year after year, and never suffer more than a flesh wound, or they can decide that sudden and complete reformations are questionable. Conversely, they can learn to recognize and praise those dramas in which the events might actually happen and in which actors act like real people. Although in their study of literature they need to learn about "the willing suspension of disbelief," and although they need to appreciate fantasy for fantasy's sake, they should vigorously condemn artistically unwarranted distortions of human portraits and the laws of chance.

## Applying Literary Tests

In their study of literature, students acquire at least partial answers to such questions as these: "What are the characteristics of a good story?" "Of a good play?" They should be taught to apply the same or similar criteria to dramatic broadcasts, even though TV drama is now recognized by some critics as a unique genre. Have them compare the techniques used by TV writers and writers of printed stories or stage plays, paying particular attention to the demands made by limitations of time, space, or dramatic conventions. In addition, have classes discuss characteristics peculiar to the medium, such as plausibility of the acting, excellence of the photography, or quality of the direction.

### Reading Books on Which Broadcasts Are Based
Comparing a book and its dramatization is educationally sound. Lively and informative discussions may result from such questions as these: "What important episodes or characters were left out?" "Why?" "What differences in characterization did you notice?" "Why were these changes probably made?" "What alterations were made in the arrangement of events?" "Why?" "What depth of meaning did you observe in the original but not in the dramatization, or vice versa?" "What other differences did you see?" "Was the ending the same in both versions?" Sarah Roody has pointed out that some movie and radio versions of *Pygmalion* end with Eliza Doolittle's marriage to Henry Higgins, although "Shaw considered that outcome most unlikely and wrote an epilogue for the express purpose of telling why such a marriage would have failed to attract Eliza in the first place or to satisfy her in the long run." "Which version, Shaw's or a later one, is preferable?" "Why?" "How does *My Fair Lady* (based on *Pygmalion*) end?" "Is this ending satisfactory?"

### Writing Radio and Television Plays
Not only does this activity provide well-motivated writing experience, but it sharpens critical acumen. As students try to avoid weaknesses to which they have learned to object, they become even more aware of those weaknesses. And, as they attempt to bring into their plays what they have learned to approve, they develop a keener appreciation of the professionals who succeed. Some of their efforts may be to create original dramas; others may involve the rewriting in play form of short stories studied in class. Both individual and group creations are possible. Some of the best work may be presented in assembly programs or in other classrooms.

### Teaching the Power and the Responsibilities of the Mass Media
Today, the television writer, the producer, and the sponsor may exert a strong influence on 40 million minds at once. Their influence may be good or bad. In the control of the unscrupulous, television can contribute toward mental and moral bankruptcy, but fortunately the potential for good is no less. A nation addicted to the mass media must learn to question ceaselessly the integrity of the purveyors. Students in the senior high school can understand and should discuss the implications of the immense power the mass media have placed in the hands of a few hundred people.

### Analyzing Speeches
*The English Language Arts in the Secondary School* says that, in listening to speeches intended to influence thought or to inform,

*"Who is speaking?"* students learn to ask. *"Why? Under what sponsorship?"* and *"On what authority?"* Ability to detect bias in point of view, unsubstantiated generalizations, or inferences inadequately drawn is particularly important in a land where freedom of speech gives equal rights to the informed and to the uninformed, to the straight and to the crooked thinker, to the sincere and to the insincere. Critical examination of what is heard is vital in today's world.[13]

### Analyzing Nonverbal Cues

Andrew Wolvin of the University of Maryland and Carolyn Coakley of the Prince George's County Public Schools consider these points in analyzing how nonverbal cues in the voice can affect the meaning a listener gets:

*What nonverbal voice elements did the students notice in the speaker's voice? What meanings did they derive from these nonverbal cues? Why were these interpretations made? How accurate do they think these interpretations are? Are there other possible interpretations? Did students listen to content, or did they concentrate on the speaker's delivery? How does concentration on nonverbal cues affect listening efficiency?*[14]

Here are some good questions that may alert students to the dangers of making unwarranted generalizations about speakers from nonverbal cues:

*Why do people categorize, label, generalize, and/or stereotype others? How often do the students make judgments about other individuals based on preconceived attitudes? How often are the students confronted with stereotypes by friends, family, school, church, and the media? What are the damaging effects of superficial judgments on the part of the listener? How can preconceived attitudes based on the nonverbal characteristics of a speaker distort or block what listeners hear? Do preconceived attitudes toward a speaker's voice ever serve as alibis for the listeners' not listening? How can students combat the tendency to stereotype? In what ways will students be more efficient listeners if they refrain from criticizing a speaker's nonverbal characteristics?*[15]

An eleventh grade English teacher used verbal and then nonverbal cues to give students first impressions of a speaker. Students first heard only the voice on a cassette and discussed "what they thought of" the speaker. Next they observed the speaker on film and were asked about gestures, facial expressions, dress, mannerisms, and so on. Finally, the teacher gave the students a rather full account of the speaker's educational background and accomplishments. In light of more complete information, some students changed their opinions drastically.

## Reporting Events

Students may profitably write or present orally, as if they were newscasters, descriptions of events that they have witnessed in person or on television. This activity will give a better understanding of the problems professional newscasters face.

## Discussing Subjects Not Treated or Seldom Treated

Mature classes may find profitable discussion of the fact that the large network shows infrequently treat realistically such topics as race relations, unfair or unethical practices of employers, abuses by labor of its privileges, the fact that the Caucasian race is numerically a minority, the fact that people are persecuted in some of the major oil exporting countries, the care with which some products are manufactured by other nations, and the like. "What are the reasons for such omissions?" "Are the omissions defensible?"

## Encouraging Variety

Just as some students read only the sports page or comic page in a daily news-paper, so some stick to the same monotonous radio and TV fare. Encourage them to shop around, to develop varied tastes. To choose the good, they must know both bad and good.

## Developing a Class List of Standards

An important goal in any series of activities dealing with the mass media—in fact, *the* goal—is the creation of a set of standards that will guide students in the future. These standards cannot be teacher-prepared or teacher-imposed. They must come from the observations and the discussions of the students themselves. To establish such standards, which can be modified from time to time, draw up a list of the major kinds of programs—drama, comedy, speeches, quiz shows, music, and so on—and have the class decide the characteristics of the programs to which they could conscientiously attach the label "good."

## Planning Units

Units on listening to the media may last for two or three days or several weeks. Brief ones may fit logically between fairly extensive units in English. Possible topics are "Advertising on TV," "Situational Comedies on TV," "The Myth of the TV Cowboy," and "Developing a Keener Ear for Media." Other units may be thematic and take in a larger scope of ideas and activities. Sue Conners, Julie Sweet, and Kay Kimbrough, teachers in Mobile, Alabama schools, have developed a thematic unit called "It's the Real Thing! (Isn't It?): Media and the Representation of Life." In their introductory comments they say, "The unit may be used as an introduction to a more fully developed media course, as a part of a course based on human values, or as a short unit in itself." Students are asked to "compile a list of TV programs, books, movies, songs, etc. which present life unrealistically, or through rose-colored glasses," and to discuss reasons for their choices. Other activities include comparing the views of life presented in selected movies and TV series depicting family relationships, creating a skit having a view of life opposite to that in the movie or series, taking a field trip to a local TV station, and writing a paper which attempts to support the contention that a chosen TV program presents life realistically or unrealistically.[16]

---

**THE IDEA BOX**

IT TAKES TWO TO COMMUNICATE

Carl Larson and others make this point: "One person can talk to another person, but until that second person attends to the first person, little in terms of competent communication will occur. This listener contributes to and, to an extent, controls the communication process."[17]

The stereotype of the teacher, unfortunately, is that of *talker* who controls the communication process. A recent cartoon depicts a teacher standing in front of a class. The teacher says, "All right, class. My job is to talk to you and your job is to listen. If you finish first please let me know."[18]

LISTENING IN BUSINESS ENGLISH

M. Lee Goddard of Bowling Green State University lists in *Business Education Forum* 15 activities that may be useful in classes or units in business English. Six of these are as follows:

1. Stress the importance of careful listening by relating accounts of costly mistakes caused by faulty listening.
2. Select a typical clerical task and ask students to suggest the next step after a sequence of steps has been completed.
3. Read a paragraph from a business letter which contains a sentence that doesn't belong and ask students to identify the sentence.
4. Give a set of instructions for a typing assignment and ask for questions about the assignment. Do not repeat the instructions later in the class period so students will be forced to rely on the original instructions.
5. Ask a student to present an account of an automobile accident and have the other class members write a report based on the information they obtained from the oral presentation.
6. Read a paragraph from a business letter that contains grammatical errors and then discuss the effect of the errors on students' perceptions of the writer.[19]

THE TEACHING OF HIGH SCHOOL ENGLISH

## LISTENING TO DIRECTIONS

Barbara Sundene Wood suggests arranging five dominoes on the teacher's desk and selecting a speaker to describe the arrangement to four listeners who arrange other dominoes the same way. Similarities and differences between the first set and the others are discussed.[20] Geraldine La Rocque suggests asking students to repeat directions given to a stranger attempting to reach an unnamed local place.[21] Careful listeners should be able to name the place (possibly the school or a store or public building in the community).

Other approaches include assembling or dismantling something after listening to oral directions; reproducing a shape or design on the board by following oral directions (no hand signals allowed); listening to directions on the telephone; and listening to a librarian's directions for locating materials, and then finding them in the library without talking to anyone.

## LISTENING PERIODS

Occasionally the teacher will designate a "listening" period during which students must depend entirely on listening to accomplish their goals and get the homework assignment. Lectures, small group discussions, oral directions, and so forth, will prepare students for detailed assignments involving several steps.

## LISTEN AND READ

To encourage interest and fluency in reading, teachers have asked some students to read silently as the teacher reads the same passage aloud. Recordings, sometimes referred to as "taped books," serve the same purpose. Although research seems inconclusive, some teachers claim that the students show improvement in reading. The teacher's attention to stress, pause, and other signals helps students to get more meaning and enjoyment from passages.

Patricia K. Lane and Margery Staman Miller have added simple but systematic instruction in critical thinking to this approach in teaching students with learning disabilities. The relaxed atmosphere of reading orally, following along, and asking questions to stimulate critical thinking resulted in increased interest and participation.[22]

Teachers should not assume that students with learning disabilities cannot respond to questions such as "How do we know?" "What made it happen?" "Will this person act this way the next time this happens?" "Has he learned anything that will make him feel or act a different way the next time?" "Would Ralph in the other story we read act or feel this way if this happened to him?" "Could this happen to you?" "How would you feel?" "What would you do?"

## LISTENING FOR THE VISUALLY IMPAIRED

The heading for this item is actually the title of a teaching manual by Claudell S. Stocker. It includes many good exercises under three headings: Listening Readiness, Development of Listening Skills, and Development of Recall and Retention.

Some readiness exercises require listening to directions to places in a building or community. After listening to described distances, directional turns, and numbers of doorways or intersections, the student repeats all details and directions in his or her own words. Discriminations between sets or words and sets of sounds are also tested. In developmental listening, students are asked to form mental images as they draw conclusions. Recall and retention are developed through follow-up discussions of taped radio programs, television newscasts, commercials, short stories, and so forth. This manual is a rich source for listening lessons for all students, impaired or not.[23]

## TV SCRIPTS MOTIVATE STUDENTS TO LISTEN

Barbara Lee, senior project director, Office of Social Research, CBS Inc., finds increased motivation in both reading and listening by students who read and discuss TV scripts before seeing the programs in the classroom. Students also read broadcast directions, discuss what they have seen, compare the script with the broadcast, and in some cases act out the scripts.[24]

You may wish to explore the possibility of this kind of activity by writing to CBS or another network. It may be the answer to the problem of using tapes without violating copyright laws, and it may broaden the base (adding scripts and broadcast directions) for critical evaluations of TV broadcasts.

## STUDENT TAPES FOR HANDICAPPED CLASSMATES

Writing in the April 1980, issue of *The English Journal,* Julie Dodd suggests asking students in English, drama, or radio and broadcasting classes to prepare audio tapes for students with learning disabilities.[25] The visually impaired will of course also benefit. Doing this for handicapped classmates should also improve attitudes and increase understanding among students who do not have these handicaps.

## IMPROVE LISTENING WITH "OLD-TIME RADIO"

Karen Hall, head of the English department at Riverview Junior High, Murray, Utah, writes of success with recordings of "old-time" radio programs in the classroom. She has "found that students' listening skills are renewed and sharpened, imaginative and creative skills expanded, involvement heightened." In one approach "to help students rejuvenate their atrophied listening skills," the teacher may ask students to prepare questions to test their classmates' ability to recall particular details of programs. Asking students to describe Fibber McGee, Colonel Lemuel Q. Stoopnagle, Henry Aldrich, or Senator Claghorn, or to describe the town of Pine Ridge, Arkansas, can stimulate imagination and creativity. Added involvement comes as students tape their own radio shows complete with sound effects.

Appended to Ms. Hall's article are 11 names and addresses of companies that sell recordings of old radio programs. Three of these are: Remember Radio, Inc., P.O. Box 2513, Norman, OK 73069; Radio Memories, 1033 Gypsum, Salina, KA 67401; Radio Reruns, Box 724, Redmond, WA 92052.[26]

Douglas Alley, another teacher who has used radio tapes with success, points to the advantage of asking students to listen to descriptive words in such radio productions as "Country of the Blind," which starred Orson Welles. "In this country of blindness there are no words dealing with sight or seeing, not even the word *sky,* because there is no need for such words in the people's environment." Through listening to radio drama, students "can also come to understand how the authors created mood, as music and voices blend in atmospheres of horror, happiness, or even dullness."[27]

## QUESTIONING THE COMMERCIALS

Jack McGarvey of Bedford Junior High School, Westport, Connecticut, has developed an interesting "TV Advertising IQ" test for students. Among his questions for students are these:

Why might Texaco look with some irritation on Mobil's claim to being "the detergent gasoline"?

What, if anything, is wrong with the sentence, "You can see how luxurious my hair feels."

Explain why "Lots of things have changed, but Hershey's goodness hasn't" is not necessarily reassuring.

What's special about the claim, "Great Lash greatly increases the diameter of every lash"?

Need answers? Almost all gasolines contain detergents; we can't really *see* how something feels; Hershey may have changed its recipe many times; all mascaras increase the diameter of eyelashes.

You can find the rest of this test, complete with answers, in "Cross-Examining the Commercial," *Media & Methods,* Jan. 1980, pp. 47–49. If you can't find the article, why not work up a TV IQ test of your own?

## STUDENTS IDENTIFY THEIR OWN LISTENING PROBLEMS

During a mini-course on listening taught by Elizabeth W. Gratz of West High School, Iowa City, students found that their own listening problems were caused by emotional reactions, lack of knowledge, and personal distractions. Ms Gratz summarizes her students' findings this way:

> About half of the items they identified can be categorized as emotional reactions that minimize effective listening. Such specifics as "blaming the other person for a lack of communication, shouting, resorting to ridicule or insults of a person's ideas or appearance, using a belligerent tone or expression, such as 'but *you* said . . . ' impatiently, not giving the other person a chance to respond, responding defensively, or feeling overpowered by a dominant personality" are all emotional traps they suggested that interfere with maximum listening. Students also identified listening difficulties that arise from a lack of knowledge or information (such as vocabulary) and those that are caused mainly by inattention to the speaker because of personal distractions.[28]

## MAYBE NOT ALL TV PRIME TIME IS A WASTELAND

David England, chair of the Committee on the Impact of Television on Children, National Council of Teachers of English, finds some worthwhile qualities in "Little House on the Prairie," "Happy Days," "All in the Family," and "Family," four prime-time series. At least characters in these programs turn to one another for help in confronting problems. This is, according to England, a hopeful swing away from the self-sufficiency of lawyers, doctors, detectives, and superheroes like Wonder Woman. Although not always convincingly realistic, these programs are better than most commercial series for small group discussions and exploratory writing.[29]

## LISTENING HAS ORGANIZED

Listening, often called the most neglected area in the English language arts, now has an international platform. During the spring of 1980, teachers, teacher educators, and researchers interested in listening assembled for the first convention of the International Listening Association. For information about this new organization, contact Dr. Lyman K. Steil, chair, Speech-Communication Division, Department of Rhetoric, University of Minnesota, St. Paul.

## WHAT DOES RESEARCH ON LISTENING SAY TO THE TEACHER?

Reviews of research in any area of education characteristically reveal studies with conflicting evidence and studies with no statistically significant evidence. Such is the case with many studies reviewed recently by Thomas G. Devine of Boston University. From 50 years of reported research, though, he has been able to draw some interesting conclusions and make some suggestions. Listening is measurable, and it can be taught. Although correlations apparently run fairly high between listening tests and intelligence tests, listening does not depend on intelligence alone. Listening is still not a generally accepted part of the standard school curriculum. Few attempts have been made through research to establish a sequential arrangement of listening skills. Skills are usually selected arbitrarily by test builders or writers of instructional materials. Scope and sequence seem to be generally predicated on the assumption that listening is like reading.[30] From this review, it would seem that research is needed to clarify the relationships between listening and thinking, to explore the similarities and differences between listening and reading, to discover what factors other than intelligence greatly affect listening, and to establish effective sequential arrangements of listening skills in school programs.

Following a rather thorough review of research related to auditory problems, Karl K. Taylor of Illinois Central College concludes that some auditory processing problems may be "nothing more than poor listening and auding skills." Pursuing this notion, he recommends that programs be developed to teach listening. "If students undergo this kind of training and are unsuccessful, then they should be diagnosed very carefully in case the problem is more sophisticated than a mere listening deficiency."[31]

# FOOTNOTES

1. *Listening*, Urbana: NCTE, 1979, p. 1.
2. *Ibid.*, p. 18.
3. Information in this paragraph was influenced by Andrew D. Wolvin and Carolyn Gwynn Coakley, *Listening Instruction*, Urbana: NCTE, 1979, pp. 7–13. The authors use the terms *appreciative, discriminative, comprehensive, therapeutic,* and *critical. Comprehensive* involves "understanding a message" and covers a wide range of pragmatic goals; *therapeutic* is "understanding a message to help the speaker solve a problem."
4. "Improving Listening in Content Area Subjects," *NASSP Bulletin,* Dec. 1976, pp. 26–27.
5. *Listening*, pp. 59–61.
6. "Listening," in *Guiding Children's Language Learning,* ed. Pose Lamb, Dubuque, Iowa: Wm. Brown Co., 1971, pp. 128–129.
7. "Listening Guide—A First Step toward Notetaking and Listening Skills," *Journal of Reading,* Jan. 1976, pp. 289–290.
8. "Profile of an English Teacher," *English Journal* 57, March 1968, p. 420.
9. "Some Suggestions for the Teaching of Listening," *The Speech Teacher,* Nov. 1975, p. 387.
10. "Listening and Auding—Activities and Research," *English Journal* 67, May 1978, p. 38. This source includes many other useful activities.
11. "Your Personal Listening Profile," *Sperry,* n.d.
12. *English Teaching and the Electric Dream,* Springfield: Illinois Office of Education, 1978, pp. 45–46.
13. P. 229.
14. *Listening Instruction,* NCTE, p. 25.
15. *Ibid.*, p. 35.
16. *Thematic Units in Teaching English and the Humanities,* ed. Sylvia Spann and Mary Beth Culp, Urbana: NCTE, 1975, pp. 61–65.
17. *Assessing Functional Communication,* NCTE/ERIC, p. 49.
18. From "The Small Society," a cartoon by Brickman, Washington Star Syndicate, Inc.
19. "Listening: Forgotten Skill in Effective Communications," Jan. 1976, p. 19.
20. *Development of Functional Competencies: Grades 7–12,* Urbana: NCTE/ERIC, 1977.
21. "In One Ear, Out the Other," *The English Quarterly,* Spring-Summer 1976, p. 78. This source includes an interesting application of the Kellogg Listening Model for students in English.
22. "Listening: Learning for Underachieving Adolescents," *Journal of Read-*

*ing*, April 1972, pp. 488–491. See also Phyllis Weaver and Fredi Shonkoff, *Research Within Reach*, St. Louis: CEMERL, Inc.; Mary K. Monteith, "Taped Books and Reading Materials," *Journal of Reading*, March 1978, pp. 554–556.

23. Springfield, Ill.: Charles C. Thomas, 1973.
24. "Prime Time in the Classroom," *Journal of Communication*, Winter 1980, pp. 175–180.
25. "Mainstreaming," p. 54.
26. "Turn Up Student Interest with Old-Time Radio," *Media & Methods*, Feb. 1976, pp. 40–41.
27. "Radio Tapes: A Resource for English Teachers," *English Journal* 68, Oct. 1979, p. 40. For a unit plan using radio tapes and other media see "Nostalgia and the Interview," by Lois Easton in *Thematic Units in Teaching English and the Humanities*, Second Supplement, ed. Sylvia Spann and Mary Beth Culp, Urbana: NCTE, 1980, pp. 37–64.
28. "Goal: Maxi-Listening," *English Journal* 62, Feb. 1973, p. 270.
29. "Television and the English Teacher," *English Journal* 68, Nov. 1979, pp. 99–102.
30. "Listening: What Do We Know After Fifty Years of Research and Theorizing?" *Journal of Reading*, Jan. 1978, pp. 296–304.
31. " 'People Hearing Without Listening': Problems of Auditory Processing in the Classroom," *Research in the Teaching of English*, Feb. 1978, p. 74.

# 15

## TEACHING FILM

## FILM STUDY

### WHY STUDY FILM?

Some high school English teachers still believe that a film should be used in the classroom only as an audiovisual aid, as an interesting and possibly motivating support to lectures and textbooks. "It would be nice to have a film on the novel if I can work it in," a teacher might say. "The kids would find it a good change of pace after working so hard on the novel in class." He or she might order a film early in the year or late the previous year without any clear idea about how to use it later, and if the film comes to the school unexpectedly (mixup in scheduling or forgetfulness on the teacher's part), the teacher might show it anyway because it might not be available again until the next year. Apparently such a teacher regards films as adjuncts and extras, not as a part of the curriculum or as genres or art forms worthy of separate critical discussions. Film study does not have much chance of success in an English department where this attitude prevails.

A student who sees a film outside the classroom does not consider it an audiovisual aid to anything. The student's attention is on film viewing as an emotional experience in itself. Because this experience appears to depend on no author to tell the viewer what to see or to think about, it can seem closer to reality. In a film, specific people seem to be in very specific places doing specific things. Recognizing one of these specific people as Jane Fonda or Paul Newman adds familiarity: there *they* are doing their thing again before the viewer's eyes. Vocal characteristics, facial expressions, bodily movements, all seem to come as first-hand clues to character, just as they do in real life.

Setting and action can also greatly affect viewers. As with characters, setting is very specific. The forest fire roars in the viewer's ears, and its smoke obliterates objects the viewer has just seen. As an airplane rolls, the viewer sits in the pilot's seat: the horizon slants, becomes vertical, seems to replace the sky, becomes vertical again, slants, and returns to its normal position. These illusions of reality carry the authority that comes with seeing and hearing for oneself. "Seeing is believing." Film promoters certainly know this. When a TV commercial for a movie about the raising of the Titanic says, "*You* will be there to raise the Titanic," many viewers will indeed be "there."

Nothing is inherently wrong about the special emotional appeal that movies have for viewers. But why study them in English classes? Why make such study part of the curriculum when English teachers are already working hard to help students to read and write? Answers lie in the English teacher's responsibility for teaching communication. Once an English teacher rejects the assumption that films are just audiovisual aids and understands that they communicate, that teacher knows that students should study film. Further, if an English teacher stops to consider how extensively directors use film to manipulate thinking, then that teacher knows students must study film. Finally, an English teacher who appreciates film aesthetically will want students to explore its artistic qualities.

## WHERE AND HOW TO BEGIN

Acknowledging film as a vehicle for communication or as an art form worthy of study in the English classroom is one thing; knowing where and how to begin film study is quite another. If you are like most junior high and senior high English teachers, you probably have had little experience with film study and no experience with filmmaking. Actually, the teaching approaches used in film study are very similar to those used in literature study. The historical or chronological approach, the introduction to terms and techniques, the study of genres, the study of selected "classics," the study of topics through the use of selected works, the study of themes in selected works, and the critical analysis of selected works are all familiar to teachers of literature and to teachers of film. Like literature, film may be approached for knowledge (facts and ideas), and for appreciation (aesthetics, feelings, experiences, and fantasies). In addition, students study film to improve receptive skills peculiar to appreciating and understanding its message (perceptive listening and viewing), and students make films to improve expressive skills peculiar to producing films (acting, writing film scripts, and directing).

The fact that film and literature share some teaching approaches should not obscure another very important fact: film and literature are not the same. Film has its own techniques and its own art forms; it "has its own language, composition and literature.''[1] With this fact in mind, let's take a look at where and how to begin.

## FILM HISTORY APPROACH

A short historical survey of film can serve as part of the introductory material for a fairly extensive unit or course, or it can be a unit or course in itself. Its purposes include recognizing film as a technological advancement in the society, becoming aware of film as an art form, understanding the great sociological and political influences of film, and realizing that the history of film is also a cultural history.

Interesting questions come to the surface as film history unfolds: "How has the invention of talking film changed the industry?" "How has it changed the public's concept of film?" "How has film affected life styles?" "How has it affected the dissemination of information?" "How has culture affected film, and how has film affected culture?" "Has film changed or influenced history? If so, in what ways?" "How has film been used by national leaders to influence people?" "In what ways has it been recognized as art, and in what ways only as entertainment?" "Why has film had difficulty gaining recognition as an art form?" "Has it enjoyed greater recognition as art in America or in Europe? Why?"

Film history that does not approach some of these important questions is probably not worth teaching. Names of producers, directors, actors and actresses; dates that mark important developments; and details about leading film companies can be as dreary and irrelevant for students as many facts about literary history. As an English teacher, you should not try to play historian; but you should have enough knowledge about film history to discuss with students answers to questions like those above. If you have not read about the history of film, a good first book is Arthur Knight, *The Liveliest Art* (rev.), New York: New American Library, 1979.

## FILM TECHNIQUES APPROACH

Uninitiated viewers may believe that film is merely fiction or nonfiction presented through the voices and actions of people before a camera. They may even believe that everything they see and hear evolves from a written script. Verbal language is often a component, but film does not make its greatest impact through the artistic arrangement of words. It makes its impact through arrangements of objects, people, and places before the lens (composition); through the use of lighting and color; through skillful, often subtle uses of sound; through movement of the camera; and through the grammar of film, the "syntax" developed by sequencing the shots. Of all steps in the process, editing is probably the most important; it is through discerning and meticulous editing that film speaks its language most effectively. The editor manipulates the images of sound and sight by "cutting the strip of film and splicing it together with other strips of film to achieve a desired effect."[2]

Film techniques are taught for several reasons. Some teachers hope that techniques such as film history will give students a good background for creative and aesthetic viewing. Teachers who plan to take students through filmmaking feel that students should learn techniques before using them. Teachers who hope to raise the level of literacy believe that some study of the manipulative devices used in directing and editing will help students develop a critical eye and mind.

A word of caution: The study of techniques can get in the way of personal experiences with film if teachers become too zealous. Lecturing on many of the techniques to look for before viewing a film, and giving students long lists of terms to memorize, may dampen enthusiasm for the film itself.

## FILM GENRES APPROACH

One of the most popular approaches to literature is the study of literary forms and types. Film also has its genres, so teachers have led students through the study of westerns, musicals, comedies, mysteries, horror films, spy films, war films, science fiction films, educational films, cultural films, and so forth. Genres in film can provide teachers with convenient pivots from which to introduce film, to study the history of film (development of the western, for example), to study other films of the same type, to study topics and themes, and to engage in film criticism. Some of these approaches no longer technically involve the study of genres. In film as in literature, the study of a genre usually focuses a student's attention on qualities and characteristics of the type of work chosen. The use of westerns to study a topic would not focus attention on that genre to the same extent as their use to study treatments of character, theme, and setting as distinguishing features of that type.

A unit on the western, a popular genre in high school, may take into account techniques of action and melodrama in silent films as well as the uses of color, sound, and widescreen in later films. The focus, though, is frequently on the stereotyping of western heroes, most often silent, romantically unattached men with strong and handsome features, strong and lean bodies, quick eyes, and fast guns. Like Shane, the stereotypic hero often rides into a situation where bad guys (often wearing black hats) are intimidating good guys (owners of small farms or ranches—sometimes a widow). He is not looking for trouble, but he is drawn into the conflict on the side of the good guys, reluctantly reveals his skill as a fistfighter and gunslinger, kills the leader(s) of the bad guys in a gunfight, and rides off as mysteriously as he came. He is apparently not interested in becoming a husband, a mayor, a sheriff, or even governor of the territory, so we suspect he has suffered a great hurt, is doing penance, or has been unjustly accused of a crime somewhere. Nevertheless, we wish him well as he rides out over the horizon. Like Beowulf or Sir Galahad, he could be the archetypal hero, the one whose deeds inspire legends. Less romantic stereotypes are the gun-for-hire gunfighter, the bounty hunter, or the avenger. He may be the cool-headed professional killer or the wronged young man bent on revenge. He may kill repeatedly, and he may be killed at the end of the movie. Other stereotypes are trail boss, wagon master, cavalry officer, sheriff, cattle baron, sheepherder, prospector, saloon girl, greenhorn, doctor, buffalo hunter, Indian scout, Indian, banker, drifter, town drunk, preacher, school teacher, and Mexican.

Ralph Amelio, media coordinator and English teacher at Willowbrook High School, Villa Park, Illinois, describes the goals of a unit on "The Western and Myth: Reality" this way: "Distinguish between the reality and myth of the Western as part of the American dream by an analysis of purpose, treatment, structure, genre, and technique of significant Western."[3] This unit, through lectures and varied student activities, treats "such topics as settings, landscape, themes, structure, myth, archetypes, characterization, acting, style, stereotypes, plot, music, motif, use of the camera, and symbols." Some of the movies chosen for study are *The Real West, My Darling Clementine, Shane, High Noon, Lonely Are the Brave, Song of the Prairie, Stagecoach, Now That the Buffalo's Gone, Home of the Brave, Ride the High Country,* and *Broken Arrow.* Through such films, students study the following mythological aspects of the American dream:

1. The freedom of great spaces
2. The closeness of nature
3. The comradeship of men with men
4. Violence
5. Defiance of the law
6. Execution of the law
7. Unceasing quest
8. Solitary, free, wandering individual[4]

Taking one point of view, students examine "such American traditions as respect for one's freedom of conscience and action, self-reliance, nationalism, and pursuit of happiness; taking another, they examine genocidal acts against the American Indian, the use of violence, unjust treatment of the Mexican and the Negro, and unlawful, brutal, or cowardly acts committed by such glorified heroes as Billy the Kid, Bat Masterson, Jesse James, Wild Bill Hickok, and Wyatt Earp.

This unit includes lectures, class discussions, small group discussions, panels of student critics, role-playing characters, and written reviews.

## FAVORITE FILMS APPROACH

The great books approach, inspired by reading lists for college entrance, has not returned to English teaching with any vigor. Yet English teachers have fossilized certain novels in the curriculum by favoring them, by purchasing anthologies containing them, and by building units around them. This can happen to films as well. *Shane* and *The Ox-Bow Incident* have become entrenched westerns; *An Occurrence at Owl Creek Bridge,* although outstanding, has become *the* perennial short film for critical discussion; and *The Red Balloon, Dream of the Wild Horses, Neighbors,* and *The Stringbean* are in the inner circle of short, silent films.

Kenneth Donelson of Arizona State University looks at such favorites in "What Films Are Worth Seeing? What Books About Film Are Worth Reading?" After examining the *Media & Methods* poll of 1400 subscribers (May 1970 issue) and the reactions of readers of the *Arizona English Bulletin,* Donelson concludes that "clearly there is danger of some sort of semi-official party-line developing in film teaching . . . both for short films and feature-length films."[5]

Film has not had a long history, and many English teachers are relatively inexperienced with film study, so they may be inclined to follow the advice of a few colleagues without previewing and without searching about for something different. Considering the number of films available even in the medium's short history, a teacher does not have to order the same ones year after year. The search for teachable but untaught films should be fairly vigorous.

## TOPICAL APPROACH

Topics such as The Western Movement in American History, The Impact of Technology on Plant and Animal Life, The Image of the All-American Athlete, and Portrayal of Women by Film might use several kinds of film, from full-length fiction to documentary and modern short film. As in the case of some topical units in literature, knowledge about the topic, and improvement in reading, writing, speaking, and listening may be principal goals. These are worthy goals indeed, but if they alone dominate a topical unit using film, teachers and students should realize that they are not participating in a unit on film study. A topical unit may have little connection with the understanding and appreciation of film itself unless topics stimulate interest in themes and unless this interest in turn leads students to look thoughtfully at the filmmaker's treatment of those themes in certain films.

## THEMATIC APPROACH

Survival, courage, heroism, love, and alienation are only a few of the many themes studied in thematic film units. Understandably, the thematic approach has a special appeal for English teachers, for in it they find a "familiarity that allows an immediate concentration on techniques and criticism." [6] Experience with literature tells them that when a work stimulates strong feelings and urges students to consider one or more points of view that they can relate to their own lives, students are more curious about the structure and art which created that impact. Questions such as "What does the theme in this film mean to you?" "Has the film changed your thinking?" and "What was there about this film that caused you to feel this way (or believe this)?" are likely to produce fruitful answers if the theme is significant to students and if it is presented effectively by the film.

Jim Kitses and Ann Kaplan, teachers at Kingsway Day College in England (a vocational school for teenage dropouts), are convinced that through the thematic approach students "find links between films they see and the life they experience outside." Also, students "recognize that films can be personally meaningful and judged on other grounds than those of 'entertainment.' " [7] It is interesting to note this kind of success with students who have not done well academically.

Frank Manchel, professor of Communication and Theater at the University of Vermont, has organized the thematic approach to film study around five general headings inspired by Dwight Burton's *Literature Study in the High Schools*. These are: (1) Coming to Terms with Self; (2) Problems of Conflict with Society; (3) Family Problems; (4) Preparing for the Future Adult Role; (5) Moral and Philosophical Problems and Issues. [8] Although Burton proposed such headings in 1959, they are still viable because they are still among adolescents' main concerns. A brief discussion of Manchel's treatment of the first three headings should serve to illustrate the approach.

## Coming to Terms with Self

In his introductory remarks about this heading, Manchel observes that teenagers, because they are self-centered and impressionable, seek comparisons between themselves and peers, adults, and heroes. Physical appearance, friendship, social status, and love relationships are main concerns. Filmmakers, he claims, have portrayed teenagers in ways that students will find superficial and unrealistic; they have also capitalized on stereotypes of adolescent behavior. These are points he suggests for discussion as students examine the filmmaker's point of view and reflect on their own behavior. Among the several films he recommends for units are *Captains Courageous* (MGM—16mm: 1937, 116 min., b/w, sound, R-FNC);[9] *Loneliness of the Long Distance Runner* (Britain—16 mm: 1962, 103 min., b/w, sound, R-WRS); and *The Member of the Wedding* (Columbia—16 mm: 1952, 91 min., b/w, sound, R-AUD, IDE).

## Problems of Conflict with Society

The adolescent's desire for independence causes conflicts with adults and with the society adults feel they must protect. Therefore, films dealing with such conflicts attract teenagers. In a unit relating to this heading, students should examine the balance between positive and negative portrayals of teenagers, the extent to which the real causes of delinquency are revealed, and the believability of solutions. One of Manchel's choices is *Blue Denim* (Fox—16mm: 1959, 89 min., b/w, sound, R-FNC). A film he does not include, but which might prove interesting, is *High School* (Frederick Wiseman, dir., 115 min. b/w, sound, Zipporah Films, 1968), a controversial documentary of students' conflicts with a social institution that plays a major role in their lives. Articles and reviews on this film appeared during 1969 in such publications as *The New Yorker, New Republic, Saturday Review,* and *Newsweek.* See also Harold Foster's discussion of this film in *The New Literacy,* Urbana, Illinois: NCTE, 1979; and Pauline Kael's review, "High School and Other Forms of Madness," in *Deeper into Movies,* New York: Bantam, 1974, pp. 24–30.

## Family Problems

A unit organized under this heading covers such themes as freedom, independence, responsibility, patience, loneliness, and love. Among possible films are *Nobody Waved Goodbye* (Canada—16mm: 1964, 80 min., sound, R-AUD) and *A Raisin in the Sun* (Columbia—16mm: 1961, 128 min., b/w, sound, R-AUD etc.). In studying these films and others, students should challenge implications made by the filmmaker. Parents, foster parents, and guardians are not always to blame, nor are teenagers. The economic and social status of the family doesn't necessarily lead to conflicts between teenagers and both parents or a single parent. The main cause of a problem may not be easy to identify, and reaching a solution may take years of effort and much patience.

Most of the films mentioned above are fairly old. In planning a thematic approach, no matter what the heading, the English teacher should be on the lookout for current films that might stimulate interest in relevant themes. If the films chosen are well made, discussions can focus on the art as well as on the social commentary.[10]

Sometimes teachers prefer to let a discussion of personal feelings, human conflicts, and social issues precede a film with a strong theme. This may have some value if the discussion is not long and truly involves students, but a more fruitful approach may be to show the film first and use it as the basis for an introductory discussion of the theme. It is important in discussions to allow students to express their feelings and reactions completely and freely; the teacher's role should be to help students make relevant connections between their personal observations about life and the treatment of life in the film. In short, a teacher's own attraction to a particular theme should not influence the discussion. Excessive and intrusive teacher talk has ruined many good pieces of literature for students; it can do the same thing in film study.

## CROSS-MEDIA APPROACH

Enlightening comparisons can be made between film and theater, film and litera-ture, TV film and cinema film, film and radio play, and so on. David Sohn effectively outlines some of the possibilities:

> *Why, for instance, did Robert Bolt omit the "common man" when he adapted "A Man for all Seasons" for the movie medium? How does the impact of "Romeo and Juliet" change from the silently read printed version to the phonograph recording to viewing the stage play to the experiencing of the movie, and then to the musical adaptation called "West Side Story" on both stage and screen? Compare and contrast the novel "Oliver Twist" with the movie and the musical stage version. Opportunities for such comparative studies are readily available to the perceptive teacher.*[11]

Not all film critics agree that there is value in comparing films with artistic works in other media. Pauline Kael, for example, has called the process an unfortunate "divide and conquer game of aesthetics."[12] This point is worth considering. When the cross-media approach is used, its purpose in film study must be clear: to further students' understandings of the art of film, not to try to conclude that art in one medium or the other is more effective in any way. In the following discussions, the focus is on film.

### Film and Theater

On the surface, both seem very similar; both use live subjects who speak and move about before the audience. Film, however, uses the pictorial arts. That is, it is a sequence of still shots, each shot dependent on a pictorial arrangement of people and objects for effective composition. To heighten drama, film also uses methods that are not available on the stage. The camera can zoom in for a closeup of telling facial expressions, or it can shoot from above or below to make a character seem insignificant or impressive. In film, faces become extremely important; in drama, voices become especially important. Finally, film creates a strong illusion of reality, and it permits viewers to probe the feelings of charac-ters with considerable flexibility. It also permits viewers to move about very quickly in time and from place to place.

### Film and Literature

Although film may have "developed its strongest bond with the novel, not with painting, not even with drama,"[13] important distinctions nevertheless exist be-tween film and novel. Although some films, such as *War and Peace* and *Gone with the Wind,* are considered to be quite long, they are limited to much greater time restrictions than most novels. A novelist does not expect a reader to com-plete a novel in the time it takes a viewer to see a movie. The reader can put a novel aside, ponder its significance so far, and return to it at will. Not so with the movie, unless the viewer possesses the tape or reel; it moves along steadily for one to two hours, and the viewer can do nothing about its pace or its time span. Some scholars point to the greater density of the novel—to its more contemplative portrayals of the human condition. This view is somewhat simplistic, though. Films, like novels, vary in their degrees of density. Although a viewer cannot vary the rate of assimilation, as can a reader, to adjust for density, the viewer should see some films repeatedly. Louis D. Giannetti makes this point in *Understanding Movies:*

> *Naive students of the film are often amazed at how a sophisticated viewer can read so much in a movie. But a viewer merely explicates the images on several levels simultaneously, just as a sensitive reader of Melville's* Moby Dick *can appreciate both the adventure and the rich texture of symbols that add such emotional and intellectual resonance to the novel. Until the student of film has at his disposal an equivalent of a text (the film itself), he must train his eyes and ears to assimilate simultaneously as much of the density of the images and sounds as possible. But no matter how sophisticated the viewer, great films—like great literature and drama—require repeated exposure.*[14]

The story is not used as often as the novel in cross-media approaches, but apparently teachers have had much success with *An Occurrence at Owl Creek Bridge.* James Wicklund of Arlington Heights High School in Illinois suggests focusing on the masterful editing and the skillful uses of sound and camera in the film version. His sample lesson seeks no comparison between the short story and the film; rather it contains observations that emphasize the uniqueness of the film as art. The situation in story and film is of a condemned Confederate spy who is hanged from a bridge. "Penetrating" closeups of the man's face and of the faces of Union officers, camera shots selected to emphasize point of view, sounds of nature contrasted with sounds of man, the use of silhouettes and slow motion, the splicing of five shots to let the viewer fall alongside the man's plunging body, and the use of sounds and movements to catch images of the man's fantasy of escape and reunion with his wife, and the quick snap back to the reality of death at the end of the rope are examples of art well worth discussing with students.[15]

Films and poems are compared even less frequently than films and short stories. Occasionally a poem and a film of that poem are compared, but a cross-media approach is more common between a particular film and one or more poems that are related thematically or artistically but are not sources for the film. Willowbrook teachers have found that students can relate *Dream of the Wild Horses* to William Blake's "The Tiger."[16] Teachers in Ontario, Canada, have discovered that the films *Free Fall, Very Nice, Very Nice,* and *A Trip Down Memory Lane* may be used effectively with poems by Dylan Thomas and T. S. Eliot.[17]

THE TEACHING OF HIGH SCHOOL ENGLISH

Another approach, one that does not necessarily include poems, is to study a film *as* poetry. For example, *Dream of the Wild Horses* is studied as a "lyrical film poem," with particular attention to the rhythmic movements of the horses. In a short film such as this one, each shot may have several metaphors, and the composition, the arrangement of shots, and especially the editing may bring all visual images together to create an artistic whole. When effective, short films of this type stimulate the viewer to expand the tight sequence of images into a flow of personal feelings and thoughts. Concrete visual images then become expanded metaphors in the viewer's imagination.

## CRITICAL APPROACH

All approaches described above have in them some opportunities for critical viewing and appraisal. The difference between them and the critical approach is that in units on film criticism the level of perception is much higher and the focus on film as art is much sharper. Film criticism calls for the highest level of film literacy; in effect, it teaches students how to view films and read critical reviews perceptively and openly, and how to judge the worth of films for themselves. In a unit of this kind, one aim would be to develop a fairly high level of literacy in reading external criticism by professional critics, but the ultimate goal would be to develop a kind of inner criticism—a strong personal intellectual curiosity about the artistic value of films and some confidence in one's own ability to evaluate both films and one's experiences with them.

Reaching such goals with even the most able students is not a task for the beginner. Film criticism is the most demanding approach, so even an experienced teacher should proceed cautiously. Knowing about students' experiences with films, their interests, their academic abilities, and many other factors, is extremely important. The teacher's knowledge and interest are no less important. In no case should a teacher attempt to teach film criticism without *much* preparation and genuine enthusiasm.

# FILMMAKING

## THE BENEFITS

Although filmmaking is not as actively pursued by English teachers as film study, it has made significant contributions to the English curriculum. Many teachers who have participated in it claim that student interest in the process has generated greater interest in reading, writing, speaking, and listening. Apparently, some students who have had very little hope of success in English have finally worked hard and have had the satisfaction of helping to produce something that has given other people pleasure. Their experience with planning, writing a script, directing, shooting, and editing has also given them insights into the importance of effective technique in filmmaking. To an extent, this experience has also helped them to become better judges of film. When literature has been the source for a student-made film, students have read the literature with greater interest and care and have been able to discuss it more thoroughly as literature. Of greatest importance, though, has been their awareness of film as communication. As one student said after listening to his classmates react to a film he had developed with his group, "I liked it because you can say something with a film."

## THE TASK

An English teacher who is convinced that a remark like the one above is worth much anxiety and hard work, who finds beauty and meaning in films, who is willing to spend a great amount of time and effort learning something new, who can work effectively with students who are doing several different tasks at the same time, and who is willing to keep an open mind throughout an experiment, might be ready for a serious encounter with filmmaking. Oh, yes, and who is willing to see something through in spite of negative comments by colleagues, and who is willing to ask the principal once more for special funds, and who is willing to ask the coaches for their video equipment when that is the only filming equipment available, and who . . . . The list grows, but so might the interest in films and filmmaking.

Lillian Schiff, a "repetitious film teacher" at Schreiber High School, Port Washington, New York, describes some of the patience and attention to detail:

> *Draw the drapes gently; keep the film off the floor, hold on to the camera even if it is on a tripod, don't pan, zoom, or move the camera, plan everything, rehearse, think in seconds, don't be late or absent, be considerate of your group members, splicing isn't editing, vary the angles, vary the distances, see with your own eyes whether there's light on the subject, say what's good about the film first, then suggested improvements.*[18]

Elsewhere in her article, Ms. Schiff departs from her diarylike chronology of the process to reflect, apparently with some awe, on the hours that students spend editing their films. These are in many cases students who "wouldn't edit their own writing." She also talks about their involvement at the outset in arranging material and determining the length of shots and scenes for the sake of rhythm, reshooting if there is time, and splicing in small segments. Her comment to other English teachers about all of this is, "That's how I write an essay, don't you?"

## THE KNOW-HOW

The day-after-day process of filmmaking is the topic of several books. A good one to pick up first is Kuhns and Giardino, *Behind the Camera,* Dayton, Ohio:

Pflaum, 1970. Among the many other helpful books are Spottiswoode, *Film and Its Techniques,* Berkeley: University of California Press, 1968; Mascelli, *The Five C's of Cinematography,* Hollywood: Cinne Graphics Publications, 1965; Walter, *The Technique of the Film Cutting Room,* New York: Hastings House, 1969; Kinsey, *How to Make Animated Movies: A Studio Handbook,* New York: The Viking Press, 1970; and Lowndes, *Film Making in Schools,* New York: Watson, Guptill Publications, 1968. The *English Journal* and *Media & Methods* are two publications teachers should consult for helpful articles. Professional sessions on filmmaking during national and state meetings, conferences with teachers who have had experience, and workshops and courses on the subject are also avenues to information. And, if you are still excited about it, by all means *do it.* Because it's a process, books, articles, and teacher talk do not substitute for trying it yourself.

---

### THE IDEA BOX

#### SIX APPROACHES WITH ONE FILM

A good film can be used in several approaches to film study. *Walkabout,* a film praised by critic Pauline Kael, is apparently that versatile. Writing in *Media & Methods,* Ralph Amelio describes six approaches: (1) cross-media (with the novel *Walkabout*), (2) functional (critical analysis of the technical uses of image and sound), (3) thematic (self-identity, culture clash, survival, etc.), (4) genre (a romantic odyssey), (5) stylistic (filmic style of director/*auteur* Nichlas Roeg), and (6) the critical-aesthetic (film's harmony, unity, integrity, vitality, emotional and intellectual involvement, and universality).[19] The novel *Walkabout* is of course already used widely in secondary schools; Mr. Amelio's article shows that the film is well worth teaching, too.

#### THE AUTEUR THEORY

This controversial theory, which originated in France and has caused conflicts among critics in America, generally proposes that the director is the main author of a film. Critics who take this point of view believe that a director's skillful treatment of the subject matter has more to do with making a good movie than does the content of the movie.

It might be interesting to ask students whether they are more impressed by the directing skill than by the content. Should technical skill and artistry be the deciding factors if the subject matter is not very significant? To what extent should films be evaluated on content? To what extent on method? Could the *auteur* theory lull a viewer into believing that all films directed by a famous director are outstanding?

## FILM CENSORSHIP IS HERE

Kenneth Donelson offers this quote from an attack on *Occurrence at Owl Creek Bridge:* "It is anti-American, anti-establishment, and filled with violence."[20]

## ALMOST 140,000 STUDENTS

A U.S. Office of Education survey shows that in 1972 to 1973 secondary school English departments enrolled 139,978 students in elective courses in film and television. The declining popularity of elective programs in the 1980s may have reduced this figure, but if teachers will address the problem of film literacy seriously in new units and courses, film could again attract large numbers of students.

## "WHAT IS THE FILM ALL ABOUT AND HOW DO YOU KNOW?"

Joy Gould Boyum, film critic for the *Wall Street Journal,* and Gordon Pradl of New York University identify the questions above as the key ones in film study. They contend that students will have the best chance of answering these questions if the teacher carries out "a sequence of study in which students are first invited to respond to film as freely and as intensely as possible, to share their responses and to test them in relation to the film that stimulated them, and to see how their perceptions and feelings parallel or diverge from the perceptions and feelings of others."[21]

## FILM STUDY: A REQUIRED BASIC

Denny T. Wolfe, Jr., director of the Division of Languages, State Department of Public Instruction, Raleigh, NC, tells of a film study unit for all ninth grade students at Githens Junior High School in Durham. In view of the so-called "back-to-the-basics" movement of the 1980s, this statement from the Githins *Film Unit Guide* is quite interesting: "Within the scope of a basic skills emphasis, it is the belief of the Githins English Department that the skill of viewing must not be overlooked. It is upon this belief that the Department offers its film unit to all ninth grade students."[22]

## BASICS THROUGH FILMS

Writing in the *English Journal,* Rebecca West tells of success in using films to teach basics.

> As an English teacher, I originally turned to media, specifically to film, to *teach my students basics,* when everything else I tried left me unsatisfied with the results. The proof I received through the thousands of papers I read, developed through the hundreds of writing activities I wrote based on films we used in the classroom, fully convinced me of the validity of film use in the English class.[23]

## ONE FILM, MANY THEMES

One short film (11 minutes) that has several interesting thematic contrasts for study is *Chromophobia*. An animated production, it satirizes Germany's occupation of

490    THE TEACHING OF HIGH SCHOOL ENGLISH

Paris during World War II. Possible contrasts for discussion are these: "prejudice versus tolerance and understanding; freedom versus oppression; regimentation versus flexibility; idealism versus cynicism; tyranny versus individual liberty; conformity versus nonconformity; despair versus hope, gloom versus wit; conflict versus peace; nature versus technology."[24]

## FILMMAKING WITH VIDEOTAPE

Before filmmaking with a movie camera, students can learn some of the fundamentals by experimenting with a TV camera. In many high schools, this equipment is used by coaches to film games for replay and discussion. Students should realize that although the TV camera offers some good beginning learning opportunities it also limits possibilities in filmmaking. Among the advantages are experimenting with sequences of shots, camera angles, perspectives, and to some extent lighting effects; learning narrative film technique (telling a story in images and sounds); training actors (rehearsing); experimenting with sound effects; experimenting with a moving camera (moving the camera instead of zooming in with a lens); learning some of the basics of lighting; learning some of the basics of pictorial composition; and editing *in* the camera (erasing segments and reshooting them for better effect). Among the shortcomings are the virtual impossibility of cutting and splicing film in editing; the restrictions of picture size (usually a 19 to 23 in. TV screen, unless a widescreen accessory is available); and the greater difficulty of achieving desired lighting effects.[25]

Two articles offer additional tips on filmmaking with a TV camera: Nancy Cromer, "Making a Videotape: A Group Experience," *English Journal*, May 1976, pp. 94–95; Stephen Moro and Donald Fleming, "Video Short Story", *English Journal*, March 1976, pp. 60–63.

## MAKE A FILM

The following exercises should interest student filmmakers:

1. An excellent type of film to make for thinking out problems in continuity is to shoot a pool game entirely and keep the audience aware of who is shooting each shot, where each ball goes, but without losing the audience's interest (as a concentration of high overhead shots might do).
2. Do a rhythmic film: a brief film centered entirely around some rhythm—natural, mechanical, human. You may want to do a film of waves that has a rhythm of cutting and camera movement which is like the waves themselves, or a film of a train that catches the rhythm of the train's wheels.
3. Write a script for an event involving at least three people. Then film it twice. One version should be an interpretation as seen through one of the person's eyes (subjective camera). The other should be more objective, but through editing build toward an exciting conclusion.
4. Make a documentary about a local incident: between 5 and 10 minutes in length. Use not more than 100 words of narration to help explain the incident.

**5.** Do a film based on a familiar cliché (the gunfight, the saloon brawl, etc.), keeping to the visual style of the cliché but changing the ending.[26]

## TWICE THROUGH

Teachers of film recognize the difficulties of showing a film twice. In most schools, doing so would consume two consecutive class periods in the week. But of course the discussion of a short story may take two days or more, and the study of a novel or a five-act play may take two or three weeks. The point is not so much the amount of time as the wise use of that time. Thus, some sort of strategy is needed. In *The Art of Watching Films,* Joseph Boggs suggests this approach:

> In the first viewing we can watch the film in the usual manner, concerning ourselves primarily with plot elements, the total emotional effect, and the central idea or theme. Then in a second viewing, since we are no longer caught up in the suspense of "what happens," we can focus our full attention on the hows and whys of the filmmaker's art.[27]

In *Film and the Critical Eye,* Dennis Denitto and William Herman suggest the same pattern, but between viewings they recommend jotting down from memory an outline, a plot sequence of "skeletal structure," that will help to organize one's responses later. Then during the second viewing they recommend recording (whispering into a tape recorder) one's reactions, including recognized details and techniques.[28] Thirty students whispering into tape recorders could overtax a teacher's sanity, if not the school's budget, but a teacher might recommend the taping procedure to students for individual viewing, especially at home with a film on television.

# FOOTNOTES

1. Frank Manchel, *Film Study,* Rutherford, N.J.: Fairleigh Dickinson University Press, 1973, p. 13.
2. Harold M. Foster, *The New Literacy,* Urbana, Ill.: NCTE, 1979, p. 10.
3. *Film in the Classroom,* Dayton, Ohio: Pflaum/Standard, 1971, p. 99.
4. *Ibid.,* p. 104.
5. *Films and the English Class,* Feb. 1971 issue of the *Arizona English Bulletin,* p. 49.
6. James Wicklund, *Film: The Moving Image in Language Arts,* Springfield Illinois Office of Education, 1974, p. 19.
7. *Talking About the Cinema,* London: British Film Institute, rev., 1974, pp. 12–13.
8. *Film Study,* p. 125.
9. The letters FNC refer to Films Incorporated, a film distributor. School media specialists have catalogs listing distributors and their addresses.

10. *Film Study,* p. 125.
11. "Film Study and the English Teacher," a booklet, Indiana University Audio Visual Center, 1968, p. 4.
12. *I Lost It At the Movies,* Boston: Little, Brown and Company, 1954, p. 276.
13. James Monaco, *How to Read a Film: The Art, Technology, Language, History and Theory of Film and Media,* New York: Oxford University Press, 1977, p. 29.
14. Englewood Cliffs, N.J.: Prentice-Hall, Inc., 1972, p. 180.
15. *Film: The Moving Image in Language Arts,* pp. 8–9.
16. *Film in the Classroom,* p. 94.
17. *The Uses of Film in the Teaching of English,* Toronto: The Ontario Institute of Studies in Education, 1971, p. 64.
18. "In-service Course Diary: An Introduction to Super-8 Filmmaking," *English Journal* 63, Oct. 1974, p. 49.
19. "Walkabout: Six Approaches to Film Analysis," Feb. 1976, pp. 22–25.
20. "The Censorship of Non-Print Media Comes to the English Classroom," *English Journal* 62, Dec. 1973, p. 1226.
21. *English Journal* 63, Dec. 1974, p. 56.
22. "Thinking Through Film," *English Journal* 68, Dec. 1979, p. 63.
23. "English Fundamentals Through Educational Films," March 1978, p. 96.
24. "Thinking Through Film," p. 63.
25. William Kuhns and Thomas F. Giardino, *Behind the Camera,* Dayton, Ohio: George A. Pflaum, 1970, pp. 166–167.
26. *Behind the Camera,* pp. 174–175.
27. Menlo Park, California: The Benjamin/Cummings Publishing Company, Inc., 1978, p. 11.
28. New York: Macmillan, 1975, pp. 6–7.

# 16

## TEACHERS WHO GROW

### THE PRESERVATION OF IDEALS

Again and again it happens. Disillusionment. Loss of ideals. The young teacher finds that not all students are eager to learn. Not all are lovable. Many are bored, some recalcitrant. Older colleagues of the teacher appear tired, blasé, indifferent. Some administrators seem to be mere paper shufflers.

The days are filled and overfilled. Much of what the young teacher learned in methods courses proves inadequate, inappropriate, unworkable, even untrue. Paperwork takes too much time. There are too few hours or even minutes for helping students individually. And students forget: What was thoroughly taught must often be retaught.

In the face of such troubles the disillusionment sets in. Many second-year teachers are less bright-eyed than the neophytes; many are on the way to thinking of teaching as only a job, on the way to indifference to students.

But, fortunately, not all. Some second-year teachers are more effective than they were before, and year after year they continue to grow. (Those who don't should resign and go to work in a shoe store, for feet are easier to serve than minds and emotions are.)

We'll glance here at a few of the aspects of professional growth, at the preservation and enhancement of ideals.

### A BALANCED PERSPECTIVE

Regardless of how much teachers of English love literature—and they must love it—they cannot afford to immerse themselves in it so deeply that they ignore reality. Literature is a reflection and an interpretation of life, but it is not life

494

itself. Teachers must not lose contact with life, must not climb into the tower of the Palace of Art. Their students are alive; the people in the community are alive. Teachers of English are living links between the life about them and the life depicted in literature. To their students they bring something fine—an enrichment of knowledge concerning themselves, their heritage, and their potential. If teachers are to succeed in effecting this enrichment, though, they must know people as they are, as they breathe, work, play, sweat, eat, drink, love, talk, and dream. Teachers who knew only literature would be like physicians who knew only medicine but were ignorant of the bodies that need strengthening.

## THE TREADMILL

So successful teachers cannot isolate themselves in the Palace of Art. No more, however, can they place themselves on a treadmill. You have perhaps seen pictures of a treadmill: One or more persons move a large horizontal cylinder by climbing steps mounted on it; as their weight pushes one step down, another takes its place. Over and over they repeat the process, hour after hour and day after day, climbing the same steps, looking always at the same monotonous fixtures, reaching no higher point, while the massive cylinder slowly turns. Those long on the treadmill lose their human qualities and become automatons—mere physical forces, part of a mechanical assemblage of weights and counterweights.

Almost any kind of work can become a treadmill. Teaching can, very readily, but it need not. The danger lies in the ease with which the teacher, after a few years, may fall into a routine.

> Today I teach as I taught before;
> Tomorrow I work as I wrought before;
> Friday I cry as I cried before;
> Monday I die as I died before. . . .
>
> Bowed by the weight of tediousness he stands
> Behind his desk and glowers at the class,
> The emptiness of ennui in his face,
> And in his eyes dull hate of all he sees.

How can a teacher avoid the treadmill? Perhaps a minister gave the clue. For more than 50 years he had followed the routine of his calling: a sermon every Sunday, prayer meeting every Wednesday, christenings, weddings, funerals—each week much like 3000 others. His hair had become white, his face wrinkled, but his eyes were still vivacious as he rose to speak at the banquet on the occasion of his retirement. "I have been excited for fifty-five years," he began. "People excite me. They interest me. During my fifty-five years in the ministry I have learned much about people. I know how they blunder, how they err, how they stumble and often fall. I know how they need leadership both human and divine. But I am perpetually excited by the sparks I find in them—sparks of goodness and kindness and self-sacrifice, sparks of promise for the future. In my small way I have spent my life fanning sparks.''

He concluded with quotations from Khalil Gibran and Elizabeth Barrett Browning:

> You have been told also that life is darkness and in your weariness you echo what was said by the weary.
> And I say that life is indeed darkness save when there is urge,
> And all urge is blind save when there is knowledge,
> And all knowledge is vain save when there is work,
> And all work is vain save when there is love,
> And when you work with love you bind yourself to yourself, and to one another, and to God.[1]

> The world waits
> For help. Beloved, let us love so well,
> Our work shall still be better for our love,
> And still our love be sweeter for our work.[2]

## TEACHERS AND STUDENTS

"Should we try to be pals to our students?'' an earnest young prospective teacher once asked one of the authors of this book.

"Heavens, no!'' was the reply. "You people are already old men and old women in the eyes of many junior and senior high school students, and every year you'll become more ancient. You can hope to become an older friend, sometimes an adviser. But a pal—never. Pals have to have much in common including similarity in age. Thirty-two and 22 may be pals, but not 22 and 15.

*Despite what I've said about your antiquity, though, some of you are young and attractive enough that one or more of your students will dream of you in a quite unorthodox teacher-student relationship. In other words, some of them may get what used to be called a "crush on you." When you suspect it, ignore it if you can. Pretend that it doesn't exist. It will probably go away. If pretense becomes impossible, if there is an open avowal, be gentle. Say how flattered you are, but how impossible the situation is. Make the break gentle, but clean and complete. Leave no room for hope. The student's pain and bitterness will last no more than a week or so—about the time it lasts when a going-steady pair breaks up.*

*While we're on the general subject of relationships with students, let me urge you to continue learning about young people. You'll never know enough. Take a graduate course in adolescent psychology. A bit of sociology and even anthropology may answer a question or two. Some fiction for teen-agers is realistic and filled with insights. You'll learn most about young people, of course, from your own students, from their writing, from their class responses, from their participation and behavior in cocurricular activities. Try to meet them socially on some occasions. Dinner at a student's home can be both revealing and pleasant.*

*All this is relevant to the original question about "palship." Give them your best efforts. You are their teacher. You can be a teacher-friend. That's the end of the line. Next year your're teacher-friend to another generation.*

## ENGLISH TEACHERS AND THEIR COLLEAGUES

English teachers have an especially strong motive for cooperating with their fellows. Because English overlaps all other fields to some extent, working with other teachers will pay large dividends to any English instructor. English teachers hope that all teachers in the school will reinforce the attitude that good English is important—that, for instance, clarity and organization are desirable in writing. Cordial relationships with members of other departments may help to translate that hope into reality.

A small but important matter: Beginners should find out about channels of communication in their school. If, for example, supplies are needed or a recommendation of some kind is to be made, should the information be channeled through a course chairman, the department head, the business office, the assistant principal, or somebody else? Sad to say, some teachers and administrators resent being bypassed; sometimes bypassing will indeed result in confusion and omission or duplication. Following channels, then, is the most sensible procedure. Only if a clearly unnecessary block develops is another procedure justified.

## ENGLISH TEACHERS AND THE COMMUNITY

Even as late as the midpoint of this century, some teachers, especially in small communities, had to sign contracts containing some rather absurd provisions: that they would not leave town for more than four weekends during the school year, that they would not use "excessive" makeup, that they would abstain from alcohol, that they would not dye their hair, and even—in at least one community—that they would not fall in love! Today such stipulations in contracts are rare. In general, though, teachers are now regarded as responsible adult citizens who are entitled to live lives of their own.

Nevertheless some communities—again predominantly small ones—still foster the notion that in their moral standards teachers should be role models for the young people they instruct. The point may be debatable, but certainly there is evidence to suggest that some students do attempt to emulate teachers they particularly admire and that they are influenced by them in ways other than purely academic. In an era when so many nonadmirable role models abound, perhaps teachers, without being excessively straitlaced or puritanical about it, should at least consider the kind of model they would like to be.

In another way, too, English teachers may affect lives in their communities. If they can act or if they have musical talent or other specialized abilities, the small community may welcome them most heartily and possibly overburden them with requests. Even teachers with no such talents may be asked to review a current book or play, give a talk to the PTA, write a feature or a review for the local newspaper, or possibly give a talk over the air. With a good subject and enough speaking ability, some teachers speak occasionally before luncheon clubs or other gatherings.

Words are English teachers' chief stock in trade, and the teachers' chief value to the community outside of school hours may lie primarily in what they do with words. They are not missionaries bringing sweetness and light to the uncultured, but some of them may bring wholesome entertainment and worthwhile information to the community through what they write and say. Although the welfare of students is their chief responsibility, they may, if they have time and energy remaining, enjoy themselves and give pleasure to others by using their skill with words.

## ENGLISH TEACHERS AND THEIR BOOKS

English teachers should be the most omnivorous readers among the faculty. Books are their specialty, and all learning is their province. Never, of course, can they catch up on their reading. The presses clatter and rumble ceaselessly.

Inevitably, much of the reading will be in Western classics that they have missed or largely forgotten: Homer, Aeschylus, Aristotle, Vergil, Ovid, Dante, Racine, and many more. Some reading is necessary to refresh memory of the giants of English and American literature. All teachers are aware of vast gaps, too: The literature of the Orient, of Australia, of Latin America may be almost unknown. Few stateside teachers can name five or ten Canadian authors. Literature by black Americans, largely ignored for many years, has now become part of the curriculum. The literature now being written in English in several African nations contains rich surprises in style and content. The teacher should at least skim books for adolescents. Philosophy, sociology, the fine arts, science for laymen, good current magazines—the list goes on and on.

Then there is professional reading. The *English Journal* tops the list, but *College English, College Composition and Communication,* and *Language Arts* (addressed primarily to elementary school teachers) have many relevant articles. *Research in the Teaching of English* affords new insights. Journals about reading, *Educational Leadership, Media and Methods*—the list may be expanded to suit special interests. *The Education Digest* gives a quick monthly overview of varied developments in education. Important new books on teaching and on literary and linguistic scholarship appear every year. The NCTE alone publishes as many as eight or ten books in a 12-month period.

A hopeless task to try to keep up with all this? Yes, for the days and the nights and the summer are never long enough. Yet, one can be thankful that there is always a book to look forward to, a magazine crying to be read, the pleasure of new knowledge to be savored. How can any English teacher's life be dull?

## ENGLISH TEACHERS AS EXPERIMENTERS

There is an easy way to teach English in the second year and forever after. That way is simply to repeat whatever was done in the first year, to follow the same outline and the same lesson plans. So easy! But so dull to teachers and students alike! So futile—for whose first year of teaching (or thirtieth) has ever been so nearly perfect as to deserve endless repetition?

The lively, exciting classroom is the one where something new is always being tried—new books, other new materials, new procedures. It is the classroom where the teacher isn't always sure how something will turn out, because part of what is being done he or she has never attempted before. At least once a week, maybe even once a day, alert teachers conduct little experiments. Some of the experiments fail; some succeed. But they all help to keep the teachers alert.

No big experiments are needed—just a substitution of this poem for that; just a little more room for student initiative this hour, an unusual kind of evaluation tomorrow, a filmstrip, a tryout of some programmed material. Sometime, perhaps, there *will* be a big experiment—*Research* maybe—with all the trimmings of control groups and coefficients of correlation and a picture in the paper. But that isn't necessary. Lots of little experiments are enough to keep the sap flowing.

## ENGLISH TEACHERS AS JOINERS

The organization that addresses itself almost exclusively to English teachers is the National Council of Teachers of English. In addition to publishing half a dozen important magazines, the NCTE has 60 or so committees and commissions working on problems of the profession, publishes pamphlets and a few books on curricular and other matters; manages a talented-student competition that has helped many young people to obtain college scholarships; works towards a reasonable teacher load; makes available to its members, at reduced cost, large numbers of cassettes, filmstrips, literary maps, and other teaching aids; and assists in the articulation of elementary, secondary, and college teaching of English. Its conventions move to a different city each year according to a set geographical pattern; the leaders of the profession are often at the speakers' tables there, but competent young persons—tomorrow's leaders—are constantly sought as participants. The NCTE is the one organization that an English teacher cannot afford not to join.

Most states and some communities or other areas within a state have English-teacher organizations, most of which are affiliated with the NCTE. Because these organizations concern themselves with state or area problems in English teaching, they are worth support. Some of them publish excellent small magazines or newsletters, and most of them hold one or more professional meetings each year.

For those especially interested in the teaching of reading, the International Reading Association has a strong program and worthwhile publications. The Association for Supervision and Curriculum Development appeals to those who do the things suggested by its title; it, too, has a good magazine, *Educational Leadership,* of which perhaps a fourth is especially pertinent to English teaching. Other special-interest associations exist and may appeal to individual teachers.

Five minutes of conversation with almost any English teacher will probably reveal whether or not that teacher is an active member of one or more professional organizations. Almost without exception the members are professionally better informed, more alert, more willing to experiment, more *interested* in their work. Eye-brightness is a significant clue: the bright-eyed are almost always professionally active.


## ADVANCEMENT IN THE PROFESSION

Devoted and hardworking teachers of English can advance professionally in several ways. Some school systems require earning additional college credits, educational travel, in-service study, or contributions to curriculum development as a prerequisite to certain upgradings in salary. Some have only automatic salary increments. But how else may teachers move upward?

There is, of course, a chance to move to a "better" school, although teacher mobility is reduced in times of teacher surplus. "Better" should not be confused with "bigger." Some relatively small schools have English departments, English programs, and salary schedules superior to those of many larger schools.

Some English teachers become interested in part- or full-time work in guidance and counseling. A graduate degree in this field is likely to be required. The penalty involved may be abandonment of the classroom in favor of individual work with students and perhaps the conduct of a largely impersonal testing program.

Administration beckons some English teachers. This is most likely to take the form of a department headship, which in large schools generally involves an increase in salary and a reduction in teaching responsibilities. Administration may also mean a principalship or even a superintendency. For either of these posts, special graduate work is essential. Although the loss of able classroom teachers to administrative posts is in a way lamentable, it is good for a school to have administrators with strong academic interests and preparation.

College teaching offers another attraction. However, decreases in student population have reduced the availability of college jobs. Also, except for positions in community colleges, a PhD degree is likely to be required.

Some universities have developed doctoral programs in the teaching of English. These degrees, which often require a major in English and a minor in education, and which have high school teaching as a prerequisite, prepare teachers to take over college methods courses and to counsel prospective teachers; they also prepare candidates for headships in large high school departments and for supervisory positions.

Committee work and writing for local, state, and national organizations of teachers offer a different road for advancement and do not take the teacher from the classroom. Able people are always needed to help with research in these organizations, and their editors are always looking for excellent manuscripts. No money, as a rule, is paid for such work or such articles, but professional prestige and personal satisfaction may be sufficient remuneration. Some school districts recognize professional contributions in their salary schedules.

Individual research is a special means of advancement, open to a few persons who are patient and thorough. Such research may be in conjunction with work for an advanced degree, but it need not be.

Writing is attractive to some English teachers. Good textbooks, which are usually developed cooperatively by teachers and representatives of a publishing firm, are always needed. Writing for children or adolescents appeals to some teachers. So do other kinds of writing: A fairly large number of today's novelists, poets, and writers of nonfiction were or are teachers of English.

Unfortunately, several of the roads to advancement may take the teacher partly or entirely out of the classroom. For most teachers the best route may be the one that keeps them in the classroom doing the job each day as well as they are able, experimenting on a small scale, working with children, spending most of a lifetime in the same community, growing old and honored in Littleville or in Bigg High. Perhaps no other road leads to greater satisfaction.

# THE IDEA BOX

## DEDICATION AND PROFESSIONALISM

Some old-timers in teaching assert that teachers in general are less dedicated to their students and to their profession than was once true. As evidence they cite teacher strikes, greater attention to wages and hours than to curriculum improvement, declining membership in some professional organizations, and unwillingness to take work home, help students outside school hours, or perform any educational task without compensation.

Certainly almost no generalization dealing with human behavior is completely true. To the extent that these old-timers are right, however, teaching has declined from a profession to a mere trade. The following definition of *profession* from Webster's *Third International* is worth pondering: "a calling requiring specialized knowledge and often long and intensive preparation including instruction in skills and methods as well as the scientific, historical, or scholarly principles underlying such skills and methods, maintaining by force of organization or concerted opinion high standards of achievement and conduct, and committing its members to continued study and to a kind of work which has for its prime purpose the rendering of a public service."

## THINKING ABOUT A RAINBOW

Think for a moment of a spectrum, of a rainbow. The colors are not just red and violet but are countless, each shading off almost imperceptibly into the next.

Most things in education are spectrumlike. They are not red or violet, black or white, right or wrong. Yet, driven by either/or thinking, educators often trumpet, "This is *the* way," and many teachers take up the new fad. To some extent the history of education is a history of fads. Teachers concentrate for a time on the red, on the violet, or on something in between, when they should be looking at the whole rainbow instead.

Education is not, for instance, a matter of subject matter *or* child. It is subject matter *and* child and the numberless potential links between them. And learning is not just cognitive, affective, or motor; it is all three, and teaching must take all three into account.

## WHO IS THE GOOD TEACHER?

"The difference between a good and a mediocre teacher," said literary critic Northrop Frye, "lies mainly in the emphasis the former puts on the exploring part of the mind, the aspects of learning that reveal meanings and lead to further understanding. . . . Mediocre teachers . . . stress memory at the expense of intelligence."[3]

## TALKING TOO MUCH: AN OCCUPATIONAL DISEASE

Some research has shown that 70 percent of the talking in classrooms is teacher talk. In a class of 30 students that leaves 1 percent for each student. Is that enough?

Are a teacher's words seventy times as important as a student's? Could we settle for 50? 40? 30?

## THE TEACHER'S VOICE

Some young teachers fail because their speaking voices are unpleasant—excessively high-pitched, monotonous, jarring, indistinct, or barely audible. Some not-so-young teachers fail because they have let once-pleasant voices and vocal mannerisms deteriorate.

Suggestion: Once a semester, make a tape of one of your classroom sessions. Listen to yourself critically, as to a stranger. Perhaps you will be satisfied, even pleased, with what you hear. If not, try to correct the defects before they become more serious.

## THE WIDENING CIRCLE

Can you use this in what must be a constant struggle, the fight against your own provincialism and that of others?

Each of us lives inside a small circle, the circumference of which is our own experience. Timidity or complacence restricts many of us to a never-expanding circle; we live our one life and die in its narrow confines. Others of us are battering constantly against the rim, seeking new knowledge and new experiences, reaching out geographically, hunting for what those younger and those older know that we do not, searching backward through time; we bulge the circle here and there, and gradually it becomes a larger circle. The seekers, the bulgers, live a richer, more exciting life than do the provincials—maybe not a happier life, but a more rewarding one. The provincials are vegetables; the seekers are Daniel Boones.

## I'VE BEEN READING . . .

A few social evenings each year may provide both pleasure and profitable interchange, especially if elementary, junior high, senior high, and nondogmatic college teachers all participate. After dinner, instead of having a formal program, each person may talk informally for no more than 5 minutes on "I've been reading . . ." Literature, professional books and articles, even popular magazine articles may be included.

## MAKING THE CLASSROOM ATTRACTIVE

1. Ideally, each English teacher should have a classroom of his or her own.
2. Enlist student aid in improving the appearance of your classroom. Students' interest will carry over into their classwork.

## TO ENCOURAGE STUDENTS

Give frequent recognition to students who contribute usefully to the work of the class. Check the class roll weekly to see that all members have had an opportunity to distinguish themselves in some way.

## THOUGHTS ON DISCIPLINE

1. If the teacher knows the subject well and is truly courteous (not merely polite), discipline problems seldom arise.
2. Troublemakers are often students who have too little to do or who cannot do what has been assigned. The cures should be obvious although not necessarily easy.
3. Potential troublemakers may be given special positions with important sounding titles: Chairman of the Classroom Library Committee. (But the positions must carry genuine responsibilities.) They may also be won over by having them do special favors for the teacher (not vice versa); a boy who has adjusted a carburetor for the teacher will seldom cause trouble in class.
4. Probably a student should never be scolded in front of the class. A friendly private conference, with an attempt to get at the cause of the difficulty, may bring much better results.

## TO KEEP THINGS IN ORDER

1. Have files for pictures, maps, notes, and other supplementary aids.
2. Return papers promptly.
3. Keep summaries of especially successful units or lessons.

## CURRICULAR MATERIALS; FREE AND INEXPENSIVE MATERIALS

Most issues of the *English Journal* devote space to information about recently developed textbooks and other curricular materials, including some that are free or relatively inexpensive. *Textbooks in Print,* frequently revised, may provide other leads. So can various NCTE books and pamphlets.

## KEEPING THE PUBLIC INFORMED

The NCTE occasionally issues pamphlets for teachers of English in the elementary and secondary schools to help them inform the public about the teaching of English. The best way to prevent problems of censorship, for instance, is an informed community; NCTE's "The Student's Right to Read," which deals with this topic, is one of the Council's all-time best-sellers. SLATE, an "action arm" of NCTE, prepares materials useful for dealing with the public.

## "I HAVE A DREAM"

"I have a dream—of a day when English teachers will help their students inquire into the use and misuse of language in human affairs . . . of a day when English teachers will use literature to help each student inquire into the problems that concern him . . . of a day when all teachers will have their students use writing every day to develop their learning and thinking process, instead of writing boring compositions for bored English teachers to correct and return." So said Gerald Kincaid, an English specialist in the Minnesota state department of education.

## FOR COMFORT ON YOUR BLUE DAYS

In a comic strip, Priscilla's Pop laments that all of Priscilla's classmates, but not she, can tell a hyphen from a comma. Priscilla comforts herself, "But can they tell a pinto from a palomino?" (Philosophical question: What knowledge is of most worth?)

## PROFESSIONAL MEETINGS

Professional conferences and conventions are valuable for exchange of points of view, getting new ideas, and examining new textbooks and other materials. Yet William A. Jenkins, a past-president of the NCTE, found that over four-fifths of English teachers have never attended a national meeting, about half never a state meeting, and about a quarter not even a local meeting.

## KEEPING UP WITH RESEARCH FINDINGS

It is difficult for a busy teacher to keep *au courant* with recent research. The *English Journal, Research in the Teaching of English,* and ERIC publications will help. (ERIC is an acronym for Educational Research Information Center, which is supported by federal funds.) Teachers find especially useful English ERIC's "state of the art" papers on specific topics. Write to NCTE for details.

## "COMPETENCY TESTING AND PR"

Instead of looking with abhorrence at proposed competency testing, as teachers often do, teachers at North Tama High School, Traer, Iowa, decided to think positively. They developed and used a writing test in which they themselves could believe. It covered central ideas, organization, sentence structure, word choice, and mechanics. They found it helped to improve public relations and emphasized for both students and school patrons the fact that good writing involves more than spelling and punctuation. Veta Hildebrand tells the story.[4]

## HISTORICAL PERSPECTIVE

The statement has often been made that the chief use of history is to help living people avoid the mistakes of the past. Dogs and lions and other animals do not know the histories of their species and therefore cannot advance beyond the status of their ancestors. It seems that many or most English teachers, too, are lacking in historical perspective; they are unaware of the mistakes—and the successes—of the past. A comprehensive history of the NCTE, *A Long Way Together,* makes perspective easier to attain.

## A TEACHER'S HAPPINESS

Happiness, according to Lin Yutang, consists of moments. A teacher cannot expect an endless series of joy-filled hours, success after success. A reasonable goal may be one or two moments a day—on the average. They will make an impressive array by retirement age.

TGIM

"Off to meet the enemy!" says a teacher, picking up an armload of books. "TGIF!"
  "Amen!" another responds.
  Thank God it's Friday! Try saying, three days later, "TGIM!"

# FOOTNOTES

1. Kahlil Gibran, *The Prophet,* New York: Alfred Knopf, Inc., 1923.
2. E. B. Browning, "Aurora Leigh."
3. *Design for Learning,* Toronto: University of Toronto Press, 1962, pp. 12–13.
4. *English Journal* 69, Dec. 1980, p. 76.

# NAME INDEX

510

512

Shaw, George Bernard, 418
Shefter, Harry, 414
Shehan, Lawrence, 414
Shelley, Percy B., 308
Sheridan, Richard B., 272
Shonkoff, Fredi, 476
Shuman, R. Baird, 347, 374, 406
Shutt, Randall, 313
Shuy, Roger, 288
Simonini, R. C., 280
Singler, Harry, 114
Slager, William R., 312
Sloan, Gary B., 280, 370
Slote, Bernice, 221
Small, Donald, 323
Smith, Blanche H., 375
Smith, Brenda G., 111
Smith, Elaine, 318
Smith, Elsdon, 280, 301
Smith, James A., 69
Smith, Richard, 89
Smith, Richard L., 362
Smith, Veta, 289
Smitherman, Geneva, 289
Snyder, F. W., 352
Sohn, David, 115, 375, 485
Sommers, Mary C., 336
Sommers, Nancy, 373
Spann, Sylvia, 45, 64, 475
Sparks, Madeleine, 401
Squire, James R., 41
Stafford, William, 201, 218
Stanford, Barbara, 137, 192
Stanford, Gene, 137, 174, 372
Stassen, Marilyn, 449
Steil, Lyman, 461, 474
Steinbeck, John, 95, 187, 361
Steinley, Gary, 194
Stensland, Anna Lee, 192
Sternglass, Marilyn, 313
Stevenson, Robert Louis, 184
Stewart, George R., 279, 301
Stocker, Claudell, 471
Stoen, Don, 403
Stone, Pat, 442
Strickland, Ruth, 358
Strong, William, 276
Stroud, Janet, 159
Struck, Herman R., 282
Stuart, Jesse, 311
Styles, Ken, 172
Suhor, Charles, 282, 317

Sutton, Gary, 276
Sweet, Johanna, 357
Sweet, John, 195, 456
Sweet, Julie, 469
Swift, Jonathan, 128, 266, 272
Swinburne, A. C., 126
Swinney, Louise, 418

Tabakow, David, 371
Tanzi, La Arigo, 444
Taylor, Gary, 187
Taylor, H. O., 205
Taylor, Karl K., 474
Taylor, Lois, 234
Taylor, Mary V., 282
Terry, Ann, 202
Thomas, Douglas, 88
Thompson, Nancy, 447
Thorpe, Janet, 356
Thurber, James, 340
Tibbetts, Charlene, 124
Tierney, Gilbert, 329
Torvik, Solveig, 309
Tovatt, Anthony, 42, 69
Towery, Gene, 94, 419
Trout, Lawana, 435
True, Michael, 235
Turner, Darwin, 131
Turner, Thomas N., 372
Twain, Mark, *see* Clemens, Samuel
Tyler, Priscilla, 365
Tymn, Marshall, 196

Vandell, Jean, 322, 374, 377, 419
VanderMeulen, Ken, 119
Van Doren, Mark, 201
Van Loon, Hendrik, 460
Veidemanis, Gladys, 200
Vonnegut, Kurt, 170

Wagner, Betty, 46, 427
Wagner, Eileen, 350
Wagner, Linda W., 355
Wagoner, David, 211
Walker, Margaret, 128
Walters, Thomas N., 350
Ward, C. H., 181
Waxenburg, Jane, 346
Weaver, Phyllis, 476
Webster, Noah, 302
Webster, S. W., 282
Weeks, Ruth Mary, 5

514

# SUBJECT INDEX

515

teaching, 292–293

Vocabulary building, 95–96, 294–300,
317–318
vocabulary games, 298
Voice, in writing, 338

Wordiness, 317
Writing, 324–373
descriptive, 363
objective *vs.* subjective, 308–
309
for self-discovery, 326